Lucy A to Z

Lucy A to Z
The Lucille Ball Encyclopedia
4th Edition

Michael Karol

iUniverse Star

New York   Lincoln   Shanghai

Lucy A to Z
The Lucille Ball Encyclopedia

Copyright © 2001–2003, 2004, 2007, 2008 by Michael Karol

iUniverse Star
an iUniverse, Inc. imprint

iUniverse books may be ordered through booksellers or by contacting:

iUniverse
2021 Pine Lake Road, Suite 100
Lincoln, NE 68512
www.iuniverse.com
1-800-Authors (1-800-288-4677)

Because of the dynamic nature of the Internet, any Web addresses
or links contained in this book may have changed
since publication and may no longer be valid.

The views expressed in this work are solely those of the author
and do not necessarily reflect the views of the publisher,
and the publisher hereby disclaims any responsibility for them.

ISBN: 978-0-595-29761-0 (pbk)
ISBN: 978-0-595-75213-3 (ebk)

Printed in the United States of America

DEDICATION

To my mother, who always joked that I had more pictures of Lucy in my apartment than pictures of her.

I miss you, Mom.

And to Craig, without whom this book wouldn't exist.

I miss you, too.

EPIGRAPH

"Who will believe that Lucy is married to a Cuban bandleader?"

—Nervous CBS executives during the filming of the I Love Lucy *pilot*

CONTENTS

ILLUSTRATIONS

Cover Illustration: Lucille Ball in 1945, by Harry Warnecke; design ©2007 by Michael Karol; image © 2007 by Nicholas Orzio.

Back Cover: Author's photo © 2007 by the Estate of Craig Hamrick; design ©2007 by Michael Karol.

Lucy A to Z covers in "Introduction" ©2007 by Michael Karol

All other photos are from Photofest, unless otherwise noted (i.e., the artist or photographer, or from the author's collection). Visit Photofest online at photofestnyc.com.

A WORD (OR TWO) FROM WANDA CLARK

I first met Michael Karol at the Lucille Ball-Desi Arnaz Center in Jamestown, New York, where I found his book *Lucy A to Z: The Lucille Ball Encyclopedia*, and quickly learned he was not only a talented writer, but also a lovely person to know. I had the privilege of working for Lucy, a beautiful and remarkable woman, for 27 years, and I've been a founding member of the Lucy-Desi Museum in Jamestown since her children asked me to participate when it was first talked about. After all those years with Lucy, I can truthfully say that every time I read through one of Michael's books I learn something new about Lucy and her career. This new Fourth Edition of *Lucy A to Z* is a wonderful read and I'm very pleased to recommend it to everyone.

—Wanda Clark, October 2007

[*Wanda was Lucille Ball's personal secretary for more than a quarter century and a classy lady. For much more on Wanda and her life with Lucy, see the entry* Clark, Wanda.]

FOREWORD

A Few Words from Lucy's No. 1 Fan: Michael Stern

Lucille Ball's most ardent supporter answered some questions for me.

How did you become Lucille Ball's Official No. 1 Fan?

I was at the right place at the right time. I lived in the Los Angeles area and I was able to receive tickets to see *Here's Lucy* being filmed (with guest star Bob Cummings). I remember Gary Morton (Lucy's second husband) introducing her and her flaming red hair as she entered through the curtains. She ran from one end of the stage to the other while waving and blowing kisses. Actor Jesse White (the former Maytag Repairman) was sitting next to me, so when she said hello to him I knew she was also looking at me.

I was able to go back a few more times over the next two years and on July 12, 1973, after the filming (with guest stars Steve Lawrence and Eydie Gorme), Lucy's mom, DeDe, took me backstage with her and I was introduced to Lucy. I showed her my scrapbook of photos, which she looked at, then she signed an autograph for me and gave me a big kiss on the cheek.

By the time I turned 15, I was able to meet her maybe once or twice a year. She finally took me backstage at a TV guest appearance she was doing with Dick Van Dyke on *Van Dyke & Company* (1976). She said it was nice that I was a big fan, but she told me, in a stern way, that if I wanted to be her No. 1 fan, I would have to stay in school and get a job. So I did; and since I got a job and was doing well in school, she called me her No. 1 fan.

What does your collection consist of?

My collection consists of over 3,000 items from as small as an autographed matchbook cover with her photo on it, to her cast from when she broke her leg in 1972, to posters that hung in her home. I would love to say the collection is all in my Lucy room but it has spilled into the living room, den, kitchen, closets, and now my parent's home as storage.

What's your favorite piece?

Asking me about my favorite piece is like asking me, "Who is my favorite child?" I like them all. But I do have special items. My copy of the 1976 book *Lucy & Ricky & Fred & Ethel* is one of my favorites, because over 60 people who either appeared on the show or worked behind the scenes autographed it. Some of the signatures include Lucy, Desi, Vivian, and all the writers, plus the directors and supporting players. I also have a beautiful 11x14-inch photo of Lucy from *The Long, Long Trailer* that she signed "Lucille Ball" for me, which as most collectors know is very rare. [Mostly, she just signed "Lucy."] And all my photos with Lucy are very special to me.

Lucy was often characterized as lonely, depressed, and strident in her final decades, especially the latter as regards her professional life. Was that the Lucy you knew?

I knew Lucy the last 15 years of her life. I knew two different Lucys. One Lucy was Lucille Ball the actress, who loved her work and loved being with people who shared her love of the work. She loved meeting fans, and it was great to be in her company. The other Lucy I knew was Lucy Morton. Lucy Morton was sometimes a little sad. She was growing older and her friends were dying. She was not working anymore, and she really wanted to work even at age 75. Lucy was very distraught after *Life with Lucy* was canceled in 1986; she thought that no one (including her fans) appreciated her any longer.

Did you get a sense of whether Lucy had any regrets in her life?

I'm sure everybody has regrets in life. I know she always thought about going back to school. She always wanted to learn new things. One of her favorite things to do was to read those 20 new words each month in *Reader's Digest* magazine. She always thought one was never too old to learn.

Did Lucy ever talk about how she wished to be remembered?

Yes, Lucy always said she'd love to be remembered for her body of work. She thought it was wonderful that anyone of any age could watch any of her shows, and they would be able to enjoy her work. Putting a smile on someone's face was the best thing that she could ask for. I also remember one time when someone asked her, "How does it feel to be an American Legend?" She answered, "I'm just proud to be an American."

Are there any other comments or anecdotes you'd like to share?

Knowing Lucy was such an honor. I didn't know it then but I do now. When I was with Lucy, we hardly discussed what she did 30 years earlier. We talked about life in the present. She wanted to know how I was doing at work or school, and about my family, my health, my friends, what I liked to do. She wanted to be an everyday type of person. I think I helped. I loved Lucy, the person.

PREFACE

Each edition of Lucy A to Z got bigger.

One begins the fourth edition of a book with some trepidation. *Lucy A to Z: The Lucille Ball Encyclopedia* was first published in 2001, the year of *I Love Lucy*'s 50th anniversary. I published it myself (well, iUniverse helped just a bit …) because I was tired of sending out manuscripts to publishers and getting them back, literally unopened, with a xeroxed message attached that read, "Sorry, we already have too many manuscripts to get through and cannot take the time to read and evaluate yours as we'd like to. Good Luck." Or sending requests to agents who invariably wrote back, "My client list is full. Good luck."

Good luck, my a—! Years ago it cost thousands of dollars to get a small, prestige print shop to produce very few copies of your book. In searching the Internet, iUniverse seemed to me to have the best package deals (and still does) of the many "Publish yourself!" companies out there. The most worthy part, to me as an author, is that iUniverse gets your book distributed by the big guns that, in turn, get you listed on Amazon, Barnes & Noble, Borders, et al. Without that Web presence these days, a book has less chance of being noticed and selling.

To my surprise and delight, the first edition of *Lucy A to Z* (a slim volume of 150 pages or so) became a best seller, at least in my eyes. Its sales remained strong enough to justify second and third editions, the latter of which was published in 2004. iUniverse noted the sales and turned it into one of its Star books, which meant a thorough re-edit and makeover for the third edition. I did a slew of radio interviews and got national publicity. It was very satisfying and told me that, clearly, I'd made the right publishing choice.

Since the first edition of *Lucy A to Z*, I've written and published three other Lucy-centric books. Therefore, I can sympathize with someone, a friend or relative for example, who might look at me—after I mentioned tackling a fourth edition of this book—as if to say, "Come on, Michael, even the subject of Lucille Ball has a limit. There's only so much to say."

Well, there was one friend who felt differently: my best friend and fellow author, Craig Hamrick, who died in September 2006. For half a year before he passed he urged me to update and redo this book. "It's your magnum opus," he said. "With the Internet and virtual publishing, you could update it every few months if you wanted to. Just take a look and see how much new information you could compile for another edition."

Honestly, the thought of going back to this particular well left me numb. Then Craig became progressively more ill and everything else in my life receded. After he died, I felt bereft and lost interest in the idea of writing anything substantial, until March of 2007, when I began to feel a bit more "normal" again. I remembered what Craig said, and that he would've wanted me to soldier on without him. Then I thought about laughter being the main thing that helped lift my depression. Lucy equals laughter.

Without even trying hard I came up with enough words to fill more than 50 new pages. And I figured since it's a new edition, let's redo the cover and the format (size) as well, literally making it a bigger book, commensurate with its subject; one that's easier to read and handle. And perhaps most important, I decided this edition would feature pictures.

So here it is. Enjoy, again. To those of you who've bought previous editions, thank you and mea culpa. If you're a Lucy completist, you'll need this, too. I promise I won't do it again....

Hmmm ... 2011 is *I Love Lucy's* 60th anniversary ...

Michael Karol
New York
Winter 2007

BREAKING NEWS! At press time, the Jamestown, New York, *Post-Journal* had reported, "Four members of the Lucille Ball-Desi Arnaz Center board of directors, including Lucie Arnaz and Desi Arnaz Jr., have left the board and have been replaced with local residents, organization officials confirmed Tuesday. Other departures include Wanda Clark, Lucille Ball's longtime personal secretary, and Mary Rapaport, a Buffalo-area resident and an active supporter of the Lucy-Desi community."

What this means is there's an internecine struggle going on within the Lucy-Desi Center board for control of the center, its activities, and its direction in the future. Lucie Arnaz, who had also served as board president, noted, "We hope to continue to work with the people of Jamestown and its beautiful surrounding community, and to be supportive of their desire to utilize the memories of Jamestown's 'first daughter' and its 'adopted son-in-law' to maximize the area's potential for revitalization and growth."

Rumors are flying, and publishing deadlines prevent me from going into details, except to note the center still plans to continue its day-to-day activities, including its two annual festivals—one over Memorial Day weekend, and one honoring Lucy's birthday in August. Visit my website, www.sitcomboy.com, for updates.

ACKNOWLEDGMENTS

Special thanks to the following for their invaluable help and support: my family; Craig Hamrick, my editor, a rock of a friend and an idea person extraordinaire (and my personal hero—I hope you're mixing it up in heaven as I write this); Judy Hill, Craig's mom, for her loving strength; copy editor Saul Fischer (the first three editions); Mark Worteck, for his friendship; actress Marie Wallace; Michael Stern; Christine W. Kitto of the Mudd Manuscript Library in Princeton, N.J.; artist and illustrator Drew Friedman; Jessica Padilla, communications associate, La Jolla Playhouse, La Jolla, Calif.; Al Hirschfeld's archivist, David Leopold; Nicholas Orzio for the information on photographer Harry Warnecke and the fabulous cover photo; Larry Gerber, editor in chief of *Emmy* magazine; artist Sonya Paz; the warm, wonderful actress Jane Connell for her valuable time; Lucy's secretary, Wanda Clark, a true gem; documentarian Garrett Boyajian for his invaluable suggestions; artist and friend Rick Carl; Howard and Ron at Photofest for all their help; Trent Clegg of Idaho State University for his biographical information on costume designer Edward Stevenson; a new friend and a helluva artist, Dave Woodman; Kelly Haigh, Teresa Barnett, and Alva Stevenson of the University of California, Los Angeles, Department of Special Collections Charles E. Young Research Library; Karen Herman of the ATAS Emmy online archive; Steven Diamond at Scholastic, Inc.; JINSA's Jim Colbert; the wonderful and extremely kind artist, Robert Risko; Lelly, for listening; and the staff and crew at The New York Public Library for the Performing Arts, at Lincoln Center, whose performer clippings and boxes of memorabilia are heaven for any entertainment fan.

To Joe Diliberto, my editor and copy editor for the Fourth Edition: my eternal gratitude for adding his expert professional touch to this book. His suggestions were invaluable, and invariably right. Joe helped me reshape, reorganize, and retool the book, all to the benefit of the reader. (And thanks also for major help with the new *Star Trek* entry.)

A shout-out to Tootsie S. for helping me to survive in a universe where "up" is "down" and "crazy" is "normal"—God bless you, Toots.

And love to Ronald White, who sometimes must feel he is living with Lucy & Co. as well as with me.

ABBREVIATIONS AND OTHER MINUTIAE

—While writing this book, I was tempted to abbreviate the name *I Love Lucy*. I resisted because Lucille Ball herself didn't like the negative connotation of its acronym, ILL.

—When someone or some*thing* has their own entry elsewhere, it is underlined within the text. For example, if you come across this while reading—See <u>Ball, Lucille</u>.—that means there is further information under the biography entry <u>Ball, Lucille</u>.

—A date after an episode title in quotes indicates the original airdate of that episode.

INTRODUCTION

INTRODUCTION TO THE 4TH EDITION

Lucy A to Z began as an outgrowth of my fondness (some might say obsession) for all things Lucille Ball. In April 1996 I set up a website (www.sitcomboy.com) to rant and rave about the media. At the start, one page was a Lucy tribute. This page proved to be the most popular part of the site, and after a year or so I restructured it to make my Lucille Ball tribute the site's main focus. After writing online about her for several years, I realized I had enough material to put together a book.

But I needed a unique perspective and a format that would differ from the traditional biographies that had already been published. I realized one thing Lucy fans have in common is a thirst for knowledge about Lucille Ball. My late friend, author Craig Hamrick, thought an encyclopedia might satisfy that thirst. I received a lovely letter from Lucie Arnaz calling the first edition of *Lucy A to Z* a "godsend" in helping her prepare for the *I Love Lucy 50th Anniversary Special* in 2001. In fact, *Lucy A to Z* made a cameo appearance in the special, during a segment chronicling Lucy memorabilia and collectibles—it was prominently displayed in a bookstore window.

For the Second Edition, published in June 2002, I spent more than a year doing research on the lives and careers of Lucille Ball, Desi Arnaz, Vivian Vance, and William Frawley, much of it at The New York Public Library for the Performing Arts. The result was a book more than twice as long as the original.

It subsequently became an iUniverse Star book (their best-seller designation). The Third Edition of *Lucy A to Z*, published in 2004, was rigorously re-edited and redesigned. All entries about Lucille Ball other than her biography were placed in the regular alphabetical listings, for example.

For this Fourth Edition … well, for my thoughts on it, see the Preface.

As an author, it has been a joy to watch the public embrace *Lucy A to Z*. It has enabled me to travel and meet people, including celebrities and behind-the-scenes folk in the Lucy universe, which have become treasured experiences for me.

Life is ever changing, but one constant is the public's interest in Lucille Ball's career—going strong for more than 50 years—and its fascination with her landmark show *I Love Lucy*. If anything, it has grown since her death in 1989. There is continued interest in collecting anything Lucy-related and it shows no signs of abating.

Three years ago, I wrote that "Lucille Ball is a part of so many of our lives most of us can't picture a world without her." Given the current fractious state of our world, Lucy's legacy on film, video, and now DVD becomes even more important. This book is a valentine, from one Lucy fan to many others. I hope you'll find yourself smiling as you read about the life of our favorite redhead. After all, what we're really celebrating when we celebrate Lucy is the gift of laughter.

—Michael Karol

A

ACTORS WHO PLAYED LUCILLE BALL

Ai Yai Yai! A rumor seems to surface every so often: Some major or minor Hollywood star is just dying to play Lucille Ball in a movie or on TV. Some years ago we heard these yearnings from Tea Leoni. (And whatever happened to her?) In 1999, the *Pretty Woman* herself, Julia Roberts, was "hinting to the press that she's hot to star in a movie based on the life of beloved carrot-top comedienne Lucille Ball." *Movieline* (now *Hollywood Life*) magazine's gossip columnist Murgatroyd reported this, and referred to any "Life of Lucy" project as "a daunting proposition for even the most skilled actor." The columnist added that, to play Lucy's loving, brilliant-but-flawed Latin hubby Desi Arnaz, Roberts wanted her beau (at the time), Latin heartthrob Benjamin Bratt. Everyone from Antonio Banderas and Lou Diamond Phillips, to Jim Carrey and Johnny Depp had reportedly been mentioned for the role.

While Roberts, like many, may have dreamed of playing the role of Lucille Ball, it appears to have been merely a rumor. In reality, few have ventured into that difficult territory. Most who have, have played the farcical Lucy Ricardo character, with mixed results. They are arranged by date of performance.

Constance Ford, as Hildy Jones in *Nobody Loves an Albatross*, Broadway, 1963
Ford played a female television executive who was also a beloved star with her own hit series in this

Many have tried, but few actresses have even come close to capturing the mix of beauty and comic perfection that was Lucille Ball.
Photofest

1

now-forgotten play about the TV industry and Lucille Ball. It was written by Ronald Alexander, who'd worked at Desilu several years earlier. For the whole story, see <u>Nobody Loves an Albatross</u>.

Gilda Radner, *Saturday Night Live*, 1976
When Desi Arnaz hosted the show to promote his autobiography, *A Book* (1974), Radner played Lucy in a funny, over-the-top sketch combining *I Love Lucy* with the violent Desilu hit *The Untouchables*. As you might imagine, there were lots of "Waaaaaaahhhhhhs!" and machine-gun volleys. Radner also played Lucy in an *SNL* interview sketch in which she charged, smoking and gravelly voiced, "Desi was a bum."

Lucille Ball, *Here's Lucy*, "Lucy Carter Meets Lucille Ball," March 4, 1974
This surreal episode had Lucy's character, Lucy Carter, meeting "star" Lucille Ball. Daughter Kim (Lucie Arnaz) enters a Lucille Ball look-alike contest and when she doesn't make the finals, her mother (Lucy Carter) appeals to Lucille Ball via split screen. Confused? The episode is not as fun as it sounds. The "Lucille Ball" character was decked out in *Mame* drag, and the episode was one long promotion for the movie.

Gypsi DeYoung, *The Scarlett O'Hara War*, 1980
DeYoung played Lucille Ball in a recreation of the search for the actress to play Scarlett O'Hara in the 1939 blockbuster *Gone With the Wind*. The legend is that Lucy was so nervous while auditioning for producer David O. Selznick that she did the entire screen test on her knees and did not realize it until she was through.

Catherine O'Hara, *Christmas with SCTV*, 1982
O'Hara, the fabulously talented mimic and comic actress, played Lucy as a talk-show guest in one of *SCTV*'s notorious "let's trash celebrity" romps on this 90-minute special. The "talk show" was cheesy kid-show host Count Floyd's (Joe Flaherty, doing his worst Dracula imitation, on purpose) Christmas special. Wearing a typical red *Lucy Show/Here's Lucy* wig, O'Hara affected a gravelly voice and croaked out the title song from Lucy's *Mame*. It was a riot.

Jane Curtin, *Kate & Allie*, "Reruns," March 2, 1987
Allie (Curtin) dreams she and roommate Kate (Susan Saint James) are the lead characters on *I Love Lucy*, with Saint James doing an affectionate tribute to Vivian Vance as Ethel Mertz.

Frances Fisher, *Lucy & Desi: Before the Laughter*, February 1991
Fisher looked amazingly like Lucille Ball in some of the scenes of this poorly done television movie, purporting to tell the "real story" of Ball and Arnaz's relationship. With Maurice Benard as a pale imitation of Arnaz, most critics (including me) found this a tacky effort, full of holes. Lucie Arnaz protested publicly when it first aired.

Roseanne Barr, as Lucy Ricardo, *TV Guide*, January 4, 1992
On the cover of this issue, Roseanne, at the height of her show's popularity, decked herself out in a red wig and makeup as Lucy, while the cover line asked: "Is Roseanne the new Lucy? Not since the '50s has one woman so dominated television." Roseanne didn't really look much like Ball, and I believe we can now safely answer that question: No.

   TV Guide returned to this well for its final digest-sized issue, dated October 9-16, 2006. It recreated eight of the magazine's most iconic covers, including country music and sitcom star **Reba McEntire** in Italian peasant dress stomping away in a grape press, mimicking a Lucy cover from 2001. Consider it an affectionate tribute, since McEntire has never expressed a desire to be the next Lucy.

Tress MacNeille, as Lucille McGillicuddy Ricardo Carmichael, *The Simpsons*, January 9, 2000
This animated character turns up on the episode "Little Big Mom" to help Lisa Simpson curb the rowdy behavior of brother Bart and father Homer while mother Marge is incapacitated with a broken leg. The "ghost" of Lucy shows up and suggests some mischief to keep them in line. MacNeille, one of *The Simpsons*' voice regulars, played a raspy-sounding Lucy. See *The Simpsons*.

Nicole Sullivan, *Mad TV*, "I Love Lucy 2000/2001," 2000 and 2001
Sullivan played "Lucy Ricardo" more than once on this outrageous sketch show, which wrung laughs out of the *I Love Lucy* foursome by placing them in incongruous setups with echoes of the original plots, e.g., Lucy and Ethel packing drugs instead of chocolate on an assembly line.

Laura Prepon, *That '70s Show*, May 1, 2001
In this episode of the series chronicling the lives of a group of teens in the groovy 1970s, Latin American exchange student Fez (Wilmer Valderrama) dreams that he's married to redheaded

Donna (Prepon) and their life is one wacky *I Love Lucy* episode. Donna's real boyfriend's parents, Kitty (Debra Jo Rupp) and Red (Kurtwood Smith), play the Mertzes. Prepon is game and had long red hair, but she's no Lucille Ball.

Many Actresses/One Actor, *Rat Race*, Summer 2001
This parody of treasure-hunting movies owed a great deal to the classic *It's a Mad, Mad, Mad, Mad World* (1963). Among the fortune hunters sent on a chase from Las Vegas to Silver City after $2 million is Cuba Gooding Jr. as a football referee. Gooding ends up piloting a busload of Lucille Ball look-alikes. See *Rat Race*.

Debra Messing, as Lucille Ball in *Entertainment Weekly*, October 5, 2001
Messing, star of the hit series *Will & Grace*, appeared on the cover of the magazine's celebrity photo issue with sitcom partner Eric McCormack. Inside, they were photographed as famous duos, including Lucille Ball and Desi Arnaz. Emmy-winner Messing, who has a knack for physical comedy, has often been called "the new Lucy" and compared favorably to her. So why hasn't anyone cast her as Lucy?

Suzanne LaRusch, Lucille Ball impersonator at various events and television programs
LaRusch lovingly, if sometimes a bit over the top, "played" Lucy Ricardo at such events as the "Loving Lucy" convention in Burbank, California, Universal Studios, and during the Home Shopping Network's special hour-long tribute to Lucille Ball merchandise on October 15, 2001. In the summer of 2007, she was voted fourth runner-up on the ABC reality series *The Next Best Thing: Who Is the Greatest Celebrity Impersonator?*

Rachel York, *Lucy*, CBS TV movie, May 4, 2003
The Broadway and soap actress tried gamely, but neither she nor Danny Pino, who played Desi/Ricky, were up to the task of re-creating TV's best-known stars. Not quite as bad as *Lucy & Desi: Before the Laughter* (see Frances Fisher above), but only because its heart is in the right place. (See *Lucy* for a full review.)

Eva Longoria, as Lucy Ricardo on *Saturday Night Live*, Nov. 19, 2006
In a sketch, the "Vincent Price Thanksgiving Special: 1958," Longoria, of *Desperate Housewives* fame, played a different sort of housewife. Broadcast in glorious black and white, "Price" introduced his celebrity guests, including "Alfred Hitchcock," "Judy Garland," "Clark Gable," and

America's "favorite illegal alien, Desi Arnaz [played nicely by Fred Armisen] and his lovely wife, Lucille Ball [Longoria]." Desi launched into a Cuban Thanksgiving song (!), forbidding Lucy to sing with him; of course, Lucy sang a few bars anyway, and then started crying when Desi shushed her. Give Longoria a 10 for effort, but a five overall; her performance consisted of being loud and whiny; certainly qualities the real Lucy gave Lucy Ricardo, but without any of the warmth.

See also Vincent, Diane.

ADDRESSES

The places Lucille Ball lived included:

*1344 North Ogden Drive, Hollywood, California. Lucille Ball's first Los Angeles home.
*19700 Devonshire Drive, Chatsworth, California. Otherwise known as the Desilu Ranch.
*1000 North Roxbury Drive, Beverly Hills, California. Lucy and Desi, weary of the 35-mile drive back and forth to the studio, moved here with the kids in 1955 and sold their beloved ranch to actress Jane Withers.
*Thunderbird Golf Club, 40-241 Club View Drive, Rancho Mirage, California. Lucy and Desi built a home here on the 17th fairway in the mid-1950s.
*Snowmass, Colorado. Lucy bought three condos here in 1970 after she took up skiing.
*East 69th Street, The Imperial House, New York. Lucy rented two apartments here in 1960 after divorcing Desi and signing on for the Broadway show *Wildcat*.

ADVERTISEMENTS FEATURING LUCILLE BALL

Lucy was featured in many advertisements besides the on-air pitches she and Desi did during the run of *I Love Lucy*. This list is meant to be representative of the kind of pitchwoman Lucy was, not all-inclusive. For example, Lucy appeared in ads throughout her film career for her many movies. Unless otherwise noted, these are print ads.

- ◆ Royal Desserts, 1940
- ◆ Shinola Lotion White shoe cleaner, 1942
- ◆ Woodbury Powder, "color controlled," 1943
- ◆ Max Factor Pan-Cake makeup, 1944
- ◆ Jergens Lotion, 1945

- Woodbury Film Finish face powder, 1945
- Max Factor lipstick, 1947
- Roma Wine, 1948
- A·S·R Lighter: "ASR carries the torch for me," 1949
- Chesterfield Cigarettes: "They're milder, much milder. It's my cigarette," 1949
- LaFrance Bluing Flakes & Scatter Pins, 1949
- Lux Toilet Soap: "Used by 9 out of 10 film stars," 1949
- SealRight Ice Cream, 1949
- SealRight Milk, 1949
- Summerettes Shoes: "Bright Colors Afoot," 1949
- Hoover Aero-Dyne vacuum, 1950
- La Crosse Manicure Instruments (also plugs the movie *Fancy Pants*), 1950
- Royal Crown Cola, 1950s
- Carling's Red Cap Ale, 1951: Lucy in graduation cap topped with velvet Carling's Red Cap
- Carling's Ale, 1951
- Easterling Sterling, 1951
- Woodbury Cold Cream, 1951
- General Electric Ultra Vision TV series, 1952
- Auto-Lite Sta-Ful car batteries, December: "Am I really Lucille Ball? Batteries also look alike," 1952
- Philip Morris cigarettes, 1952-'53
- Western-Union Bunnygrams, kids/Easter promo: Lucy is shown with Richard Keith (aka Keith Thibodeaux), Little Ricky on *I Love Lucy*, 1957
- Owens-Corning Fiberglas Curtains & Draperies: "No sun rot," circa 1960
- Kroger Foods: In support of Lucy's and Bob Hope's 1960 film *The Facts of Life*, Kroger Foods published a four-color, seven-page ad supplement featuring Ball, Hope, and their

co-stars Don DeFore and Ruth Hussey preparing a "Fun Feast" using all Kroger brands, like Star-Kist tuna and Royal Crown Cola, 1960

♦ CBS Radio *Let's Talk to Lucy* promotional spots, 1964

♦ See also <u>Games</u>.

ADVERTISEMENTS FEATURING LUCILLE BALL AND DESI ARNAZ

Again, please note this list is not exhaustive.

♦ Philip Morris cigarettes, 1952-'53

♦ Philip Morris Holiday cigarette cartons, 1952

♦ General Electric Ultra Vision TV, 1952

♦ *I Love Lucy* Pajamas by Harwood, 1953

♦ Lucy & Desi present: the *I Love Lucy Baby* doll: a blond-haired doll selling for $9.98; no manufacturer prominent in ad, 1953

♦ Nursery items, 1953

♦ In a 1954 Newsreel, Lucy and Desi, in a living room setting, spoke of the urgency surrounding the need for funding the polio inoculations.

♦ New Moon Mobile Apartment Homes, in conjunction with Lucy and Desi's film *The Long, Long Trailer,* 1954

♦ Bigelow Carpets: "We're mighty proud of our beautiful Bigelow carpets," 1955

♦ Window shutters, in *House Beautiful*, April 1955

♦ Dodge, 1956

♦ Allen Karpet-Squares, with photo of "magnificent 'New' Desi Arnaz Western Hills Hotel, Indio, California," 1957

♦ Allen Rubber-Top carpet cushion, 1957

♦ Illustrated faces on cover of "Pocket Encyclopedia of Alaska (the 49th State), Your reminder of Westinghouse Lucy-Desi Wonderama Days," 1959

♦ Apple Computer: "Think Different" campaign, print ads and billboards, 1990

- ◆ *The Nuevo Herald/The Miami Herald* used a headshot of Lucy and Desi with the tagline, "In half the households in Miami, she's the one with the funny accent," to target the Spanish-speaking market, 1995
- ◆ U.S. Postal Service, print ads and billboards featuring the Lucille Ball/Desi Arnaz 1950s-era stamp from its Celebrate the Century series, 1999. See U.S. Postage Stamps.

ADVERTISING ICONS

The May 24, 1999 issue of *Advertising Age* offered a thought-provoking column, illustrated with Lucille Ball and Desi Arnaz: "Virtual Ads, Real Problems." The cartoon showed Lucy and Desi hawking products not available when they were alive. *Ad Age* was not one of the first places I'd look to find Lucy and Desi, but this is a perfect example of how one is likely to find Lucy almost anywhere. Indeed, with the prolific licensing of characters and stars that have become icons, *Ad Age* may be the perfect place to find the *I Love Lucy* crew. (I'm thinking of the 1990s Apple Computer "Think Different" campaign, which featured huge billboards of Lucy and Desi in a famous profile kiss.)

The *Ad Age* column concerned a new trend that was brewing (which, thankfully, hasn't happened yet) called virtual product placement. Thanks to the same digital technology that brings you films like *Star Wars*, *The Matrix* movies, and 3-D video games, the ad industry was talking about inserting a modern product into a syndicated show. Syndicators, according to the column, were "intrigued" with the idea of being able to sell a product over and over, and even replace it with a different product over time. There would be much to iron out, including what might happen if a product placed in a show competes with one of the show's paid advertisers, for example.

But leaving that issue behind, it's no coincidence that Lucy and Desi were chosen to illustrate the article. Imagine Desi popping Advil or Lucy with a Diet Pepsi in her hand (as illustrated). It's a powerful acknowledgment of Lucy and Desi as highly recognized (and the most frequently aired) icons of syndicated TV. They, and the characters they created, make the point, easily, without encumbrance, and they're much beloved.

AGING GRACEFULLY

Much has been made of Lucy's increasingly haggard appearance as she aged, especially post-*Here's Lucy* (1974). Those close to her maintain that her fair skin, which bruised easily, could not suffer plastic surgery. (Though it is noted in the 2003 biography *Ball of Fire* that Lucy did have an eye job, and spent one year concealing the redness as it healed with heavy makeup.) Add to that the raucous shenanigans of her 25 years in television, a 56-year career that included more than 80 films, Broadway, radio, and decades of smoking, and Lucy's wrinkles become badges of honor.

Another complication was that Lucy was 40 years old when she began *I Love Lucy*, but during the entire decade of the 1950s, she appeared easily 10 years younger on camera and in photos. It was destined to catch up with her. Unfortunately, fans only wanted to see her as Lucy Ricardo, or perhaps Lucy Carmichael.

Lucy, however, was very conscious of this. Perhaps that explains the lengths she allowed makeup and craftspeople to go in disguising the ravages of time in *Mame* (1974), a ploy that backfired. She was occasionally shot in such soft focus that it detracted from the film itself, making it difficult to watch, and became the focus, so to speak, of many negative reviews.

New York Daily News columnist George Rush described one of Lucy's hide-the-wrinkles techniques in 1994: "Convinced her fans didn't want to see her age, Lucy ironed out her wrinkles with a headache-inducing skull-fracture bandage, hidden under an orange wig."

In real life, Lucy kept her distance from fans in public as she aged. Photographers (and film cameramen) were directed to stay a certain distance from her before shooting, not to shoot any close-ups, and so on. What did Lucy *really* look like toward the end of her life? Here's an account from *The Village Voice*'s Guy Trebay, who attended one of her New York Museum of Television and Radio (now known as The Paley Center for Media) seminars on May 1, 1984, five years before Lucy died.

"Photographers attending an earlier press conference had been required to distance themselves 60 feet from the stage, a situation that inconvenienced them to the extent that they uncased their telephoto lenses. In pictures taken that day, she doesn't fare well, but no worse than any 72-year-old woman could expect to, whose face has been subjected to a lifetime of harsh lights, putty, Pan-Cake, and cream pies.

"The heavily lined forehead and cheeks are nonetheless taut. Her hair is a gentle tousle of pale red curls. Most charming is the theatrical stencil of her overarched brows and the famous lip line.... Her profound gift for mime is naturally aided by a latex-expressive face and large eyes. Her upper lip, though, is small, with a delicately old-fashioned sweetheart bow. The crimson inner tube she paints over it is pure circus."

(Note that Lucy shaved her eyebrows for an early career assignment and they never grew back; she drew them on every day thereafter.)

ALL IN THE FAMILY

In 1976, Lucille Ball was asked how she felt television had changed since the 1950s. She responded: "I don't really know that much about how television has changed; it's just that there's a helluva lot more competition. It shocked me a bit when *All in the Family* was first shown. Not from its content, only from its introduction of some words back into our vocabulary that should have been forgotten."

ALLYSON, JUNE

A perky, diminutive, blonde musical-comedy star whose husky voice and girl-next-door persona made her popular in the 1940s. She overcame several years of being confined in a steel brace (after a childhood accident) by exhaustive swimming and dancing lessons. The latter especially proved a boon to her career. Married from 1945 until his death in 1963 to fellow actor, crooner, and director Dick Powell, Allyson appeared in three of Lucy's MGM movies: *Best Foot Forward* (1943), *Thousands Cheer* (1943), and *Meet the People* (1944), the last also starring her husband (see Film Career). She curbed her career following Powell's death, and was largely inactive after the late 1970s, except for hosting a segment of the compilation film *That's Entertainment III* (1994). Allyson died on July 8, 2006, of respiratory problems, at the age of 88.

AMERICAN FILM INSTITUTE *DIALOGUE ON FILM*

Just before Lucille Ball ended her weekly TV series *Here's Lucy* in 1974, she participated in the American Film Institute seminar series. On January 18, 1974, Ball answered questions, aided by her husband Gary Morton and publicist Howard McClay. The AFI, as it did with all such Q&A sessions, printed a transcript as part of its *Dialogue on Film* series, dated May-June 1974. The 20-plus page document reveals much about many aspects of Lucy's career, particularly her views on comedy; her film career and why she actually *wanted* to be typecast; how she shot her television series and why she was perceived by some as an "ogre"; why *I Love Lucy* was an international success; her work ethic; the "Lucy" character; running Desilu Studios; being a woman in "the business"; predicting the success of a sitcom; and much, much more. The AFI, in making the transcript, got some of the facts wrong (they have Lucy saying she's from "Jenkinstown, New York," as opposed to Jamestown), but overall, this is highly recommended reading. See The Quotable Lucy for some gems.

ANDES, KEITH

Lucille Ball's handsome co-star on TV (*The Lucy Show*) and Broadway (*Wildcat;* see <u>Stage Career</u>), Andes was an actor with classic movie-star looks who said playing Marilyn Monroe's leading man in the 1952 film *Clash by Night* was a highlight of his 30-year career. He died on November 11, 2005, at the age of 85. The Los Angeles County coroner's office ruled the death suicide by asphyxiation. Andes, who had been fighting bladder cancer and several other ailments, was found dead in his Santa Clarita, California home, said Marshall LaPlante, a longtime friend.

Though Andes rarely spoke about his career, the walls of his apartment were lined with memorabilia, according to his *Los Angeles Times* obit, including an album cover from *Wildcat*, the 1960 Broadway musical in which he played Joe Dynamite, opposite Lucille Ball. A framed, handwritten note from Ball alludes to their sharing close quarters onstage: "I ate onions, ha-ha, love, Lucy." Lucy liked the tall, blond actor with the booming voice; on four episodes of *The Lucy Show*, he played Lucy Carmichael's rugged boyfriend/date.

Everyone "always, always, always" asked about Andes' friendship with Monroe, said Ryan Andes, his grandson. "There was always a murmur about them having a relationship, but he said that wasn't the case." A friend who was the UCLA valedictorian in the mid-1950s asked Andes if he could get Monroe to attend the graduation reception. She agreed—only if Andes would go as her date, his grandson recalled.

Andes came to Hollywood after studio head Darryl F. Zanuck saw the understudy perform in the Broadway production of *Winged Victory* and offered him a minor part in the 1944 film version. After World War II, he appeared on Broadway in *The Chocolate Soldier*—earning the Theatre World Award for the outstanding breakout performance of 1947—and later starred in *Kiss Me, Kate*. Andes went on to appear in about 20 movies, including playing one of the brothers in 1947's *The Farmer's Daughter* and Gen. George C. Marshall in the 1970 block-buster *Tora! Tora! Tora!*.

On television I recall him as Glynis Johns' improbably studly husband on the short-lived 1963 Desilu sitcom *Glynis*; as the original voice of Harvey Birdman, a cartoon hilariously updated for the Cartoon Network's Adult Swim programming block; and as the sexy alien, Akuta, on an episode of the original *Star Trek*, "The Apple," fondly remembered by fans for its "space hippies." He also made guest appearances on more than 40 shows, many of them Westerns.

Andes bought a house in the 1950s and kept Arabian horses on a three-acre ranch in Chatsworth, which then was considered far from Hollywood. Lucy and Desi Arnaz lived there for more than a decade before relocating to Beverly Hills in the mid-1950s. In addition to his grandson, the twice-divorced Andes was survived by his son, Mark, an original member of the rock bands Canned Heat and Spirit, and another son, Matt.

AR SOUND

These two letters found themselves into the name of every Lucille Ball sitcom character—Lucy Ricardo (*I Love Lucy*), *The Lucy Show* (Lucy Carmichael), *Here's Lucy* (Lucy Carter), and *Life with Lucy* (Lucy Barker)—because Lucille Ball believed they were good luck for her. They were also, of course, in her first husband's last name and in mentor Carole Lombard's first and last names.

ARDEN, EVE

A popular, wisecracking supporting player in movies beginning in the 1930s, Arden found lasting fame on radio and TV in the 1940s and 1950s with the sitcom *Our Miss Brooks*. Arden's sardonic delivery led to success in all the major media and she even co-starred with Ball, a similar "type," in several early films (*Stage Door* [1937] and *Having Wonderful Time* [1938]). Ball referred to them both as the "drop-gag" girls, meaning that the types of characters they'd play in movies would walk into a scene, drop a gag, and exit.

Arden found success (and an Oscar nomination for *Mildred Pierce* in 1945) in more prestige pictures as a supporting player, whereas Ball was a star player in many "B" movies. An accomplished stage and musical performer as well, Arden appeared with Vivian Vance in the hit musical *Let's Face It* on Broadway in the 1940s (and appeared in the film version, though Vance was too little known at the time to repeat her role).

In another interesting career intersection, Arden played Vance's signature role of Olive Lashbrooke in the movie version of *The Voice of the Turtle* (1947). It was in this role, on stage, that Vance was "discovered" by Desi Arnaz, Marc Daniels, and Jess Oppenheimer. (See entries for each.) Arden chose to take her popular radio show *Our Miss Brooks* to Desilu when it moved to TV. The role of teacher Connie Brooks brought Arden increased fame and success (and an Emmy award). She repaid Ball by doing a cameo in the well-remembered "L.A. At Last!" episode of *I Love Lucy*, in which Lucy and Ethel, lunching at The Brown Derby, scope out the stars' caricatures and confuse Arden's with Judy Holliday's. Arden dryly sets them straight. (Lucy then goes on to memorably interrupt William Holden's lunch.)

Arden acted in films through the 1980s, and also did a two-year stint for Arnaz as the star of his late-sixties sitcom *The Mothers-in-Law* (1967-'69). She is perhaps best remembered in the latter arc of her career for her wry turn as the principal in the film version of *Grease* (1978). Arden died in 1990.

ARNAZ, DESI

Birth name: Desiderio Alberto Arnaz y de Acha III
Born: March 2, 1917, Santiago, Cuba
Died: December 2, 1986, Del Mar, California (of lung cancer)
Cremated, ashes scattered.

Desi Arnaz. Photofest

Arnaz was Lucille Ball's first husband, a Cuban refugee who popularized the Conga line in America and then swept a soon-to-be-legendary redhead off her feet. In fact, his contribution to her legend is inestimable. His wealthy, privileged youth (dad was mayor of Santiago, mom was heiress to the Bacardi rum fortune) ended during the Batista revolution in 1933, and a teenaged Arnaz fled to Florida with his mother (his father came later). He cleaned birdcages for a while to make spare change, and eventually put together a band. This won the attention of Xavier Cugat, the reigning king of Latin music, who hired him. Arnaz's performing bug led him to strike out on his own, and using his mentor's name in the band (for a fee), Arnaz eventually made it to New York City, where he was a smash.

Legendary Broadway producer George Abbott saw his act and hired him to play a supporting role in the Broadway show *Too Many Girls* (1939). Arnaz parlayed the role into a ticket to Hollywood, where he repeated the role in the film version and fell in love with the star of the picture, Lucille Ball. They married in 1940, but their separate work and his army service during World War II kept them apart more often than they were together. That, plus Arnaz's reputation as a Latin lover, kept Lucy anxious through much of the first decade of their marriage.

Reports like this from UPI in September 1940, months before Lucy and Desi wed, didn't help: "Since Desi Arnaz arrived in Hollywood, half the feminine hearts have been turning flip-flops, much to the embarrassment of the handsome Cuban. Arnaz is the Cuban conga king who made a hit on Broadway in *Too Many Girls*, and is currently playing the same role in the screen version at RKO.

"Arnaz isn't a woman hater, but when strange, beautiful girls slip him notes reading 'I think you're wonderful, I love you,' he is embarrassed." The article notes that Arnaz dated Ann Miller, Gene Tierney, Betty Grable and others when he first hit Hollywood, but was now exclusively dating Lucille Ball, his *Girls* leading lady ... "though they both deny any romance exists." Arnaz was said to especially hate being called "glamorous.... He doesn't want to be compared to any Latin screen favorite of the past, but wants to succeed on his own merits merely as Desi Arnaz." Which, of course, he did, eventually. But not before suffering through seven feature films and several shorts that presented him mostly as an exotic ethnic type.

Lucy eventually helped Arnaz and his band land a steady gig as Bob Hope's radio orchestra, with a bonus: finally, they were both based in Hollywood. At this time, Lucy began thinking of projects they could do together, eventually homing in on a television version of her successful radio show, *My Favorite Husband.*

CBS balked at Arnaz being cast as her husband; no one would believe it, executives thought. A Cuban who mangled his English and a redheaded all-American gal? To prove people accepted them as a couple, Lucy and Desi put together a vaudeville act in 1950 and toured the country to much acclaim. CBS executives finally relented, agreeing that Arnaz might be acceptable as Lucy's TV husband. A pilot was shot, an advertiser found, and the show was on its way, except ...

Ball and Arnaz insisted on filming the show and performing it before a live audience, necessitating a much higher cost-per-episode than the normal, kinescoped show of the day. CBS agreed on both counts, as long as the Arnazes paid the difference, which they did. Desi and Lucy ended up owning what Lucy had figured might be, at worst, a year's worth of "home movies." The rerun was effectively invented, thanks to the superior quality of the filmed episodes (kinescopes, shot off a television monitor, tended to deteriorate after time).

Arnaz proved to be a genius at TV production. He hired the best people, like cinematographer Karl Freund, who perfected a special three-camera technique to film three separate angles of an episode at the same time, as Arnaz wanted (a long shot, medium shot, and close-ups); the three films were spliced together from the best takes. Freund also figured out how to uniformly light the show's set. Arnaz wanted a studio audience because he knew from the audience response at her radio show that was how Lucy responded best as a performer: to live feedback. Special bleachers were built, and the show became one of the hottest tickets in town. Arnaz was also renowned as a top "script doctor"—he knew what worked and what didn't—and not just for situation comedy.

Arnaz's adept business sense did not, unfortunately, extend to his private life. After the phenomenal run of *I Love Lucy* and the explosive growth of Desilu Studios, Arnaz's drinking and womanizing caught up with him. Ball divorced him (in 1960, a month before filming their final scenes as the Ricardos) and the duo went their separate ways—at least, as separate as the co-owners of a major Hollywood studio could be. Arnaz settled down to making sparse public appearances and following racehorses with pals like Jimmy Durante.

Still, Lucy was never far from his mind, as this 1962 report by Lloyd Shearer notes: "One morning this past summer when Lucille Ball reported for work on the new *Lucy Show*, ex-husband Desi Arnaz (president of Desilu, which is producing the show) was on hand with good-luck greetings, a friendly cheek-kiss, and the gift of a small, costly four-leaf clover made of antique emerald jade. Desi seemed his usual cheery, jaunty self, wishing aloud in his Cuban-American accent that 'this new show does as well as *I Love Lucy* … which he and Lucille sold to CBS in 1958 for $6 million."

Desi told reporter Shearer that he missed being with his family the most since his divorce from Ball: "A funny thing. I do not have the image of being a family man. The public does not think of me as a homebody. I don't really know what the public image is. I guess they think I am a 45-year-old playboy or bongo beater, or Lucy's husband Ricky, or somethin'. But the truth is I am a family man, and I love the family life.

"Lucy and I—we have two of the most wonderful children, a boy and a girl, and they spend the whole summer with me at Del Mar, and that makes me very happy. I think what I miss most is the home life—a wife and children around most of the time."

The man who was the "I" in *I Love Lucy* and helped transform television into the industry we know today had a much less publicized life after the sitcom went off the air. Arnaz eschewed most TV work after he and Ball separated, although he was the producer for the first year of *The Lucy Show*, until Ball installed her second husband, Gary Morton, in his place.

Arnaz remarried (to Edith Hirsch, another redhead). Hirsch had just been divorced herself, from Clement Hirsch, a millionaire who owned a racing stable and a successful dog food business, among other companies. In 1977, while promoting his autobiography, he told reporter Marian Christy of the Mansfield, Ohio *News Journal*, "I knew Edie when she was this gorgeous cigarette girl. Gorgeous! Stacked! I tried everything to land her. Every trick. It didn't work. She married Hirsch. Then I met Lucy, loved her and married her. Finally, when Edie and I got together, I said, 'Honey, darlin', you're a fool. You could have had me when I was young and handsome.'"

"The man talks as if he and Lucy are still in love," Christy wrote. "He talks as if he and Edie are still in love. He says Lucy and Edie are friends, play cards together, and the three of them are more 'like family' than anything remotely connected to the eternal triangle. Well, for heaven's sake, why did he and Lucy split?" she finally asked.

Arnaz's reply: "Desilu got to be such a big business. There was too much togetherness. It was a seven-day workweek. Little things that didn't matter became big things." He was mainly content to stay at his Del Mar ranch and play the horses. Eventually, he sold his share of Desilu to Ball (who, in 1967, sold it to Paramount for $17 million).

Arnaz briefly returned to TV from 1967 to 1969 for two seasons as the producer (and occasional guest star, as bullfighter Rafael Del Gado) of *The Mothers-in-Law*, a lukewarm sitcom obviously patterned after *I Love Lucy* (but then, weren't most of them?) in its interplay between two married couples. But the only reason to watch was the comic chemistry between stars Eve Arden and Kaye Ballard. He also guest-starred occasionally on shows like *The Kraft Music Hall* and *The Tonight Show*, and even took a rare dramatic role when offered (*The Virginian*, *Ironside*).

He memorably hosted *Saturday Night Live* with the original cast (and son Desi Jr.); Gilda Radner played Lucy in one funny sketch that melded *I Love Lucy* and *The Untouchables*, another Desilu show; Desi Jr. joined his dad in a huge conga line around the studio. His final sitcom appearance was *Alice* in 1976, as Paco in an episode called "The Cuban Connection." *Lucy* scribes Madelyn Pugh Davis and Bob Carroll Jr. produced the show.

Arnaz also found time to write a best-selling autobiography, called simply *A Book*.

In his 60th year, decades of drinking, carousing, and smoking cigars had already done their part to make Arnaz look like a shell of his former robust self. The *News Journal's* Christy was so taken aback by Arnaz's appearance she led her May 24, 1977 article about *A Book* with these gasping, short sentences:

"It can't be Desi Arnaz. My God, it is. An old battered hat. A smelly cigar. Obviously false teeth. A liquid lunch of ice-cold beer. Period. Runny nose. Hard of hearing. ('What darlin'?' he asks of perfectly audible questions.)" After the initial shock, she continues: "Arnaz, who alternately grins and pouts, clearly loves an audience. He's 'on' all the time." Desi got a $125,000 advance for writing his autobiography. When he told his children he'd have to tell all about their parent's famous divorce, "They said I should tell it like it is," he noted.

If there was any doubt Desi still loved Lucy, he erased it in this interview. He told Christy he still carries a torch for the redhead: "We talk to each other on the telephone often. On my 60th birthday, she sent me a present." Pause. "Jeez, that's a big one. Six-O. Wow! I send Lucy flowers on our anniversary. Even though we're divorced, she gets 'em every year. I still love Lucy. Yes. Very much." He told Christy that in his two big romances, Lucy and Edie, he had regrets, regrets he'd "rather not specify. Just say in some areas I goofed. Really goofed."

In December 1981 he made brief headlines after being hospitalized in La Jolla, California. Edie said he was suffering from diverticulitis, an intestinal problem for which he'd undergone surgery four times from 1969 to 1970. This was not an unusual illness for someone of his age, 64.

His last film role was as a mayor with a problem son (Raul Julia) in *The Escape Artist* (1982). Interviewed to publicize the movie by AP's Bob Thomas, Arnaz said it was doubtful he'd "return to television, especially with the retirement of 'our last friend,' William S. Paley, CBS founder and chairman. I love the business, and I may make a tour with my band. We had a reunion in March [1982] at the Orange Bowl for Cuban refugee relief, and forty thousand people were there. I had a terrific time."

At this point in his life, Arnaz had some time to enjoy his family, including grandchildren from Lucie Arnaz. The Emmy-winning documentary Lucie made, *Lucy & Desi: A Home Movie*, poignantly shows Ball and Arnaz swimming with their grandchildren and bantering like their divorce never happened. He tried to undo some of the physical damage the years of drinking and partying had caused by quitting, but it was too little, too late. His beloved Cuban cigars, coupled with all his excess drinking over the years, were what finally did him in; he died of lung cancer in 1986.

According to friends who knew Arnaz, he never got over Ball during his lifetime (and apparently, she felt the same way). They were constantly in touch, and saw each other on family occasions. Ball told Arnaz she loved him one last time via phone days before his death. After Arnaz passed away in 1986, it was then that he was acknowledged as a true television pioneer.

Arnaz was never nominated for an Emmy during his lifetime. He was posthumously inducted into the TV Academy Hall of Fame in 1992, alongside his first wife, the love of his life (one of the initial inductees, in 1986) and their fabulous brainchild, _I Love Lucy_ (inducted in 1992 with Arnaz, the only TV show thus honored to date).

Arnaz remained grateful to America for having given him opportunities he never could have found elsewhere. "When I think of the fortune I made," he reflected in 1977, "I find nothing to squawk about." He maintained he was able to succeed by following some sage advice his father had given him: "If a ship leaving New York Harbor thinks of all the storms it will meet, it will never leave New York. A man is like a ship. He must meet one wave, one storm at a time."

ACCIDENT-PRONE: A 1950 newspaper article headlined "Desi Arnaz Hurt as Waiter Drops Tray on Head" reported that Arnaz, "bandleader-husband of actress Lucille Ball, was recovering yesterday from a scalp wound suffered when a waiter dropped a tray of dishes on him at a crowded Sunset Strip nightclub. 'It wasn't anything at all,' Miss Ball explained afterward. 'Desi and I were sitting at a table with Red Skelton and his wife, near a service table. The place was very crowded, and suddenly this waiter tripped or something and spilled the tray on Desi.'

"The incident occurred at the Chanteclair Restaurant at a party following the inauguration of comedian Ed Wynn's new Hollywood television show. Many celebrities attended." Desi was escorted to Citizen's Emergency Hospital by sheriff's deputies and took three stitches in his scalp. Lucy and Desi subsequently guest-starred on Wynn's variety show.

Many years later, in 1967, it seemed he had remained accident-prone. A serious one almost sidelined him permanently. Arnaz chatted with AP reporter Cynthia Lowry on August 23, 1967, as he prepared to launch his new series, _The Mothers-in-Law_, from his home in Del Mar, California. He was recuperating "from a freak accident which almost took his life. A veranda on which he was sitting collapsed and threw him against a metal stake, puncturing his side and requiring emergency surgery."

ADVERTISEMENTS FEATURING DESI ARNAZ: The June 4, 1953 edition of *The New York Times* featured a quarter page ad showing Arnaz modeling a shirt from Browning King Fifth Avenue. In one picture, he's tying a bow tie to go with the shirt; in the other, he is tieless. The text reads: "Desi Arnaz wears the new convertible Sportshirt by Sea Island. It has a handy, detachable bow tie, which changes it from a casual to a more formal shirt. This dressy look is carried out by the white panel. Navy, charcoal, brown. Dad, too, will like this versatile and completely washable shirt."

Arnaz, announcing the sale of his thoroughbred breeding stock, placed a center spread, two-page ad in a show business trade magazine (October 9, 1968). The headline read, "Desi Arnaz Announces: 100% Sale of Corona Breeding Farm Broodmares, 2-Y-O, Yearlings, Sucklings, at private Treaty." The ad featured a headshot and message from Arnaz, a listing of the horses for sale, and information on the Corona Breeding Farm. It measured 12.25x18.5 inches.

You could also see Arnaz in movie ads spotlighting his films.

BOOKS: Arnaz wrote an autobiography, entitled *A Book*, which was a best seller when initially released in 1977. Long out of print, it was republished in 1999. Most interesting are the initial chapters detailing the Arnazes' somewhat privileged life in Cuba before the family was torn apart and forced to flee due to the Batista revolution in 1933. Including Arnaz's personal views on everything from cleaning birdcages in Miami to popularizing the conga line in America, to creating the most enduring sitcom of all time, this is must-read material on the Lucy phenomenon. Sadly, he never completed his planned sequel, tentatively titled *Another Book*.

Desi Arnaz also played in clubs around the country, many in Los Angeles. This souvenir postcard caricature was from the L.A. hot-spot Ciro's, circa the 1940s. Author's collection

CLUBS PLAYED: The following list of clubs played by Arnaz in the late 1930s/early 1940s in New York comes from newspaper clippings and advertisements of the time. It becomes apparent from the various descriptions of him that Arnaz (and any ethnic entertainer, for that matter) was sold as an "exotic" entertainer with lots of sex appeal.

*Central Park Casino, October 11, 1938, 151 East 57th Street.

*The Copacabana, 10 East 60th Street. Arnaz was a frequent entertainer here. One ad for a "late night show and rumba fiesta" referred to him as "The Town's New Dream-Boat." Tickets, which included a "full-course table d'hôte dinner," were $2.75!

Another quarter-page newspaper ad for the Copa touts Arnaz on one side and Peter Lind Hayes on the other. Both headshots have been doctored to add a Carmen Miranda-style fruit basket and large earring! One must assume it was all done in good fun. Under Arnaz's picture is the review, "One of the most likeable entertainers you've ever seen."—Lee Mortimer, *Mirror*

*La Martinique, 57 West 57th Street.

*The Versailles, 151 E. 50th Street. In the *New York Journal-American*, November 7, 1940, Louis Sobol reviewed Arnaz's performance here and noted: "The whip-like Cuban Desi Arnaz, now at the Versailles, dashes to a booth to receive a long-distance call from Lucille Ball of Hollywood.... Upon his return: 'Twenty-two minutes and she pays for all this herself—I guess we're gonna get married.'" Less than a month later, they did.

*La Conga, Broadway.

*Windsor Theater, The Bronx, November 1941: "Havana Fiesta, the greatest rumba-conga show ever assembled, with Desi Arnaz, the Ciro Romac Band, and Harry Savoy."

*Loew's State Theater, November 1941, along with the movie *Dr. Jekyll and Mr. Hyde* (the Spencer Tracy version). "A vaudeville featuring Desi Arnaz: Latin America's Romantic Singer of Songs. Señor Arnaz brings the house down with his indisputable glamour and his vibrant Latin singing and dancing."

When Arnaz was signing autographs after a Loew's matinee one day in 1940, a newspaper asked Dorothy Rogers of Brooklyn, a finalist in that night's Loew's State Starmaker Contest, what she thought of him. Roger's response: "You may quote me as saying I think he is the Oomph Boy!" Offstage noise from Desi Arnaz: "Owwwwww!"

COMEDY: In 1967, as he prepared to return to TV with *The Mothers-in-Law*, Arnaz told reporter Cynthia Lowry that, "I didn't know anything about comedy shows with gimmicks where the people take pills or live in bottles.... Comedy is where you pile one joke on top of another joke and people laugh."

CONFIDENTIAL-LY ... Arnaz and Ball, like all other big stars of the era, were not safe from the salacious (and often true) articles published in the sleazy but mesmerizing top tabloid magazine of the 1950s, *Confidential*. In August 1957, Arnaz, pictured in the *San Mateo Times* holding the *Racing Form* at the Del Mar track, said he "didn't remember" ever meeting a Hollywood prostitute who'd recently testified during the trial of *Confidential* and *Whisper* magazines that she and Arnaz had a "tryst" in 1944 and later sold the story to *Confidential*. In fact, Arnaz called her story "a lot of baloney…. I don't remember meeting the lady, and I guess I'm being kind in calling her a Lady." The "lady" placed her and Arnaz in Palm Springs for the rendezvous in October 1944, but Desi countered, "I was in the army in 1944 and I think I was somewhere up north. I don't remember being in Palm Springs. From the pictures I've seen of her I don't think I could have done anything like that."

DESI ARNAZ PRODUCTIONS: Company formed by Arnaz three years after he sold Desilu to Lucille Ball; its projects included *The Carol Channing Show, Land's End, Gussie My Girl, Brother Bertram*, and, the only pilot that sold, <u>*The Mothers-in-Law*</u>.

FBI FILE: Arnaz considered himself a friend of J. Edgar Hoover's, but that didn't stop the FBI from watching the Cuban immigrant. Thanks to the Freedom of Information Act, you can see some of Arnaz's FBI files online at various websites. In 2002, one of these sites, Apbnews.com—now defunct, the site specialized in crime and justice stories—reported that, "… Bureau files contained overwhelming documentation concerning [Arnaz's] childhood, his father, and his various productions. In 1953, the Bureau decided that Arnaz 'probably' was not a Cuban Communist Party card-carrying member because he was too young at the time and his father's political affiliation did not support those views."

Much of Arnaz's file, of course, deals with his Desilu television show *The Untouchables* (see separate entry). The FBI closely monitored all media portrayals of the agency, and was not happy at all with the Desilu version of its crime-stopping capabilities. Agent Elliot Ness, for example, was not employed by the Bureau (he was an agent for the Bureau of Prohibition, under the jurisdiction of the Justice Department), and the FBI tried desperately to convince the public of this. The FBI considered *The Untouchables* "a perversion of FBI history." It collected copious clippings on the show and monitored every episode and piece of publicity about it, much of which is in the Arnaz file.

Of special interest is a letter Arnaz wrote to Hoover ("Dear Edgar," it began) in April 1959 asking Hoover if the FBI would be opposed to Desilu producing a one-hour series called *FBI Story*. The teleplay (a pilot episode) was already written; Arnaz noted, "Obviously under no conditions would we proceed with such a project unless we had the complete sanction of you and your department," but added that Desilu would be "very unhappy" if another company bought the pilot and did a series based on it, "with or without your approval." He signed off, "with best regards from Lucy and myself."

Hoover responded in May 1959 that he appreciated Arnaz's motives and respected him as a producer but the teleplay's title was too similar to a Warner Bros. picture called *The FBI Story* (1959), which the Bureau was totally "committed to." Thus, Hoover objected to "any television series at this time, which would use as a base the activities of this Bureau." He added that this did not mean the FBI was "shutting the door entirely" on a TV project, but that the time was not right. He ended with, "It was good to hear from you, and I want to extend my warmest regards to Lucy."

Another seven or eight pages of memos follow, including one to "Director" from Clyde Tolson, Hoover's longtime "companion" and associate director of the FBI, regarding a *Desilu Playhouse* adaptation about the "Apalachin Meeting," a famous mob-related bust that took place in 1957 in and around a mansion in the sleepy southern New York State town.

BETTY GRABLE: Arnaz dated the musical comedy star in 1939 when she was appearing on Broadway in *DuBarry Was a Lady* at the same time he was appearing a few blocks away in *Too Many Girls*. (Lucy starred in the movie version of *DuBarry*.)

HAIR RAISING: Hairstylist Irma Kusely told this tale of working with Desi Arnaz on *I Love Lucy* to Karen Herman for the Emmy AAT Archive (see The ATAS Archive of American Television):

"Desi's [hair] was prematurely grey. And he always looked very young with his dark hair, but that was my doing. I had to tint his hair for the shows. And [it] lasted for a period of weeks before you had to redo it, but this was a very difficult show that he was directing and acting in, and running back and forth. And he knew he had to get his hair colored, so once he came dashing upstairs to my quarters. I had everything ready to put on and I said, 'Desi you take your gabardine shirt off and I'll, you know … [He said,] 'Well no, it's all right. So it's a cape that just goes on, and they're open all down the back. And he was busy doing and doing, I'm getting it on his head and the phone on my counter rings.

"And he lunges forward to take the receiver and at that time the plop of hair that was on the brush went right down onto his gabardine shirt. Oh, he was so upset. And I said, 'Well, it's your own fault. I asked you to remove it.' And he was going to take it off; with all the hair full of color, it would've been all over the shirt. [I said,] 'No, you have to wait until you wash it out. And then we'll work on the shirt.' [He said,] "Can you get it out?' And that's the one time I said something that I had no idea how to do, and claimed I did. I said, 'Sure I can get it out.'

"And I had no idea, because my peroxide would eat the threads. It wouldn't work. And water wouldn't remove it and carbon tet wouldn't remove it, so I was dead in the water, but I said I would be able to get it out. I got the wardrobe girl and asked her what about [it]: 'Can we get this out?' And she said, 'No. Clorox would eat the threads.' So we thought and I said, 'Oh, boy, this is bad.' She said, 'Well, we have a weaver down here on Melrose and we can cut that spot out of there, take it to the weaver and she can weave that closed.'

"I said, 'You're sure they can do that?' And she said, 'Sure.' So I pulled the spot together, took the scissors, and cut it off. I took the shirt to the set brave as a warrior and Des said, 'Irma, how about my shirt?' And I hold it up with a hole in it and I said, 'I got the spot out.' And Lucy passed out on the floor, laughing like the dickens. He didn't think that was funny…. He went into orbit. But then he got the funny part of it, he realized that we could fix it. So that was all right, but for a moment he was ready to kill me (*laughs*). But I got the spot out.

"I didn't cut his hair. He had his own barber. Where he is [now] I didn't know. But he may not have been a union man, so he wasn't on the set."

IN THE ARMY NOW: When Arnaz was inducted into the army, he was quoted as saying, "I have my heart set on becoming a bombardier in the Air Force." Unfortunately, he broke his kneecap in basic training; he was placed in limited service, and assigned to entertain hospitalized GIs at Birmingham Hospital in Southern California.

MUSIC: Arnaz's contributions to *I Love Lucy* are often overlooked, so it's no surprise to learn his music suffered a similar fate. In fact, Arnaz never saw the popularity (especially in Latin circles) of Mambo Kings like Tito Puente. However, he has to be given credit for keeping Latin music in the consciousness of millions of Americans through his orchestra in the 1940s and his participation in *I Love Lucy.*

Today, Latin music is more mainstream than ever, thanks to the popularity of *The Buena Vista Social Club* (1999), a Grammy Award-winning album and documentary focusing on a group of Cuban musicians, and crossover pop phenomenons like Puente, Celia Cruz, Ricky Martin, Enrique Iglesias, and Marc Anthony.

Arnaz combined a strong, clear voice with popular Latin and American songs of the day.

He integrated "traditional Latin sounds with American orchestration" and "melded a true blend of cultures" according to his contemporary reviewers, especially on such numbers as "I Come from New York" and "The Straw Hat Song," which was described by RCA at the time as a "boogie rumba."

The Arnaz repertoire tended to be more upbeat than down, and his crowning glory was, of course, the thunderous "Babalu," which he performed many times on *I Love Lucy* (it was also the butt of many jokes on the show). But listen to the real joy in "Cuban Pete," or the warmth in "We're Having a Baby," and you'll know there was much more to Arnaz the musician than a hot mambo.

Finally, if you doubt Arnaz's importance in the Latin American music canon, note this: On *The I Love Lucy 50th Anniversary Special* (2001), comedian Paul Rodriguez remarked that Latin music legend Puente once said to him that there were two periods for Latin music in the United States: before Desi Arnaz, and after Desi Arnaz.

Recommended listening: *The Best of Desi Arnaz, The Mambo King*, BMG

Desi Arnaz performing for NBC radio in the 1940s. Photofest

STAGE CAREER: The vehicle that bought Arnaz to the attention of Hollywood was also his first and only Broadway effort: 1939's *Too Many Girls*. Prior to the show, Desi had made a big hit first with Xaviar Cugat's orchestra, and then on his own as a bandleader, popularizing the conga in Miami and New York.

In the Big Apple, the legendary George Abbott caught Arnaz's act and had Arnaz audition for a role in his new show. Desi won the part.

As Danton Walker told it in his Broadway column in 1940: "When George Marion was discussing difficulty of getting an actor for the role of the young Spaniard in *Too Many Girls*, Larry Hart remembered [Arnaz, whom he saw at La Conga in New York] and recommended him to George Abbott, who had danced frequently to the music of his band."

Too Many Girls, 1939

Rehearsals for the new George Abbott/Richard Rodgers/Larry Hart musical (as it was invariably referred to) were set to begin in August of 1939, according to a June 3, 1939 item in *The New York Times*.

Nine days later, the *New York Mirror* reported, "Larry Hart, Dick Rodgers, and George Marion Jr., after a conference with producer George Abbott, have decided on *Co-Ed* as a working title for their new musical comedy."

Three days after that a *New York Post* gossip column began, "This Latin rhythm fad grows. George Abbott [will] feature rumbas in his next tune show ..."

On June 19, 1939, the *New York Daily News* announced this casting tidbit: "Although the new Rodgers and Hart musical for George Abbott may be called *Co-Ed* and concerns colleges and football, Abbott has signed another Latin for a leading role. The player is Desi Arnaz, rumba band leader at La Conga, who has been a professional entertainer for only one year." (The first hired 'Latin' alluded to was Desi's co-star and fellow La Conga performer, Diosa Costello.)

But things were obviously fluid as the musical took shape. A few days later, the *New York Herald-Tribune* reported that Abbott was back from the country after a creative rest, "So far, the producer and author [Marion] have decided to change the title of their new Rodgers and Hart musical from *Co-Ed* to *Yale Bait*. The original title was *The More the Merrier*."

Finally, in early August 1939, the *Times* noted, "*Too Many Girls* is the latest and final title of the one-time *Yale Bait*, George Abbott's proposed musical production for next fall." Set to open on October 18, 1939, the show traveled to Boston's Shubert Theater for a two-week preview beginning on October 2. *The Boston Traveler* wrote about the show on September 13, 1939, in an article titled "Rehearsals Under Way for *Too Many Girls*": "The musical numbers include several of the Latin-American type. Mr. Abbott has not revealed how the rumba and conga found their way to Pottawatomie, but has assigned Diosa Costello and Desi Arnaz, recently featured at La Conga in New York, to the task of executing these numbers."

Reviews of the preview performances were positive, indicating a hit:

"*Too Many Girls* re-lighted the Shubert Theater and declared open season for song, dance, and the kindred merriments of musical comedy. Diosa Costello and Desi Arnaz [are] two new-comers who justify the Pan-American policy."—John K. Hutchens, *Boston Transcript*

"Desi Arnaz from the nightclubs plays his first stage role with assurance. Last night's audience loved his scene with Leila Ernst, a local debutante, in which he tried to discover her brand of lipstick."—Helen Eager, *The Boston Herald*

The buzz on Arnaz was hot even before the show opened, as evidenced by this *Voice of Broadway* column written in the summer of 1939 by Dorothy Kilgallen. Titled "The Glamor Boys" and subtitled "Today: Desi Arnaz—King of Conga," Kilgallen wrote rapturously of Arnaz's sex appeal:

"Desi Arnaz is a black-eyed, slim-hipped rhythm-conscious young Latin on the threshold of becoming a fad…. It takes no well-oiled crystal ball to predict that the days in which Desi may stroll down Broadway unmolested by feminine throngs are numbered. He is a lad destined to belong to the stage-door Susies.

"Now he operates in the comparatively dim and sheltered confines of La Conga, where there are loyal waiters, headwaiters, musicians, and some few conventions to protect him from coat-ripping, handkerchief-stealing women. But this autumn he is going into the George Abbott show, and once he steps on a brightly lit stage, and is exposed to the predatory multitudes of the matinee ticket buyers, he is a cooked Cuban.

"All this past season, Desi has been getting a preview of the penalties paid by dream boys. He is almost recovered from the embarrassment he felt the first time a girl slipped a note into his hand as she danced past his bandstand, [which] read: 'I think you're wonderful. I love you.'" Kilgallen also noted, apropos of Arnaz's later *I Love Lucy* character, that, "He at first tried to get rid of his amusingly bad Cuban accent, but stopped when they told him he would need it for his role in *Too Many Girls*."

The show premiered on October 18, 1939, at The Broadway Theater in New York. It ran for 249 performances. Ticket prices ranged from $1.10 to $2.75, with a top of $5.50 for the December 30, 1939 performance. Songs included "Pottawatomie," "'Cause We Got Cake," "Spic and Spanish," "I Like to Recognize the Tune," "She Could Shake the Maracas," "Give it Back to the Indians," the title tune, and "I Didn't Know What Time It Was." The last, with its wistful, haunting lyrics, went on to become a standard and one of the best-remembered songs of the era. (The song was added to the score of the 1957 movie version of Rodgers' and Hart's *Pal Joey*.)

The plot revolved around a wealthy father who hires a group of football players to keep an eye on his wild daughter in college (Pottawatomie, in Stopgap, New Mexico). It had a book by George Marion Jr., music by Richard Rodgers, lyrics by Lorenz Hart, and was directed by Abbott. Writing in the September 2001 *Playbill*, in an article titled "The Sporting Life ... On stage," Louis Botto noted, "Rodgers' and Hart's 1939 musical *Too Many Girls* ... concerned three jocks (one of them played by Desi Arnaz) and their pursuit of co-eds who didn't wear a 'beanie' (and were, therefore, no longer virgins)." That was a decidedly racy plot for the time.

It starred, in addition to Arnaz, who played a Cuban football sensation, Eddie Bracken, Van Johnson, Ivy Scott, Richard Kollmar (who later married Dorothy Kilgallen), Mildred Law, Leonar Sola, LaVerne Lipton, Diane Sinclair, Key Taylor, Vera Fern, Hal LeRoy, Clyde Fillmore, Hans Robert, Marcy Westcott, Byron Shores, Mary Jane Walsh, Leila Ernst, Libby Bennett, Diosa Costello, James MacColl, Harry Pederson, Edison Rice, and Harry Jackson.

Arnaz was a newcomer to the legitimate stage, but his exuberance and performance got him an expanded role; his character, Manuelito, was given the finale of Act I, in which, taking off from his nightclub act, Arnaz led the entire cast in a conga line. It reportedly stopped the show out of town, and continued to do so when the show opened on Broadway.

Arnaz's *Playbill* biography read: "Desi Arnaz is Cuba's contribution to the musical comedy stage, on which he is now making his debut. He was born in Santiago, where his father was mayor for some 10 years. His serious interest in the entertainment world began when the revolution of 1933 in Cuba forced the family into exile in Florida. Living in Miami, he was asked to lead a rumba band at the Roney Plaza Hotel 'just for fun.' So popular did he become that agents from New York induced him to come to the big city to lead a Cuban orchestra at La Conga, a fashionable nightclub. There, George Abbott, producer of *Too Many Girls*, and Larry Hart, who wrote the lyrics for the Richard Rodgers songs, saw him and corralled him for a leading role in their play."

Well, it may not have happened exactly like that, but it makes good reading. When the show finally hit New York, reviewers were more or less ecstatic:

"The important virtue of *Too Many Girls* is, of course, the score. Almost every number is a delight. My own favorite is 'I Didn't Know What Time It Was.' Desi Arnaz is a handsome young leading man of the Latin type who achieves the feat of being bearable to the men in the audience."—Richard Watts, *New York Herald-Tribune*

"The first musical hit of the season has just reached Broadway. It has everything that's needed for a smash hit—good music, an excellent cast, and an amusing story. Most important for a musical, it has a talented and beautifully costumed chorus. A pair of fiery Latins gives zest to the show: Diosa Costello and Desi Arnaz. The first act finale is really terrific: Building up to a climax, Desi and his conga drum, and Diosa, dance and dance, the curtain falling on a scene as colorful and exciting as these eyes have yet seen on a stage."—*Gotham Life*

"A Latin lad named Desi Arnaz turns out to be a particularly appealing personality, and a very versatile and extraordinarily able musical comedy performer."—Eugene Burr, *The Billboard*

"It's set in New Mexico, which brings it near enough to the Rio Grande for Desi Arnaz and Diosa Costello to supply Latin lilt and Conga color to the sum total. They're the personality standouts and both mark their legit production debuts. For a rumba bandleader, Arnaz, as the juvenile center of *Too Many Girls*, handling the title song, among others, does all right. He's a personable Cuban and deports himself well."—Abel, *Variety*

"It is a musical comedy with Mexican flavor. The Hispanic artists who appear in this cast, as well as the touch and color which it has of our neighbor republic south of the Rio Grande, make this an out-of-the-ordinary production. Desi Arnaz, one of the [student] bodyguards, is shown as a stupendous 'Don Juan.'"—*La Prensa*, translated from the Spanish

Well after the show's debut, Arnaz continued to get positive press, as shown in an excerpt from this *Gotham Life* magazine article on La Conga, dated January 7, 1940. After waxing eloquent about Arnaz's co-star Diosa Costello, also "discovered" at La Conga, the article notes, "A word, too, about Desi Arnaz, the handsome glamour boy who leads the famous Conga line. Desi is also a La Conga protégé, and, like Diosa, is featured in *Too Many Girls*. He leads the conga line beating on his goatskin drum, dancing and shouting like a tribal chieftain. See among Desi's followers in the snake line such sane citizens as Brenda Frazier, Errol Flynn, Bruce Cabot, Mae Murray, Doris Duke Cromwell, and others."

Arnaz and Costello, by the way, rushed off after each performance of *Too Many Girls* to continue playing at La Conga, just up Broadway.

Arnaz was among several in the original cast who toured with the show when it went to Chicago (just after the movie was filmed). By this time, Van Johnson had graduated to playing one of the leads. Again, reviews were superlative:

"Youth has its fling and an intoxicating fling it is, in George Abbott's expertly produced musical comedy of life at the mythical campus of Pottawatomie College. [It features] a lot of Larry Hart's best rhymes. Desi Arnaz, an ingratiating Cuban, who sings, acts, and pounds a drum well, and Diosa Costello, furnish the Latin touch most satisfactorily."—Cecil Smith, *Chicago Tribune*

"George Abbott has assembled young people with plenty of zip. Desi Arnaz as the Latin-American hero, has a South American way with him, and pounds a mean conga drum at the blazing finale of the first act."—Robert Pollack, *Chicago Times*

Too Many Girls Postscript

When RKO made the movie in June 1940, also directed by Abbott, Lucille Ball was cast in the leading role, and it was only natural, given such success onstage, that Arnaz (among several others in the original cast) was plucked to repeat his role in the movie version.

A newspaper article dated June 9, 1940, noted that, "Spring training for the football players of *Too Many Girls* has already gotten under way. Though Desi Arnaz is the first of the Broadway boys to arrive, he will be joined any day now by Eddie Bracken, Hal LeRoy, and others of George Abbott's sprightly contingent.

"Abbott, aware of the differences between stage and screen, is determined to put some real gridiron scenes in the film version of his musical. Furthermore, he will tolerate no substitutes or doubles.... As a matter of fact, he has a coach who is already working on Desi Arnaz.... The Cuban song-and-dance man played some soccer in his childhood but American football is a stranger to him. Jim Blewett, noted mentor of the UCLA backfield, is knocking the soccer out of him and laying the groundwork for some homegrown passing, blocking, and tackling.

"Arnaz ... has not neglected other aspects of California life. He has been seen at the racetrack, the beach, nightclubs, and on boulevard promenades in the space of a few crowded hours. He confesses he has fallen in love with Hollywood life and its sub-tropical allure."

It was apparent just after their first meeting on the soundstages at RKO that Ball and Arnaz had fallen head over heels for each other. Each left a committed relationship to be with the other. When the movie finished filming and Arnaz was on tour with the show in Chicago, a

Chicago Herald-American article on September, 1940, said it all. Accompanying a large photo of Lucy eyeing Desi as if he were the prize bull in a herd, and headlined "Cupid Eyes Lucille Ball," the text read, "You can take it from today's *Town Tattler* that there's as much as meets the eye here in the visit to Chicago of Lucille Ball of the movies to see Desi Arnaz of the *Too Many Girls* show. They are in the Pump Room [a popular Chicago watering hole]."

♥ **Lucy Trivia** *Too Many Girls*, the movie, was rereleased in 1952 to capitalize on the success of *I Love Lucy*. The poster advertising the film showed headshots of Lucy and Desi over the title with the words: "Lucille and Desi together on the screen … in a sizzling college comedy set to the music of Rodgers and Hart!" Also starring in the film were Ann Miller, Eddie Bracken, Richard Carlson (who got Lucy onscreen), and Hal LeRoy. Van Johnson can be seen in the chorus numbers; it was his film debut.

Yours for a Year

The season after Desi Arnaz made his Broadway splash in *Too Many Girls*, several New York papers, including *The New York Times*, reported he was starring in another show, *Yours for a Year*. In September 1940, the *Times* noted, "George Marion Jr. has signed Desi Arnaz for a role in *Yours for a Year*, for which he has written the book and lyrics, and Arthur Schwartz the music. The producing auspices have not yet been arranged."

Marion wrote more than 100 screenplays and also wrote the book *for Too Many Girls*. Schwartz wrote the songs for more than a dozen movies, including *The Band Wagon* (1953). A month later, on October 8, it was reported that Eddie Dowling "will sponsor *Yours for a Year*. This is the musical comedy with book and lyrics by George Marion Jr. and melodies by Arthur Schwartz, rehearsals of which will start toward the end of the month with Desi Arnaz prominent in the cast. Others mentioned for roles are Hal LeRoy, Betty Bruce, and Olympia Bradna. A motion picture company is understood to be interested in the production, too."

LeRoy appeared with Arnaz in *Too Many Girls*. Dowling was a sometime playwright and screenwriter who penned *Sally, Irene and Mary* (filmed in 1925 and 1938) among others. When the play was delayed, Arnaz bowed out and took a gig at the Roxy Theater. The show was never produced.

WHITHER FAME: Arnaz had been "retired" from TV for three years when he brought *The Mothers-in-Law* to the small screen in 1967. Still, he was off the canvas long enough for a comeback article in the Salisbury, Maryland *Daily Times* to misspell his famous last name in the headline: "Desi Arnez Returns to Television."

ARNAZ JR., DESI

Born: January 19, 1953, Los Angeles, California

The son of Lucille Ball and Desi Arnaz, and sometime entertainer, Desi Jr. became instantly famous for being born in real life on the same night the fictional Ricardos welcomed their son, Little Ricky, to television.

When Lucy became pregnant during the second season of her hit show, producer Jess Oppenheimer and Arnaz hit on the idea of writing it into the script as a way of keeping the show going without interruption. At that time performers couldn't even say the word "pregnant" on the air. "Expectant" or "expecting" was about as risqué as it got. Arnaz smartly decided to give script approval to a select group of clerics and thus won the CBS network's okay to go ahead with the storyline.

The night Lucy gave birth to Little Ricky on the air (January 19, 1953), Desi Jr. was delivered by Caesarian section in Los Angeles. "The Birth of Little Ricky" episode was the sitcom's most watched ever, eclipsing Eisenhower's inauguration the next day, and remained a benchmark for "most sets tuned to one show" until the 1960s. It reportedly garnered 44 million viewers, a figure that would be coveted today by any TV executive.

The proud mom and her "$50 million" baby

Lucy with her children, Desi Jr. and Lucie. Photofest

graced the cover of *TV Guide*'s first national edition (it commands a hefty price in the collectibles market).

It's no secret that Desi Arnaz Jr. had problems growing up in the shadow of his famous parents and such a famous TV counterpart. His birth made him the most famous baby boomer in the country and was a catalyst for the continued success of his parents' long-running sitcom. But the confusion and angst Desi Jr. suffered at being constantly mistaken for "Little Ricky" left emotional scars that led him to substance abuse.

As Desi Jr. aged and lost his baby fat, he became a teen idol (playing drums in the band <u>Dino, Desi & Billy</u>), and sex symbol, dating all the then-hot starlets, such as Linda Purl, Liza Minnelli, and Patty Duke, and giving the tabloids much fodder. Mama Lucy tried her best to put the kibosh on anything remotely scandalous.

When Duke gave birth to son Sean Astin in 1971, the tabloids had a field day suggesting the baby's father was Desi Jr. Many years later, Desi Jr. took a blood test that proved definitively he was *not* Astin's dad (that would be biological father Michael Tell, a music promoter, and adoptive dad John Astin, whom Duke married in 1972). Astin became an actor himself, and is best known for his role as Samwise (Sam), friend to Frodo in the *Lord of the Rings* movies.

Desi Jr. appeared for several years with his mother and sister in the sitcom *Here's Lucy* (1968-'71) but left to pursue a promising movie career that never quite took off. His first film, 1971's *Red Sky at Morning*, remains an excellent "coming of age" flick, in which Richard Thomas grows up in desolate New Mexico with the help of friends Desi Jr. and Catherine Burns. Desi Jr. won the 1972 Most Promising Newcomer Golden Globe award for this film.

An article at the time noted, "He still lives at home with his mother and sees his father frequently. 'I saw the picture first with my father at a projection room at Universal,' Desi Jr. said. 'We both were somewhat emotional.' Desi Sr. wept, shouted and laughed throughout the screening. He could not have been more proud of his son. 'Dad flipped out,' Desi Jr. said, pleased.

"Lucille Ball held a screening at home for friends. Less mercurial than her ex-husband, Lucy just studied her son's face intently and—unable to articulate her feelings—hugged him for fifteen minutes, tears streaming down her face."

Desi Jr. said he couldn't have done the picture "without the years of experience I had [acting] on mother's television show [*Here's Lucy*]. It gave me confidence, I felt at home in front of the camera. When I was younger, I wanted to be a psychiatrist. Then I met a few of them and

I think they're all nuts. So I decided to stay with music [Dino, Desi & Billy] and now with acting. So far, I haven't regretted it for a minute."

The article also noted that Desi Jr. "may be hip, but he doesn't swear, drink, or even indulge himself in the patois of his companions. So far as is known, he has never been heard to utter 'Like, yeah man,' or 'I gotta make more bread for this chick I dig." (Did *anyone* ever talk like that besides *Dobie Gillis'* beatnik friend, Maynard G. Krebs?!)

The above is ironic because Desi Jr. himself has admitted to drinking as early as age 11, and doing a variety of drugs while still a teenager, all of which no doubt helped screw up his personal relationships, and pretty much ruined his career as an actor. He credits his climb out of the downward spiral to involvement with Vernon Howard's Success Without Stress organization. Beginning in the mid-1970s, Desi Jr. was a spokesperson for the group, although he's no longer associated with it, since Howard's death in 1992. He met his future wife, Amy Bargiel, through the seminars in the early 1980s; they married in 1987.

By 1988, with six years free of drug, alcohol, and other dependencies, Desi Jr. was conducting seminars on behalf of the group.

In 1992, publicizing his last film, *The Mambo Kings*, he noted that there wasn't much in show business that made him want to pursue a career: "In television comedy now, men are made to look weak. Children are sarcastic toward their parents. That's not funny; it's not even humor. It kind of undermines the American family. One reason I'm not pursuing an acting career is that I don't think there's anything worth pursuing, other than a handful of projects that rarely come along."

Desi Jr. said he respected the artistry involved in making *I Love Lucy*, but felt that "… its incredible impact helped misrepresent his parents—particularly his father—to the American public." He pointed out that his dad was funnier and smarter than his TV persona, and that his parents, despite their divorce, "didn't shout at each other at home as they did on television."

Desi Jr. and sister Lucie appeared along with other veterans of classic TV shows in *TV Road Trip*, a 2002 Travel Channel production. In late October 2003, Ricci Martin was performing in a salute to his father, Dean, at the Boulder Theater with "guest star Desi Arnaz Jr."

Currently, Desi Jr. lives in Boulder City, Nevada. He and his wife manage the nonprofit Boulder City Ballet Company. They have acquired and remodeled the Boulder Theatre and stage a variety of productions there. On March 3, 2007, Desi hosted the third of sister Lucie's "Legacy of Laughter" seminars there (see Laughter and Lucy). Sean Astin was a guest.

Desi Jr. also joined his sister in accepting, on behalf of their mother, the TV Land Legacy of Laughter Award on April 22, 2007, during the fifth annual TV Land Awards.

AUTOMAN: Short-lived (13 episodes in the 1983-'84 season) sci-fi television show on ABC starring Desi Jr. as Walter Nebicher, an inept police officer who is assigned to his precinct's computer room to keep him out of trouble. To show his mettle, he creates an artificial human called Automan by entering a large quantity of data into the computer system. Automan could actually appear outside the computer as a human figure at night, when the city's energy usage was low. Together, the two fought crimes along with a "holograph" called Cursor, who was able to create objects out of nothing.

TEMPER: At one of Desi Jr.'s "Success without Stress" seminars in the 1980s, a reporter hit on a still-stressful topic. Author Craig Hamrick (*Barnabas & Co.*, *Big Lou*), a reporter then on the scene at Coffeyville (Kansas) Community College, says that Desi Jr. used prepared responses for almost any question. Except for this one:

"The other reporter tried to warm up to Desi by saying, 'I was watching *I Love Lucy* when they showed the episode you were born on …'

"Desi slammed his fist on the table, exhibiting a bit of the stress he was lecturing about. 'That was *not* me!' he said. He explained he was born by C-section and the doctor did C-sections on Mondays. It was planned to coincide with the *I Love Lucy* episode about the birth of Little Ricky."

NOTABLE CREDITS: 1960s Band: <u>Dino, Desi & Billy</u>. Movies: *Red Sky at Morning* (1971), *Marco* (1973), *The Wedding* (1978), *House of the Long Shadows* (1983), *The Mambo Kings* (1992). Stage: *I Love My Wife*, January 17, 1986, Coconut Grove Playhouse, Miami. TV: *Automan* (1983, see above); <u>Here's Lucy</u>.

ARNAZ, LUCIE
Birth name: Lucie Desirée Arnaz
Born: July 17, 1951, Hollywood, California

The daughter of Lucille Ball and Desi Arnaz, this initially awkward TV performer grew into a sturdy, self-assured musical comedy lead player.

Little Lucie first appeared with her famous mom on one of her series in the episode "Lucy Is a Soda Jerk" of *The Lucy Show* (March 4, 1963). She played a friend of Lucy's TV daughter, Chris. She made similar appearances on *The Lucy Show* and then her mother cast her and brother Desi Jr. in a new sitcom, *Here's Lucy*, as, what else, Lucille Ball's (excuse me, Lucille *Carter's*) daughter and son, in 1968.

She was briefly married to Phil Vandervort (they met in 1967, married in 1971, separated a year later, and divorced in 1977). He was an aspiring actor who played mostly small parts on Lucille Ball's shows from 1967 to 1972.

Desi Jr. was the more self-assured performer, but Lucie grew into her role and by the end of the show (1974) was carrying entire episodes with charm to spare. Certainly, this experience enabled her to pursue a stage career, and a successful one at that, in musical comedy. Lucie has always professed a great love for live theater, and attributed much of her fervor to the encouragement of Vivian Vance. Vance always said she preferred the stage to any other medium. (Lucie helped contribute the fee that enabled Vance to get her own—posthumous—star on the Hollywood Walk of Fame.)

Some people, no matter what she does, will always think of her mainly as "Lucille Ball's daughter." She maintains a healthy attitude about that: "It's not their fault," she said in a December 1992 interview. "I go into many directions. I'm a singer; I'm a dancer a little bit. I do a straight play and then I go do a little series. Then I'm on a talk show. They don't know what the hell I do."

Then of course, there's the baggage she's carried all her life, her mother being a national icon and all—and her dad was no slouch either—making them "a very difficult act to follow." Lucie has acknowledged her mother and father "were rarely home, and when they were usually had little time to spend with her and her brother." Again, she's very forgiving: "It's not their fault. It's what comes with the territory."

At the time she had just replaced Mercedes Ruehl as Bella in Neil Simon's *Lost in Yonkers* on Broadway. She'd written longtime friend Simon (her oldest son's namesake) before she got the role that, "I'm sure every woman comes up to you and says something about how she feels like she's Bella. But this is my life! How did you know? But since then every woman who's met me at the stage door has said that to me in one way or another, so it's not just me."

Lucie's movie and TV careers have been more problematic. She's performed well in a handful of TV movies, and starred in her own short-lived sitcom (*The Lucie Arnaz Show*, 1985). A family-type drama (*Sons and Daughters*, 1991) didn't fare much better. In films, she's been in the much-maligned Neil Diamond version of *The Jazz Singer* (1980), the critically panned but financially successful sequel to Billy Jack (*Billy Jack Goes to Washington*, 1977) and had a supporting role in the Freddie Prinze Jr. flick *Down to You* (2000). She filmed the Western-based noir *Wild Seven* in 2006, and *The Pack*, about the dangers of secondhand smoke, in 2007.

But Lucie is resilient, and has extended her talents to newer media: she created a wonderful CD-ROM series based on the lives of her famous folks, but the project was in limbo after one CD was released in 1997—*Lucy & Desi: The Scrapbooks, Volume 1: Made for Each Other*—chronicling Lucy and Desi's lives in the 1930s and 1940s.

Much more successful was a two-hour documentary Lucie produced for TV in 1992 about her parents, using extensive home movies she'd found and interviews with their closest friends and business associates. Genuinely moving, <u>*Lucy and Desi: A Home Movie*</u> won her a deserved Emmy.

Married to actor Laurence Luckinbill since 1980, Lucie has three children: Simon, Joseph, and Katherine. In 2001, she performed on the London stage as one of the lead witches in a new musical version of *The Witches of Eastwick*. In 2003 she guest-starred on *Law & Order* as a Martha Stewart-type accused of murder. In 2006 she replaced Joanna Gleason in the successful Broadway musical *Dirty Rotten Scoundrels*. She continues to tour the country when time permits with her seminar on the value and importance of laughter in our lives (See <u>Laughter and Lucy</u>).

And as far as forever being associated with her famous parents is concerned: "It's not so bad to be associated with someone who's brought joy to millions and millions of people."

"Heaven Knows": A song recorded in November 2001 by Lucie and friends with proceeds going to The Twin Towers Fund, set up to help victims of the September 11, 2001 World Trade Center tragedy and their families. Lucie said, in a press release dated November 6, 2001, "My father always said: 'If you don't know what to do, don't do anything!' And I believe what he meant by that was that, sometimes if you wait a little bit, another part of the puzzle will fall into place and you *will* know what to do."

Lucie, in Los Angeles to finish editing the *I Love Lucy 50th Anniversary Special*, helped pull a recording session together.

Notable Credits: Albums: *Just in Time*, Concord Jazz label, 1993; *The Witches of Eastwick*, original London cast recording, 2000. Movies: *Who Is the Black Dahlia*, 1975 (TV), *The Jazz Singer* (1980), *Down to You* (2000), *Wild Seven* (2006), *The Pack* (2007). TV: *Here's Lucy, The*

Lucie Arnaz Show (1985), *Sons and Daughters* (1991). Theater: *On Broadway, Seesaw* (first national tour); *They're Playing Our Song* (Broadway, 1979); *My One and Only* (first national company); *Lost in Yonkers* (Broadway, summer 1992); *Grace & Glorie* (Off-Broadway, 1996); *Dirty Rotten Scoundrels* (Muriel, replacement, May-September 2006). Magazine Cover: *Cue New York*, with Robert Klein, March 2, 1979.

ART

These are some well-known, and not so well-known, pieces of art that feature images of Lucille Ball or are related to *I Love Lucy*. It is not meant to be all-inclusive. For Al Hirschfeld's Lucy output, see <u>Hirschfeld, Al</u>.

Neal Adams, *Superman vs. Muhammed Ali* Collector's Edition, cover, Vol. 7, No. C-56, 1978. Popular comic artist Adams did the cover for this oversized special comic book, with Superman and Ali duking it out in the center, surrounded by a mob of special celebrity fans, real and otherwise, including Lucille Ball in the lower left corner, near Batman's right ear.

Julian Allen, "The CEO of Comedy," *Working Woman*, October 1986. Allen, who passed away in 1998, specialized in celebrity illustrations, and this is a full-page piece of Lucille Ball circa the mid-1980s in color, with Lucy, Ricky, Fred, and Ethel in black and white behind her.

Richard Amsel, *TV Guide* cover, July 6-12, 1974, "End of an Era, Lucy Bows Out." Amsel (1947-'85) was an extraordinary commercial artist whose work appeared on

Lucille Ball in a glamorous 1950's pose, by artist Rick Carl. Courtesy of the artist.

magazine covers, posters, ads, and record album jackets. His style was extremely influential, immediately identifiable, and his originals continue to be in great demand today.

Rene Bouché, a well-known French painter and portrait artist, drew Lucille Ball and Desi Arnaz in the mid-1950s for CBS (as well as many more of the network's stars). The black-and-white sketch has Ball on top left and Arnaz on bottom right. Bouché was known for his *Vogue* fashion illustrations from the 1940s through the early 1960s.

George Bungarda, color oil painting entitled *Hollywood Drive-In*, 1995. In the style of the classic poster "Boulevard of Broken Dreams"—which features James Dean, Marilyn Monroe, Humphrey Bogart, and Elvis at the counter of an otherwise desolate café—this painting offers a drive-in (playing *Gone with the Wind*) parking lot studded with Hollywood immortals. These include Dean, Monroe, Garbo, Chaplin, the Marx Brothers, Hitchcock, John Wayne, Frankenstein, the four principals of *The Wizard of Oz*, and Laurel & Hardy. Ball is slightly left of center sitting in a vintage convertible with Marlon Brando leaning next to the driver's seat in full biker regalia (à la his film, *The Wild One*).

Rick Carl is an artist, designer, and decorator who drew a series of black-and-white pencil sketches of Lucy, circa 1986, among many other Lucy-related sketches, drawings, and paintings. Most recently, he illustrated Lucy (magnificently) for the 2004 book *I Love Lucy Paper Dolls*. (See illustration.)

Xavier Cugat, Original Oil Painting of Lucille Ball; lithograph featuring caricatures of Ball and dozens of other stars, in a style reminiscent of Al Hirschfeld; others? We all know that Cugat was a well-known Latin bandleader who helped launch the career of Desi Arnaz; lesser known is his output as an artist. Cugat's paintings featured brilliant colors and humorous caricatures in comical scenes. The oil painting is in a private collection; a lithograph (one of a run of 350) was sold on eBay in April 2002.

Shelley Daniels, *Scholastic Math Magazine* cover, September 12, 1986. Sculptor Daniels created a Claymation-type sculpted Lucy Ricardo sitting atop a TV set, juggling numbers and math symbols. Inside was an *I Love Lucy* game that helped kids learned to add and subtract.

A picture of Daniels' Lucy can be found in <u>Magazine Covers</u>. Daniels later worked as a sculptor for the animated films *Toy Story* and *The Nightmare Before Christmas*.

Drew Friedman, Xavier Cugat, Lucille Ball, Vivian Vance, and Michael Richards. Drawn in the early 1990s for an *Entertainment Weekly* parody article on recasting classic TV shows. On-the-money comic artist and illustrator Friedman is known for his wild celebrity and political caricatures. This odd but somehow endearing picture features Cugat leading a band with Lucy, Viv, and Richards (Kramer on *Seinfeld*) doing duty as the Andrews Sisters, dressed in period (1940s) outfits. Friedman reports that he's drawn Lucy several other times, "including a rather rude comic strip for Howard Stern's book *Private Parts* [1995] and Lucy in a cheesecake pose for *TV Guide*, in 2000."

Lucy by Jacques Kapralik. Author's collection

Clark Hanford, Lucille Ball doll/Statuette. 1993. Hanford specialized in celebrity likenesses. The one he did of Lucy, all glamour circa the 1950s, was 34 inches tall and wore a pink and black evening gown accented with jewelry and a fur wrap. It sold for $4,500.

Edith Head, Pastel Sketch of Lucille Ball, 24x36 inches. The legendary Hollywood costume designer signed this illustration showing Lucy in a long, flowing evening dress. This piece is listed on the Internet as "stolen art" by the Los Angeles Police Department.

Ralph Hodgdon, mid-1990s, Lucille Ball Paper Doll Coloring Book. Hodgdon created a 12-page tribute to Lucy, featuring a doll figure and 11 pages of carefully researched costumes from Lucy's movie and television work.

Jacques Kapralik, 1943 Shadow Box caricature of Lucille Ball and trumpeter Harry James, pictured, from the movie *Best Foot Forward*; possibly others. This was one of a series of shadow box illustrations Kapralik did spotlighting various MGM stars in movie roles for publicity purposes (lithographs of the art were sent to trade magazines for insertion) and in-house use, i.e., the cover of MGM's magazine *The Lion Roars*. This color piece is 9.25"x12.5", on heavy paper stock with "spectacular" silver embossing, likely removed from *The Lion Roars*—and sold on eBay in September 2003 for $69.

Jim Kritz, Hamilton plate collection. Series of eight plates, depicting Lucille Ball and the cast of *I Love Lucy* in various scenes, beginning 1988.

Stanley Livingston, art glass rendition of Lucille Ball and Desi Arnaz, framed in wood, 37x25x1.5 inches. The technique was described as, "Glass-to-glass fusion, acrylic-to-glass fusion, hand-stained colors, and color fusion. Artwork also has a number of jewels and eye-catchers." This "stained glass"-look piece was done by California artist Livingston, better known as Chip on the long-running TV show *My Three Sons* (1960-'72), which not so coincidentally co-starred Lucy's Fred Mertz (William Frawley) from 1960 to 1965. The piece was priced at $400 on eBay in June 2002.

Clement Micarelli, a realist, a fashion, commercial, fine, portrait, and pop artist since the mid-1950s, who lately has relished putting famous people of a similar stripe (i.e., actors, musicians, sportspeople) together on canvas. His oil/gesso panel, "Gone With the Stars," is a 25x32-inch takeoff of *Gone With the Wind*, uses staircase scene as a backdrop, but with Clark Gable eyeing Marilyn Monroe as Vivien Leigh looks on behind them. Surrounding them are other stars of the era, including Fred and Ginger, John Wayne, Henry Fonda, Cary Grant, Audrey Hepburn, and, of course, Ball, looking glamorous with long hair and a white stole.

Sir Eduardo Paolozzi, *Meet the People*, Screen print, lithograph, and collage, approximately 10x14 inches. Hanging in the Victoria and Albert Museum, England, this fascinating piece features a picture of Lucille Ball advertising the 1944 movie *Meet the People*. Minnie Mouse, a can of tuna, a glass of orange juice, and a fruit plate are also featured in this work. The Pop (and popular) artist also works in ceramics and sculpture; the Queen made Paolozzi "Her Majesty's Sculptor in Ordinary for Scotland" in 1986.

Sonya Paz, *Lucille Ball Tribute*, December 1996-January 1997, Gordon Biersch Brewery, San Jose, California. The artist recalls, "The concept was one woman, many faces—I had a great time doing it and I was proud of the exhibition. There were 15 acrylic paintings of Lucy in the series—sort of Warhol-esque, but no two were alike. Each had its own name and personality. One was called 'Polka Dot' and had dots painted around the image. One of my favorites is called 'Jewel'; it's an image of Lucy on a two-tone golden/yellow background, and it has vintage earrings and a necklace attached to it, very three-dimensional. Another one was done on a silver gray movie-screen background, and it sparkles." See Paz's art at her website, Sonyapaz.com.

Lucy by Robert Risko. Courtesy of the artist.

Bob Peak, *TV Guide* cover, July 16, 1967, "Lucille Ball: Redhead with a Golden Touch." Peak (1927-'92) is often called the father of the modern movie poster and the king of illustrators. He was a prolific and respected artist and painter.

Penelope, *Babalu*, circa mid-1980s. This artist/illustrator did a wonderful color airbrush illustration of Lucy and Ricky Ricardo with the word "Babalu" colorfully spread across the bottom.

Mike Peters, Pulitzer Prize-winning cartoonist and creator of *Mother Goose & Grimm*, uses celebrities often in his drawings. A "Grimm" comic from the early 1990s with the caption "Desi and Lucy" had a figure of Arnaz pounding on drums singing "Babalu" while observed by Lucy … from the cartoon strip *Peanuts*, thinking "Oh, Good Grief."

Robert Risko, a widely popular caricaturist whose retro style is "painted with designer's gouache in airbrush," according to the artist, drew Lucy in 1981 for the New York *Daily News* (shown); in 1985 for *The Village Voice*; in 1986 for *In Style* (not *InStyle*, which debuted in 1995); in 1988 for a *VarBusiness* cover story on AT&T's bungling employees; and finally for the July 2003 VH-1 TV and Web special, "The 200 Greatest Pop Culture Icons" (Lucy came in at No. 4 behind Oprah, Superman, and Elvis). He's also drawn Ball with *I Love Lucy* partner Harpo Marx for a DVD cover in 1996. Ball is featured in *The Risko Book*, a 2000 collection of his work.

Marcia Salo, *Lucy #3*, photo/collage. Salo's large format photographs typically depict pop-culture icons in bizarre settings to question social mores.

Ronald Searle, *TV Guide* cover, April 30-May 6, 1966 "Ronald Searle Sketches Lucille Ball." Searle (b. 1920) is an illustrator, cartoonist, caricaturist, and much more; his wild renderings have delighted the public for more than half a century. This issue features Searle drawings of Lucy inside as well.

Ernest Shelton, life-size bronze sculpture of Lucille Ball, unveiled in the Academy of Television Arts & Sciences (Los Angeles) courtyard on Dec. 9, 1991. Guests at the ceremony included Milton Berle, Steve Allen, Jayne Meadows, and Gary Morton. Shelton created "Lucy" using photos and tapes of her TV shows, according to Larry Gerber, editor in chief of *Emmy* magazine, the academy's publication. Shelton also sculpted likenesses of Johnny Carson and Jack Benny for the courtyard. Jan Scott, an Emmy-winning (11 times) production designer who was Academy vice president at the time, oversaw the design, creation, and placement of the Lucy statue and 24 other sculptures of TV pioneers in the plaza, Gerber noted.

Red Skelton, the actor and comedian (see also separate entry) was a friend of the Arnazes and a painter. He loved to paint clowns, and he did a pair of paintings of Ball and Arnaz in clown-face, titled *Crazy Quilt Clown* and *Amigo*, respectively. The Lucy clown vaguely resembles our favorite carrot-topped comedienne (especially if you know it's supposed to be her), but the Desi clown is more ambiguous-looking.

Emmanuil and Janet Snitkovsky, life-size bronze sculpture of Lucille Ball as Lucy Ricardo, located on North Palm Canyon Drive in Palm Springs, California, sitting on a bench outside Leed's Jewelers.

Wach Steter, *Lucy Da Vinci*, caricature of Lucille Ball painting Vivian Vance, pen and ink; released February 1, 1963 by CBS to publicize *The Lucy Show*. See the picture under that entry.

Drew Struzan, 2001 Lucille Ball *Hollywood Legends* Postage Stamp, USPS. Struzan, of Pasadena, California, painted this color image of Lucy circa 1955 from a black-and-white photo of the era. Known for his movie posters (*Raiders of the Lost Ark, Star Wars, E.T.,* and many others), books and album covers, and celebrity illustrations, the popular and collectible Struzan also did the Edward G. Robinson stamp from this series.

L. Supino, *Lucy*, 26x41 inches, graphite on paper, 1989. Black-and-white head shot of Lucy.

Dave Woodman has been drawing Lucille Ball (and other celebrities) since the 1970s. She's one of his favorite subjects. Ball admired Woodman's work so much she bought several pieces from him while he was still in high school at Alamosa, Colorado. The professional cartoonist—he worked on Walt Disney's films *The Little Mermaid* and *Aladdin*, among other projects, during an almost 20-year stay at the Mouse House—also designed the posters for the "Loving Lucy" Conventions held by the We Love Lucy fan club (his drawings were featured in the club's annual magazines for many years) and the Official 50th Anniversary Lucy Reunion Poster. You can see several samples of his work under the entry The Lucy Character. Visit Woodman's website at www.softniche.com/keepcom.

Artist Unknown, Family portrait in oil of Lucille Ball, Desi Arnaz, and their children, circa the mid-to-late 1950s, currently on display in the Holiday Inn lobby, Jamestown, N.Y. The painting is pictured opposite the title page in the book *Love, Lucy*. According to Ric Wyman, executive director of the Lucille Ball-Desi Arnaz Center, "I can tell you that it did hang in Lucy's Palm Springs home (the sign at the Holiday Inn cites the Beverly Hills home). It was Palm Springs for certain and possibly Beverly Hills, too."

ARTHUR, BEA

Best known as the infuriating but lovable liberal title character of the hit TV series *Maude* (1972-'78), and as *Golden Girl* Dorothy Zbornak (1985-'92), gravel-voiced Arthur began her television career as a regular on *Caesar's Hour* (1956-'57). Her first real fame came as heavy-drinking Vera Charles in the Broadway musical *Mame*, which starred Angela Lansbury (1966). Arthur repeated her role in the movie version with Lucille Ball (1974), and their moments together onscreen are the best parts of the movie, especially the duet "Bosom Buddies." Arthur also saluted Lucy onstage (along with Valerie Harper and Robert Stack) when the Kennedy Center in Washington, D.C., honored the redhead in 1986.

In 2002 Arthur played the Great White Way in her one-woman show, *Bea Arthur on Broadway: Just Between Friends*, and made these comments about working with Lucille Ball in *Mame* for an interview in *Next* magazine: "Lucy was a brilliant, brilliant clown, but she was terribly miscast. But we would never have gotten the money for the production if she hadn't wanted to do it. Lucy was lovely [to work with]. She was really the reason I did it, she insisted I do it. I really didn't want to, but I was married to the director [Gene Saks] who said, 'Look, as my wife you owe it to me to do the part.' So I did."

For more on *Mame*, see Connell, Jane; Kahn, Madeline and Lucy's Film Career entry.

ASHER, WILLIAM

Solid TV director who began working on *I Love Lucy* in its second season and stayed through the final one. He wouldn't take any bull from the demanding Lucy and that's what she needed on the set. Asher subsequently married Elizabeth Montgomery, and produced and directed her hit show *Bewitched* (1964-'72). Perhaps that's why Montgomery used some Lucy shtick, such as the drawn out "Welllllll...." whenever she had a problem explaining things. (See also Ball, Lucille and *I Love Lucy*.)

ATAS ARCHIVE OF AMERICAN TELEVISION (AAT), THE

This unprecedented project by the Academy of Television Arts & Sciences (ATAS), the folks who bring you the Emmy Awards among other industry events and seminars, is an online archive of video interviews that is part of the ATAS Foundation in partnership with Google. According to the ATAS website, "To date, more than 2,000 hours of videotaped conversations have been completed with over 475 television legends and pioneers. Working under the auspices of the Television Academy Foundation, AAT contains interviews with actors, writers, producers, directors, craftspeople, executives, and many others. With the help of industry volunteers, historians, journalists, and students, we are achieving our broad goal of becoming the world's largest, most advanced interactive encyclopedia covering the history of television."

Just a short list of Lucille Ball-related people interviewed in the AAT includes Steve Allen, Bea Arthur, William Asher, Milton Berle, Carol Burnett, Dann Cahn, Richard Crenna, Bob Carroll Jr. and Madelyn Pugh Davis, Mike Douglas, Irma Kusely, Sheldon Leonard, Art Linkletter, Dick Martin, Jayne Meadows, Howard Morris, Jay Sandrich, Bob Schiller, George Schlatter, Mel Shavelson, Doris Singleton, Aaron Spelling, Bob Weiskopf, and Betty White.

Here are a few choice nuggets from the AAT Archive interview with Lucille Ball's hairstylist of many years and close friend, Irma Kusely, done on June 14, 2001, by ATAS' Karen Herman in Glendale, California:

—"Everyone thought Lucille was foolish to go into television. 'Don't lose your whole career. You're just getting it going.' ... She didn't care. She wanted to do it. I met her [at MGM] when she was [doing] a second read with Katharine Hepburn [for] *Without Love*. She knew me and I knew her, but [when she was] cast with Katharine in the second lead, I had to have someone special to stand by for [Lucy], because Katharine was a [full]-time job for me. And I enjoyed it, I really did. But Lucille was definitely a good friend, right from the beginning. Coincidentally, she wanted to have a baby. And I found out that I was going to have a baby, so every day she wanted to have a touch [to] get the same vibes going for her."

—"[Lucy] was a talented person, very talented and much respected. And sometimes, you know, talent gets in the way. It never did with me but there are people to whom it did happen. She always really tried to present herself as a very fine person, but sometimes someone would tell her they knew what to do and they had no idea; that was not the right thing to say. So she would get lost but people would say she's bitchy or she's that, she isn't at all. She just want[ed] you to know your work. And don't say something you can do [that] you can't do."

—"I did [Vivian Vance] every show. When I did Lucy with the wig [post-*I Love Lucy*], I could do Vivian in between.… She was an absolute angel, just a wonderful lady. She suffered too [much] at the end. She and Lucy? Of course, they had differences of opinions; everybody does, but their relationship was something that you'd treasure yourself. It was that nice.… Vance was glad to be working but there was a lot of scuttlebutt because she would fight with William Frawley.… She didn't like that he never rehearsed with them, he would come in and botch up everything, and it would just disturb her terribly.… They wanted her to be dowdy at first and then gradually they just forgot all about that and she was a regular gal."

Go to the ATAS website—www.emmys.org/foundation/archive—for more information. See also Kusely, Irma.

AWARDS

There are too many to list them all, but some of the major honors given to Lucille Ball during and after her lengthy career include the following. (See also Golden Globe Award.)

1952: Emmy: Best Comedienne

1955: Emmy: Best Actress in a Continuing Performance, *I Love Lucy*

1961: Golden Laurel, Second Place, Top Female Comic Performance, *The Facts of Life* (1960). The Laurels were given out by the trade magazine *Motion Picture Exhibitor* from 1958 to 1971. There was no ceremony.

1967: Emmy: Outstanding Lead Actress in a Comedy Series, *The Lucy Show*

1968: Emmy: Outstanding Lead Actress in a Comedy Series, *The Lucy Show*

1968: Golden Laurel, winner, Top Female Comic Performance, *Yours, Mine and Ours* (1968). The film itself won a Laurel for best General Entertainment.

1977: Women in Film: Crystal Award

1979: Hollywood Foreign Press Association: Cecil B. DeMille Award

1984: An initial inductee (and the first woman so honored) into the Television Academy Hall of Fame

1986: Kennedy Center Honors: Lifetime Achievement Award

1987: American Comedy Award: Lifetime Achievement

1988: Harvard Hasty Pudding: Woman of the Year

1989: Eastman Kodak Second Century Award

1989: On July 6, The Presidential Medal of Freedom was awarded to Lucy, posthumously, by President George W. Bush. The Medal of Freedom, according to the website www. medaloffreedom.com, is "the nation's highest civilian award, [and] recognizes exceptional meritorious service. The medal was established by President Truman in 1945 to recognize notable service in the war. In 1963, President John F. Kennedy reintroduced it as an honor for distinguished civilian service in peacetime."

1989: Academy of Television Arts and Sciences: Governor's Award

1990: The Women's International Center Living Legacy Award, posthumously

1994: The industry organization Women in Film (WIF) began presenting the Lucy Awards. They were founded by Joanna Kerns, Bonny Dore, and Loreen Arbus and "are presented in association with the Lucille Ball Estate," according to a WIF spokesperson. "They were named for Lucille Ball, who was not only a legendary actress and comedienne, [but] a producer, studio owner, creator and director. They are given to recognize women and men who exemplify the extraordinary accomplishments she embodied; whose excellence and innovation have enhanced the perception of women through the medium of television." Past recipients include Elizabeth Montgomery, Imogene Coca, Angela Lansbury, Diahann Carroll, Phyllis Diller, Debra Messing, Megan Mullally, Geena Davis, and in 2007, Shona Rhimes, creator, executive producer, and writer of *Grey's Anatomy*. Go to www.wif.org for more information.

2001: Inducted into the National Women's Hall of Fame

2007: Cable network TV Land presented Lucy with the first Legacy of Laughter Award on April 22, given to her children, Lucie Arnaz and Desi Arnaz Jr. The award honors Ball's "groundbreaking career and body of work, including her enduring sitcom, *I Love Lucy*." TV Land noted, the Legacy of Laughter award "is presented to honor an entertainer whose awe-inspiring work continues to serve as an inspiration and a guiding force: Lucille Ball. Her comedy always delivered, from the broadest slapstick to the most nuanced verbal reaction. Her gift is indeed a legacy. It serves as both an ideal for those who have followed her, and also in and of itself—timelessly providing the invigorating, healing power of laughter.

"Named by *TV Guide* as the 'Greatest TV Star of All Time,' Lucille Ball's groundbreaking work in film and television continues to touch the funny bones of viewers all over the world. Today, *I Love Lucy* is one of the most successful and longest-running programs in television syndication."

Lucy became a force behind the TV camera as well: She became the first woman to run a major Hollywood Studio—Desilu Productions—when her husband, Desi Arnaz, sold her his shares following their 1960 divorce. Desilu produced such television hits as *Star Trek, The*

Andy Griffith Show, *Mission: Impossible*, and *Mannix*. She was one of television's first major stars, and since her death in 1989 has only become more popular as an icon of laughter.

2007: In its November 23 issue, *Entertainment Weekly* joined with cable channel TV Land to announce "The 50 Greatest TV Icons of all Time." Johnny Carson was No.1, and while his importance to many TV genres cannot be denied, for me, the magazine's No. 2 choice, Lucille Ball, will always be No. 1, for obvious reasons. And the public agrees with me: in the accompanying Internet poll, voters chose Lucy as the No. 1 icon. (Carson was #2).

B

BABALU MUSIC

"Weird" Al Yankovic, known for his on-target pop-music video parodies, produced this affectionate tribute to *I Love Lucy* and especially Desi Arnaz's music, which gave the series its unique Latin flavor. The CD features the best-remembered musical bits from the show, some short dialogue scenes, and a new music video of the title tune, Arnaz's signature song.

BABY FIGURES

44,000,000—Estimated number of viewers who watched the "birth of Little Ricky" episode of *I Love Lucy.*

1,000,000—Total number of responses to Lucille Ball and Desi Arnaz's blessed event, including phone calls, telegrams, gifts, and so on.

30,000—Number of fan letters received by Lucy expressing joy over her new son.

27—Number of letters written disapproving of showing a pregnancy on television.

BACKGAMMON

Board game played with dice and round chip counters in which players try to be the first to gather their pieces into one corner, and then systematically remove them from the board. The game was popularly revived in the 1970s. Lucille Ball was an enthusiastic player and engineered many tournaments and games, sometimes played for charity. Ball played backgammon in character on her final sitcom, *Life with Lucy* (1986).

BADMINTON

You might know Lucille Ball was generally considered a good sport early in her career, but did you know she was actually good at one sport: badminton? A 1939 publicity shot of Ball shows her with a racket on the court and notes, "Lucille Ball, RKO star, plays an extremely fast game of badminton. And not just for the exercise. She's crazy about the game."

BALL, DEDE

See **Peterson, Desirée 'DeDe' Hunt Ball**.

BALL, FRED

Lucille Ball's younger brother, by three years, benefited from Lucy's devotion to keeping her family together once her Hollywood career had taken off. He was the first family member to join her in California (in 1933) and served in various capacities throughout Lucy's career. He was the road manager for Desi Arnaz's band in the 1940s and worked at Desilu until Arnaz fired him in a fit of anger after Fred expressed concern about Desi being able to run the company (this was after the Arnaz marriage had soured). Once Lucy bought out Arnaz, she brought back Fred as an investor in real estate for the company, mostly in Arizona.

Fred died at the age of 92 on Feb. 5, 2007, at his home in Cottonwood, Arizona. I met Fred at the May 2005 Lucy festival in Jamestown, N.Y. (his birthplace) and though obviously dealing with some of the problems associated with aging, he was sharp as a tack when his memory was prodded.

He told his niece Lucie Arnaz in 1992 that he and Lucy were "latchkey children" who had "less than an idyllic upbringing. I asked him, 'How did you play when you were little?'" Arnaz asked, as she was preparing *Lucy and Desi: A Home Movie*, "and he said, 'We didn't play. We worked.' So she became an adult at a very young age…. It was like, 'Get on with it, move on,' which is what she had to do."

Fred and his wife, Zo, were videotaped visiting the house he (and Lucy) grew up in, in Celeron, which is being lovingly restored to its original condition (see <u>Lucy's Celeron, New York House</u>). They operated The View motel in Cottonwood. Fred is survived by Zo, four children, seven grandchildren; several great-grandchildren; and nephew Desi Arnaz Jr. and niece Lucie Arnaz and their families.

From her home in New York City, Lucie Arnaz said, "It was always special to us that Uncle Fred and I shared the same birthday. In addition to being my mother's brother, he was also a close friend of my father. I like to think that they are all enjoying a wonderful reunion right now." Fred wanted his ashes interred in Jamestown's Lake View Cemetery along with his sister, parents, grandparents and other family members. See also Lucy's biography, below.

BALL, LUCILLE

Birth name: Lucille Desirée Ball
Born: August 6, 1911, Jamestown, New York
Died: April 26, 1989, Los Angeles, California (after surgery for a heart ailment)
Cremated, remains were interred at Forest Lawn (Hollywood Hills), Los Angeles; relocated along with mother, DeDe, by Lucie Arnaz and Desi Arnaz Jr. in October 2002 to Jamestown's huge Lake View Cemetery, where many members of Lucy's family are buried (including maternal grandparents Florabelle and Fred Hunt, her father, Henry Ball, and brother Fred Ball).

She's the wackiest redhead we ever let into our living rooms. Her face, it's been said, has been seen more times, by more people, than any other face in the history of the human race. She is one of those rare celebrities (well, super-mega stars) identifiable by just her first name: Lucy. As with many comedians, her early life was not entirely a happy one.

Born Lucille Desirée Ball in 1911, in Jamestown, New York—near Lake Erie in the western part of the state—Lucy's first years saw her traveling with her impoverished mother Desirée (DeDe), and father, Henry, a telephone lineman, to wherever Henry could find

The lady known as Lucy. Photofest

work. This included Montana and Michigan. The vagabond existence instilled in the young Lucille a strong desire to always have her family close to her, ideally all in one house. This was a mission she wouldn't be able to complete until after she'd become a minor success in Hollywood.

Lucy's dad died of typhoid fever when she was just 3 years old and her mother was pregnant with Fred. Perhaps as an escape from the dreary reality of her life, Lucy expressed an early love for putting on shows (she used to do so in her family's living room) and being on the stage. Her grandfather, Fred Hunt, would take her to see the vaudeville shows that passed through Jamestown, and it was said Lucy was particularly mesmerized by the monologists, like Harry E. Humphrey, and how they kept the audience glued to every word.

Lucy acted in real plays, too, in elementary school, high school and throughout her little theater community in Jamestown and the region. She'd got it in her head that she wanted to command an audience from the stage, like the vaudeville performers she'd loved. According to her brother, Fred, who spoke at one of the Lucy Jamestown festivals in 2005, "As a young girl she was always on the go, always doing something, and kept every one of us busy worrying about her. Everything was a playhouse to her. Mom was supportive from day one … as long as Lucy was honest, and we were all honest with each other. We were all called on every day." Called on to help with Lucy's various productions, that is.

With mom DeDe's blessing Lucy attended the John Murray Anderson School in New York City to learn about acting. The star pupil at the time was Bette Davis, and Lucy was intimidated by her; Lucy, however, needn't have worried: She was told to go home—she was "wasting her mother's money" as she "had no talent."

Lucy's subsequent career is proof that there's an actual reason not to take "No" for an answer. Within a year, circa 1927, Lucy was back in New York, getting modeling jobs (like billboard work as the Chesterfield girl) and live gigs for designer Hattie Carnegie.

She would have to bear several more personal tragedies as a youngster: the accidental shooting death of a Jamestown boy with a gun given to Fred by her beloved Grandpa Hunt (after which trial the Hunts lost everything, and the family had to split up, Lucy's worst nightmare); and a bout with rheumatoid arthritis, after which she needed to learn how to walk again.

Being back in New York in the early 1930s, unemployed during the Depression, was no fun—when she wasn't looking for work, Lucy scoured diners to find leftover donuts; when she found one she ordered a cup of coffee—which was all she could afford—and sat down at the counter as if she belonged. That became lunch or dinner.

Eventually, her perseverance and modeling experience paid off. It was just such experience that an agent was looking for one summer day, when she ran into Lucy on the street. It was

1933. One of the girls going to Hollywood to test for Sam Goldwyn was pulled out of the running by her mother. Would Lucy be interested in taking a train trip west? Would she?!

On arrival in Hollywood, Lucy was christened a Goldwyn Girl and signed to a contract. She immediately sent for her family to come west and live with her. "She always had to have family around her," brother Fred noted in 2005 at one of the Jamestown Lucy festivals. "When she brought us all to Hollywood that was the first time the family had gotten back together since splitting up in Jamestown. She also treated the people she worked with as family." Fred ended up working for Lucy, then Lucy and Desi, in a variety of capacities. Eventually, Fred was put in charge of a lot of the accounting/financial operations. He also set up the [Desilu] transportation department.

Lucy was cast in her first movies, including an Eddie Cantor vehicle called *Roman Scandals* in 1933. Though it was little more than a glorified extra part, she straight away made herself stand out from the crowd of other girls by agreeing to take a mud pie in the face, or do whatever anyone asked of her. She didn't care how her looks held up on camera; she just wanted the experience. Director Busby Berkeley noticed her and told Sam Goldwyn to watch out for "that one," she was going to be big.

One of the other "girls" was blonde, beautiful Barbara Pepper (see <u>Pepper, Barbara</u>). Lucy and Barbara became great friends, and when Pepper fell on hard times later in the 1940s and early 1950s, Lucy made sure she had work by casting her in *I Love Lucy* bit parts, six times between 1952 and 1955. Pepper, who also appeared in more than a hundred films, ended her career on a high note: as the formidable Doris Ziffle on the TV hit *Green Acres*. (See also <u>Keefer, Vivian</u>.)

Back in the '30s, Lucy racked up bit part after bit part, graduating to co-starring roles in unmemorable comedy shorts and supporting roles in better pictures, like Fred Astaire and Ginger Rogers' *Follow the Fleet* (1936). She was working steadily under contact at RKO and finally made a real impression in the prestige picture *Stage Door* (1937), in which Lucy held her own against Katharine Hepburn, Rogers, and Eve Arden. After this film, Lucy would never be lower-billed than "co-star."

RKO gave her a two-film B series in which she played Annabel, an actress whose press agent has grand dreams for her. (See the entry <u>Osborne, Robert</u> for more on those films.) She made more of an impression in the low-budget but tense *Five Came Back* (1939) as the proverbial hooker with a gold heart who survives a nasty plane crash in South America and then has to survive the other survivors. The next year, she filmed one of her best roles, as the cynical dancer/stripper Bubbles, in *Dance, Girl, Dance*, one of the few mainstream films to that time directed by a woman (Dorothy Arzner). RKO then cast her as the lead, a college cutie, in *Too Many Girls* (1940). Though the film is a decent enough college caper of its era, it's more important for being the film on which Lucy met future husband (and love of her life) Desi Arnaz, repeating his stage role as a Cuban college football star. (See <u>Arnaz, Desi</u> for more.)

Lucy in the 1940s, by Howard Montiel. Author's collection

Lucy and Desi immediately fell in love and were married just months after the movie was completed. After leads in several forgettable comedies, Lucy filmed one of her last RKO pictures, *The Big Street*, a 1942 Damon Runyon sudser co-starring Henry Fonda as a busboy in love with a hardened night-club singer (Lucy). When her gangster lover cripples her, Fonda vows to give Lucy everything she wants. Brittle as cut glass and beautiful to boot, Lucy tore up the screen and finally proved she could, indeed, act.

As a result, she was offered a contract at MGM, then the Tiffany of movie studios, where she followed her pal Ann Sothern (who also toiled at RKO and then Columbia), playing many of the same roles. In fact, Lucy's first MGM role, as "herself" in 1943's *Best Foot Forward*, came about because Sothern got pregnant and couldn't do the film. This led to a series of Technicolor show-cases for Lucy, including *DuBarry Was a Lady* (1943) and my favorite Lucy film of this era, *Easy to Wed* (1946). If you've ever wanted to see Lucy as a true drop-dead gorgeous movie star, those are the three pictures to see.

In between, she was loaned out occasionally to do tight little films noir like *The Dark Corner* in 1946, and *Lured* in 1947, and filmed the occasional MGM prestige black-and-white pic (1945's *Without Love*, which ostensibly starred haughty Kate Hepburn and lively Spencer Tracy but in reality showcased Lucy and Keenan Wynn, her *Easy to Wed* co-star, who easily steal the picture). Bored with the choices of movies she was being given, Lucy took a big leap and signed to do a national stage tour of *Dream Girl*, a comedy/fantasy in which her character was onstage and talking nearly 100 percent of the time. *Dream Girl* was a country-wide smash during 1947, and reinforced the fact that Lucy was happiest when performing in front of a live audience (see Stage Career).

To prove her point, she took on a weekly radio sitcom, *My Favorite Husband*, which ran for three successful years (1948-'51). Co-starring the likeable Richard Denning as her long-suffering spouse, it was here that Lucy began to fashion the character that would become the crowning achievement of her career: Lucy Ricardo. With the help of head writer Jess Oppenheimer (formerly of Fanny Brice's *The Baby Snooks Show*), and writers Bob Carroll Jr. and Madelyn Pugh, Lucy and her fellow actors fashioned a weekly playlet involving the schemes of a slightly daffy housewife who always wanted just a little more than she had. Sound familiar?

All three scribes would follow Lucy from the radio show to television when CBS suggests the move.

♥ **Lucy Trivia** Lucy's first appearance on television was as a panelist on the game show *Pantomime Quiz* in 1949. The show was later known as *Stump the Stars*.

At the same time, Lucy had been dabbling a bit more than usual in slapstick in her movies, such as *The Fuller Brush Girl* and *Fancy Pants* (both 1950), to great success.

Lucy was adamant that Desi play her TV husband; she wanted to work with him side-by-side after nearly a decade of having separate (and often geographically distant) showbiz careers. CBS balked at first; who will believe, execs asked, that Lucy was married to a Cuban bandleader? "But I am!" she insisted. Lucy and Desi took to the streets (actually, a series of movie theaters) with a vaudeville act to prove that audiences did accept them as a duo. They were a smash success.

But more was necessary in order to make it work: Desi wanted the series filmed, which would make it look a lot nicer and more polished than the grainy kinescoped product most of the country saw (a show was normally produced and then filmed off a studio monitor; those copies were what the rest of the country saw). And Lucy needed to perform in front of a live audience. Film and live audiences meant more money (a studio with bleachers had to be built, for example). Lucy and Desi agreed to salary cuts with the stipulation that they owned the films. CBS agreed. When Lucy and Desi sold those films back to CBS for about $4.3

million in 1956 (as reported by the Museum of Broadcast Communications in Chicago), the rerun was born.

A pilot version of *I Love Lucy* was filmed in 1950. Lucy and Desi played Lucy and Larry Lopez; the showbiz theme was very much in evidence, but best friends and landlords Fred and Ethel Mertz were nowhere in sight. Perhaps that was because everyone assumed that sponsors could be sold solely on Lucy and Desi. They were right. Still, as late as May 1950 Lucy was doing typical, if not outright ridiculous, publicity like kissing the soldier voted "Prettiest GI" in the army's first-ever beauty pageant. That stuff would end with the mammoth success of *I Love Lucy.*

I Love Lucy was sold, and casting commenced. First choices for the neighborly and co-meddling Mertzes were Lucy's radio co-stars, Gale Gordon and Bea Benaderet, but both had already begun long runs on hit TV shows, Gordon in *Our Miss Brooks* (1952-'56), Benaderet in *The Burns and Allen Show* (1950-'58). Every character actor and actress of a certain age was considered, including Oscar-nominee James Gleason (for 1941's *Here Comes Mr. Jordan*), but it was said he demanded too much money.

Barbara Pepper, Lucy's Goldwyn Girl pal, desperately wanted to play Ethel Mertz, but Desi had already hired a known alcoholic (and suspected troublemaker) to play Fred Mertz: movie and stage veteran William Frawley. Desi made Frawley promise that his drinking and offstage escapades would never affect the series, and they never did. But the thinking was, why risk working with *two* drinkers? (Pepper had lost her husband several years before in a tragic accident, and her drinking had escalated.)

Desi ended up hiring Vivian Vance after seeing her perform in San Diego as the sarcastic best friend, Olive Lashbrooke, in *The Voice of the Turtle*, at the suggestion of *I Love Lucy's* first-year director Marc Daniels, a friend of Vance's. Desi saw her and lit up, proclaiming, "That's our Ethel!"

Several problems: Vance had just completed small parts in two movies and was optimistic about a film career. She'd starred on Broadway and toured in both plays and musicals. She wasn't sure she wanted to do a television series. But she said yes, tentatively. A bigger problem: She and Lucy had never met; they did so several days before filming the first episode of *I Love Lucy.* Though Lucy initially thought Vance was too pretty and sophisticated looking to play frumpy Ethel, Vance convinced her that she "filmed frumpy." That attitude, plus Vance's willingness to rehearse as much as was needed to perfect the comedy they performed, ultimately won Lucy over.

♥ **Lucy Trivia** Vance's contract did not stipulate, as legend has it, that she remain 20 pounds overweight while playing Ethel. That urban legend is a result of a "gag contract" Lucy presented to Vance in the 1950s, which Vance read during an appearance with Lucy on *Dinah!* in April 1975.

When *I Love Lucy* debuted on October 15, 1951, it was an instant hit. Everything that Lucy and Desi had put together clicked, from the cast to the innovative filming technique using three cameras (and employing Oscar-winning cinematographer William Freund) to the writing and direction. For a detailed examination of the show and its success from some of the people who were part of it, see *I Love Lucy*.

Lucy had her own beliefs as to the initial and continuing success (in reruns) of her show. She had wanted to create a female lead character the audiences could identify with, someone who wasn't out of reach of Mr. and Mrs. America, but could have lived next door. Thus, Ricky Ricardo was always just *this*close to immense fame. The things that Lucy wanted (a new hat, dress, dishwasher, or furniture) were what audiences of the 1950s also desired. But mostly, she told *TV Guide* in 1959, "It's so important to have what I like to call the enchanted sense of play. Many, many times you should think and react as a child in doing comedy. All the inhibitions and embarrassments disappear. We did some pretty crazy things in *I Love Lucy*, but we believed every minute of them. It's like getting drunk without taking a drink."

Around the same time, hoping to give back to younger actors what she had learned working in Hollywood, Lucy ran an actors' workshop under the Desilu banner; the most famous alumni were Carole Cook, Ken Berry, Majel Barrett (*Star Trek*), and Hollywood columnist and Turner Classic Movies host Robert Osborne. The only TV program to emerge from the workshop was the seldom-seen "Desilu Review," a Christmas Special that aired December 25, 1959, showcasing the talents of all the "kids" in the workshop. It featured the *I Love Lucy* cast and other Desilu guest stars (Danny Thomas, Ann Sothern) to bolster viewership.

Lucy and Desi had bought the former RKO Studios (where both had worked in B movies early in their careers) for a bargain $6 million in 1957 to expand the Desilu facilities. By 1960, Desilu was grossing more than $20 million a year, more than some of Hollywood's big movie studios. Desilu produced more than 30 series in its heyday, including *Our Miss Brooks*, *December Bride*, all the Lucy series up through *The Lucy Show*, and the controversial, violent success, *The Untouchables* (1959-'63).

Sadly, also in 1960, Lucy and Desi finally divorced after 20 tumultuous years. Oh, they still loved each other, all right, they just couldn't live together. Each picked a less fiery, more domestic-type partner within several years: Lucy chose Catskills comic Gary Morton, introduced to her by *Wildcat* co-star Paula Stewart, and Desi wed another vibrant redhead, Edie Hirsch.

Lucy's movie career effectively ended in the 1950s, except for successful anomalies like *The Long, Long Trailer* (1954), *Facts of Life* (1960), and *Yours, Mine and Ours* (1968). The latter

Lucy in the 1960s. Photofest

was no doubt her biggest commercial success, earning $25 million in 1968 bucks.

After divorcing Desi, Lucy made a total break and took the kids to New York, planning to star in her first Broadway musical, *Wildcat*. Though she worked her butt off and got wonderful personal reviews, the book of the musical was savaged by critics. (One of the show's hit songs, "Hey, Look Me Over," became forever associated with Lucy.) Even though *Wildcat*'s story was weak, as long as Lucy starred in it, it made money. But she overestimated her own energy and emotional state, which led to a physical collapse. When Lucy left the show, *Wildcat* closed. (See the extended entry under <u>Stage Career</u>.)

Once recuperated, Lucy decided to return to what she did best: TV. She insisted she wouldn't come back without her pal and sidekick, Vivian Vance, and after months of cajoling, Vance was convinced to do *The Lucy Show*. In it, her character would be called Vivian and she'd get to wear nice clothes. This was a big plus for her, a step away from Ethel Mertz. In the two years since finishing *The Lucy-Desi Comedy Hour*, Vance had returned to her first love, the stage, had a facelift, and remarried. She and book editor husband John Dodds lived in Connecticut, so Vance commuted every week to Los Angeles to do the series, starting in the fall of 1962.

Though basically *I Love Lucy* without the men, *The Lucy Show* was an immediate hit and ran for six years. The first two seasons, in glorious black and white, showcased some of the best Ball/Vance slapstick ever, as they attempted to install a TV antenna, fix a broken shower, find a lost contact lens in cake batter, and sleep in bunk beds with the use of stilts, among other wacky stunts. Those early shows, in fact, preserve a record of the fine comedy team Ball and Vance had become. The kids are more prominent than in the following years, but that doesn't stop the episodes from focusing on the two people everyone tuned in to watch: Lucy and Vivian. Each was the comic yin to the other's yang. These episodes remain a delight to watch.

The Lucy Show was in the top five programs for four years, and finished its run in 1968 at No. 2. By then, Vance had left, tired of commuting, and was only an occasional guest. Lucy, who realized she could not replace her comedy pal, survived on guest stars for the remaining three years, and expanded the role of the blustery banker, Mr. Mooney, played by Gale Gordon.

At this point in her career, without Desi's instinctive knowledge of what worked and what didn't, and without her original directors and writers, Lucy began to take charge of her set. She knew everything there was to know about producing a sitcom, but her insecurities reportedly turned her into an unthinking sergeant who barked orders at everyone, no matter how big or small. Guest stars as varied as Joan Crawford, Richard Burton, Jack Benny, and George Burns commented on her unnecessarily gruff behavior.

William Frawley died in 1966; ironically, his final TV appearance was a cameo on *The Lucy Show*. Frawley had gone from *The Lucy-Desi Comedy Hour* to a supporting role in the Fred MacMurray hit *My Three Sons* (1960-'72). Frawley stayed as long as he could be insured (1965), and was then forced to leave. At his passing, Desi took out a full-page ad in the trade paper *Variety* that showed a picture of Frawley and read, "Buenos Noches, Amigo" (Goodnight, my Friend).

In 1962, Lucy had bought out Desi's share of Desilu (spending more than $2.5 million for 300,350 shares of stock), becoming the first woman to head a major Hollywood studio and the highest-ranking TV executive in the world. She often complained about running the business end, and eventually sold it to Paramount in 1967 for a then-hefty $17 million. Two of her final acts at Desilu were giving the go-ahead for pilots called *Star Trek* and *Mission: Impossible*. Some have surmised that since *The Lucy Show* was a Desilu Production (its final one) Lucy ended it and changed formats in 1968 to avoid paying any money to her old studio.

In any case, she set up Lucille Ball Productions and went ahead with *Here's Lucy*, her third sitcom hit, in which her kids, Lucie and Desi Jr., played major supporting roles (along with Gale Gordon, this time playing "Uncle Harry"). Desi Jr. left after three seasons to pursue a movie career, and Lucy and the rest held out for three more years, by which time the show had sunk from a high of being the No. 3 program (the 1970-'71 season) to dropping out of the Top 25 in its final season (1973-'74).

During the filming of *Here's Lucy's* second season, in September 1969, Lucy gave an interview to the AP's Cynthia Lowry that ran in the *Lima* (Ohio) *News*, among other papers. In it, she waxed philosophical: "Gary and the children are always asking me what I want, and the other day I told them. I want a lodge, on a mountain, in the trees. I want a place with privacy, deep woods, rough beams, and where you can chop wood." Gary and Desi Jr. would be doing the chopping, she clarified.

Desi Sr., meanwhile, had formed his own company, Desi Arnaz Productions, and had a minor hit in *The Mothers-in-Law* (1967-'69), which starred Eve Arden and Kaye Ballard. It was the only pilot he produced that went on to become a series. He made the occasional guest appearance (hosting *Saturday Night Live* in 1976) and movie, and wrote a best-selling autobiography (*A Book*), but mostly seemed happy out of the public eye. Eventually, he and Lucy warmed up and bonded all over again with their grandchildren from Lucie's marriage to actor Laurence Luckinbill.

Once Lucy stopped filming a weekly series—the final new episode of *Here's Lucy* aired on March 21, 1974—she remained on TV for a series of successful specials and the rare TV movie, such as 1985's *The Stone Pillow*, in which she played way against type as a homeless bag lady; viewers chafed at not seeing her play the Lucy character. During this period she lost two people who were very important to her personally and professionally: her mother, DeDe (in 1977), and her comic partner, Vance (in 1979). Her mom had sat in the audience of every show Lucy had ever done except her final one, *Lucy Calls the President*. (Lucy and Vance last appeared together on that 1977 special.) It is said Lucy broke up and couldn't go on for a moment when she realized that, for the first time, her mother was not out there cheering her on.

The public mostly wanted to see her as lovable buttinsky and show business wannabe Lucy Ricardo, and refused to accept her in almost any other role. Her final film, *Mame* (1974), was a disastrous misstep (Desi warned her not to take the role and was right, as he usually was about business decisions). It may have been doomed from the start once Angela Lansbury, who created the role on Broadway, was passed over by Warner Bros. for the part because she wasn't a big enough "star." *Mame* unfortunately capped Lucy's long film career. (For more, see Connell, Jane; Film Career, Kahn, Madeline, and DVD Reviews.)

Vance, meanwhile, having done sporadic TV work but mostly performing on stage, had found happiness (via residuals) as Maxine, the Maxwell House Coffee spokesperson, in a series of TV commercials. She'd already suffered a stroke by 1977, and was fighting breast and bone cancer on top of that. Lucy and fellow comedienne (and friend) Mary Wickes trekked to San Francisco, where Vance was living with her husband, for one final, bittersweet goodbye to the woman who defined the sitcom's nosy but lovable neighbor. After Vance's death, Lucy would often tear up or cry when asked to speak about her invaluable sidekick.

Lucy found she missed working, and grew tired of just showing up to accept awards and honors. When the opportunity to star in weekly sitcom came up, courtesy of Aaron Spelling (who, as an actor, had a bit part on an episode of *I Love Lucy*), Lucy grabbed it. But audiences did not want to see Lucy as a frisky grandmother in *Life with Lucy*, and the writing and format were stuck back in the 1970s, the last time she was on a weekly series.

For the first time on TV, reviews were horrific for Lucy personally, and ratings dropped precipitously after the first airing. Though guest star Audrey Meadows and Lucy had real chemistry when Meadows played her sister in one episode, by then it was too late. The series was yanked in the fall of 1986 after only eight episodes; the rest are stored with the entire series at The Lucille Ball-Desi Arnaz Center in Jamestown (they were donated by Spelling), where they are occasionally shown at the Center's biannual Lucy festivals.

On December 22, 1986, Lucy was honored by the Kennedy Center in Washington, D.C., which must have helped ease the pain of the cancellation of her final series, but couldn't have helped much to console her after the loss of the true love of her life, Desi, who died of lung cancer earlier in December. After *I Love Lucy*, Ball never hesitated to give the lion's share of credit for the show's success to Desi, something Hollywood only did after his death: "At his death," recalled Dann Cahn, *I Love Lucy* film editor, "there were only a handful of us that went down to the funeral from Hollywood [to scatter his ashes]—the two writers, Bob and Madelyn, Danny Thomas, Bill Asher and myself. Very few people [in the Hollywood community] acknowledged their respect for Desi at the time."

Desi's remembrances of Lucy for the Kennedy Center tribute—read by Desilu star Robert Stack (*The Untouchables*)—were particularly touching, especially his sentiment that *I Love Lucy* was "never just a title." Desi and the show itself were posthumously enshrined in the Television Academy Hall of Fame, several years after Lucy was honored as one of the first inductees (1984). After the Kennedy Center, Lucy would make public appearances mostly to accept awards, honor other performers, or for charity. Her last public appearance, fittingly with longtime co-star (four movies, lots of TV) and pal Bob Hope, was at the 1989 Academy Awards (held on March 29). Looking positively radiant in a gown slit up to her thigh showing

off her still-shapely gams, Lucy and Bob entered to a prolonged standing ovation, bantered and presented the "stars of the future," including Ricki Lake, Tracy Nelson, Corey Feldman, and Christian Slater. It's unlikely any of them will ever have the impact Lucy or Hope has had.

Lucy was rushed to Cedars-Sinai Medical Center in Los Angeles several weeks later, and died a week after that, on April 26, of a ruptured aorta. Her condition was reported to have been improving, so Lucy's death was a shock to the world, which mourned her for weeks.

Her passing was treated with the kind of coverage reserved for presidents and royalty. TV networks cleared their slates for several nights, offering tributes and reruns (see *Entertainment Tonight*). Dan Rather began a special hour-long CBS tribute the evening of her

Lucy in 1986, around the time of her final series and the Kennedy Center tribute. Photofest

death with, "We lost a member of the family today." There were public memorial services on both coasts.

We all felt as though we had lost a dear friend. *People* magazine reported that its May 8, 1989 memorial issue with Lucy on the cover was "far and away *People*'s best-seller of the year" (and the fourth largest-selling magazine of 1989 in the category of 400,000-plus subscribers). It's no wonder, too, that *People* was just one of many to try to cash in on the public mourning by publishing a *second* Lucy memorial issue, in the summer of 1989.

Longtime co-star Gordon noted, "My grief, although it is deep … is nothing compared to what her family must feel, and, in her case, the entire world." Friend Danny Thomas said, "She was the best female clown that ever lived, no question…. Lucy did everything."

Lucy, who wanted to do *I Love Lucy* in order to be close to her husband, ended up preserving *I Love Lucy* on film, creating, in essence, the modern situation comedy and reruns that became a staple of TV programming around the world. She *was* a member of the family to many people, and that explains the utter sadness at her passing better than anything else.

The press coverage of her death and funeral also served notice that Lucy needn't have worried that the public had abandoned her. She had been in our lives for so long, and brought so many so much happiness, that she had become a trusted and beloved friend. Television had given Lucy the outlet she'd been waiting for: a chance to perform her slapstick before a live audience; yet the comedy was always based on the character, and the characters in *I Love Lucy* left plenty of room for engaging situations. The fearless performer she became endeared her to the hearts of an America that needed a laugh after World War II. Her wife-trying-to-be-more-than-a-housefrau subtly expressed the emotions percolating underneath many women of the era.

The honors and tributes continue, year after year (Cable network TV Land honored Lucy as a TV Legend in April 2007, for example). For, in truth, who has given the world more laughter than Lucille Ball? Who has made people forget their troubles and smile in the worst of situations more than Lucy and company? And who is needed, perhaps more than ever, to shine an uplifting light on all of us? In a world where we deal with death and destruction and poverty and sadness on an hourly basis, we can say of Lucy, "She made us laugh." She still does. And that's all she needed to do.

Postscript: From the Amazon.com page of a new book called *The Last Days of Dead Celebrities*, a Booklist review notes, "And when Fink [the author] quotes an expiring Lucille Ball remarking, 'I'm so tired of myself' (to which veteran couch potatoes may breathe a silent 'You and me both'), he imparts insight into what it must be like to end life with a celebrity-crazed public raptly watching."

The "dying quote" (I haven't read the book) is sad if nothing else. What's sadder still to me is the reviewer thought he needed to add his own two cents about how "veteran couch potatoes" are just plain sick of Lucy. Honestly, in all the years I've spent writing about Lucy I've certainly heard some negatives about her behavior on the set (especially after she split with Desi and took control of her own production company). But even those who had not-so-nice things to say never said anything remotely like they were sick of her. And judging from the continued popularity of *I Love Lucy*, *The Lucy Show*, and *Here's Lucy*, as well as Lucy's own iconic status, it seems just the opposite is true: We regular fans (many of whom are veteran couch potatoes) will never get sick of her, or tired of hearing about her. So to that reviewer, I humbly suggest—if you're not interested, change the channel.

BALLARD, KAYE

Born in 1926, Ballard played in vaudeville and appeared in television and movies from the early 1950s. Short, stout, and with a foghorn voice, she was limited to comic roles, but she found success on TV partnered with Eve Arden in the sitcom, *The Mothers-In-Law*, produced and occasionally directed by Desi Arnaz. Ballard also shined spitting out one-liners as a semi-regular on the original *Hollywood Squares* (circa 1968) and in support of Doris Day on *The Doris Day Show* (1970-'71).

The dark-haired comic actress noted in her 2006 biography, *How I Lost 10 Pounds in 53 Years: A Memoir*, that she and Carol Burnett had both worked with, and admired, Lucille Ball: "If it hadn't been for Lucy (and Martha Raye) leading the way, our careers, along with those of so many other comediennes, would have been a lot more difficult." Ball had called Ballard to her table after seeing the latter's nightclub act in the sixties, and said two words—"You're funny"—that "coming from her" left Ballard speechless.

Kaye reported that Ann Sothern was the first choice for Ballard's role on *The Mothers-In-Law*, but that Sothern's and Arden's comedy styles were deemed too similar. (Sothern claimed she turned down the part, and that it was one of her "most regretted decisions," in her bio, *Cordially Yours*). Once Ball recommended Ballard to Arnaz, he sent writer Bob Carroll Jr. to Detroit to see Ballard's act, and she got the part of Kaye Buell.

Ballard became a friend to Ball and Arnaz. She has said one of the great joys of working on the show was the opportunity to get to know Ball, but notes that the redhead was not easy to get to know. Ballard describes Ball as no-nonsense offscreen, with a strong will and the desire to be in control. She could be cruel, Ballard notes, but in Ball's mind she was just stating the truth or the obvious. Ballard added that games were Ball's passion. If you liked to play them, you were fine with her; if you didn't, no dice.

Arnaz, by contrast, was much more accessible and lovable, personally. He let Ballard weekend at his second home at the Palm Springs Thunderbird Country Club (he bought one near Ball and Gary Morton, after he married Edith Hirsch in 1963). She told writer Allene Arthur that, "He always left the refrigerator stocked with champagne and caviar." After *The Mothers-in-Law* ended in 1969, Arnaz sold the home to Ballard (in 1970), who is still in residence as of this printing, along with some of Arnaz's furniture.

A gossip item from the 1970s notes: "Not too long ago robust comic Kaye Ballard was complaining to her pal Lucille Ball that she was feeling too robust for her own good. Always one to lend a helping hand, Lucille bluntly told her weighty pal, 'Enjoy yourself during the day—but eat very lightly at night!' The best part of the diet, admits Kaye, is, 'in the morning, I start each day by getting on the scale and finding I haven't gained! What joy.' Don't worry, Lucy, we're sure Kaye doesn't mean an Almond Joy!"

Ballard stated in her bio that Ball and Arnaz remained in love with each other all of their lives.

BALL OF FIRE (BOOK)

This 2003 biography of Lucille Ball by Stefan Kanfer got a lot of initial publicity, including the cover of the *New York Times Book Review*, which is about as big as it gets. But any national publicity is good for all Lucy fans. The "warts-and-all" portrait of Ball and Arnaz, and their cherished sitcom *I Love Lucy*, doesn't ignore the negative aspects of their personalities, which led to the dissolution of their marriage, their TV show, and their empire.

But the author, in his painstaking research, provides a balanced portrait of the biggest star television has yet produced. The one area in which I can find fault is that Kanfer doesn't really do much to explain his stated thesis: why Ball didn't click until she moved from the big screen to the small screen. I believe the answer is there in Ball's story—she found her calling, if you will, performing in front of a live audience onstage and on radio, and wanted to be able to do that on TV—but it's never overtly stated in the book.

Still, I am prepared to be especially kind to Kanfer because he's done his homework: I was surprised (and pleased) to find my name in the book's index. On the page specified, Kanfer calls *Lucy A to Z* an amalgam "of insight, fact, and trivia," and quotes an item from this book that illustrates the *I Love Lucy* influence on sitcoms that followed it (see The *I Love Lucy* Influence, of course).

BALL OF FIRE (FILM)

Classic Howard Hawks comedy from 1941 that *almost* starred Lucille Ball. Producer Sam Goldwyn offered the lead female part of Sugarpuss O'Shea, a singer on the lam from the Mob, to Ginger Rogers, who turned it down. He next went to Carole Lombard, who was otherwise engaged, but went to bat for Ball, based on her performance as the stripper in *Dance, Girl, Dance*. But Gary Cooper was already cast as the male lead, and Goldwyn wanted a female star of Cooper's magnitude, so he gave the part to Barbara Stanwyck.

BARBERSHOP QUARTET

This unique type of four-part harmony was featured in the *I Love Lucy* episode "Lucy's Show Business Swan Song," in which the pregnant Ball, hidden under the towels in a barber's seat, replaces the fourth partner in the quartet, surprising the other singers (Ricky, Fred, and Ethel, naturally) who do their best to keep her from singing off-key by sticking their shaving brushes, full of lather, in her mouth every time Lucy opens it. Lucy returned to this theme in a *Lucy Show* episode called "Lucy's Barbershop Quartet."

BARRETT, RONA

A pioneering female broadcast journalist (1967's *Dateline: Hollywood*, a precursor to *Entertainment Tonight* et. al.; 1973's *ABC Late Night*; and 1975's debut of *Good Morning America*), Barrett is better remembered as *the* Hollywood gossip columnist of the 1970s and 1980s. Taking over where Hedda Hopper and Louella Parsons left off, Barrett was basically the only (big) name in the game during her reign, which included presiding over several fan magazines, each with her name in the title, guaranteeing sales. Barrett knew many stars, but was friend to only a handful, and Ball was one of them. Always featured prominently in Barrett's magazines or TV segments (and pictured on at least a half-dozen covers between 1971 and 1976), Ball was invariably accorded a measure of respect that Barrett gave only a select few. In 1981, Barrett broadcast an exclusive: the first footage of the "lost" *I Love Lucy* Christmas episode on her short-lived series, *Television: Inside and Out*.

BASIL, TONI

The video of choreographer/actress/singer Basil's hypnotic hit "Mickey" (1982) was added to the Rock & Roll Hall of Fame in Cleveland as an illustration of a "one-hit wonder" (an artist who climbs to the top of the charts only once in his or her career). In 2001 VH1 named it "the No. 1 one-hit wonder of all time." It has also received another unique honor: a parody version by "Weird Al" Yankovic, called "Ricky," using, of course, *I Love Lucy* themes in the lyrics.

BEAUMONT, HUGH

Best known as Beaver's patient, loving dad on *Leave it to Beaver* (1957-'63), Beaumont had a bit part in Ball's 1943 movie, *DuBarry Was a Lady.*

BENADERET, BEA

A beloved character actress who co-starred with Lucille Ball in *My Favorite Husband* on radio, Benaderet was supposedly Ball's first choice to play Ethel Mertz, but Benaderet was already a TV regular, as neighbor Blanche Morton on George Burns and Gracie Allen's hit sitcom.

Benaderet's remarkable voice characterizations gave her an enviable career in radio (*Jack Benny, Fibber McGee and Molly*), and she also often provided female voices for the classic Warner Bros. cartoons of the 1940s and 1950s.

Benaderet guest-starred once on *I Love Lucy*, as the Ricardo's memorably romance-minded older neighbor. She subsequently starred in *The Flintstones* (as the original voice of Betty Rubble), *The Beverly Hillbillies* (as Cousin Pearl, Jethro's mom), and perhaps her best-remembered sitcom, *Petticoat Junction* (as Kate). She died of lung cancer in 1968 during the run of that show.

BENNY, JACK

Born in 1894, Benny was a radio, movie, and television comedian, known for his expert comic timing and his carefully crafted image as a cheapskate. His sitcom remains one of the longest-running shows in TV history (1950-'65).

Benny was a friend and neighbor of Ball's in Beverly Hills, and performed with her many times on TV, on her show, on his show, and on various specials. Of his performances on *The Lucy Show*, the best remembered is "Lucy Gets Jack Benny's Account," which aired October 16, 1967. A scene in which Lucy shows Benny the special bank devised to hold his money was, at the time, the most expensive one-shot television gag in history; the vault featured a guillotine, tomahawk-throwing Indians, a gorilla, piranhas, snapping turtles, and quicksand.

Benny also appeared four times on *Here's Lucy* and had a cameo in *A Guide for the Married Man* (1967), as did Lucy. After one of his appearances, Benny reportedly told Ball to "calm down, you already have the job," referring to her bossy behavior during filming. The beloved comic died in 1974.

BERLE, MILTON

The comedian known as "Mr. Television" and "Uncle Miltie," famous for his onstage drag and the facility to do anything for a laugh, actually dated the Queen of Comedy in 1937, early in their careers. His suffocating stage mother, who, Ball said, "was around all the time," thwarted the affair. Berle and Ball remained pals; he was a guest on *The Lucille Ball-Desi Arnaz Show*, and appeared many times on Ball's later series (see Guest Stars for actual show dates). He also appeared on the special *CBS Salutes Lucy: The First 25 Years* (1976) and with Lucy on an HBO magic special in 1981. Berle died at the age of 93 in March 2002.

BERMAN, PANDRO

Starting off in the 1920s as a script clerk, Berman rose to become a film editor and producer under David Selznick's reign at RKO studios. There, he was well respected and credited for pairing Fred Astaire and Ginger Rogers, and turning Katharine Hepburn into a star. He also took a young starlet named Lucille Ball under his wing, and was responsible for Ball getting many of her first big breaks in the movies (such as *Stage Door* in 1937).

Berman had tried to get Ball cast in the original Broadway production of *Stage Door* without success. This led to his helping her get cast in the short-lived play *Hey, Diddle Diddle*, which got only slightly further than the McCarter Theater in Princeton, N.J. (See Stage Career.)

Ball accompanied Berman (who was a married Catholic with kids) to industry functions, but refused to become the other woman when he confessed his love for her in the late 1930s. At that point, he lost interest in her career. Berman moved on to a successful stint at MGM and produced movies until 1970. He died in 1996.

BEVERLY PALMS HOTEL

Fictitious Beverly Hills hotel where the Ricardos and Mertzes stayed during the California episodes of *I Love Lucy*—probably derived from the actual Beverly Hills Hotel, which Ball and Arnaz did visit on occasion.

BICENTENNIAL MINUTE

Premiering on July 4, 1974, and running through July 4, 1976, the United States' 200th birthday, these one-minute spots aired on CBS in prime time. Each of the 732 minutes celebrated a moment from American history that took place 200 years before, on that day. Lucille Ball's *Bicentennial Minute* was about the corn-shucking parties New Englanders held to relieve themselves of the monotony of everyday life, and aired November 28, 1974. It was taped on October 15, 1974.

BIOGRAPHY

This cable show on the A&E network offers biographies of well-known personalities from all walks of life. In the 1990s, *Biography* offered a two-hour special on the life of Lucille Ball; it was subsequently yanked and the film *Lucy & Desi: A Home Movie* by Lucie Arnaz was played on occasion as the Lucy bio. In January 2002, to celebrate its 15 years on the air, the show began a series of specials with *TV's 15 Greatest Comedians*. Picked by a panel of more than 250 critics and comedians, our favorite redhead was No. 1 (the rest of the list, in order from top to bottom, was Jackie Gleason, Sid Caesar, Johnny Carson, Jack Benny, Carol Burnett, Milton Berle, Groucho Marx, Bill Cosby, Ernie Kovacs, Richard Pryor, Robin Williams, Bob Hope, Steve Martin, and Steve Allen). On *Biography*'s website (Biography.com), surfers were encouraged to vote for their own favorite "all-time greatest TV comedian," and in late January 2002 Ball was the top choice of 33,901 voters with a whopping 63 percent. Her closest competitors were Carol Burnett (seven percent of the vote) and Bob Hope (six percent).

BODY LANGUAGE

Mid-1980s game show based on Charades and hosted by Tom Kennedy, in which celebrities helped contestants compete for cash prizes. Ball guest-starred several times, including the week of December 24-28, 1984, with Isabel Sanford, Richard Simmons, and Robert Morse.

BOOKS

A treasure trove of books exists detailing the behind-the-scenes drama and events of the life of Lucille Ball and *I Love Lucy*. Among the best are, in alphabetical order:

Ball of Fire, The Tumultuous Life and Comic Art of Lucille Ball, by Stefan Kanfer (Knopf, 2003). The latest and one of the best; see separate entry.

But Darling, I'm Your Auntie Mame! A 1998 book by Richard Tyler Jordan that covers all the book, stage, and movie productions based on Patrick Dennis' 1955 novel *Auntie Mame.* One long chapter dissects what was wrong with Lucy's 1974 film version in a mostly objective and fair manner. This is a must for those who need every bit of writing and criticism about Lucy.

Desilu: The Story of Lucille Ball and Desi Arnaz, by Coyne Steven Sanders and Tom Gilbert (1993). A solid look at the Ball/Arnaz story from the perspective of the studio they built and nurtured.

For the Love of Lucy: The Complete Guide for Collectors and Fans, by Ric B. Wyman (1995). A great book spotlighting Ball collectibles in many categories and what they're worth. Wyman is the executive director of The Lucy-Desi Center in Jamestown, N.Y.

Forever Lucy: The Life of Lucille Ball, by Joe Morella and Edward Z. Epstein (1986). Hastily assembled bio interesting mainly for being one of the earliest attempts to chart Lucy's life. First published as *Lucy: The Bittersweet Life of Lucille Ball* (1973).

The I Love Lucy *Book,* by Bart Andrews (1985). See separate entry.

The I Love Lucy *Book of Trivia,* by Ric B. Wyman (2001).

I Loved Lucy: My Friendship With Lucille Ball, by Lee Tannen (2001). A memoir by a cousin of Lucy's second husband, Gary Morton, that concentrates on the last decade or so of Lucy's life.

I Love Lucy: *The Complete Picture History of the Most Popular TV Show Ever* by Michael McClay (1995). Photos and plots from every episode, with a special spotlight on the "35 best" episodes. McClay is the son of one of Lucy's publicists.

I Love Lucy: *The Official 50th Anniversary Edition, Celebrating 50 Years of Love and Laughter*, by Elisabeth Edwards (2001). Oversized official 50th anniversary book, long on pictures and a true inside look at the classic show (Edwards is Lucie Arnaz's personal assistant).

Laugh with Lucy, by Joel H. Cohen. Long out-of-print 1974 paperback published by Scholastic for kids/teens. With a straightforward, short (92 pages) positive-role-model look at Ball's career to that point, collectors covet this rare volume.

Laughs, Luck … and Lucy: How I Came to Create the Most Popular Sitcom of All Time, by Jess Oppenheimer (1996). Completed by Jess's son Gregg, this meaty volume goes way behind the scenes of the creation of *I Love Lucy*. It comes with an audio CD.

Love, Lucy, by Lucille Ball and Betty Hannah Hoffman (1996). Of historical interest as it contains Ball's own memories of the events in her life, but do not expect any angst or horror stories; also, the book ended in the 1960s when Ball shelved the project. Published posthumously with great fanfare in 1997.

Loving Lucy: An Illustrated Tribute to Lucille Ball, by Bart Andrews and Thomas J. Watson (1980). See *The I Love Lucy Book*.

Lucille: The Life of Lucille Ball by Kathleen Brady (1994). If I had to pick just one favorite Lucy bio not written by an insider, this would be it; well written and revealing.

Lucy, by Annie McGarry (1993). Slim (less than 90 pages) hardcover with lots of full-page pictures.

The Lucy Book: A Complete Guide to Her Five Decades on Television, by Geoffrey Mark Fidelman (1999). The most complete archive of Ball's television career that I've ever seen. See separate entry.

Lucy: The Real Life of Lucille Ball, by Charles Higham (1986). Breezily written, serviceable biography.

The Real Story of Lucille Ball, by Eleanor Harris (1954), Ballantine Books. A first-edition paperback, now a rare find, this came out at the height of Lucy's early TV fame and features headshots of the *I Love Lucy* cast on the back cover. Containing one long interview with Ball, there is little scandal here but lots of revealing quotes.

Stay Tuned: Television's Unforgettable Moments (2003), by Joe Garner, focuses on 36 landmark events in news, sports, and show business. Opening with Ball's spiel for Vitameatavegamin, the book devotes four pages to Ball and *I Love Lucy*. It comes with a companion DVD and two audio CDs that offer picture and sound to complement the 36 watershed events. Ball (giving her pitch) is also on the cover of this book, which offers nothing new for fans, but is a must-have for the collectible completist.

Finally, there are my three companion books to *Lucy A to Z*: *Lucy in Print* (2003), which examines the life and career of Ball, Arnaz, and their co-stars via the press coverage they received over the past 60 years; *The Lucille Ball Quiz Book* (2004), which is self-explanatory; and the most recent, *The Comic DNA of Lucille Ball: Interpreting the Icon* (2005), a look at how Lucy's status with her fans and the public has amazingly grown more solid since her passing.

The above books will get you started (and keep you busy!) reviewing the "Lucy" pantheon. My favorites tend to be the more obscure or unusual books, such as the Eleanor Harris book, the small-format *I Love Lucy Guide to Life*, or the campy Whitman hardcover novel based on the characters from *The Lucy Show* called <u>*Lucy and the Madcap Mystery*</u>.

BORN YESTERDAY

It's been written that Ball was considered, however briefly, for the role of Billie Dawn, the dumb blonde that Judy Holliday made famous in 1950. There's no record of Ball playing the role onstage, but according to the *N.Y. Herald Tribune* on July 2, 1949, "Lucille Ball is coming east to play the Judy Holliday role in *Born Yesterday* at the Henry Miller Theatre." That would have been a hot ticket.

BOYAJIAN, GARRET

Garret Boyajian is an Emmy-winning producer/director and <u>Lucille Ball</u> authority. The GAB Entertainment president's love of Lucy began at the age of three. As an adolescent he became a member of the *Loving Lucy* fan club, participated in Ball Q & A's, and even had the rare opportunity to enjoy Ball as she performed live the legendary "Lucy" character. Through the years, Boyajian has become close friends with many of the behind-the-scenes professionals and character players associated with Ball's long career. It was *I Love Lucy* creator/producer Jess Oppenheimer who encouraged Garret to pursue a career in producing. Along with producing associate <u>George Ridjaneck</u>, Boyajian has spent years preserving the legacy of Ball, <u>Desi Arnaz</u>, and <u>Desilu</u>. To date, GAB Entertainment's Lucille Ball Library contains more than 200 interviews. Stay tuned for GAB's feature-length documentary on Ball and her fans, as well as the forthcoming film *You Know the Face*, about Charles Lane, Hollywood's oldest actor and frequent Lucy/Desi character player, which GAB is producing with Jeff MacIntyre. Boyajian promises "many Lucille Ball-related projects to come." Visit gabentertainment.com for more.

BREAKFAST

Such was the publicity grind of the movie studios in the 1940s that a star could be photographed in virtually any situation. One picture of Ball beautifully made up and coiffed, wearing a stylish hat of the era at a rakish angle, shows Ball sitting at a booth lifting a fork to her lips, with a plate of bacon and eggs before her. The caption: "Lucille Ball believes in breakfast. Here, in a studio commissary, she eats what a dietician suggests: orange juice, eggs, bacon, buttered toast, and coffee."

BUNGLE ABBEY

A TV sitcom pilot directed by Ball in 1981, this never made it as a series. Starring Gale Gordon as "The Abbott," and produced by Lucille Ball Productions, the show was about a bunch of screwball monks (including the always-wacky Charlie Callas) in a monastery.

BURNETT, CAROL

Another legendary redheaded comedian, Burnett was befriended by Ball backstage on the second night of Burnett's early Broadway success, 1959's *Once Upon a Mattress*; it was then, Burnett often recalls, that Ball told her, "Listen kid, if you ever need anything, just call." Burnett took Ball up on the offer for a special she did several years later. The two formed a mutual admiration society that flourished for more than three decades. Burnett guest-starred a half-dozen or so times on *The Lucy Show*, and Ball returned the favor by guest-starring on Burnett's hit variety show and several specials.

Burnett has always dealt very reverently with her friendship with Ball. She introduced Lucy when Ball was inducted into the Television Academy Hall of Fame, and she spoke very lovingly of Ball for the PBS documentary *American Masters: Finding Lucy* (2000), noting that Ball never forgot her birthday, and always sent flowers. Ball died on Burnett's birthday in 1989, and, sure enough, flowers came for Burnett later that day. Most recently, Burnett contributed priceless commentary along with Lucie Arnaz to the 2004 *Here's Lucy* DVD package. She introduced the TV Land Legacy of Laughter Award, given to Ball (and accepted by her children) in 2007.

BUTTE, MONTANA

Rustic western town which young starlet Lucille Ball appropriated as her hometown for publicity purposes. Ball and family spent almost a year in Montana when she was very young, due to her father's work on the telephone lines. But aside from a short stop near Detroit, they were home to Jamestown soon thereafter. Nonetheless, Ball must have thought Butte sounded better than Jamestown as a birthplace, for Butte is what ended up in her publicity as late as the 1940s—except for what was written by a few journalists who had done their homework and knew she was a New York State native.

One inventive biography, for the color magazine of the *New York Daily News* in 1940, added another fib (in italics): "Lucille was born in Butte, Mont. 28 years ago. When she decided she wanted to be an actress, she went about it the hard way—*working in stock in Cleveland*, [italics mine] acting as a showgirl on Broadway." As far as I can determine, Ball never did stage work in Cleveland before landing in Hollywood. But, again, it must have sounded good to someone.

Another reporter, New York columnist E.V. Durling, swallowed the Butte line whole. He ran this item in a column in the late 1930s: "Lucille Ball. Flaming tressed cinema cutie. First girl from Butte, Mont. to achieve national prominence since the days of Mary MacLane." (MacLane was a prominent proto-feminist writer from Butte who was popular around the turn of the last century.)

Even at the height of her fame in 1953, Ball was still promoting the idea that she was from Butte. In an interview with *Cosmopolitan* magazine in January of that year, writer Albert Morehead noted, speaking of her early career failures, Lucy's "only stage offer was from a burlesque impresario who wanted to gild her like a statue and bill her as 'the Beaut from Butte' (Lucy was born there)."

C

CACTUS FLOWER

A 1969 movie comedy in which philandering dentist Walter Matthau enlists the aid of his shy receptionist (Ingrid Bergman) to pose as his wife, to ward off the attentions of a particularly attached girlfriend (Goldie Hawn, who won an Oscar). Ball was reportedly offered the Bergman role, but turned it down because she saw the movie as a vehicle for the girlfriend, and, in retrospect, she was right; if the film is remembered at all, it is for Hawn's debut performance.

CAREER STATS

29 miles: length of the film from Ball's three major series—*I Love Lucy, The Lucy Show*, and *Here's Lucy*—would stretch.
479: number of episodes of the three series.
257 hours, 30 minutes: total viewing time of all three series.

CAHN, DANN

Cahn was the talented and quick-to-learn film editor for all the *I Love Lucy* episodes, the movie *Forever Darling*, and the *I Love Lucy Movie*. Recommended by friend and director William Asher for the editing job at Desilu when Asher declined (he was already directing), Cahn took to Desilu's revolutionary filming and editing techniques (created by Desi Arnaz and film legend Karl Freund) like a duck to water.

I was lucky enough to meet Dann in Jamestown during one of the Lucy festivals and we kept in touch. He is an incredible personality, vibrant, funny, and a fascinating interview subject. I asked him, among other things, if he ever worked with Ball and Arnaz after *I Love Lucy*. "Not much," he responded. "But life has a funny way of happening. Some years later, in the 1980s, I wound up as the vice president of post-production at 20th Century Fox, and Lucy and Gary Morton had their offices there. (Lucille Ball Productions produced Tom Cruise's *All the Right Moves* in 1983 while at Fox.) I'd see them a lot, and Lucy would always kid with me. A couple of times she'd come up with a golf cart behind me, I'd be walking down the street and she'd yell, 'I never let you walk anywhere!' And then I'd get in the golf cart and we'd talk. Desi and I had one get-together after they divorced. Desi came up on the train from Del Mar (California, where he lived), and along with Jess Oppenheimer and Marc Daniels and their wives, we all met at the American Film Institute, and had a big reunion party in the early 1980s."

Cahn worked on everything from TV shows (*The Beverly Hillbillies, Branded,* and much more) to TV movies and theatrical films, including the cult classic *Beyond the Valley of the Dolls.* He recently wrote the Preface for my book, *The Comic DNA of Lucille Ball: Interpreting the Icon* (2006). When I spoke to him in the summer of 2005, he was preparing a 10-minute film honoring the men of the First Motion Picture Unit of the Army Air Corps in World War II, of which he was a member. He received a Career Achievement Award from the American Cinema Editors (ACE) in 2000. See also <u>Ball, Lucille</u>, <u>*Forever Darling*</u>, <u>I Love Lucy</u>, and <u>*The I Love Lucy Movie*: Lost…and Found!</u>

CARMEL, ROGER C.

The man who played Kaye Ballard's husband in the first season of Desi Arnaz's *The Mothers-in-Law* (1967-'68) was a big fellow with a matching personality, who could play comedy or drama. He was also very troubled, and it was widely rumored that he had a drug problem. The official line was Carmel walked away from the show because the producers wouldn't give the cast more money for its second season. (See <u>*The Mothers-in-Law*</u> for more.) But legend has it that Arnaz, tired of Carmel coming in late and then sitting in his dressing room until he was ready to work, fired him using the morals clause of his contract. Richard Deacon replaced him.

Around the same time, Carmel appeared in two popular episodes of the Desilu show *Star Trek*, including the original series' only sequel episode. Carmel was in his element playing blustery space con man Harry Mudd in *Mudd's Women* (October 13, 1966) and *I, Mudd* (November 3, 1967). He'd worked in TV and movies (*Gambit*, 1966) beginning in the late 1950s, and was active until the mid-1980s, doing mostly voice work at the end.

In 1986, Carmel died of a heart attack due to an enlarged heart, though there were rumors he'd committed suicide. Drug abuse, specifically cocaine abuse, certainly could have made a heart problem worse. At the website findadeath.com, both the salary dispute and Carmel's drug abuse are discussed, citing different sources.

CARROLL JR., BOB AND MADELYN DAVIS

These two writers are most closely associated with Lucille Ball during her radio and subsequent television successes. They began writing for Ball on the radio (when Madelyn was still Madelyn Pugh) as part of the *My Favorite Husband* team and followed her into TV, often cribbing plots from the radio show and fleshing them out for the more visual medium of TV.

It was while working as a staff writer for CBS Radio in Hollywood that Carroll was teamed with fellow writer Pugh. Their partnership lasted more than 50 years, and included approximately 400 TV shows and 500 radio shows. Carroll and Pugh submitted a script and ended up writing for *Husband* for the entire three-season run, along with head writer and producer Jess Oppenheimer. The three then created the format for Ball's long-running sitcom (after helping to create the vaudeville act for Ball and Desi Arnaz that they took on the road to prove audiences would accept them acting together, and which became the basis for the *I Love Lucy* pilot).

Ball often marveled at how Carroll and Pugh could nail the antics of two married couples (the Ricardos and the Mertzes) while they remained single. The writers used their instincts about relationships to help formulate scripts, and routinely acted out bits of business that Ball and company would be doing, to make sure they could be done.

Carroll and Pugh wrote (with Oppenheimer) 39 episodes per season for the run of the series, aided in the final years by "the two Bobs," Schiller and Weiskopf. They were nominated for three Emmys but never won. In helping to create the "Lucy" character, which Ball played in one form or another for almost 40 years, Carroll and Pugh's legacy can be seen and felt to this day on TV.

The pair insisted that Ball was the easiest person to write for because she never refused to do any bit that the two could create. "And this does not only refer to her great comedic talents," Pugh told a reporter in 1962. "There is almost nothing she won't attempt, and as a result, we can let ourselves go, in the knowledge that at least Lucy will give it a try." Ball returned the compliment by publicly crediting her writers for her TV success many times.

The team continued to write for Ball through the first few seasons of *The Lucy Show*, and from then on whenever Ball asked for special help, such as the Elizabeth Taylor/Richard Burton episode that opened *Here's Lucy* in 1970-'71. (For that episode, the writers recycled a famous bit from *I Love Lucy* Episode No. 39, "The Handcuffs," which in turn had been used previously on *My Favorite Husband*.)

In the *I Love Lucy* episode, Lucy Ricardo handcuffs herself to her husband to keep him at home, then, when they can't find a key, ends up performing with Ricky (her right hand only, from behind a curtain) that night. In the *Here's Lucy* segment, Liz's 64-carat diamond ring (a real-life gift from Burton) gets stuck on Lucy Carter's finger, and Liz ends up greeting the press and showing off the ring on Lucy's not-so manageable hand, reaching from behind a curtain through Liz's sleeve.

Carroll and Davis, who wrote the story for Ball's 1968 hit *Yours, Mine and Ours*, and also did duty on Arnaz's sitcom *The Mothers-in-Law*, worked post-*Here's Lucy* on the sitcom *Alice* (as writers and producers, for which they won a Golden Globe award), *The Paul Lynde Show*, and Ball's 1977 TV special, *Lucy Calls the President*. They appeared as talking heads on the *I Love Lucy 50th Anniversary Special*.

Carroll died on Jan. 27, 2007, after a brief illness. He was 88. One of his last writing jobs was as co-author of Pugh's 2005 autobiography, *Laughing with Lucy*. Carroll's death leaves Pugh one of the few surviving key *I Love Lucy* creators.

♥ **Lucy Trivia** After Burton died, his memoirs stated that he had hated the whole process of filming *Here's Lucy* due to what he called Ball's tyrannical behavior on the set. Burton reportedly used slightly more colorful language, as did his wife, who allegedly referred to Ball as "Miss C—t" during the rehearsal process, according to Geoffrey Fidelman in <u>*The Lucy Book*</u>. A Burton biographer pointed out that he had a habit of making a bigger mess out of things than was actually so.

CARROTS

Item, from Hedda Hopper's *Hollywood* column, 1943: "When Lucille Ball was planting her victory garden she was handed carrot seed, and shrieked, 'Take them away! Since they made me dye my hair a cross between carrots and strawberries, I haven't been able to look either of them in the face.'" Ball's picture was captioned "Can't stand carrots."

CBS EYE

Ball and *I Love Lucy* will forever be associated with the show's original network, CBS. On October 15, 1951, a Monday evening, *I Love Lucy* debuted. Two days later, the network unveiled its original "CBS Eye," which became its official on-air logo. Both were winners for CBS, with the series becoming the most popular sitcom of all time, and the Eye celebrating its 50th anniversary in the same year as *I Love Lucy* (2001).

Bill Golden, at the time CBS's art director, designed the original Eye. Golden's careful attention to detail helped create a look for CBS that earned it the title of the "Tiffany Network."

Golden's Eye lasted nearly 15 years with minor changes until CBS began broadcasting all its programs in color, in 1965. Thereafter, the Eye changed, becoming glitzy, sedate, or more classic looking as the times demanded. It is still part of CBS, and you can see it as a "bug," in the lower right corner of the screen, ghosted over most of the network's programs.

CBS SALUTES LUCY: THE FIRST 25 YEARS

I'd wanted to see this twenty-fifth anniversary tribute (which aired on CBS November 28, 1976) for many years. It ran on Thanksgiving weekend that year, and I missed it because I was out of town in that era before the VCR. I'd kept it in my head for more than 20 years; that's what obsession is all about. Over all that time, I had a chance to build up in my head what the show would be like; I pictured a very fancy live affair, with the women in designer gowns and the men in tuxedos. Sort of like one of The Dean Martin Celebrity Roasts, but with lots of clips.

Wrong!

When I finally saw the show, at The Paley Center for Media in New York, I discovered it was a taped tribute, starting with CBS boss William Paley and moving through Desi Arnaz, Dick Van Dyke, Carol Burnett, John Wayne, Vivian Vance, and a dozen others (including Dean Martin). This was a clip show, with different segments set up by each of the guest stars (on videotape themselves). Arnaz (shot in front of the studio stage where *I Love Lucy* was shot) talked about his favorite clips; Vance introduced a segment about Lucy and Ethel, and so on. Since it was a two-hour show, the clips were generously long. The viewer got to see the whole Vitameatavegamin routine, not just a few lines. Still, I was disappointed it wasn't a live show. The special is now available on DVD.

CEDARS-SINAI MEDICAL CENTER

This Los Angeles hospital played a significant role in Lucille Ball's life from 1950 on. Ball was taken there after a miscarriage in July 1950. She delivered Lucie there in July 1951, and delivered Desi Jr. at Cedars of Lebanon via Caesarian section in 1953. In July 1960, she was rushed there to recuperate from a nine-foot fall off a dock while filming *The Facts of Life* with Bob Hope. (The hospital became Cedars-Sinai the following year when it merged with the Mount Sinai Home for the Incurables.) Cedars-Sinai Medical Center was where Gary Morton took Ball after she'd apparently had a stroke in May 1988. Less than a year later, on

April 26, 1989, Ball died there after heart surgery from a burst aorta; she'd been in Cedars-Sinai for a week after suffering a heart attack on April 18.

CHAPLIN, CHARLIE

Silent film comedian and creator of the "Little Tramp" persona. Ball greatly admired Chaplin for his attention to character and detail. She eventually paid homage to him in a silent sketch on *The Lucy Show* in the mid-1960s, in which she played the tramp character opposite Vivian Vance's flapper.

Three first ladies: Mary Pickford, first lady of the cinema; U.S. first lady Eleanor Roosevelt; and TV's first lady, Lucille Ball, together for a good cause in 1944. Photofest

CHARITY WORK

The *New York Daily Courant* of January 23, 1944, reported Lucille Ball was one of many "prominent screen personalities" who would be participating in President Roosevelt's birthday celebrations on behalf of the Infantile Paralysis Foundation in Washington, D.C. The other celebrities included Brian Donlevy, Jinx Falkenburg, John Garfield, Maria Montez, Mary Pickford, Walter Pidgeon, and Red Skelton, Ball's friend and co-star.

In the early to mid-1940s, Ball and Desi Arnaz both did as much charity work for U.S. men in uniform as they could.

In the next decade, thanks to her incredible television success, Ball and Arnaz were able to help any number of charitable organizations. For example, in 1954, the American Heart Association gave them an open-car parade in New York to honor their efforts to raise money. The New Orleans Recreation Department (NORD) reported in 1956, "Lucille Ball, Desi Arnaz, Vivian Vance, and William Frawley were in town for the annual Crippled Children's Hospital benefit ball, held on November 30, 1956, at the Roosevelt Hotel's International

Room. Earlier in the day they made a public appearance at NORD's Lyons Center, where they entertained (on stage) informally for a half hour. Before that they were given keys to the city at the City Council meeting and had lunch on the yacht Good Neighbor."

In 1965, Ball was the National Easter Seal chairman, leading more than half a million volunteers in her appeal for support of the handicapped

Ball was a loyal and giving person, especially to friends, and often at unexpected moments. Paradoxically, she was most circumspect when it came to herself, refusing to splurge on expensive items she could obviously afford. She gave to charities all her life, and was especially kind to the Heart Fund, cerebral palsy, and her favorite, Childrens Hospital Los Angeles.

CHATEAU MARMONT

Desi Arnaz made the legendary Los Angeles hotel his home base when he was in town after he split from Lucille Ball and left their Beverly Hills home in 1960. Vivian Vance also took an apartment there while she was shooting the first three seasons of *The Lucy Show* (1962-1965). Vance lived at the time with her husband, John Dodds, in Long Ridge Village, Connecticut. Long Ridge Village was designated a historic district on June 2, 1987.

CHER

Cher's mom, Georgia Holt (born Jackie Jean Crouch), was working with Lucille Ball doing bit parts (she had appeared in the *I Love Lucy* European Tour episode, "Lucy Gets a Paris Gown," March 19, 1956, as one of the models wearing Lucy and Ethel's sack dresses) when Cher (with partner Sonny Bono) hit it big with "I Got You Babe." After Holt told Ball who her daughter was, Ball demanded she get her to the set immediately because, "My kids want to meet her!"

CHILDHOOD HOME OF LUCILLE BALL, SOLD

Unbelievable as it may sound, Lucy's childhood home in Celeron, New York was "sold" on eBay, the online auction house, on June 25, 2001. (eBay is usually the marketplace for much smaller items, such as collectibles.) There were four bidders, and the winning bid was $100,201. Sitting at 59 West Lucy Lane (formerly Eighth Street), the house was described as a "one-family frame dwelling, with one-car detached garage situated on 4 lots with an approximate total of 100 x 200 feet. Zoned residential." This has to be the ultimate Lucille Ball collectible!

This is the house once owned by Ball's maternal grandparents, Florabelle and Fred Hunt. Lucy lived in it for a time when she was growing up. In the backyard, a gun given by Hunt to his grandson Fred Ball accidentally discharged; a neighbor's child was hit, paralyzed, and died several years later. The Hunt family lost the house in the ensuing lawsuit.

When Lucie Arnaz visited the house with her brother Desi as part of the *I Love Lucy 50th Anniversary Special,* a curtain rod on the first floor was noted as having been used by Ball to hang a sheet when she'd give impromptu performances for high school friends.

However, real estate transactions on eBay are not set in stone. The winner doesn't have to buy, and the reason for doing it in the first place is to basically let the public know that the property is available. The house was re-listed on eBay on February 6, 2002, for $98,500. A spokesman for the broker reported 23,107 people viewed the auction.

♥ **Lucy Trivia** On March 8, 2002, during a news conference at the Holiday Inn in Jamestown, Lucie announced that her family had bid on Ball's former home. In late March, it was announced that Lucie's bid was "too low" and that an unidentified Lucy fan from Florida had bought the house to use as a summer home. There was no confirmation on the final price tag. The house is now in the hands of fans and is being restored and donated to Jamestown's Lucille Ball-Desi Arnaz Center. For the full story, see Lucy's Celeron, New York House.

CLARK, WANDA

Wanda Clark was Lucille Ball's personal secretary for more than 25 years (1963-1989). Did she like the job? Let's put it this way: Clark told me in an interview in 2002 that if the Queen of Comedy were still alive, she'd more than likely still be working for her. "I can't put into words what I miss about her—she was a great force in my life that I appreciated, and miss very much," she noted. Clark worked with Lucy's cousin Cleo Smith (whom Ball thought of as a sister) at *Look* magazine. When Ball needed a secretary, she asked Smith if she knew anyone, and Smith recommended Clark for the job. No interview was necessary; Ball told Smith, "If *you* like her, she's good enough for me." As Clark reminded me, Ball liked having her family and people she trusted in her immediate circle.

Clark's first day at the studio went something like this: "We went to 780 North Gower—now Paramount; there was just a little fence between Desilu Gower and Paramount. It was a regular office and office duties; it just happened to be for a very wonderful and well-known celebrity." Part of her job was taking phone calls, and preparing the mail for Ball to look at; "When she had time, she would," she says. Running interference is what any secretary does for the boss, of course. Clark adds, "I've never had a job I could put a description on, and working for a celebrity like Lucy, the duties were whatever happened to come up: travel, setting up interviews with the publicity department, making doctor's appointments and seeing that she would get to them." And fielding many, many phone calls: "Some Lucy couldn't possibly take and some she had to—it was a busy job but I had a good time doing it."

As you might expect, Clark met many other celebrities during her time with Lucy; as any self-respecting fan already knows, shows during the last few seasons of *The Lucy Show* and throughout *Here's Lucy* featured an army of guest stars. "Carol Burnett was everyone's favorite," Clark says. "She was just a joy—and everyone loved it when she would guest star; when Lucy would do her show, I got to go there with her and watch. Ernie Ford, Mel Tormé—all the musical stars were fun. I fell in love with Donny Osmond when he guest-starred on *Here's Lucy*. He had a crush on Lucie Arnaz at the time, and he was just a darling young man."

Bob Hope and Jack Benny were particular favorites of Ball's, Clark says, and they were always "so much fun to be around. I enjoyed meeting them all." Ball "just adored Dean Martin," Clark adds, "but Dean [guest-starring on *The Lucy Show*] didn't work the way Lucy did—he tried to get off without any rehearsal and Lucy insisted on a lot of it. Still, they liked and respected each other so much it turned out to be a great show." Clark's one regret is not collecting all their autographs. "I wish I had. Actually, I have very few pictures of Lucy and me together—it's just one of those things I didn't think about when it was happening. But I sure wish I did now!"

Ball always spoke kindly of those "other stars" she worked with for so many years—you know, her co-stars on that little show called *I Love Lucy*. "She was so respectful of them all, she appreciated their talents," Clark says. "She thought Vivian [Vance] was the best script doctor in town; she counted on Vivian to help fix something whenever a script problem came up." She recalls a "heartbroken" Lucy going to visit Vivian just before Vance passed away. "She relied on Desi [Arnaz] for his good advice and ability to recognize good and bad material. She liked [William] Frawley because he did his job, did it well, never caused a problem." She adds that if Frawley had a drinking problem, it never impacted his work.

There were many memorable experiences working for Ball over more than a quarter of a century, but several stick out for Clark. She actually got to perform on an episode of *Here's Lucy*, which, she says, "was memorable for me because that wasn't my thing—I didn't do well in front of a camera. But it was a wonderful experience." Episode No. 38 aired on December 22, 1969, in the second season. It was called "Lucy Protects Her Job." Uncle Harry (*Lucy* regular Gale Gordon) thinks Lucy needs some help in the office, but she fears he is going to replace her. Clark plays the secretary Lucy interviews in the first scene.

Clark explains how she got the part: "The actress Lucy hired for the part couldn't type, and to Lucy the important part of the character was having someone who could type fast, like a demon. Lucy wouldn't allow her to fake it, she wanted the real rhythm, and she thought it was something I could do, because she knew I was a good typist." One thing Ball hadn't taken into account: Clark had been typing on an electric for many years, and she "wasn't used to working with the carriage [of a non-electric typewriter], and thrusting the carriage return back at the end of a line and all that, so I had to kind of fake it myself, but at least I had the rhythm down."

Another unforgettable experience for Clark happened after Ball broke her leg skiing in Snowmass, Colorado, near Aspen, where Ball had a condo, in the early 1970s. Ball asked Clark to help her close up the place so she could come home to L.A. Clark recalled, "Lucy was in a huge, full-leg cast. She was practically helpless in that huge cast, but it was great being there and helping her out. Eventually they shortened the cast, and gave her a walking cast so she could move around. She ended up doing a dozen *Here's Lucy* shows with the broken leg written into the show."

What was the "real" Lucille Ball like? She was warm and wonderful and generous, Clark says, "to all of us that worked with her, and her family, of course. And she was loyal—that's why we were all so loyal to her." Though Ball's writers were an important element of her career, and she always gave them credit for her success, Lucy herself was a funny lady, Clark says, refuting what Ball herself often claimed, that she wasn't a particularly funny person. "She didn't go around doing *shtick*, but she had a great sense of humor and she loved to have a good laugh." Clark's favorite moments spent with Ball included the parties Ball threw at her Beverly Hills house, "especially when the kids were still at home. They were a lot of fun, planning them; she'd do themes, like a hoedown, with traditional music and costumes. Those were great parties."

Clark especially enjoyed the times she got to spend alone with Ball. Wanda says that every Thursday night after the show taped Lucy and Gary Morton, her second husband, would head for Palm Springs. "For one reason or another she might want me to come down the next day, to bring her dog to her, or maybe to drive back with Lucy if she was not driving with Gary, and that was always fun. There were a lot of word games; when she couldn't play backgammon, she used to love to play Jotto. It boggled my mind—and still does—that she could keep all those letters in her head while she was driving, but we played it all the way from Palm Springs to L.A."

I asked Clark if Ball ever expressed any regrets about her career or life, and the answer was a firm no: "I never heard Lucy say she was sorry she did or didn't do something. She was always sorry she didn't finish school, but she was so well-read and could spell better than anyone I ever worked for. But as far as her career goes, I can't say she ever discussed any regrets about it with me. I know it hurt a lot to hear the reviews of *Life with Lucy* [Ball's only TV misfire]. She took pride in her work and she worked so hard—she just couldn't find the right material for a character of her age." At the time of the show, Ball was 75.

Clark last spoke to Ball the morning she went into the hospital: "We just thought it was another regular day—and Lucy was looking forward to a trip to Jamestown, where she was getting an honorary degree. She had the reservations made, Irma [Kusely, Lucy's hair stylist] had been alerted—and Fred Williams, her makeup man—they were all set to go. That day she was stricken with a ruptured aorta, and they rushed her to the hospital. They repaired that one and she was on her way to recovery; her children were with her, she knew they were there, and was happy they were all right. Then she had a second rupture and was taken instantly."

Asking Clark what she misses most about Ball is probably not a fair question for someone who became a close friend over more than 25 years. Still, when prompted, she gives the answer you expect: "Everything about her—it was a very long and happy association."

For the Fourth Edition of *Lucy A to Z*, Clark gave me some not-too-surprising answers to a few quick questions:

Favorite actress: Lucille Ball.
Favorite singer: Desi Arnaz.
Favorite movie: *Yours, Mine and Ours* … or maybe *Casablanca*.
Favorite TV show: *The Lucy Show*.
Smartest thing I ever did: Moved to California in 1960 and took my job with Lucy.
What I would title my autobiography: *Life with Lucy*.

CLUB BABALU

A New York club-bar-restaurant that celebrated Latin music and heritage, Club Babalu opened in midtown in August 2003. One advance reviewer noted, "With its tropical art deco bar and savory Cuban flair … you may well feel you've stumbled upon the reincarnation of Ricky Ricardo's famed Latin nightclub." On *I Love Lucy*, Ricky ultimately bought the Tropicana nightclub, where he had always had a steady gig, and renamed it … Club Babalu, no doubt after Arnaz's best-known song. The New York club was closed as of this writing, though a Google search in August 2007 found Club Babalus in San Diego, Dallas/Ft. Worth, and Chicago.

COLLECTIBLES

Being a collector is serious business. As Vincent Price once noted, the collector has a responsibility to the community at large as well as to himself. He was talking about fine art, but you get the drift.

Lucille Ball collectors are indeed a serious bunch. Interest in memorabilia associated with Lucille Ball has never been hotter. Her various TV series (*I Love Lucy*, *The Lucy-Desi Comedy Hour*, *The Lucy Show*, *Here's Lucy*, *Life With Lucy*); her co-stars—especially Desi Arnaz, Vivian Vance, and William Frawley, but literally anyone who ever made an appearance on any Lucy-related program; her TV specials; her movies; her personal life; her children; and so on ad infinitum, all are grist for the collectible market.

Search the online auction house eBay for "Lucille Ball" on any given day and you're likely to find more than 2,000 items. Visit Cathy's Closet online (Lucystore.com) and revel in the amount and types of items related to all of the above that you could buy.

There are several cardinal rules for collectors. Collect what you like, not something you intend to sell; then you'll never be disappointed with what you buy. Always keep looking; you never know where you're going to find a valuable collectible. Don't always buy an item the first time (and at the first price) you see it; given some time, nearly everything is bound to turn up again, and likely at a much better deal.

A case in point: I found a long-sought prize—the pre-national edition of *TV Guide* with William Frawley and Vivian Vance on the cover for a story called "Lucy's Neighbors Exposed"—at an antique flea market outside of Ft. Lauderdale, Florida. The issue is dated March 20-26, 1953, actually a mere two weeks before the national edition (with you-know-who and her bouncing baby boy on the cover) debuted. I noticed the cover staring at me, partially hidden in a small booth that featured all sorts of movie/TV star memorabilia. The price on it was $45, a steal considering that I'd seen it at other flea markets and *TV Guide* "specialists" for $300 or more. What's more, it was in like-new condition.

See also <u>Dolls</u>.

COMIC BOOKS

From February 1954 through April/June 1962 Dell published the *I Love Lucy* series of comics. Thirty-five issues were produced. As any Lucy lover knows, that means you could still buy an *I Love Lucy* comic a full five years after the original half-hour series ended (1956-'57). Some of the stories were based on themes or episodes from the show, but many are originals.

As an example, one of the stories, called "The Steps of the Stars," places our fab foursome in Hollywood. The boys drop Lucy and Ethel off at Grauman's Chinese Theatre, where Lucy gets the idea to add Ricky's footprints to the gallery of stars memorialized in cement. She and Ethel end up striking oil (by tapping into the city's underground pipes) and trapping half the Hollywood police force in concrete. This comic story is a riff on the famous two-part *I Love Lucy* episode in which she and Ethel steal John Wayne's footprints from the front of Grauman's.

The artwork in these comics was fabulous, and captured the essence of the characters of Lucy, Ricky, Fred, and Ethel. Indeed, the lunacy of *I Love Lucy* was a perfect candidate for transition to a comic series, and many of the stories prove just that. The artist is unknown, but could have been Bob Oksner, a well-known comic book artist who drew the comic strip (see next entry).

A random check on eBay in September 2007, revealed the Dell original-run *I Love Lucy* comics were being auctioned at prices ranging from $9.99 for a worn but readable copy of No. 19 (1958), to $1,095 for a near-mint, Certified Guaranty Company (9.4)-graded copy (10 is the highest grade) of No. 5 (1955). CGC is considered the leading comic book grading authority.

Dell also published a comic book based on Ball and Arnaz's movie *Forever Darling*, in 1956. In the early 1990s, Eternity Comics collected some of the *I Love Lucy* comics in a paperback book. In 1990, Malibu Graphics published *I Love Lucy: A Comic Retrospective*, reprinting 15 of the Dell stories in scruffy black and white, and offering a few pages of commentary on the art.

The Lucy Show comics from Gold Key had a much shorter run: June 1963 to June 1964, during the show's second season. Only five issues were published. In September 2007, eBay was auctioning all five issues of this series, from a low of $.99 for No. 3, with only three-quarters of its cover but otherwise intact, to a high of $795 for No. 1, touted by its seller as "near-mint" with a 9.2 grade, but no CGC certfication. As always with collectibles, do your homework and buyer beware.

COMIC STRIP

A daily comic strip appeared in newspapers during the run of *I Love Lucy*, beginning on December 8, 1952. It was drawn by Bob Oksner, similar in tone and illustration to the Dell *I Love Lucy* comic books also released during the period (see previous entry), and ran in as many as 132 newspapers. Oksner (born in 1916) is a beloved comic artist, having drawn everything from *Supergirl* to *Dondi*; he is perhaps best known for the comics he drew based on popular performers, including the Bob Hope and Jerry Lewis series for D.C. His style has been described as "loose, supple, sure-handed, and pleasantly goofy." He drew the *I Love Lucy* strip for King Features Syndicate from 1952 to 1955. In the early 1990s, Eternity Comics published six issues of a comic book reprinting the strips.

COMIC TIMING

"You can't really teach timing, but you *can* explain something that might make [a student understand] timing.… [Don't] learn *my* timing, *his* timing, *her* timing, Joan Davis' timing, Jack Benny's timing, it's all different. But to learn [about] timing for yourself, try *listening*, reacting, and then acting."—Lucille Ball, 1974

CONNELL, JANE

A stage, television, and film actress born in 1925, Connell began performing with husband and actor Gordon Connell in San Francisco clubs like The Purple Onion. A busy stage performer, Connell's film and TV careers were more erratic, though she is remembered for seven performances on *Bewitched*; from 1964 to 1972 Connell played a diverse group of historical and fantasy figures, including Mother Goose, Queen Victoria, and Martha Washington.

Connell also co-starred in a late-1950s television comedy called *Stanley* (1956) with an intriguing cast: Carol Burnett, Buddy Hackett, and Paul Lynde. In 2001, she joined the Broadway cast of *The Full Monty*. Connell took time out of her busy schedule to speak with me about the making of *Mame* (1974), in which she repeated her signature stage role of Agnes Gooch.

Ball had seen Connell doing the musical version of *Mame* (as the perennially put-upon Agnes Gooch) at the Dorothy Chandler Pavilion, in Los Angeles. "When you make a movie from a play or musical, it's a new toy," Connell notes. "I'm not offended by not being cast in a part I might have created." She got the movie part by default—Madeline Kahn had been cast as Gooch. "I was a fan of hers," Connell says. "But Lucy felt quite threatened by Madeline;

she did a different kind of comedy. Lucy was used to the old-school style and Madeline was a wonderfully eccentric young comedian."

The company had been rehearsing the movie version of *Mame* for about two weeks, when Ball stopped the production. According to Connell: "She said, 'Get me that girl I saw [as Gooch] at the Dorothy Chandler!'"

Connell and her husband were at their country house when her agent called and asked if she was ready to go to California. Connell went west thinking she had the role, but Ruth Buzzi was also in the running. "We had known each other earlier in New York," Connell explains, "and found ourselves being rushed around the set, in one door and out the other." Perhaps this was to avoid them seeing each other. "I said to Ruth, 'Well, if I don't get the part, I hope you do!'"

Both actors did a screen test that day, and that's how Connell got the part. "I think they gave [Madeline] $50,000 to get out of her contract—which was more than I got paid for the movie!" Connell refers to it understatedly as "a less than glorious casting process."

Ball in fact was threatened by the whole project, Connell believes. She thought that Theodora Runkle (the costume designer) was out to get her; she was disappointed that she couldn't sing well. She and director Gene Saks were *not* bosom buddies, and Connell says Saks had a terrible time. "It was overall an unhappy experience for Lucy," she adds. "I think she wanted me to spy for her, to see who was out to get her and who wasn't." Connell believes Ball was paranoid because she sensed she wasn't the greatest choice for the role of Mame Dennis: "It was unnerving for Lucy because Angela [Lansbury] had done so well in the role on Broadway."

Connell took the experience in stride. Her future didn't depend on Ball. She wasn't living in Los Angeles at the time. "I felt secure and could sense her insecurity, so the things I might have taken exception to, I didn't," Connell says. "She was a very powerful lady, but I couldn't have cared less whether I worked with her again and whether I impressed her, so she didn't have to play any roles with me.

"She sensed that I appreciated what she did to get me the job, but could see I wasn't taken in by it. As soon as she realized I wasn't about to do any snooping, she respected me for that. I was her pet. She wanted me to be good and be her friend, because I don't think she had many friends."

Ball was "kind in many, many ways," says Connell, but Ball did feel a strong sense of responsibility for the movie. In truth, without Ball's name to guarantee a strong opening at the box office, *Mame* would never have been made.

Connell tells a funny story that happened during the filming of the final sequence, in which Mame brings in a busload of pregnant women to draw out her prospective in-laws' true feelings. Lucy smoked continually, Connell says. "We were standing there waiting for the lights to be adjusted, and she thrust a cigarette in my mouth, quite belligerently, to be funny, and I started saying, 'How dare you! Just because you're a big star!' And we did a whole scene for 15 minutes, riffed on it and pulled it off. She took the 'I'm a bad little girl' role. The cast was laughing and loved it."

Ball liked Connell, and had her to dinner at the Beverly Hills house, where they'd watch movies; Ball even took Connell to the dailies. "Once, Gary Morton was at home," Connell recalls, "when a very elaborate lobster all cut up beautifully was taken over to him, and Lucy said, 'Don't worry, he's the only one having that—we're having leftovers.'"

Another set incident resulted in a misused word that ended up in the film. One day, someone asked what the word "pregnant" was in French. Connell suggested "encien," pronouncing it wrong so that it sounded like "ancien," which means ancient. "It got into the movie!" Connell says, laughing. "That always tickled me; everything in a film is so well-prepared and researched, but they took the word of a supporting actress on the French for 'pregnant.'" (The correct French word is "enceinte." Ironically, the word was misspelled decades ago as a famous episode title on *I Love Lucy*: "Lucy Is Enciente.")

Filming took about six months. The crew had typical problems for some of the scenes— during the title song, for example, they had to wait for the weather to cooperate. "If Lucy had just been herself in the movie it might have worked," Connell believes. "It was too bad she felt she had to look the way she did 30 years before. She should have relaxed a bit, because Mame could be any age. But she had that old-school feeling that she had to look the way her fans remembered her from TV."

The film itself is "rather horrifying to me," Connell admits. "It looks better on the small screen and it's got kind of a cult following." In the 1980s, she requested the film at a video store on the Upper West Side in New York. The clerk said, "Oh, lady, you don't want to see that one, you want the really good one with Rosalind Russell." Connell explained who she was, and says, "He was embarrassed, but I felt he should know, with all the actors living in that area, he should probably be more circumspect about his opinions!"

At the first screening for the cast and crew, Connell's teenaged daughters Melissa and Margaret were sitting on either side of her. "The titles were kind of clever," Connell says. Indeed, some critics singled out the art deco-inspired title sequence as one of the best things in the film. "My billing is not the greatest," she notes. "I couldn't have Madeline's billing, of course; the opening scenes were quite wonderful and then the movie started and it was clear that it just didn't work. My daughters started making remarks and both my arms shot out to silence them. They had known the show from the beginning, but I had to remind them where they were."

In the end Connell was very disappointed certain things were left out. The "St. Bridgette" number, which Gooch sings to young Patrick (played in the film by Kirby Furlong) as they prepare to arrive at Mame's residence, was filmed in a church, with both actors kneeling. It ended up being used over the credits. "But it was thrilling in a way," Connell says. She enjoyed the end credits, a montage of all the characters rushing to hug Mame, one after the other.

After it was over, though, Connell says, "There was kind of a feeling of 'Oops.' I leaned over after to Bea [Arthur, who co-starred as Vera Charles, Mame's bosom buddy] and said, 'I wish Angie had done it.' And she looked at me as though I'd slapped her in the face. Perhaps it was because Bea had long desired to play the role of Mame herself. All in all, I think Lucy put up with a lot and had to assume a certain role because of who she was, which put her between a rock and a hard place, sometimes. I went along for the ride; it was my first big movie and I had a ball."

Connell saw Ball once after the film was completed: "Her daughter had a party; I did *The Guardsman* with Lucie Arnaz and her husband Laurence Luckinbill. Lucy was a good guest; she wasn't trying to be the center of attention. She'd been around a long time and was a presence. But Lucy didn't push it and she was awfully proud of her children and grandchildren. She was at the time still angry at Desi Jr. for dating Patty Duke."

Ball was coping with power, fame, the female image, her own image that she believed in and maintained, and she had a lot to deal with that we'll never know about, Connell points out. Much of her life required a certain acumen and poise she had to maintain. In the end, Connell says, "My hat's off to her. She was a genius with what she did on TV. She was a very bright woman. She had great respect for talent. All in all she was a terrific person."

CONGA CRAZE OF THE 1930S

A New York newspaper article by Henry Lee circa the late 1930s describes a trip to the Big Apple by Ball, "a somewhat brisk and voluptuous actress" of Hollywood. Interviewed in the Plaza Hotel's Oak Room, Lucy waxes enthusiastically about New York, noting, among other things, that, "I haven't been in New York in three years and it's kon-gah, kon-gah everywhere, and my head's going round-and-round." Future husband Desi Arnaz, who at that same time was appearing at the club La Conga and possibly on Broadway in his debut, *Too Many Girls*, popularized the conga, of course. There's no mention of Arnaz, so apparently the two hadn't yet met, but they would meet and marry within a year.

COOK, CAROLE

A protégé of Ball's circa the late 1950s, when Ball ran an actor's workshop at <u>Desilu</u>, Lucy took Cook under her wing, changing her first name from Mildred to Carole (in honor of Ball's mentor, Carole Lombard); Cook even lived in Ball's Beverly Hills home for a while. Cook blossomed into a funny, if occasionally overblown, comedic actress.

She appeared in such films as *The Incredible Mr. Limpet* (1964), *American Gigolo* (1980), and *Sixteen Candles* (1984). She also dubbed Ball's singing voice on *The Lucy Show* and afterward when Ball's voice had lost its range due to heavy smoking. Cook has remained active on TV, guest-starring in a variety of series, including Comedy Central's outrageous *Strip Mall* (2000) and the medical hit *Grey's Anatomy* (2006).

Married to actor Tom Troupe, Cook brought him along when she appeared as the headliner during the August 2006 Lucille Ball Birthday celebration in Jamestown, New York. She shared anecdotes about growing up in Texas, how she first met Ball (who was the matron of honor at her wedding) at a dinner/audition for the Desilu Workshop, and answered questions. Most interesting were her comments about Ball's second husband, Gary Morton. Morton was no favorite of Cook's and, on the verge of tears, she voiced her opinion that Morton had kept many of Ball's friends away from her toward the end of Ball's life.

Mostly, though, she kept it light and breezy, as in this comment about her forty-plus year marriage: She's never considered divorce, she noted … *homicide*, yes, but not divorce. Cook also tells a funny story about meeting two elderly Lucy fans who mistook Cook for the wacky redhead herself. As this happened after Ball had passed away, Cook gently as possible informed them that Lucy was dead. Oh, she couldn't be, they chimed—we just saw her on TV last night!

CRAWFORD, BRODERICK

Gruff, blustery Oscar-winning (*All the King's Men*, 1949) star of stage and screen, best known for his work in *Born Yesterday* (1950) and on the TV series *Highway Patrol* (1955-'59), Broderick was also Lucille Ball's fiancé for a time early in her career. In June 1938 a picture of the couple appeared in *The New York American* with the caption, "Their Engagement

Announced—Lucille Ball, film player and Screenland's Best-Dressed Girl, and her fiancé, Broderick Crawford, actor." The wedding never happened. Crawford died in 1986.

CROFT, MARY JANE

Lucille Ball's acting pal and friend, born in 1916, had a career spanning more than 50 years in radio and TV. The distinctive-voiced Croft began her television career as a regular on Eve Arden's *Our Miss Brooks* (1952-'54). During the same period, she was also a regular on *I Married Joan* (1952-'55). Croft was hysterical as the nasal voice of Cleo, the basset hound on *The People's Choice* (1955-'58), commenting on the frivolous actions of the human characters. She played neighbor Clara Randolph on *The Adventures of Ozzie and Harriet* for 10 years, from 1956 to 1966 (TV husband Lyle Talbot was a *Here's Lucy* guest star).

On *I Love Lucy*, she will be remembered as Lucy's seatmate with a baby on the flight home from Europe; as a snooty friend in the Martian episode; and as Connecticut neighbor Betty Ramsey in the final group of *I Love Lucy* episodes.

She made a number of appearances on *The Lucy Show* (in 1963 and 1964) before becoming a regular. Taking over Vivian Vance's role as Lucy's pal, Croft appeared with Ball on *The Lucy Show* and *Here's Lucy* as Audrey Simmons (1962-'65) and then Mary Jane Lewis from 1965 to 1974, once *The Lucy Show* format changed. Her second character name was her married name; husband Elliot Lewis, was an executive producer of *The Lucy Show* and a producer of *The Mothers-in-Law* (1967-'69, along with Desi Arnaz), as well as a writer and director. He died in 1990.

Croft, an unsung but talented actress and comedienne, died of natural causes at 83 in 1999.

CUGAT, XAVIER

Xavier Cugat's flair for music came from a dual Spanish/Cuban heritage that eventually led the young maestro to Los Angeles, where he worked the requisite hours in clubs and finally got a break in 1928 at the Coconut Grove.

Thereafter, he was responsible for a minor musical revolution: a public fascination with the Latin beat. Cugat popularized the rumba in the 1930s, was nicknamed the Rumba King, and appeared in several dozen films.

Cugat recognized young Desi Arnaz's talent after seeing Arnaz perform. According to one tale, Cugat had a hiring stipulation: that Arnaz complete high school before he would accept him as a member of the Xavier Cugat Orchestra. The 16-year-old Arnaz completed school and as soon as he graduated joined Cugat and his band for $25 a week.

Arnaz toured with Cugat for a year, learning the music business and honing his stage act before striking a deal to license the Cugat name for his own band. Launching Desi Arnaz and his Xavier Cugat Orchestra, Arnaz single-handedly created a craze for "La Conga" in the top clubs of Miami. Arnaz became known as "The Rumba King" (he had to fight Tito Puente for the sobriquet, "The Mambo King") and Arnaz eventually conquered the nightclubs of New York, which led to his successful audition for the musical *Too Many Girls*.

Cugat was sometimes mentioned on *I Love Lucy*, either to make Ricky jealous or as the butt of a joke. Cugat had a stroke in 1971, after which he retired. He lived until 1990. His last wife was Latin bombshell Charo.

CUMMINGS, BOB

A genial light comedian and dramatic actor, Cummings appeared in scores of movies from the 1930s through the 1970s. He starred in some classics like *Saboteur* and *King's Row* (both 1942) and *Dial M for Murder* (1954) but never really became a top-rank star, though he had the chops for it (he won an Emmy for the original 1954 television production of *12 Angry Men*).

Cummings graced television almost from its inception, and starred in a well-remembered sitcom in the 1950s, *Love That Bob* (1955-1959) in which he played a bachelor photographer cum ladies man. The show centered on Bob's efforts to woo his models, while providing a role model for his nephew (Dwayne Hickman), and was a kind of antidote to most of the sexless sitcoms of the era. He guest-starred on two of Lucille Ball's series: first, on *The Lucy-Desi Comedy Hour* called "The Ricardos Go to Japan," November 27, 1959; and twice on *Here's Lucy*, playing a romantic interest for Lucy in "Lucy's Punctured Romance" (February 7, 1972) and an antiques dealer in "Lucy and Her Genuine Twimby" (January 15, 1973). Cummings died at 82 in 1990.

D

DANIEL, ELIOT

Daniel was the composer who wrote the *I Love Lucy* theme song. He received an Oscar nomination in 1949 for "Lavender Blue" from Disney's movie *So Dear to My Heart*. Jess Oppenheimer asked him to write theme music for the *I Love Lucy* pilot; they had met at CBS Radio in the early 1940s. Daniel wrote the theme around the phrase "I love Lucy and she loves me," in a single afternoon. (Harold Adamson added the complete lyrics to the song for the episode "Lucy's Last Birthday," May 11, 1953.)

Daniel did the incidental music for the first few seasons, and supplied the songs for "The Pleasant Peasant" in the episode "The Operetta" (October 13, 1952); the dream sequence in "Lucy Goes to Scotland" (February 20, 1956); and wrote "Nobody Loves the Ump" for the Bob Hope episode (October 1, 1956). He also scored another successful Desilu series, *December Bride* (1954-'59). Daniel died in 1997.

DANIELS, MARC

Director for the first season of *I Love Lucy*, 1951-'52, Daniels is also credited with getting his friend Vivian Vance seen by Desi Arnaz at a San Diego production of *Voice of the Turtle*, after which Arnaz hired her for the part of Ethel Mertz.

Daniels left the show early in the second season due to issues of control on the set, but it was an amicable parting. His last episode was the classic "The Operetta." He also directed *I Married Joan* (1952-'55) and installments of many other sitcoms and dramas—more than a dozen episodes of Desilu's *Star Trek*, for example—including *Hogan's Heroes*, *Ben Casey*, *The Flying Nun*, *Hawaii Five-0*, *Barnaby Jones*, *Alice*, and *Eight Is Enough*.

He directed Lucille Ball again in the special *Lucy Calls the President* (1977) and on her final show, *Life with Lucy*, in 1986. Daniels died a few days before Ball did in 1989.

DARIN, BOBBY

Popular singer and actor of the late 1950s and 1960s, Darin was considered by many to be the best interpreter of standards since Frank Sinatra. Doomed to die young of a bad heart, Darin was well established in many media by the time he passed away in 1973; his *Darin at the Copa* album was Ball's favorite.

DAVIS, JOAN

A rubber-limbed slapstick comedian, Davis was Lucille Ball's forerunner in radio and motion pictures, and follower on TV. The hilarious Davis, who enlivened many a "B" picture during the

1930s and 1940s, got her start in vaudeville. Born in 1907 (some sources say 1912), she was working with Mack Sennett by 1935 in the first of almost 50 movies; many of her films were forgettable but they always shined during Davis' screen time. Her best vehicles included Abbott and Costello's *Hold That Ghost* (1941) and the wacky *She Gets Her Man* (1945), in which Joan played a sheriff. Davis was also a popular radio star, the highest paid broadcast comedienne of her era.

Gary Covile of *Radiogram*, reviewing the Davis biography *Hold That Joan*, noted, "Comparison with Lucille Ball was always a source of contention for Davis. Jim Backus, who co-starred with

Lucille Ball and Joan Davis in a rare shot together circa 1949; both were publicizing their CBS radio shows: Lucy's was *My Favorite Husband*, Joan's was *Leave it to Joan*. Photo courtesy of Ron Wright.

Davis in the 1952-1955 television series, *I Married Joan*, once wrote, 'Lucille Ball was to Joan Davis what Moriarty was to Sherlock Holmes.' *I Married Joan* premiered exactly one year to the day after *I Love Lucy*. For some of us who actually remember the series, the opening signature always seemed something of a dig at Lucy. Viewers were assured each week that they were about to see 'America's favorite comedy show, starring America's queen of comedy, Joan Davis.' Lucy and many critics might have disagreed with the royal pecking order, but, after all, it was Joan's show."

If Davis really felt that Ball was her Moriarty, her grand competitor (I doubt Backus meant that Davis looked on Ball as an evil murderess …), the fact is there were few who could match either's sublime slapstick. Ball's movie comedy was often more dependent on the written word, and Ball was generally sold to the public as a glamour girl. Davis' movies were often silly and just plain bad when dependent on the written word, but shined whenever she kicked her up her heels; Davis was also never considered "pretty" enough to be marketed as a glamorpuss.

By the 1950s, television was a natural place for Davis to land, and she did so in *I Married Joan* (1952-'55), as the exasperating, screwball wife of a judge (played solidly by Backus). In 98 episodes Davis proved she could pratfall with the best of them. While the show was marred by its familiarity (at the time, *TV Guide* called it "a show with more than a faint resemblance to *I Love Lucy*"), it's an injustice to Davis to dismiss her as merely a Ball clone. Marc Daniels (the first *I Love Lucy* director) directed the show.

Davis died of a heart attack in 1961, at age 54. She had lost much of her career memorabilia in a fire several months earlier. In an unbelievable tragedy, her daughter, her mother, and her grandchildren were killed in another fire soon after Davis' death. That, coupled with the fact that Davis never had the chance to keep showing her form in sitcom after sitcom, as Ball did, explains why Davis is not as well remembered, or revered, as Ball. (See also Six Degrees of Lucille Ball.)

DAVIS JR., SAMMY

Known as the "world's greatest all-around entertainer," Sammy Davis Jr. was a friend of Ball's who made a memorable *Here's Lucy* appearance in 1970; Ball returned the favor on his mid-1970s variety show, *Sammy and Company*. Davis paid a heartwarming tribute to Ball on the 1984 NBC special, *An All-Star Party for Lucille Ball*. After noting the many exotic and foreign locales where Lucy viewing was the one constant, Davis spoke directly to the redhead, noting, "Laughter crosses friendly and unfriendly borders…. Joy requires no translation. God wanted the world to laugh, and He invented you, Lucy. Many are called, but you were chosen."

DEACON, RICHARD

Deacon was a busy character actor in movies and films beginning in 1953, who, like William Frawley, seemed to always look the same, no matter his age or role. He is best remembered as Fred Rutherford (Lumpy's dad) on *Leave it to Beaver* (1957-'63) and as Carl Reiner's flunky, Mel Cooley, on *The Dick Van Dyke Show*, 1961-'66 (where he was the butt of Morey Amsterdam's constant "bald" jokes). Deacon guest-starred on nearly every memorable sitcom of the 1960s and 1970s, and also did dramatic duty on such shows as *Perry Mason* and *Night Gallery*.

Usually playing an officious or snobby (or both) clerk or public servant, Deacon enlivened anything he was in. That included a *Lucy-Desi Comedy Hour* (starring Tallulah Bankhead, airing December 3, 1957) and two episodes of *Here's Lucy* (he was an unemployment clerk in "Lucy and Carol Burnett," February 8, 1971, and Mr. Zelderbach in "Lucy Sublets the Office," January 31, 1972). Deacon also had a minor role in Ball's 1963 movie *Critic's Choice*, and replaced Roger C. Carmel in the second season of Desi Arnaz's sitcom *The Mothers-in-Law* (the 1968-'69 season). He died in 1984.

DENNING, RICHARD

Affable Denning played Lucille Ball's patient, loving husband in the radio hit *My Favorite Husband*, the prototype for *I Love Lucy*. CBS wanted him to reprise the role on television, but Ball had other ideas, and, of course, won that battle.

A "B" picture leading man and then character actor, Denning appeared in films beginning in the late 1930s, when he won a screen test at Warner Bros. thanks to a radio contest, "Do You Want to Be An Actor?" Warners passed, but Paramount picked him up, and he was rarely out of work after that.

Denning also worked on TV (*Mr. and Mrs. North*) and in movies through the 1950s and 1960s, ending up playing the governor of Hawaii for 12 years on the hit *Hawaii Five-O*. He retired after that show was cancelled in 1980. Denning was married for more than 40 years to 1940s "Scream Queen" actress Evelyn Ankers, and died of a heart attack in 1998.

DESI/DESIRÉE

The names have a special significance in the lives of Lucille Ball and Desi Arnaz, and they mean the same thing in Spanish and French. Ball's mother was named Desirée (shortened to DeDe), and Ball's full name is Lucille Desirée Ball. Desilu (the combination of their first names) became the name of their ranch and studio. The couple named their daughter Lucie Desirée Arnaz and their son Desi Arnaz Jr.

DESILU STUDIOS

This is the studio that Arnaz and Ball built. The couple had first given their combined names to their beloved ranch in Chatsworth, California, and later bestowed it (in 1950) on their fledgling production company. The ranch served as an anchor for the couple, often separated due to their careers, and is well remembered by many in Hollywood as the scene of informal barbecues and costume parties.

There was a natural watering hole that became a pool, and the Arnazes even attempted to raise chickens and cows; ultimately, the animal farming was discontinued because Ball couldn't bear to kill any of them, and they all ended up becoming pets.

The same hominess and sense of family Ball strived to create at the ranch was applied to Desilu, the studio. Even when it grew to include more than a thousand employees, the Arnazes tried to maintain a family atmosphere. This included annual company picnics, birthday parties and the like.

Once *I Love Lucy* took off, stars visited Desilu to find out the "secret" of

The house that Lucy and Desi built: Desilu. Photofest

the Arnazes' sitcom success. Many stayed on and starred in successful vehicles of their own, including Eve Arden (*Our Miss Brooks*), Danny Thomas (*Make Room for Daddy*), Spring Byington (*December Bride*), and Robert Stack (*The Untouchables*).

Desilu grew to such an extent that in 1957 Ball and Arnaz were able to buy the ailing RKO studios, where both had toiled in "B" pictures, for a reported (bargain) price of $6 million.

In a May 14, 1955 *Cue* magazine cover story titled "Young Man of Property," Arnaz talked about Desilu and how his studio was doing. It's noted that prior to *I Love Lucy*, Ball was earning $125,000 per movie, and made $86,000 for four days' work in *The Magic Carpet* (1951). Arnaz had averaged $4,000 a week over the last several years from his orchestra engagements. They were "managing," as writer Philip Manoff pointed out.

Desilu Productions was at the time grossing $10,000,000 annually and producing more filmed product than MGM, Warner Bros., and 20th Century Fox combined. The Sunday reruns of *I Love Lucy* alone were bringing in $35,000 weekly (other sources note the reruns were leased at a fee of $30,000).

Arnaz is quoted as saying, "I wouldn't take 5 million bucks for those films," referring to his and Ball's ownership of the 160 episodes of *I Love Lucy* produced to that date. Well, something changed his mind, as the Arnazes ended up selling the rights to their sitcom for a reported $4.5million-$5 million in October 1956.

By 1956, a newspaper article reported that Desilu output surpassed that of six of Hollywood's major studios combined. There were 1,000 employees working on 16 stages. Ten were on lots owned by Desilu.

After their 1960 divorce, Arnaz sold out to Ball, who became the first woman in Hollywood to run a major film/TV production company. Ball always professed uneasiness at being in such a position of power, but from all accounts she acquitted herself admirably.

In a November 17, 1962 special report, *The Winnipeg Free Press* noted that Ball, "long famous on television in the role of a ditzy redhead, became one of the most important business figures in Hollywood yesterday. Buying out her former husband, Desi Arnaz, for something in excess of $2.5 million, Miss Ball became president of Desilu Productions," described as one of the world's "largest producers of television programs." At the time, Desilu was producing 12 weekly series, including Ball's (then) No. 2-rated program, *The Lucy Show*.

Desilu announced Ball "will purchase" 300,350 shares of stock owned by Arnaz "at a price considerably in excess of the current market price [$7.63]. The purchase would bring Ball's total shares 600,650, "or 52 percent of the total outstanding stock." A studio official noted Desilu operated the largest physical plant in Hollywood at the time: 36 sound stages in three separate studios.

In 1967, after green-lighting *Star Trek* and *Mission: Impossible* over Desilu executives' objections, Madame Chairperson sold the studio to Paramount for $17 million and stock, making her one of Los Angeles' wealthiest citizens.

DESILU GOULASH: Quiet dinners at home were likely to find Ball and Arnaz noshing on a "nourishing dish of hamburgers, onions, and tomatoes … called Desilu Goulash," reported *Look* magazine in its June 3, 1952 issue.

DESILU MEMORABILIA: As with any large company, Desilu created its share of promotional pieces as client giveaways and to entice sales. The difference is, on a Desilu piece, you were as likely as not to find some reference to Ball or *I Love Lucy*. These pieces could be anything from ashtrays to watches, and are highly valued by collectors. One interesting item, described by an eBay auction seller: a "vintage promotional piece from Desilu Sales, Inc. It's a lithographed ceramic plaque with a caricature of Ball saying "Hi!" and signed Love, Lucy. It measures 3.5 inches in diameter and has a cork backing. (It came out of the estate of a television writer …)" This piece, probably a coaster, was sold on eBay in November 2001, for at least $280 (the last bid I caught). The caricature, by the way, was taken from the original animated openings of *I Love Lucy*, and shows the stick figure Lucy Ricardo posing seductively.

DESILU PLAYHOUSE

Dramatic anthology TV series—also called *The Westinghouse Desilu Playhouse*—that ran for two years (1958-'60), hosted by, and occasionally starring, Desi Arnaz. He, Lucille Ball, Vivian Vance, and William Frawley, among others, appeared in "The Desilu Review" in 1959, while Arnaz himself guest-starred in the episodes "So Tender, So Profane" and "Thunder in the Night," both airing in 1959. Ball offered a rare dramatic stint in "K.O. Kitty" in 1958. Frawley turned in a guest dramatic performance in the episode "The Comeback" in 1959.

The guest-star roster of this series reads like a Who's Who of the dramatic acting community, including Eddie Albert, Pier Angeli, John Drew Barrymore, Ed Begley, William Bendix, Lloyd Bridges, Lee J. Cobb, James Franciscus, James Gregory, Jean Hagen, Earl Holliman, Sam Jaffe, David Janssen, Cloris Leachman, Robert Loggia, E.G. Marshall, Lee Marvin, Dina Merrill, Lloyd Nolan, Hugh O'Brian, Tony Randall, Aldo Ray, Jane Russell, Dick Sargent, Red Skelton, Susan Strasberg, Barry Sullivan, Claire Trevor, Robert Vaughn, Eli Wallach, Adam West, James Whitmore, Cara Williams, Jane Wyman, and Ed and Keenan Wynn.

The Untouchables debuted as part of this series, a two-parter in the spring of 1959. The hour-long *Lucille Ball-Desi Arnaz Show* (also known as *The Lucy-Desi Comedy Hour*) also ran in its time period, on a very irregular basis during its final two seasons.

THE DESILU STORY (TV Movie, 2003)

Much like the "Desilu goulash" Ball claimed was her and Arnaz's favorite dinner (tasty, simple, and easy to make comfort food; see entry under Desilu), *The Desilu Story*, which ran on the Bravo cable network, Sunday, August 24, was a nicely put-together but familiar comfort food package examining the lives of Ball and Arnaz from the perspective of the powerhouse movie and TV studio they built in the 1950s, Desilu.

The Desilu Story was basically a talking heads documentary—with some little-seen film of Ball, Arnaz, and even William Frawley and Vivian Vance doing promos for Westinghouse (the sponsor of *I Love Lucy* and *The Lucille Ball-Desi Arnaz Show* in the late 1950s). It succeeded as a not-too-in-depth look at Desilu product from the early 1950s (*Our Miss Brooks*, *Private Secretary*, *The Danny Thomas Show*), to the mid-1960s (*The Untouchables*, *Star Trek*, *Mannix*, and *Mission Impossible*).

The problem is, since many of the stars of those shows had passed away, the documentary covered them by showing promos or clips from the shows, many of which remain mired in 1950s sentiment and pacing, and thus don't really reveal what made the shows so successful. To the filmmakers' credit, it was stressed throughout that Arnaz's business acumen and sharp producer's eye was responsible for the success of many Desilu offerings. And many ex-Desilu executives were found, very willing to talk about the good old days; to a man, they all praised Arnaz as being the best in the business, a true visionary, and a crack producer.

Lucie Arnaz was on hand, too, to offer a personal perspective (as was Fred Ball, Lucy's brother), and indeed, the most touching moment of the show came as she described her mother's final phone call to her dying father. Lucie had noted earlier in the film that she could now say, since all her parents' spouses were dead, that Ball and Arnaz were always the loves of each others' lives. Any diehard fan would have already known that, but it was fascinating and meaningful to hear it from their daughter.

Several other bits of information were (surprisingly) new to me, and they make *Desilu* worth catching when it's repeated. The one caveat: don't expect too much on the show that made Desilu possible: *I Love Lucy* is relegated to the background even though, without its huge success, Desilu Studios would not have been possible.

DESILU TOO LLC

Desi Jr. and Lucie are the managing directors of Desilu too llc, the licensing organization supervising the estate of their parents, including any new Lucille Ball, Desi Arnaz, and *I Love Lucy*-related merchandise.

DILLER, PHYLLIS

Pioneering stand-up comedienne who made a name for herself by making fun of herself, becoming increasingly more outrageous—specifically, her hairdos and outfits—through the 1960s and 1970s. Her career was boosted by a friendship with comic and icon Bob Hope, who put her in several of his 1960s films. Diller stood in front of an audience and snapped out one-liners, which is quite different from what Ball did, yet it's arguable that one (Diller) might not have existed had not the other (Ball) pioneered raucous female slapstick comedy for an earlier generation of TV viewers.

Diller had the utmost respect for Ball, and praised her to the skies whenever she got the chance—like an appearance, via long-distance telephone, talking to female impersonator Jim Bailey at the beginning of his act in Jamestown, New York, during one of the town's Lucille Ball birthday celebrations. Bailey had impersonated Diller on one of the *Here's Lucy* shows, and was about to run the episode for the audience. Diller was kind enough to participate, though she said she always wondered why Ball didn't just ask *her* to be on the show!

Diller puts female comics into three categories: comic actresses (Ball, Carol Burnett); comediennes (Joan Davis, Kaye Ballard); and stand-up comics (herself, Totie Fields). Regardless, a reviewer of one of Diller's solo films, 1968's *Did You Hear the One About the Traveling Saleslady?*, noted that, "Miss Diller is following the well-worn path trod by Lucille Ball in *The Fuller Brush Girl* back in 1950...."

Diller "appeared on 32 of Bob Hope's TV specials (more than anyone)," according to *USA Today* in its 100th-birthday salute to Hope. "During a show on an aircraft carrier in 1967, Hope said: 'To give you an idea how long these guys have been at sea, they just made Phyllis Diller their pinup girl.'"

She turned up several times on television with Ball, though only once did they perform together: fittingly, on a Hope special that aired May 26, 1986: *Bob Hope's High-Flying Birthday Extravaganza*. Hope toasted his 84th birthday and the 40th anniversary of the United States Air Force in a show taped at Pope Air Force Base in North Carolina. In one segment, Diller played Lucy's daughter (as did Brooke Shields and Barbara Mandrell); Lucy was their hillbilly mom with a shotgun, protecting their innocence. Ball and Hope duetted, touchingly, on "I Remember it Well," (from *Gigi*) with special lyrics written for them. Diller, who was and remains in awe of Ball, says it was during this special that Ball directed Diller on making a memorable stage entrance, using the simple command: "Phyllis: Take stage!"

Diller also appeared with Ball on the 1970 patriotic special *Swing Out, Sweet Land*, and on *Bob Hope's Unrehearsed Antics of the Stars* (which aired September 28, 1984), and saluted Ball on the Feb. 7, 1975 *Dean Martin Roast of Lucille Ball* (along with Totie Fields, Vivian Vance, and many others).

Diller turned 90 on July 17, 2007, and was still painting and performing at this writing.

DINO, DESI & BILLY

Decidedly minor teen band that aimed for Pop Idol status, it succeeded mainly because the members had the right showbiz connections (Dean Martin, Frank Sinatra, Desi Arnaz, Lucille Ball, et al).

Dino was Dean Paul Martin Jr., Desi was, of course, Lucy and Desi's boy, and Billy Hinsche was a friend and the son of a wealthy furniture manufacturer. They were managed by Mack Gray (see Gray, Mack), a Dean Martin employee, and ushered into the recording studio by Sinatra, a Martin compadre of many years. Sinatra reportedly heard the boys jamming at Dino Sr.'s house and insisted they record the tune they were playing at the time, on his record label, Reprise. The song was "I'm a Fool" and it sold eight hundred thousand copies.

But these kids were no Rat Pack; they were just new hunks of boy meat for teen females to gobble up, even though Gray insisted their parents told him, "The most important thing in the lives of these boys is their schoolwork. That counts most." Um, yeah … for their parents, at least.

As Richie Unterberger writes online in the All Music Guide, perhaps somewhat harshly, "A Hollywood trio that were barely into their teens when they hit the charts in 1965, Dino, Desi & Billy anticipated the bubblegum fad with records that usually featured none of their own contributions, except their characterless vocals. That may be phrasing matters too kindly. The best bubblegum is far more distinctive and catchy than the lowest-common-denominator L.A. session pop-rock that they recorded. But they knew the right people, as they say in the business, which made them stars for a brief time, although they never had an ounce of credibility."

This was acknowledged even in 1966, when a two-page article by Lloyd Shearer, which ran in the *Modesto* (California) *Bee*, among other places, on February 2, 1966, began with this alarming sentence, which would have been a curse for most pop bands: "There are at least a thousand music combos in this country playing better rock 'n' roll music than Dino, Desi & Billy." Though this was followed by noting no other band was "as unique" or "in demand," the damage was done.

Allowing they had "the best show-biz contacts in the world," the band had, at that point, recorded four singles, and sold 1.5 million records. The boys, not quite 15 at the time, were getting $7,500 per TV gig, and averaging 7,000 fan letters a week. Pretty heady for some kids who got together to jam and just wanted to have a little fun.

In a sidebar to Shearer's article titled "What Lucille Ball and Jeanne Martin Think About Their Sons' Success," Ball is quoted as follows: "Frankly, I'm concerned. For years, I've patiently explained to young Desi that success requires painstaking perseverance, years of practice and hard work. Over and over I've drummed that into his head. Suddenly he comes along with two other cute-looking boys, darling boys. They form a trio, and wham, right out of the bag they're a tremendous success. It's been too easy, too quick, too unrealistic, and too atypical. And worse yet, it's disproved everything I've taught him about success in life.

"I've tried to point out [his] success … may turn out to be a flash in the pan. They will have to constantly work on and improve their act. Right now they're cute and the young girls go gaga over them. Tomorrow it may be different, and they've got to plan for tomorrow.

"I've also told Desi [that] his first responsibility is to his schoolwork. He's a 'B' student, and if he falls below that grade his drums and tambourines and the rest of his equipment go right into the garage and stay there.

"Our big problem is preventing him from getting spoiled. This is what ruins most kids who meet with too-early success."

Considering Desi Jr.'s almost two-decade-long love affair with addictive substances, it seems in retrospect that mama Ball's comments were, unfortunately, on the mark.

Ball remarked about the boys' success: "Youngsters identify with them. They're the heroes of their own age group. They know what sort of music they like, and what appeals to them also appeals to millions of others." Um, maybe. But not for long. The band's chart success only lasted for a year or so, roughly 1965 into 1966, and only two charted singles: "I'm a Fool," which made the Top 20, and "Not the Loving Kind," which broke into the Top 30 a few months later, both in 1965. Dino, Desi & Billy never had another Top 40 hit, though they recorded through 1970.

Once the trio disbanded, Hinsche went on to a steady career playing with the Beach Boys for a quarter century and Desi Jr. broke into TV and movies. Handsome Dino Jr. tried a bit of everything, but unfortunately his potential was snuffed out when he died in a plane crash while serving in the National Guard in 1987 (he was 35).

In 1999, Desi Jr. regrouped the band, with Ricci Martin replacing his brother, Dino. Renamed Ricci, Desi & Billy, the group made a new CD, has a website—Riccidesibilly. com—and began playing together live in 1999. It has toured sporadically since then.

DIRECTORS

These film directors worked with Ball during her 40-year film career. Where more than one director is credited on a movie, it indicates that both had a hand in directing it.

Frank Tuttle, *Roman Scandals*, 1933

Lowell Sherman, *Broadway through a Keyhole*, 1933

Raoul Walsh, *The Bowery*, 1933 and *Hitting a New High*, 1937

Rowland Brown, *Blood Money*, 1933

Sidney Lanfield, *Moulin Rouge*, 1934 and *Sorrowful Jones*, 1949

Dorothy Arzner, *Nana*, 1934 and *Dance, Girl, Dance*, 1940

David Butler, *Bottoms Up*, 1934 and *That's Right, You're Wrong*, 1939

Roy Del Ruth, *Bulldog Drummond Strikes Back*, and *Kid Millions*, both 1934; *DuBarry Was a Lady*, 1943

Gregory La Cava, *The Affairs of Cellini*, 1934 and *Stage Door*, 1937

James W. Horne, *Perfectly Mismated*, 1934 and *His Old Flame*, 1935 (comedy shorts)

Lambert Hillyer, *Men of the Night*, 1934

Frank Capra, *Broadway Bill*, 1934

Ray McCarey, *Three Little Pigskins*, 1934 (comedy short) and *You Can't Fool Your Wife*, 1940

Roy William Neill, *Jealousy*, 1934

Hamilton MacFadden, *Hold That Girl*, 1934

Albert S. Rogell, *Fugitive Lady*, 1934

Walter Lang, *Carnival*, 1935

John Ford, *The Whole Town's Talking*, 1935

William A. Seiter, *Roberta*, 1935, *Room Service*, 1938, and *Lover Come Back*, 1946

Leo Bulgakov, *I'll Love You Always*, 1935

Edward Ludwig, *Old Man Rhythm*, 1935

Mark Sandrich, *Top Hat*, 1935 and *Follow the Fleet*, 1936

Rowland V. Lee, *The Three Musketeers*, 1935

John Cromwell, *I Dream Too Much*, 1935

Ben Holmes, *The Farmer in the Dell*, 1935

William Hamilton and Edward Killy, *Bunker Bean*, 1935

Leslie Goodwins, *One Live Ghost*, 1935 (comedy short)

Alfred Santell, *Winterset*, 1936 and *Having Wonderful Time*, 1938

Leigh Jason, *That Girl from Paris*, 1936

George Nichols Jr., *Chatterbox*, 1936 and *The Marines Fly High*, 1940

Christy Cabanne, *Don't Tell the Wife*, 1937

Tay Garnett, *The Joy of Living*, 1938

Benjamin Stoloff, *The Affairs of Annabel*, 1938 and *The Marines Fly High*, 1940

Lucille Ball and Tommy Dix take some direction from Eddie Buzzell for the school dance scene in *Best Foot Forward*, **1943. Photofest**

Lew Landers, *The Affairs of Annabel*, 1938 (uncredited), *Annabel Takes a Tour*, 1938, *Twelve Crowded Hours*, 1939, and *The Magic Carpet*, 1951

Garson Kanin, *The Next Time I Marry*, 1938

Edward F. Cline, *Go Chase Yourself*, 1938

Glenn Tryon, *Beauty for the Asking*, 1939

John Farrow, *Five Came Back*, 1939

Jack Hively, *Panama Lady*, 1939

George Abbott, *Too Many Girls*, 1940

Richard Wallace, *A Girl, A Guy, and A Gob*, 1941

Alan Dwan, *Look Who's Laughing*, 1941

George Marshall, *Valley of the Sun*, 1942 and *Fancy Pants*, 1950 (Marshall also directed Ball in *Here's Lucy*)

Irving Reis, *The Big Street*, 1942

Tim Whelan, *Seven Days' Leave*, 1942

Edward Buzzell, *Best Foot Forward*, 1943, *Easy to Wed*, 1946, and *A Woman of Distinction*, 1950 (cameo; Gale Gordon had a bit part in this film)

George Sidney, *Thousands Cheer*, 1943

Charles Reisner, *Meet the People*, 1944

Harold S. Bucquet, *Without Love*, 1945

S. Sylvan Simon, *Abbott & Costello in Hollywood*, 1945 (cameo) and *Her Husband's Affairs*, 1947

Edward Sedgwick and Buster Keaton, *Easy to Wed*, 1946 (uncredited)

Vincente Minnelli, *Ziegfeld Follies*, 1946 and *The Long, Long Trailer*, 1954

Jules Dassin, *Two Smart People*, 1946

Henry Hathaway, *The Dark Corner*, 1946

Douglas Sirk, *Lured*, 1947

Lloyd Bacon, *Miss Grant Takes Richmond*, 1949 and *The Fuller Brush Girl*, 1950

Jacques Tourneur, *Easy Living*, 1949

Alexander Hall, *Forever Darling*, 1956

Melvin Frank, *The Facts of Life*, 1960

Don Weis, *Critic's Choice*, 1963

Gene Kelly, *A Guide for the Married Man*, 1967 (cameo)

Melville Shavelson, *Yours, Mine and Ours*, 1968

Gene Saks, *Mame*, 1974

DODDS, JOHN

Veteran book editor and fourth husband to Vivian Vance, Dodds is alleged in Vance's biography, *The Other Side of Ethel Mertz*, to have been gay prior to his relationship with her (other sources say Dodds was bisexual). They met on a blind date in Santa Fe, New Mexico.

Dodds, a California native, worked for many years at G. P. Putnam's Sons (now a division of Penguin Publishing), eventually becoming vice president, editor in chief, and general manager of the Trade Division.

When Vance was commuting to the West Coast to film *The Lucy Show* (1962-'65), Dodds would fly from their Connecticut home once a month for a ten-day stay that included seeing his wife, of course, but also doing business. At the time he owned the literary agency McIntosh, McGee and Dodds (later sold to the Harold Matson Co. of New York), and out West he would visit with some of his authors, and talk to the movie studios about selling their properties to film.

Vance insisted at the time she was happiest just being a normal gal at home. One reporter was invited to the couple's New England house and noted, "Vance arranged potato chips around a cocktail dip. Dodds filled a bucket with ice cubes. The doorbell rang and a group of neighbors trooped into the living room for a cocktail party. 'Look at me,' said Vivian, gaily dressed in a pink flannel muumuu over green leotards. 'A regular Connecticut housewife!'"

By 1968, the Doddses had a house in Santa Fe, New Mexico as well as a New York residence, and he was working for Holt, Rhinehart & Winston. In 1975, they were living in California, and Dodds had taken a position as West Coast editor for Simon & Schuster. It was reported, as she guest-starred on *Rhoda* that year, that Vance was "going back to her real love": TV!

"Back East," she said, "I did a lot of stock and dinner theaters, but now, since we'll be living on the West Coast, I can do television comedies again. I'm at home on a television set where I spent so many years doing the *Lucy* shows." Of course, she'd said the exact opposite (she was going back to her true love, the stage), when she exited *I Love Lucy*.

Vance said that Dodds was a wonderful man and she was happily married, with a bonus—his literary background: "I love books and respect writers highly. You can be an excellent actress, but without good material, you can't win."

Dodds reportedly had abandoned his former (gay) lifestyle and devoted himself to Vance for many years, through her death in 1979. By all accounts, it was the actress' most successful marriage (of four). Dodds died of cancer in 1986. See also the biography entry under <u>Vance, Vivian</u>.

DOLLS

Once *I Love Lucy* became a raging success the merchandising of the show and its characters began in earnest. There was everything from a duplicate of Ricky's smoking jacket, to Ricky and Lucy Ricardo matching pajama sets, to dolls.

In 1954, the Ball-Arnaz movie *The Long, Long Trailer* was released. To generate publicity at movie theaters across the country, a cloth doll was given away as a promotional prize to the person who could name the most movies that Ball appeared in to date. The 24-inch doll has a cloth body with a molded plastic face and yarn hair. It wears a red striped shirt with red pants and a yellow apron adorned with two red hearts and the words *I Love Lucy* (the name "Desi" is underneath). The doll, a true rarity, sold on eBay for well over $200 in June 2001.

There have been paper doll sets of the Ricardos, dating from the early 1950s (with an inappropriately *blond* Little Ricky in one of the sets); another blond Little Ricky, this time a plastic doll from American Character, now a prized collector's item; Ball and her *Lucy Show* cast were also honored with paper dolls.

Since the 1980s, there have been many opportunities for Ball collectors to purchase dolls based on their favorite redhead and her cohorts in comedy. One of the first was the Lucy doll from Effanbee in 1985. It was the seventh in the series of "Celebrity Collectible" groupings, and the first living legend. The doll pictured Ball as she appeared in the animated opening to *Here's Lucy*, in top hat and tails, wearing shorts instead of slacks. This doll is now a rare find and sells for $100 or more.

The now-defunct Cascade Pictures of California, a company that specialized in animation and special effects, created the doll/puppet used in the opening credits of *Here's Lucy*. Cascade used a process called Magnascope to provide multi-plane depth perspective, allowing the doll to "perform" in front of blue curtains. The doll wore a tuxedo top. Cascade kept the doll after it was used to produce the credits, but the company owner's widow noted in 1994 that its entire collection had been stolen.

The Hollywood Walk of Fame and Desilu too llc put out a porcelain Lucy doll in a limited edition of 3,000. Featuring Ball all dolled up, so to speak, in a shimmering dress with feathers, the face on this one is fairly accurate but looks a tad scary from certain angles, and the hair is rather stiff.

Madame Alexander has released several dolls in her trademark style (somewhat eerie, to me), adult-as-child, small size. They include Ball as Carmen Miranda, from the "Be a Pal" episode, and Lucy Ricardo in her trademark polka-dot dress. Madame Alexander dolls, especially those no longer made, tend to sell for high prices, $100 on up.

The Hamilton Collection doll series began in the late 1980s and continued for about a decade. Starting with Ball in a polka-dot dress, the series went on to include her as Queen of the Gypsies (from "The Operetta" episode) and in several other costumes from I Love Lucy, such as Sally Sweet and the Italian grape stomper. Two Ricky dolls were also marketed, one with him in a suit, the other with Ricky in ruffled shirt and accompanied by a bongo drum. All are rather rare and no longer produced; they sell for $100 or more, depending on the condition of the doll (mint in box is best, as always).

A set of four rubbery vinyl/cloth I Love Lucy cast dolls was first available in 1988 from Presents, a division of Hamilton Gifts. These dolls are now a true find. The set featured the first dolls made to resemble Vivian Vance and William Frawley (not including the hundreds of ceramic collectibles made in the past decade). Lucy and Ethel are 14 inches tall, Ricky and Fred are 16 inches tall. A set of all four in good condition sells for anywhere from $300 up.

In the summer of 2003, my sister was antiquing in Seekonk, Massachusetts, on the Rhode Island border. Fortunately, she had her cell phone with her. I got a call on a Saturday morning which began, "I'm looking at a set of four I Love Lucy dolls …" "Hold on, let me get my book," I said. I read her the previous paragraph, and added details that I knew from seeing pictures of the dolls—for example, the Fred doll was in suspenders with a white shirt. In a minute, she confirmed that she had indeed found this elusive set of dolls. And she picked them up for me at the relatively bargain price of $140. So once again, I stress, as a collector, never give up. Never stop looking. (And have your family and loved ones looking out for you, too!)

Mattel took its "celebrity Barbie" concept and applied it to Lucy Ricardo beginning in the late 1990s. These are amusing dolls that retailed for $39.99 each but now sell for more depending on where you buy them: you can still buy them fairly cheap on eBay, but beware of the condition; and Cathy's Closet, the online Lucy store, was at this writing selling the first 10 in the series for $125 to $149, but keep in mind they're probably "mint in box," which always adds to the price. The doll series began with Ball as Ricardo doing her Vitameatavegamin commercial; on the candy conveyor belt (with a picture of Vance as Ethel in the background of the box); and Ball stomping grapes for her Italian movie role. All dolls are accurately costumed and come with cute accessories attached (e.g., the Vitameatavegamin bottle, high-heeled shoes, a purse).

The fourth (and fifth) dolls in the series, on shelves in fall 2000, were Ball and Arnaz (or, as Mattel bills them, Barbie and Ken as Lucy and Ricky) from the "We're Having a Baby" episode. This is the first (and to this date only) Ricky doll in the series, and was released in honor of the *I Love Lucy* 50th anniversary in 2001. The first edition sold out quickly. In the fall of 2001 Mattel released its sixth doll in the *I Love Lucy* series, featuring Ball in full Carmen Miranda drag from the "Be a Pal" episode.

The latest dolls in the series feature Ball in her Paris "burlap" fashion gown; Ball disguised in glasses, a bandana, and her fake "burned" nose, from the William Holden "L.A. at Last" episode; Ball in her familiar dark blue polka-dot dress and vacuum cleaner from the "Sales Resistance" episode; Ball as the Queen of the Gypsies from "The Operetta"; "Lucy Gets in Pictures," with the redhead as a showgirl with a too-heavy headpiece; Ball as Santa (a 2006 special edition) from the long-missing Christmas episode; and the first 2007 doll, called "The Audition," inspired by Lucy's clowning and trick cello act in the series pilot.

Available later in 2007 was a Lucy and Ethel pairing from the episode "Lucy and Ethel Buy the Same Dress" (October 19, 1953), in which they sing "Friendship" while ripping said dress off each other. This was the first Ethel (Vance) doll in the series, and unfortunately, the doll was crafted without a care as to Vivian Vance's appearance; it looks more like Marilyn Monroe than Ethel Mertz.

In 2001 came the Lucille Ball Vinyl Portrait doll from the Franklin Mint. Lucy was memorialized in a short-sleeved navy and polka-dot dress, with an accompanying apron. In articulated (you can move the arms and legs) vinyl and selling for well over $200, this doll at 17 inches high is one of the largest. It was authorized by CBS Worldwide Inc. and Desilu, too, llc. The Franklin Mint has also issued a Porcelain Baby *I Love Lucy* Doll. It stands approximately 6.5 inches high and is a nicely executed piece of a (literally) baby-faced Ball.

The Home Shopping Network, during its hour of selling *I Love Lucy* merchandise celebrating the show's 50th Anniversary on October 15, 2001, debuted a porcelain Ball doll in a limited edition of 1,951. The doll sold out almost immediately at $99.50. The doll portrayed Lucy Ricardo in a typical navy and polka-dot dress, and was also authorized by CBS Worldwide Inc. and Desilu too llc.

Classic Collecticritters released the Ball and Arnaz Bobblehead Doll Set in March 2002. The company debuted an entire line of Lucy products in honor of the 50th anniversary of *I Love Lucy* (October 15, 2001). The bobblehead dolls are approximately six inches high, and have oversized, springy, bouncy heads. They are patterned after the Ball and Arnaz animated figures that opened and closed the original *I Love Lucy* show. Each set of figures is individually numbered on the bottom. Collecticritters limited total production of these sets to 10,000. These dolls came in a decorative box, for storage and protection or display.

And the dolls just keep on coming. Newer items include a set of four limited-edition Vitameatavegamin nesting dolls (which fit inside each other) from Newcrafters; and a rare set of the Fab Four from *I Love Lucy* as 8-inch action figures (each has 14 to 16 movable joints). Someone will make a stop-motion animated video using these, mark my words.

DOTTIE GETS SPANKED

Short (27-minute) film from independent filmmaker Todd Haynes in 1994, about a young boy obsessed with a Ball-like TV star. Steven Gale's world revolves around *The Dottie Frank Show*, a sitcom reminiscent of *The Lucy Show*. The comic misadventures of its heroine inspire endless fascination for Steven, who becomes a Dottie expert, and fantasizes about her all the time. Eventually, he wins a contest and meets Dottie, discovering that she is nothing like her screwball character; she's a tough commander on the set. Called by turns heartfelt, compelling, hilarious, and unsettling, the film drew this response from critic Amy Taubin: "Todd Haynes may well be the best filmmaker of his generation."

DRAW 50 FAMOUS STARS

Large-format book by Lee J. Ames published in 1982 that shows the reader how to draw 50 celebrities, including Ball.

DREAM GIRL

Comic play in which Ball toured the country in 1947, garnering rave reviews. See entry under "Stage Career."

DUKE, PATTY

Duke is an Oscar- and Emmy-winning actress who had a tabloid-worthy affair at the age of 24 with Desi Arnaz, Jr. (then 17), in 1969-'70. She acknowledged him from the Emmy podium after winning the award for Best Actress in a Drama for 1970's *My Sweet Charlie* at the June 7, 1970 ceremony. During the preshow warm-up for the *Here's Lucy* episode "Lucy and Sammy Davis Jr.," which aired September 28, 1970, Gary Morton affectionately introduced Duke from the studio audience. But it wasn't all smiles and sunshine; mama Ball ordered Desi to stop seeing the older and troubled Duke. He complied. Duke was pregnant at the time, and rumors flew that the child was Desi Jr.'s. DNA tests subsequently proved otherwise. (See Arnaz Jr., Desi.)

E

EL CAPITAN THEATER

This is the Hollywood Boulevard theater in which Desi Arnaz and his band played for Bob Hope's radio show in 1947.

EDEN, BARBARA

Eden, on a 2002 Lifetime *Intimate Portrait*, recalled that Lucille Ball was a dream to work with, kind and warm, and actually offered Eden a contract with Desilu, since, as she put it, there weren't that many "pretty gals" who could also do comedy. Eden signed with 20th Century Fox instead, and then went on to fame as the title character in the sitcom *I Dream of Jeannie*. She says she'll always wonder what might have happened careerwise had she taken Ball up on her offer.

ELAINE'S

Celebrated New York celebrity watering hole on the Upper East Side of Manhattan, where Ball often went to eat and play backgammon in the 1980s, after she took an apartment in the city to be near her grandchildren. According to owner Elaine Kaufman, Ball "was a warm, nice lady."

EMMY AWARDS

Over the years, The Academy of Television Arts and Sciences frequently honored Ball. *I Love Lucy* won for Best Situation Comedy in 1952 and 1953, while Ball herself won four Emmys for individual performance (in 1952, 1955, 1966, and 1967). In 1989, the Academy's Governor's Award was presented to Lucy posthumously.

Vivian Vance was the first Best Series Supporting Actress Emmy winner, in 1953, and was nominated for most of the years *I Love Lucy* was on. William Frawley was consistently nominated year after year as Best Supporting Actor for playing Fred Mertz, but never won. And in a shameful oversight, Desi Arnaz was never even nominated for an Emmy during his entire career.

The latter mistake was somewhat rectified when Arnaz and *I Love Lucy* were (separately) inducted into the Television Academy Hall of Fame (also run by the Emmy organization) in 1991. Ball herself had been among the first inductees in 1984.

Lucie Arnaz won an Emmy for Best Documentary after producing the heartfelt *Lucy & Desi: A Home Movie* (1994).

Author Craig Hamrick, who wrote the 1995 biography, *Big Lou*, about the life of actor Louis Edmonds (*Dark Shadows*, *All My Children*), recalled this anecdote about the Emmys: "Louis was nominated for the Emmy Award for his portrayal of Langley [on *All My Children*] in 1984, 1985, and 1986. He told me once that, at one of the Emmy telecasts, he found himself seated next to Ball. He related, 'I turned to her in awe, and said, "My God, it's like sitting next to the Queen Mother!" Lucy looked at me, rolled her eyes, and said, "Oh, brother!" She got up and moved to sit somewhere else.'"

ENGRAV-O-TINTS

These black-and-white movie star portraits were popular in vending machines of the 1940s. Ball (with "Metro-Goldwyn-Mayer" under her name) was featured on these cards, made by "Peerless Weighing & Vending Machine Corp., N.Y." They were sold via machines on which you could weigh yourself for a penny and get a card. The collectible cards had a horoscope or fortune on the back and measured approximately 1.25x2.25 inches.

ENTERTAINMENT TONIGHT

Magazine-style television show that covers Hollywood and the entertainment scene. *ET* has been on the air since 1981. On the night of Lucille Ball's death, the show devoted its entire half hour to her life. Staff member Ben Herndon described what transpired in creating the show for *Emmy* magazine's July/August 1989 issue. Here are some of his comments:

"Oddly, the first reaction [on hearing of Ball's death] for many in the *ET* offices was to phone their families." Maybe that wasn't so odd, considering millions of people considered Ball family after having her in their living rooms for 50 years..

About a dozen sleepy people attended the original 6:30 a.m. *ET* staff meeting to determine that day's program contents. More than 50 staffers, everyone "wide-awake, high-strung," and on "ready-alert" attended a new production meeting called in light of the news of Ball's passing. Senior producer Jim Van Messel made a short announcement: "The whole show will be Lucy. Everything will be for Lucy."

Herndon notes *ET* wasn't in such bad shape, having prepared an obituary for Ball in 1988 when she had suffered a heart attack. But new segments had to be ready by noon, since *ET* had a 12:30 p.m. satellite feed to its affiliates, "some of which broadcast the show in the early afternoon." The staff managed to put its tribute together, frantically completing it in half the time it took to produce a regular show.

Noting that *ET* had only once before devoted an entire show to a celebrity passing (Henry Fonda, in 1982), Herndon stipulated this one was different: "Coming out of the 'Lucy Classics' piece, *ET* anchor John Tesh is chuckling and grins broadly on camera, obviously charmed. Same for the stage crew. This is not your average obituary.... There is no mention in the script of death or dying. Words like *loss*, *passing*, and *mourning* are used instead."

Co-anchor Mary Hart noted at the end of the show that Ball "lived the most remarkable career in show business history." After the final segment, a longer-than-usual clip montage of Ball's antics ran to the tune "Be a Clown" sung by Judy Garland and Gene Kelly, a curtain dropped and instead of end credits there was this text: "We Love You … We'll Miss You and We'll Never Forget You … Thank You, Lucy."

"ETHEL TO TILLIE!"

Famous phrase from an early *I Love Lucy* episode (No. 7) called "The Séance." In the episode, Lucy Ricardo, having read the wrong day's horoscope and mistakenly cancelled an important appointment for Ricky (with a Mr. Meriweather), enlists neighbor Ethel (as Madame Mertzola) to conjure up Meriweather's beloved but deceased Tillie; what the Ricardos and Mertzes don't know is that Tillie was Meriweather's cocker spaniel. During the séance, Ethel goes into a trance and intones "Ethel to Tillie" several times, in the crisp manner of an overseas telephone operator, wholly unsuited to a somber séance (but wildly funny).

F

FACTOR, MAX

Makeup artist extraordinaire, Factor began applying cosmetics to the faces of the czar of Russia and his family, eventually immigrating to the United States and becoming a sought-after makeup artist in Hollywood. Considered the father of modern makeup, Factor invented the first "pancake" that looked good under the heavy klieg lights necessary for filmmaking, had many other patents, and came up with the "bee-stung" lip look.

Lucille Ball signed her first promotional agreement with Max Factor in 1935, and again in 1942. She appeared in many print ads during those decades for Factor products. Factor's name is listed in the credits of *I Love Lucy* as well. Of all film stars, Ball had the longest professional association with Max Factor.

FAN CLUB

We Love Lucy offers a wealth of information on all things Lucy, thanks to the expertise of president Tom Watson, also the author or co-author of several books about Ball (see Books). On the Internet, visit welovelucy.com. E-mail the fan club for information at info@lucyfan.com.

"A FAN OF LUCY'S"

This article, written by Thomas J. Cottle and published in *Television Quarterly* as a tribute to Ball just after her death in 1989, is a mere two pages, but brims with everything one needs to know to understand why Ball was so popular with all ages, races, and creeds, and why she will remain so. The article was an interview with Hattie Dinsmore, a descendant of slaves who had died two years earlier at age 87.

Dinsmore was a great fan of television and really loved comedies, and in particular, Lucille Ball's shows. She was quoted as saying she threw out all her medications (except the one for her blood pressure) later in life, because she was, "Better off with Lucy any day. [That] woman isn't just *on* the television, she comes into this room here with me, with those long legs of hers, and all that red hair jumping about. Second she shows up, you hear all those people laughing. Has to make you laugh, no matter how sick you are."

Dinsmore credited Ball with bringing her close to her family, like her great-granddaughter, who would lie with her and laugh at Ball's antics, though not louder than Dinsmore. If she was depressed, Dinsmore would put in a videotape of Ball: "Lucille Ball [would] come on the television and everybody and I mean everybody in the country forgets all the bad things that happened to them that day, and they just laugh.... Doesn't nothing hurt in my body when I hear her screaming at Ethel and Fred, and, mister, *everything* hurts when the commercials come back on."

Dinsmore's devotion was all the more poignant for this fact, which Cottle reveals in the last sentence: "Surely the great comedian renowned for her pratfalls, sight gags, and mime, would have been especially intrigued by the bond [she had with Dinsmore] had she known that the late Hattie Dinsmore was born blind."

FASHION PLATE

Like every movie star of her era, Ball was obliged to do publicity stories tied to a variety of themes, including fashion. One such article from 1942 called "Lucille Ball's Fashions for Fun" featured three pictures of Ball in casual outfits. One is a three-piece playsuit (shirt, shorts, and a skirt) with a "Roman-inspired red-and-white border on a navy linen pinafore and white linen blouse." In this outfit "Lucille's all set for summer fun ... whether she wants to play the game or just watch.... Pinafores are an advancing style this year."

What the well-dressed traveler was wearing in the 1940s, as modeled by Lucille Ball; Lucy seems ready for anything as she studies a map of New York harbor. Photofest

Pictured at home on her San Fernando Valley ranch, "Lucille fits right in with the landscape in her Mexican-inspired costume. The skirt is bright red cotton; vest is white felt, blouse of yellow jersey. Appliqués continue to be favorite trimmers, Lucille's being large, felt flowers."

Ball is referred to as "one of Hollywood's most naturally beautiful stars," and though she counts no day complete "without her time in the sun," she has had to "limit her leisure hours to make time for home-front duties." Still, she has "insured her fun by selecting the three gay costumes pictured on these pages." Further, "Lucille feels right at home in her Mexican play costume.... She has found, as you too may discover, that you can have fun in your own front yard if there's color and variety in your playtime costumes!"

Though Ball always professed not to be interested in the "glamour girl" part of the business, she went through her paces exceedingly well, with the looks and a figure that were made for modeling (see photo).

FBI FILE

After World War II, with the Germans and Japanese soundly defeated, America needed another villain to spur patriotism among its citizenry. Who better than the Russians, whose Communist agenda frightened as many as had the Nazis? Thus began the Red Scare and the infamous rise of Sen. Joseph McCarthy.

The Federal Bureau of Investigation (FBI) was notorious for keeping files on celebrities and politicians, and when the Red Scare was going on, along with the paperwork generated by blacklisting and government hearings, the Bureau's cabinets must have been overstuffed.

One of those files was on Lucille Ball and, thanks to the Freedom of Information Act, you can see some of the documents that occupied it. In fact, there's more than one site on the Internet that publishes some of the documents (see also <u>FBI File</u> under <u>Arnaz, Desi</u>).

Why did the FBI keep a file on Ball? It turns out that her socialist grandfather Fred Hunt had pressured the family to register to vote as Communist Party members once they moved to Hollywood. Ball claimed she and the family only did it to please Grandpa, and, luckily for her, by the time the news hit nationwide (broken as a blind item in then-powerful Walter Winchell's national broadcast), *I Love Lucy* was already a phenomenon.

The public not only believed Ball's disclaimer, many were indignant that the FBI went after someone who was, even at that point, so obviously an American institution. And there were others, including newspaper columnists, who went in the opposite direction, claiming, after Ball was cleared of any wrongdoing, that she got special treatment because she was a big, popular star.

Desi Arnaz was quoted at the time (1952-'53) as saying, "The only thing red about Lucy is her hair, and even that's not real."

Ultimately, the scandal had no effect on Ball's career or *I Love Lucy*. For Ball personally, it was just one more example of how everything wonderful you had could immediately be taken away in an instant, and reinforced her determination to hang on to all she did have.

♥**Lucy Trivia** By the late 1950s, the family had warmed enough toward Winchell that Arnaz asked him to do the staccato narration for *The Untouchables*.

FERRER, MEL

Born in 1917 in New Jersey, Ferrer was half-Cuban and wore many hats during his long career: actor, writer, producer, and director among them. An actor's actor, Ferrer was one of the co-founders of The La Jolla Playhouse in 1946 (along with Dorothy McGuire and Gregory Peck) and was a good friend to Vivian Vance. He persuaded her to perform there in *The Voice of the Turtle*, during which she was seen and hired to portray Ethel Mertz in *I Love Lucy*. Previous to that, he gave Vance one of her few screen roles, in the 1950 film noir, *The Secret Fury*.

Ferrer was married to Audrey Hepburn for 14 years and, to some, is best known for that; his most famous film role is the self-pitying puppeteer in the charming fable *Lili* (1953) with Leslie Caron. Ferrer also appeared with Ball co-star William Frawley (and Marlene Dietrich) in Fritz Lang's classic Western, *Rancho Notorious* (1952). Though he made more than 60 movies, he never broke through the ranks as a big star.

FILM CAREER

Those who only know Lucille Ball from her TV appearances are missing a huge treat: the 80-plus films she made during her 50-year career. These ranged from potboilers to hysterically funny comedies, and even a few surprisingly moving dramas.

1. *Roman Scandals* (1933), Slave Girl, uncredited. As one of the Goldwyn girls, Ball can be glimpsed as a scantily clad long-haired blonde among dozens in Eddie Cantor's dream sequences. She also appears in the modern-day scenes.

Ball's strong desire to make it in show business first reared its head during this picture, generally acknowledged as the redhead's (then a willowy blonde) first film appearance. Noel Holston, of the *Minneapolis-St. Paul Star Tribune*, wrote in 1989 after Ball's death that, "In 1933, six years before television was introduced at the New York World's Fair, eighteen years before a comedy called *I Love Lucy* made millions of Americans more eager than ever to own a TV set, comedian Eddie Cantor was filming a musical romp called *Roman Scandals*.

"The script called for a villain to hurl mud at Cantor who, with perfect comic timing, would duck, allowing the mud to hit one of the Goldwyn Girls in the face. But none of the chorines was willing to be the target. No one, that is, except leggy, young Lucille Ball, who volunteered. She wasn't afraid of looking silly. Cantor loved Lucy for this, and so, eventually, did everyone…. Absolute comic courage—that's Lucille Ball's legacy."

♥ **Lucy Trivia** In a December 8, 1969 episode of *Here's Lucy* called "Lucy and the Generation Gap," Ball and Gale Gordon play parents to Lucie and Desi Jr. in a series of sketches charting the generation gap through the ages. The first setting is Rome, and Gordon (as Caesar) is carried on stage by six beauties while reading a magazine called … *Roman Scandals*. Later in the sketch, Ball is also seen flipping through the fake magazine.

2. *Broadway Through a Keyhole* (1933), Girl at the Beach, uncredited. In his intimate biography of Ann Sothern—*Cordially Yours, Ann Sothern*, 2005—Colin Briggs noted of this film, Sothern's ninth uncredited bit, "A blonde Lucille Ball was seen with Harriette [Lake, Ann's real name, used initially in her career] in a brief beach scene. Lucille had some lines, but H.L. [sic] did not get to speak. Harriette and Lucille formed a friendship then that lasted throughout their lifetimes."

3. *The Bowery* (1933) Bit part, uncredited.

4. *Blood Money* (1933) Bit part, uncredited.

5. *Nana* (1934, aka *Lady of the Boulevards*) Chorus Girl, uncredited.

6. *Men of the Night* (1934) Peggy.

7. *Jealousy* (1934) Girl.

8. *Hold That Girl* (1934) Girl.

9. *Fugitive Lady* (1934) Beauty Operator.

10. *Moulin Rouge* (1934) Chorus Girl in the nightclub scenes. A true bit part, though her legendary TV character, Lucy Ricardo, aspired to be a showgirl in one of the series' funniest episodes.

11. *Bottoms Up* (1934) Girl.

12. *The Affairs of Cellini* (1934, aka *The Firebrand*) Lady-in-Waiting, uncredited.

13. *Perfectly Mismated* (1934).

14. *Kid Millions* (1934) Goldwyn Girl, uncredited, in the harem scene. Ball backed up future television co-stars and chums Ethel Merman and Ann Sothern.

15. *Bulldog Drummond Strikes Back* (1934) Girl.

16. *Broadway Bill* (1934, aka *Strictly Confidential*) Ball's onscreen for less than a minute as a blonde telephone operator; uncredited.

17. *Three Little Pigskins* (1934) Daisy Simms. This was Lucy's one and only appearance with The Three Stooges. It was the Stooges' fourth film.

18. *A Night at the Biltmore Bowl* (1935). This was a two-reel RKO musical short also featuring Betty Grable, Pert Kelton, Anne Shirley, and Edgar Kennedy.

19. *His Old Flame* (1935). Eighteen-minute two-reeler in which a former girlfriend and some steamy love letters sideline a candidate running for mayor.

20. *Carnival* (1935, aka *Carnival Nights*) Nurse. Lucy as a nurse is background atmosphere (along with 60 or so other bit players) in this Jimmy Durante feature about the goings-on at a carnival.

21. *The Whole Town's Talking* (1935, aka *Passport to Fame*) Girl, uncredited.

22. *Roberta* (1935) Fashion model, uncredited. This part was a natural for Ball, who began her career as a model in New York.

23. *I'll Love You Always* (1935) Lucille. Ball's part was of the "blink-and-you'll-miss-her" kind in this George Murphy vehicle. She would later co-star with him, as his love interest in 1941's *A Girl, A Guy, and A Gob*, one of her final pictures for RKO. (See No. 57.)

24. *Old Man Rhythm* (1935) College Girl. Ball has a bit part in this romantic comedy featuring Buddy Rogers and Betty Grable, about a father and son competing for the same girl at college. Don't worry, this was the 1930s and it was all *trés innocente*.

25. *Top Hat* (1935) Flower Clerk. One of Ball's more famous early bit parts in a classic movie; even though she's not on for long, she makes an impression.

26. *The Three Musketeers* (1935) Extra, uncredited. Ball's walk-on may have been cut from this picture; she's impossible to spot.

27. *I Dream Too Much* (1935) Dated musical dramedy noteworthy for Ball playing a small role as a gum-popping tourist, Gwendolyn Dilley, in support of future co-star (two movies and television) Henry Fonda. Fonda plays opera singer Lily Pons' neglected husband.

28. *That Girl from Paris* (1936) Claire Williams. Ball's supporting part is a jealous "best friend" to star Lily Pons. Tagged by studio PR as "that brilliant, sparkling, witty, song-and-dance musical comedy," opera-star Pons was an acquired taste, and Ball's small role as the "other woman" exists merely to keep the comedy moving along.

29. *So and Sew* (1936) A comedy short, this farce centers on mistaken identity, with Ball as a decorator's wife who gets confused when he's asked to pose as a client's husband.

30. *The Farmer in the Dell* (1936) Gloria Wilson. In this bottom half of a double bill, Fred Stone plays the titular farmer, "a son of the soil," as one review described him, and Jean Parker is his daughter, looking to become a star. When they go to Hollywood, though, dad is the big success. Ball is not mentioned in the reviews or advertising.

31. *Dummy Ache* (1936) Actress. A short starring Edward Kennedy (a slapstick silent film comedian who also scored in talkies, known as the master of the slow burn), this comedy was nominated for an Oscar in 1937 as Best Short Subject, two-reel.

32. *Chatterbox* (1936) Lillian Temple. According to the online *Classic Film Guide*, blonde Ball is a "sophisticated urbanite" stage actress who just wants to get the back pay that's owed her. Star Anne Shirley aspires to be on the stage, but learns that dreams are sometimes not at all what they seem to be.

33. *Bunker Bean* (1936) Miss Kelly. Bunker Bean is a shy employee at an aircraft company who learns to be more assertive and win the boss' daughter after discovering he's the reincarnation of Napoleon and then an Egyptian Pharaoh. (Of course, the fortune-teller he consults is a fake.) Ball is the company receptionist who's somewhat helpful to Bean.

34. *Follow the Fleet* (1936) Kitty Collins. Ball's parts began to get larger during this period. In this film, her wisecracking blonde friend to lead Ginger Rogers drew the following comment from a preview audience member: "You might give the tall gum-chewing blonde more parts and see if she can't make the grade. A good gamble."

♥ **Lucy Trivia** Ball took acting lessons from Ginger's mother Lela at the RKO lot, and Lela's influence is credited with getting Ball some of her first big supporting spots.

35. *One Live Ghost* (1936) An RKO comedy short. Star Leon Errol is a wise guy who fakes his death in order to see how his family will react. Ball plays Maxine, the maid.

36. *Winterset* (1936) Girl. Ball has yet another bit part in this potboiler of a crime movie that was Burgess Meredith's screen debut. Meredith searches for the truth of his father's (John Carradine) involvement in an earlier robbery/murder.

37. *Don't Tell the Wife* (1937) Ann "Annie" Howell. Ball plays a secretary for a sextet of cons in support of "stars" Guy Kibbee, Una Merkel, Thurston Hall, Guinn Williams, and William Demarest. The plot is a stock scheme involving an innocent wife (Merkel) as the front, which inevitably goes awry. Ball would soon be beyond such roles (and she'd be billed above Demarest in her 1949 film, *Sorrowful Jones*).

38. *Hitting a New High* (1937). This musical was Ball's final bit part, once again in support of Lily Pons. The film is missing from some lists of Ball's films, and I couldn't prove or disprove she was in it. Interesting note: Pons only did three films in her career, all for RKO, but the

studio couldn't turn her into another Jeanette MacDonald and gave up. Ball was in all three films.

39. *Stage Door* (1937) Judy Canfield. The first big movie (or "A" picture) in which audiences and reviewers took notice of Ball's characterization, no mean feat in a cast that included Ginger Rogers, Eve Arden, Ann Miller, and Katharine Hepburn. Ball plays a young, hopeful actress in a boarding house full of the same; Ball's character is just as content, however, to run off to the security of marriage, which she does at the end. Until then, she cracks wise with the best of them. Ball will not go back to playing bit parts after this film. Unfortunately, for the next few years, she will be cast in mostly average comedies or potboiler dramas in which she invariably transcended the material.

Lucy consults with acting coach Lela Rogers (Ginger's mom) on set in the 1930s. Photofest

40. *The Next Time I Marry* (1938) Nancy Crocker Fleming. Enjoyable trifle in which Ball plays an heiress pretending to be "one of the people" so she won't be fleeced by a man after only her money. The first picture in which the credits read: "Starring Lucille Ball."

41. *Joy of Living* (1938) Salina. Ball is Irene Dunne's little sister in a comedy about a Broadway star who learns to enjoy life and distance herself from her money-grubbing family. Ball was cast in this movie when Ann Sothern bowed out. Ball recalls after that, whenever Sothern turned down a script or wasn't available, they gave it to her: "I got a whole career out of Ann Sothern's rejects."

42. *Go Chase Yourself* (1938) Carol Meely. Lame comedy wastes pretty Ball as the girlfriend of comedian Joe Penner. Penner had heard Ball on radio and requested her as his co-star in this film.

43. *Having Wonderful Time* (1938) Miriam. This poor excuse for a comedy can be blamed on the fact that all the ethnicity (read: Jewishness) was taken out of the original play when it was filmed, leaving a bunch of WASPs running around a Catskills-type camp for adults. Ball tries

gamely, but she's stuck in a pre-PC supporting role that requires her to constantly demean herself. Pal Ginger Rogers stars, and Red Skelton makes his film debut.

44. *The Affairs of Annabel* (1938) Annabel Allison. Recognizing Ball's audience appeal, RKO gave her a (short-lived) movie series, about a young actress at the mercy of her publicity man (Jack Oakie). Critic Frank Nugent noted, "Miss Ball, who is rapidly becoming one of our best comediennes, plays it broadly and without a disruptive touch of whimsy." Another critic, Irene Thirer, wrote, "We doubt a big-name luminary would have lent herself to this bolt of celluloid slapstick. But Lucille Ball is practically a beginner, and a right good sport—besides which, she has it on many movie mighties when it comes to looks. The gal should go places."

45. *Room Service* (1938) Christine Marlowe. Wasted as the female lead in this Marx Brothers adaptation of the hit Broadway play about producers trying to put on a show without any money, Ball does as well as she can in a straight role while Groucho, Chico, and Harpo chew the scenery around her.

46. *Annabel Takes a Tour* (1938) Annabel Allison. The second and final picture of Ball's RKO "series" offers more wacky doings with actress Annabel and her publicity man. RKO offered Ball and co-star Jack Oakie contracts for another "Annabel" film, but Oakie demanded too much cash and killed the deal (see Osborne, Robert).

47. *That's Right You're Wrong* (1939) Sandra Sand. Ball plays a secondary role to bandleader Kay Kyser in this overripe making-it-in-Hollywood tale.

48. *Panama Lady* (1939) Lucy. Downbeat noir picture in which Ball gets stranded in Panama, all for the love of her guy. Co-star Allan Lane was later the voice of Mr. Ed on TV. A tad cliched, but tight and well structured. In several important ways—gloomy and dark, first-person narrative, and guilt-ridden characters—this could be considered one of the first film noirs.

49. *Beauty for the Asking* (1939) Jean Russell. An office melodrama, in which Ball, jilted by her fiancé, invents a face cream that becomes wildly successful, thanks to her wealthy rival's investment in it. This is a cut above her usual "B" picture.

50. *Five Came Back* (1939) Peggy Nolan. One of the earliest "disaster" pictures, this taut drama has 12 people stranded in a South American jungle (with headhunters on the loose), after a plane bound for Panama (a popular destination of the time; see no. 48) goes down in a storm. The damaged plane can only take five of them back to civilization. Ball is a strong woman of dubious past (1930s-speak for prostitute) who fights to be one of the survivors. Her Peggy Nolan is pegged a shady lady strictly by her dress and sarcastic manner, it appears. Other than this, one might think Nolan is just a typical tough 1930s movie dame.

Her true character is revealed when the father of the young boy on the plane is murdered, mob-style (the passengers hear of it via a radio broadcast) and Peggy goes to comfort him. "He needs a woman," she says to Allan Jenkins, playing the tot's uncle. Jenkins' withering reply: "He needs a *lady*." Don't worry, though, by the end of the film she is the kid's "Aunt Peggy" and will likely be taking care of him back in the states along with newfound beau, pilot Bill Brooks, played by Chester Morris.

Jenkins of course, was a familiar character actor of the era who appeared in over 100 movies and guest-starred three times on *I Love Lucy*, twice playing a police officer and once a police sergeant. Morris, according to Turner Classic Movies host and Ball's friend Robert Osborne, made Ball miserable during the shoot by constantly chasing after her. And the director, John Farrow (Mia's father) was known for his argumentative behavior.

The movie is a tight 75 minutes, the characters are all well drawn, and Ball is especially vibrant in an early role that brought her positive reviews and attention in Hollywood.

51. *Twelve Crowded Hours* (1939) Paula Sanders. Amiable crime "dramedy" with Ball in a typical wisecracking supporting role.

52. *The Marines Fly High* (1940) Joan Grant. Average war flick in which two marines duke it out for the attention of pilot (!) Ball.

53. *You Can't Fool Your Wife* (1940) Clara Hinklin/Mercedes Vasquez. Ball plays two roles in this fair farce about a husband and wife whose marriage goes sour.

Critic Wanda Hale praised our favorite redhead: "Lucille Ball and James Ellison, who were seen together some time ago in *Next Time I Marry*, again are having domestic trouble in the new RKO comedy *You Can't Fool Your Wife*. These two young players are good at comedy, and it's bad that the picture lets them, as well as us, down with a climax that I thought had been put in mothballs for good. That old business of a wife wearing a mask to fool her husband and another woman in identical costume at the same party is as old as sin. Yet up to this commonplace ending the picture furnishes quite a few hearty laughs at the expense of an average married couple with mother-in-law trouble."

The plot device was later used on an *I Love Lucy* episode, when Lucy dons a black wig to test Ricky's faithfulness.

54. *Dance, Girl, Dance* (1940) Bubbles, aka Tiger Lily White. One of Ball's best roles, as one of two dancers (along with Maureen O'Hara) who choose different paths in life; jaded Ball becomes a stripper and has much success, while O'Hara chooses the high road and ends up poor, eventually becoming Ball's onstage stooge.

Produced by Erich Pommer, the film was originally directed by Roy Del Ruth. After a month or so of filming starting in May 1940, however, it became obvious the project was in trouble; the characters and the plot had no focus. Pommer shut down the film, fired Del Ruth, and hired Dorothy Arzner, one of the few female directors working in Hollywood at the time. Arzner threw out the footage already filmed, tightened up the story, worked with Ball and O'Hara on their characters, and defined the central conflict of the story. The movie portrayed one woman's drive for independence and self-worth, and another's for crass commercialism, without denigrating either character. It's become a minor classic.

A public relations release from 1940 noted, "When Lucille Ball first [performed] as Tiger Lily in *Dance, Girl, Dance*, a spontaneous roar of applause went up from the Hollywood premiere audience. Now, as fast as the picture is being shown from coast to coast, critics everywhere acclaim a new star. She's a star who has been five years and more in rising. Trouble is that going up like a skyrocket has its disadvantages. You're liable to come down a dead stick. Lucille Ball is well aware of that danger. Said she: 'If my Lily White brings me bigger chances in pictures, I'll have the seasoning to help me handle them....

"'I believed in Tiger Lily when I played her. She wasn't a [pillar] of nobility, but a regular woman who yielded to her impulses, sometimes good and sometimes bad.'"

55. *Too Many Girls* (1940) Consuelo "Connie" Casey, desirable college co-ed. Bubbly but dated college musical, a filmed version of the stage hit that made Desi Arnaz famous; the movie is more famous now for being the film on which Ball and Arnaz met and fell in love.

56. *Look Who's Laughing* (1941) Julie Patterson. Who's laughing? No one. This tired attempt to transfer Edgar Bergen's radio magic to the screen wastes Ball as a foil for dummy Charlie McCarthy.

57. *A Girl, A Guy, and A Gob* (1941) Dot Duncan. Love triangle with staid Edmund O'Brien falling for Dot, who's marrying long-in-the-tooth sailor George Murphy. Some funny spots, but the film suffers from a typically vacuous Murphy performance. One New York reviewer noted, "Lucille Ball may not be made of India rubber, but she has as much bounce.... The cast is giddy as can be."

58. *Seven Days' Leave* (1942) Terry. Ball wants to marry her soldier boy but he only has … you guessed it, seven days' leave. Average at best.

59. *The Big Street* (1942) Gloria. This might be Ball's best film performance; she plays a chanteuse and gangster's gal who values money at the expense of all else, including Little Pinks (Henry Fonda), the busboy who loves her. When she tries to leave her mobster beau, he

pushes her down a flight of stairs, crippling her. Pinks takes her in, and despite Gloria's awful treatment of him and his friends, he stands by her, making her last wish come true.

Melodramatic and often silly to the point of being surreal (Pinks pushes Gloria to Florida in her wheelchair so she can be with the "smart set" at the end of the movie), the picture still resonates due to the performances of its leads, especially Ball, playing way against type, and looking gorgeous. This is the role that cemented Ball's MGM contract. *LIFE* magazine, in October 5, 1942, wrote that, "Lucille Ball bounced around a lot before winning her new long-term contract with MGM. Not until this summer when she played 'Her Highness' in Damon Runyon's *The Big Street* did anybody face the truth about Lucille: the girl can really act. As Runyon's tough little crippled night-club queen, Lucille is superb."

♥ **Lucy Trivia** Ball apparently had a screen reputation or persona as a comedienne by this time. *The Big Street*, a Damon Runyon melodrama in the strictest sense of the word, and a sentimental one at that, was advertised with a poster that showed a big head shot of a pretty Ball, proclaiming, "That Laugh-A-Minute Gal! ... In a Thrill-A-Minute Movie!"

60. *Valley of the Sun* (1942) Christine Larson. Entertaining low-budget Western, with a sub-plot about the mistreatment of Indians that was ahead of its time. Ball's the girl at the center of all the action. Adding to the film's authenticity, it was shot on location near Taos, New Mexico.

61. *DuBarry Was a Lady* (1943) May Daly/Madame DuBarry. Ball stepped into this role when Ann Sothern, who was scheduled to film it, became pregnant with daughter Tisha Sterling. The film is a Technicolor extravaganza—in many ways, it's typical MGM 1940s fluff—filled with everything but the kitchen sink in order to make wartime audiences forget their troubles. Hatcheck boy Red Skelton and dancer Gene Kelly both long for nightclub performer May Daly's heart. When Red is accidentally slipped a Mickey, he dreams he's Louis XV and May is Madame DuBarry. Ball sings (well, she's mostly dubbed, but I'd swear it's her voice in the final song, "Friendship"). She dances. And she's never looked more spectacular, given the full MGM glamour treatment.

This was the first time audiences saw Ball in color, and she was made a redhead for the occasion. It's a defining moment in her career, and the red hair became her trademark over the next decades, though the actual color ended up more apricot/orange-y than red. Ignore the plot and watch for several novelty acts, plus Tommy Dorsey and band in full French Revolution drag, the screen debut of Zero Mostel, a cameo by Lana Turner, and the always-wonderful, deadpan Virginia O'Brien as the cigarette girl who loves Skelton.

♥ **Lucy Trivia** Ball reprised "Friendship" to great comic effect on an episode of *I Love Lucy* with Vivian Vance; they end up performing in The Wednesday Afternoon Fine Arts League talent show in the same dress, singing about friendship while ripping apart each other's dress.

62. *Best Foot Forward* (1943) Lucille Ball. When Lana Turner became pregnant, Ball replaced her in this rousing college musical. Her agent has secured Ball some top publicity, he assures her, when he responds to a fan letter written by a cadet to Ball inviting her to the Winsocki Military Academy's big dance. Then the cadet's girlfriend shows up. Though dated (as are all college musicals of this era), there's good music (courtesy of Harry James) and dancing, the screen debut of Nancy Walker, and Ball looking exquisite and delivering her trademark sarcasm. Ball's singing voice was dubbed by actress and singer Gloria Grafton.

A slice of one of MGM's "More Stars Than There Are in Heaven" promotional shots, circa 1944, shows Lucy with, clockwise from top left, Red Skelton, Mickey Rooney, William Powell, and Hedy Lamarr. Author's collection

♥ **Lucy Trivia** As a result of her spectacular looks and success in her first MGM films, Ball was dubbed "Technicolor Tessie," and chosen as the star who photographed best in Technicolor by industry experts. A profile of her appeared in *LIFE* magazine at this time, attesting to the honor.

63. *Thousands Cheer* (1943) Cameo as herself. Thin plot is the format for a dozen or so songs/ sketches featuring the top MGM talent of the day. Ball joins Ann Sothern in a sketch of dubious taste starring Frank Morgan (*The Wizard of Oz*) as a lecherous doctor who gets his jollies examining women for the Armed Service.

64. *Meet the People* (1944) Julie Hampton. Another wartime effort in which Ball plays an actress interested in Dick Powell's patriotic play. Can she convince him to turn it into a musical? Well, this is MGM, after all.

65. *Without Love* (1945) Kitty Trimble. Ball pairs nicely with Keenan Wynn (and walked off with the best reviews) in support of Katharine Hepburn and Spencer Tracy as two who marry without love. The plot was rather modern for 1945—Hepburn and Tracy decide to marry for companionship, convenience, and their careers rather than love, and, of course, end up falling in love. As a real estate agent, Ball is the epitome of the modern (circa mid-1940s) woman and steals every scene she's in. Future Oscar-winner Gloria Grahame cameos as a flower girl.

66. *Abbott and Costello in Hollywood* (1945) Cameo, uncredited. Ball appears for about a minute as herself, when the boys run roughshod through the MGM studios.

67. *Two Smart People* (1946) Ricki Woodner. Ball's a grifter who hooks up with fellow con John Hodiak, who's being taken into custody via train to New York. Can they escape the law? Neither comedy nor drama, this film succeeds only if you're a diehard fan who can suspend disbelief in the mundane plot twists. Sold with the tagline "Adult: Heartbeats and Gunplay! A Thrill Romance!" the picture didn't garner great reviews. Frank Morriss wrote, in his "Here, There and Hollywood" column, that, "Ball and Hodiak, as the two crooks who fall in love, are able to do very little with the material that has been handed them. The same goes for [Lloyd] Nolan as the detective hired to bring Hodiak back to New York. The best acting in the movie is contributed by Elisha Cook Jr., [who is] well versed in the art of malignant characterization, and can suggest enough depravity to give any fan the creeps."

68. *Lover Come Back* (1946) Kay Williams. Decent trifle with Ball as a fashion company executive who gets even with her philandering husband. Ball didn't care for the title: "That title shouldn't happen to a dog," she told columnist Sheilah Graham just after its completion.

69. *The Dark Corner* (1946) Kathleen. Atmospheric film, which finds Ball in top form, this pleasant film noir surprise has Ball as faithful secretary/lover to down-on-his-luck investigator Mark Stevens. With a plot cribbed from any number of the dark thrillers of that era, and a prissy reenactment by Clifton Webb of his menacing portrayal in *Laura*, Ball gives the movie an added kick, and it's a treat to see her in such forbidding surroundings.

70. *Ziegfeld Follies* (1946) Specialty act. After Ball's 13 years in movies, it was obvious MGM still didn't know how to best use her, as evidenced by casting Ball as a glamorous dominatrix with a bullwhip, lording it over a chorus of pretty girls dressed as jungle cats at the beginning of this typical, cameo-infested spectacle.

♥ **Lucy Trivia** William Frawley performs with another great comedian, Fanny Brice, in a sketch called "The Lottery Ticket." Ball could have done it with her eyes closed, and wouldn't that have been interesting?

71. *Easy to Wed* (1946) Gladys Benton. Though this is technically an Esther Williams vehicle, you can't take your eyes off Ball as the wronged woman in this remake of *Libeled Lady* (Ball has the Jean Harlow role). Ball is again paired with Keenan Wynn, and one reviewer suggested starring the pair in their own movie series. Alas, this was not to be, and this film signaled the end of Ball's brief MGM contract. From now on, it was free-agent time. Though uncredited, Buster Keaton reportedly wrote and directed this movie. That might explain why this is one of Ball's best comedy showcases.

In a column by Sheilah Graham at the time of its release, Graham noted Ball "and her husband Desi Arnaz were taking off by plane to New York, and Lucille was in a jubilant mood, because she had finally proved her point—that she is a comedienne. And if you have any doubts on this, I advise you to see *Easy to Wed*, in which Lucille sweeps all before her—and the 'all' includes Van Johnson, Esther Williams, and Keenan Wynn. 'I waited 10 years for *Easy to Wed*,' said Lucille. 'What makes me happy is that I knew I could do it if I had the chance.'

"Her drunk scene with Van Johnson alone is worth the admission price. At three previews in California, the scene elicited spontaneous applause from the audiences. And she did it all on ginger ale—'It makes me ill,' said Lucille."

72. *Lured* (a.k.a. *Personal Column*, 1947) Sandra Carpenter. In this atmospheric thriller, Lucy plays a chorus girl tapped by Scotland Yard as bait for a serial killer who preys on women through personal ads. George Sanders is her love interest (but is he also the killer?) and Boris Karloff has an odd, disturbing cameo. This is a well-done and little-seen gem directed by Douglas Sirk, who graduated to glossy melodramas over the next decade.

A remake of a 1939 French movie called *Personal Column*, the film's title was changed, midway through its run, as the Hays Code (also known as the Production Code)—which monitored what it considered morally offensive in films—posited that *Lured* sounded too much like *Lurid*. Sirk posited that this title change confused potential audiences and sank the film's chances of being a success.

73. *Her Husband's Affairs* (1947) Margaret Weldon. Ball gets involved in her husband's wacky experiments in order to save her marriage in this enjoyable situation comedy.

74. *Sorrowful Jones* (1949) Gladys O'Neill. Returning to Damon Runyon territory (see *The Big Street*), Ball's character is much more likeable this time around, in a remake of Shirley Temple's *Little Miss Marker*. Ball helps Sorrowful Jones (Bob Hope) keep an orphan (Mary Jane Saunders) off the streets. The kid was left with Hope as a marker for a bet. Though Saunders is cute and not too saccharine, this is Ball and Hope's movie; they clicked so well

together (as noted by the increased box office receipts of this movie versus the typical Hope vehicle), they reteamed many times in the future, both in movies and on TV.

♥ **Lucy Trivia** Co-star William Demarest replaced Ball's *I Love Lucy* co-star William Frawley on *My Three Sons* in 1965.

75. *Miss Grant Takes Richmond* (1949) Ellen Grant. Dim-bulb secretary Ball squares off against bookie William Holden, ultimately winning his heart in this solid comedy. This comedy and *The Fuller Brush Girl* (see below) served notice to viewers that Ball and comedy were a perfect fit, and hinted at the slapstick to come in *I Love Lucy*. With cranky but lovable James Gleason, who was a candidate for Fred Mertz, in support, and bit parts for future *Lucy* TV regulars Charles Lane and Roy Roberts (See Guest Stars).

♥ **Lucy Trivia** Holden would later appear in one of the most famous episodes of *I Love Lucy*, "L.A. at Last!" See Holden, William.

76. *Easy Living* (1949) Anne. In a throwaway part that was a step backward, football team secretary Ball wants Victor Mature, but he has eyes for bad-girl Lizabeth Scott. Ball deserved better than this dated look at relationships between men and women by this point in her career.

77. *The Fuller Brush Girl* (1950) Sally Elliot. One of the few movies to actually use Ball's slapstick talents. Ball and co-star Eddie Albert get involved with murder, not to mention brushes, but it's all solved in a tight 85 minutes. Watch Ball hone her comedic skills as a klutzy phone operator. Pal Barbara Pepper has an uncredited bit as Wife Watching TV. Silly but enjoyable.

78. *A Woman of Distinction* (1950) Ball had a cameo in this Rosalind Russell picture.

79. *Fancy Pants* (1950) Agatha Floud. Ball's second teaming with Bob Hope is a winner all around and a solid hit. In a remake of *Ruggles of Red Gap* cowardly actor Hope poses as an English butler to give Ball's Southwestern family some class. Good slapstick, songs, and action abound. Filmed at the Paramount ranch in Agoura, California, as well as Santa Fe, New Mexico, Hope fell off a mechanical horse while making this raucous film and suffered a mild concussion. Ironically, Ball was injured in the next film they made together, 1960's *The Facts of Life*.

80. *The Magic Carpet* (1951) Narah. This is the awful potboiler that Ball did to get out of her Columbia contract. Studio chief Harry Cohn never thought she'd do it; she proved him wrong and the rest is television history. Ball obviously is having a great time despite the woeful material.

The story goes, Columbia chief Harry Cohn offered Ball the part expecting her to turn it down, so he could get out of paying her the $85,000 he still owed Ball on her contract. When

Ball got wind of the rumor, she accepted the part graciously: "I think it's a wonderful part," she supposedly said. While shooting the film she was offered a role she coveted: the Elephant Girl in Cecil B. DeMille's circus extravaganza for Paramount, *The Greatest Show on Earth*. While doing wardrobe tests for the latter, the costumer mentioned Ball was getting bigger. Turned out she was pregnant, and, with just a few days of filming left on *The Magic Carpet*, decided not to say anything to anyone until that film was in the can. Then she went to apologize to DeMille and explain why she couldn't take the part in his film. His famous response: "Lucille, you're the only woman I know who screwed Desi Arnaz, Harry Cohn, Paramount Pictures, and C. B. DeMille all at the same time!"

81. *The Long, Long Trailer* (1954) Tacy Collini. At the height of their TV success, Ball and Arnaz returned to MGM for this lush, romantic comedy about a trailer that almost destroys a honeymooning couple's marriage. Directed by Vincente Minnelli, the film also works as a travelogue; the vistas are stunning, and the Arnazes were never better together onscreen. A huge success and MGM's biggest grossing comedy at the time. Movie ad tagline: "Now— They're in the Movies—and in Color!"

Ball and Arnaz did a lot of co-op advertising for this family-friendly flick, including full-page ads sold in local newspapers headlined "[Town Name Here] Welcomes Lucille Ball and Desi Arnaz in their Technicolor MGM hit *The Long, Long Trailer*." The entire page would be filled with ads by companies that supplied products for the film, like Mercury ("The Perfect Complement for the 'Long, Long Trailer.' See Lucille Ball, Desi Arnaz and the Power-Packed Mercury in this laugh-filled riot at the [local theater name here]." Other ads were run by Crosley Refrigerator ("Displayed in the trailer appearing in …"); Youngstown Kitchens ("Featured in …"); and P. & T. Trailer Sales.

♥ **Lucy Trivia** Ball and Arnaz's duet on the hit song "Breezing Along with the Breeze" from this movie was rereleased on the 1997 CD *Romantic Duets from M-G-M Classics*. Lucy and Desi are pictured on the cover. Though Ball's singing is often dubbed in films, I believe (and so does daughter Lucie) that it's her mother's voice on this song.

82. *Forever Darling* (1956) Susan Vega. This second big-screen teaming of Ball and Arnaz was more problematic than the first, not helped by a skimpy script that had to deal with a weighty subject: guardian angels. There are a few trademark "Lucy" moments here and there, but most of the film will leave you empty. See <u>Forever Darling</u> for film editor Dann Cahn's take on the movie.

83. *The Facts of Life* (1960) Kitty Weaver. An adult topic (for 1960) as friends Ball and Bob Hope contemplate having an affair, but never quite consummate it. The two stars are

fabulous, and the script is witty. They couldn't consummate the affair for two reasons: it just wasn't done on film in a light comedy of that era, and both Ball and Hope were wary of their public images and did not want to anger their fans. Ball was injured when she fell nine feet off a dock while filming one of the boat scenes. This film won the Oscar for best costume design (which went to Edith Head and Edward Stevenson; see Stevenson, Edward), and was nominated for four other Oscars. It was filmed in and around Pasadena and Monterey, California, and Acapulco, Mexico.

♥ **Lucy Trivia** Phil Ober, Vivian Vance's third ex-husband, had a small role in *The Facts of Life*.

84. *Critic's Choice* (1963) Angela Ballantine. The only Ball/Hope movie misfire, this one is just plain blah. Lucy writes a play; her husband's a critic. Watch the fireworks … *not*. The source material was rather clichéd and wooden to begin with.

85. *A Guide for the Married Man* (1967) Technical Adviser. Don't let the character name confuse you. All that means is Ball played a role (opposite Art Carney) in one of the sequences Robert Morse uses to illustrate to pal Walter Matthau how to cheat on his wife. A chauvinistic movie, with dated values, Ball plays it straight the few minutes she's onscreen. She did the part as a favor to director, friend, and former film co-star Gene Kelly.

86. *Yours, Mine and Ours* (1968) Helen North Beardsley. Ball's final film hit, this was a big success—making $25 million in 1968 bucks—reteaming her with Henry Fonda (as Frank Beardsley) in the true-life story of two middle-aged people with a total of 10 and eight kids (Frank and Helen, respectively), who marry to make up an even bigger family. The film gives a positive spin on the term "family picture," dealing with situations in a realistic, often wry, comic way. Rarely has a romance between two middle-aged lovers been portrayed so honestly. The kids, bless 'em, are not the least bit annoying. Ball is restrained and appealing, and her drunk scene—Fonda's kids spike her drink repeatedly when she's invited to dinner and she ends up zotzed at the dinner table—is a masterpiece of comic timing.

That drunk scene, "One of the funniest parts of the [original] movie, never could have happened, according to Greg Beardsley. In the film, when Helen North meets the Beardsley children at a family dinner, the older boys spike her cocktail with extra alcohol and get her drunk. 'If I had done that, I wouldn't be alive today,'" Beardsley told *Monterey* (Calif.) *Herald* reporter Brenda Moore, in a November 22, 2005 article, revisiting some of the Beardsleys/ Norths as a "modernized" remake of the film—starring Dennis Quaid and Rene Russo—was released.

"From what they've heard about the new movie," Moore reported, "the Beardsleys and Tom North expect more slapstick and [the characters to be] even less like them. The lead actors keep the names of Helen North and Frank Beardsley. But that may be where the similarities end. The children all have new names, six of the Norths are adopted and there are different ethnicities among them. [Tom] North also noted that his parents were perpetually 'exhausted and overwhelmed. Lucy portrayed that really well in the film. Imagine running a dorm for [18] kids.'

"'It was very exciting for us,' Louise (Beardsley) Ingram recalled. Lucille Ball came to Monterey for the premiere [of the original], a red-carpet affair at the Del Monte Center, where the entire Beardsley family joined her onstage. There was a dinner party with the actress in Pebble Beach and she also made an appearance at the Beardsley's candy shop, Morrow's Nut House.

"This time around the family isn't getting that red-carpet treatment," the *Herald* noted. "They weren't even contacted by the movie's producers. But because the Beardsleys sold the rights to their story years ago there's nothing they can do except sit back and watch it. They don't expect it to hit very close to home. The first one didn't and this one is even more removed. They clearly have affection for the first version."

All of which brings to mind the question "Why?" as in, Why remake a film that was almost universally loved and a hit to boot? The traditional Hollywood reason: cash. With a somewhat similar plot but vastly boring presentation, the remade *Yours, Mine & Ours* stalled before it got out of the gate. Here are snippets from one of the awful reviews:

"At once so bland and so frantic that it's almost unendurable. Will no one save us from this plague of alternately messy and mawkish comedies about oversized families?"—Frank Swietek, One Guy's Opinion

But perhaps the *Hollywood Reporter* best pinpoints the shortcomings of the remake: "Officially owing its existence to the 1968 Lucille Ball-Henry Fonda comedy of the same name but clearly going after [the 2003 remake of] *Cheaper by the Dozen*'s $138.6 million good fortune, *Yours, Mine & Ours* adds up to a blandly wishy-washy proposition…. Taking its cue, but not the winning tone, from the original [the movie is] unable to decide whether it wants to be a rambunctious family comedy or a tender romantic comedy. The Dennis Quaid-Rene Russo vehicle strains to be both and ends up falling short of both marks."

My advice: rent the original. You'll love it. (See also <u>Shavelson, Mel.</u>)

87. *Mame* (1974) Mame Dennis. Ball had wanted to play Mame ever since Rosalind Russell found success with the part on Broadway and in the 1958 movie version, *Auntie Mame*. But the film version of the popular Broadway musical has its problems. It's not as awful as some critics crowed, and certainly was not responsible for the death of the big-screen musi-

cal (that was just changing tastes; and despite the odd success like *Chicago*, musicals mostly remain box-office poison. The one exception: animated musicals like *The Lion King*). *Mame*'s problems start with the kid who plays young Patrick (he's got a decent singing voice but all the childlike charisma of Ted Koppel) and continue through Ball's attempts to talk/sing the score.

There were also rumors, categorically denied, that Ball and co-star Bea Arthur did not get along, and that Ball's singing was dubbed (if the latter was true, wouldn't a sweeter voice have been piped in?). Ultimately, though, it was the need to camouflage the age of its star that did in this movie; the use of layers of makeup and gauzy filters were what most of the reviews centered on. One of the reasons for Ball doing *Mame* was her ostensible dislike for the movies being produced in the mid-1970s, as evidenced by this quote from 1974: "I really hate the sick stuff they're putting in films today."

She continued in this vein during an April 2, 1974 interview with Robert Taylor of the *Oakland* (Calif.) *Tribune*, headlined "Lucy in Distress," for his column "Stage and Screen." "Lucille Ball said she was 'amazed,' after an opening night audience had cheered her every kick and shout in Mame. 'And now—to get up the next morning and [have] this reviewer calling it *the ultimate in vulgarity....*'

"Miss Ball was distressed but not really angry," Taylor wrote, "confident that her 42 million fans would vindicate her judgment about leaping into a $10 million movie musical at an age when many actresses are drifting into *Long Day's Journey Into Night*. 'I shouldn't be talking about the half-dozen reviews that have been unfavorable,' Ball added, 'because there have been many others. But I can't imagine anyone calling it vulgar, compared with what else is out today. Where is it vulgar? One line?'

"Reminded of the movie's PG rating, which suggests Parental Guidance before dumping the kids at the theater for a Saturday matinee, Miss Ball had a ready explanation. 'I fought for that rating,' she said, 'so we could leave in two lines.' One is little Patrick's discovery of Mame's philosophy: 'Life's a banquet, and most SOB's are starving to death.' The other is Bea Arthur's shout to a preening, stage-struck Mame, who's missed her cue to begin 'The Man in the Moon' number: 'Get your ass on that moon!' [If memory serves, after Mame screws up the number, Arthur, as Vera Charles, hisses, "I have an astronomical discovery for you. The man in the moon is a bitch," which might be a third reason for the PG rating.]

"'I don't mind being naughty and up-to-date,' Miss Ball explained, 'but the far-out things filling our young people today are outrageous.' In *Mame* she dances, she sings ('Don't ask about my singing, just accept it,' she cracked), and she wears $300,000 worth of outlandish costumes created by Theadora van Runkle.

"As spectacular as it appears, *Mame* is no farewell to the movies. Among the pictures Miss Ball has been offered is a script by Norman Panama identified in the trade papers as *Further Adventures in the Erogenous Zone*. 'My God!' gasped Lucy. 'Is that the title? What does that mean … it's not sexual, is it?'"

Yes, it was sexual, and Mame was, in fact, Ball's farewell to the big screen, other than a posthumous documentary or two. It is possible (and this is just a guess) that *Further Adventures in the Erogenous Zone* was eventually made into a movie in 1976 as *I Will, I Will…For Now*, written and directed by Panama, and starring Diane Keaton and Elliott Gould. One poster tagline read, "They set out to try everything in the book … what happens next you won't find in any book …" Another quotes a review noting the couple heads "for a hang-up clinic in California, which is three time zones and one hundred erogenous zones from home."

This was Panama's final film, not counting a 2007 movie called *Are We Done Yet?*, based on his screenplay for 1948's *Mr. Blandings Builds His Dream House*. If *I Will, I Will … was* initially called *Further Adventures in the Erogenous Zone*, one can hardly imagine Ball appearing in it, or taking a part that could have been played by the much-younger Keaton, given Ball's frank opposition to open sexuality in the movies and her age (63).

Panama wrote and produced one of Ball's best films, 1960's *The Facts of Life* (see No. 83.)

For much more on *Mame*, see Connell, Jane, Kahn, Madeline, and Lucy on DVD.

88. *Stone Pillow* (1985) (Made for TV) Florabelle. Ironically, Ball's final film finds her deep in aging makeup to convey a homeless woman on the streets of New York. Ball acquitted herself more than admirably, and by the end of the film you really care for this dame. Ball filmed this movie, which takes place in the winter, during a particularly hot New York summer, which is often blamed for weakening her physically toward the end of her life.

The week it aired, *The Stone Pillow* came in at No. 9 in the Nielsen ratings; with a 23.3 rating and 33 share, the show reached about 20 million households and 30 million viewers. The movie received the "Golden Halo" award from the Southern California Motion Picture Council in 1986 as Best TV Special.

FILM ROLES THAT NEVER WERE: Like many actors and actresses, Ball was considered for roles but not cast, for various reasons. Here are several of the more interesting possibilities.

—Orson Welles proposed a film version of *The Smiler and the Knife*, a C. Day Lewis spy novel to RKO in 1939; he wanted Ball to star in it. The plot concerned a madcap heiress who is enlisted by the government to expose a wealthy businessman believed to be a Nazi collaborator. Welles later told a reporter he thought Ball "was the greatest female clown around." The studio, unfortunately, disagreed, telling him, "What do you want Lucille Ball for? She's practically washed up in this town," Welles recalled. "Imagine how idiotic they were. They didn't know what they had."

—On June 27, 1941, *The New York Times* ran a blurb that announced, "Erich Pommer will produce Lucille Ball and Joseph Cotten in *Passage to Bordeaux*. Robert Stevenson will direct." *Photoplay*, in a February 1942 article about Ball titled "Stop Crying!" noted, "There is much bating of breath around the lot these days over the picture they whisper will make [Lucy] a full-blown star, *Passage to Bordeaux*, film on which William L. Shirer of *Berlin Diary* fame is acting as technical director."

—In 1947 it was reported that Ball would play "a very hard-boiled and wicked woman" in a film called *Too Late for Tears*. In the movie, "Lucy's character murders her husband and finally gets her comeuppance in a very dramatic scene. When Lucille read the story in a popular magazine she couldn't rest until she was assigned the part." The film, now considered a film noir classic, was eventually made in 1949 with Lizabeth Scott tackling the role Ball wanted, and Arthur Kennedy playing her husband. Ball flirted with the noir genre in two of her best films, *The Dark Corner* (1946) and *Lured* (1947), but she was the "good girl" in both those films; it would have been fascinating to see her play the bad girl.

THE FILM 100

Book by Scott Smith (subtitled "A Ranking of the Most Influential People in the History of the Movies") listing his choices, "ranked in order by the sheer magnitude of their impact on the motion picture industry." The book emerged from the author's website, Film100.com. One might not expect Lucille Ball to make this list, given the checkered nature of her movie career, but there she is solidly at No. 68. Admittedly, the list can seem rather capricious: Why Bette Davis (58) and not Joan Crawford? Louella Parsons (48) and not Hedda Hopper? Why is Roger Corman (49), noted for his low-budget horror and exploitation movies, ahead of Steven Spielberg (82), Federico Fellini (80), and Billy Wilder (57)? Well, all such lists are subjective, and part of the fun is reading someone else's perspective.

The author says Ball was the first movie star to make the transition to television and back to the movies successfully: "And [after scoring on TV] her subsequent film work in *The Long, Long Trailer* (1954) and *Yours, Mine and Ours* (1968) demonstrated television's ability to make saleable stars for future full-length features." Smith also gives Ball credit for making television a more comfortable place for established movie stars (William Holden, John Wayne) and technicians (Karl Freund, Max Factor) who might have been wary of working on the small screen. Many of them worked on *I Love Lucy* because of the friendships made by Ball during her movie career. (Smith reports that Alfred Hitchcock adapted Freund's unique three-camera shooting technique for his movies.)

Ball, of course, also ran a major studio in the early sixties, after Desi Arnaz sold his shares in Desilu to her, becoming the first woman in Hollywood to do so. (Mary Pickford, No. 4, is the only other contender; she was one of the owners of United Artists early in Hollywood history). Smith should be congratulated for being one of the few to put Ball in her proper movie-land context.

FIRST HOLLYWOOD CONTRACT

Ball's full signature on her very first Hollywood contract is a historic document that finally found its way to The Lucy-Desi Museum, it was reported in February 2006. The contract—indicating Ball would receive "railroad transportation including lower berth from New York to Los Angeles" and $60 per week for a "role to be selected by the producer in a photoplay to be designated by the producer"—was discovered at an autograph dealer's business in California by Bill and Mary Rapaport, major donors to The Lucille Ball-Desi Arnaz Center in Jamestown, New York (Mary is also on the board).

Lucy looking glamorous in the 1956 film, *Forever Darling*. Elois Jenssen's costumes for this film were her final work with Lucy. Photofest

"When my husband and I found these contracts in California we knew that we not only had to purchase them but we also had to immediately donate them to the center," Mary said. "Ball's first Hollywood contract is historic and something that should not be retired to a private collection but instead shared with the tens of thousands of visitors the center welcomes each year to Jamestown." The document will be archived until a proper display can be arranged.

Ball's first role was as a blonde showgirl in 1933's *Roman Scandals*. The contract further stipulated that, should "the producer" choose, it could be extended for up to seven years, with a final salary of $500 per week. (Otherwise, return transportation from Los Angeles to New York would be provided.) Of course, Ball never returned to New York until after she'd become a movie star.

FORD, BETTY

The former first lady and the first lady of Comedy conversed in an unusual *Parade* magazine cover feature dated January 13, 1980, called "Conversation Piece: The *I Love Lucy* and Betty Show." Billed as a feature where "*Parade* listens in as celebrities, many of whom have never met, ask each other about fame, family, and fortune." The phone conversation is a light-hearted chat that concentrates largely on the ladies' husbands and families, what they think of current mores in society, and a small bit of career recapping. Ball begins by telling Ford, "You're harder to connect with in Palm Springs than you were in the White House." There's talk about Ball's upcoming special [*Lucy Moves to NBC*, which aired February 8, 1980] and some about Ford's work with cancer patients, but for the most part it's a decidedly upbeat talk, with the two feeding each other questions that lead to mostly pat answers.

FOREVER DARLING

This Technicolor fantasy-comedy that Lucille Ball and Desi Arnaz made in 1956 was finally released on DVD in April 2006, in a "Lucy-Desi" set along with *Too Many Girls* (1940; the movie on which Ball and Arnaz met) and *The Long, Long Trailer* (1954). Though not a smash hit in the vein of *Trailer*, *Darling* has its moments, and the whole "broken marriage needs fixing" plot becomes oddly touching in retrospect, considering the state of the Arnazes' marriage (though film editor Dann Cahn notes, "They weren't breaking up yet, they were fine."). Here are excerpts from a conversation I had with Cahn in 2005 at the Lucy-Desi Days festival in her hometown, Jamestown, New York.

"The movie was a bit maudlin even with all the comedy shtick we put in it," Cahn recalled. "Al Hall directed it. It got a little heavy handed, sentimentally, and Bud Molin [a Desilu film editor] and I worked closely with Hall. We got his cut—it was summertime (1955); and we all got together in a bus, Lucy, Desi, Al, myself, Jerry Thorpe, the associate producer; we ran the film [for a preview audience], it was somewhat long, and it got a little overly-sentimental, those were the comments from the preview cards.

"So we get out of there, get into the bus to head home—Lucy had it catered so there was a lot of food and booze, and we had to drive up to L.A. from San Diego. Lucy was in the back of the bus, I was somewhere in the middle and Al Hall was up front. He'd been a film director for a long time [since the early 1930s, though he'd worked in silent films as an editor and assistant director; Hall was Oscar-nominated for *Here Comes Mr. Jordan*, a 1941 classic that also had a heavenly theme; *Forever, Darling* was his final film]. He also owned a turkey farm. The Arnazes' previous film, *The Long, Long Trailer*, had been a smash hit, and Lucy was making low-key comments along the way home. At one point, she yelled out, 'Al, why don't you go back to your turkey ranch?!' And Al responded, 'After this turkey, Lucy, that's just what I'm gonna do.'"

"That precipitated myself and an assistant going to Del Mar, California; Desi got us a hotel on the beach [this was probably the famous Hotel Del Coronado], and we spent the rest of the summer working with Desi on the picture, recutting it and reworking it. He actually let us shoot a few little things. [By this time Cahn's title at Desilu was editorial supervisor.] So we finished it and I had to deliver it to MGM. The second time around we took it to the Rowena Theater in Sherman Oaks on Ventura Boulevard to preview—the box office is still there but it's now part of a mall. Clark Gable and his wife, lots of stars came … and the press. We'd done quite a bit with the movie, and the reviews came way up. But to my mind, it's still a little maudlin in spots."

FOUNTAIN OF YOUTH, THE

For Desilu Productions, Arnaz executive-produced this half-hour pilot for an anthology television series hosted by Orson Welles. Airing on September 16, 1958 as part of NBC's *Colgate Theater*, the short film, also directed by Welles, was not picked up as a series. According to one reviewer, "Welles used stills and stop-motion to tell a very witty tale." The cast included Nancy Kulp and Joi Lansing, both *Lucy* guest stars, as well as Marjorie Bennett, Billy House, Rick Jason, and Dan Tobin. Other production credits include: cinematography by Sidney Hickox; film editing by Bud Molin; art direction by Claudio Guzmán; Maurice Seiderman, makeup artist; Argyle Nelson, production manager; Marvin Stuart, assistant director; Sandy Grace, property master; Dann Cahn, editorial supervisor; and Julian Davidson, music supervisor. Welles also wrote the script (from a story by John Collier), helped out with the production design, and arranged the music. The show won a special Peabody Award in 1958.

FRAWLEY, WILLIAM

Birth name: William Clement Frawley
Born: February 26, 1887, Burlington, Iowa
Died: March 3, 1966, Hollywood, California (of a heart attack)
Buried at San Fernando Mission Cemetery, Mission Hills, California

A durable character actor making appearances in vaudeville and on Broadway, Frawley was at the tail end of a long movie career when he approached Desi Arnaz about the Fred Mertz role in Arnaz's new situation comedy for television. Frawley rarely had the lead role in a film; he

William Frawley. Photofest

was a solid supporting player, often playing the best friend of the male lead. He had one of the most easily recognized film faces of the 1930s and 1940s. But due to a bad reputation (mostly centered on his appetite for booze and his gruff disposition), few offers were coming in by the end of the 1940s.

Arnaz gave Frawley the part, on the condition that the latter's drinking never become an issue. It didn't, and the two became fast friends. Not so Frawley and his TV wife, Vivian Vance. They detested each other. After Frawley overheard Vance mumbling that he was old enough to be her father, war was declared. (See <u>The Mertzes' Real-Life Relationship</u>.)

It must be said, however, despite the real ill-will Frawley had toward Vance, and vice versa, it was never evident in the series. That makes Frawley and Vance truly worthy of the term "consummate professionals."

Frawley *was* Fred Mertz. Literally. He wasn't acting, just being his curmudgeonly self, as he had been in scores of movies. Frawley had the odd habit of reading only his parts of the *Lucy* script, and tearing out all the pages that didn't involve him. Often, he'd enter in character and say a line, get a big laugh, and wonder what it was all about; without the rest of script, he was ignorant of the entire setup to the gag.

He was also the rare (only?) actor to complain if a script featured *too much* for Fred Mertz to do. All Frawley was concerned about was exiting the studio as early as possible so he could drink with his buddies. According to *Lucy* writer Bob Schiller, Frawley was also "a bigot."

Frawley lasted the run of *I Love Lucy* and its successor, *The Lucy-Desi Comedy Hour*, but never forgave Vance for refusing to do a spin-off based on the Mertzes. A veteran of more than 100 movies (not to mention vaudeville and Broadway) by the time of the series, Frawley was nominated many times for an Emmy for his role as Fred. He never won, and the fact that his nemesis Vance did was proof to him that the awards were "meaningless." (At least, that was his story in public.)

Frawley briefly returned to his vaudeville roots (and capitalized on his sitcom success) in 1958 with the album *Bill Frawley Sings the Old Ones* on the Dot label. Frawley always got sentimental recalling his vaudeville days, and it was reported in a 1960 article that he, not Al Jolson, introduced "My Mammy" on the New York stage. Frawley also claimed to be the one who introduced "Carolina in the Morning," which he and Vance performed in an episode of *I Love Lucy*.

But he was most proud of having debuted another song. As he told the story to a reporter in 1960, it was "a night in 1914 when he was singing at the Mozart Café in Denver, where his buddies Damon Runyon and Gene Fowler had been heckling him nightly to sing something new.

"A couple of friends, Ernie Burnett and George Norton, had just that afternoon scribbled an original tune. So I pulled their lead sheet out of my pocket, handed it to the piano player, and yelled to Runyon and Fowler, 'All right, you fatheads, here's something so new it hasn't been published yet!' The song was such a hit, I sang it every night. But Paul Whiteman took all the bows for introducing it." The song was "Melancholy Baby," which, along with "Carolina," "Moonlight Bay," and eleven other standards were on Frawley's 1958 album.

After *I Love Lucy*, Frawley performed in *Fit as a Fiddle* (1959), a sitcom pilot about a dance academy that didn't sell (Eddie Foy Jr. and *Night Court*'s Florence Halop were also in it). Then he joined *My Three Sons*, in 1960. He stayed there for the next five years. In fact, Frawley was signed for *Sons* before star Fred MacMurray (who took some convincing)—he was the first actor to be signed to the show, period.

He didn't need the work; he was well-off, he freely admitted, thanks to perpetual residuals from the *I Love Lucy*'s reruns, which never stopped. (Vance had no such arrangement, though Ball and Arnaz did.) According to *Sons* producer Don Fedderson's 2005 book, *From My Three Sons to Major Dad: My Life as a TV Producer*, Frawley's agent, Walter Meyers, insisted on a similar deal for *Sons*: "In those days, residuals ended after six shows [reruns]. Bill would get residuals for all the reruns of *I Love Lucy* and *My Three Sons*. They still go to his estate to this day."

The role of Bub on *Sons*, described in one 1960 report as "chief cook, bottle washer and 'den mother' to three grandsons," was created by producer Fedderson with Frawley specifically in mind. "Bub's a lovable old coot and just my type of guy," Frawley told Charles Leavy in a July 1961 *Gettysburg Times* article. "He's rough, has a voice like an old buzz saw, and he's always recalling his vaudeville days. He howls like a lovesick wolfhound at the slightest incident. But he has no bite at all. I think I'd like Bub if I ever met him face-to-face." In fact, Frawley might as well have been describing himself.

Except for Bub's prowess in the kitchen, Frawley agreed the character fit him well. "It's embarrassing," he noted, "when women write in for my recipes. I can't even boil an egg." Peter Tewksberry, a *Sons* producer and director, had a hard time getting Frawley to be comfortable using props on the kitchen set: "Pete has me pulling things out of the oven, picking up toys, stirring a pot of goulash. I just can't be telling a gag while kneading dough or waxing the floor," Frawley said.

Frawley, who lived in a hotel in Hollywood, always ate in restaurants, he growled to AP reporter Cynthia Lowry in June 1961, over "a breakfast consisting of a whiskey sour, made healthful by extra orange juice (!), a Crenshaw melon, and black coffee." You can be sure *that* recipe was never leaked to fans of the show.

But on rare occasions the show provided Frawley with recipes to send out or give to interviewers, for publicity purposes, such as this one for Mulligan Stew. "It seems," Frawley told *TV Guide* on March 3, 1962, "that of the 34 million people watching *My Three Sons*, 33 million want our recipe for Mulligan Stew." The show's "official recipe" came from a Los Angeles newspaperman who loved to cook, *TV Guide* reported. Frawley added, "It has everything in it but a leprechaun." Here's the recipe:

Ingredients: three pounds stewing beef, cut in cubes; handful of seasoned flour; one cup peanut oil; liquid to cover meat; two bay leaves; salt and pepper; one chopped onion; a pinch of thyme; two cloves of garlic; six whole allspice; one tablespoon of parsley; any vegetables but turnips.

To cook: "Roll meat in flour and shake off excess. Heat oil in Dutch oven or skillet and brown meat. Cover meat in Dutch oven with water or three cups bouillon, or half water and half bouillon. Add bay leaves, onion, thyme, garlic, allspice, parsley, and salt and pepper. Simmer for at least two hours or until the meat is tender.

"A half hour before serving, add any or all of these vegetables: fresh carrots, peas, tomatoes, potatoes (cubed and partially precooked), small onions (canned and frozen vegetables require less cooking time; see label directions), and lentils (presoaked). Canned hominy and precooked rice may be added if desired. Serves about eight."

Frawley stayed with *Sons* until ill health forced him out in the middle of the show's fifth season (1965); by then, he was reportedly reading all his lines off cue cards.

Frawley become much more part of the family at *Sons* than on the *I Love Lucy* set. He was a perfect foil for the low-key MacMurray (who had the unusual practice, set in his contract, of filming *all* his scenes at the beginning of the season; everyone else filmed around him for the rest of the season).

By the show's second season, it became obvious that "Bub" was feeling his age. Then in his mid-70s, Frawley would on occasion fall asleep standing up while waiting for a cue, which would come when one of the show's kid actors would tug on his pants cuff to wake him.

MacMurray biographer Chuck Tranberg revealed to me that Frawley was beloved by the kids on the set: "I can say that all the kids on *My Three Sons* loved him. He was just like the characters he played, according to them, except that he had a soft spot for kids. He and Stan Livingston (Chip) used to go to ball games together. He loved to make Don Grady laugh. But as the years went on Bill's memory was going and he had to rely on cue cards. By the start of the *Sons* fifth season he was uninsurable but Don Fedderson Productions decided to use him anyway, betting that he would make it thru the season. He made it half way and then they had to write him out of the show." [When the studio's physician refused to okay him—"I can't figure out how the man is still breathing!" he commented—Frawley was replaced by similarly gruff character actor, and hated rival, William Demarest.]

Tranberg continues, "According to my sources, he came back to visit the set after Demarest took over as 'Uncle Charley,' and they had strong words for each other. Unfortunately, after that, Frawley was barred from the *Sons* set."

Fittingly, his final TV (and show business) appearance was a cameo as a stableman on *The Lucy Show* in 1965. Lucy and her friend "the Countess" (guest Ann Sothern), are shopping for a racehorse when Lucy spies Frawley sweeping up in a stable (to thunderous applause), pauses, and says, "He sure looks familiar."

TV's best-known landlord died the next year of a heart attack while walking down Hollywood Boulevard. "I've lost one of my dearest friends," Ball said when she learned of his death. "Show business has lost one of the greatest character actors of all time."

Frawley had a good life, and he knew it. A few years before his death, he commented, "It has been interesting, and I've enjoyed life. I still do. I don't know what you think success is, but I think it's working steady and making money. I'm doing both those things, and I like it fine."

ADS FEATURING WILLIAM FRAWLEY: Although a favorite curmudgeon on TV, Frawley was more problematic as a spokesperson. His reputation as a heavy drinker probably didn't help. The only ad I could discover featuring him was a "*My Three Sons* Premieres Tonight" trade ad, from 1960. Frawley's name no doubt appeared in ads for some of his many movies, but rarely was he so prominent a character that his picture would be included.

Although Vance used her *I Love Lucy* fame to generate profits as a commercial spokesperson (see Ads Featuring Vivian Vance under Vance, Vivian), I found little evidence that Frawley ever did. It's a shame he missed the modern era, in which fame of almost any kind is used to hawk almost any product. PacifiCare Health Systems Inc. of Cypress, California, understood this, and launched a national marketing campaign in October 2005 for its new Medicare Part D program, Prescription Solutions from PacifiCare. It starred none other than Vance and Frawley.

Created by Deutsch Inc., the "Choice is Swell" campaign aired on all the major networks beginning Oct. 15, and was directed by Academy Award winner Rob Legato (Best Visual Effects for *Titanic*). It featured digital-imaging technology never before used in a commercial.

Through digital magic, famously cheap Fred Mertz and his famously exasperated wife Ethel were used in a series of vignettes about—what else?—inexpensive Medicare coverage. "Innovative production techniques combine body doubles, voice impersonators, original sets and computer-generated imagery to enable Fred and Ethel to 'speak' once more," the company reported.

According to Howard Phanstiel, PacifiCare's chairman and chief executive officer, Fred and Ethel created a memorable message that resonated with seniors, an audience that values choice, quality, and affordability. "We are confident the 'Choice is Swell' campaign will effectively highlight our plans' affordability and quality," Phanstiel noted at the time. "Fred and Ethel are American icons that capture the essence of a generation and its desire to get the best value for its money. After exploring numerous advertising options, we chose Fred and Ethel because of their enduring popularity and strong appeal, not only with seniors, but also with baby boomers and people of all ages."

BARTENDING: Frawley was no friend of the legitimate theater or motion pictures by the time he was finished with *I Love Lucy*. While starring in *My Three Sons* (1960-'65), he was pretty much stuck in curmudgeon mode, according to a *New York Times* article from May 14, 1961. "There's nothing much to see on Broadway anymore," Frawley told reporter Murray Schumach. "*South Pacific* was lousy and *Guys and Dolls* stinks." He forsook the movies "because of what they did to me." Even television, which brought him his greatest fame, had no real place in his heart: "To tell you the truth, I don't give much thought to television as a field of endeavor. It's a place—an art, let's call it—where I'm making a livelihood. If something happens to television, I'll tend bar, something I enjoy doing."

BASEBALL: Frawley's true passion, baseball, was the one thing about which he got excited. When he first arrived in New York and was playing Broadway in the 1930s, he "knew all the top ball players," he told the *New York Journal American* on May 4, 1961. For a long time, there was a clause in his contracts "permitting me time off for every World Series." Frawley became part owner of the minor league San Francisco Missions in 1938; the team was part of the Pacific Coast League. The team was renamed the Hollywood Stars and sold 20 years later to Salt Lake City when the major leagues expanded into the Los Angeles area.

BOOKS: The actor who played the gruff but lovable landlord to Lucy and Ricky Ricardo finally got his due in 1999. In *Meet the Mertzes*, by Rob Edelman and Audrey Kupferberg, you'll learn more about Frawley's life than about co-star Vance. There is nothing else of length published on him, and Vance's biography, which preceded publication of this book, covers her life in detail.

To the Lucy connoisseur, the more interesting part of *Meet the Mertzes* is Frawley's story, which hasn't really been documented anywhere except briefly in the many Lucille Ball bios and *I Love Lucy* books.

If you've read those, you know that Frawley *was* Fred Mertz. As Lucy herself often commented, "What you saw is what you got." Fortunately, his cranky, gravel-voiced persona fit that of the penny-pinching Fred Mertz to a "t" (or a "tz," if you will).

There's much to the man that remains a mystery, especially how he turned into such a grandfatherly figure on the set of *My Three Sons*. Frawley lived a solitary life, never marrying except for one brief union in the 1920s, though he did form an attachment to actress Patricia Barry in the early 1960s (she was in her 30s). Pretty Barry was a TV regular who appeared in dozens of movies and more than a hundred shows (including *My Three Sons* in 1960). She also co-starred with Frawley in his final film, *Safe at Home* (1962). Barry's most recent TV appearance was as a recurring character on the soap opera *Loving* in 1993.

Frawley remembered Barry in his will.

Chicks to Chase: In an interview with Vernon Scott in the *New York World-Telegram and Sun* on October 15, 1960, Frawley bemoaned the lack of women on *My Three Sons*, except as potential love interests for lead Fred MacMurray. When asked if he missed his former TV wife, Vivian Vance, Frawley growled, "Only because I don't have a nagging wife to bounce the comedy off of. There's nothing better than a battleaxe as a foil for laughs.... So far, the only girls who have shown up [on *Sons*] are romantic interest for MacMurray. There aren't any girlfriends written into the script for me, though. Maybe it's just as well. I might end up with another old-crow type. On the other hand, it wouldn't be bad if they brought in some young chick for me to chase around the set."

Fame: "I don't mind admitting my movie career was in a bit of a lull when *I Love Lucy* came along," Frawley told *New York Journal American* columnist Jack O'Brian on March 3, 1953. "Now the movie moguls are after me again, and somehow I can't help but gloat inwardly that I can't make movies while I'm playing Fred Mertz."

Gruff Exterior: "So far, the gravel-voiced [Frawley] has been complaining about television for 10 years," wrote Kay Gardella in the New York *Daily News*, August 17, 1961, "eight of which he starred as the crusty Fred Mertz in *I Love Lucy*. By some reverse law that only another Irishman would understand, when this warm, wonderful character gripes it's a sure sign everything is going okay. And admittedly this is the case [with *My Three Sons*]."

Horse Sense: Desi Arnaz loved the races, and so did William Frawley. Indeed, the *Newark* (New Jersey) *Evening News* reported on March 2, 1964, that Frawley had purchased a race-horse for $15,000, one he'd never seen, called French Evidence. Noting that he had, in his lifetime, "spent enough dough to buy 'em all," and in particular had "spent so much on Sea Biscuit in his day I feel like an owner," Frawley's horse was an English racer that had won twice and came in second once in England. His sense of humor still intact, Frawley said, "I'm not going to tout my friends on French Evidence. But I might telephone some producers who refused to hire me and say he's a cinch to win every race."

The Mertzes' Real-Life Relationship: Television producer Sherwood Schwartz once noted he received letters lamenting the situation of those poor folks marooned on *Gilligan's Island*. There's something about television, perhaps hinging on the fact that it's in our living rooms, that makes people think what they're seeing is real, despite any evidence to the contrary. William Frawley and Vivian Vance knew this all too well.

Any Lucille Ball fan worth his or her salt knows the actors playing Fred and Ethel Mertz didn't really care for each other. And that's putting it mildly. Vance detested being thought of as the wife of a man who, as she put it, was old enough to be her father. She would pick up the new script to *I Love Lucy* each week and rip through it, praying there were no scenes in it where she had to climb into bed with that "square-headed Irishman."

Frawley, meanwhile, being a vaudevillian, thought Vance (and Ball, for that matter) had no business trying to sing and dance. Reportedly, he overheard Vance's "old enough to be my father" comment early in the run of the show, and from then on it was war.

They were not kindred spirits, but both were professional enough (and smart enough) to realize the value of pretending they were, at least for one half hour every week. Longtime *I Love Lucy* director William Asher noted, "Bill and Vivian didn't get along, but I never had to step in."

The two actors had to endure lots of joint publicity, and both good-naturedly submitted to this chore. A pre-national edition of *TV Guide* dated March 20-26, 1953, with Fred and Ethel on the cover, features a story called, "Lucy's Neighbors Exposed."

The cover looks suspiciously like two separate photos superimposed on each other, itself a giveaway of the actors' real feelings. The article features a picture of the four co-stars from the Barbershop episode with a caption: "Close harmony, which from all reports, prevails both on and off the *Lucy* set." But in the center of the second page is a strip with small pictures of

Vance and Frawley scowling at each other with the caption, "Don't be so sure the Mertzes are just play-acting."

For the most part, though, the article errs on the side of positive PR: "In more serious moments, Bill adores Vivian. He says, 'She's one of the cleverest actresses I've ever known. And one of the funniest dolls in the world—both on and off stage.'" He's also quoted as saying, "I don't care much for women. Of course, I'm wild about those two gals [Lucille and Vivian]." Vance is a bit less enthusiastic: "Vivian thinks [Frawley]'s a 'darling'" and "We really shouldn't spend all our free time together. After all, we may be in business together for 30 years," are two quotes attributed to her. The latter, in actuality, was Vance's worst nightmare.

In fact, as early as 1954, three years into the run of *I Love Lucy*, there were public pronouncements that indicated Vance and Frawley were not each other's favorite people. A *TV Guide* article from the period, about the public confusing TV husbands and wives with the actors' real-life spouses, quotes them both: "The widespread impression that he is Fred Mertz, the character he plays on *I Love Lucy*, is a minor plague in the life of William Frawley. So many strangers have hailed him as Fred Mertz that he is inclined to go along with the gag—at least until they start asking him where his wife Ethel is.

The Mertzes (a.k.a. Vivian Vance and William Frawley) mug for the camera. Photofest

"Then Frawley, a gruff, hearty bachelor, is likely to snort, 'Ethel! That hag! I wouldn't take her to a snake dance. She's home doing the laundry.'

"As for Vivian Vance, the other half of the celebrated Mertz couple, she has a stock answer for people who scrutinize her husband, actor Phil Ober, and demand: 'But aren't you Mrs. Mertz?'

"'Only on the show, thank goodness,' Vivian snorts."

Hmmm. There was a lot of snorting going on …

During an interview in February 1955 at Chasen's in Hollywood, writer Florabel Muir noted the gangs of people coming up to ask Frawley for an autograph. One of them lagged behind after the others had left, and asked Frawley how he got his job on *I Love Lucy*. The man was thinking of settling down in Hollywood, and thought it would be nice to "get on TV so the folks at home could see us." "You an actor?" asked Frawley. "No," the Texan answered. "Do you gotta be an actor to get on a television show?" "It helps," was Frawley's reply. "It sure helps."

"Gee, I didn't know you were an actor," the Texan persisted. "I thought you were just yourself."

"That's what's so fascinating about television," Frawley commented to Muir. "The people think you're just one of them, coming into their living rooms to visit with them. They go to a movie theater or a stage show and they expect to see actors, but not on television."

As the man walked away he said, "Give our love to your wife. We think she's wonderful, too." Frawley added, "They believe Vivian Vance, who plays Ethel Mertz, is my wife and it wouldn't do any good to disillusion them. They'd never believe me anyway."

Vance, interviewed in the same article, had similar problems. She noted that sometimes when she and husband Ober were out, "The women give me suspicious looks as if they've caught me stepping out. I can't always stop and tell them that Phil is my real husband."

Lucille Ball was tickled to find out all this: "That's why we picked Bill Frawley and Vivian Vance. They look and act like people you'd meet every day."

Almost the minute the hour-long *Lucy-Desi Comedy Hour* left the air, in April 1960, the gloves were off. Ball and Arnaz had just divorced, and in an AP article titled "Desi, Lucy Sidekicks Weren't Happy Either," Frawley noted, "I knew Lucy real well before the show started, Desi not so well. I never heard of Vance. She came up like a mushroom."

The article continued, "When told Vivian was going back to the stage now that the *I Love Lucy* team has disbanded, Bill replied, 'That's okay. It doesn't matter one iota to me. She could go to Budapest and I wouldn't care.' He added, however, that he believed she was a fine performer.

"Informed of Bill's remarks, Vivian asked, 'Was he drunk?' Told he didn't seem to be, she commented: 'Bill and I got along fine—like a couple of Irish. We worked together, fought together, cried together and made up together. I think we did very well, considering we were not the best-mated pair in the world.'

"Their co-workers agree that the pair acted professionally in their relations with each other. There were no scenes, no name-calling. But the coolness between them was always apparent. That made their TV-screen bickering all the more realistic. But it also made their lovey-dovey scenes more difficult.

"Both she and Frawley feel no remorse that the series is over," the article concluded.

What put the icing on the cake was Vance's refusal to do a spin-off featuring the Mertzes after being approached by Arnaz following the run of *I Love Lucy*. Frawley thought (rightly so) that this was denying him a chance at lots of dough, and never forgave her. Vance ran like hell when *Lucy* finally ended in 1960.

(See <u>Mitchell, Shirley</u> for another perspective.)

PALLBEARERS: Frawley's pallbearers after his funeral service at the Church of the Blessed Sacrament in Hollywood included Arnaz, MacMurray, *My Three Sons* producer Don Fedderson, actor pal William Lundigan (who appeared with Ball in the *Westinghouse Desilu Playhouse* episode "K.O. Kitty," airing October 21, 1958), and Richard Whorf, a *Sons* director.

STAGE CAREER: The death of vaudeville had been greatly exaggerated, for even in the 1960s a lot of old stage shtick was being used on television variety shows, especially in the late 1940s and 1950s, television's infancy. *I Love Lucy* was not a vaudeville show by any means, but one of its lead foursome honed his singing, dancing, and acting skills on vaudeville stages through the early 1900s.

By 1910 Frawley was appearing in vaudeville with his brother Paul (who beat Frawley to Broadway as a "singing juvenile"), and then joined pianist Franz Rath in an act they took to San Francisco and toured with for four years. It was during the latter period Frawley later claimed to have introduced the song "Melancholy Baby."

In 1914, with wife Edna Louise Broedt, as "Frawley and Louise," they toured the Orpheum and Keith circuits until they separated in 1921. They divorced in 1927.

After splitting with his wife, Frawley toured in various revues and finally ended up in his first New York show. Here are his major Broadway appearances:

The Gingham Girl April 20, 1923, Central Theater, short run. Frawley played Jack Hayden.

Merry Merry September 24, 1925, Vanderbilt Theater, 176 performances. Frawley played Horatio Diggs. Frawley's first legit stage hit saw him in a tailor-made role: a singing and dancing vaudevillian. In this show, Frawley got reviews that would become familiar, citing him as the source of much of the show's levity.

Bye, Bye Bonnie January 13, 1927, Ritz Theater, 125 performances. Frawley played Butch Hogan.

Talk About Girls June 14 1927, Waldorf Theater, 13 performances. Frawley played Henry Quill.

She's My Baby January 3, 1928, Globe Theater, 71 performances. Frawley played Meadows. Legend has it Frawley was thrown out of the show for punching snobbish star Clifton Webb in the nose.

Here's Howe! May 1, 1928, Broadhurst Theater, 71 performances. Frawley played Sweeny Toplis.

Sons O' Guns November 26, 1929, Imperial Theater, 295 performances. Frawley played Hobson, a playboy's valet who becomes his gruff top sergeant in an ironic role reversal. It was a role that fit him perfectly, and the show was a big hit.

She Lived Next to the Firehouse February 10, 1931, Longacre Theater, 24 performances. Frawley played Harlan Smith.

Tell Her the Truth October 19, 1932, Cort Theater, 11 performances. Frawley played Mr. Parkin.

20th Century, 1932, Broadhurst Theater, December 29, 1932, 152 performances.

20th Century was a highly anticipated show, thanks to its pedigree: authors Ben Hecht and Charles MacArthur, who had previously collaborated on the hit *The Front Page*, and producers Philip Dunning and George Abbott.

On November 19, 1932, *The New York Times* announced *20th Century* was going into production. On December 11, the *New York Herald Tribune* reported *20th Century* had begun rehearsals with Russian actress Eugenie Leontovich (previously seen on Broadway as the dancer in *Grand Hotel*) as the female lead. And on December 22, 1932, a "completed casting" notice in the *Times* reported the play, "opening next Thursday, includes Moffat Johnston, Eugenie Leontovich, and William Frawley." The cast also included Roy Roberts.

William Frawley as he appeared in *20th Century.* **Author's collection**

The hit production of *Dinner at Eight* was also on Broadway at the time. It featured Conway Tearle, the actor whose illness would help KO Lucille Ball's production of *Hey, Diddle Diddle* a few years hence.

The basic plot of *20th Century* has a bankrupt producer trying to enlist a former protégé, now an award-winning star, to appear in his new show. He has to; it's the only way he'll get it produced. Johnston played the producer, Leontovich the star, and Frawley played Owen O'Malley, an acerbic press agent.

The show opened on December 29 and was an immediate hit, both critically and with the public. The reviews uniformly picked out Frawley as an outstanding contributor to the show's merriment. His show-bill biography noted that, "William Frawley is playing his first straight dramatic role in *20th Century*. He has long been associated with the musicals, and is remembered as the belligerent Hobson of *Sons O' Guns* with Jack Donahue. Some of the lyric comedies in which his jaw has protruded are *Here's Howe*, *She's My Baby* with Beatrice Lillie, *Merry, Merry* and *Gingham Girl*."

Here are highlights from some of the major reviews:

"The lash of caricature, rather than the sting of satire, is in this new Hecht-MacArthur collaboration. It moves with the simulated speed of the train that bears its name. Sustained, rounded, biting, it is a tour de force. There are a couple (or three) of too-good-to-be-true three-dimensional cartoons in [it. One] is the easily recognizable press agent of William Frawley. Each, in its own way, is perfect. In the weeks to come you will hear much of the Oscar Jaffe of Mr. Johnston. You will also hear of Mr. Frawley's Owen O'Malley. You will love him."—Robert Garland, *New York World Telegram*

"So long as Broadway holds out to laugh, *20th Century* is a hit. It is another of those bright satires on show business…. There is uncommon skill in both the acting and directing. An amusing comedy role for William Frawley."—Burns Mantle, *The New York Daily News*

"There are so many laughs in *20th Century* that there isn't much point in treating it pontifically as a subject for review. So let's forget that it turns into a story of such incredibility as to pass even the point of being fantastic. And let us take *20th Century* for what it's worth. Which is roughly about 90 or 100 loud laughs and any number of snorts.

"Most of the big laughs fall to William Frawley to deliver, and they couldn't have fallen into better hands. His gratuitous abusiveness (he starts calling people names before he even knows whether he likes them or not) and his instinct to refer to even the most inoffensive objects as foul make him one of this department's favorite characters in fiction, although rumor has it that he is not fiction at all."*—Robert Benchley, *The New Yorker*

* A December 24, 1950 article called "*Twentieth Century* Memoir" was published in *The New York Times*. It was the opening day of the revival of the show, and Richard Maney, the publicist on whom Hecht and MacArthur based Frawley's character of O'Malley, wrote a brief piece about the genesis of the show and its intersection with his life.

"It was Helen Hayes [MacArthur's wife] who informed me of my intrusion on the play's plot. She called me on a May morning, jarred me with, 'Dick, you have been immortalized. Charley and Ben have written you into the play down to your last truculent threat. They have caught all your fevers and folderols in the character of a press agent named Owen O'Malley. The boys have done you proud.' I was a little shaken by this intelligence. If Hecht and MacArthur told all they knew about me, it might be wise to flee for the border before the posse got ugly."

Maney noted several other major characters were composites of real-life theater people also known by Hecht and MacArthur.

"The acting comes glibly to the point. William Frawley as the aggressive press agent [gives a] brisk and excitable performance."—Brooks Atkinson, *The New York Times*

"… A press agent [is] acted to the limit, but not beyond, by William Frawley, whose slang and fruity utterances, while frequent, are never tiresome. It is Mr. Frawley and Matt Briggs, as the feverish entrepreneur's business manager, who give needed life and light to the proceedings when they threaten to become overly fantastic."—Percy Hammond, *New York Herald Tribune*

"William Frawley comes into his own as O'Malley, who likes his licker [sic] but is indispensable to his 'chief.' Frawley has all the laugh lines, and he does handle 'em. It is frothy wordage [sic] that should be irresistible not only to those of the theater but the average playgoer. The show was given privately several times, but at the premiere Frawley discovered there were more laughs than were expected. After the first night he took his time."—*Variety*

The show's run was unexpectedly interrupted for nine days in March 1933 due to "disagreements between the managers and the stagehands," *The New York Times* reported on March 25, the day it reopened. An article in the next day's paper recounted what the players did during the "hiatus." Bill Frawley, "… who impersonates the brash publicist, spent three days with his midirons and his putters…. Then he took to coming to the office, making veiled inquiries about the reopening of the rumpus in which he had so lately stormed. In between visits he went to other theaters and ran a freelance Mardi Gras on his own." Whether this is a reference to Frawley's well-known (even then) penchant for drinking and carrying on remains a mystery.

Ultimately, the show would close unexpectedly early on May 20, 1933, after 154 performances. It was done in by the Depression. Though it was reported Frawley and several others would appear in a West Coast production of the play, Frawley did not.

A *New York Sun* item from July 25, 1933, reported "William Frawley, who gave a grand performance as the press agent in *20th Century*, has a Paramount contract. He has already left for the Coast." On the 20th Century Limited train, appropriately.

In a perfect world, Frawley would have repeated his delectable Broadway performance on film, but that was not to be. On April 18, 1933, the *New York Sun* announced Columbia Pictures had acquired the rights to the play. Frawley had snubbed a song peddler named Harry Cohn during a previous stage run some years before. Cohn visited him backstage during *20th Century* as the head of Columbia Pictures Corp., to report that he had just bought the rights to the show and Frawley was *not* going to be in it.

The movie was made into a raucous farce starring John Barrymore and Carole Lombard (a favorite and friend of Ball's), with another dependable character actor, Roscoe Karns, in the O'Malley role. It remains a model of screwball comedy and one of the best-remembered films of the 1930s.

A successful revival in New York at the ANTA Playhouse opened on December 24, 1950, starring Jose Ferrer and Gloria Swanson, who were both up for Oscars at the time. Robert Preston and Binnie Barnes replaced them in mid-June 1951, and the play closed on July 3.

In 1978, the show conquered Broadway once again, this time as a musical called *On the Twentieth Century*. Winner of five Tony Awards, including Best Book and Score, *On the Twentieth Century* featured a book and lyrics by Betty Comden and Adolph Green, and music by Cy Coleman (who had done the same chores for Ball's *Wildcat*). Madeline Kahn, John Cullum, Imogene Coca, and Kevin Kline starred in the production, a smash hit that is still revived and played in stock.

The Ghost Writer June 19, 1933, Masque Theater, 24 performances. Frawley played Joe Gordon. This flop turned out to be a minor blip in Frawley's career. He signed a seven-year contract with Paramount pictures around this time, and in late July headed out to California.

TRAFFIC INSPECTOR One of the world's best-known and funniest character actors took to the stage quite by chance, but almost ended up as a traffic inspector for the railroad. Frawley told the *Brooklyn Daily Eagle* on March 5, 1939, "My dad was a railroad man, and as soon as I started wearing long pants, he saw to it that I got a job with the railroad company. So after I left high school, I found myself traffic inspector for the Burlington (Iowa) Railroad, with headquarters in Chicago.

"One night, I was with a bunch of fellows in a little café on the south side and we started singing our repertory of old railroad favorites. Pretty soon, a stranger came up to me and said, with a voice like mine, I should be in show business. I thought it was a gag at first, but he left me his card and I decided the next day it would do no harm to find him. Well, the upshot of the matter was that he got me into the chorus of a little show running at the LaSalle Theater, called *The Flirting Princess*.

"I was crazy about the theater from the first moment I set foot in it. It awed me, excited me, and thrilled me beyond anything I'd ever done." When his parents sent brother Paul to Chicago after him, Frawley did another stint with the railroad in St. Louis, but both brothers found the siren call of the stage too strong, and ended up back in Chicago. They worked on a vaudeville act, which they performed in East St. Louis. "It clicked, and we took it out on the road."

The act split when Paul went east and found success on Broadway, while William tried the West Coast. After a series of revues, he ended up in New York, where Broadway (and, later, movies and television) beckoned.

FREEMAN, KATHLEEN

Versatile comic character actress in more than 120 films since 1948, Freeman is perhaps best known for her work opposite Jerry Lewis in many of his classic comedies of the 1960s, including *The Errand Boy* (1961) and *The Nutty Professor* (1963). Her wide, familiar face and gruff, take-no-prisoners persona graced scores of movie comedies and television shows from the 1950s through the 1990s. Freeman made a handful of appearances on *The Lucy Show* (see Guest Stars). Freeman was also a regular for two years on *The Donna Reed Show* (1958-'60) and a semi-regular late in the run of *The Beverly Hillbillies* (1969-'71). She was the voice of Peg Bundy's battle-ax mother on *Married ... With Children* (1995). She died on August 23, 2001, five days after leaving her Tony-nominated role in the Broadway musical hit *The Full Monty*. (Another Ball co-star, Jane Connell, replaced her. And Ball pal Kaye Ballard took the role in a touring company.)

FREUND, KARL

Born in 1890 in Austria-Hungary and known in the film industry affectionately as "Papa," Freund was the Oscar-winner (for Best Cinematography, *The Good Earth*, in 1937) and some-time director—*The Mummy* (1932)—actor, producer, and writer who was tapped by Ball and Arnaz to work on *I Love Lucy*. He had worked with Ball on several films at MGM, including *DuBarry Was a Lady* and *Without Love*, and Ball knew he would make her look good for the TV cameras.

Freund was intrigued by the idea of filming for a new medium, and he perfected a special three-camera technique to Arnaz's specifications that captured the action from three angles; the best takes could then be spliced together. It is a style of shooting that revolutionized the sitcom and is still in use today. He also designed the lighting for the sets, a not inconsiderable task that meant making sure everyone (and everything) looked good through the lens at all times. Freund also worked on several other Desilu series, including *December Bride* and *Our Miss Brooks*. He died in 1969.

FRIAR'S CLUB

New York-based private show-business club founded in 1904, famous for its risqué "roasts" of celebrities, in which friends of the roastee insult him with jokes as dirty as possible. Not to be confused with The Beverly Hills Friar's Club, with which it is not associated. The latter was begun by Milton Berle in 1947 and serves basically the same purpose. Lucille Ball and Desi Arnaz were roasted by a legend-filled dais in 1958, but their roast is best remembered for being the one during which Parkyakarkus—called a "beloved radio comic" by former Friar's Club Abbott Alan King—performed a fantastic routine, returned to his seat, put his head down, and died of a heart attack. As the late King told the story, "George E. Jessel shouted to performer Tony Martin, 'Sing something!'" during the chaos that followed. Martin, said King, started to sing "There's No Tomorrow." Arnaz finally spoke: "This was an evening that comes to you once in a lifetime. It means so much, then all at once it doesn't mean a damn thing." Parkyakarkus was the stage name of Harry Einstein, father of comedian Albert Brooks.

FURNITURE

When Ball moved to New York in the early 1960s, to do the Broadway show Wildcat, four huge vans were needed to get all her California furniture to the Big Apple, and into a seven-room rented apartment in the East 60s (the neighborhood of the Ricardos in *I Love Lucy*). According to columnist Sheilah Graham, Ball told her at the time, "I brought all the terrace furniture, five TV sets, a piano that was sitting out there doing nothing, the toys for my daughter, Lucie, little Desi's bongo drums, all my paintings, and all my books. Plus a limousine with chauffeur, and a big package of courage."

G

GAMES

Lucille Ball loved to play games, especially backgammon, and in the 1970s she appeared in TV and print commercials and on game boxes endorsing various board games for Milton Bradley. These included *Pivot Pool*, which had a picture of Ball and the phrase "This is my favorite family game"; *Body Language*, which had Ball twisted in various poses on the box; and *Solotaire* ("plays like solitaire, scores like poker"), with a picture of Ball on the front of the box. In 1976 she was on the cover of Milton Bradley's *Cross Up*, billed as "The Competitive Crossword Game."

Ball and the gang are featured in games including jigsaw puzzles, an *I Love Lucy* board game, and the *I Love Lucy* Trivia Game.

Finally, there's the Monopoly *I Love Lucy* 50th Anniversary Collector's Edition. Ball would've loved this: a deluxe edition of the classic Parker Bros. board game Monopoly with an *I Love Lucy* theme. The board has a gorgeous colorized photo of the Fab Four on the way to California; Chance and Community Chest cards are replaced with sets of cards called The Ricardos and The Mertzes. Houses and hotels transformed into red "set" pieces and white "studio" buildings. Six special pewter tokens include a bottle of Vitameatavegamin, a convertible, Ricky's conga drum, Ricky's straw hat, a vat of wine, and a loving cup. Instead of properties, players are wheeling and dealing for 28 of the series' best-known episodes. The game, though out of print, is still available as of this writing (2007) and generally sells online for around $40. Check your local flea markets, too.

There was a second *I Love Lucy* Monopoly game produced, variously called The Travel Edition or The California, Here We Come! Edition, with a different box cover and board graphics. The pewter tokens are also different (i.e., a derby hat, a harp) and properties featured the California episodes. This edition was available as of this writing on Amazon.com, also for $40.

GARRETT, JIMMY

This wholesome, wisecracking child actor played Lucille Ball's younger child on *The Lucy Show*. Prior to his work on with Ball, Garrett was cast as one of the children in the doomed Marilyn Monroe version of *Something's Got to Give*. He was also in the Desilu pilot <u>*The Victor Borge Comedy Theater*</u>.

Garrett, by virtue of his strong personality and unique delivery, added some zest to *The Lucy Show*, and lasted a few episodes longer than the other kids, who were written out once Vivian Vance left the show after the 1964-'65 season. He was cast in the pilot for *The Carol Channing Show* (produced by Desi Arnaz Productions), but it didn't sell, and that was his last acting job, according to a 1992 interview. At that time, Garrett helped his wife run the Helen Garrett Agency, a Los Angeles-based agency for child actors, still in existence as of this printing.

GAVIN, JOHN

Gavin was one of a handful of handsome, up-and-coming male stars who was making his way on TV in 1965 (he'd starred in 1960's Psycho and a handful of melodramas and comedies, like 1961's *Back Street* and *Tammy Tell Me True*) when a unique opportunity came his way: the chance to sing live on national TV, with … Vivian Vance. Gavin was then starring on the NBC series *Convoy* when he made a guest appearance on *The Mike Douglas Show*, one of TV's pioneer talk-fests. James Bacon reported in the October 9, 1965 *Gettysburg* (Pennsylvania) *Times*, that Gavin "stopped off in Cleveland to plug [Convoy] on Mike Douglas."

Gavin continued the story: "You might say a funny thing happened to me on the way to meet the NBC bosses. Vic Damone was the guest [host] of the week, and Vivian Vance and I were the guests for the day. Douglas almost knocked me off my feet when he asked if I would sing with Vivian—and with no rehearsal. And to top it off, he picked 'You're Just in Love,' from *Call Me Madam*. You know the one where the boy sings different words than the girl? It's the toughest song there is and I had never sung before without water running on my back. But I got through it okay. It was the first time I had ever sung in public.

"One of the viewers of the show was producer Leland Hayward who is going to make a Broadway musical out of the movie *Roman Holiday*. The next day I got a call from Leland asking me if I would be interested in playing the Greg Peck part on Broadway. He liked my singing.

"So now I'm studying singing—and watching the television ratings. If the show goes off, Broadway, here I come." (I could find no evidence the show went anywhere.)

GAY-FAY SCHOOL

A "private school for children" in Van Nuys, California, where Lucie Arnaz took dancing lessons in 1955. (Lessons cost $1.25 each.)

GENEROSITY

According to the *Philadelphia Daily News* on June 6, 1942, Ball sent a $25 war bond to each of 10 chorus girls who were fired from backing her up in *The Big Street*.

"GETTING ALONG WITH OTHER WOMEN"

In a fan magazine article in the 1940s, Lucille Ball and other stars of the day (Loretta Young, Ida Lupino), gave readers advice on how to get along with women. Ball's subject was "Don't Criticize."

"Never criticize a woman to a woman if you *don't* want it to reach her ears," Ball was quoted. "People never fail to find out when you talk about them behind their backs. If you have a criticism to make, tell it directly to the woman, not to her friends."

GHOST

The website LegendsofAmerica.com reports that Lucille Ball has haunted her ex-home at 1000 North Roxbury Drive in Beverly Hills since her death: "New owners tell of unexplained broken windows, loud voices being heard from an empty attic, and furniture and other objects moving around inside the house." Another source, the 1999 book *Hollywood Haunted: A Ghostly Tour of Filmland* by Laurie Jacobson and Mark Wanamaker, devotes a chapter to Ball's afterlife activities, called "I Love Roxbury." Ball's specter is described as "despondent." It should be noted that after Ball's death, the house was demolished and totally rebuilt.

GLAMOUR GIRL

Lucille Ball was not fond of being tagged a "glamour girl," reports a 1940 newspaper article by Burdette Jay. Ball, Jay writes, "was known as one of the most beautiful commercial models in the world before she came to the screen," and "now wants to be regarded as an actress, not a glamour girl. To prove it, Miss Ball sheds smart clothes and becomes a drab, colorless house-wife in the name of art in her new RKO Radio Picture, *You Can't Fool Your Wife*."

Actually, Ball plays two roles to try to trick her husband, one of which is Mercedes Vasquez, a very glamorous woman indeed. Just a few years later in *The Big Street* (1942), Ball would prove that being glamorous and being able to act did not have to be mutually exclusive. See <u>Fashion Plate</u>.

GLEASON, JAMES

A popular film character actor from a theatrical family in New York, Gleason was born in 1886. He co-starred with Ball in the comedy *Miss Grant Takes Richmond* (1949). Ball considered him for the role of Fred Mertz when Gale Gordon was not available, but Gleason asked for too much money.

Gleason was in the theater (as a writer and actor) in the early 1900s and in more than 100 movies from 1922 until his death in 1959. He specialized in playing tough, wiry ethnic characters with a hidden heart of gold, and was nominated for an Oscar for just such a part: the fight trainer in 1941's *Here Comes Mr. Jordan*.

GOLDEN GLOBE AWARD

Often-maligned movie and television honor awarded by the Hollywood Foreign Press Association, the Golden Globe has survived accusations of being "meaningless" and that it could be bought (especially in 1981, when wooden actress Pia Zadora won "New Star of the Year" over Kathleen Turner and Howard Rollins Jr., among others). Mostly, though, the awards have been a decent indicator of who will be nominated and win the Oscar. Their broad sweep (i.e., categories for Best Musical and Comedy Film, and Actor and Actress) has acknowledged great performances that Oscar never would.

Lucille Ball and Desi Arnaz were among the five people honored in 1955 for the "Television Excellence" award, the first time the HFPA acknowledged the new medium. Significantly, it was the only major industry award Arnaz ever won for his contribution to TV during his lifetime. Ball was nominated as Best Actress in a Comedy or Musical film, for *The Facts of Life* (1960), *Yours, Mine and Ours* (1968), and, believe it or not, *Mame* (1974); she also received several nominations in the television Best Comedy Actress category for *The Lucy Show* and *Here's Lucy*. In 1971, Desi Jr. won "New Male Star of the Year" for his work in the film *Red*

Sky at Morning. In 1978, Ball won the HFPA's Cecil B. DeMille award, a career-achievement honor.

GORDON, GALE

Born Charles Aldrich in 1906, Gordon was a blustery comic foil for Ball over four decades, beginning with the radio show *My Favorite Husband* in 1948 through Ball's final series in 1986, *Life with Lucy*. He was a busy supporting player in radio and television, but only made a dozen or so movies in his long career.

Onstage by 1923, he settled in Hollywood by 1925 and in 1926 began a long radio career. In 1933 he was the highest paid radio actor in Hollywood. His roles included Flash Gordon and Inspector Lestrade with Basil Rathbone in *Sherlock Holmes*. He joined the *Fibber McGee & Molly* show in 1941 and stayed on for 12 seasons.

Gale Gordon in typical simmering mode. Author's collection

His role on radio as the principal on *Our Miss Brooks* (1948) led to four years of starring in the TV version (1952-'56), and was the reason he was unavailable to play Fred Mertz (he was Ball's first choice) on *I Love Lucy*. He was on *Pete & Gladys*, the spin-off of *December Bride*, for a year, and also replaced Joseph Kearns, the original Mr. Wilson, on the hit show *Dennis the Menace*. Gordon was known for playing excitable, low-boiling-point buffoonish figures of authority, whose power was always being threatened.

A Copley News Service article that ran in the Hayward, California *Daily Review* on July 4, 1971, pinpointed Gordon's appeal: He "sputters better than anyone around. He may well be the best sputterer who ever fumed on cue, an Old Faithful of emotional geysers."

Gordon himself noted, "The sputter started years ago, on radio, in the old Fibber McGee & Molly days when I was playing Mayor LaTrivia. Don Quinn, who wrote the show, would give me these alliterations to say and then I was supposed to build to the big sputtering blowup. If I do say so, I've always played a blowhard rather well.

"A good sputter must be more than technique. It's not a static maneuver and it can't be timed. Working before a live studio audience, as we do, I work my sputter in accordance with the audience's reaction. If they're receptive, if the laugh is building, I keep sputtering and I delay the high point until I sense the rightness of the moment."

Gordon has always played the boss, or men of importance, even if they're actually only self-important. He told the *Daily Review*, "Years ago—and I mean many years ago—I was on a radio show starring Joe E. Brown. Now I've got a few accents in my back pocket. I've played all sorts of parts. But even as a young actor, I could play Joe E. Brown's boss. I even remember my name in the script—a very bossy name, Mr. Bullhammer.... If you're disliked and pompous, then it's tragedy," Gordon theorized. "But if you're pleasantly pompous, then it's comedy."

Being the foil for the beloved Ball, and playing her boss, necessitated that Gordon always be aware of the intensity of his character's pomposity: "Being pompous as the boss of a woman calls for a fine line between bellowing out orders and being plain nasty. Deep down, I have to be careful not to shout at Lucy with a certain edge in my manner. The audience must know that no matter how fierce I sound, I really don't mean it."

Off screen, Gordon was anything but pompous, and in fact was known for being one of the nicest people in the acting profession, with little or no ego and a quiet, soft-spoken demeanor. He chalked it up to circumstance: "It's all a matter of money, you see. In reality, I'm far from bossy. I have not much temper to speak of. But for the money they pay me, I'm only too happy to play the blowhard, which is a role that has kept me out of the ranks of the unemployed and living rather well...."

When Gordon wasn't acting, he was likely doing some kind of construction on his ranch in Borrego Springs, California, where he lived with his longtime wife, Virginia, and, among other things, farmed carob trees. "When I'm away from acting, I'm really away," Gordon said. "I'd no more think of 'acting' in front of friends than a plumber would thread a pipe on a social visit to a friend's living room. I leave Gale Gordon at the studio and I immediately become Charles Aldrich, which is still my legal name." He was also the honorary mayor of Borrego, though he referred to himself in typical self-deprecating style, as the "ornery" mayor.

Gordon guest-starred on *I Love Lucy* as Ricky's Tropicana nightclub boss. He came on board *The Lucy Show* in its second season (1963) and stayed with the redhead as her second banana until *Here's Lucy* ended in 1974. He was nominated four times for an Emmy, but never won.

He basically retired from the business in the seventies, returning mostly for Ball-related specials (*Lucy Calls the President*, *Lucy Moves to NBC*), and for a final curtain call with the redhead on the short-lived *Life with Lucy* in 1986. He made a cameo appearance in the film *The 'Burbs* (1989). He died at 89 of lung cancer in July 1995, about a month after his beloved wife, Virginia.

GOREY, FRANK

After 33 years of driving Lucille Ball, from the mid-1950s on, Gorey, also Ball's de facto personal assistant and confidante, has plenty of stories to tell. The redhead's chauffeur had to deal with Ball wanting him to play word games on the way to and from Palm Springs, among other things. (He'd remind her that he was driving, and she'd often suggest a game that required no writing or handwork.) Gorey was with Ball when she moved to New York after her 1960 divorce from Desi Arnaz, to get away from Los Angeles and star in *Wildcat*. He was with her back in Beverly Hills on Roxbury Drive when she returned to television soon after. Lee Tannen describes weekly phone calls to Lucy in his book *I Loved Lucy: My Friendship with Lucille Ball*, and notes that if Gorey answered the phone, it usually meant Ball was in a bad mood and the conversation would be short.

I had the pleasure of sharing breakfast with Gorey in Jamestown, New York in 2006, where he was leading a seminar and promoting his upcoming book, tentatively titled *Being Frank with Lucy*. He told fascinating tales of screenings at Ball's house where the invited guests typically included Milton Berle, Jack Carter, and other classic stand-ups. "Jack was a normal guy one-on-one," Gorey recalled, "but if there was another comic around, he was 'on.' They were all like that." He says that Berle, surprisingly, was the most down-to-earth of the bunch. Unfortunately for any non-showbiz guests at these occasions, like Gorey, Ball "expected everyone to hold their own, humor-wise, for example, or they weren't invited back." How does Mr. Joe Average Fan hold his own with the likes of Berle and Carter? "Bring a funny joke along with you," Gorey says. "And if it's a bit off-color, but not outrageously so, that's even better." Then, deliver it like your life depended on it! (Your invitation back *did* depend on it.)

GOULD, SANDRA

Comic actress Gould, best known as the second Mrs. Kravitz (the nosy neighbor) on *Bewitched*, played Liz Cooper's bridge partner, Marge, on a 1950 episode of *My Favorite Husband*. Fans also remember her as the wife of the "oil tycoon" in an episode of *I Love Lucy*, and as the woman on the train platform in "Lucy and the Loving Cup." She also guest-starred on *The Lucy Show*. Gould made more than 20 feature films and logged hundreds of other TV appearances, as recently as *Veronica's Closet* in 1999. She died on July 20, 1999, of a stroke at the age of 73.

GRAY, MACK

File this under "Don't always believe what you hear … or read." Shirley MacLaine, in her 1995 book, *My Lucky Stars—A Hollywood Memoir*, wrote that Dean Martin's "longtime assistant and loyalist, Mack Gray"—Martin started out as a boxer; Gray, a.k.a. Maxie Greenburg, used to manage fighters—and Ball were very close. Gray, she wrote, "had had a long affair with Lucille Ball. I used to ply him with questions about his relationship with Lucy because I admired her so much. He would only say her red hair was real. I teased him that he blew it. He could have been one half of 'Mackilu.'"

Cute story. True? Well, anyone who knew the wacky redhead, even many of her fans, knew her flaming hair was the product of henna and a decent hairstylist, first tried on Ball in the early 1940s at MGM. She was a natural brunette who went blonde in Hollywood, then red. Gray, who appeared in bit parts, usually uncredited, in more than 40 movies from 1929 to 1962, was actor George Raft's assistant before he hooked up with Martin circa 1952. According to Martin biographer Nick Tosches, Gray was a known supplier of drugs (like Percodan) to Martin and others.

Gray was an escort for young starlets in Golden Age Hollywood, as this gossip item from August 27, 1936, shows: "If our eyes don't deceive us, that was Mack Gray who escorted Lucille Ball and Barbara Pepper to greet dancers Tony and Renee de Marco at the Cocoanut Grove."

So Gray knew Ball, dated her, and may have even had an affair with her—though I could find no concrete evidence of that—in which case his comment was likely a snide aside to MacLaine indicating that he had slept with the queen of comedy. (For more on Gray, see Dino, Desi, & Billy.)

GUEST STARS

Lucille Ball and Desi Arnaz knew from the beginning that guest stars meant an audience larger than the norm, and used them liberally, especially later on in the run of *I Love Lucy*. Guest stars were prominent throughout the runs of *The Lucille Ball-Desi Arnaz Show*, *The Lucy Show*, and *Here's Lucy*.

Here's a selection of my favorite *Lucy* guest stars. For the purposes of this list, a "guest star" is an entertainer who was well known to the audience of the time, who subsequently became a star in his/her own right, or who is strongly identified with Ball's life or career. Character names are in parentheses.

I Love Lucy 1951-'57

Claude Akins: "Desert Island" 11-26-1956 (Indian) Akins played Sheriff Lobo in *BJ and the Bear* (1979) and his own spin-off.

Jack Albertson: "Bon Voyage" 1-16-1956 (Helicopter Dispatcher) This durable character actor won an Oscar for *The Subject Was Roses* (1968) and co-starred with Freddie Prinze in the sitcom *Chico and the Man* (1974-'78).

Elvia Allman: "Job Switching" 9-15-1952 (Factory Foreman) A familiar character actress in TV and movies, Allman's famous line in this episode is, "Speed it up a little!" Allman would appear again on "Fan Magazine" 2-8-1954 (Minnie's neighbor) and "The Homecoming" 11-7-1955 (Nancy Graham), and later on *The Lucy Show*.

Eve Arden: "L.A. At Last" 2-7-1955 (Herself) One of the best remembered *Lucy* episodes.

Desi Arnaz Jr.: "The Ricardos Dedicate a Statue" 5-6-1957 (Extra at Unveiling, uncredited) This is the only time Lucy's real-life son appeared on *I Love Lucy*.

Parley Baer: "Ricky Needs an Agent" 5-16-1955 (Mr. Reilly) Familiar comic character actor who appeared in hundreds of movies and TV series, Baer was a regular on *Ozzie and Harriet* (1955-'61) and *The Andy Griffith Show* (1962-'63). Baer would make about a dozen appearances with Lucy on all three of her major series.

Florence Bates: "Pioneer Women" 3-31-1952 (Mrs. Pettebone) Bates played society matrons by the dozens in the movies, including the Alfred Hitchcock classic *Rebecca* (1940).

Bea Benaderet: "Lucy Plays Cupid" 1-21-1952 (Miss Lewis).

Madge Blake: "Ricky Loses His Temper" 2-22-1954 (Mrs. Mulford); "Lucy and Superman" 1-14-1957 (Martha) Blake is best known for playing Bruce Wayne's Aunt Harriet on the campy 1960s TV series *Batman* (1966-'68).

Gloria Blondell: "The Anniversary Present" 9-29-1952 (Grace Foster) Blondell was the sister of future Ball co-star Joan Blondell.

Roz and Marilyn Borden, aka The Borden Twins: "Tennessee Bound" 1-24-1955 (Teensy and Weensy).

Charles Boyer: "Lucy Meets Charles Boyer" 3-5-1956 (Himself).

Hillary Brooke: "The Fox Hunt" 2-6-1956 (Angela Randall) Brooke's good looks were often deployed as the "other woman" in films, but she was a deft comedienne: she co-starred on the *I Love Lucy* summer replacement series *My Little Margie* (1952-'54) and was Abbott & Costello's female sidekick on their TV show (1952-'53).

Kathryn Card: "Fan Magazine" 2-8-1954 (Minnie Finch) Card would later turn up on the series as Lucy's mother, Mrs. McGillicuddy, beginning in episode 110, "California, Here We Come" (1-10-55). She played the role through 1959.

Hans Conried: "Redecorating" 11-24-1952 (Mr. Jenkins) Conried was a distinctive-voiced character actor best known as Uncle Tonoose on *The Danny Thomas Show* (aka *Make Room for Daddy*) from 1958 to 1964. Also in "Lucy Hires an English Tutor" 12-29-1952 (Percy Livermore).

Ellen Corby: "Lucy Meets Orson Welles" 10-15-1956 (Miss Hanna) Corby went on to play Grandma in *The Waltons* (1972-'81).

Richard Crenna: "The Young Fans" 2-25-1952 (Arthur) Crenna was a regular on *Our Miss Brooks* and *The Real McCoys*, and subsequently became a respected dramatic actor. He talked about what it was like to work with Lucy on *The I Love Lucy 50th Anniversary Special* in November 2001.

Mary Jane Croft: "Lucy Is Envious" 3-29-1954 (Cynthia Harcourt) After promising snooty friend Cynthia more money for charity than they can afford, Lucy and Ethel dress up as Martians as part of a movie publicity stunt to earn extra cash (one of the best-remembered *Lucy* episodes). Also in "Return Home from Europe" 5-14-1956 (Airline Passenger with Baby) and "Lucy Gets Chummy with the Neighbors" 2-18-1957 (Betty Ramsey), after which Croft and Frank Nelson played the Ricardo's Connecticut neighbors for the rest of the series.

Barbara Eden: "Country Club Dance" 4-22-1957 (Diana Jordan) One of Eden's early bit parts; she later starred as the title character in *I Dream of Jeannie* (1965-'70).

Verna Felton: "Sales Resistance" 1-26-1953 (Mrs. Simpson) Felton later co-starred in the Desilu series *December Bride* (1954-'59). Also in "Lucy Hires a Maid" 4-27-1953 (Mrs. Porter).

June Foray: "Little Ricky Gets a Dog" 1-21-1957 (Voice of the dog) Foray provided voices for Warner Bros, and most of the major cartoon studios, but is perhaps best known as the voice of Rocky, the Flying Squirrel on *Rocky and His Friends* (1959-'61) and *The Bullwinkle Show* (1961-'73).

Tennessee Ernie Ford: "Tennessee Ernie Visits" 5-3-1954; "Tennessee Ernie Hangs On" 5-10-1954; "Tennessee Bound" 1-24-1955 (all as Cousin Ernie).

Gale Gordon: "Lucy's Schedule" 5-26-1952; "Ricky Asks for a Raise" 6-9-1952 (Mr. Littlefield).

Sandra Gould: "Oil Wells" 2-15-1954 (Nancy Johnson); "Lucy and the Loving Cup" 1-7-1957 (Subway Passenger).

Florence Halop: "Redecorating" 11-24-1952 (Woman on Phone) Best known as the crusty bailiff on *Night Court* in its second season (1985-'86), Halop also guested on *Here's Lucy*.

William Holden: "L.A. At Last" 2-7-1955 (Himself) This is one of the best remembered *Lucy* appearances by any guest star.

<u>Bob Hope</u>: "Lucy and Bob Hope" 10-1-1956 (Himself) In this baseball-themed episode, Hope, Lucy, and Ricky sing "Nobody Loves the Ump."

<u>Hedda Hopper</u>: "The Hedda Hopper Story" 3-14-1955 (Herself).

Edward Everett Horton: "Lucy Plays Cupid" 1-21-1952 (Mr. Ritter) Horton was a very popular supporting comic actor in films, known for his fluttery, dyspeptic performances. Vivian Vance toured with Horton in his stage vehicle *Springtime for Henry*.

Rock Hudson: "In Palm Springs" 4-25-1955 (Himself).

Allen Jenkins: "New Neighbors" 3-3-1952 (Police Sergeant); "Ricky and Fred Are TV Fans" 6-22-1953 (Cop); "Too Many Crooks" 11-30-1953 (Cop) Jenkins was a familiar character actor from the movies, including Ball's *Five Came Back* (1939), who specialized in playing policemen.

<u>Van Johnson</u>: "The Dancing Star" 5-2-1955 (Himself).

Joseph Kearns: "The Kleptomaniac" 4-14-1952 (Dr. Tom Robinson); "Lucy's Night in Town" 3-25-1957 (Theatre Manager) Character actor Kearns, also on radio and an *Our Miss Brooks* TV regular, was the first Mr. Wilson on *Dennis the Menace* (1959-'63). Kearns died in 1962 and was replaced by Gale Gordon in the final *Dennis* season. Coincidentally, another recurring *Dennis* character was police sergeant "Theodore Mooney," Gordon's character name on *The Lucy Show*.

<u>Nancy Kulp</u>: "Lucy Meets the Queen" 1-30-1956 (Maid) Kulp shows Lucy how to properly curtsy for the Queen.

Elsa Lanchester: "Off to Florida" 11-12-1956 (Mrs. Edna Grundy) Lanchester was *The Bride of Frankenstein* (1939) and married to Charles Laughton.

<u>Charles Lane</u>: "Lucy Goes to the Hospital" 1-19-1953 (Expectant Father); "Lucy Tells the Truth" 11-9-1953 (Casting Director); "The Business Manager," 10-4-1954 (Mr. Hickox); "Staten Island Ferry" 1-2-1956 (Passport Clerk) Lane was a familiar character actor from

movies, and was a semi-regular as the crusty banker Mr. Barnsdahl on the first season of *The Lucy Show* (see that show's guest-star list for details).

Joi Lansing: "Desert Island" 11-26-1956 (Herself).

Sheldon Leonard: "Sales Resistance" 1-26-1953 (Harry Martin) Leonard was a character actor specializing in gangster types; he went on to become one of the most successful TV producers of all time.

Don Loper: "The Fashion Show" 2-28-1955 (Himself).

Sheila MacRae: "The Fashion Show" 2-28-1955 (Herself) MacRae, best known for her TV stint as Alice Cramden in the musical "Honeymooners" sketches on *The Jackie Gleason Show* (1966-'70), was musical star Gordon's wife, actress Meredith's mother, and a friend of Ball and Aranz.

Hal March: "Lucy's Fake Illness" 1-28-1952 (Himself); "Lucy Is a Matchmaker" 5-25-1953 (Eddie Grant) Actor and game-show host March later emceed *The $64,000 Question* (1955), one of the only shows to knock *I Love Lucy* out of the No. 1 ratings spot. March was the first Harry Morton on *The Burns & Allen Show* (1950-'51), where he played opposite Ball co-star Bea Benaderet. He was the "boyfriend" on television and stage of other funny ladies like Joan Davis, Marie Wilson, Eve Arden, and Imogene Coca. March also appeared on *The Lucy Show*.

Strother Martin: "Off to Florida" 11-12-1956 (Cafe Waiter) Martin became a familiar character actor in the 1960s, especially in Westerns like *Cool Hand Luke* (1967), where he introduced the line, "What we have here is a failure to communicate."

Harpo Marx: "Lucy and Harpo Marx" 5-9-1955 (Himself) The mirror routine with Harpo and Lucy in this episode is a classic that Harpo had to learn, since he previously had done it slightly differently every time.

Howard McNear: "Little Ricky Gets Stage Fright" 10-22-1956 (Mr. Crawford) McNear played "Floyd" the barber on *The Andy Griffith Show* (1960-'67).

Edith Meiser: "Lucy's Schedule" 5-26-1952; "Ricky Asks for a Raise" 6-9-1952 (Mrs. Littlefield) Meiser co-starred on Broadway with Vivian Vance in the hit *Let's Face It* (1942). See Stage Career under Vance, Vivian for details.

Shirley Mitchell: "Lucy and Ethel Buy the Same Dress" 10-19-1953; "Lucy Tells the Truth" 11-9-1953; "Lucy's Club Dance" 4-12-1954 (all as Marion Strong).

Frank Nelson: "The Quiz Show," 11-12-1951 (Host); "Lucy Gets Ricky on the Radio" 5-19-1952 (Host); "Lucy Changes Her Mind" 3-30-1953 (Waiter); "Ricky and Fred Are TV Fans" 6-22-1953 (Cop); "The Million Dollar Idea" 1-11-1954 (TV Announcer); "Return Home from Europe" 5-14-1956 (Orchestra leader); "Lucy Gets Chummy with the Neighbors" 2-18-1957 (Ralph Ramsey) After this episode Mary Jane Croft and Nelson played the Ricardo's Connecticut neighbors for the rest of the series.

Jay Novello: "The Séance" 11-26-1951 (Mr. Meriweather); "Visitor from Italy" 10-29-1956 (Mario) Novello was known for his comic Italian immigrant portrayals.

Philip Ober: "The Quiz Show," 11-12-1951 (Arnold); "Don Juan Is Shelved" 3-21-1955 (Dore Schary) Ober was Vivian Vance's third husband.

Jess Oppenheimer: "The Audition" 11-19-1951 (Cameo).

Elizabeth Patterson: "The Marriage License" 4-7-1952 (Mrs. Willoughby) Patterson would become a semi-regular on *I Love Lucy* as neighbor Mrs. Trumble starting in the episode "No Children Allowed" 4-20-1953.

Barbara Pepper: "Breaking the Lease" 2-11-1952 (Extra); "The Freezer" 4-28-1952 (Grocery Shopper); "Lucy Goes to the Hospital" 1-19-1953 (Nurse); "The Girls Go Into Business" 10-12-1953 (Customer); "The Tour" 5-30-1955 (Bus Tourist); "The Homecoming" 11-7-1955 (Neighbor).

Pepito "The Clown" Perez: "Lucy's Show Business Swan Song" 12-22-1952 (Pepito) Desi Arnaz's friend Perez appeared in the *I Love Lucy* pilot and helped teach Ball and Arnaz the vaudeville routines they took on the road (and used in episode No. 6).

George Reeves: "Lucy and Superman" 1-14-1957 (Superman) TV's *Superman* from 1952 to 1957, Reeves died two years later; his death was originally ruled a suicide, but some now believe it was murder. He was the subject of a 2006 movie, *Hollywoodland*, in which Reeves was played by Ben Affleck.

Elliott Reid: "The Ricardos Are Interviewed" 11-14-1955 (Edward Warren) Remembered as Jane Russell's boyfriend in *Gentlemen Prefer Blondes* (1953), Reid also appeared in *Here's Lucy* and more recently *Seinfeld*.

Hayden Rorke: "New Neighbors" 3-3-1952 (Tom O'Brien) Rorke had toured with Lucy in the play *Dream Girl* (1947), and went on to create the exasperated Col. Dr. Alfred Bellows on *I Dream of Jeannie* (1965-'70). Vivian Vance's third (and ex by this time) husband Phil Ober was a regular on *Jeannie* during its first season. Rorke also appeared on *Here's Lucy*.

Natalie Schafer: "The Charm School" 1-25-1954 (Phoebe Emerson) Schafer became a TV immortal as Mrs. Howell on *Gilligan's Island* (1964-'67).

Doris Singleton: "The Club Election" 2-16-1953; "The Camping Trip" 6-8-1953; "Lucy and Ethel Buy the Same Dress" 10-19-1953; "Baby Pictures" 11-2-1953; "Lucy Tells the Truth" 11-9-1953; "Lucy's Club Dance" 4-12-1954; "The Dancing Star" 5-2-1955; "Lucy and Harpo Marx" 5-9-1955; "Lucy and Superman" 1-14-1957 (all as Carolyn Appleby). The last was Singleton's final appearance as Carolyn Appleby, though she would act with Lucy in the future.

Aaron Spelling: "Tennessee Bound" 1-24-1955 (Gas Station Man) Yes, this is *the* Aaron Spelling, who went on to become one of TV's most successful producers (including Ball's short-lived final sitcom, *Life with Lucy*).

Lurene Tuttle: "The Club Election" 2-16-1953 (Club President) Tuttle co-starred on the sitcom *Julia* (1968-'71).

Norma Varden: "The Ricardos Change Apartments" 5-18-1953 (Mrs. Benson) Varden was a familiar character actress, usually playing upper-crust types.

Janet Waldo: "The Young Fans" 2-25-1952 (Peggy) Waldo was the voice of Judy Jetson on *The Jetsons* and Josie in *Josie and the Pussycats*, plus many other animated characters, and played Lucy's sister in one episode of *The Lucy Show*.

John Wayne: "Lucy and John Wayne" 10-10-1955 (Himself).

Orson Welles: "Lucy Meets Orson Welles" 10-15-1956 (Himself).

Mary Wickes: "The Ballet" 2-18-1952 (Madame Lamand).

Richard Widmark: "The Tour" 5-30-1955 (Himself) The exterior of Ball's (then) new Beverly Hills home was featured in the exterior shots as Widmark's home in this episode.

Cornel Wilde: "The Star Upstairs" 4-18-1955 (Himself) One of Vivian Vance's best comic moments comes in this episode, as Ethel distracts Ricky so he won't see Lucy hanging from a palm tree outside their Beverly Palms hotel balcony window.

The Lucy-Desi Comedy Hour 1957-'60

Tallulah Bankhead: "The Celebrity Next Door" 12-3-1957 (Herself) One of the funniest *Lucy* shows, period. The Mertzes put in time as the Ricardo's servants to impress Connecticut neighbor Bankhead. Lucy persuades Bankhead to act in their community show, with hysterical results. This script was originally slated to star Bette Davis.

Milton Berle: "Milton Berle Hides Out at the Ricardos" 9-25-1959 (Himself) Perhaps the worst of the hour-long episodes. Uncle Miltie does everything he can to enliven the proceedings, including donning a dress. Silly and pointless.

Maurice Chevalier: "Lucy Goes to Mexico" 10-6-1958 (Himself) Routine episode unless you're a Chevalier fan.

Bob Cummings: "The Ricardos Go to Japan" 11-27-1959 (Himself) Cummings' natural charm and some great slapstick holds this one together.

Paul Douglas: "Lucy Wants a Career" 4-13-1959 (Himself) One of the better hour-long episodes. Lucy is believably human and caring in this one: she tries to reconcile showbiz success (as a morning show hostess) with the decreased time it means spending with her family.

Gale Gordon: "Lucy Makes Room for Danny" 12-1-1958 (Judge).

Betty Grable: "Lucy Wins a Racehorse" 2-3-1958 Grable and husband Harry James play themselves in an overlong, typical episode about a racehorse Fred Mertz wins and gives to Little Ricky. James had appeared with Ball in the movie *Best Foot Forward* (1943).

Hedda Hopper: "Lucy Takes a Cruise to Havana" 11-6-1957 (Herself). This show originally ran 75 minutes, and Desi Arnaz convinced the sponsor of the following show to give up 15 minutes of airtime so the entire episode could run. For syndication, the episode was pruned to fit a 60-minute format, and all of Hopper's scenes ended up on the cutting room floor. It has since been restored; see Lucy on DVD.

Ernie Kovacs: "Lucy Meets the Moustache" 4-1-1960 Kovacs and wife Edie Adams played themselves. The comedy is overshadowed by the sadness of Ball and Arnaz getting a divorce, and this being the final time they would play Lucy and Ricky Ricardo. There was much crying and angst on the set of this one.

Fernando Lamas: "Lucy Goes to Sun Valley" 4-14-1958 (Himself) Lucy uses Lamas to make her Latin hubbie jealous in the amusing hour-long episode.

Joi Lansing: "Lucy Wants a Career" 4-13-1959 (Starlet).

Ida Lupino: "Lucy's Summer Vacation" 6-8-1959 Lupino and husband Howard Duff play themselves and get more than they bargained for sharing a summer house with Lucy and Ricky. The Mertzes are hardly in this episode, and it suffers as a result. Lupino, a fine actress and director, was not a broad comedian. This one falls flat.

Fred MacMurray: "Lucy Hunts Uranium" 1-3-1958 MacMurray and wife June Haver play themselves in this funny episode that takes the Ricardos and Mertzes into the desert to stake their claims.

Cesar Romero: "Lucy Takes a Cruise to Havana" 11-6-1957 (Carlos Garcia) Romero played Ricky's Cuban pal. Suave Romero was a second banana and "B"-movie leading man at 20th Century Fox from the 1940s who is best known for his appearances as the Joker on the *Batman* TV series of the 1960s. He also appeared on *Here's Lucy*. Romero, who was "outed" after his death by Boze Hadleigh in *Hollywood Gays*, dated Lucy for a time in the late 1930s, Stefan Kanfer reports in *Ball of Fire*. One night when both were drunk, Lucy asked him why he never made a pass at her. Romero's response, before breaking down, reportedly was, "I'm strange."

Red Skelton: "Lucy Goes to Alaska" 2-9-1959 (Himself) Some funny bits in this one, especially the hammock scene as the gang tries to get some sleep.

Ann Sothern: "Lucy Takes a Cruise to Havana" 11-6-1957 (Susie) Sothern played her *Private Secretary* (1953-'57) character, Susie McNamara.

Danny Thomas: "Lucy Makes Room for Danny" 12-1-1958 Thomas and his TV family (Marjorie Lord, Rusty Hamer, and Angela Cartwright) guest star on the best of the hour-long shows. The Williamses (Thomas et al.) rent the Ricardos' house, but Lucy and Ricky end up staying when his movie is cancelled. They move in with the Mertzes, but Lucy just can't stay out of her home, causing inevitable friction. It ends up in a snow fight free-for-all that takes them to court. Listen for Ethel's "We raise chickens" line in court. Lord (actress Anne Archer's mother) was Vance's friend; the two had appeared onstage together. Thomas, whose long-running sitcom filmed at Desilu, was forever loyal to Ball and Arnaz for his success, and spoke at Arnaz's funeral.

Rudy Vallee: "Lucy Takes a Cruise to Havana" 11-6-1957 (Himself) Long past his prime, Vallee's role was written as a big, romantic star that Lucy and Ann Sothern swoon over. It was hardly believable.

The Lucy Show 1962-'68

Edie Adams: "Mooney's Other Wife" 1-22-1968 Adams and husband Ernie Kovacs guest-starred on the final *Lucille Ball-Desi Arnaz Show*.

Claude Akins: "Lucy Meets the Law" 2-13-1967.

Mabel Albertson: "Lucy and the Missing Stamp" 12-21-1964 Sister of Jack, Albertson played Darrin's mother on *Bewitched* (1964-1972).

Elvia Allman: "Lucy Bags a Bargain" 1-17-1966; "Lucy the Babysitter" 1-16-1967.

Keith Andes: "Lucy Goes Duck Hunting" 11-7-1963 (Lucy's boyfriend); "Lucy and the Winter Sports" 10-5-1964; "Lucy and Joan" 10-11-1965; "Lucy the Stunt Man" 10-18-1965 Andes played Lucy's rugged boyfriend on this series, though two different characters, since by the final two shows he did, the series had changed format and moved its setting from Connecticut to California.

Desi Arnaz Jr.: "Lucy and the Scout Trip" 3-30-1964 (Scout).

Lucie Arnaz: "Lucy Is a Soda Jerk" 3-04-1963; "Lucy and the Ring-a-Ding Ding" 10-10-1966; "Lucy Gets her Diploma" 10-9-1967; "Lucy and Robert Goulet" 10-30-1967 (Dot) Lucie and brother Desi Jr. showed up at various times in bit parts throughout this series.

Frankie Avalon: "Lucy the Star Maker" 10-2-1967 (Tommy).

John Banner: "Lucy and Bob Crane" 2-21-1966 Banner played Schultz, his *Hogan's Heroes* character.

Vanda Barra: "Lucy and Robert Goulet" 10-30-1967 The wife of *Lucy Show* regular Sid Gould, Barra appeared many more times on this show and *Here's Lucy* in small parts. She also guest-starred on Desi Arnaz's sitcom, *The Mothers-in-Law*.

Majel Barrett: "Lucy Is a Kangaroo for a Day" 11-12-1962 (Secretary) Barrett, a student in Lucy's Desilu Workshop, went on to *Star Trek* (1966-'69) as Nurse Chapel and married its creator, Gene Roddenberry.

Ed Begley: "Lucy the Bean Queen" 9-26-1966 (Mr. Bailey) Begley was an Oscar-winning supporting character actor.

Jack Benny: "Lucy and the Plumber" 9-28-1964 The plumber looks suspiciously like Jack Benny. Also "Lucy and George Burns" 9-12-1966 (Cameo) and "Lucy Gets Jack Benny's Account" 10-16-1967 (Himself).

Milton Berle: "Lucy Saves Milton Berle" 12-6-1965; "Lucy Meets the Berles" 9-11-1967 (both as himself).

Ken Berry: "Lucy Helps Ken Berry" 2-19-1968 (Himself) Berry was part of Lucy's Desilu Workshop in the late 1950s.

Joan Blondell: "Lucy and Joan" 10-11-1965; "Lucy the Stunt Man" 10-18-1965 (Joan) A musical and comedy star in films in the 1930s and 1940s, Blondell was tried out as Lucy's new neighbor and pal in these episodes. When Ball criticized Blondell's line readings as not funny, Blondell was offended, according to *The Lucy Book*; when Ball mimed a toilet flushing—as if to indicate "What you did stunk,"—Blondell caught part of it, cursed Ball and stormed off the set, never to return.

John Bubbles: "Main Street, U.S.A" 1-23-1967; "Lucy Puts Main Street on the Map" 1-30-1967.

Carol Burnett: "Lucy Gets a Roommate" 10-31-1966; "Lucy and Carol in Palm Springs" 11-7-1966 (Carol Bradford) This two-parter is Burnett's first appearance (of many) on Lucy's shows. Also: "Lucy and Carol Burnett, Parts 1 and 2" 12-4-1967, and 12-11-1967 (Carol Tilford).

George Burns: "Lucy and George Burns" 9-12-1966 (Himself) Lucy and Burns do a lovely soft-shoe routine.

Sid Caesar: "Lucy and Sid Caesar" 3-4-1968 (Himself).

LUCY AND VIV THROUGH THE AGES: Although many stars guested on the various *Lucy* shows, everyone's favorite was Lucy's best partner and pal, Vivian Vance. Here they are, from the top, in the '50s, '60s, and '70s. All photos, Photofest

Jack Carter: "Lucy Sues Mooney" 11-27-1967 Comedian Carter was a friend of Ball's who dated her *Wildcat* co-star Paula Stewart.

Jack Cassidy: "Lucy and the Undercover Agent" 11-22-1965 Musical comedy star Cassidy was husband to Shirley Jones, and father of David, Shaun, and Patrick.

Pat Collins: "Lucy and Pat Collins" 11-28-1966 (Herself) Collins billed herself as the "hip hypnotist."

Hans Conried: "Lucy's Barbershop Quartet" 2-4-1963 (Voice teacher).

Jackie Coogan: "Lucy and the Military Academy" 12-09-1963 (Drill Sergeant); "Lucy Gets Involved" 1-15-1968 Coogan was the former child star who played Uncle Fester on *The Addams Family* (1964-'66).

Carole Cook: "Lucy and Viv Are Volunteer Firemen" 1-14-1963 (Fireperson) The first of many Cook appearances on *The Lucy Show* and *Here's Lucy*.

Wally Cox: "Lucy Conducts the Symphony" 12-30-1963 (Harold) One of several Cox appearances. Cox was TV's *Mr. Peepers* (1952-'55), the voice of *Underdog* in the cult cartoon series (1964-'73), and an original *Hollywood Squares* regular.

Bob Crane: "Lucy and Bob Crane" 2-21-1966 (Himself) Crane was at the height of his *Hogan's Heroes* fame.

Joan Crawford: "Lucy and the Lost Star" 2-26-1968 (Herself) Crawford famously remarked after her stint on the show, "And they call me a bitch!" Lucy verbally mistreated the star during rehearsal, especially after she found out about Crawford's secret vodka flask.

Mary Jane Croft: "Lucy the Music Lover" 11-19-1962 (Audrey Simmons) This is Croft's first appearance post-*I Love Lucy*. Her character will return many times—a total of 24—during in the show's run, with a name change to Mary Jane Lewis once the show moved its setting to California for the 1965-'66 season.

Dennis Day: "Little Old Lucy" 10-23-1967 Day was a regular on the *Jack Benny* show.

Kirk Douglas: "Lucy Goes to a Hollywood Premiere" 2-7-1966 (Himself).

Vince Edwards: "Lucy Goes to a Hollywood Premiere" 2-7-1966 (Himself) Edwards was TV's *Ben Casey* (1961-'66).

Jamie Farr: "Lucy the Rain Goddess" 1-3-1966 (Indian Brave) Farr became famous as the transvestite Klinger on television's *M*A*S*H* (1972-'83).

Tennessee Ernie Ford: "Lucy and Tennessee Ernie Ford" 2-27-1967. (Himself).

William Frawley: "Lucy and the Countess Have a Horse Guest" 10-25-1965 Frawley's cameo as a stableman was his final TV appearance.

Kathleen Freeman: "Lucy Plays Florence Nightingale" (1-6-1964); "Lucy and Viv Open a Restaurant" (2-17-1964); "Lucy Takes a Job at the Bank" (2-24-1964); "Lucy Enters a Baking Contest" (4-27-1964); and "Lucy Gets Her Maid" (11-30-1964).

Arthur Godfrey: "Lucy and Arthur Godfrey" 3-8-1965 (Himself).

Sid Gould: "Lucy Is a Kangaroo for a Day" 11-12-1962 (Waiter) Gould's first appearance on a *Lucy* show. Gould appeared (sometimes with wife Vanda Barra) in dozens of small parts on Ball's shows after this one. He was (Ball husband No. 2) Gary Morton's cousin, and died in 1996.

Robert Goulet: "Lucy and Robert Goulet" 10-30-1967 (Himself).

Buddy Hackett: "Lucy and the Stolen Stole" 1-29-1968.

Alan Hale Jr.: "Lucy Puts Out a Fire at the Bank" 12-2-1963 (Fireman Academy Instructor) Hale would soon become famous as the lovable Skipper on *Gilligan's Island*.

Phil Harris: "Lucy and Phil Harris" 2-5-1968 (Himself).

Helen Hayes: "Lucy and the Little Old Lady" 1-3-1972 (Mrs. Kathleen Brady) Oscar winner Hayes credited Lucy with giving her career new life on TV by casting her.

Bob Hope: "Lucy and the Plumber" 9-28-1964 (Cameo).

Danny Kaye: "Lucy Meets Danny Kaye" 12-28-1964 (Himself).

Jane Kean: "Lucy and the Soap Opera" 1-31-1966 Kean played Trixie on Jackie Gleason's hour-long musical *Honeymooners* shows in the 1960s.

Nancy Kulp: "Lucy Becomes an Astronaut" 11-5-62 (Jane Corey).

Charles Lane: "Lucy Misplaces $2,000," 10-22-1962; "Lucy Buys a Sheep," 10-29-1962; "Lucy Is a Kangaroo for a Day," 11-12-1962; "Vivian Sues Lucy," 12-3-1962 (all as banker Mr. Barnsdahl).

Ruta Lee: "Lucy's Substitute Secretary" 1-2-1967 (Audrey Fields) Lee schemes to take over Lucy's job. Also: "Lucy Meets the Berles" 9-11-1967.

Sheldon Leonard: "Lucy Meets Sheldon Leonard" 3-6-1967 (Himself).

Art Linkletter: "Lucy and Art Linkletter" 1-10-1966 (Himself).

Barry Livingston: "Lucy and the Scout Trip" 3-30-1964 (Scout) Livingston replaced one of the original sons on *My Three Sons* (1960-'72).

Hal March: "Mooney the Monkey" 12-5-1966.

Peter Marshall: "Lucy's Sister Pays a Visit" 1-7-1963 (Hughie) Marshall was the host of the original *Hollywood Squares* (1966-'82).

Dean Martin: "Lucy Dates Dean Martin" 2-14-1966 Martin plays two roles in this one, himself and a stuntman named Eddie Feldman who looks just like Dean Martin. Wacky Lucy gets mixed up with both of them. Ball always claimed this as her favorite *Lucy Show* episode.

Dick Martin: "Lucy Digs Up a Date" 10-8-1962 (Harry Conners) This was comic Martin's first of 10 appearances on the show, all during the first season, after which his character disappeared.

Ethel Merman: "Lucy Teaches Ethel Merman to Sing" 2-3-1964; "Ethel Merman and the Boy Scout Show," 2-10-1964. Herself.

Jan Murray: "Lucy and the Soap Opera" 1-31-1966 (Peter Shannon) Stand-up comedian Murray was reportedly unnerved by Ball's insistence on giving a full performance from the first reading.

Jim Nabors: "Lucy Gets Caught in the Draft" 11-14-1966 Nabors does a cameo as Gomer Pyle.

Wayne Newton: "Lucy Discovers Wayne Newton" 12-27-1965 Playing a farm boy, Newton is "discovered" by Lucy in one of the series' best-remembered episodes. Newton says he was offered a series based on his performance in this episode but turned it down, not wanting to be typecast at such an early age.

Jay North: "Lucy the Robot" 2-28-1966 The former *Dennis the Menace* played the nephew of Mr. Mooney (Gale Gordon). Gordon had played the second Mr. Wilson on North's show.

Lew Parker: "Lucy Sues Mooney" 11-27-1967 (Garfield) Parker played Ann Marie's dad on *That Girl* (1966-'71). Also: "Lucy Helps Ken Berry" 2-19-1968.

Michael J. Pollard: "Chris Goes Steady" 1-20-1964 (Ted Mooney) Pollard, who specialized in weird, oddball characters on film, played it straight as Gale Gordon's son. He went on to co-star in *Bonnie and Clyde* (1967) and dozens of cult horror-drama films.

Don Rickles: "Lucy the Fight Manager" 2-20-1967 (Eddie) Rickles' trademark insult humor is squashed on this episode.

Roy Roberts: "Lucy and the Submarine" 9-19-1966; "Lucy's Substitute Secretary" 1-2-1967 (the latter is Roberts' first appearance as semi-regular Mr. Cheever).

Edward G. Robinson: "Lucy Goes to a Hollywood Premiere" 2-7-1966 (Himself).

Kasey Rogers: "Lucy Helps Ken Berry" 2-19-1968 Rogers, best known as the second (and longer-lasting) Louise Tate on *Bewitched* (1966-'72), died in July 2006.

Mickey Rooney: "Lucy Meets Mickey Rooney" 1-24-1966 (Himself).

Dan Rowan: "Lucy and Carol in Palm Springs" 11-7-1966 Rowan was the straight man to Dick Martin's goofy comic and starred with him on the hit *Laugh-In* (1968-'73), which seriously cut into Ball's Monday night ratings. On this show, when the players' names in a golf tournament are posted, one of them is "Dick Martin." Also: "Lucy Puts Main Street on the Map" 1-30-1967 (TV Reporter).

William Schallert: "Lucy and the Little League" 4-15-1963 (Coach); "Lucy and Viv Play Softball" 10-15-1963 One of several Schallert *Lucy Show* appearances, he has been a guest star or regular on more series than just about any other actor. Perhaps he is best remembered as the father ("Martin Lane") on *The Patty Duke Show* (1963-'66). His most recent sitcom appearance was on *How I Met Your Mother* in January 2007. Schallert is 85 as of this writing, and says he never thinks about retiring, the IMDbPro reports.

Dick Shawn: "Lucy and the Pool Hustler" 1-8-1968 (Ace).

Phil Silvers: "Lucy and Phil Silvers" 12-12-1966 (Himself) As an efficiency expert, Silvers puts Lucy in charge of a toy assembly line, with predictable results.

Doris Singleton: "Lucy and Art Linkletter" 1-10-1966 (Helen Cosgrove). This is Singleton's first post-*I Love Lucy* appearance with Ball. Also: "Lucy Gets her Diploma" 10-9-1967 (Doris).

Ann Sothern: "Lucy and the Countess" 2-1-1965 The first of several episodes guest-starring Sothern as the broke Countess Framboise. Vivian Vance is not in these episodes, and Sothern was being tested as a replacement. Also: "My Fair Lucy" 2-8-1965; "Lucy and the Countess Lose Weight" 2-15-1965; "Lucy and the Old Mansion" 3-1-1965 In which Vance returned; this was the only time she acted with Sothern, and Sothern recalled there was tension on the set as a result of Vance leaving the series at the end of that season; "Lucy and the Countess Have a Horse Guest" 10-25-1965; "Lucy Helps the Countess" 11-8-1965; "Lucy and the Undercover Agent" 11-22-1965.

Robert Stack: "Lucy the Gun Moll" 3-14-1966 Stack essentially did his Elliot Ness *Untouchables* role here.

Danny Thomas: "Lucy Helps Danny Thomas" 11-1-1965 (Himself).

Mel Tormé: "Lucy in the Music World" 9-27-1965 (Mel Tinker) The first of several Tormé appearances as "struggling" songwriter Tinker. His jazzy, smooth singing voice brought Tormé the nickname "The Velvet Fog." Also: "Main Street, U.S.A" 1-23-1967 and "Lucy Puts Main Street on the Map" 1-30-1967.

Vivian Vance: "Viv Visits Lucy" 1-9-1967 (Vivian Bagley Bunson) Vance's first return after leaving *The Lucy Show* as a regular. Also: "Lucy and Viv Reminisce" 1-1-1968 Features flashbacks with Ball and Vance from the entire run of *The Lucy Show*; and "Lucy and the Lost Star" 2-26-1968.

Phil Vandervort: "Lucy Gets her Diploma" 10-9-1967 (Alan) Vandervort and Lucie Arnaz, who met on this show, would eventually marry for a short time.

Janet Waldo: "Lucy's Sister Pays a Visit" 1-7-1963 (Marge).

Clint Walker: "Lucy and the Sleeping Beauty" 11-15-1965; "Lucy and Clint Walker" 3-7-1966 (Frank) Western star Walker played Lucy's boyfriend in several episodes.

John Wayne: "Lucy and John Wayne" 11-21-1966 (Himself).

Mary Wickes: "Lucy and the Runaway Butterfly" 4-22-1963 This is Wickes' first post-*I Love Lucy* appearance. Also: "Lucy and Viv Play Softball" 10-15-1963 (Fran); "Lucy Plays Cleopatra" 9-30-1963 (Fran); "Lucy Puts out a Fire at the Bank" 12-2-1963 (Fran); "Lucy the Babysitter" 1-16-1967 (Mrs. Winslow); "Lucy and Robert Goulet" 10-30-1967 (Miss Hurlow); and "Lucy's Mystery Guess" 11-16-1967 (Aunt Agatha).

Paul Winchell: "Lucy and Paul Winchell" 10-3-1966 (Himself) Lucy ends up as ventriloquist Winchell's dummy. Literally. Also: "Main Street, U.S.A" 1-23-1967 and "Lucy Puts Main Street on the Map" 1-30-1967.

William Windom: "Lucy Digs Up a Date" 10-8-1962 (Mr. Taylor) Windom is a prolific TV actor, familiar to audiences as the star of *The Farmer's Daughter* (1963-'66), *My World and Welcome To It* (1969, based on the life and work of writer James Thurber, for which Windom won an Emmy), and *Murder, She Wrote* (1985-'96). He also guest-starred on hundreds of other series, including *The Desilu Playhouse* episode "In Close Pursuit" (1960), and was Commodore Decker on "The Doomsday Machine" episode of Desilu's *Star Trek*, which aired November 20, 1967.

Here's Lucy 1968-'74

Eddie Albert: "Lucy Gives Eddie Albert the Old Song and Dance" 10-15-1973 (Himself). Albert co-starred with Lucy in *The Fuller Brush Girl* (1950). On TV, he starred in the long-running *Green Acres* (1966-'71) as perpetually harried Oliver Douglas. Albert, who excelled at both comedy and drama in films and TV, died at the age of 99 on May 26, 2005.

Robert Alda: "Lucy, the Coed" 10-19-1970 (Dean Butler) Actor and Alan's dad. Also: "Lucy Goes Hawaiian: Parts 1 and 2" 2-15-1971 and 2-22-1971 (Captain McClay).

Patty Andrews: "Lucy and The Andrews Sisters" 10-27-1969 (Herself) In the inevitable Andrews Sisters routine, Lucy and daughter Lucie filled in for missing sisters Laverne and Maxine.

Ann-Margret: "Lucy and Ann-Margret" 2-2-1970 (Herself) The vivacious singer, dancer, and actress had only nice things to say about working with Ball.

Desi Arnaz Jr.: "Lucy and Joe Namath" 10-9-1972 (Craig Carter) Arnaz had left the show for the movies by this time, but returned for a one-shot.

Frankie Avalon: "The Carters Meet Frankie Avalon" 11-19-1973 (Himself).

Parley Baer: "Lucy's Vacation" 1-4-1971; "Lucy's Bonus Bounces" 12-27-1971 (both as Dr. Cunningham).

Jim Bailey: "Lucy and Jim Bailey" 11-6-1972 (Himself, as Phyllis Diller) Female impersonator Bailey became a friend of Lucie Arnaz.

Lucille Ball: "Lucy Carter Meets Lucille Ball" 3-4-1974 (Lucy Carter, Herself) Odd episode indicating the writers had totally run out of steam, in which Lucy Carter meets Lucille Ball. This episode was one long plug for Lucy's upcoming movie, *Mame*.

Kaye Ballard: "Lucy and Harry's Italian Bombshell" 9-27-1971 (Donna).

Jack Bannon: "Lucy, the Conclusion Jumper" 10-21-1968 (Man In Line) Bannon is the son of actress Bea Benaderet and was a regular on *Lou Grant* (1977-'82).

Jack Benny: "Lucy Visits Jack Benny" 9-30-1968; "Lucy and Jack Benny's Biography" 11-23-1970; "Lucy and Carol Burnett" 2-8-1971; "Lucy and the Celebrities" 11-8-1971 (Himself).

Milton Berle: "Lucy and the Used Car Dealer" 11-17-1969 (Cheerful Charlie) This is what you call typecasting. Also: "Milton Berle Is the Life of The Party" 2-11-1974 (Himself).

Whit Bissel: "Lucy Goes on Strike" 1-20-1969 (Ted Crystal) Bissell was a familiar character actor from movies and TV.

Lloyd Bridges: "Lucy's Big Break" 9-11-1972 (Dr. Paul Murray).

Foster Brooks: "Tipsy Through the Tulips" 11-12-1973 (David Benton Miller) Brooks was known for his comedic "drunk" act, and died in 2001.

Philip Bruns: "Lucy and the Gold Rush" 12-30-1968 (J.C. Tompkins) Bruns played the title character's father on *Mary Hartman, Mary Hartman* (1976-'77).

Victor Buono: "Lucy Gets Her Man" 2-24-1969 (Mr. Vermillion) Portly Buono is best known for the 1962 film, *Whatever Happened to Baby Jane?* and for his many appearances as the foppish King Tut on *Batman* (1966-'68).

Carol Burnett: "Lucy and Carol Burnett" 1-27-1969; "Lucy and Carol Burnett" 3-2-1970 (Herself); "Lucy and Carol Burnett" 2-8-1971 (Carol Krausmauer).

George Burns: "Lucy and Jack Benny's Biography" 11-23-1970 (Himself).

Richard Burton: "Lucy Meets the Burtons" 9-14-1970 (Himself) This casting coup was the highest rated *Here's Lucy* episode ever. Lucy gets Liz's huge diamond ring stuck on her finger after trying it on. Made headlines years after Burton's (and Ball's) deaths when his diary supposedly revealed how much he loathed working with authoritative Ball. Joyce Adams, Army

Archerd, Jim Bacon, Vernon Scott, Cecil Smith (real-life members of the Hollywood press, the latter married to Lucy's cousin, <u>Cleo Smith</u>) also played themselves in this episode.

Ruth Buzzi: "My Fair Buzzi" 12-11-1972 (Annie Whipple) Comedian Buzzi was a *Laugh-In* regular (1968-'73), and in the running for the part of Agnes Gooch in Ball's *Mame* (1974). See <u>Connell, Jane</u> for details.

Johnny Carson: "Lucy and Johnny Carson" 12-1-1969 (Himself) Lucy's mom DeDe makes a cameo in this episode, as part of the Carson *Tonight Show* audience.

Petula Clark: "Lucy and Petula Clark" 10-30-1972 British pop singer Clark played herself.

Chuck Connors: "Lucy and Chuck Connors Have a Surprise Slumber Party" 12-17-1973 (Himself). Connors was TV's *The Rifleman* (1958-'63).

Hans Conried: "Lucy and Danny Thomas" 9-10-1973 (William Barkley) Conried was a semi-regular on Thomas' TV series.

Mike Connors: "Lucy and Mannix Are Held Hostage" 10-4-1971 (Joe Mannix) Connors' series *Mannix* ran from 1967 to 1975. Lucy saved *Mannix* from cancellation during her final year as president of Desilu.

Jackie Coogan: "Lucy's Tenant" 10-22-1973 (Kermit Boswell).

<u>Carole Cook</u>: "Lucy the Crusader" 10-12-1970 (Mrs. Sheila Casten); "Lucy, Part-Time Wife" 12-14-1970 (Lillian Rylander); "Lucy and Ma Parker" 12-21-1970 (Ma Parker); "Lucy and Carol Burnett" 2-8-1971; "Lucy Carter Meets Lucille Ball" 3-4-1974 (Cynthia Duncan).

Wally Cox: "Lucy and the Ex-Con" 1-13-1969 (Rocky Barnett) Also: "Lucy and Wally Cox" 2-9-1970 (Wally Manley) Cox was known for playing "milquetoast" characters, so his character's name was an inside joke; "Lucy, the Diamond Cutter" 11-16-1970 (Gustav Vandemeer); and "Lucy Sublets the Office" 1-31-1972 (Tommy Tucker, The Toy Tycoon).

Mary Jane Croft: "A Date for Lucy" 2-10-1969 (Mary Jane Lewis, in all episodes); "Lucy Protects Her Job" 12-22-1969; "Lucy and Lawrence Welk" 1-19-1970; "Lucy the American Mother" 10-26-1970; "Lucy's Wedding Party" 11-2-1970; "Lucy Cuts Vincent's Price" 11-9-1970; "Lucy Loses Her Cool" 12-7-1970; "Lucy and Aladdin's Lamp,"2-1-1971; "Lucy and Mannix Are Held Hostage" 10-4-1971; "Won't You Calm Down, Dan Dailey?" 11-15-1971; "Lucy's Bonus Bounces" 12-27-1971; "Lucy and the Chinese Curse" 1-10-1972; "Lucy's Punctured Romance" 2-7-1972; "With Viv as a Friend, Who Needs an Enemy?" 2-14-1972; "Lucy and the Franchise Fiasco" 2-5-1973; "The Not-So-Popular Mechanics" 2-19-1973; "The Big Game' 9-17-1973; "Mary Jane's Boyfriend" 2-18-1974 The only series episode that was centered around Croft's character.

Gary Crosby: "Lucy Plays Cops and Robbers" 11-26-1973 (Officer Riggs) He is one of Bing's sons.

Robert Cummings: "Lucy's Punctured Romance" 2-7-1972 (Bob Collins). Cummings' character's name was the same as in his hit show *Love That Bob* (1955-'59). Also: "Lucy and Her Genuine Twimby" 1-15-1973 (Robert Henning).

Dan Dailey: "Won't You Calm Down, Dan Dailey?" 11-15-1970 (Himself).

John Davidson: "Lucy and the Professor" 1-29-1973 (Professor John Kleindorf).

Sammy Davis Jr.: "Lucy and Sammy Davis Jr." 9-28-1970 (Himself).

Richard Deacon: "Lucy and Carol Burnett" 2-8-1971 (Unemployment Office Clerk); "Lucy Sublets the Office" 1-31-1972 (Mr. Zelderbach).

Jack Donohue: "Where Is My Wandering Mother Tonight?" 3-11-1974 (Dirty Jack) Donohue began as a dancer in the Ziegfeld Follies and went on to choreograph, write, produce, act, and direct, including long directing stints on *The Lucy Show* and *Here's Lucy*. He died in 1984.

Totie Fields: "Lucy, the Other Woman" 10-23-1972 (The Milkman's Wife) Fields was a pioneer female stand-up comic.

Jerry Fogel: "The Carters Meet Frankie Avalon" 11-19-1973 (Emcee) Fogel played one of the kids on Desi Arnaz's sitcom *The Mothers-in-Law.*

Tennessee Ernie Ford: "Lucy and Tennessee Ernie Ford's Fun Farm" 3-10-69 (Himself).

David Frost: "Lucy Helps David Frost Go Night-Night" 11-29-1971 (Himself).

Allen Funt: "Lucy and the Candid Camera" 12-13-1971 (Himself).

Eva Gabor: "Lucy and Eva Gabor" 11-11-1968 (Eva Von Gronyitz) Gabor starred with Eddie Albert in *Green Acres* (1965-'71). Also: "Lucy and Eva Gabor Are Hospital Roomies" 9-18-1972 (Herself).

Beverly Garland: "Lucy Goes to the Air Force Academy, Part 1 and 2" 9-22-1969 and 9-29-1969 (Secretary) More familiar as a cult film and "B"-movie actress, Garland guested on *The Desilu Playhouse* episode "In Close Pursuit" (1960); co-starred on *My Three Sons* for its final three seasons; and co-starred with Kate Jackson in *Scarecrow and Mrs. King* (1983-'87).

Jack Gilford: "Lucy Helps Craig Get a Driver's License" 3-17-1969 (Wilbur Harlow) Funny-man Gilford did the well-remembered "Cracker Jack" commercials in the 1960s.

Jackie Gleason: "Lucy Visits Jack Benny" 9-30-1968 Gleason cameos as Ralph Kramden, his signature role from *The Honeymooners.*

Andy Griffith: "Lucy and Andy Griffith" 10-29-1973 (Andy Johnson).

Alan Hale Jr.: "Lucy and the Ex-Con" 1-13-1969 (Moose Manley).

Florence Halop: "Lucy, the Sheriff" 1-28-1974 (Old Woman).

Phil Harris: "Lucy and Phil Harris Strike Up the Band" 2-25-1974 (Himself) Harris was a Palm Springs golfing pal of Desi Arnaz.

Bob Hastings: "Lucy the Crusader" 10-12-1970 (Martin Phillips) Hastings was a regular on *McHale's Navy* (1962-'66) as the cowardly Lt. Carpenter, and on *All in the Family* (1973-'77) as bartender Tommy Kelsey.

Jerry Hausner: "Lucy Gives Eddie Albert the Old Song And Dance" 10-15-1973 (Jimmy) Hausner played Ricky's agent on *I Love Lucy*.

Arte Johnson: "Lucy Is a Bird-Sitter" 1-7-1974 (Sir Osbird Beechman Place).

Van Johnson: "Guess Who Owes Lucy $23.50?" 12-9-1968 (Imposter and Himself).

Kurt Kasznar: "Lucy and The Group Encounter" 12-18-1972 (Dr. Henderson) Kasznar was a regular on the cult TV series *Land of the Giants* (1968-'70).

Don Knotts: "Lucy Goes on Her Last Blind Date" 1-8-1973 (Ben Fletcher) Knotts won five Emmys playing nervous deputy Barney Fife on *The Andy Griffith Show* (1960-'65).

Jack LaLanne: "Lucy and the Bogie Affair" 12-15-1969 (Himself) LaLanne carved out a career as one of the first fitness gurus.

Elsa Lanchester: "Lucy Goes to Prison" 1-22-1973 (Mumsie Westcott).

Marc Lawrence: "Lucy and Mannix Are Held Hostage" 10-4-1971 (Rudy) Lawrence, a prolific character actor and director who appeared in close to 200 movies, mostly as a crook or thug, died November 27, 2005 at the age of 95. Among his many TV appearances was this guest role, co-starring Mike Connors as his fictional detective alter ego, Mannix. Lawrence played … what else, a gangster. He remained active in his 90s; his most recent credit was *The Shipping News* (2001).

Steve Lawrence & Eydie Gorme: "Lucy, the Peacemaker" 9-24-1973 (Themselves).

Al Lewis: "Lucy Plays Cops and Robbers" 11-26-1973 (Lionel Barker) Lewis was Grandpa on *The Munsters* (1964-'66).

Liberace: "Lucy and Liberace" 1-5-1970 (Himself) As if he could play anything else!

Art Linkletter: "Lucy Loses Her Cool" 12-7-1970 (Himself).

Rich Little: "Lucy and the Celebrities" 11-8-1971 (Himself).

Ruth McDevitt: "Lucy, the Diamond Cutter" 11-16-1970 (Mrs. Cornelius Whitmark III) Character actress McDevitt also had a small role in Lucy's film *Mame* (1974).

Ed McMahon: "Lucy and Johnny Carson" 12-1-1969 (Himself); "Lucy, the Wealthy Widow" 10-1-1973 (Ed McCallister) McMahon also co-starred in one of Lucy's TV specials, *Lucy Calls the President* (1977).

Tim Matheson: "Kim Moves Out" 1-24-1972 (Peter Sullivan) Matheson was one of the kids in Lucy's hit movie, *Yours, Mine and Ours* (1968). It was one of the first high-profile roles for the future *Animal House* star.

Marilyn Maxwell: "Lucy, the Coed" 10-19-1970 (Gloria Pendleton) Former 1950s starlet.

Jayne Meadows: "Lucy Stops a Marriage" 12-28-1970 (Laura Trenton) Jayne's sister Audrey would guest star on Ball's final series, *Life with Lucy*.

Ricardo Montalban: "Lucy and Her Prince Charming" 11-27-1972 (Prince Phillip Gregory Hennepin Of Montalbania) Montalban is best known for playing Mr. Roarke in *Fantasy Island* (1978-'84).

Gary Morton: "Lucy and The Andrews Sisters" 10-27-1969 (Announcer); "Lucy and Sammy Davis Jr." 9-28-1970 (Actor); "Lucy Makes A Few Extra Dollars" 10-18-1971 (Carnival Barker); "Lucy Carter Meets Lucille Ball" 3-4-1974 (Himself).

Joe Namath: "Lucy and Joe Namath" 10-9-1972 (Himself).

Wayne Newton: "Lucy Sells Craig to Wayne Newton" 11-25-1968; "Lucy and Wayne Newton" 2-16-1970 (Himself).

Donny Osmond: "Lucy and Donny Osmond" 11-20-1972 (Himself) Lucie Arnaz recalls that Osmond, who was 15 at the time, had a big crush on her at this time.

Lew Parker: "Mod, Mod Lucy" 9-23-1968 (Mr. Caldwell); "Lucy and Her All-Nun Band" 11-1-1971 (Mr. Adams).

Eve Plumb: "Lucy and Donny Osmond" 11-20-1972 (Patricia Carter) Plumb played Jan on *The Brady Bunch* (1969-'74).

Don Porter: "Meanwhile, Back at the Office" 1-14-1974 (Ken Richards) Porter was a regular on Ann Sothern's Desilu series *Private Secretary* and *The Ann Sothern Show* (1953-'61); played *Gidget*'s father on the Sally Field series (1965-'66); and co-starred in Lucy's film *Mame* (1974).

Vincent Price: "Lucy Cuts Vincent's Price" 11-9-1970 (Himself).

Tony Randall: "Lucy, the Mountain Climber" 9-20-1971 (Rudolph Springer III).

Elliott Reid: "Milton Berle Is the Life of the Party" 2-11-1974 (Telethon Emcee).

Charles Nelson Reilly: "Lucy the Crusader" 10-12-1970 (Elroy P. Clunck) Stage actor (who won an 1962 Tony award for *How to Succeed in Business Without Really Trying*) and a respected stage director and acting coach, Reilly is best remembered for his supporting role in the sitcom *The Ghost and Mrs. Muir* (1968-'70) and his hysterical ad-libbed game show appearances (as on *The Match Game*) in the 1970s. He died on May 29, 2007.

Stafford Repp: "Lucy and Ma Parker" 12-21-1970 (Police Detective) Repp was Chief O'Hara on the 1960s *Batman* TV series.

Buddy Rich: "Lucy and Buddy Rich" 10-5-1970 (Himself) A young Rich soloed on the drums in Tommy Dorsey's orchestra in Ball's 1943 movie, *DuBarry Was a Lady*.

Joan Rivers: "Lucy and Joan Rivers Do Jury Duty" 11-5-1973 (Herself).

Roy Roberts: "Lucy Goes to the Air Force Academy, Part 1 and 2" 9-22-1969 and 9-29-1969 (General); "Lucy and the Astronauts" 10-11-1971 (Dr. Jensen); "Lucy Goes to Prison" 1-22-1973 (Warden Magenetti); "Lucy Is N.G. as an R.N." 1-21-1974 (Dr. Honeycutt).

Ginger Rogers: "Ginger Rogers Comes to Tea" 11-22-1971 Rogers and Ball had known each other since they worked at RKO in the 1930s.

Hayden Rorke: "Lucy and The Raffle" 1-18-1971 (Judge Gibson).

Cesar Romero: "A Date For Lucy" 2-10-1969 (Tony Rivera). The suave (and gay) Romero died on January 1, 1994, at age 86. A friend of both Ball and Arnaz, he appeared in more than 100 movies, and an equal amount of TV, though best known as the Joker on *Batman*. He reportedly refused to shave his trademark mustache for the role, despite needing a heavy application of the Joker's white clown-face makeup each time he played it.

Dick Sargent: "Lucy Plays Cops and Robbers" 11-26-1973 (Officer Spencer) He was the second Darrin on *Bewitched* (1969-'72).

Reta Shaw: "Lucy and the Group Encounter" 12-18-1972 (Mrs. Rita Forrester) Portly character actress Shaw specialized in comic matrons, especially those with a haughty demeanor. Also: "Lucy's Tenant" 10-22-1973 (Mrs. Witherspoon).

Dinah Shore: "Someone's on the Ski Lift with Dinah" 10-25-1971 (Herself) Lucy guest-starred a number of times on Shore's popular daytime talk show, *Dinah!* (1974-'80).

Doris Singleton: "Mod, Mod Lucy" 9-23-1968 (Miss Singleton); "Lucy and Petula Clark" 10-30-1972; "Lucy Gives Eddie Albert the Old Song And Dance" 10-15-1973 (Eddie Albert's Secretary); "Lucy Carter Meets Lucille Ball" 3-4-1974 (Lucille Ball's Secretary).

Craig Stevens: "Dirty Gertie" 11-13-1972 (Lieutenant Egan) Stevens starred as *Peter Gunn* on TV (1958-'61).

Lyle Talbot: "Lucy Takes Over" 2-23-1970 (Harry's Lawyer) Veteran of close to 200 movies and innumerable TV shows, character actor Talbot is best known for his long stint as neighbor Joe Randolph on *The Adventures of Ozzie and Harriet* (his wife was played by longtime Lucy pal and co-star Mary Jane Croft) and for being in gonzo director Ed Wood's *Plan 9 From Outer Space* (1958). Also: "Lucy's Wedding Party" 11-2-1970 (Freddy Fox).

Elizabeth Taylor: "Lucy Meets the Burtons" 9-14-1970 (Herself).

Danny Thomas: "Lucy and Danny Thomas" 9-10-1973 (Danny Gallupi).

Mary Treen: "Lucy Fights the System" 3-18-1974 (Mary Winters) Supporting actress in hundreds of films since the 1930s, and lots of TV, Treen was a Mary Wickes-type of character actress; no great beauty, but solid and reliable no matter what the role in more than 150 movies. She died in 1989. This was the final *Here's Lucy*.

Rudy Vallee: "Lucy and Rudy Vallee" 11-30-1970 (Himself).

Vivian Vance: "Lucy, the Matchmaker" 12-16-1968; "Lucy and Lawrence Welk" 1-19-1970; "Lucy and Viv Visit Tijuana" (a.k.a. "Lucy and Vivian Vance") 1-26-1970; "Lucy Goes Hawaiian: Part 1 and 2" 2-15-1971 and 2-22-1971; "With Viv as a Friend, Who Needs an Enemy?" 2-15-1972 (all as Vivian Jones) Vance had a mastectomy and suffered a stroke shortly after her final *Here's Lucy* appearance.

Phil Vandervort: "Lucy and Rudy Vallee" 11-30-1970 (Steve); "Lucy's Replacement" 1-17-1972; (Joe Hackley); "A Home Is not an Office" 10-2-1972 (Tommy). He was Lucie Arnaz's first husband.

Lawrence Welk: "Lucy and Lawrence Welk" 1-19-1970 (Himself).

Jesse White: "The Case of the Reckless Wheelchair Driver" 10-16-1972 (Mr. Hickey) Character actor White became the Maytag repairman in a series of well-remembered commercials.

Mary Wickes: "Lucy Goes On Strike" 1-20-1969 (Isabel); "Lucy Gets Her Man" 2-24-1969 (Isabel); "Lucy and Harry's Tonsils" 10-20-1969 (Nurse); "Lucy, the Diamond Cutter" 11-

16-1970 (Mrs. Whitmark's maid); "Lucy and Her All-Nun Band" 11-1-1971 (Sister Paula Carter; Wickes played a nun in 1966's *The Trouble with Angels* and its 1968 sequel, *Where Angels Go, Trouble Follows*, and a *singing* nun in both *Sister Act* movies, 1992 and 1993); "Lucy's Big Break" 9-11-1972 (Nurse Sylvia Ogilvy); "Lucy and Eva Gabor Are Hospital Roomies" 9-18-1972 (Nurse); "Lucy Plays Cops and Robbers" 11-26-1973 (Violet Barker); "Lucy, the Sheriff" 1-28-1974 (Clara Simpson).

Flip Wilson: "Lucy and Flip Go Legit" 9-13-1971 (Himself).

Shelley Winters: "Lucy and Miss Shelley Winters" 10-14-1968 (Shelley Summers).

Life with Lucy 1986

Dick Gautier: "Lucy Gets Her Wires Crossed" 10-18-86 (Fred Dunlap) Gautier was the lovable Hymie the Robot for three years on *Get Smart* (1966-'69).

Peter Graves: "Love Among the Two-by-Fours" 10-4-86 (Ben Matthews) The *Mission: Impossible* star (1967-'73) played a credible love interest for Grandma Lucy.

Dave Madden: "Lucy Makes Curtis Byte the Dust" 11-1-86 (Stanley Bigelow) Madden was a regular cast member on *Laugh-In* (1968-'69), *The Partridge Family* (1970-'74), and *Alice* (1978-'85). *Alice* was written and produced by *I Love Lucy* scribes Bob Carroll Jr. and Madelyn Davis.

Audrey Meadows: "Mother of the Bride" 11-15-86 (Audrey) The Emmy-winning Alice of *The Honeymooners* (1955-'56) brought a much-needed lift to this sagging series, and she and Ball performed well together; there was talk of Meadows becoming a regular on the show, but by then the show's fate was sealed. This was the final episode aired.

John Ritter: "Lucy Makes a Hit with John Ritter" 9-27-96 (Himself) Ritter was one of Ball's favorite slapstick comedians, and she lets him have it in this physical episode.

GUILAROFF, SIDNEY

Hairdresser to the stars, Guilaroff coiffed many of classic Hollywood's best-known and beloved leading ladies, including Lucille Ball. He was the head hairdresser at the MGM studios beginning in 1935. Ball was a natural brunette, and had been a blonde early in her Hollywood career. She was rechristened a redhead when she was signed by MGM in the early 1940s and cast as the lead in her first Technicolor movie, *DuBarry Was a Lady* (1943).

The color was brassy red, but it wasn't until *Ziegfeld Follies* (1946) that Guilaroff "dyed Ball's hair that famous golden red," as he put it in a 1996 interview. "I felt she needed to stand out [from her apricot costume] so I mixed a variety of hair dyes into a henna rinse that transformed her into a shimmering golden redhead." That color (longtime hairstylist Irma Kusely called it apricot) became Ball's trademark for the rest of her career.

Guilaroff wrote a dishy memoir in 1996, *Crowning Glory: Reflections of Hollywood's Favorite Confidant*. The very first hairdresser listed in a film's credits, Guilaroff worked on more than 2,000 films.

See also <u>Hair Color</u>, <u>Henna Rinse</u>, <u>Kusely, Irma</u>, and <u>Wigged Out</u>.

H

HAIR COLOR

Born a brunette, Lucille Ball was turned into a platinum blonde by Hattie Carnegie, the New York designer for whom Ball modeled in the late 1920s and early 1930s. Carnegie thought Ball resembled (then-blonde) actress Joan Bennett, a Carnegie client. Her hair remained blonde and became gradually darker (brownish) until she arrived at MGM in the 1940s. It was there that famous hair designer Sydney Guilaroff created the flaming red-orange shade with which Ball became forever identified. Ball herself said her career was basically blah until she became a redhead, and then things took off.

In her book, *The Encyclopedia of Hair: A Cultural Study*, Victoria Sherrow writes that, "Red hair became more popular in the twentieth century both in Europe and the United States. Some historians say that color films and television [i.e., Ball?] played a key role, since blond and red shades show up well in those media. Other analysts point out that red hair was often associated with a passionate personality type." This begs the fascinating question: which came first: Lucy Ricardo's red hair or her passionate desire to get out of the house and into show business?

Finally, Sherrow notes, "Studies have show that, in general, female actors with red hair tend to be more popular with audiences than male actors with this hair color."

Ball's longtime hair stylist, Irma Kusely, had her own opinion of the color of Ball's hair: "[It's] apricot, but a lot of people think of it as red. It's not red at all," she told Emmy archivist Karen Herman in 2001. "It's a golden apricot color. [I used] regular hair dye when I did her own hair. And then I used a henna rinse as a balance, which she was famous for. She had a safe [full] of [henna] in my garage. She loved to gamble, and when we did a show in Las Vegas, she met a very wealthy sheikh and he heard about her [need for] henna, and said he would send her the henna. And he did.... There was a lot of it left when she left this world, but I had to give it to the estate because it wasn't mine. I don't know what little Lucie did with it, maybe sold it for a million dollars. Just for a spoonful, can you imagine what I could've made with that?"

See also the entries <u>Guilaroff, Sydney</u>; <u>Henna Rinse</u>, <u>Kusely, Irma</u>; and <u>Wigged Out</u>.

HALL, ALEXANDER

Hall was a film editor and director from the 1930s through the 1950s who had a serious relationship with Ball. Hall was known for a string of light comedies in the 1940s. Perhaps the best of these is *Here Comes Mr. Jordan* (1941), a charming fable about a boxer who, having died before his time, is given another chance at life in a different body by his guardian angel. It has been remade twice: *Heaven Can Wait* (1978) with Warren Beatty and *Down to Earth* (2001) with comedian Chris Rock.

Hall's long-term relationship with Ball began in 1937 and ended when she met Desi Arnaz. Hall was nearly 20 years older than Ball, but that did not seem to be an impediment. They were seen and photographed all over Hollywood, sharing a shrimp cocktail, attending a premiere, at The Brown Derby, and so on. Hall directed Ball and Arnaz's final film, *Forever Darling* (1956, coincidentally another guardian angel picture), which was also his last directorial effort. He died in 1968.

HARPER, VALERIE

Four-time Emmy-winning comedian for her portrayal of neurotic Rhoda Morgenstern, first on *The Mary Tyler Moore Show* (1970-'74) and then on her own spin-off *Rhoda* (1974-'78). Early in her career, Harper danced in the chorus of several Broadway musicals, including Lucille Ball's *Wildcat* (1960). Vivian Vance made one of her final television appearances in an episode of *Rhoda*, playing Rhoda's new neighbor. Harper was one of the celebrities saluting Ball in song when the redhead was presented with the Kennedy Center Honor in 1986. See also <u>Wildcat</u> under <u>Stage Career</u>.

HART, RALPH

Good-natured blond child actor who played Vivian Bagley's son, Sherman, on *The Lucy Show* (1962-'65). He was out of a job when Vivian Vance (who played Bagley) decided not to return as a regular for the 1965-'66 season. Vance had advised Hart's mother not to allow her son a career in show business. He took a few more professional acting jobs after The *Lucy Show* (on *The Outer Limits* and *My Three Sons*) and then apparently left show business. Website IMDbpro.com notes that as of 1999, Hart was working as hydrogeologist in California.

HAUSNER, JERRY

Hausner appeared on *I Love Lucy* during its first three seasons as Ricky Ricardo's agent. Desi Arnaz fired him after an intense argument over a missed cue during the filming of the episode "Fan Magazine Interview" (episode 83, February 8, 1954). Hausner remained bitter about it the rest of his life. However, he did guest-star in small parts on Arnaz's *The Mothers-in-Law* (1969) and *Here's Lucy* (1973), and performed a number of bit parts on *The Dick Van Dyke Show* (1962-'63), a series filmed at Desilu Studios. He subsequently voiced characters for the successful United Artists' *Mr. Magoo* cartoon (1953-'59). He passed away in 1993.

HENNA RINSE

A rinse that colors and conditions the hair, made from the *Lawsonia inermis* plant, which "grows in hot climates and is indigenous to North Africa, the Middle East, and possibly India," according to Victoria Sherrow in *The Encyclopedia of Hair: A Cultural Study*. Often associated with the ancient Egyptians, who used it to color hair, cure hair loss, and as make-up, henna has been in use for more than 6,000 years. Ball, who used henna to get her unique red hair color, popularized the use of it through the many references and jokes about her "henna rinse" on *I Love Lucy*.

HERE'S LUCY

Debuted: September 13, 1968, Monday night, 8:30 p.m., CBS
Final Airing: March 18, 1974, Monday night, 9:00 p.m., CBS
Stars: Lucille Ball (Lucille Carter); Gale Gordon (Harry Carter); Lucie Arnaz (Kim Carter); Desi Arnaz Jr. (Craig Carter); Mary Jane Croft (Mary Jane Lewis)
Awards: Nominated for two Emmys (Gordon for Outstanding Performance by an Actor in a Supporting Role in Comedy) and writers Bob Carroll Jr. and Madelyn Pugh Davis for Outstanding Writing Achievement in Comedy (for "Lucy Meets the Burtons"), both in 1971; and Ball received two Golden Globe nominations for Best TV Actress/Musical Comedy, in 1970 and 1972.
Based On: The premise and plots for *Here's Lucy* were heavily "borrowed" from Ball's other shows, and were basically "Lucy gets into trouble" plopped into a new setting. This one had

Ball widowed with two children, played by her real-life children (Desi Jr. only stayed for three seasons) and working for her brother-in-law (Gordon) at the Unique Employment Agency. To its credit, at least the situation gave Lucy ample opportunity to find herself in strange spots and commit her trademark slapstick. Croft took over as the "best friend" from Vivian Vance, who guest-starred six times through the 1972 season.

Ratings: The ratings for *Here's Lucy* started relatively low, for Ball; very high for anyone else (No. 9 for the 1968-'69 debut season), and improved for the next two seasons (No. 6 in 1969-'70 and No. 3 in 1970-'71, no doubt helped by the Richard Burton/Elizabeth Taylor appearance in the season opener). Then they went steadily down (No. 11 in 1971-'72, No. 15 in 1972-'73, and No. 29 in 1973-'74, after which Ball quit the weekly series grind). It should be noted that a show positioned at No. 29 as of this writing (2007) would be considered a minor hit.

Trivia: Ball broke her leg skiing before the fifth season began, and played half the episodes in a leg cast.

The problems in Ball's third half-hour sitcom were the same as in the latter years of *The Lucy Show*, but amplified: the Lucy character has no one to play off except Gordon, and the banter between them gets tired after one episode. How many times can you see Lucy jump and drop something as Uncle Harry enters? Or try to hide the fact that she's destroyed his favorite desk/office/plant? Or ruin his suit with a squirting pen/pie/you-fill-in-the-blank? Vance's presence was sorely missed.

The Lucy Carter character was idiotic, sympathetic, smart, dumb, clever, and nonsensical, sometimes all in the same episode. The writers cobbled together old routines and bits whenever they could. The most successful and best-known episode, guest-starring Richard Burton and Elizabeth Taylor (September 14, 1970), recycled an *I Love Lucy* gag for the big finale. Lucy gets Taylor's huge diamond ring stuck on her finger and has to substitute her hand for Liz's through a curtain at a big press conference; On *I Love Lucy*'s "The Handcuffs" (October 6, 1952), Lucy Ricardo playfully handcuffs herself to Ricky and then can't get unattached; she ends up behind the curtain as he performs "Santiago Chile," doing a similar hand/arm substitution routine. When all was lost, the *Here's Lucy* writers had the cast stage a show. Still, as noted by the generally decent ratings, audiences would watch Ball in almost anything.

The kids' characters were not written with any personalities, leaving Lucie and Desi Jr. operating on pure charm. The only "character development" that occurred during the series involved Lucie, who steadily became more and more polished as a comic/musical performer.

In fact, she eventually carried entire episodes with charm to spare. Desi Jr. left after the third season to pursue a movie career.

Ball's plan, she revealed to AP writer Cynthia Lowry in 1969, at the start of the show's second season, was to keep her children in the show "for three years. That's enough for experience and enough to build up enough shows for syndication later [actually, three years at that point wasn't enough, but the show went on for six, so it's a moot point]. I wanted them in the show for the same reason I want them out of it after three years. Then they can decide what comes next." She hoped it would be college if that's what they wanted.

Ball brushed off "carelessly" questions about *Laugh-In*, her toughest TV competition ever, probably because her show remained high on the charts until its final season. The coming summer, Lowry reported, Ball and company would move out of the studio to film the show in distant locales. "It gives the show a new look and does something for the performances," noted its star.

HIRSCHFELD, AL

The famous Broadway and Hollywood caricaturist Al Hirschfeld was also known as "The Line King" for his masterful way of capturing the essence of a subject in pen and ink. Performers considered it the highest honor to show up in one of the master's drawings. He died at the age of 99 in January 2003. Hirschfeld did many drawings of Ball at various stages of her career. The following list is as complete as possible, but there are probably more Hirschfeld "Lucys" out there, according to the artist's archivist, David Leopold.

For MGM:
1943: 34 Portraits from *Thousands Cheer*, including Lucille Ball
1943: Publicity Campaign: *Best Foot Forward*
1944: MGM Map of the USA
1944: Campaign: *Meet the People*
1940s: Lucille Ball in Headdress, circa 1945
1946: Campaign: *The Ziegfeld Follies*

For Other Studios:
1960: *The Facts Of Life* with Bob Hope and Lucille Ball, 1960
1974: Lucille Ball in *Mame*, 1974

For CBS Nationwide Newspaper Inserts:

1962: CBS's New Season: Garry Moore, Lucille Ball, Vivian Vance, Danny Thomas, Andy Griffith, and Don Knotts

1962: Specials on CBS

1963: CBS's New Season, 1963: Phil Silvers, Lucille Ball, Garry Moore, Danny Thomas, Jack Benny, Andy Griffith

For Publications:

4/30/54: Lucille Ball & Desi Arnaz in *I Love Lucy*, *Colliers*

10/29/54: TV Totem Pole, Gouache, *Colliers* cover, 10/29/54

5/27/55: Television Personalities, *Colliers*

11/2/57: Lucille Ball, Gouache, *TV Guide*

12/11/60: *Wildcat* with Keith Andes, Lucille Ball, Don Tomkins, *The New York Times*

3/3/74: Lucille Ball and Robert Preston in *Mame*, *The New York Times*

1975: Lucille Ball with Fur Stole and Purse, for limited-edition lithograph

1985: Lucille Ball in *I Love Lucy* from Viacom (syndication); included Desi Arnaz

1986: Kennedy Center Honorees: Lucille Ball, Yehudi Menuhin, Jessica Tandy, Hume Cronyn, Ray Charles, Anthony Tudor

1989: Lucille Ball and Desi Arnaz

1989: *I Love Lucy* with Lucille Ball and Desi Arnaz, for limited-edition lithograph

6/1/98: Top 100 Artists and Entertainers of the 20th Century: Lucille Ball, Steven Spielberg, Bob Dylan, and Picasso, Gouache, for *TIME* magazine cover

6/98: Top 100 Artists and Entertainers of the 20th Century: Lucille Ball, Steven Spielberg, Charlie Chaplin, Louis Armstrong, and Picasso, Gouache, unpublished *TIME* magazine cover

Dates Unknown:

Lucille Ball and Desi Arnaz, watercolor

Lucy and Desi with Lucille Ball and Desi Arnaz [sic]

Information copyright © Al Hirschfeld. Courtesy of the Al Hirschfeld Archives.

Update As of this printing, Hirschfeld's works had dramatically risen in value beginning a mere eight months after he passed away, as a result of most being limited editions. Plus, Hirschfeld's own celebrity added to those he drew. According to his official gallery, Margo

Feiden in New York, prints that used to run $70 to $150 in the 1970s fetch as much as $10,000, and original drawings can go as high as $35,000.

I bought a print of the 1975 litho described above (Ball in fur and purse) when I first moved to New York in the early 1980s. Alex Goodstadt, of the George J. Goodstadt gallery in Ridgefield, Connecticut—which also sells authorized Hirschfeld lithos—wrote to me in June 2004 after I'd sent her a picture of it: "We are happy that you have such a fine 'vintage' etching from our collection of editions. We are happy also to inform you that this particular print is sold out, but the last one sold for $4,500. If we had one available today for sale it would probably be in the $8,000-$10,000 range." That's probably a low-ball estimate now.

HOLDEN, WILLIAM

The Oscar-winning actor made 80 films and co-starred with Ball in 1948's *Miss Grant Takes Richmond*.

Holden also made a rare television appearance on *I Love Lucy*, and the episode ("L.A. at Last," February 7, 1955) is one of the series' best remembered. When the Ricardos and the Mertzes arrive in L.A., Ricky has to go to the studio, so the others immediately head for the famous Brown Derby restaurant and some star spotting. Who should sit in the next booth but William Holden?

Soon tiring of Lucy Ricardo's manic staring, Holden decides to turn the tables and stare at her. The result: Lucy can't concentrate on her meal (at one hilarious point, Ethel has to cut her spaghetti with a pair of manicure scissors) and, embarrassed, leaves the Derby in a rush—but not before spilling a platter of pies on Holden.

Later that day: Guess which movie star Ricky's invited to the hotel? Bill Holden, of course, and the shenanigans Lucy goes through to disguise herself from Holden, including a putty nose that accidentally catches fire, are some of Ball's best comedy moments.

♥ **Lucy Trivia** Ball, Gale Gordon, and guest stars Johnny Carson and Ed McMahon did a minor recreation of the Brown Derby scene in a 1969 *Here's Lucy* episode. In it, Lucy gets excited to see Gregory Peck and Cary Grant while dining with Carson and McMahon (she won a Stump the Band contest on Carson's *Tonight Show*), and jumps up, knocking a plate full of dishes, food and liquids on the unruffled Carson. It can't hold a candle to the original.

HOLDING MY OWN IN NO MAN'S LAND

Book by film and culture critic Molly Haskell published in the late 1990s. Subtitled "Women and Men and Film and Feminists," the book posits the thesis that Ball (as her "Lucy" character) "cut a wide swath through the [formerly exclusive] preserves of maledom," from husband Ricky (dubbed her "sweet sitting-duck Babalu husband") to various Hollywood male icons such as John Wayne and William Holden. Haskell also wrote an appreciative essay on Ball for the Museum of Television and Radio's (now known as The Paley Center for Media) tribute booklet *Lucille Ball: The First Lady of Comedy* in 1984.

HOLLYWOOD BOND CAVALCADE

In 1943, the cavalcade crossed the country as part of a massive war bond-selling campaign. Lucille Ball was among the traveling stars.

HOLLYWOOD VICTORY CARAVAN

The caravan toured the United States in the early 1940s entertaining in major cities to raise money for the army and navy relief funds. A few dozen stars participated, including Desi Arnaz and Bob Hope.

HOLLYWOOD WALK OF FAME

Tourist attraction in Hollywood that places the names of stars from all walks of entertainment along with symbols of their specialty (i.e., a microphone if they starred on radio) inside five-pointed stars in plaques on Hollywood Boulevard. The specialty icon and name are in bronze; the rest of the star is pink terrazzo outlined in bronze. All the *I Love Lucy* principals have stars; Arnaz and Ball have two each. Interestingly, William Frawley's star is for his movie career, not his extensive television career. The stars can be found at:

Desi Arnaz' stars: Motion pictures, 6325½ Hollywood Boulevard; Television, 6254 Hollywood Boulevard

Lucille Ball stars: Motion Pictures, 6346 Hollywood Boulevard; Television, 6100 Hollywood Boulevard

William Frawley star: Motion Pictures, 6322 Hollywood Boulevard

Vivian Vance star: Television, 7000 Hollywood Boulevard

OPE, BOB

American comedic institution in vaudeville and then films from the mid-1930s, Hope's greatest impact came on television. He had a decades-long, fruitful relationship with NBC, which aired his poignant overseas trips to entertain the troops in Vietnam in the 1960s as well as innumerable, popular specials from the early 1950s on.

Hope co-starred with Ball in four films (He said 1960's *The Facts of Life* was his favorite) and many television specials. Their personalities meshed nicely and both were skillful physical comics. An early Ball connection of Hope's: He co-starred with Ethel Merman and Jimmy Durante in the Broadway musical *Red, Hot and Blue* (1936) which featured an up-and-coming bit player named Vivian Vance as a reporter. Vance and Hope's future wife, Dolores, also sang on the same New York supper-club circuit.

Later, on one of his many variety appearances in the 1950s, Hope played Ricky Ricardo—with Desi Arnaz playing Fred Mertz, and Ball and Vance in their traditional roles—in a take-off of *I Love Lucy*. A highlight was a smoldering kiss between Ethel and her newly handsome "Fred." Hope also contributed a memorable guest-star turn on *I Love Lucy*.

Ball guest-starred on many of Hope's specials through the 1960s and 1970s, and Hope made a cameo on *The Lucy Show* in 1964. A few months after Ball's death in 1989, Hope created a 90-minute tribute to her featuring many of their variety-show appearances, called *Bob Hope's Love Affair with Lucy*. He was one of the hosts on *CBS Salutes Lucy: The First 25 Years* (1976) and he was with Ball as a presenter at the Oscars for her last public appearance on March 29, 1989.

Shortly after Ball's death, reporters looking for quotes and stories sought out Hope. He didn't disappoint. Noting that Ball "was the First Lady of television and may never be surpassed," he added that she was one of his favorite co-stars, someone who "never let me down." They met in the 1940s when Ball persuaded Hope to use Arnaz's orchestra in his act, replacing the departing Stan Kenton.

And he told a touching, if dated, anecdote that illustrated Ball's worldwide fame back in the 1950s: "Something she got the biggest kick out of happened years ago in Japan. Lucy and Desi went to this little restaurant way up on a mountain. They drove for hours. And it was this little shack of a place, but it had a TV antenna. And an elderly Japanese gentleman greeted them, blurting out, [keep in mind the era] 'I ruv rucy!' It just put her away."

Hope died shortly after his 100th birthday in July 2003.

HOPPER, HEDDA

Golden Age gossip columnist Hopper, along with rival Louella Parsons, ruled the Hollywood roost for decades. A complicated character, Hedda began her career as an actress and starred in more than 100 films, beginning in the silent era, and her carefully cultivated upper crust diction carried her nicely into talkies, up through the early 1940s. She and Ball both appeared in *Bunker Bean* (1936), and Hopper appeared as herself in one of Ball's starring vehicles, *That's Right, You're Wrong* (1939).

When movie work dried up, she reinvented herself as a columnist and became a powerful voice to average Americans agog with the antics of the movie community. Many stars curried her favor, but Ball appears to have genuinely liked her and became a close friend. Hopper appeared on *I Love Lucy* (during the Ricardos' trip to Hollywood) in the aptly titled "The Hedda Hopper Story" (1955), in which Lucy tries to drum up some publicity for Ricky. She made another appearance in the debut *Lucy-Desi Comedy Hour* episode, "Lucy Takes a Cruise to Havana" (1957), also as herself. The mother of actor William Hopper (*Perry Mason*), she died in 1966.

"HORSES AND WATER"

In her early attempts to make a splash in show business, Ball was at one time enrolled at John Murray Anderson's dramatic school in New York. She told the story that the admissions director asked her what her prior experience was. "School plays and summer stock," was her nervous reply. Then the diction coach ordered her to say "Horses and water." Ball complied, offering "Horr-ses and watt-er," in the flat accent of western New York State, where she grew up. Ball says the diction coach shuddered, and for the next six months her nickname was "Miss Horr-ses and Watt-er."

HOT AND COLD

At the height of their popularity in the 1950s, Ball said there was only one thing that she and Arnaz couldn't agree on: the temperature. "Desi is a great thermostat sneaker-upper, and I'm a thermostat sneaker-downer. Cold is the one thing that isn't great with him."

HOTEL DEL CORONADO

Located in San Diego, this National Historic Landmark hotel has been the host to society, showbiz, and political notables for more than 100 years (It's also reputed to be haunted)—

and it was the setting for the comedy *Some Like it Hot* (1960). Lucille Ball and Desi Arnaz rehearsed the pilot episode of *I Love Lucy* here with Arnaz's friend, Pepito the Clown. Arnaz and *Lucy* film editor Dann Cahn came to the Coronado in 1956 to re-edit and reshoot *Forever Darling* after its initial test screening. See <u>Forever Darling</u> for the full story.

HOW TO CAST AN ESKIMO

Saxophonist Anthony Ortega recalled an unusual request from 1974, for an interview 20 years later by Steven L. Isoardi for the University of California Department of Special collections: "[Lucille Ball's musical director] Marl Young (See <u>Young, Marl</u>) called me one day. He said, 'Hey, Tony. How would you like to play an Eskimo on *The Lucy Show?* I was thrilled but yet insulted at the same time (*laughs*). You called me to play an Eskimo? … An Eskimo (*more laughter*)? So I said, oh, yeah. Sure, man. I'll do it…. I had a few lines."

Phil Harris was the guest star on this episode, which aired during the final season of *Here's Lucy*. When Ortega was asked to do the show, it was likely phrased to mean the current Ball series, i.e., the *Lucy* show that's on CBS.

Ortega continued, "So it ended up that we walked into the studio to do the prerecording, Henry Miranda, who play[ed] a Mexican guy, myself—I played Ooka Lanooka the Eskimo—Phil Harris, and Lucy. We were all walking in to do the prerecording, and sitting in the studio in the sax section was Jackie Kelso and Ted Nash. They were looking at me and … they were laughing. But I felt pretty good about it, because I'm walking in the studio with Lucy, and we were going to go into the booth. You know … like, I'm an actor now, man. And I was wearing my combat boots. I almost stepped on Lucy's toe in the booth there.

"After the thing was over she gave me a kiss on the cheek, and she said, 'Oh, you did a good job. I must tell you, though, when I first saw you I thought to myself, "Where in the heck did they find this guy?" And I hear that you are a very fine saxophone player.' I guess Marl Young had probably told her that.

"This was her final series, so I got in on the tail end. But that was a real kick. In fact, I still have the script, 'Lucy and Phil Harris Strike Up the Band,' January 9, 1974," Ortega noted. This was Harris' second appearance with Lucy; he also guest-starred on a 1968 episode of *The Lucy Show*. The episode of *Here's Lucy* that Ortega talks about aired on February 25, 1974, and was indeed in the tail end of the final season.

For the full text of the interview with Ortega, visit the University of California's Special Collections online, at www.oac.cdlib.org/texts/and type in "Anthony Ortega" in the search field.

HUNT, FRED

Lucille Ball's maternal grandfather was an opinionated socialist and not very effective at providing a serene life for his family. When Ball, her brother Fred, her mother, and stepfather were all living at his house in Celeron, New York, a neighborhood child, Warner Erikson, was paralyzed in 1927 by an accidental shot from a gun Hunt had given Fred for his birthday (Erikson died five years later). The resulting publicity and lawsuit forced Hunt to sell his house and enter bankruptcy. He was even jailed for a time. This was referred to in the family as "the break-up," because they had to split and never lived together in one place again.

Hunt was not the same after the incident, and Ball began to feel responsible for the old man, who worked odd jobs around the Celeron area. She eventually persuaded him to move to California, where he read *The Daily Worker* incessantly and pressured Lucy, her brother, and mother to register as Communist Party members—a decision that would come back to haunt Ball during the Red Scare of the 1950s (see FBI File for details). He died in 1944.

I

ICON

In a 2001 *New York Times* article celebrating American landmarks, writer Rick Lyman focused on Hollywood Boulevard in California. Noting that no big star would be caught dead in sleazy downtown Hollywood, Lyman also pointed out that the fabled street remains a huge tourist draw, not least because of landmarks like Grauman's Chinese Theatre (renamed Mann's Chinese Theatre from 1973 to 2001) and the Hollywood Walk of Fame.

He noted, "At souvenir shops all along the street, and there are dozens of them, it is easy to see from the faces emblazoned on the T-shirts which icons still speak most loudly to the passing parade; Marilyn Monroe, of course, but also Lucille Ball, Betty Boop, James Dean and The Three Stooges."

See also my book, *The Comic DNA of Lucille Ball: Interpreting the Icon.*

IDEAL MAN

United Press syndicated an item headlined "Lucille's Ideal" in 1940 in which Ball talks about her perfect guy: "About all I would ask of a man is that he be interesting, have a grand sense of humor, and be a ready conversationalist. I'd like him to be intelligent, able to talk on a variety of subjects, but not necessarily be brilliant … capable of earning a good living [but not] so eager to become wealthy that he gave over all his life and thoughts to that aim."

I LOVE LUCY

Debuted: October 15, 1951, 9:00 p.m., CBS
Final Airing: May 6, 1957, 9:00 p.m., CBS
Stars: Lucille Ball (Lucille McGillicuddy Ricardo); Desi Arnaz (Ricky Ricardo); Vivian Vance (Ethel Louise Mae Roberta Potter Mertz); William Frawley (Frederick "Fred" Hobart Edie Mertz)
Awards: Emmy for Best Situation Comedy in 1953, 1954, and 1955; Emmy for Best Comedienne, 1953 (Lucille Ball); Emmy for Best Series Supporting Actress (Vance),

1954; Emmy for Best Actress, Continuing Performance, 1956 (Ball); Voted No. 2 on *TV Guide*'s list of the Top 50 Shows of All Time; inducted into the ATAS Television Academy Hall of Fame in 1992, the only show thus honored (Ball and Arnaz are also in the Hall of Fame).

Based On: The premise for *I Love Lucy* was heavily "borrowed" from Ball's hit radio show, <u>*My Favorite Husband*</u>, by head writer/producer Jess Oppenheimer and writers Bob Carroll Jr. and Madelyn Pugh Davis; on occasion entire episodes from *Husband* were rewritten or reworked for *I Love Lucy*. One major change: Lucy insisted her real-life Cuban husband, Desi Arnaz, play the husband role, replacing Richard Denning from the radio show. It was the first interracial marriage depicted on television, but caused nary a bleep on anyone's radar, perhaps because the show was an instant hit and viewers fell in love with Lucy (and all those associated with her) at first sight.

Ratings: *I Love Lucy* was never lower than No. 3 in the ratings (during the first season, 1951-'52), and except for the 1955-'56 season, when it was No. 2 (thanks to *The $64,000 Question*), it was the No. 1 show on TV (1952-'53, 1953-'54, 1954-'55, and 1956-'57) throughout its run. It is one of only a handful of shows to leave the air while it was No. 1.

Picture this: a Cuban bandleader in 1950s Manhattan—not struggling, not super successful—has a scheming, redheaded wife who wants to get into show business any way she can. Their best friends are a more mature couple who are also their landlords. Each week, the conflicts center on the redhead's scheming, and the husband's frustration at extricating her from said shenanigans. Would you watch that show? Doesn't it sound like the basic plot of dozens and dozens of sitcoms you've seen throughout TV history?

That's because it's the basic plot of the most influential sitcom in TV history, *I Love Lucy*, which shaped every other situation comedy that followed (see <u>The I Love Lucy Influence</u>).

Here's what it was like, according to two people who were there: Dann Cahn, the film editor for *I Love Lucy*'s entire run, and William Asher, who directed most of the episodes. I spoke to both in Jamestown during the 2005 and 2006 Lucy festivals.

Cahn got the job through his friend, Asher. Asher was initially approached about the editing job, but he'd already graduated to directing, and recommended Cahn for the position; they'd interned together in the production department at Universal.

Cahn recalled, "The first half-hour show, we shot four cameras on it. After that show, we dispensed with the fourth camera and it became a three-camera show, because it suited our purposes to have one camera getting a master, or full shot, of the scene, and the other two cameras getting over-the-shoulder, or medium shots, and close-ups." Cahn was the person who (along with assistant Bud Molin) edited the multiple camera scenes together on a unique moviola device created for Desilu, which Cahn jokingly referred to as the three-headed monster. It now rests at The Lucille Ball-Desi Arnaz Center in Jamestown.

Cahn knows that "The reason for my success in editing the show was getting a good handle on the three-camera editing technique, and quickly. As for Arnaz's input, he and Jess [Oppenheimer, a producer as well as head writer] usually went over the scenes to determine the exact edits—with Desi and Lucy's approval, of course."

The mood during the first executive screening was tense. A lot of money had been invested, and careers were on the line, says Cahn: "I remember sitting in the projection booth, and it was very quiet after we ran it. We had all these advertising people there, and all the CBS executives along with Jess. No one said a word after we ran that first picture. Lucy broke the silence, and she said, 'Danny, that's a good first cut.' Then everyone chimed in and said, 'Yeah, the picture looked really great.'"

When Cahn realized he and Molin would need help to get a finished product filmed, edited, copied, and distributed each week, he asked Arnaz to hire his friend Quinn Martin (who later married Ball's writer, Madelyn Pugh) to be the sound editor. Arnaz joked to Cahn that his editing department would soon be as big as his band, but the joke became a prophecy one year later.

I Love Lucy was that rare series: an immediate hit. The power of that "little box in the living room" was a surprise in those first years of television, and eye opening, according to Ball in an interview with *U.S. News & World Report* on September 22, 1986: "I remember when we took our first tour and saw how people reacted. We'd made an instant, into-their-living-room connection. The closeness with the audience was unbelievable. I'd been in pictures for 12 years or more and made 40 or 50, and most people hardly knew who I was. Then after three months on TV, everybody in the country knew us and felt so close to us. That has never changed."

Asher came to the series in its second year; the first episode he directed was "Job Switching" (a.k.a. "The Candy Factory"), which is often cited as *the* classic *I Love Lucy* episode. Asher stayed on to direct another 105 episodes. He helped launch *Make Room for Daddy* and *Those Whiting Girls* for Desilu, and is perhaps best known as the creative force and director behind *Bewitched* (1964-'72; he was also married to the show's star, Elizabeth Montgomery, at the time).

I Love Lucy was a family affair; Ball loved to put her family and people she'd worked with previously into positions at Desilu. Even Asher's first wife, Danny Sue Nolan, was put to work, playing the MGM secretary in the William Holden L.A. episode. Asher himself had a walk-on in the Richard Widmark Hollywood episode. Still, families argue, and everyone found him or herself in the hot seat at one time or another.

Asher, for example, found out on his first day of work that rumors of Ball "testing" co-workers to see how much moxie they had were true. Asher remembers the encounter as Lucy giving him too much direction. "Lucy," Asher recalled saying during a Jamestown seminar, "'There's one director here and that's me, and you're paying me to do it. If you want to direct, go ahead, and you won't have to pay anyone!' Lucy broke down in tears and ran off the set, and I retired to the men's room—I didn't yet have an office! I finally returned to the set and met Desi, who started yelling at me in Spanish, until I said, 'Desi, give it to me in English, please.' After hearing the story, Desi was very understanding, and agreed with me, but told me 'to find Lucy in her dressing room and bring her back to the set.' I did, she and I hugged and cried for a few minutes; then Lucy pulled herself together and went back to work. After that," Asher concluded, "I never had another problem with Lucy."

One of Cahn's most important bits of business was editing the episodes so they'd fit the required running time (about 25 minutes with commercials, to fill a half hour). The problem was, the show was too funny, and audience laughter and reaction would inevitably stretch it three or four minutes longer than it was supposed to be. Cahn needed to trim these laughs very carefully in order to preserve the momentum of the show. He was a success—CBS and the William Morris Agency both hired Desilu for production responsibilities on other shows.

"What stands out the most for me," says Cahn, "is editing *The I Love Lucy Movie*. The success of the show inspired Desi to string three episodes together and release it as a feature film." Cahn was the logical choice to edit it (see *The I Love Lucy Movie*: Lost … and Found!).

Cahn's personal favorite *Lucy* scene is "Vitameatavegamin. When she gets progressively drunk, I thought it was a memorable piece of acting above and beyond the pratfalls and the pies in the face and all the obvious things. Being onstage all by herself with no cards or anything, it stands out. I also loved the bread-making episode, and the ones where we went cross-country and they decided to open the show up, instead of just three walls, so we could go outside."

Asher said this about Ball: "She was a great gal, and a great lady. As a comedian, she was a natural. Her instincts were sharp, and she loved to work. She worked to perfection in all she did." That included after she found herself pregnant following the first season. According to Asher, when "you discover your leading lady is in the *family way*," it became a juggling act—once Desi fixed it so that the pregnancy could be part of the show, a first for a nationally broadcast series—to film as many episodes as possible before Lucy "showed" too much. Then cast and crew had to film wrap-around scenes for a half-dozen or so flashbacks, essentially repeats that would be aired to give Ball time off. "It was difficult for her, but she managed very well," Asher recalled in Jamestown. "It was hard for her [as big as she got] to get around and make all the moves, but she did."

The pregnancy episodes (late 1952 to early 1953) brought Ball (and Desilu) to new heights of success and viewership (44 million viewers, or 71 percent of the viewing population, watched Lucy Ricardo give birth to Little Ricky). As Desilu expanded, Cahn found himself doing more than just editing: "I came across country when the characters went to Hollywood, and I drove that Pontiac with a crew, for the episodes in which the Ricardos and the Mertzes traveled to Hollywood. Then there was another trip, to Florida, for the episode in which Elsa Lanchester guest-starred. Desi and Jess had me go on all those excursions with second-unit cameramen and doubles for the actors, and it was a lot of fun.

"Everyone had their own personal triumphs; mine was when I shot the second unit of the helicopter landing on the *USS Constitution* in New York harbor (for the "Bon Voyage" episode). I went to New York and did it [a friend of his wife Judy doubled for Ball when Lucy Ricardo was dangling from the helicopter]. Also, I was sent to Havana, Cuba, to pick up location shots for the debut of *The Lucy-Desi Comedy Hour*, 'Lucy Takes a Cruise to Havana.' I got there just as Castro was busting out big-time and Desi was screaming at me over the phone, 'Get the film and get back home!' That Havana trip, getting involved with the mob and Castro making *I Love Lucy*, was my personal highlight of the 10 years I was there."

Regarding the personalities involved in *I Love Lucy*, Cahn told me that, "Lucy was as demanding a perfectionist as we've heard. Desi was more laid-back … except when he got mad, his eyes popped out and he could be a terror. Vivian and Bill had their differences. The feud with her and Frawley is overblown. She was about the same age as Lucy, and Viv didn't like the image of being a stuffy old lady. In the next series [*The Lucy Show*], which I wasn't involved with, Viv got to slim down and wear different kinds of clothes, and she felt better about it, but we (*laughing*) usually had her looking like the sloppy wife of Bill Frawley. She didn't love doing that, but she did it."

The Fab Four (Desi Arnaz, Vivian Vance, Lucille Ball, and William Frawley) pose with a few of the many awards they earned for a little sitcom called *I Love Lucy*. **Photofest**

♥ **Lucy Trivia** Vance, in fact, hated working with Frawley so much that she refused to consider the idea of a Mertz spin-off, which no doubt could've run for years and brought her enough money that she'd never have to work again. Turning it down was the final break in her relationship with Frawley.

Arnaz explained very succinctly why he and Ball ended the half-hour run of *I Love Lucy* in a 1957 *TV Guide* article: "You've got to change in this business. You can't stand still. I would rather make a big change while we are still ahead. It would be ridiculous for us to wait until people got sick and tired of the regular half-hour Monday night [show]."

Desi Jr. reflected on the series' continuing popularity as he publicized his role in 1992's *The Mambo Kings* (in which he played his father): "Situation comedies are abominable and comedy itself has degenerated," he told Lou Gaul of the Calkins Newspapers. "We still love *I Love Lucy* because right, moral, old-fashioned values were in the humor, and the characters were laughing with each other and at themselves, not at other people."

Why does *I Love Lucy* still resonate with the viewer? The simple answer to that is because it's funny. And the humor is based in reality: *I Love Lucy* producer and head writer Jess Oppenheimer once said he thought "The funniest single line ever uttered on *I Love Lucy* came when Lucy (Ricardo) summed up smartly what happens to a lot of marriages: 'Ever since we said, "I do" there are so many things we don't.'" *I Love Lucy* held up a mirror to viewers of their own lives, not necessarily a true mirror, but a twisted mirror, leavened with laughter at the quirks and daily lunacy of life. And laughter always makes a situation easier to take.

I Love Lucy has never been off the air. No other show even comes close. No wonder almost everyone in show business aspires to *Lucy*'s success. For example, among the extras in the complete season one DVD collection of the popular NBC superhero drama *Heroes* (2006-?), series composer Wendy Melvoin (of Wendy & Lisa fame) expresses hope that *Heroes* "runs as long as *I Love Lucy*. That'd be hot!"

I Love Lucy was also known as *The Lucy Show* and *The Sunday Lucy Show* when rerun in 1955; *The Top Ten Lucy Shows* when rerun in 1958; and *Lucy in Connecticut* when rerun in 1960.

♥ **Lucy Trivia** You know that *I Love Lucy* is responsible for many broadcast firsts. But did you know it was the first sitcom to appear on British TV, in 1955, on the ITV network?

THE I LOVE LUCY BOOK: Written by one of the premier Lucille Ball fans and authorities, Bart Andrews, this book (originally published in 1976 as *Lucy & Ricky & Fred & Ethel: The Story of I Love Lucy*) was the first compilation of facts about the sitcom. Covering each episode and filled with backstage tidbits, it's a must-have for any fan. Andrews also wrote, with Ball friend and fan-club president Thomas Watson, *Loving Lucy: An Illustrated Tribute to Lucille Ball* (1980). The book is filled with pictures, many stemming from her early career. These books constituted the first major literary coverage of Ball and their success allowed for the dozens of tomes that followed.

I LOVE LUCY COMIC BOOKS: See Comic Books.

I LOVE LUCY COMIC STRIP: See Comic Strip.

***I Love Lucy* 50th Anniversary Celebration:** October 15, 2001 marked the 50th Anniversary of the debut broadcast of *I Love Lucy*. There were a number of special events and celebrations, ranging from live shows to reruns of the original series uncut and with the original animated credits. These included:

♥ *TV Guide*, always a big Ball fan, celebrated the week of October 15, 2001, with eight separate black-and-white covers of Lucy. A ninth, special cover, featuring the Ricardos and Mertzes, was available only through the *TV Guide* website, for $12.99. The special issue featured the Top 50 *I Love Lucy* episodes and a rare interview with Desi Jr., the cover subject of the first national edition of the magazine.

♥ *The I Love Lucy 50th Anniversary Experience* toured the country; see separate entry below.

♥ TV Land, a cable network, celebrated its acquisition of *I Love Lucy* by airing the Top 50 episodes listed in *TV Guide* over five nights, uncut, using the original animated opening and closing credits. The openings were edited slightly: original sponsors like Philip Morris were replaced with "TV Land" logos. The TV Land website (tvland.com) offered a salute to *I Love Lucy* teeming with wonderful surprises. Surfers could click on many different hearts that offered categories like Postcard Gallery, Screen Saver, Lucy and Ricky, The Mertzes, and Pioneers of Television, to see more pictures, hear audio, and view animations.

♥ The Home Shopping Network aired a special hour of Lucy-related products, including a limited-edition porcelain doll (in an edition of 1,951, which sold out almost instantly); a 50th anniversary bracelet; a special *I Love Lucy* edition of Monopoly (see Games); and an *I Love Lucy* Power Picture, with four separate panels that rotated, revealing best-loved *Lucy* scenes with matching audio. Lucy impersonator Suzanne LaRusch clowned during the hour.

♥ *The I Love Lucy 50th Anniversary Special* aired November 11, 2001, executive-produced by Lucie and Desi Jr., featuring many Hollywood stars paying tribute to Ball, Arnaz, Vance, Frawley, and the show; performances and new interviews with Lucie and Desi Jr.; and interviews with director William Asher, writers Madelyn Pugh Davis, Bob Carroll, Jr., and Bob Schiller; and Greg Oppenheimer, son of the show's creator Jess Oppenheimer. For more, see the separate entry.

♥ Columbia House Home Video began issuing its *I Love Lucy* DVD collection, four shows per disc. That collection was complete as of October 2007; see Lucy on DVD for details.

♥ *The New York Times* ran a group of articles celebrating Ball, Arnaz, and *I Love Lucy* in the *Sunday Times* Arts & Leisure section, October 14, 2001.

THE I LOVE LUCY 50TH ANNIVERSARY EXPERIENCE: In honor of the 50th anniversary of *I Love Lucy* on October 15, 2001, S.E.S.P. (which created and developed The I Love Lucy 50th Anniversary Experience) and SFX (billing itself as "the world's largest producer and marketer of live entertainment events") gave fans the chance to "reach out and touch all of the magic that changed television history" in a multimedia, interactive attraction. The tour made its debut at the Milwaukee Summerfest on June 28, 2001.

"With this tour, our family wanted to give the legions of *I Love Lucy* fans throughout America a way to celebrate along with us and join in the fun that was the *I Love Lucy* experience 50 years ago," said Lucie at the time. "Now they can experience the action and excitement that existed on the set 50 years ago as Lucy, Ricky, Fred, and Ethel made television history."

The I Love Lucy 50th Anniversary Experience featured a plaza with three interactive games in which audiences could step into Ball's shoes (i.e., work the chocolate factory conveyor belt); everyone was videotaped and some would air on *The I Love Lucy 50th Anniversary Special*, broadcast on CBS on November 11, 2001. The *Experience* also gave fans their first chance to visit exact replicas of the most famous sets in television history—Lucy and Ricky's New York apartment, their Beverly Palms Hotel room, and the Tropicana Nightclub.

The nightclub was converted into a theater where fans could view a highlight reel created especially for this experience, featuring great moments from the show. Display cases of cherished original props, costumes, scripts, and rare photographs were located at almost every turn, offering fans an up-close, personal look. "This tour is the culmination of two years of intense research and development, resulting in the largest collection of *I Love Lucy* material ever assembled," said S.E.S.P. executive producer Steve Kahn.

The tour wound its way across the country. The sets eventually ended up as part of the Lucy-Desi Center, in the Desilu Playhouse building. To find out how they got there, see <u>The Lucille Ball-Desi Arnaz Center</u>.

THE *I LOVE LUCY* 50TH ANNIVERSARY SPECIAL: On November 11, 2001, CBS celebrated the 50th anniversary of *I Love Lucy* with a two-hour special hosted by Whoopi Goldberg and Dick Van Dyke. It featured a rundown of the Top 10 episodes of the show, as picked by online votes at CBS.com ("Lucy Does a TV Commercial," otherwise known as the Vitameatavegamin episode, was No. 1); a generous helping of clips from those episodes and others; interviews with many of the original people behind the scenes who worked on *I Love Lucy*; a special trip to Ball's home in Jamestown, New York, with Lucie and Desi Jr.; tributes to Vivian Vance and

William Frawley; and commentary by many celebrities (including Cher, Roseanne, Arturo Sandoval, Barbara Walters, Richard Crenna, Paul Rodriguez, and Antonio Banderas).

The highlight for me was the energized version of "Babalu" sung in tribute to Desi Arnaz by Cuban heartthrob Jorge Moreno, assisted by Lucie and Desi Jr. on vocals and bongos, and set to a video complement featuring Arnaz doing the song on *I Love Lucy*. It was fine, fun, and well-done. In a segment about Lucille Ball collectibles and merchandise, the camera panned across a row of books about Ball, and, to my surprise and delight, *Lucy A to Z* (the first edition) was featured prominently at the center of the display.

Audiences proved they still loved Lucy by watching to the tune of 17.6 million people, making the special the second-highest-rated show of its night.

THE *I LOVE LUCY* INFLUENCE: *I Love Lucy* has been called the most influential sitcom ever made for a variety of reasons. The first modern sitcom remains important because it continues to influence sitcoms more than 50 years after its debut. Here are some reasons:

♥ The *three-camera technique*, developed by Desi Arnaz and cinematographer Karl Freund, which allowed the action to be filmed from three different angles. The best of these could then be spliced together for the final show.

♥ Use of a *live audience*. Lucille Ball responded with her best performances when there was an audience for her shtick. This was discovered during the run of her radio show *My Favorite Husband*. Arnaz knew that *I Love Lucy* had to be performed like a play, before an audience, and spent lots of time and money figuring out how to put bleachers into the soundstage while respecting the studio fire code.

♥ The episodes were *filmed* at the Arnazes' request (and using money out of their own pockets). The films enabled the show to be rebroadcast time after time, and earned Desilu a tidy sum when they were sold to CBS. This was not possible with many other shows of the era, which were recorded, if at all, on kinescopes, that is, movies filmed from a TV screen during a broadcast. These were often of such poor quality they could not be repeated.

An article in *TV FAN* magazine in October 1954 called "How Do You Like Your TV Shows?" by Paul Marsh speculated the reason Ball and Arnaz filmed *I Love Lucy* sprang "from a sheer commercial point of view, since Arnaz is the president of Desilu productions, the outfit which makes their films. You'll agree it wouldn't make sense to do a *live* show from one of the best-equipped TV *film* studios in Hollywood." No doubt, there's a kernel of truth to that, but the decision to film the show, resulting in the birth of the rerun, was one of the Arnazes' most profitable ideas.

♥ The *main characters* were four people, one older married couple and one younger, best friends and neighbors (in fact, the older couple was the younger couple's landlord) who interacted with each other, and had different ideas, personalities, and goals. This concept has been rehashed so many times over the past 50 years that it would be impossible to list all the shows that owe *I Love Lucy* a debt in this area. As Vivian Vance recalled to Ridder News Service reporter Ron Miller in 1974, "We always tried to keep our characters human—even though we were a bunch of clowns.... Lucille had more ambition than I had and made me work harder than I ever wanted to work. She pulled me along and taught me a lot of things.... Lucille and I always wanted our routines to look like we were doing them for the first time. But we might have done that routine for 72 hours before we got it right."

♥ *Everyone had a vote.* "There was no boss on that set," Vance noted. "He would have been trampled by the crowd. Everybody was allowed to have his say at every conference. We rehearsed for three days, then sat in a room sometimes until 4 a.m. and fought out every word, every scene. Desi was the arbiter of taste for the show, and often these arguments were settled democratically by a vote of the principal performers."

For a more specific kind of influence, the text below illustrates just one plot point that first surfaced on *I Love Lucy* (on television at least; Lucy actually used it in one of her movies, *You Can't Fool Your Wife*, 1944) and was later modified by other hit sitcoms.

1950s
I Love Lucy Plot: Lucy tries on a black wig at a salon and is amazed at how different she looks in it. She buys it to see if she can fool Ricky and prove that he flirts with other women. Ricky, of course, discovers what's going on and decides to teach Lucy a lesson.

1970s
All in the Family Plot: Gloria (Sally Struthers) buys a blonde wig as a lark to see how husband Mike (Rob Reiner) will react, only to find out he likes her in it too much; she accuses him of enjoying her in the wig because it's like sleeping with another woman. After lots of screaming, the two make up and rush upstairs to make love, much to Archie Bunker's (Carroll O'Connor) disgust.

1990s
Just Shoot Me Plot: Maya (Laura San Giacomo) buys a long blonde wig in an effort to make boyfriend Elliott (Enrico Colantoni) notice her more, and gets upset when she finds out he

likes making love to her in it. The politically correct solution: She likes him in uniform, so she's happy to wear the wig as long as he'll dress up for her.

***I Love Lucy* In Outer Space:** It's possible that if aliens ever contact Earth, it will be because Lucy and the gang will have alerted them to our presence. On a 1999 Learning Channel show about alien contact and the SETI (Search for Extra-Terrestrial Intelligence) program, several scientists noted that the main stumbling block for contact of any kind is the vast distance between our solar system and stars in different galaxies.

They added something they've known for years: that one way to zip through those distances at the speed of light is via an electronic signal. Radio and TV signals, of course, have been beamed into space for more than 70 years (these signals are known as "earth leakage"). They mentioned *I Love Lucy* specifically, perhaps because it's the best-known TV program ever produced, and added that it was unlikely the aliens would actually be able to see the program unless they had decoded our specific TV technology. But at the very least, they would notice the signal.

This brings to mind an episode of the Steven Spielberg *Amazing Stories* anthology series called "Fine Tuning" (which aired November 10, 1985), in which three geeks set up an antenna that starts receiv-

We know these people well. But did you know it is possible aliens are familiar with their faces, having had the potential to see them for more than half a century? It's true! Photofest

ing alien broadcasts. What do they find? Cute, pudgy aliens who worship all the Golden Age comedians, because they've been receiving their signals for many years. The highlight of the show: an alien performance of several scenes from *I Love Lucy* in which the characters are clearly defined and even Ricky's accent is discernible! Talk about *universe-al* humor …

THE *I LOVE LUCY MOVIE*: LOST … AND FOUND!

In 2005 Dann Cahn, *I Love Lucy*'s film editor, introduced the *I Love Lucy Movie* at the Reg Lenna Civic Center in Jamestown, New York. He noted it had not been seen since it was originally produced in 1953, except for a single showing at one of the West Coast We Love Lucy fan club conventions. The only other time it was ever shown in public was in Bakersfield, California, where the Desilu crew went to take a look at it after it had been put together. The movie was a result of the show's success. As Cahn pointed out, "You have to remember there were no such things as reruns or tapes or DVDs back then, so it was also kind of a nice way to preserve the show."

What the movie did was string together three *I Love Lucy* episodes from the first season, directed by Marc Daniels—"The Benefit," where Lucy upstages Ricky singing "Underneath the Bamboo Tree" at the end; "Breaking the Lease," in which an argument between the Ricardos and the Mertzes leads Ricky and Lucy to try to break their lease so they can move out; and "The Ballet," wherein Lucy tries to learn ballet in order to, of course, get into Ricky's act. The episodes were framed by scenes of a couple viewing a taping of *I Love Lucy*.

The new footage was shot by Ed Sedgwick, a director and old pal of Ball's, who helmed her best MGM comedy showcase, 1946's *Easy to Wed*. It was Sedgwick who suggested making the movie a "show within a show," framing it around what it would be like to be in the *I Love Lucy* audience, so that the laughter and applause on a typical Lucy episode wouldn't seem out of place.

The movie opens as the audience files in to see the show, and ends as they leave. At the start, Arnaz is seen warming up the crowd and introducing his three co-stars. At the end, the actors break character to take a bow. We follow a couple in the audience (Ann Doran and Benny Baker) as they watch the movie.

The I Love Lucy Movie is a fascinating artifact of its time, with an even more interesting backstory. Cahn said the movie never saw the light of day, because when the Arnazes previewed it at Bakersfield in 1953, the chief of MGM, Dore Schary, and the producer of their movie *The Long, Long Trailer*, Pandro Berman, were in the audience. They noted afterward to Lucy and Desi, "We're going to be releasing [*Trailer*] this upcoming Valentine's Day, 1954, and we don't want this little *I Love Lucy Movie* to steal our thunder." Ball and Arnaz graciously put their movie aside and then apparently forgot about it. Cahn spent years trying to find it in various vaults and archives before it turned up.

Cahn remarked that he had searched for five years to find a print of the movie, which even insiders like original *I Love Lucy* writers Bob Carroll and Madelyn Pugh thought might not exist. He finally found the print in a Paramount Studios vault, listed as a *Westinghouse Desilu Playhouse* production. [Ball sold Desilu to Paramount in 1967.]

Cahn recalled, "I went through all the *I Love Lucy* footage and couldn't find it. And then one day I was at Paramount Studios, and I thought, 'It's just got to be here. It's not something we'd throw away, although we threw away too many things we shouldn't have, proofs and masters, whatever. There was a vice president at Paramount who was putting everything in the entire studio [vaults] on a computer. And I said, 'Let's just look in the *Desilu Playhouse* files,' which had nothing to do with the movie; the series was made several years later. And sure enough, the movie popped up, under a different title." It was lost all those years because no one thought to look for it in a Desilu series archive.

There was one inconsistency I found … the subplot that was part of the new footage was about Ethel's club giving a plaque to Lucy and Ricky for their performance at the benefit. When we saw them at the benefit, the sign that introduced them from the original episode had the benefit being presented by The Middle East 68th Street Woman's Club. On the plaque, which Lucy shows off after the second episode ["Breaking the Lease"], it says, "In Appreciation [from] The Wednesday Afternoon Fine Arts League." So somebody in the continuity department was asleep at the switch....

The **I** *Love* **Lucy** *Quiz Book:* This hard-to-find paperback trivia exercise, compiled by Ball aficionado Bart Andrews in 1981, often sells for $100 or more, and collectors prize it.

I Love Lucy **30 Years Later** …? In September 1982, the AP's Bob Thomas interviewed Desi Arnaz, and reported, "Arnaz for many years has lived in Del Mar with his second wife, Edith. He enjoys the seaside life, especially during the racing season, and travels to Baja, California where he has another home and business interests. His visits to Hollywood are rare, and often frustrating.

"I had a lot of talks with CBS about doing a special looking back at *I Love Lucy*," Arnaz told Thomas. "Lucy (Lucille Ball) was willing and so was Gary (Morton, Miss Ball's second husband and producer). But CBS wanted the show to be 'Lucy and Ricky Ricardo 30 Years

Later.' I said it wouldn't work because Fred and Ethel (the late William Frawley and Vivian Vance) are not around. How could we explain it? That they had died? That's no way to start a comedy show.

"My idea was to have Lucy and me tell the kids (Desi Jr. and Lucie) what it was like during the *I Love Lucy* years. It would be a way of paying tribute to Bill and Vivian, the writers and directors, and stars like Maurice Chevalier, John Wayne, and William Holden who appeared on the show for scale. CBS wanted me to prepare the special both ways. I said forget it."

I Love Lucy **Trivia:** In no particular order, here are some fun facts not everybody knows about the show:

♦ *I Love Lucy* was filmed on a converted movie soundstage (part of the old RKO Studios, which Arnaz and Ball ultimately bought).

♦ The pilot episode cost $19,000 to produce, and starred Ball and Arnaz as Lucy and Larry Lopez, with the Mertzes nowhere in sight.

♦ Ball and Arnaz together took home $4,000 a week during the first season of *I Love Lucy*. By comparison, Roseanne Barr was taking home $30,000 an episode in the early 1990s. According to The Inflation Calculator at www.westegg.com/inflation, the Arnaz's salary equals $22,669.42 in 1992 dollars.

♦ Ball and Vivian Vance had met on September 3, 1951, only five days before filming the first episode.

♦ A live audience of 300 attended each filming, the first of which took place on September 8, 1951.

♦ Furniture was marketed in the 1950s patterned after Lucy and Ricky Ricardo's living room and bedroom pieces.

♦ Vitameatavegamin contained 23 percent alcohol.

♦ More people watched the "Birth of Little Ricky" episode of *I Love Lucy* than watched Queen Elizabeth II's coronation that same year.

♦ Ball never thought of herself as funny, only as an "honest" actress.

♦ Ethel Mertz had three middle names during the course of *I Love Lucy* (Louise, Mae, and Roberta) thanks to the writers.

♦ Baseball fan William Frawley's contract had a clause allowing him time off if the Yankees were playing in the World Series.

♦ Writers Bob Carroll and Madelyn Pugh offered silver dollars to any cast member who caused a spontaneous audience reaction.

♦ Pugh performed Ball's routines before presenting them to Ball to ensure that a woman could do everything demanded of Lucy Ricardo.

♦ *I Love Lucy* scripts usually ran about 50 pages.

♦ Arnaz "warmed up" the studio audience before each show.

♦ In its second season, *I Love Lucy* had 45 million steady viewers.

♦ Not only was the eight-foot loaf of bread used in the episode "Pioneer Women" real, the show had a metal shop custom-design a special pan for it.

♦ An average of 93 people worked on each *I Love Lucy* episode.

♦ "Fred and Ethels" became a slang phrase for older American couples, e.g., tourists, in Europe.

♦ The New York *Daily News* reported, on October 6, 2007, that Ricky Ricardo was one of the names the Yankees used at hotels on the road to avoid recognition. The News speculated the name might be used by Yankees catcher Jorge Pasado. Along with the article ran a picture of Desi Arnaz as Ricky, superimposed inside a baseball-card frame.

♦ The Los Angeles city council voted September 12, 2007 to rename the Melrose Avenue and Plymouth Boulevard intersection near Paramount Studios I Love Lucy Square, cbs2. com reported, "in honor of Desilu Productions, which Ball and Arnaz founded there in 1951."

IMPERIAL PALACE AUTO COLLECTION

The Imperial Palace Hotel & Casino in Las Vegas features a special exhibit of more than 200 rare "classic, antique, muscle, and special-interest automobiles." Included is Ball and Gary Morton's 1962 Silver Ghia coupe. Billed as "The World's Largest Classic Car Showroom," all the autos are available to buy, sell, trade, or just gawk at. The Morton's car is described as a "dual-Ghia L6.4 coupe, serial number 0318, one of 26 built. Assembled in Italy, the chassis and drive were supplied by Chrysler, and the end result was a very popular car with celebrities." Ball's car can be yours for a mere $165,000 as of this writing.

INFLUENCE ON OTHER PERFORMERS

Lucille Ball and Desi Arnaz invented the sitcom we know today. Therefore, it's not surprising that hardly a day goes by when I don't hear, see, or read a reference to Ball, *I Love Lucy*, or its wonderful cast. From *Seinfeld* to *Third Rock from the Sun*, from *Ellen* to *Designing Women*, the Ball influence is consistently acknowledged and sometimes even remarked on.

In an issue of *TV Guide* celebrating the Top TV stars of all time, Ball was crowned No. 1, and readers agreed. She is still chosen in poll after poll as television's top comedian (as in 2002, by the TV show *Biography*). The wacky redhead's influence is pervasive, and not likely to end any time soon. *TIME* magazine picked *I Love Lucy* as one of the "17 Shows That Changed TV" (and one of the Top 100 TV shows ever) in its September 17, 2007 issue and a companion online feature. For details, see <u>Tributes, 2000 and Beyond</u>.

Those who would dismiss her as a whiny, silly complainer, or worse, have never really watched the show or given Ball a fair chance. Feminist treatises have been written noting that Ball's anarchic personality sowed the first seeds of women trying to escape their traditional boundaries, and in the 1950s, yet.

Lucy Ricardo was a homemaker who wanted more. A loyal friend. A loving wife and mother. She had a genius for screwing up things. That just made us love her more, for she had flaws and foibles (like all of us).

The four *Lucy* principals were actors of the finest caliber. If you doubt it, consider the fact that Vance and Frawley loathed each other from the start, and that Ball and Arnaz were acting out a very traumatic marriage in real life while they filmed the most popular TV show of all time, one *that centered on the lead characters' wonderful marriage.*

In real life, Ball was nothing like Lucy. Noel Holston, of the *Minneapolis-St. Paul Star Tribune*, commented in 1989, that, "In person, Miss Ball was brassy, opinionated, tough and bawdy, more like Mae West than Lucy Ricardo. It was obvious that this was a woman who knew the score, knew what she wanted and would drive a hard bargain.

"Although she always gave credit to [Desi] Arnaz, she, too, exhibited great foresight by casting her lot with the untried medium of TV, and by having *I Love Lucy* done on film."

Ball *was* serious, and believed in hard work. Her career became one any woman trying to make it in Hollywood—hell, any person, period—would kill to have. She was a model, chorus girl, movie star, radio star, television star, stage star, and studio owner.

So the next time you see someone on TV using a disguise to spy on someone else, or *Laverne & Shirley* doing just about anything, or someone cry, "You got some 'splainin' to do," remember: Ball was there first, and she probably did it better.

THE INTERNET

Lucille Ball is all over the Internet. Gracenote.com maintains a short but solid list of Ball sites (including my own, www.sitcomboy.com). The best way to find Ball & Co. on the Internet is to go to Google, Yahoo or your favorite search engine, enter "Lucille Ball websites," and follow the links to the literally hundreds of pages and thousands of mentions of Ball online.

J

JEFFERIES, WALTER M.

A Desilu set designer, Jefferies was working on *The Lucy Show* (1962-'68) when Gene Roddenberry approached him in the mid-1960s about designing a spaceship that would anchor the new series *Star Trek* (1966-'69, one of the final shows Ball okayed as president of Desilu). Jefferies' design for the starship Enterprise has become a science fiction classic, reworked and tinkered with (but never abandoned) over *Star Trek's* 41-year (so far!) television and movie history. The Jefferies Tubes aboard the Enterprise are named for him. Jefferies died in 2003. See *Star Trek*.

JENSSEN, ELOIS

Oscar-winner Jenssen (Best Costume Design, Color, in 1951, for the movie *Samson and Delilah*) did the costumes for Lucille Ball's film *Lured* (1947), and for the Ann Sothern show *Private Secretary* (1953). Jenssen is credited as costumer designer on almost 20 films, all but one made before or during her run with Ball.

Ball in costume for *Lured* (1947) with designer Elois Jenssen; note costume sketch bottom left. Photofest

229

Jenssen was too busy when Ball first approached her to do the costumes for *I Love Lucy*, but she joined up in 1953. Before that, the show took its costumes wherever it could get them, especially from then-fashionable department store Ohrbach's (credited as *Fashions by Ohrbach's* for the first year of the show). Ohrbach's, a Macy's-type clothing store, specialized in knockoffs of high-fashion dresses.

Jenssen was responsible for making Lucy Ricardo as lovable looking as she was likeable, and Jenssen's designs offered just the right mix of 1950s middle-class housewife and, when needed, glamorous wife of a nightclub performer; showgirl trying to break into the business; et. al.

Jenssen also created specialties like the costumes Ball wore when starched ("Bonus Bucks," March 8, 1954) or dolled up as Marilyn Monroe ("Ricky's Movie Offer," November 8, 1954). She worked on *I Love Lucy* from 1953 to 1955, episodes 65-127. She also did the costumes for the Arnazes' 1956 movie *Forever, Darling*. She was let go over a salary dispute and replaced in episode 128 (October 3, 1955), the start of season five, by Edward Stevenson (see Stevenson, Edward).

Post *Lucy*, Jenssen basically retired, working on only one other TV series (*Bracken's World*, 1969, a nighttime soap that purported to provide an inside look at Hollywood), and one movie, Disney's innovative *Tron* (1982), which took its lead characters inside a computer. For the latter, her final film, Jenssen was again nominated for an Oscar. She died in 2004 at the age of 81.

JEWELRY

A 1947 article appearing around the time of Lucille Ball's *Dream Girl* tour noted that Ball carried with her "a collection of jewelry which was given to her by her admiring husband. 'He has good taste, hasn't he?' says Lucille fondly. She was wearing an aquamarine ring with a stone the size of a bread-and-butter plate; Desi has given her many other aquamarines including a cross made of the stones and held together with gold.

"There is a bracelet which spells out 'I Love You' in gold letters, but on the other side is engraved in his own writing, 'Te quiero mucho, mucho, mucho,' which is his Spanish way of saying the same thing. 'It's corny, but we have all our jewelry engraved with some message or date or initials,' Miss Ball smiles with a tenderness you wouldn't believe if you saw her in some of her hard-boiled roles.

"One of her favorite bracelets is a charm circlet with each charm a replica of one of her husband's records, in gold. Her favorite tunes, as played by his musicians, are 'I'll Never Love Again' and 'Tia Juana.'"

A few years later, Ball was robbed of some of those possessions. A report on June 30, 1950, trumpeted, "Lucille Ball Robbed of Gems." Ball told the police, "$6,000 in jewelry was stolen from her suite at the Ambassador East Hotel [in Chicago] while she was out with her husband, Desi Arnaz, last night. The loot included a 40-carat aquamarine engagement ring, a 62 carat aquamarine pendant, a gold choker chain, gold earrings, and other valuables."

On October 16, 2007, the New York auction house Christie's featured 10 lots of Lucille Ball's jewelry as part of its Magnificent Jewels auction. According to The Lucille Ball-Desi Arnaz Center in Jamestown, New York (which was to receive a portion of the proceeds), the pieces included "a tiger's eye and gold wristwatch; an onyx, emerald and diamond pendant necklace; a 46.92 carat cabochon star sapphire and diamond ring; a diamond and gold evening bag that Lucy used on her White House visit in 1986 [when she accepted the Kennedy Center Honor]; a Cartier diamond and gold 'tonneau' wristwatch; and a sodalite, diamond and gold pendant necklace by Van Cleef & Arpels." Lucy's jewelry sold for a whopping $256,375, Christie's reported. The best-selling item was described by Christies as "a unique-shaped pendant necklace that has an oval-cut sapphire surrounded by and topped with diamonds in a cartouche panel," by Van Cleef & Arpels, which sold for $82,600.

JOHNSON, ARTE

Diminutive, lovable character comedian who co-starred on *Laugh-In* (1968-'73). The show aired Monday nights opposite *Here's Lucy* and damaged Ball's ratings. Johnson would often end the show as his German soldier character, cooing slyly, "Goodnight, Lucy." He also guest-starred on *Here's Lucy*.

JOHNSON, VAN

Star of mostly light, airy musical comedies who debuted on Broadway (in the chorus) with Desi Arnaz in *Too Many Girls* (1939; also his film debut in 1940), Johnson appeared with Ball in one of her best films at MGM (*Easy to Wed*, 1946). He guest-starred on *I Love Lucy* during the Hollywood shows. In "The Dancing Star," May 2, 1955, Johnson played himself, and with Ball performed "I Like New York in June" to a soft-shoe routine. Johnson played a supporting role in Ball's 1968 movie *Yours, Mine and Ours*, and was a guest star on *Here's Lucy* that same year.

JOSEFSBERG, MILT

Script doctor, writer, and producer who was hired by Ball to supervise the scripts on the third season of *The Lucy Show* (1964-'65) and stayed through the fourth season of *Here's Lucy* (1971-'72). He later worked on *All in the Family*. Josefsberg was also the author of *Comedy Writing for Television & Hollywood*, subtitled "A book to be read for fun and possibly profit," from Harper & Row (1987).

K

KAHN, MADELINE

A vivacious and unique comedian in films, stage, and television, Kahn, born in 1942, made her first big splash as the frumpy Eunice Burns in Peter Bogdanovich's screwball comedy salute, *What's Up, Doc?* (1972), upstaging star Barbra Streisand. That part also brought her to the notice of Lucille Ball, whose movie *Mame* was in the casting process. Kahn was signed to play frumpy Agnes Gooch, but when she showed up Ball was surprised at how different Kahn appeared in person.

Lucy dismissed Kahn (to the tune of $50,000) and hired Jane Connell, who had played Gooch in the stage version of the musical. Kahn spoke with critic Rex Reed after her dismissal and noted, "I'm not exactly sure what happened. They showed Lucille Ball *What's Up, Doc?* and she liked me in it, but then I walked on the set and I guess I don't exactly look like frumpy Eunice in the movie.

"It was just a part. I don't look like that in real life. But I thought that's what the movies were all about. I can look like 40 different people with makeup and padding. I think when Lucille Ball met me, she thought, 'What kind of casting is this?' And I must admit I'm no Agnes Gooch. I planned to play it differently from the way Jane Connell had played it on Broadway, and I thought they wanted a different approach, too.

"The problem was, do we go in a different direction, or do we do what's already been done? They got Jane Connell, and there's your answer. But I didn't take it as a personal insult or rejection. That's show business." (For Jane Connell's memories, see Connell, Jane.)

The gracious Kahn moved on to great success in movies like *Paper Moon* (1973) and *Blazing Saddles* (1974), both of which earned her Oscar nominations, and *Young Frankenstein* (1974), as well as stage hits including *On the Twentieth Century* (1978) and *The Sisters Rosensweig*, which earned her a Best Actress Tony award in 1993. She was a cast member of Bill Cosby's sitcom *Cosby* (1996-'99) when she died of cancer in 1999.

KALLMAN, DICK

Born on July 7, 1933, in Brooklyn, New York, handsome comedic actor Kallman was part of Lucille Ball's Desilu repertory company (Ball had handpicked the members from auditions, and they included Carole Cook, Ken Berry, Majel Barrett, and Robert Osborne). According to the website TVParty.com, "One musical number from the special featured some wild art direction and garnered excellent reviews for performances by Cook and Kallman as singing/dancing coffeehouse beatniks."

Kallman also appeared in the final *Lucy-Desi Comedy Hour* playing a bellboy in the episode, "Lucy Meets the Mustache," which aired April 1, 1960 and guest-starred Ernie Kovacs and Edie Adams. He is remembered for the sitcom *Hank* (1965-'66) in which he played a nice guy trying to take care of his younger sister while preventing anyone from finding out they were both orphans; and several performances as Little Louie Groovy on *Batman* (1966-'67).

Kallman eventually left Hollywood and began doing stage work, touring in such musicals as *How To Succeed in Business Without Really Trying* and *Half a Sixpence*. In 1975, reports Kallman's bio on the Internet Movie Database, "He joined a partnership to manufacture women's play clothes and party clothes, and began working as a dealer in antiques, silver, and art. On February 22, 1980, Kallman and business associate Steven Szladek of Brooklyn were found shot to death in Kallman's posh Manhattan apartment." The killer was found, convicted, and sentenced to 25 years-to-life. The stolen property—paintings, jewelry, and antiques—was never recovered.

KEATON, BUSTER

Silent film genius whose career stalled in the talkie era, Keaton ended up at MGM in the 1940s, where his talent was misused and overlooked even more than Ball's. When not filming, Ball used to clown around with him and another silent great, comedian/director Harold Lloyd, and said that she learned how to handle props from Keaton.

"Buster was a personal friend," Ball told the American Film Institute in a 1974 seminar. "I never got a chance to work with him until two months before he died.... He taught me about props, about the value of taking care of them and checking them yourself, and even how to make some of them, but how to make them work especially."

Ball said Keaton also helped her get the "cello act" together, which she used in her 1950 vaudeville tour with Arnaz. The act was also featured on an early episode of *I Love Lucy*.

Although uncredited, Keaton reportedly wrote and directed one of Ball's best film comedy showcases, *Easy to Wed* (1946).

KEEFER, VIVIAN

Blonde, pretty Chesterfield Girl chosen to come to Hollywood alongside Barbara Pepper and Lucille Ball, Keefer was a chorus girl or "chorine" in four films with Ball, like 1933's *Roman Scandals* and 1934's *Kid Millions*. According to We Love Lucy president Tom Watson, Lucille and Keefer also "shared a large apartment in Hollywood with three or four other showgirls." But not for long … Keefer left Hollywood after a year, married, and disappeared from show business. In a famous 1933 publicity still for *Scandals*, star Eddie Cantor is surrounded by a "bevy of beauties," eight in all, including Keefer, Pepper, and Ball.

A 1933 article in the *Oakland* (California) *Tribune* on January 16, 1934, reported that, "When *Roman Scandals* gets into the Roxie in the near future, those who know their ads may recognize seven faces in the ranks of the hundred chorines in support of Eddie Cantor. The special seven were recruited by Samuel Goldwyn for purposes of publicity: … 4. Vivian Keefer, known to every famous photographer and commercial artist as the inspiration for the Listerine ads. 5. Barbara Pepper, the 'Fisher Body Girl.' … and 7. Lucille Ball, whose dark smile lights up ads for Camels."

In another publicity stunt, some of the girls are quoted in Dan Thomas' "Hollywood Gossip" column, as it ran in the *Burlington, N.C. Daily Times-News* January 20, 1934, on the subject of millionaires and chorus girls. Keefer supposedly noted that, "Millionaires marry showgirls because … showgirls are smarter than most millionaires."

Keefer, who hailed from Spokane, Washington, according to one report, also appeared on Broadway in Earl Carroll's 1931 and 1932 *Vanities*, plus the 1930-31 hit *Girl Crazy*, in which Ethel Merman made her first big impression. She died in 1978 at age 69 on August 6 … Ball's birthday.

KELLY, GENE

One of classic Hollywood's top male dancers, also a premier musical comedy performer and director, Kelly made an early screen appearance in Ball's film *DuBarry Was a Lady* (1943) as Ball's love interest. Best known for his musical classics *An American in Paris* (1951) and *Singin' in the Rain* (1952), Kelly was a choreographer and dancer matched only by his elder peer Fred Astaire (in whose films Ball played bit parts at RKO in the 1930s). Kelly's career also connected with Ball's in two other MGM spectaculars, *Thousands Cheer* (1943) and *Ziegfeld Follies* (1946). As a favor to Kelly, Ball made a cameo appearance in his 1967 picture, *A Guide for the Married Man.*

KENWITH, HERBERT

A prolific stage and television director—everything from the original *Star Trek* (a well-remembered episode called "The Lights of Zetar") to *Sanford and Son, Good Times,* and *Diff'rent Strokes,* the latter of which he also produced. Kenwith directed Ball in her successful stage tour of *Dream Girl* in 1947. He returned to direct the redhead in *The Lucy Show* and *Here's Lucy,* but was apparently put off by her late-career habit of directing the director and only did a handful of episodes. Kenwith directed the infamous Joan Crawford episode of *The Lucy Show* ("Lucy and the Lost Star") and according to the website joancrawfordbest.com, it was Kenwith who begged Ball to give his old friend, Crawford, another chance after Ball discovered Crawford passed out from drinking on the set. Ball did, Crawford finished the show, and Ball subsequently tagged it one her "worst" series episodes. He fared better with the 1970 "Lucy the Crusader" episode of *Here's Lucy,* in which Ball actually works in tandem with co-star Gale Gordon (and funny guest star Charles Nelson Reilly) to make a manufacturer pay for his defective products. Ball protégé Carole Cook and movie co-star Jerome Cowan (1950's *The Fuller Brush Girl*) were also in the episode.

KING, HAL

Lucille Ball's extraordinary makeup artist, King worked on *I Love Lucy* from the beginning, and stayed with Ball through the fifth season of *Here's Lucy.* He had the daunting task, as *The Lucy Book* author Geoffrey Mark Fidelman noted, of "making 40-year-old Lucille look 28, 42-year-old Vivian Vance look 50, covering Desi's acne scars, making 64-year-old Bill Frawley look healthy, and keeping them all looking well under the hot lights." His first onscreen credit was "Lucy Visits Grauman's," October 3, 1955, the fifth season opener.

King was makeup director of the Max Factor Salon in Hollywood beginning in 1945, once he completed his World War II service. King did the makeup for many motion picture stars over the years, but by 1964 was working pretty much exclusively for the Factor Salon in Hollywood and had let go of individual clients.

"With one exception, that is!" noted a 1964 article in the *San Antonio Express* by Mildred Whittaker. "Years ago he made up Lucille Ball for [a] motion picture role. He has been her personal makeup advisor throughout her successful television, cinema and stage careers—and is still on hand each week before the cameras roll on *The Lucy Show*."

King also worked on *The Lucy-Desi Comedy Hour* and at least three of her later films: *The Facts of Life*, *Yours, Mine and Ours*, and *Mame*. He became known as "the only man whom Lucille Ball would permit to do her makeup."

Whittaker listed four must-adhere-to makeup tips King told her, for those who wanted to improve their complexion care:

1. "Most women don't take enough time to cleanse their skin thoroughly."
2. "Too many women seek cosmetic advice from friends instead of a professional beauty specialist."
3. "The woman who is not sure of herself tends to use too much or too little makeup."
4. "Every woman of every age should protect her skin before retiring. Creams and lotions do more good when a woman is sleeping that at any other time."

KRAFT MUSIC HALL

This variety series was broadcast from 1967 to 1971, and featured revolving hosts. The February 4, 1970 host was Desi Arnaz, who welcomed Vivian Vance, Lucie, and Desi Jr., along with Bernadette Peters. Arnaz and Vance were featured with Lucie in the song "Under the Bamboo Tree," which he had performed with Lucille Ball on *I Love Lucy*.

KRUSTYLU

The studio owned by Krusty the Clown on *The Simpsons*, Krustylu is one of the series' affectionate tributes to Ball, who, with husband Desi, formed Desilu.

KULP, NANCY

Ball knew comedy, and, apparently, on occasion, she could predict a success. Kulp (1921-'91) was a comic actor who usually played bookish, spinster, or snooty roles. She guest-starred once on *I Love Lucy* (as the maid who teaches Lucy how to curtsy in the 1956 episode "Lucy Meets the Queen"); played a maid in the Arnazes' movie *Forever Darling* (1956); and was a regular as bird-watcher Pamela Livingstone on *Love That Bob* (1955-'59) before achieving TV immortality as Miss Jane Hathaway on *The Beverly Hillbillies* (1962-'71). She also guest-starred on an early episode of *The Lucy Show* ("Lucy Becomes an Astronaut," which aired November 5, 1962).

In a 1984 interview on *Entertainment Tonight*, Kulp mentioned that she and Ball were friends. When Ball heard that Kulp was appearing on a new sitcom (*Hillbillies*) she asked Kulp about the plot. Kulp recalled that after explaining the premise, Ball gave it a "thumbs-up" and predicted it would be a hit. The show was indeed a hit, running for nine seasons.

KUSELY, IRMA

Lucille Ball's hairdresser from the time they first met on a movie set in 1942 until Ball's death in 1989. Kusely described her famous client's tresses as "studied carelessness" when Ball was named one of the "Best Coiffed Women of 1971" in the 15th annual judging of the Helene Curtis Guild of Professional Beauticians. "When working with such a famous person, deviating from her established look can cause havoc," Kusely noted at the time. "While we keep her basic look, I use different approaches to achieve a modern, up-to-date hairstyle for Lucy."

Though initially given her raging red hair while at MGM in the 1940s, Ball "used a written formula that was given to her" by Kusely, that "required an application of chemicals, followed by a henna rinse," according to *The Encyclopedia of Hair: A Cultural Study*.

On disc one of the *I Love Lucy: The Final Seasons* collection, Kusely discusses creating Ball's "artichoke cut," after the short style popularized by Italian star Gina Lollobrigida, which Ball wore beginning on the *Lucy-Desi Comedy Hour* episode "Lucy Hunts Uranium" and forever after. This and other anecdotes like it, according to Penelope Green of *The New York Times*, are "cultural history," such as when Kusely "describes the making of Lucille Ball's signature wig," in the 2002 book *Hair Heroes*, by Michael Gordon: "First the hair was bought from nuns in Europe, then it was pieced together and the curls were boiled in; finally, the wig was dyed with Tintex fabric dye. Ball had a wardrobe of wigs, at $1,500 each, for her television show, to save time redoing that enormous red artichoke of hair."

Wanda Clark, Lucy's personal secretary, became close friends with Irma; Clark's first day on the job happened to include a photo shoot for *Look*; the photographer and interviewer came to Ball's house. "I basically sat and listened," Wanda recalled for me in a phone interview. "I didn't need to do anything, but Lucy thought if I was interested in being there, I should be. So I watched Irma do her hair. Lucy's home salon consisted of a dryer and shampoo bowl. Lucy could do her own hair color and hair, which she did frequently.

"But in fact she wore wigs at most appearances, because her own hair was fine and soft, and the hot lights would make it wilt. Putting on a wig is a very specialized thing—it has to be done right or it won't look good. And hers always looked wonderful. Irma put them on so carefully. Lucy's own hair had to be pin-curled up tight, as close to the scalp as possible, and over that was wrapped some material, and then the wig was attached."

Kusely is credited with perfecting what became known as the "non-surgical facelift," a procedure that involved pinning back Ball's hair with tightly wound rubber bands secured by pins, covering the whole mess with a skull fracture bandage, and then plopping the wig on top of it. Supposedly, it was a painful process. But Ball, whose skin was described as 'too fair" to survive a true surgical facelift, adhered to the process whenever she wore a wig. Jenny Lewis, who played Ball's granddaughter on the legend's final (and failed) sitcom attempt, *Life with Lucy*, affirms, "She would pull her face back with tape, sort of like a cheap face-lift."

Kusely styled Ball's hair for all of her series, four of her movies, many of Ball's TV specials, and also worked on the original *The Dick Van Dyke Show*. A documentary about Kusely is coming from GAB Entertainment's Garret Boyajian and George Ridjaneck. "It's said that only a hairdresser knows for sure, and star stylist Irma Kusely knows plenty, as she shares the story of her amazing 50-year career shaping the locks of Hollywood's biggest stars," Boyajian shares. For more details, visit gabentertainment.com.

See also Guilaroff, Sydney, Hair Color, Henna Rinse, and Wigged Out.

L

LANE, CHARLES

Prolific character actor described accurately on the Internet Movie Database Pro as "skinny, hatchet-faced, bespectacled … with a prominent nose, rimless eyeglasses and [a] permanent scowl. [Lane] typically portrayed short-tempered and often loudmouthed bureaucrats, yes-men and other minor minions, principally in lighter fare." Lane died July 11, 2007, at the age of 102½. His remarkable career in entertainment stretched from initial uncredited appearances in films from the early 1930s to supporting or bit roles in dozens of classics, like *Mr. Deeds Goes to Town* (1936) and *It's a Wonderful Life* (1946). He met Lucille Ball while she was a chorus girl at RKO, and they became friendly. Lane appeared in several movies with Ball, including *Joy of Living* (1938), *You Can't Fool Your Wife* (1940), *Look Who's Laughing* (1941), and *Miss Grant Takes Richmond* (1949).

Subsequently, on TV, he made four appearances on *I Love Lucy* (he was the harried father of nine girls in the hospital waiting room as Ricky Ricardo awaited the birth of Little Ricky); was a semi-regular during the first season on *The Lucy Show* (he played cranky banker Mr. Barnsdahl when Ball couldn't get Gale Gordon, who was committed to *Dennis the Menace*); and made regular appearances on such shows as *Bewitched, The Beverly Hillbillies, Petticoat Junction, Soap,* and literally dozens of others. You would know Lane's face even if you hardly ever watched TV or went to the movies … he was *that* ubiquitous. In fact, he's the subject of a documentary called *You Know the Face*, by Garret Boyajian and George Ridjaneck, in post-production at this writing. I met Garret and George in Jamestown, New York, in 2006 when they were filming interviews for a different documentary, on Ball, and they were filled with amazing stories about Lane, his career, and his amazingly good condition and *joie de vivre* despite his advanced age.

Boyajian notes, "Charles Lane was Hollywood's oldest actor, with over 600 film and television performances. Not a day goes by that someone around the world isn't enjoying a Charles Lane performance. At the age of 97, Lane came out of retirement for an amazing third act of his career. He participated in our upcoming Lucille Ball fan documentary, hosted a TV retrospective of his work with Lucy and Desi to raise money for the Lucille Ball-Desi Arnaz Center, and gave his first performance of the 21st century in George's soon-to-be-released holiday treat 'The Night Before Christmas.'" Lane is one of the few actors about whom it can honestly be said, there'll never be another like him; he was still working when he passed away. For more information, visit charles-lane.com.

LANSING, JOI

Born in 1928 as Joyce Wassmansdoff, this voluptuous blonde model and actress was at first better known for her figure than her talent; when she was cast in *Love that Bob* (the final three seasons, 1956-'59) she proved herself a capable light comedienne with more to offer than her looks. She joined Ball and Arnaz first on *I Love Lucy* (playing herself in the episode "Desert Island," November 26, 1956), and later on one of the better *Lucy-Desi Comedy Hours*, "Lucy Wants a Career," April 13, 1959, playing "Miss Low Neck," one of Lucy's job rivals. She also guest-starred on Arnaz's show *The Mothers-in-Law*, in the episode "Take Her, He's Mine," airing March 23, 1969. She continued in movies and television (she's especially remembered as Lester Flatt's wife Gladys in a handful of *Beverly Hillbillies* episodes). Lansing died of breast cancer in 1972.

LAUGH TRACK

Situation comedies routinely "sweeten" their soundtracks with prerecorded laughter, but back in the '50s *I Love Lucy* pioneered the use of a live studio audience, because that's how star Lucille Ball performed best: with feedback. With a live audience came, of course, laughter, and all sorts of sounds, which were edited for broadcast by sound man Cameron McCullough.

You may not recognize the name Charles Douglass, but he was responsible for the invention of the Laff Box, creating canned sitcom laughter as we know it today. (Douglass died in April 2003 at 93.) Ball always used a studio audience, but the laughs from *I Love Lucy*—including such recognizable sounds as Ball's mother DeDe's high-pitched laugh and wary "Uh, oh" when something was about to happen—were recycled and have been used over and over again thanks to Douglass' invention.

A major plot point turned on a device similar to the Laff Box in the Broadway play <u>*Nobody Loves an Albatross*</u>, which featured a lead character based on Ball.

LAUGHTER AND LUCY

There are many things one can do to add humor to life on a daily basis. There's watching Lucille Ball on TV, for instance. Ball, by the way, embraced the philosophy of the late Rev. Norman Vincent Peale, espoused in his classic book, *The Power of Positive Thinking.*

Lucy was that rare combination: a clown with glamour. Detail of soft sculpture circa mid-1980s by Jim Dale of ol' softies, Salt Lake City. Author's collection

Lucie Arnaz has organized (and moderated) a series of panel discussions under the rubric "Legacy of Laughter," and sponsored by The Lucille Ball-Desi Arnaz Center in Jamestown, New York. As of this writing, there have been seminars across the country, several held in Ball's hometown, Jamestown. Lucie's Web page (luciearnaz.com) has more information. Panelists include those who create or perform comedy, who use it in their work, or who have been healed by it. In this way, Lucie is continuing her parent's legacy by making people aware of the power, magic, and healing properties of laughter.

But how do we keep laughing in the face of the myriad problems life throws at us at any given time?

First, retrain your brain to not take life so seriously. Find the humor in the flat tire, the misprint in the report at work. Don't go overboard. Certain aspects of your life *should* be taken seriously. But never forget that we only come around this way once, and what's the better way to spend it: laughing at the ironies of our life, or cursing at everything that comes our way?

Michael Miller, M.D., director of the Center for Preventive Cardiology at the University of Maryland Medical Center led a March 2005 panel on the potential health value of humor and notes that the most significant study finding was, "People with heart disease responded less humorously to everyday life situations." In general, they were more hostile and angry than the norm. Miller added, "We know that exercising, not smoking, and eating foods low in saturated fat will reduce the risk of heart disease. Perhaps regular, hearty laughter should be added to the list."

To help us out, the University of Maryland's Medical System website writer Michelle Weinstein has put together a list of methods to increase the health-pumping humor in our lives. Weinstein spoke to Judy Goldblum-Carlton, a humor therapist at the University of Maryland Hospital for Children's Division of Pediatric Hematology/Oncology. Carlton's suggestions are in boldface; mine follow.

1. **Figure out what tickles your funny bone.** Does slapstick ring your bell? Or perhaps something a bit more cerebral? *I Love Lucy* offers both in the same package.

2. **Rent a funny movie.** *Fancy Pants, Easy to Wed, The Long, Long Trailer,* and *Yours, Mine and Ours* are my favorites from Ball's oeuvre.

3. **Add comedy to your commute**. If you're in a car, turn off public radio; that will only depress you further. Put in a comedy tape. Ball's radio show, *My Favorite Husband*, will do fine. If you get satellite radio, there's a 1950s channel that features lots of Ball audio clips (and other classic comedians) on a regular basis.

4. **Start a humor library**. Have scissors, will travel. Cut out any item from papers and magazines that makes you laugh. Post them on the wall at home and at work. Look at them frequently. Smile, laugh. Ball and company graced the covers and insides of many magazines, humor and otherwise, in the 1950s and beyond.

5. **Laugh with others.** Goldblum-Carlton says, "People laugh more with other people. It gives you permission to laugh." Invite friends over for an *I Love Lucy* marathon.

6. **Find humor in seemingly ordinary, everyday things**. Releasing your inner child will help. Ball did it as her Lucy character all the time. Her childlike reactions to something new, or attempts to get something that she wanted, drove her humor, and kept us from viewing the character as selfish or egotistical. Say something nonsensical. Rhyme like Dr. Seuss. Make a funny face. You'll be surprised—it helps.

7. **Learn the basics of humor.** Visit comedy clubs instead of bars. Take notes. Take a class. Watch *I Love Lucy. The Dick Van Dyke Show. All in the Family. Mary Tyler Moore.* Take more notes.

8. **Remember a funny moment....** Such as any of hundreds of Lucy moments. Or that time you were about to pin a corsage on your prom date, for example, and a huge sneeze necessitated a change of plans (not to mention a change of dress)?

9. **Laugh at yourself.** See all of the above, especially No. 6.

10. **Conquer your fears.** Those witches in the Halloween House aren't real witches. In fact, they're Lucille Ball and Vivian Vance (see *The Lucy Show* episode "Lucy and the Monsters" which aired January 25, 1965. In it, after seeing a scary movie, Lucy dreams she and Viv visit a haunted house and turn into witches.) And that ghost in the house you just moved in to isn't out to frighten you ... he wants romance (see any episode of *The Ghost and Mrs. Muir*, 1968-'70).

11. **Act silly.** Ball was the champ at this. Create a costume to make a loved one or friends laugh. Take up ventriloquism. Black out your front teeth. Talk to yourself in a strange voice (but not in front of people who don't know you).

12. **Learn to play.** Playing games with kids and adults can be lots of fun. Charades-type games would seem to offer the best chances to purposely act silly. Ball loved charades and, of course, backgammon, plus word games of any kind.

13. **Visit the zoo and watch the animals, especially the monkeys.** Or, gain some perspective on your situation by watching the animals at work and play. Ball worked with all kinds of animals, from baby elephants to chimps, seals, and dolphins. She knew what a tonic they were.

14. **Lighten up!** The worst thing you can do is take yourself too seriously. Take a deep breath and don't be afraid to act the fool on occasion ... though not in a board meeting in front of your entire company. This was, perhaps, Ball's greatest gift as a comic actress: she was not afraid to act the fool, be it dressing up as a ridiculous-looking Martian, or getting drunk selling a health tonic. The difference was, though she loved doing it, she was really doing it for all of us, her fans.
See also "A Fan of Lucy's."

LET'S FACE IT

A 1940s war-era musical comedy co-starring Vivian Vance, *Let's Face It* had many other Lucy connections. See <u>Stage Career</u> under <u>Vance, Vivian</u> for more.

LIFE WITH LUCY

Debuted: September 20, 1986, 8:30 p.m., Saturday night, CBS
Final Airing: November 15, 1986, 8:30 p.m., Monday night, CBS
Stars: <u>Lucille Ball</u> (Lucille Barker); <u>Gale Gordon</u> (Curtis McGibbon); Larry Anderson (Ted McGibbon); Philip Amelio (Kevin McGibbon); Ann Dusenberry (Margo Barker McGibbon); Jenny Lewis (Becky McGibbon); Donovan Scott (Leonard Stoner)
Awards: None
Based On: A tired premise: Lucy, now a hip, New Age grandma, moves in with her daughter's family and becomes co-owner of her brother-in-law's (Gordon) hardware store, to lethal effect.
Ratings: Lethal is the right word here, unfortunately, for Ball's first sitcom misstep. It started out at No. 23 (that was the first shock; many expected it to be a Top 10 show) and went downhill from there. It was cancelled after airing only eight episodes.

Lucille Ball's final stab at the sitcom format in 1986 was her only TV series flop. The problems were many, but they all began with this: Ball was afraid to do, or determined not to try, anything different from <u>The Lucy Character</u> she'd honed over 25 years in her three other successful series. Coupled with the star's demands—creative control, big salary, guaranteed time slot, and no pilot, all of which were agreed to by producer Aaron Spelling—the show creaked along for eight episodes until the network mercifully gave it the ax. Five filmed episodes were never aired.

The setting had Ball as health-conscious grandmother Lucy Barker moving in with her daughter's family (played by Ann Dusenberry, Larry Anderson, and cute kids Jenny Lewis and Philip Amelio), and butting heads with her ex-husband's business partner and in-law (Gale Gordon) in his hardware store. Ball was in her mid-70s and Gordon was in his 80s; and the viewers cringed every time either of them had to perform anything physical.

Producers Bob Carroll and Madelyn Pugh Davis (Ball's veteran writing team, see separate entries) gave their star weak scripts that depended on Ball's trademark slapstick, instead of letting Ball play a warm, likeable and less loud/annoying older person, something à la Betty White in *The Golden Girls*.

Ball could be found on talk shows lamenting the show's cancellation afterward, complaining, "People don't want me to grow old!" That might have been part of the problem, but the main stumbling block was the unimaginative writing, coupled with the fact that the actors, except for Ball, Gordon, and the guest stars, simply did not bring much to the party. Even so, the press was much harsher on Ball than it needed to be. Critics jumped on the anti-Ball bandwagon with a vengeance not seen since her ill-fated movie, *Mame*.

Producer Aaron Spelling donated all 13 episodes of the series to The Lucille Ball-Desi Arnaz Center, where they are occasionally shown to fans during the center's twice-a-year Lucy festivals.

LIFE WITHOUT GEORGE

This book by Irene Kampen became the basis for *The Lucy Show*.

Kampen was a reporter and author whose work was characterized by her wry humor, wrung from real-life experiences. She was born in Brooklyn in 1922, attended the University of Wisconsin, and edited its humor magazine, *Octopus*. She had a degree in journalism when she graduated in 1943, became a copy girl at a New York paper, and subsequently married Owen Kampen, a World War II pilot. They were one of the original families to settle in Levittown, the haven built on Long Island for GIs.

With her husband and daughter, she moved to Connecticut in 1954, after which her marriage of 15 years fell apart. Forced to work to support her daughter, Kampen took in a divorced woman who had a son to help pay the mortgage. (Sound familiar?) *Life Without George* (1961) was the result, subtitled "The Struggles of Two Whacky [sic] Dames in a Suburban Jungle" and chronicling what it took to raise a child in a small New England town. At the time, divorce was still uncommon, and speaking about it was a social no-no.

It was her first book, and it caught the eye of Desi Arnaz, still at Desilu and looking for a new property for ex-wife Ball. Louis Ferioli, Kampen's companion of 25 years, noted, "It happened that Lucille Ball had just gotten divorced from Desi Arnaz. She was looking for a new TV show [premise] about a divorcée. Irene's book just fit the bill." Ball didn't want to do another show in which she and pal Vivian Vance had husbands.

Ball's character was made a widow, as divorce was an untried topic for TV comedy in 1962, and Vance became TV's first series regular divorcée. The TV series followed Ball and Vance (as Lucy Carmichael and Vivian Bagley) as they dealt with life after their husbands. The first few seasons were genuinely funny and warm, following the spirit of the book, as the two stars played off each other and were forced to do things that "the man" traditionally took care of, e.g., putting up a TV antenna, fixing the shower, and so on.

After Vance left and the kids were written out in 1965, the show became more focused on Lucy's job and her fractious relationship with her banker, Mr. Mooney (Gale Gordon). As it veered from the initial premise of the early years, it became less home-centered and more formulaic.

Kampen went on to write 10 books, including *Europe Without George* (1965), a sort of sequel in which she described a six-week trip to six countries with her daughter, *Due to Lack of Interest Tomorrow Has Been Canceled*, and *Nobody Calls at This Hour Just to Say Hello*. She also wrote for many magazines, and in her later years became a popular lecturer.

Kampen wrote in 1975, "Every time *The Lucy Show* appears on a TV screen, and it appears a lot, I get a royalty check. I love Lucy." She died in 1998.

LITTLE SHOP OF HORRORS

This musical comedy was about Audrey II, a man-eating plant, and Seymour, the shy young man who takes care of it. Based on the screenplay by Charles B. Griffith, it debuted off-Broadway in July 1982 and became a huge hit. Audrey, the female lead, yearns for a picture-perfect place to live with Seymour, one that's like all the shows on TV, which she describes in the song "Somewhere That's Green." The lyrics, by Howard Ashman, include this snippet: "Between our frozen dinner, and our bedtime, nine-fifteen, we snuggle watchin' Lucy on our big, enormous 12-inch screen." The show was revived in 2003 on Broadway.

LOUIS-DREYFUS, JULIA

The actress who created the neurotic but lovable Elaine Benes in *Seinfeld* (and won an Emmy and a slew of other awards for it) might just be a contender for Lucille Ball's comedy crown. Louis-Dreyfus is exercising her comic chops starring on the CBS sitcom *The New Adventures of Old Christine*, in its third season as of this writing. One critic compared her shenanigans on a first-season episode to Ball herself. Tom Shales wrote in *The Washington Post*, "Louis-Dreyfus has a priceless moment in the second episode, with a mustachioed Andy Richter guest-starring as a (potentially) one-night stand that Christine picks up at the supermarket. Attempting earlier to seduce another shopper, she nervously babbles out her entire autobiography, and then stumbles awkwardly into a would-be come-hither wiggle that looks more spasmodic than erotic.

"It's a combination of physical and verbal humor that evokes memories of—and one can never say this lightly—the immortal Lucy herself." The article was headlined "Juicily Lucy-ish, Zanily Elainey." In another episode, with Christine trying to impress a date played by

Scott Bakula, Louis-Dreyfus mulls over how best (ladylike, sophisticated) she should sit on the restaurant's round banquette to meet her date in her tight black dress. She goes from sitting on the edge to lying back and stretching out, leaning on one arm, and finally falling on the floor with a huge thud. This was not only hysterical, it revealed a mastery of physical comedy that not too many younger actresses possess.

Dreyfus won her second Emmy for Best Actress in a Comedy several months after *Christine* premiered in the spring of 2006.

LOUISE, TINA

The beautiful, red-haired starlet of the 1950s and 1960s gained television immortality as sexy "movie star" Ginger Grant on *Gilligan's Island* (1964-'67). Louise has said that she was initially hired to play a combination "Marilyn Monroe—Lucille Ball" type, and successfully fought back when the producers asked her to play the role sexy without the comedy.

LUCILLE BALL AND VIVIAN VANCE

The real-life relationship between Lucille Ball and Vivian Vance was complicated. Desi Arnaz and producer/head writer Jess Oppenheimer hired Vance for the Ethel Mertz role on *I Love Lucy* before she and Ball met. Ball was wary of working with anyone new, especially someone she'd never heard of. There was a bit of friction between the two at the start. Once Ball realized that Vance's Broadway stage and musical-comedy experience made her an invaluable comedy partner, she loosened up. The two enjoyed the many

Lucy and Viv share a laugh at dinner, as a reporter takes notes. Photofest

hours they spent together on the set, and would spend lots of extra time rehearsing routines to make sure they got them right.

In the 1950s, after the success of *I Love Lucy*, the public couldn't get enough information about the show and its stars. This resulted in more than one fan magazine article written "by Vivian Vance," although it was possible the authors were reporters or editors who reshaped quotes from interviews with Vance. One of these articles, "Life with Lucy On and Off Screen," from *TV FAN*, October 1954, is quite revealing about Vance's feelings toward Ball.

Vance wrote that Ball "is one star who will not try to play both parts simultaneously. Lucy loves her part and I love mine. Believe me, I've worked with women stars who tried to play *all* the parts!" (Vance may have been referring to her time in *Skylark* with Gertrude Lawrence. See <u>Stage Career</u> under <u>Vance, Vivian</u>.)

She said that the best way to get along with Ball was "to be adamant.... So we settled into a comfortable routine of respecting each other's acting ability, depending on each other in a crisis.... The screaming meemies we have are always about the characters or the script. There's never anything personal about them."

About Ball's personality and behavior, Vance wrote, "[Lucy] has never realized she's a natural comic, and when we first started the show, her lack of confidence was appalling for such a great talent. It has been wonderful to watch her growth in confidence since then.

Ball and Vance take a cigarette break (and some direction) between scenes on the set of *The Lucy Show*. **Photofest**

"Lucy is inherently funny. She doesn't have to depend on a characterization.

"She is also a manager of people and situations. She has a never-ending supply of suggestions for everyone. You must have a strong backbone and a strong head to evade the helpful intentions of Lucy."

Vance noted that she and then-husband Phil Ober socialized with Ball on Thanksgiving and Christmas when they were home ("The happiest I've ever seen her is when she's standing by the Christmas tree giving out the presents she's chosen with such care and love"), but limited other social activities "because we're together so much."

Finally, Vance sounded as if she had already accepted her role as TV's best-loved friend and neighbor. "One of the deep wells to be filled in all of us is to belong. And in show business, it is hard to belong. But now I know years from now I'll always feel that I did something that belongs to the people. No matter where I go, people recognize me. We've both given our all to the show, and the show has given us something wonderful in return."

Another fan magazine in 1954 featured an article by Vance called "Here's Why I Love Lucy!" In it, Vance waxed enthusiastic about being close with Ball on and off the set: "We're the best-known 'best friends' in the country I guess, Lucy and I. We're the present-day feminine version of Damon and Pythias, and it's 'for real' off-screen as well as on. Our friendship is just as real, cozy, and next-door-neighborly as that between Lucy Ricardo and Ethel Mertz. And a heck of a lot more peaceful. For Mrs. Ricky Ricardo and Mrs. Fred Mertz have their fallings-out, but Mrs. Desi Arnaz and Mrs. Philip Ober have yet to have their first one!"

How often the two socialized is a moot point, since they spent almost every waking hour working together. Though Ball could be a stern taskmaster on the set, Vance's attitude quickly became one of tolerance; she realized that if the show was a hit, it would be good for her, and decided early on to take anything that Ball might throw at her.

By the time they finished with the *I Love Lucy* format in 1960 (after the hour-long *Lucy-Desi Comedy Hour* specials) Vance was eager to get back to stage and movie work, and bury the character of Ethel Mertz; she really did "have issues" with co-star William Frawley, and the feeling was mutual.

Ball had often said she never would have gone back to series television (in 1962) without Vance alongside her, and she spent a lot of energy persuading Vance to leave her happy Connecticut home and new husband to co-star in *The Lucy Show*. That partnership only lasted for three seasons, as Vance tired of commuting from coast to coast every week. She deliberately asked for much more money (half a million dollars!) than she knew Ball could spend, and her redheaded friend, puzzled, withdrew the offer. But there was no animosity between the two that would stop them from working together.

A *TV Guide* article in 1963 perfectly captured what made Vance and Ball different from other comedy teams: "The Lucy and Vivian team doesn't fit the classic pattern [of comedy teams]. [They were] two comedians who were not only lifelong friends, but who both got laughs, a lack of which is the fundamental frustration of the straight man that drove Bud Abbott to misanthropy and Dean Martin to acting [without Jerry Lewis]."

"Basically, we like each other," is how Vance explained her chemistry with Ball to the *Cedar Rapids Gazette* in 1963. "That's important on television. On the stage, two performers who loathe each other can get away with playing together—but television is like an X-ray."

In 1966, retired from *The Lucy Show* and celebrating her return to the theater, Vance had nothing but nice things to say about her comedic partner to the *Ada* (Oklahoma) *Evening News* on September 26. "Lucille has the greatest talent; it never stops and it's so inventive. I never ceased to be amazed at the exuberance of her talent. We have fun when we work but we both like to work hard. Fourteen years together, yes, it's amazing. But each year we didn't think we'd go on for another year. We were in at the beginning, when television was fresh, and we had great writers.

"It's a good thing I was on the Lucy shows—it gave me something to do. I was in analysis part of the time. Lucy and I will work together again—there's been a lot of mail about it. We hope once in a while to do a big hour special."

Though that never materialized, Vance guest-starred on Ball's TV series through the 1970s, and appeared with Ball a final time in the special *Lucy Meets the President* in 1977. By then Vance had suffered a mastectomy and a stroke. It's been reported that Ball was unnecessarily cruel to Vance during the rehearsals for that show. But it's also been reported that Vance was one of the few people who could talk back to Ball and get away with it. Perhaps Ball, aware of Vance's deteriorating health, didn't want to make her think she was taking it easy on her.

Through the years, Ball continually credited her writers and co-stars for the success of *I Love Lucy*, especially Vance, and after Vance's death in 1979 Ball often cried when speaking about her and what a wonderful comedy partner she was. The two appeared in nearly 300 TV episodes together, making them the medium's top comedy team. It's clear they loved and respected each other, but like any close relationship involving two strong-willed people (such as sisters), there were times when they just didn't agree or get along.

THE LUCILLE BALL-DESI ARNAZ CENTER

Situated in Jamestown, New York, 58 miles south of Buffalo, New York, where Ball lived for much of her childhood, the storefront museum celebrating Ball's career opened in 1996. Now much more than a storefront, the Center includes The Lucy-Desi Museum, still in its original storefront location but as of this writing about to be expanded to a former Jamestown commercial building acquired by the Center; Ball's childhood home in nearby Celeron, bought by fans Bill and Mary Rapaport, and in the process of being restored and, ultimately, donated to the Center (see Lucy's Celeron, New York House); and The Desilu Playhouse, which offers re-creations of the familiar studio stage sets from *I Love Lucy*, such as The Tropicana Nightclub, plus displays of memorabilia from the 1950s, and hosts screenings.

Center board member Mary Rapaport recalled in 2006, "We heard the recreated sets from the 2001 50th anniversary *I Love Lucy* traveling exhibit were available." Bill continues: "We met with them in Denver and the Museum made arrangements to get them at a very good price, but they needed to raise the cash to purchase them, and a place to put them, because the new Museum space isn't available yet—and even when it is, if they put the sets in there, there won't be room for much else.

"At about that same time, the old Rite-Aid building in downtown Jamestown became available, and Ric Wyman [the Center's executive director] had the idea of putting the two together. He approached us…. What I like about the location is [the new Museum will be] very close by. The two will be anchors for the entire downtown area when they're done. We had been planning to help with the sets anyway, so this was something just a little bit extra for us to do."

The Center also presents some of the Legacy of Laughter events—panel discussions with audience interaction that explore and celebrate the inestimable value of laughter. The Center holds a Lucy-Desi Days Festival each year in the spring, and another celebration around the time of Lucy's birthday, August 6. Original Ball/Arnaz art and memorabilia is always on display and special guests abound. Its website is www.Lucy-Desi.com.

THE LUCILLE BALL-DESI ARNAZ SHOW

Debuted: November 6, 1957, CBS (Note: 13 episodes aired at different times, on different days.)
Final Airing: April 1, 1960, CBS
Stars: <u>Lucille Ball</u> (Lucille McGillicuddy Ricardo); <u>Desi Arnaz</u> (Ricky Ricardo); <u>Vivian Vance</u> (Ethel Louise Mae Roberta Potter Mertz); <u>William Frawley</u> (Frederick "Fred" Hobart Edie Mertz)
Awards: None.
Based On: *I Love Lucy*. The further adventures of the Ricardos and the Mertzes, in Connecticut, expanded to an hour in length. The quality of the episodes widely varied; a few were excellent, most were average, and some really caught the format (and the stars) showing their age.
Ratings: Ratings were good, holding at around 40 percent share of the audience or higher, indicating the public still loved Lucy (and Ricky, Fred, and Ethel, too). Details below.

Lucille Ball and Desi Arnaz halted production on the half-hour *I Love Lucy*, still No. 1 in the ratings, after the 1956-'57 season, because they felt they had taken the half-hour format as far as it could go. Still, as evidenced by the ratings, the public hadn't had enough of the Ricardos and the Mertzes, so it was decided to continue their adventures in a new, hour-long format.

"When we filmed the first show, it was like a New York opening," Vivian Vance told her "hometown" paper, *The Albuquerque Journal*, in 1957. "We shot on three stages, so our studio audience had to move three times. I'm sure this program will be as popular as the weekly series—and this way we all have a chance to slow down and breathe."

Judging by the ratings for the first four outings, Ball and Arnaz made the right decision. In paring down the weekly appearances of the Ricardos and the Mertzes but lengthening each individual one the Arnazes maximized audience interest and anticipation. The Nielsen ratings for the first four hour-long episodes were:

"Lucy Takes a Cruise to Havana," airing November 6, 1957: 47.0 rating; 18.828 million homes reached.

"The Celebrity Next Door," December 3, 1957: 39.2; 15.738 million homes. The Scripps-Howard syndicated writer Harriet Van Horne wasn't fond of this episode. She wrote, "When Tallulah [guest star Tallulah Bankhead] in priceless mink and beat-up slacks, trips next door to use the phone, Lucy is so excited she rips it out of the wall. Though the laugh track emitted one of its lunatic roars, it was right there that the show began to sag. This was overplaying, and so was virtually all that followed…. The writers had dealt Lucille Ball a poor hand this time around. They made her faintly vicious…. The plot demanded too much jousting between Lucy and Tallulah. As Fred and Ethel, Bill Frawley and Vivian Vance are as wonderful as ever."

"Lucy Hunts Uranium," January 3, 1958: 43.6; 18.190 million homes.

"Lucy Wins a Race Horse," February 3, 1958: 41.6; 17.383 million homes.

These four episodes, as of March 19, 1958, were also the four top-rated television shows of the season up to that point, reported *Variety*.

The longer format allowed the Arnazes to take the characters on location to more exotic locales than had been done on *I Love Lucy*. It was also more expensive to produce, so only five episodes were done in the 1957-'58 season, and they were aired as "special programming." For the next two seasons, the show aired occasionally in the time slot of the *Westinghouse Desilu Playhouse*—five more episodes during the 1958-'59 season, and the final three episodes during the 1959-'60 season.

In a review of the episode "Lucy Wants a Career," the fourth (of five) shows in the second season (it aired April 13, 1959), Van Horne nailed the reason some of the comedy hours didn't gel. Headlined *Lucille Ball: Great Clown*, Horne wrote, "Now we know what ailed all those clumsy, clamorous Lucy-Desi specials … for the past year, complete with banshee laugh tracks…. They starred the Ricardos and the Mertzes and wandering guest stars [when] plainly, they should have starred, in all her wild glory, our girl Lucy.

"Last night's special from Desilu Land was the best of the year…. It concentrated all attention where it rightly belongs—on the star. Ricky, Fred, and Ethel slipped neatly in and out of the story, expertly setting up the laughs for Lucy. Even guest star Paul Douglas was there simply as foil … to show how a normal, confident male can become hopelessly enmeshed in the divine lunacies of Mme. Lucy.

"No matter how often you see her, the comic genius of Lucille Ball seems fresh and new. She makes each mad scheme seem completely spontaneous; she doesn't caricature, she doesn't satirize. Lucy is an original [and also] an innocent, even when scheming like the fox in the hen yard. It's this innocence that makes Lucy's humor so appealing."

That year also featured an hour-long holiday-themed special called "The Desilu Review," with actors from Ball's Desilu Workshop, including Carole Cook, Dick Kallman (see separate entries for both), Majel Barrett of *Star Trek* fame, and future Hollywood columnist and Turner Classic Movies host Robert Osborne (see <u>Osborne, Robert</u>).

These 60-minute shows were very diverse in quality and humor. Some were good ("Lucy Wants a Career"), some were bad ("Lucy's Summer Vacation," with Howard Duff and Ida Lupino), and some were downright awful ("Milton Berle Hides Out at the Ricardos"). But a couple of gems made it through (specifically, the "Celebrity Next Door" with Bankhead, and "Lucy Makes Room for Danny," with Danny Thomas and his TV family).

The first show in this series, "Lucy Takes a Cruise to Havana," timed out at 75 minutes, and Arnaz managed to convince the occupant of the next hour to give up fifteen minutes; Arnaz knew the audience would be huge and it would spill over into whatever followed. And he was right. But the economics of TV caught up with it when the series was purchased by CBS in 1962 to run as a summer replacement show. The show began with Ball and Arnaz welcoming columnist Hedda Hopper into their home, and telling her—via flashbacks—how they first met and fell in love. CBS cut Hopper's scenes entirely and severely shortened other scenes so the episode would fit a 60-minute time slot. The cut footage was finally restored for the series' 2007 DVD release (See Lucy on DVD).

COMEDY IS HARD: Desi Arnaz was proud of his work, and routinely voiced displeasure of the fact that critics often gave comedy performances short shrift in favor of heavy drama. By the time of *The Lucy-Desi Comedy Hour*, he had become an expert and success in his chosen field, and felt comfortable speaking out. Comedy, he noted in a July 22, 1959 article in *Variety*, "is all black or all white. It's either funny or it's not. In dramatic shows there are all kinds of shades of gray, but comedy has to be just right."

From his *I Love Lucy* and Desilu producing experience, Arnaz believed that good comedy has to derive from the situation, not just show up in a script: "If you throw a pie in a man's face there's got to be a good reason for doing it, if it's going to be funny."

Ironically, in establishing this theme—the need for a believable premise to set up a good comedy sequence—as a way of explaining why he and Lucille Ball were then concentrating on hour-long shows (allowing for more time to set up the comedy), Arnaz ignored the fact that most of the half hour *Lucy* episodes were primers in how to write and perform comedy, and at least half of the hour-long episodes suffered by being too noticeably padded.

HEAT WAVE: William Frawley had no love of the cold, according to a CBS press release dated January 29, 1959. "Frawley, whose complexion turns blue when anyone even mentions a temperature below 72 degrees, was most unhappy during rehearsals for the *Westinghouse Lucille Ball-Desi Arnaz Show* airing Monday, February 9, 'Lucy Goes to Alaska.' [It] is filled with scenes of snow, ice and wintry blasts, reminding Frawley all too vividly of the 'Lucy Goes to Sun Valley' episode, another frosty production that revived his dormant Iowa chilblains.

"'Just for kicks,' Frawley groused, 'I'd like the next few episodes to be something like 'Lucy Goes to Tahiti,' 'Lucy Goes to the Belgian Congo,' and maybe 'Lucy Goes to Palm Springs.'"

LUCILLE BALL ROSE

Jackson & Perkins, promising a color-match close to Lucy's "orange-pink" hair, created this rose in the early 1990s. Its varietal name: JACapri; Apricot Hybrid Tea. Pictures reveal it could range from white with an orange center to all orange-pink.

LUCY (TV Movie, 2003)

Watching "Lucy," the three-hour biopic of Lucille Ball, Desi Arnaz, and *I Love Lucy*, I was prompted to ask a few questions about the motives behind this movie, but I kept coming back to one question: Why?

As in, why bother? We have the original show, still running several times a day on television, and if that's not enough, the entire series is now available on DVD. So why go to the trouble of recreating classic *I Love Lucy* scenes when the originals, which I'm sure even *Lucy* star Rachel York would admit couldn't be topped, are still with us?

That said, the obvious answer is that the public can't get enough of the lovable redhead. Or perhaps the stellar performance of *The I Love Lucy 50th Anniversary Special* in 2001 convinced network executives there was yet life (i.e., ratings and money to be made) in the classic sitcom.

Those who know the life story of the couple who created Desilu will not learn much from this retelling. In fact, they might learn a few wrong things. The movie depicts Desilu buying RKO Studios in 1958 (it actually happened a few years earlier), and gets small things wrong, like having Vivian Vance refer to her husband as Paul, when it was in fact Phil (Ober). Buster Keaton is shown teaching Ball about props on a Columbia set, when in fact he was her mentor at MGM.

The supporting characters are all drawn with wide strokes, so Ball's mom and Arnaz's mom come off as American and Cuban, and that's about it. Madeline Zima makes a spunky young Ball, but she's only in the telepic for the first 20 minutes or so, barely enough to register an impression, other than her dimpled chin, which the real Ball did not have. The actors playing Vance and William Frawley are used mostly in the re-creation scenes, and though vaguely physically reminiscent of the originals, have neither the charm nor spark that Vance and Frawley brought to the show.

Which brings us to Arnaz and Ball. Danny Pino is an excellent actor, as anyone who saw his raw performance as an unapologetic drug dealer on the FX series *The Shield* in 2003 can attest. He pretty much gets Arnaz right, but he's too tiny physically to suggest the more substantial Arnaz. Still, it's a nice tribute performance.

Rachel York tries hard to become Ball, and she gets the voice uncannily right much of the time. But York is hampered by a blandly attractive face that does not match the real beauty Ball bought to her portrayals, in the movies and on TV. She simply does not look like Ball (which is a problem because she has a long face, not Ball's round, expressive one, and a lanky body, not Ball's full figure). Her acting only references Ball; she does not create a complete, rounded, believable portrait of the redhead. Judy Davis, for example, caught some of the spark that was the real Judy Garland when portraying her in a similar type of TV movie (produced, incidentally, by some of the same people who did *Lucy*).

Much of the spice of *I Love Lucy* derived from the fact that movie star Ball, complete with her movie star look, could become such a complete (and successful and funny) clown without sacrificing her beauty. You believed in Ball and Arnaz's love because you believed in the Arnazes.

All you get in *Lucy* are echoes, approximations of the real thing. And so, I ask "Why?" Why not dissect the relationship between Vance and Ball? It was complex and fascinating, and it's never been done. Why not focus on the show itself, so that major players like Jess Oppenheimer, Bob Carroll Jr., and Madelyn Pugh Davis don't get stuck with a few scenes showing them cheering on Ball and company? Why bring up Ball's lifelong phobia of birds, as opposed to other traits that might have better explained why she became a comic?

Why … oh, well, there's no point in asking. By trying to squeeze lives like Ball's and Arnaz's, not to mention their creation *I Love Lucy*, into three hours, the producers necessarily had to leave out a lot, or limit things to one scene or even one line.

As a result, the only goodwill generated by *Lucy* happens when the viewer, already knowing what's coming up next, invests the movie with a backbone and sentiment it doesn't have. Familiarity might allow many viewers to fill in the blanks and come away believing they've seen a good movie. Buy or rent an *I Love Lucy* DVD instead.

LUCY AND DESI: A HOME MOVIE

Lucie Arnaz and husband Laurence Luckinbill produced this 1992 Emmy winner as a response to the poorly done TV movie *Lucy & Desi: Before the Laughter*. The two-hour documentary was made up entirely of candid, original home movies (some in color) shot mostly between 1940 and 1960, supplemented with interviews of famous friends and family. Lucie noted at the time she'd inherited an enormous amount of home-movie footage and wanted to do something with it. "I realized there were 10 years of things I'd never seen—all the early stuff. I saw this side of my parents which was unique, and very sexy and romantic. Plus, there are all these people in them like the Van Johnsons."

She described her mom as a pack rat who "saved every love letter she wrote to my father while he was in the army, and every one he wrote to her. When she died, I found them all. I never read any of them, and for this movie we photographed and read them." A conscious decision was made not to focus too much on *I Love Lucy*, since so much had already been done on it.

The result is a touching, heartfelt tribute to a love affair that never died. One look at Grandma and Grandpa playing together with their grandkids in the family pool, and the way Ball brushes Arnaz's wet hair off his forehead, speaks volumes. As Lucie noted, "I don't think there is anybody I interviewed who knew them who didn't say something to the effect that they never fell out of love with each other. Everybody felt that way. It wasn't just me."

LUCY & DESI: BEFORE THE LAUGHTER (TV Movie, 1991)

This poor effort tried to squeeze TV ratings out of the stormy relationship of Ball and Arnaz. In a *TV Guide* article at the time, Lucie Arnaz and others lambasted the movie as a sorry attempt to make money off falsehoods and rumors about Ball and Arnaz's marriage. Frances Fisher looked amazingly like Lucy in several scenes, but try as she might, she (and soap actor Maurice Bernard as Arnaz) could not overcome the clichéd script, and the fact that the public knew how Ball and Arnaz looked and sounded after four decades of reruns. Avoid this mean-spirited trip down memory lane.

LUCY AND THE MADCAP MYSTERY

Whitman Publishing Co.'s breezy 1963 adventure novel written (by Cole Fannin) for teens and based on characters from *The Lucy Show*. Lucy Carmichael and Vivian Bagley take their kids on a camping trip and get involved with bears, the military, and the FBI. Illustrated throughout, this is a campy, fun excursion.

One of my favorite passages: *"You make such a fuss about things, Viv,"* Lucy said. *"And you ought to be glad of a chance for Harry to admire you in a bathing suit. You look very nice."* This *was true. Viv did look nice. She was blonde and had a good figure. So did red-haired Lucy. They were both very youthful in appearance and spirit, too.*

THE LUCY AWARDS

See Awards.

THE LUCY BOOK

The Lucy Book, by Geoffrey Mark Fidelman (1999), billed as "A Complete Guide to Her Five Decades on Television," lived up to its name, and then some. It documents every TV appearance by Ball up to that time, starting with the 1947 TV season and moving to the years beyond her death.

If it had just done that, the book would be an excellent reference manual on the most unique TV career ever. But there's more. For every episode, Fidelman documents behind-the-scenes happenings, interviews cast and crew who worked on the episode, and offers a real picture of what was going on at the time. A kind of *You Are There* for Ball fans, it shows what was necessary to produce the series from every angle. Temper tantrums, fears, sorrows, writers' conferences, and production problems are covered in detail.

THE "LUCY" CHARACTER

She is, by turns, childish, spiteful, envious, glamorous, kind, loving, pitiable and a million other identifiable characteristics. She is Lucy, the character played by Lucille Ball first in *I Love Lucy* (Lucy Ricardo), then in *The Lucy Show* (Lucy Carmichael), *Here's Lucy* (Lucy Carter), and, finally, in *Life with Lucy* (Lucy Barker). Given Ball's enormous success, it is safe to assume there is something about this character that rang true with the public and made people wanted to see her over and over again.

What was it about Lucy that we all loved? As created initially by Jess Oppenheimer and writers Bob Carroll and Madelyn Pugh Davis for the radio show *My Favorite Husband*, Liz Cugat was the prototype for Lucy Ricardo—essentially lovable, loyal to a fault, a bit envious of things that others had, and a dreamer who always wanted *more*. Her desire could be as simple as wanting a new Easter outfit that husband George couldn't afford or a lead part in the "Young Matrons" annual show.

As the character grew over three years in radio, the question became whether or not CBS would put the show on the new medium, television, and, if so, how it could be reworked for television. Ball's express desire was to work with her husband Desi Arnaz on TV, and the network's desire to work with her was ultimately stronger than its desire *not* to work with Arnaz. On *I Love Lucy, more* became not only material things that Lucy wanted but also the character's fight to get out of the house, to liven

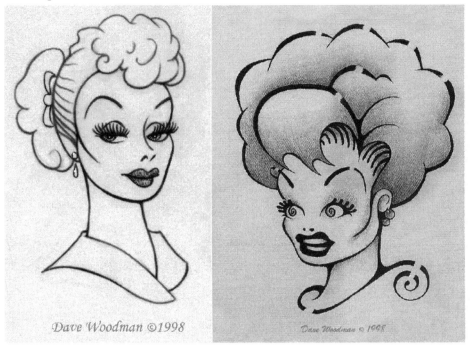

Dave Woodman ©1998

Dave Woodman © 1998

Ball, as Lucy Ricardo (left) and Lucy Carmichael (right), was fearless, and not afraid to make fun of her glamorous self. Caricatures by Dave Woodman; courtesy of the artist.

up her humdrum existence, and to make it in show business. This latter desire was especially convenient since husband Ricky Ricardo happened to be a successful bandleader, allowing Lucy many opportunities to "try out" for a showbiz career.

In many senses, Lucy and Ricky were following the American Dream, as were many other families post-World War II. The 1950s, despite the nostalgia often shown for the era, was actually a rather oppressive, restrictive time, when people were encouraged not to rock the boat, and sameness was a goal. And then along came Lucy: a pretty housewife who could handle the household, albeit with budget problems here and there. But she wanted … *more.*

The zaniness comes out of Lucy's expression of her desire to free herself from the trap of conformity, to let one and all know she will not be stereotyped: She could be a star, after all!

Many felt stifled by the 1950s, as paranoia ran rampant on many fronts, and fad after fad tried to convince Americans they were happy with their lives. Lucy Ricardo went out and did something about her life, which is what we all want to do. Americans in the 1950s, and especially housewives, identified powerfully with Lucy's instincts. The writers kept the plots grounded in reality: as America fanned out to the suburbs, so did the Ricardos.

Keeping it most real, of course, was Ball herself. As Thomas Wagner, writer of the December 2000 PBS *American Masters* special on Ball called "Finding Lucy," noted, "She is extraordinarily consistent in her portrayal of that character. In fact, consistency was a hallmark of the entire series. The writing, the production values, the performances—it's just remarkable."

By 1960, Ball and Arnaz were divorced. No one expected Ball to succeed again on television, especially without Arnaz's behind-the-scenes genius. After a brief gambit on Broadway (*Wildcat*), Ball, missing the daily work and stability a series brought her, coaxed sidekick Vivian Vance to co-star with her (as Vivian Bagley) in *The Lucy Show* (1962).

In the beginning, it was *I Love Lucy* without Fred and Ricky. But the magic of the two female co-stars, and Ball's gift for physical comedy, surprised everyone: the show was a big hit, never leaving the Top 10 in its six-year run, and more often than not in the top five. Those first three years, 1962-'65, were the golden ones, whether Lucy and Vivian were installing a new TV antenna, trying to reach the top bunk bed on stilts, losing a contact lens in a cake, putting in a shower, or getting stuck in a pile of coal in the basement. The audience believed in these characters, and rooted for them.

Lucy Carmichael and Vivian Bagley were, in those first years of *The Lucy Show*, portraying the first solid relationship ever featured in a TV series, much less a sitcom, between two middle-aged women, leavened with comedy. Both were mothers, one was widowed, and the other divorced. As we had followed the friendship of Lucy Ricardo and Ethel Mertz in the first series, so we followed the two characters as they "grew up." The situations mostly grew out of Lucy's need for money, and her schemes to get it. The show business theme was trotted out regularly, too, even more so after Vance left the series in 1965.

Up until the mid-1960s, the Lucy character remained a lovable if klutzy and sometimes not-too-shrewd mother who would do anything she could for her kids and her best friend. That changed somewhat with a new format in 1965: Lucy's kids and Vivian's son were written off the show after Vance left, and Gale Gordon, as Mr. Mooney, head of the bank, moved out to Los Angeles with Lucy Carmichael. The confrontations between blustery Mooney and unreliable Lucy soon became tiresome; the writers ran out of situations for her, so they reworked every old bit they could find. One week Lucy was smart, the next week coquettish trying to get a man, the following week starstruck over one of the innumerable guest stars who filled in for (but could never replace) Vance.

It became harder to care for Lucy Carmichael as her character became more whiny and just plain idiotic, but there was a well of 15 years' emotion that the public had bestowed on Ball, and it willingly hung onto the cherished character of Lucy despite the changes. Perhaps it did so *because* society was changing so desperately and Lucy was the one of the few constants we all had.

And change Lucy did not. When she'd had enough of *The Lucy Show*, Ball devised a new show in 1968 called *Here's Lucy* that allowed her real-life children to participate as regulars, playing Lucy's kids, of course. Lucy Carter was indeed a continuation of the Lucy character, this time as an older single mom trying to do her best for her kids' sake. The series was spiked with many guest stars, as well as Gordon, once again playing the (absent) father figure, Uncle Harry.

Warmth and good writing were consistently missing from the Lucy character by this point. Whatever warmth came through the small screen stemmed from Ball's genuine care for her children, or her continuing ability to squeeze real moments out of the Lucy character's child-like zest for life. The ongoing arguing with Uncle Harry over money was beyond tiresome, and the plots that veered away from that fared better.

Finally, even Ball's biggest fans grew bored: *Here's Lucy* steadily slipped downward in the ratings and finished its run at No. 29 (1973-'74; in 2007 that would be considered a decent rating). That year Ball retired her Lucy character, though it continued to pop up in some of the specials she did for the various networks through the 1970s and early 1980s. Ball had done her job so well over 25 years of weekly home visits that most people assumed she *was* lovable Lucy Ricardo (or Carmichael or Carter) in real life. Nothing could have been further from the truth.

In real life, Ball was serious, not funny (by her own admission) and looked nothing like the various Lucy personas.

As she tried to resurrect Lucy one more time, Ball's age became an issue. In *Life with Lucy* (1986), the Lucy character was rewritten as a meddling New Age grandmother, moving in with her daughter and family, and helping her brother-in-law (yep, blustery Gordon) run a hardware store. Or, more often than not, destroying the store. At this point audiences were unsure what to make of Ball or "Lucy." On the one hand, fans were delighted to have her back on a weekly basis and the audience applauded every entrance and line as if it were classic comedy. On the other hand, even her staunchest fans couldn't argue that it was difficult to watch a woman in her mid-70s doing physical comedy. When she fell, would she be all right? Critics were predictably harsh, sending the series packing after less than two months.

If Ball had played a more realistic older character with some humor, she might have been able to pull off a success. But then, she wouldn't have been Lucy, either. Perhaps 25 years was a nice long run, never to be equaled anyway, and it's best to leave such things as they are. Her legacy is many hours of film footage stocked with classic comedy courtesy of a character named Lucy. As we watch her, she inspires us to be inventive, to dream with her, to stick our necks out for a crazy scheme that just might be a success, and most of all, to laugh, at her foibles, sure, but more often at her humanity and ever-optimistic nature, which we like to think we see in ourselves.

THE LUCY-DESI COMEDY HOUR

Summertime rerun and syndicated name for *The Lucille Ball-Desi Arnaz Show* hour specials that began in 1957 after production ended on the half-hour *I Love Lucy* series.

LUCY ON DVD

There hasn't been much to choose from until recent years, but now there's a true abundance of product featuring Ball available on DVD. What should you buy? We'll discuss Lucy's TV output first, then her movies.

♥ *I Love Lucy* is now available on DVD in one set: *I Love Lucy: The Complete Series* was released on October 23, 2007, by CBS Home Entertainment and Paramount Home Entertainment. According to Paramount, "*The Complete Series* is a 34-disc set that includes hours of bonus material from the individual complete season releases [previously available on DVD], plus all-new special features such as *The I Love Lucy Movie* (1953), with never-before-released scenes and Spanish subtitles; the first fully colorized *I Love Lucy* episode; rare kinescoped highlights of Lucy and Desi's first joint television appearance on *The Ed Wynn Show*; excerpts from the earliest existing Emmy Award telecast in 1954 featuring Vivian Vance accepting the award for Best Series Supporting Actress, and Lucy and Desi accepting the Emmy for Best Situation Comedy, and an on-set commercial from the series premiere."

Available for $199.99, *The Complete Series* is offered in full-screen mode and English mono, with the choice of Spanish subtitles, and Spanish audio on most of the half-hour episodes.

The total running time is a whopping 89 hours and 54 minutes. The set features the 180 half-hour episodes of *I Love Lucy* (on four, five, or six discs per season); the 13 *Lucy-Desi Comedy Hour* episodes (on four discs); and the once-lost *I Love Lucy* pilot, all digitally remastered and magnificently restored.

Of particular interest to fans will be the color episode, "Lucy Goes to Scotland," which was prepared "using color publicity stills, color home movies of the dress rehearsal and the latest in colorization technology," Paramount reports. The episode "is presented just the way it was originally seen by those who were lucky enough to be in the Desilu studio audience on the evening of January 6, 1956."

Extras and bonus features also include 37 episodes of Lucy's radio show, *My Favorite Husband*, which inspired *I Love Lucy*; flubs, lost scenes, restored music, and deleted footage; and audio commentary by Keith Thibodeaux (who played Little Ricky), Doris Singleton (a.k.a. Caroline Appleby), writers Madelyn Pugh Davis and Bob Schiller, and others.

Other than Lucy, Ricky, Fred, and Ethel appearing in one's living room via holographic projection, I can't imagine anything else a fan would want on such a collection.

♥ Beware anything called *The Lucille Ball Collection* until you've examined it closely. There are several repackaged versions of *The Lucy Show* under this umbrella title. There are no extras, and quality is varied. *Lucy Show* episodes have been packaged and repackaged for years under many different titles, first on VHS and now DVD. I'll wait until an "official" *Lucy Show* DVD is released.

♥ You'll be happier buying the boxed *Here's Lucy: Best-Loved Episodes from the Hit TV Series* set, produced by Lucie and Desi Jr. This nicely done package offers 24 of the "best" episodes, plus loads of actually interesting extras (rehearsal footage, bloopers, rarely seen clips) and commentary from Lucie, Desi Jr. and some of the guest stars. Featured in the boxed set are three episodes guest-starring Vivian Vance. Highly recommended.

♥ Several TV specials that feature and/or salute Ball are also available and worth looking at. They include *CBS Salutes Lucy: The First 25 Years*; several of the *Dean Martin Celebrity Roasts*, but especially the one honoring Ball; Ball's 1985 TV movie, *The Stone Pillow*; and the *I Love Lucy 50th Anniversary Celebration*.

♥ More of Ball's films are available on DVD than ever, including gems like *Yours, Mine and Ours*, *Fancy Pants*, *The Facts of Life*, *Lured*, *The Dark Corner*, *Best Foot Forward*, and *Too Many Girls*. Best of all, a Ball film collection was released in June 2007 by Warner Bros., and features (finally!) some of her best pictures and at least one of her campiest. The best include the plush *DuBarry Was a Lady* (1943; Ball was rarely photographed lovelier than in this wartime escapist musical); *Dance, Girl, Dance* (1940; a pioneering feminist vision from gay director Dorothy Arzner that pits cynical stripper Ball against naive "dancer" Maureen O'Hara); and *The Big Street* (1942, in which Ball shows her dramatic chops as a selfish, greedy lounge singer idolized by busboy Henry Fonda). The mediocre is *Critic's Choice*, the least effective of Ball's four pairings with Bob Hope; don't blame the stars, the script was old-fashioned even for 1964.

And then there's the camp-fest that was Ball's big-screen farewell: 1974's *Mame*. Many people, even Ball's most ardent fans, have problems with this movie. I don't. The critics hated it, and years later people still ask, "Why didn't they get Angela Lansbury to do it? She was a star." Not so much, at least in the eyes of Warner Bros. Lansbury may have had a rapt Broadway following at the time, but in Warners' eyes, she lacked the star wattage to put across a major motion picture musical. They'd bought the property for Ball, and Ball would play it. In fact, Ball was considered the *only* bankable Hollywood star "of a certain age" who could play Mame Dennis. They even waited for Ball's broken leg (from a skiing accident) to heal. Lucy's singing voice, or what was left of it, is a moot point. If you have a problem with her low, basso rasp, then don't watch, or listen. Her performance, however, is pretty damned good. Notice that even when doing slapstick she is *not* being Lucy Ricardo (such as the bit on skates at the department store).

Another sore point: Ball got rid of Madeline Kahn (initially signed to play Agnes Gooch) when it became apparent Kahn was going to take her time getting into character. Lucy wanted to see the frumpy Eunice character Kahn created for *What's Up, Doc?* up front, but Kahn was less a comedienne than a comic actress and needed to prepare, to get "into" her role. Finally, Ball demanded, "Get me the Gooch I saw in L.A.!" which happened to be the original stage Gooch, Jane Connell.

P.S. Don't feel bad for Kahn. See <u>Connell, Jane</u>, and <u>Kahn, Madeline</u>.

Critics savaged the movie, but more to the point, they savaged Ball personally—which devastated her—as if to say, "How dare you take on this role? How dare you use gauze and Vaseline and makeup to tame your years?" Come on—Hollywood's been doing that since the get-go with movies and publicity stills. Face it, would you have wanted to see Bette Davis without makeup? Trust me, the answer's no. Or the forest of blonde hairs that grew on Ginger Rogers' face? Uh-uh. Or have Claudette Colbert revealed as the no-neck she was? Probably not.

So give Ball a break, enjoy the fabulous Technicolor art direction and color, the incredible costumes, and a generally top-notch cast (excepting the unfortunately charmless Kirby Furlong, who plays the young Patrick … I never could understand how such a bland kid actor was cast). Open a new window. You might find the picture an enjoyable period piece. And even if you don't, you'll never stop me from loving it!

LUCY'S CELERON, NEW YORK HOUSE

[In May 2005, during Lucy-Desi Days over Memorial Day weekend, Mary and Bill Rapaport—she's a Lucy-Desi Center board member and both of them are big fans and Jamestown area supporters—were kind enough to invite me to sit in on an interview they did with Jamestown's Post-Journal. *My transcript follows.]*

Mary: I was sick about six years ago with cancer, and I started watching a lot of Lucy on TV during the night … I always watched Lucy, but I was watching more because it was always on during the night—and it got me through a lot of stuff.… My husband got me a membership to The Lucy-Desi Museum, which I found on the Web, and our involvement just grew and grew. I started collecting Lucy memorabilia and current merchandise as well. I come down to Jamestown often on weekends and help out in the Museum gift shop, which I love to do.

Lucy's (Celeron, New York) house [where she lived during part of her childhood] went up for sale, and Bill and I decided we didn't want anyone else to have the house except the museum, so we put in an offer and bought the house. We're renovating the house back to 1922, when Lucy lived there, as original as we can get it. Fred Ball and Cleo Smith (Lucy's brother and cousin) [helped] us get the inside of the house perfectly correct, with their memories, and then we're going to donate the house back to the Museum so that everyone can enjoy it.

New York interior designer Eric Cohler (who's also designing the new Museum headquarters) is coming tomorrow to help us with colors and period furniture, draperies, fabric and wallpaper, so that we can get the house as close to a 1920s look as possible. Bill and I talk a lot about how Jamestown needs a lot of help coming back; there are beautiful buildings downtown and such nice people here. We really wanted to help in some way.…

Bill: I used to live in Jamestown, in the late 1970s, early 1980s, and at that time Jamestown was still a vibrant small town. Twenty-five years later, it's a shell of its former self. When someone told me, 25 years ago, that Lucille Ball was born here—and asked "How come they don't do more to celebrate that?—none of my friends knew or cared about it at the time. So I have a kind of personal link to all of it. The various foundations have been very positive. It's all going to help open up downtown, get more people jobs, etc. It needs to happen now. That's what will bring people and businesses into town.

Mary: After reading a lot of the books about Lucy, and then you walk into the house, go upstairs and stand in her bedroom, and you look out the back window … right now you can see the lilacs, they're in bloom. You are *her* standing there, looking at exactly what she said she saw, because it's still there. Her linoleum is still on the bedroom floor. She walked on that with her bare feet. And so … you're there. Soon it'll be everyone's view. When you walk in the front door of Lucy's house, and you know that the curtain rod that's there separating the hall and the living room was used to hang a curtain, for when she would come downstairs and perform, you cannot walk in the house without stopping, looking at the rod, and envision it happening.

And then, of course, I have pictures of her in the house from [much later] where she was explaining to Desi about all that. It's been a series of discoveries. There's a story, in fact, Lucie Arnaz told me last night: There was always a mirror hanging over the kitchen sink, and Lucy used to do the dishes while acting into the mirror, with DeDe (her mother) admonishing Lucy to finish the dishes. But Lucy was having too much fun contorting her image in the mirror. When we bought the house, we found there wasn't a mirror above the sink, there's a window. Our carpenters took the back siding off (the house), and found from the frame there were two original windows, but neither in the middle, which means that someone had replaced the middle section with a window (where the mirror hung in Lucy's day) and took the other two windows out. We've now reversed that, so there will be a mirror above the kitchen sink, and the other (surrounding) windows are back in now.

Little details like that add to the original feeling we're trying to give the house. I heard a story today that Lucy's father had made her a dollhouse. And while the guys were digging up the front porch, they found a tiny cast-iron frying pan, all rusted, and a child's doll house. We have no way of knowing, of course, but we're going to assume (*laughing*) it was Lucy's.

THE LUCY SHOW

Debuted: October 1, 1962, 8:30 p.m. Monday night, CBS
Final Airing: March 4, 1968, 8:30 p.m. Monday night, CBS
Stars: <u>Lucille Ball</u> (Lucille Carmichael); <u>Vivian Vance</u> (Vivian Bagley); <u>Gale Gordon</u> (Theodore J. Mooney); <u>Candy Moore</u> (Chris Carmichael); <u>Jimmy Garrett</u> (Jerry Carmichael); <u>Ralph Hart</u> (Sherman Bagley); <u>Mary Jane Croft</u> (Audrey Simmons/Mary Jane Lewis)
Awards: Emmys for Outstanding Continued Performance by an Actress in a Leading Role in a Comedy Series (Ball) in 1967 and 1968.

Based On: The book _Life Without George_, by Irene Kampen. A divorced woman with one child (Vance) moves in with her widowed friend who has two kids (Ball) to make ends meet. The setting is the fictitious Connecticut suburb of Danfield.

Ratings: _The Lucy Show_ was never out of the Top 10, and grew more popular in its final three years: It ranked (in order of its six TV seasons) No. 5, No. 6, No. 8, No. 3, No. 4, and No. 2.

Trivia: When Lucy won the first of her two Emmys for this series, in 1967, she was overwhelmed and cried at the podium, telling the audience how meaningful it was because she always thought they gave her the (_I Love Lucy_) Emmys for "being pregnant."

This show, filmed in black and white in the first season, was basically a continuation of Lucy and Ethel's adventures … without their husbands. It was ballyhooed as Ball's big return to TV, though no one in the industry actually expected it to do as well in the ratings as it did. But they underestimated the public's affection for Ball. Vance played the first divorced woman on prime-time TV. The first season episodes gave both characters boyfriends (including Dick Martin's character, friendly neighbor Harry), and dating was a frequent theme.

CBS announced Ball's return to series television in a press release that trumpeted, "Lucille Ball, the animated redhead with a unique knack for reducing the most sober situations into a hilarious shambles, returns to television Monday October 1 (8:30-9:00 p.m. EDT) in _The Lucille Ball Show_." Ball, described as "a colorfully wrapped bundle of energy," was then profiled for three pages, with no further mention of the show, its plot, or its co-stars.

Vance commented in 1963 to reporter Cynthia Lowry, "Before we started the new show, I kept talking with the writers, begging them to keep [my] part more feminine—I didn't mean that I didn't want to be funny, but I wanted to get away from those tough, hard-bitten, masculine-sounding jokes [that were a trademark of Ethel Mertz]. And this character gives me a chance to wear some nice clothes, too."

The reviews were mostly loving and appreciative of Ball's return to TV, despite the series being referred to as "a variable" where "you might have to wait between the great moments." Gilbert Seldes in _TV Guide_ (March 2, 1963) wrote a valentine to Ball: "How hard it is to be a beautiful woman I can only guess from certain commercials. From my own observation, I know that to be a beautiful woman and, at the same time, a great slapstick comedian is one of the rarest things in the world. A generation ago, Mabel Normand made it, and later Carole Lombard. Since then the incomparable practitioner of this double art has been Lucille Ball."

Interestingly enough, Seldes admits he lambasted _I Love Lucy_ as "the worst program of the year" when it debuted. That was because he was angry that it "used only about one-fifth of

Miss Ball's armory of talents. More of them are visible on *The Lucy Show*." He might be the only critic ever to compare this show favorably to its predecessor.

Variety was bit more sober in its assessment. Noting that in the first episode of *The Lucy Show* Ball "pranced, clowned, jumped, ran, walked, was elated, and crushed," the reviewer said, "It all didn't add up to hilarious comedy, but there were enough yocks to keep the fans' eyes dancing on the screen." Complaining that the major characters weren't delineated well enough, *Variety* conceded that Ball "is a winning performer" and the show "surely has the quality of what could be a happy romance, and a love affair that might grow between viewers and the series with time." Calling Vance "a fine performer" who assisted Ball in her hijinks, the reviewer hoped Ball's character would not be pegged as a "worrisome mother" and that the introduction of Dick Martin as a male foil for Lucy in future episodes might help.

CBS used this caricature by Wach Steter to publicize *The Lucy Show* **in 1962. Author's collection**

Two years later, in 1964, *Variety* reviewed the third season opener, noting, "Lucille Ball and sidekick Vivian Vance are providing the same mixture as before. While the ladies, aided and abetted by Gale Gordon, are not making much of a contribution to theatrical history, no one can accuse them of loafing while a guest star carries the load as some other programs have done.

"A collection of third, fourth, and fifth bananas, including Candy Moore, Jimmy Garrett, and Ralph Hart, make their own contributions to the fun or wisely stay out of the way of the daring duo." The conclusion: "For the third straight season, CBS is having a Ball!"

The kids (Moore and Garrett were Lucy's, Hart was Vivian's) were innocuous, and often shunted to the side or not used at all, especially after the first season. Ball and Vance's comedy could still work well, and the first few seasons' episodes are worth watching for that.

Once Gordon came aboard as the head of the bank (Theodore J. Mooney) in the second season, things subtly changed. The show's humor was less character-driven and more situation-oriented. Without a humanizing influence like a partner or husband, Ball's character was often merely shrill or, even worse, stupid.

Vance tired of commuting from Connecticut every week and called it quits after the 1964-'65 season. The format changed: Lucy Carmichael (along with banker Mooney) moved to California. The kids were sent away to school. Lucy and Gordon fenced every week, occasionally with Lucy on Mooney's side as they faced the wrath of his boss, Mr. Cheever (the estimable <u>Roy Roberts</u>). Almost weekly, various guest stars helped the show stay afloat, and actresses like Joan Blondell and <u>Mary Jane Croft</u> subbed for Vance as Lucy's co-conspirators. Vance herself popped in once or twice a year for a visit, but it just wasn't the same.

The AP's Cynthia Lowry noted, in a 1966 review in the *Indiana Evening Gazette* (a year after Vance left the show), that, "Since Lucy lost her co-star, Vivian Vance, the show occasionally reaches pretty far for laughs."

The country was going through drastic changes, and Ball's comedy was rooted in an old-fashioned mentality. Still, audiences loved watching her, and the show left the air rated No. 2.

THE LUCY SHOW GAME

Board game released in 1962 by Transogram, and copyrighted by Desilu Productions. "It's a real merry-go-round!" the box proclaimed. It featured a color headshot of Ball plus black-and-white headshots of Vance and their TV kids. The game itself was surprisingly mercenary in nature (or maybe not, since Lucy and Viv were always short of cash on the TV show): Four players, two "Lucys" and two "Vivians" (they are cardboard cutout figures) vie for $1 million. To get the prize, they must spend exactly $100,000; not a penny more or less. Players can spend their money on jewelry (at "Sniffany Jewelry"), exclusive fashions (at "R.H. Lacy"), and so on.

LUCY'S NOTEBOOK

Lucy's Notebook was a promotional item released in the mid-1950s; there are "realistic" illustrations of Ball and Arnaz on the cover, along with a note that promises, "inside secrets on favorite menus, recipes, and good entertaining by the star of *I Love Lucy*." There are items like the "housewife's secret weapon," what to do on the cook's night off, suggestions about outdoor cooking, and how to have extra fun at your "television parties." Also featured are pictures of the Mertzes with the Ricardos, old dinnerware like Candlewick, and many recipes in the 40-page booklet. The back cover is a color ad for Philip Morris cigarettes.

M

MACMURRAY, FRED

An actor in movies from the mid-1930s through the 1970s, MacMurray moved easily from light comedy to hard-boiled drama. Two of his best performances are as the murderous insurance man in the classic *Double Indemnity* (1940), and the hapless polltaker run afoul of a murderous hillbilly family in the screwball comedy *Murder, He Says* (1945), also featuring Ball pal Barbara Pepper.

He co-starred in one of the funnier *Lucy-Desi Comedy Hours*, "Lucy Hunts Uranium," which aired January 3, 1958. And in 1960, he fully committed to television by taking a starring role in *My Three Sons* (1960-'72), which also happened to co-star William Frawley (for the first five seasons) in his only major post-Fred Mertz role. MacMurray didn't really want to work by then, and he filmed all of his scenes at the beginning of the season, so the other actors had to work around his schedule.

According to MacMurray biographer Chuck Tranberg, "I spoke with director Mel Shavelson for my book (*Fred MacMurray: A Biography*) and he said that before he came aboard [on the film *Yours, Mine and Ours*] Fred was slated to co-star with Lucy, but due to Henry Fonda's Navy connections it was decided to cast Fonda instead. I read elsewhere that John Wayne and Jackie Gleason were also considered for the role of Frank Beardsley.

"When Fred did 'Lucy Hunts Uranium,' Lucy thought he was 'nice enough' but she had to really work with him on the comedy—particularly the phone booth sequence—because of his apparent lack of timing. I found that interesting since Fred had been one of Paramount's top light comedy leading men during his [movie] heyday, but obviously he and Lucy had different styles."

MacMurray died in 1991; he was married for 37 years to actress June Haver.

MAGAZINE COVERS

The following selection of some of the hundreds of magazine covers on which Ball was featured—everything from the *National Enquirer* to *Rolling Stone* to *Scholastic Math* magazine—offers an idea of the type of popularity attained by the comedienne. See also the separate list of *TV Guide* covers under <u>TV Guide</u>. Type in quotes is the actual cover line.

   Ball of course, appeared in many magazines from the 1930s on, not on the covers, but inside in various advertisements, for anything from Max Factor makeup to cigarettes to Lucite wall paint. (See <u>Ads Featuring Lucille Ball</u>.)

♦ March 5, 1938 *Radio Guide* Full-page black-and-white picture of Ball.

♦ July 2, 1938 *The Billboard* (now known simply as *Billboard*) A young, radiant Ball takes up the full cover. (Back then, the magazine covered all areas of entertainment.)

♦ July 18, 1943 *New York Sunday Mirror Magazine* Color cover shot of Ball in a navy bathing suit captioned "Beauty and the Beach: Lucille Ball."

♦ September 1943 *Silver Screen* Ball dressed as a lathe worker supporting the war effort.

♦ November 1943 *Movie Show* Ball is pictured in a blue gingham-check dress with a basket of cats on her lap.

♦ June 1944 *Big Song Magazine* Black-and-white headshot of Ball with the caption, "Lucille Ball stars in MGM's *Meet the People*."

♦ August 1944 *The Homemaker* (Combined with *Better Cooking*) Nice Technicolor-type saturated photo of Ball sewing a blouse with a spaniel next to her.

♦ 1945 *Yank* Easter British edition, Ball is the Yank Pin-up Girl, for the Armed Services.

♦ June 1947 *The American Magazine* Ball is pictured with costumer Elois Jenssen.

♦ June 19, 1949 *Chicago Sunday Tribune Picture Section* Full-color cover, head and neck shot of Ball.

♦ April 1950 *Radio and Television Mirror* Full-color shot of Ball on the cover promoting *My Favorite Husband*.

♦ November 27, 1950 *Quick* Ball and Arnaz are on the cover.

♦ January 30, 1952 *People Today* Black-and-white picture of Ball.

♦ May 6, 1952 *TIME* Color Head shot of Ball. "Rx for TV: A Clown with Glamour."

- June 3, 1952, *Look* With Marilyn Monroe and others. How Ball bounces back from real-life tragedies.

- October 13, 1952 *Quick* Ball and Arnaz pictured: "Why do They Love Lucy?"

- January 19, 1953 *Newsweek* "Who Doesn't Love Lucy?"

- April 5, 1953 *LIFE* "TV's First Family."

- April 13, 1953, *Quick* Ball and Desi Jr.

- April 21, 1953 *Look* Ball, Arnaz, Lucie, and Desi Jr.

- September 1953 *Family Circle* "Lucy and Desi Make a Movie."

- October 29, 1954, *Collier's* Totem pole illustration by Al Hirschfeld, with Ball and Arnaz at the top.

- December 28, 1954 *Look* An Arnaz family portrait.

- January 1955 *Confidential* "Does Desi Really Love Lucy?"

- May 1956 *TV Star Parade* Nice full-color headshot of Ball with the cover line, "Lucille Ball—I Talk to God."

- December 25, 1956 Ball, Arnaz, and Keith "Little Ricky" Thibodeaux

- February 1957 *Tip-Off*, "The Magazine of Inside Exclusives" Black-and-white pictures of Ball and Arnaz on the right with the headline: "The Nite Desi Proved He Really Loves Loosely!"

- 1957 *Color Television* Ball's face adorns eight small color TVs.

- July 1958 *Western Family* "Lucy and Desi at Home on the Range."

- May 1960 *The Lowdown* "Desi Has a 'Ball' for Himself."

- September 27, 1960 *Look* "10 Years of TV" Ball is on the cover with Robert Stack of Desilu's *The Untouchables*. Her story is headlined "Lucy Leaves TV for Broadway."

- December 1960 *The Theater Magazine* Spotlight on Lucy in *Wildcat*. Ball gets a full-cover dramatic headshot, though not in character as Wildcat Jackson.

- January 5, 1962 *LIFE* "Lucy Is Back" Three merged headshots of Ball clowning.

- March 25, 1962 *Family Weekly* "Lucy Loves Easter Hats" Ball in profile in an Easter hat.

- October 9. 1962 *Look* "TV's Comeback Season" featuring Ball, Jackie Gleason, and Jack Parr on the cover.

◆ April 1963 *TV-Radio Mirror* Ball shares the cover with Carol Burnett for the story "The Tragedy of Being Funny: What They Paid for Love—And What They Didn't Get."

◆ May 1965 *TV Star Parade* Full-color shot of Ball surrounded by "balloons" with feature story blurbs on them.

◆ February 1969 *Modern Screen* Ball shares the cover with Doris Day; the story is, "How They've Been Hurt by Their Children."

◆ June-July 1971 *Films in Review* Assessment of Ball's film career through 1971.

◆ 1971 *Photoplay* Ball and Desi Jr. pictured. Cover line: "Now Lucille Ball tells her version of the Baby scandal: 'Patty Duke Used My Son and Victimized Us!'"

◆ September 7, 1971 *Look* "TV: Turn-on or Turn-off?" Picture of Ball on a TV screen seemingly watching as a hand moves to change the channel.

◆ April 1973 *TV Radio Mirror* Ball hugging Bea Arthur: "Maude & Lucy: They're Bosom Buddies!"

◆ October 1973 *After Dark* Ball in art deco-type get-up, winning the magazine's Ruby Award.

◆ Circa 1974 *Who's Who in Night-Time TV* No. 1 Ball with other stars.

◆ February 1976 *Rona Barrett's Gossip* Big, garish wonderful full-cover picture of an older Ball.

◆ 1976 *LIFE* Special: "Remarkable American Women." Separate pictures of four "remarkable" women, including Ball.

◆ October 1979 *Camera* Ball jumping, by Philippe Halsman (this same picture appeared on a *TV Guide* cover).

◆ February 11, 1980 *People* "Lucy: Still Lovable and Loudmouthed." Small inset pic at top right of cover.

◆ February 1981 *Home Video* Drawing of the origins of TV on a Greek vase features Lucy and Ricky Ricardo, among others.

◆ June 23, 1983 *Rolling Stone* Cover line only, color feature inside.

◆ January 1984 *Ladies Home Journal* "Stars of the Century" Cover line only, feature inside.

◆ May 1984 *Architectural Digest* Ball's New York apartment.

◆ March 4, 1985 *People* "TV's Rerun Madness" Ball is one of several stars highlighted.

◆ May 1986 *Video Times.*

◆ May 20, 1986 *The Star* "Lucy Dearest."

◆ June 17, 1986 *National Enquirer* "Desi Arnaz Fights Lung Cancer."

Lucy helps teach kids math on the cover of *Scholastic Math Magazine*, **Vol. 7, No. 1, September 12, 1986, one of Lucy's many cover appearances. Photo by Galante/ Marzelli, sculpture by Shelley Daniels.** *Scholastic Math* **Cover © Scolastic, Inc. Used by permission. Other copyrights held by Shelley Daniels and Galante/ Marzelli. Author's collection**

◆ September 1, 1986 *People* "Hits and Misses for Fall TV" *Life with Lucy* is called a probable hit.

◆ September 12, 1986 *Scholastic Math Magazine* "Bring Lucy Up-to-Date" Features a Claymation-type figure of Ball as Lucy Ricardo on the cover (pictured).

◆ September 16, 1986 *The Star* "Star of the Century" Ball, of course.

◆ October 1986 *Hollywood Then & Now* (formerly *Hollywood Studio Magazine*).

◆ May 2, 1989 *National Enquirer* "Lucy's Brave Battle for Life."

◆ May 8, 1989 *People* "Lucy, 1911-1989" Memorial issue.

◆ May 8, 1989 *The Star* "Thanks for the Memories."

◆ July 1989 *Hollywood Then & Now* "Goodbye to a Magical Clown."

◆ Summer 1989 *People* Extra "Television's 50th Anniversary" issue features Ball with other stars.

◆ August 14, 1989 *People* "Remembering Lucy" (Second memorial cover, done perhaps because the May 8 issue was its biggest seller of the year.)

- August 29, 1989 *National Enquirer* Vivian Vance's "lost" memoirs.

- March 1990 *Joe Franklin's Nostalgia* No. 1 "Classy Clowns."

- 1990, *Celebrity Sleuth*, Vol. 3, No. 3 Cool Ball pictures and bio along with purported nude photo that in reality could be almost anyone.

- March 1990 *Reader's Digest* "Unforgettable Lucy!" Ball and Bob Hope on the cover.

- July 20, 1990 *Entertainment Weekly* "TV's 20 Best Golden Oldies" Famous profile picture of Ball and Arnaz kissing, on the cover; it was later used for Apple Computer's *Think Different* ad campaign.

- August 6, 1990 *People* "Casting a New Lucy" Inset picture of Ball in upper right corner of cover.

- September 3, 1990 *People* "Desi and Lucy: The Love Story."

- February 18, 1991 *People* "The Untold Story of Lucy and Desi."

- March 1991 *Hollywood Then & Now* "Lucy & Desi's TV Movie: Real or Unreal?"

- January 10, 1992 *Entertainment Weekly* The magazine's 100th issue has Ball, Elvis, Marilyn Monroe, and others celebrating "The 20th Century's Greatest Entertainment Moments."

- June 1997 *Pop Culture Collecting: Memories & Memorabilia* Full color Lucy picture on cover (from 1950s): "Memories of Lucy."

- June 8, 1998 *TIME* 100 Artists, Entertainers of the Century (drawn by Al Hirschfeld are Ball, Bob Dylan, Steven Spielberg, and Pablo Picasso).

- April 1999 *LIFE* "The Shows that Changed America" Full figure of Ball on the cover along with other TV icons.

- December 2000, *Thirteen Magazine* Full-color portrait of Ball in conjunction with the *American Masters* special "Finding Lucy."

- Fall 2001 *USA Philatelic*, Vol. 6, No. 3 The United States Post Office's official stamp collecting magazine ran a black-and-white cover shot of Ball from *I Love Lucy* to honor issuing the "Hollywood Legends" series stamp of her, released August 7, 2001, along with the stamp.

- *Modern Maturity*, September/October 2001 Gorgeous black-and-white shot of Ball in a bathing suit. "Why We Still Love Lucy: 50th Anniversary Special."

◆ Winter 2002 *The Franklin Mint Catalog* Cover features three pictures of its exclusive "Lucille Ball Vinyl Portrait Doll."

◆ January 2002 *Palm Springs Life* Cover story on Ball and Arnaz, and their love affair with the desert vacation spot; cover shot is the same as on *LIFE* magazine's January 5, 1962 issue.

◆ *TIME*, September 17, 2007 Postage stamp-size picture of Ball as Lucy Ricardo touts the magazine's "Top 100 TV Shows of All Time" feature.

MAGAZINE COVERS, WILLIAM FRAWLEY AND VIVIAN VANCE

Though Ball and Desi Arnaz appeared on hundreds of magazine covers, and still do, the same cannot be said for co-stars William Frawley and Vivian Vance. The two cover appearances by the Mertzes I could document are:

TV Guide, March 20-26, 1953 "Lucy's Neighbors Exposed" The cover showed headshots of Vance smiling and Frawley frowning down at her. This regional issue came out two weeks before the national edition debuted.

TV-Radio Life, May 30-June 5, 1953 This was a regional magazine published in the Southern California area. Frawley and Vance are pictured holding "Little Ricky" with the caption "Fred, Ethel and Ricky Jr." The article inside is called, "What We Mertzes Know about Lucy and Desi."

The Mertzes did a bit better separately, as they moved on and joined other TV series. Frawley made the cover of *TV Guide* after being cast in *My Three Sons*, on August 5, 1961. The photo shows *My Three Sons* star Fred MacMurray, Frawley, and Stanley ("Chip Douglas") Livingston cheering in the stands at a baseball game, one of Frawley's great passions. *Sons* also garnered him lots of "Sunday TV supplement" covers, such as the *Sunday TeleVues*, the "television log" of the *Sunday News* and the Long Beach, California *Independent Press-Telegram*, dated September 25, 1960, which offered a caricature of MacMurray, Frawley, and the three sons of the title. Tellingly, the caption of the cover pic described Frawley as an actor "… of *I Love Lucy* renown."

Vance also appeared on multiple covers of weekly TV supplements during the first few seasons of *The Lucy Show* (1962-'65), such as *The Sunday Previewer* ("Serving Southern Alameda County"), which on January 6, 1963, ran a caricature of Ball, Vance, and their TV kids, by Robert Thompson, noting Bally's popularity whether she was "devilishly crafty or angelically innocent." And the December, 1962 *Sunday TeleVues* opted for a full-page color photo of Vance on the cover, looking chic and wearing a pearl necklace.

No doubt there are more out there waiting to be dis*cover*ed.

MAGNIFICENT AMBERSONS, THE

A 1942 film by Orson Welles, the follow-up to his classic *Citizen Kane* (1941), *Ambersons* is often called one of the great lost films in the history of cinema. This is because RKO took control of the film away from Welles; a 132-minute rough edit was trimmed to 88 minutes, and a new happy conclusion was tacked on, filmed by assistant director Freddie Fleck.

There are those who insist, including the head of RKO's film stock library at the time, the footage was indeed destroyed. However, the idea that it still exists is so intriguing to film buffs it has led such believers as directors William Friedkin and Peter Bogdanovich to finger the likely resting place as the vaults of Paramount Studios. Part of Paramount is comprised of the former Desilu Studios, which in turn was the original main lot of RKO Studios when purchased by Ball and Arnaz in 1957 (see Movie Studios).

Unsubstantiated rumors suggest that Desilu itself discarded many of the RKO materials it inherited (including the *Ambersons* footage) into Santa Monica Bay. For the full story, see the intriguing article by David Kamp "Magnificent Obsession," in *Vanity Fair*, January 2002.

MAMBO KINGS, THE

Wonderfully evocative film made in 1992 that traces the fortunes of two Latin musicians (played by Armand Assante and Antonio Banderas) in the late 1940s and 1950s as they come to America to carve out a career. The highlight of the film has them meeting Desi Arnaz (played affectionately by his son, Desi Jr., in his last film role to date) who invites them to appear on an episode of *I Love Lucy*. The boys are spliced neatly (in black and white) into an episode of the show in which Lucy meets some of Ricky's Cuban friends. This is one of the few vehicles in any medium to address the uniqueness of the Latin flavor in *I Love Lucy*.

MAME

Ball's final big-screen effort, this lavish, Technicolor extravaganza suffered from many flaws; it's become something of a cult film and a camp classic. One either loves it, or hates it. Find out why at the following entries: Connell, Jane; Film Career; Kahn, Madeline; and Lucy on DVD.

MAN WHO CAME TO DINNER, THE

The Lux Radio Theater presentation (pruned down to one hour) of the classic George S. Kaufman and Moss Hart play aired on March 27, 1950. Starring Clifton Webb as the title character and Lucille Ball as Maggie Cutler, his personal secretary, Ball was introduced at the beginning of the show as, "A vivacious young lady who has quite a flair for comedy herself," by producer William Keeley. Unfortunately, her part (the one Bette Davis played in the film version) is pretty much straight woman to Webb and calls for her to sound little more than world-weary throughout. Still, this is an interesting career artifact from Ball's immediate pre-*I Love Lucy* career.

MARTIN, DEAN

Relaxed, easygoing crooner, Rat Packer, actor, and (with Jerry Lewis) half of one of the most popular comedy teams of all time, Martin was a friend of Ball's whose career and life intersected with hers many times. For example: Ball guest-starred on the Martin and Lewis radio show on December 22, 1948. Martin was one of the performers at the Friar's Club Roast of Ball and Arnaz on November 13, 1958. His son Dean Jr. (also known as Dino) performed in the 1960s teen boy-band Dino, Desi & Billy with Ball's son, Desi Jr.

He played a dual role on what Ball said was her favorite episode of *The Lucy Show*, "Lucy Dates Dean Martin," which aired February 14, 1966. Ball returned the favor by appearing on *The Dean Martin Show* (February 10, 1966). Martin "roasted" Ball on one of his popular series of specials, *The Dean Martin Celebrity Roast* (February 7, 1975), and Ball was on the dais at Martin's roasts of Danny Thomas (December 15, 1976) and Jimmy Stewart (May 10, 1978).

Martin co-starred with Ball in one of her post-*Here's Lucy* specials, "Lucy Gets Lucky" (March 1, 1975), which took place at the MGM Grand Hotel in Las Vegas, one of Martin's favorite haunts. In addition, he was one of the stars who honored Ball on *CBS Salutes Lucy: The First 25 Years* (1976) and on "An All-Star Party for Lucille Ball" (December 29, 1984). Even though he and Ball had polar opposite rehearsal styles (he went in cold and preferred not to rehearse; she wanted everything rehearsed to death), Ball adored him and put their different work ethics aside. Martin died in 1995.

MARTIN, DICK

The funny half of the comedy team Rowan & Martin, whose wild, rapid-fire, topical comedy sketch/variety show *Laugh-In* (1967-'72) revitalized TV (and cut into Ball's ratings as well). Martin was a recurring character on *The Lucy Show* during its first season, 1962-'63, as a romantic interest for the divorced Lucy Carmichael. His genial character, Harry Connors, worked nicely within the situations created, was a good foil for Lucy, and should have been kept on the show. But Martin was written out after the first season, and when Gale Gordon was added to the cast in the second season as blustery banker Mr. Mooney, the show shifted in tone entirely. Martin turned up to salute Ball on her *Dean Martin Celebrity Roast* (see above), and made a rare appearance talking about Ball on the excellent PBS *American Masters* documentary, *Finding Lucy* (2000). At this writing, Martin is 85, and spent much of his later career directing sitcoms, most notably good friend Bob Newhart's hits, *The Bob Newhart Show* (1972-'78) and *Newhart* (1982-'90).

♥ **Lucy Trivia** Martin's partner Dan Rowan made a rare appearance without him on a *Lucy Show* episode in 1966 that also featured Carol Burnett.

MARY KAY AND JOHNNY

Lucille Ball and Desi Arnaz weren't the first married couple to play a married couple on a sitcom, and Little Ricky wasn't the first sitcom baby born on TV, either. Those honors go to a little-remembered show called *Mary Kay and Johnny*.

Generally acknowledged as the first television sitcom, the show debuted on November 13, 1947, and ran through March 1950. It had both 15-minute and 30-minute formats, and aired on three different networks during its run: Dumont, NBC, and CBS.

Actor Johnny Stearns told the Associated Press in 1997 that the idea came to him because he'd seen "a lot of very successful domestic comedies on radio, but nothing had ever been done like that on TV." Stearns died in December 2001, and his wife Mary Kay (they were married for 55 years) took the occasion to note, "[*Mary Kay and Johnny*] was tremendously popular at the time, because there was very little else on TV."

The show starred the real-life couple as a bank employee and his zany, but not dumb, housewife. Situations revolved around daily problems one might encounter in real life, such as getting stuck in an elevator, or Mary Kay leaving a cake in the oven for Johnny to finish baking.

More significantly, when Mary Kay became pregnant, it was written into the show and the TV birth occurred on an episode that aired the same day (December 18, 1948) as the real-life birth of their son, Christopher (who soon became, via filmed segments inserted into the live show, the youngest performer, at the time, ever on TV). On live TV, Stearns was shown pacing in the hospital waiting room, waiting for news of the birth.

Most of the episodes took place in the Greenwich Village (New York) apartment of Mary Kay and Johnny. No films or kinescopes exist of the show, which explains why it is so rarely remembered. These days, if thought of at all, *Mary Kay and Johnny* is pointed to as the first show to put a married couple in the same bed on TV. Interestingly enough, almost every sitcom that followed for more than a decade reverted to separate beds for spouses.

Obviously, *Mary Kay and Johnny* set a few firsts, many of which are normally associated with *I Love Lucy*, which debuted in 1951. This does not take anything away from the pioneering *Lucy*, which remains a benchmark in sitcom development because it popularized the sitcom format, moving television from baggy-pants vaudeville-style comedy to situation-based laughter (see The *I Love Lucy* Influence).

Mary Kay Stearns told the AP on December 18, 2001, that her husband considered the show the "centerpiece of his life," and was "proud of his role as a TV pioneer," though he was on occasion "frustrated ... because a lot of publicity was concentrated on *Lucy*." Stearns went on to produce the original *Tonight* show with Steve Allen, and produced and directed the *Arthur Murray Dance Party*. In later years he was a producer of public affairs programming.

MAXIM

Popular new-millennium-era men's magazine high on testosterone, *Maxim* has a fun feature called "Head to Head" that, in December 2001, proved the iconic power of the *I Love Lucy* characters. "Head to Head" pits two well-known cultural icons—whose names are similar, sound alike, and so on—against each other in such categories as "Unsettling Project Title" and "Fashion Statement." Points are awarded for each win. In December 2001 it was Fred Durst vs. Fred Mertz. Durst is the front man for the band Limp Bizkit. Some sample nuggets (category in italics):

"*Fashion Statement* Durst: Baseball cap turned backward; Mertz: Trousers hiked up to armpits. Edge: Draw

"*Spawned* Durst: A generation of angry white kids who think they're tough; Mertz: Generations of wacky sitcom neighbors who think they're funny. Edge: Mertz."

MCNULTY, BARNEY

The king of the cue card, McNulty is credited with being the first person to use them on a national TV show, *The Ed Wynn Show* (1949-'50), when the star, ill and taking medication that affected his memory, requested McNulty, then a PA, to write entire scripts on large sheets of cardboard. One job led to another, and by 1952 McNulty had started his own business, Ad-Libs. McNulty did cue cards (also known derisively as "idiot cards") for many major celebrities and TV shows of the 1950s through the 1990s, also branching out into films.

Even after the TelePrompter became many stars' reading device of choice, there were those who preferred cue cards. "We are more adaptable to the rapidly changing conditions of the script than TelePrompter," McNulty told *The Daily Intelligencer* of Doylestown, Pennsylvania on May 27, 1967.

McNulty is credited with flipping the cards for Lucille Ball and company on the *I Love Lucy* episode "The Girls Want to Go to a Nightclub," the first broadcast, though the second one shot, and other Ball shows. His associate, Tommy Tucker, worked with Ball for more than 20 years, beginning in1963. McNulty said the best cue-card reader of them all was Lucille Ball; "Hardly anyone realizes that the madcap redhead has cue cards on the set," the *Intelligencer* reported. McNulty died in December 2000 at the age of 77.

MEDINA, RHONDA

A veteran stage, commercial, and variety actress, talent agent, commercial coach, teacher, and celebrity impersonator—Mae West, Marilyn Monroe, Dolly Parton—Medina (also known as Rhonda Richards) is best known to Ball fans as Ethel Mertz, whom she portrays with love and a twinkle in her eye for Jamestown, New York's Lucy-Desi Center twice-a-year festivals, held in May and August. During Lucy-Desi Days (Memorial Day) and Lucy's Birthday Celebration (held the weekend closest to August 6), Medina can be found, often in tandem with Ball impersonator Diane Vincent, entertaining fans, having her picture taken, reenacting classic Lucy-Ethel moments, shepherding a trivia contest … the truth is, you just never know *where* she'll show up, but you'll be glad she did. A spiritual person (currently leading a Drama Ministry in a suburb of Dallas), I've had the pleasure of meeting Rhonda at various Lucy fests, and can say without doubt she is one of the most genuine people I've ever met. Look for her when you visit Jamestown. See Vincent, Diane.

MEMOIRS

An item in Hedda Hopper's *Hollywood* column on November 1943, notes, "The writing bug has hit Lucille Ball. She whipped up a thing called *That Was Yesterday*, telling about her early days as a model and her life as queen of the B's at RKO." If that was indeed the case—and why Ball would write her memoirs at such an early age is a mystery—it is a manuscript that has never surfaced.

MERMAN, ETHEL

Brassy, distinctive-voiced musical comedian, Merman had a minor film career before and after her stage successes. However, her larger-than-life personality was better suited to the stage, where she filled many an outsized role (Annie Oakley, Reno Sweeney, Mama Rose) to perfection.

Born Ethel Agnes Zimmerman in 1908, Merman met Ball early in her movie career, when she starred in *Kid Millions* (1934); Ball was in the chorus. Merman's stage career intersected with Vivian Vance's early on; Vance supported and understudied her in *Anything Goes* (1934) and *Red, Hot & Blue* (1936), and in both cases took over the lead roles when Merman was out sick.

Merman memorably guest-starred on two consecutive episodes of *The Lucy Show* in February 1964—"Lucy Teaches Ethel Merman to Sing" and "Ethel Merman and the Boy Scout Show"—in which Merman moves to Lucy Carmichael's hometown undercover, but Lucy "discovers" her and tries to teach her to sing like Merman for a local Boy Scout show.

These episodes are two of the best in the series, and the rapport between the three leading ladies is evident onscreen. After the shows filmed, Merman told the story that she and Vance went to Ball's house for some girl talk, and Ball, an amateur hairstylist, did their 'dos, to disastrous results, but all in good fun. Ball also threw Merman a shower for her notorious one-month marriage to Ernest Borgnine in 1964. Merman died in 1984.

MITCHELL, SHIRLEY

A comic actress whom Ball took from radio to television, Mitchell played Lucy and Ethel's friend Marion Strong in three episodes of *I Love Lucy*, most notably in "Lucy Tells the Truth" (November 9, 1953). Mitchell's loud braying/cackling is memorable, as Lucy—embracing the idea of telling the truth for 24 hours, since it will win her a bet with Ricky, Fred, and Ethel—tells her, "Marion, stop cackling, I've been waiting 10 years for you to lay that egg!"

Mitchell had a long career on radio (*The Great Gildersleeve*), television and the movies, appearing as a semi-regular on the series <u>*Pete and Gladys*</u>, *Bachelor Father* and *Petticoat Junction*, and logging dozens of guest shots on dramas and comedies (including two appearances on Desi Arnaz's 1967 sitcom, *The Mothers-in-Law*). Her most recent film appearance was in *The War of the Roses* (1989).

Mitchell was a special guest at the 2006 Memorial Day Lucy convention in Jamestown, New York. We Love Lucy fan club president and author Tom Watson reported from the event: "I especially enjoyed the Sunday morning appearance of Shirley Mitchell. She had great memories of working on the show. She's the first person to speak of the Vivian Vance-Bill Frawley relationship and speak up for Bill. Everyone in the past has painted a picture of 'Saint Vivian' and 'mean old Frawley.' Shirley said Viv was always picking on Bill—and often tried to direct their scenes together, which is usually what caused Frawley to explode. Shirley added that Viv even tried tell Shirley herself how to do a scene or two—so Shirley knew from whence she spoke. Hearing different sides to [an oft-told] story is what makes these celebrity seminars so interesting—and valuable!"

With regard to Mitchell's comments, I tend to agree with Watson: There are two or more sides to every story, and hearing a new side after many years of being fed the same dish is fascinating. That said, it's been reported so often that Frawley was continually insulting Vance, Ball, and Arnaz about their performing skills, I feel confident writing that Vance probably gave back what she got. As for trying to direct Mitchell, perhaps a bit of Ball rubbed off on Vance after all that time together. And keep in mind Mitchell's *I Love Lucy* experience extends to only three episodes.

MODELING

A lot of the early publicity in Lucille Ball's career centered on the fact that she had been a model who made the difficult jump to an acting career. While Ball had certainly put in her dues as far as her career was concerned, it didn't quite happen as quickly as a 1938 article noted: "From manikin to movie star in two years is the record of Lucille Ball, who has an important role in *Having Wonderful Time*."

In fact, throughout the 1930s and into the 1940s Ball was still modeling for a variety of products, as an advertising spokesperson or just for the publicity. For example, she was featured in many articles written by someone pen-named *Mignon* for a column called "Beauty Spots." These breezy items featured stories about nail care, skin tonics, and the like. There would be a picture of Ball, usually wearing or showing off the product, with the caption, "Posed by Lucille Ball."

MOLIN, BUD

Henry D. "Bud" Molin was <u>Dann Cahn</u>'s first editing assistant on *I Love Lucy*, starting in 1951. Molin had been a friend of Cahn's and fellow editor at Republic Studios, one of the lesser Hollywood film factories, where speed was valued above all else, the better to produce low-budget pics that would bring in quick cash. This turned out to be invaluable experience for Molin and Cahn, who ended up working 14-hour days on the first *I Love Lucy* shows. Molin eventually become the sitcom's editor as Cahn supervised him and an ever-growing editing staff, and ultimately moved on to other positions at Desilu. Molin also was film editor on *The Lucy-Desi Comedy Hour* and other sitcoms like *Andy Griffith*, *Dick Van Dyke*, and *Barney Miller* (where his title became Post-Production Executive). He directed episodes of the short-lived 1976 sitcom *Good Heavens*. Molin moved into films in 1956 with Ball and Arnaz's *Forever Darling*, and edited more than 25 films through 1993, most of them comedies like *Where's Poppa?*, *Oh, God*, *The Jerk*, and *Police Academy 3: Back in Training*. In February 2007 Cahn and Molin reunited with their former assistants, Gary Freund and Ted Rich, to privately screen *Forever Darling* in Hollywood, celebrating the film's golden anniversary.

MOORE, CANDY

Child and teen actress of the late 1950s and 1960s who played Lucille Carmichael's eldest child on *The Lucy Show*. As with many teen stars of the era, she tried to use her sitcom fame to jump-start a recording career. It didn't take off. (Has anyone ever heard of the record "It's Your Turn Now"?) Moore was dumped, as were the other child actors, when the show's format changed in the 1965-'66 season. Her career never took off after *Lucy*, though she did have a minor role in *Raging Bull* (1980). The first wife of character actor Paul Gleason, Moore most recently made an appearance in 2007's *You Know the Face*, a documentary about actor Charles Lane (see <u>Lane, Charles</u>).

MORGAN, KEN

First husband of Ball's close cousin Cleo Mandicos, Morgan was often referred to as Ball's brother-in-law, as she considered Cleo more a sister than a cousin. Winner of a Silver Star in WWII, Morgan worked as an associate in the public relations firm that represented Ball in the

1940s, and handled PR and occasionally other duties for the Arnazes during the run of *I Love Lucy* and into the 1960s. He also appeared in the 1951 *I Love Lucy* episode "Men Are Messy" (billed as Kenny Morgan).

Eric Gans, author of an upcoming biography of actress Carole Landis, reports that circa 1939 to '41, "Morgan was the publicity agent and sometime boyfriend of Landis; there was talk of marriage in 1939, before she married Willis Hunt in July 1940, and they continued to see each other after the marriage broke up in September (!), as late as summer 1941."

Cleo eventually divorced Morgan. She blamed it largely on the stress caused by his working for Desilu. "I didn't think [Ken] should work for Desi," she is quoted as saying in the book *Desilu: The Story of Lucille Ball and Desi Arnaz*. "They wouldn't pay him anything and they would take advantage." (Morgan took the job despite her advice.) See Smith, Cleo.

MORTON, GARY

Catskills comedian introduced to Lucille Ball in 1960 by co-star Paula Stewart when they were in New York, appearing on Broadway in *Wildcat*. Ball eventually married Morton, and was extremely happy in her second marriage, allowing Morton to treat her deferentially, and becoming noticeably more "feminine" and "giggly" when he was around.

She was less successful integrating him into her business life; made the head of Lucille Ball Productions, Morton, who had no TV administrative or managerial experience, was reportedly disliked and mocked by many who worked for him. He was better received in his two movie roles, *Lenny* (1974) and *Postcards from the Edge* (1990), in which he is a riot as Meryl Streep's agent.

Morton dated Eva Gabor, a Ball co-star, for a short time after Ball's death in 1989. She said they broke up because he was more interested in his golf game. He was married to golf pro Susie McAllister from 1994 until his death in 1999.

Frank Sinatra was a longtime friend of Ball's (see Sinatra, Frank). Author J. Randy Taraborelli, who wrote *Frank Sinatra: Behind the Legend*, included an anecdote about Morton told by James Wright, a butler in the Sinatra household. Speaking of the entertaining the Sinatras used to do, Wright is quoted as saying, "Everybody came to visit. The Gregory Pecks, the Chuck Connors, Merv Griffin, Steve and Eydie … One person I did not care for who came often was Gary Morton [Lucille Ball's husband]. He'd talk badly about Lucy. Why talk about her [like that] when she's dead, I wondered?"

Why, indeed? Carole Cook, Ball's protégé and friend, admitted tearfully during her 2006 onstage performance in Jamestown, New York, that she never cared for Morton, and that she believed Morton kept Ball from seeing her friends at the end of her life.

We'll never know why, though Morton is consistently portrayed as being interested in golf and collecting things (like expensive cars) more than anything else. Still, he kept Ball going for better than a quarter century after her divorce from Arnaz, helped raise her kids, and must have been some kind of comfort to the red-haired legend. He also had to endure the scorn of those he worked with, on behalf of Ball, since by all accounts he lacked the showmanship, behind-the-scenes talent, and warmth of Arnaz. No doubt Morton had to put up with a lot himself, being branded "Mr. Lucille Ball."

Lucie admitted, after Morton's death, that Arnaz and Ball were the loves of each others' lives.

♥ **Lucy Trivia** Morton and Ball's company produced one of Tom Cruise's early efforts, *All the Right Moves* (1983).

THE MOTHERS-IN-LAW

This semi-successful sitcom, which ran for two years and 56 episodes from 1967 to 1969, was the brainchild of Arnaz under the auspices of Desi Arnaz Productions. Arnaz wanted to get back to a business he'd helped revolutionize in the early 1950s. The show's producer, Elliott Lewis (husband of Ball pal Mary Jane Croft; see Croft, Mary Jane), had worked on *The Lucy Show*.

According to a report from *All Florida* magazine in 1967, "During a rehearsal of the second episode of NBC TV's new *The Mothers-in-Law* series, which bows on Sunday, September 10, executive producer and director Desi Arnaz had occasion to question the quality of a gooey mess called 'chocolate malt' in the script, which was to be thrown in Kaye Ballard's face.

"He asked the prop man to whip up a darker, thicker concoction and then asked volunteers for a 'dry' run. Up spoke Roger C. Carmel, who plays Kaye's husband in the show. 'Captain,' he said, quite straight-faced, 'I am sure you wouldn't ask us to do anything you wouldn't do yourself.'

"'That is absolutely right,' Desi replied. Tying a towel around his neck, he hand the 'malt' back to the prop man and told him to do his duty. The prop man reared back and let Desi have it in the face. From that moment on, Desi Arnaz was the unquestioned leader of the group."

It's too bad the show itself wasn't as enjoyable as the above story might indicate.

Ballard's friend Vivian Vance had some advice for the sitcom newcomer as she prepared to go West: Vance urged Ballard to make sure it was in her contract that they use Ballard's first name for her character on *The Mothers-In-Law*. Vance said she had spent a "fortune in analysis," according to Ballard's biography, because, no matter what she did in show business, people always identified her as Ethel Mertz. Ballard took the advice to Hollywood, and ultimately all four characters' first names corresponded to the actors' real names.

Unfortunately, the situation in this comedy was hackneyed: Two feuding couples—Eve Arden and Herbert Rudley, and Kaye Ballard and Roger C. Carmel—are forced to get along when their children wed and they become in-laws. The writing, though slapsticky enough, was mired in sitcom traditions that even by 1967 were repetitive.

Not helping matters was the fact that Carmel left after the first season and Richard Deacon replaced him (see separate entries for both). The chemistry between Deacon and Ballard wasn't as real but was funny in a different way. Carmel and Ballard felt like a real couple; Deacon and Ballard were more like the *Odd Couple*. (It's been reported that NBC received not one letter or phone call questioning the switch of actors.)

Arnaz was totally involved in the series (and was referred to in the *All Florida* article as "the most active executive producer currently at large in the world of television"). He consulted on all the scripts (by *I Love Lucy* veterans Bob Carroll and Madelyn Davis); directed seven of the first eight episodes; acted on the series; and supervised the editing, set, costumes, and camera angles (as many as 200 per show). Arnaz also did the audience warm-up and directed all the promotional spots.

Arnaz created the series, cast it with Arden and Ballard (the latter was not his first choice; see <u>Ballard, Kaye</u> for more), and at the time was shuttling between three offices he maintained, two at Desilu Cahuenga and one at Desilu Culver (see <u>Movie Studios</u>, below).

Regardless, the main reason to watch the show was to see the interplay between the always wonderful Arden and Ballard. Jerry Fogel and Deborah Walley played the kids, and were not given much to do except look embarrassed at their parents' antics. Arnaz himself made a handful of appearances as bullfighter Raphael del Gado, joined on occasion by his son, Desi Jr.

Though Ballard claims in her book the series debuted at No. 2 in the Nielsens and was never out of the Top 15, the real story is a bit different. Even though it aired between *Bonanza*, the No. 6 show for the 1967-'68 season, and *Walt Disney's Wonderful World*, a long-running success, *The Mothers-In-Law* never took off. NBC only agreed to renew it at the same price as the first season. Carmel was the only actor who objected to not getting a raise—raises were specified in the actors' contracts if the show was renewed—and thus was replaced (for another take on why he left, see <u>Carmel, Roger</u>). The show did no better ratings-wise in its second season, and was canceled.

At its best, *The Mothers-in-Law* can be remembered as a fond chestnut, out-of-date before its time. It wasn't sitcom gold, but it wasn't dross either.

MOVIE STUDIOS

Columbia Pictures Studios (now Sunset-Gower Studios), 1438 North Gower Street, Hollywood, California. Ball filmed five of her early movies here in the mid-1930s; worked with The Three Stooges in 1934's *Three Little Pigskins*; and returned in the late 1940s to film four of her better comedies here. Her last movie at Columbia was the bomb *The Magic Carpet* (1950).

Culver Studios, 9336 W. Washington Boulevard, Culver City, California. Formerly RKO and Desilu. Ball and Arnaz purchased the RKO-Pathé lot (along with RKO's space on Gower Street in Hollywood) in 1957 from General Tire & Rubber for the bargain price of $6 million; GT&R had bought the studio from Howard Hughes in 1955 for $25 million. It became the final home of <u>Desilu</u> Studios. Ball had a long tenure at RKO in the 1930s and early 1940s, and filmed more movies here (31) than at any other studio. Arnaz had also been an RKO contract player. The Gower Street location (now part of Paramount Studios, which was bought by Viacom in 1999; see below) became known as Desilu-Gower.

General Service Studios (now Hollywood Center Studios), 1040 North Las Palmas Avenue, Hollywood, California. The first two seasons of *I Love Lucy* were filmed here, until Desilu rented nine soundstages at the Motion Picture Center in 1953 to suit Desilu's expanding needs.

MGM Studios (now Sony Pictures Studios), 10202 W. Washington Boulevard, Culver City, California. Ball was under contract here in the 1940s. She made nine films at MGM from 1943 through 1946.

The Motion Picture Center (now Ren-Mar Studios), 846 N. Cahuenga Boulevard, Hollywood, California. This is where *I Love Lucy* moved after it left the General Service Studios. Desilu originally rented here and ultimately Ball and Arnaz bought controlling interest in the studio, renaming it Desilu Cahuenga.

The Paramount Ranch, Paramount Ranch Road (off Cornell Road), Agoura Hills, California. Ball worked on her hit *Fancy Pants* (1950) with Bob Hope here.

Paramount Studios, 5555 Melrose Ave, Hollywood, California. Paramount absorbed its neighbor Desilu Studios physically and literally when it purchased Desilu in 1967. The old RKO/Desilu lot is featured in the studio tour, where you can see "Lucy Park," a small area that commemorates Desilu Studios. Also on the tour you can see the New York Street, a row of fake brownstone fronts used in several *I Love Lucy* episodes (exteriors of the *Laverne & Shirley* basement apartment were filmed there). Ball filmed *Sorrowful Jones* (1949) at Paramount.

Twentieth Century Fox Studios, 10201 Pico Boulevard, Century City, Hollywood. Ball filmed several early bit parts here in the 1930s, and in 1946 came back to film one of her best films, *The Dark Corner*, a noir detective story. In 1981, Lucille Ball Productions signed a deal with Fox and Fox TV that resulted in one project: Tom Cruise's *All the Right Moves* (1983), for which Ball and husband No. 2 Gary Morton were executive producers.

United Artists (now The Lot), 7200 Santa Monica Boulevard, West Hollywood, California. Formerly Warner-Hollywood Studios, United Artists, and the Samuel Goldwyn Studios, where Ball made *Roman Scandals*, her first movie in 1933, and a handful of other early bit parts.

Universal Studios Hollywood, Studio Tour, 100 Universal City Plaza, Universal City, California. Ball filmed *Lover Come Back* (1946) at Universal. Her Lucille Ball Productions moved here in the 1970s after being associated with Paramount. Sound Stage 27 is where *Here's Lucy* was filmed. This is adjacent to "Lucy: A Tribute," a museum with memorabilia from Ball's career.

MUSEUM OF TELEVISION AND RADIO

See <u>Paley Center for Media, The</u>.

MY FAVORITE HUSBAND

A radio situation comedy that ran on CBS from 1948 to 1951, this proved to be the prototype for *I Love Lucy*.

All the elements are in place in this funny show, from the characters—two married couples, one younger, one more mature, the situation often setting the men against the women—to the producer/creator (Jess Oppenheimer) to the writers (Bob Carroll, Jr. and Madelyn Pugh).

Ball starred as Liz Cugat, with Richard Denning as Liz's banker husband, George, and Gale Gordon and Bea Benaderet as George's boss and his wife, Rudolph and Iris Atterbury, the latter a friend to Liz (see separate entries for all). Many scripts from this show served as the basis for *I Love Lucy* plots.

A trip to the Museum of Television and Radio in New York (now known as <u>The Paley Center for Media</u>) offered an opportunity to hear an episode of the series. It was obvious that the *I Love Lucy* creative team was on the mark well before the classic sitcom made its debut.

This particular episode dealt with Liz and Iris trying to wangle new Easter outfits out of their cheap husbands. Sound familiar? It was, in a wonderful way; the situation was not specifically done on *I Love Lucy*, but certainly, variations were shown throughout its run.

Liz has already gotten a bonnet out of George, but Rudolph warns him that agreeing to a bonnet means a whole outfit isn't far behind. Then the girls get the bright idea to diet their way to new outfits: when the men insinuate the women have gained weight (Liz: You used to love to take me out and show off my nice figure. Whatever happened to that husband? George: He went the way of the figure …) the women bet them they can diet into size twelves, and, if they do, the men have to buy them new suits.

Frank Nelson, an *I Love Lucy* semi-regular, voiced the part of a store security guard who thinks the girls are shoplifting. Even the orchestrations by Wilbur Hatch sounded just like the between-scenes music on *I Love Lucy*.

This show was Ball's first attempt at doing situation comedy in front of an audience, and she loved the live response. The actors would be in costume and perform on a stage, so in a sense it was like live theater, which is what *I Love Lucy* became every week. Listening to *My Favorite Husband* makes it clear that something funny was being mined. You can imagine the tumblers clicking into place as Ball decided to transfer the show to TV. Visit the Paley Center, and don't stop with the video collection. The next sound you hear could be that of the creation of a classic sitcom.

In 1953, apparently with the hope that anything associated with Ball would be a success, CBS brought *My Favorite Husband* to television, where it ran for two and a half years. Ball, of course, was busy, so Joan Caulfield was cast as Liz Cooper, with Barry Nelson (see <u>Nelson, Barry</u>) playing her husband George, a New York banker. In the last season, September to December 1955, Vanessa Brown replaced Caulfield.

MY LITTLE MARGIE

An unpretentious sitcom starring Gale Storm as a spunky young woman and Charles Farrell as her exasperated father, *My Little Margie* ran for 126 episodes, most relying on the innate charms and wacky adorability of Storm, an underrated actress and comedienne.

Running from 1952-'55, this show took over the *I Love Lucy* Monday-night spot as a last-minute summer replacement; it landed consistently among the top five shows during the weeks it aired, and CBS renewed it for the fall and the following three years. *Margie*, like *I Love Lucy*, was sponsored by Philip Morris in the summer of 1952, and in September featured lengthy promos heralding the return of *I Love Lucy*.

Margie only ran in Lucy's spot during the summer of 1952 (June to September); it ran on three other days and in three different time slots for the remainder of its run. Storm's second hit sitcom, *The Gale Storm Show* (1956-'60)—which co-starred Roy Roberts, a *Lucy Show* semi-regular—filmed its final season at Desilu Studios.

MYSTERIES AND SCANDALS

This was a compulsively watchable E! cable network show (1998-2000) about Hollywood. In 1999, an entire episode of the show focused on Vivian Vance. There was no real mystery or scandal put forward, except perhaps her years in psychoanalysis and her complex relationship with Lucille Ball. But there were interviews with Vance's close friends and her youngest sister, plus clips that are rarely, if ever, shown, including my favorite, Vance's Emmy win in 1954 (for the 1953 season), including her acceptance speech.

N

NATIONAL WOMEN'S HALL OF FAME

Located in Seneca Falls, N.Y., the birthplace of women's rights and site of the first Women's Rights Convention in 1848, the National Women's Hall of Fame honored Lucille Ball as one of 13 inductees on October 6, 2001. Due to the events of 9/11, however, Ball wasn't actually inducted until 2002. Part of the text about Lucy on the NWHF website reads:

"Proving that her talents extended beyond the realm of comedy, the entrepreneur became the first female studio head in Hollywood. As president of Desilu Productions, she broke the glass ceiling for women executives in the film and television industry."

According to the Hall of Fame, "Selection criteria for induction include the enduring value of a nominee's contribution to society and her significant contributions to the arts, athletics, business, education, government, humanities, philanthropy, or science." For more information, visit its website, Greatwomen.org.

NELSON, BARRY

Genial comic actor of movies, television and stage, Nelson died on April 7, 2007, just days before his 90th birthday. Known for his Broadway performances in such comedy hits as *The Moon Is Blue*, *Mary, Mary*, and *Cactus Flower*, Nelson had an extensive TV and movie career. He was the first James Bond in an hour-long adaptation of *Casino Royale* on CBS's *Climax Mystery Theater* in October 1954, and he played the level-headed George Cooper, husband to the ditzy Liz (Joan Caulfield) in the TV adaptation of Lucille Ball's hit radio show (and the inspiration for *I Love Lucy*), *My Favorite Husband*, which ran for two and a half seasons, from September 1953-December 1955.

NELSON, FRANK

Anyone with a radio in the 1930s and 1940s, or a television set from the 1950s onward, saw or heard Frank Nelson.

His versatile and hilarious radio voice was on the air from 1934 supporting every major star who ever had a show (including Ball's *My Favorite Husband*). He followed Ball to TV on *I Love Lucy*, and he is remembered as quizmaster Freddie Fillmore (whom he played three times), the host of "Females Are Fabulous"; the exasperated conductor of the train the Ricardos and the Mertzes take home from California; and as Connecticut neighbor Ralph Ramsey in the show's final season. His last appearance with Ball was on a Jack Benny special in 1970.

Nelson helped found performer's union, AFTRA (the American Federation of Television and Radio Artists). He died of cancer at 75 in 1986.

NEW YORK, NEW YORK

The state and city played a prominent part in the real and reel lives of Lucille Ball. She was born in Jamestown, New York, and left there while a baby as the family moved around the country following father Henry's job as a telephone lineman. The family eventually moved back to Celeron, New York, a tiny hamlet near Jamestown, and ultimately Jamestown itself.

There, Ball spent many hours honing her gift for making others laugh, and escaped on several occasions to New York City, where she was determined to carve out a career for herself. She eventually became a known model in the Big Apple, for Hattie Carnegie and others. One summer, at a slow point in her young career, an agent stopped her on the sidewalk and persuaded her to take a train to Hollywood and become a Goldwyn Girl.

Later, of course, the East Side of New York became well-known as the neighborhood where Fred and Ethel Mertz owned a brownstone apartment building, 623 East 68th Street; their tenants included best friends Lucy and Ricky Ricardo. This fictional address would have put the building smack in the middle of the East River.

Ball also starred in a Broadway show, *Wildcat*, shortly after ending her marriage to Desi Arnaz, and much later, in the 1980s, took an apartment in New York so she'd have a place to stay while visiting her grandchildren by daughter Lucie.

NICKNAMES

During the early 1940s, Lucille Ball was known as "The 'Hello' Girl," and Desi Arnaz was tagged the "Glamour Boy" by the press. In a 1942 column, Sidney Skolsky explained how Ball got her nickname: "She has made it practice, when at the studio, to shout or wave hello to practically everyone. It doesn't matter who the person is, they get a hello from her. In this way, people she wants to know get to know her.... Now she is the star of a big musical picture, but she still gives with the hello."

In a *New York Post* article on December 31, 1940, the headline ran "'Glamour Boy' Desi Married to Lucille Ball." The article read: "Cuba's 'Glamour Boy' Desi Arnaz, 25, and Lucille Ball, 26, secretly drove to Greenwich yesterday morning, got a waiver of the five-day law, and were married by Justice of the Peace Joseph P. O'Brien at the Beagle Club there.... The chauffeur, who was one of the witnesses, drove them back to New York in time for Desi to appear for the second show at the Roxy Theater. It was the first marriage for both. Lucille gave her birthplace as Jamestown, N.Y."

Several interesting things to note here: Ball's age was not given correctly; she was 29. And Ball admitted that Butte, Montana was not her birthplace (she'd used Butte as a birthplace for years in publicity pieces). Also, in most reference sources the date for Ball and Arnaz's marriage is given as November 30, 1940, not December 30. Yet at least half a dozen newspapers of the era reported the date as December 30.

NIGHTTIME CALENDAR

Evening version of a daytime magazine show called *Calendar* that ran for two years from October 1961 to August 1963 on CBS. Hosted by Harry Reasoner and Mary Fickett (who would be better known starting in 1970 later for a long run as Ruth Martin on the soap *All My Children*), the show covered news and current events. On July 7, 1962, CBS ran a special prime-time version, taking a look at the daytime activities of the average American home. Vivian Vance, then co-starring in *The Lucy Show*, guest-starred in one of the sketches, about the "proper" management of children.

NOBODY LOVES AN ALBATROSS

I refer to this as the "lost" play about Lucille Ball. In 2000, when I was doing research for the first edition of this book, my friend Craig Hamrick introduced me to an actress named Marie Wallace, who, he said, had "been in a Broadway play that was about Lucille Ball." Craig knew Wallace through his chronicling of the gothic soap opera *Dark Shadows* (for many years, in many articles and the best-selling book, *Barnabas & Co.*). Wallace had co-starred on *Dark Shadows* from 1968 to 1970, in several roles.

I was intrigued because, as a huge fan about to write a book on Ball, I had never seen mention of *Nobody Loves an Albatross* in any reference to Ball, online or in print. Here's what I found, thanks to Wallace's tip and the archive at the New York Library for the Performing Arts: In 1963, television was barely out of its 20s. But people were already writing about the profound effect that this upstart medium had on the public. One person, in fact, had written a play about television, and one of its characters seemed suspiciously familiar. She didn't have red hair, but she was the head of a major studio starring in her own situation comedy.

Can we say "Lucille Ball"?

Ronald Alexander (1916-'95) was a writer who had minor success as a playwright in the 1950s. His works included *Time Out for Ginger*, which was made into a pilot for TV, and *Holiday for Lovers*, filmed in 1959, plus the movies *Return to Peyton Place* (1961), *Johnny Shiloh* (1963), and *Billie* (1965).

In the late 1950s, Alexander took a break from the stage and decided to try his luck in Hollywood. He ended up writing for television at <u>Desilu Studios</u>—a period which, apparently, he did not enjoy … *at all*. According to a UPI interview with Alexander in 1963, he went to Hollywood to write the pilot for the Desilu sitcom *Guestward Ho!* (See entry under <u>Vance, Vivian</u>.)

In the UPI interview, Alexander complained that, "Out there [in Hollywood] you have to write with one or more others. You keep regular office hours but nothing ever seems to get accomplished. So much time is wasted. And you can never be sure just what you have contributed."

Alexander used his real-life Desilu experience as fodder for his next few shows. One, called *The Smallest Show on Earth*, featured a "lead character who bears more than a passing resemblance to Ronnie's partner [at] Desilu, Cy Howard," noted the *Hollywood Reporter* on December 11, 1961. Howard, best known for the *My Friend Irma* radio show, movies, and TV series, worked at Desilu in the early to mid-1960s.

The other play, *Nobody Loves an Albatross*, would star Robert Preston, who was cast on September 12, 1963. A month later, the *N.Y. Journal American* noted Peggy Cass was "up for the [female] lead," but that intriguing bit of casting never happened. Later that fall Constance Ford was cast as Hildy Jones, "the role of a TV star who operates a Hollywood studio."

Others cast in the show included Tony-winner Barnard Hughes, of the show and movie *Da* and TV series *Doc* (1975); Richard Mulligan, Emmy winner for *Soap* (1977) and *Empty Nest* (1988); character actor Frank Campanella; and soap opera and stage actress Marie Wallace (*Dark Shadows*, 1969).

An October 1963 press release noted that the playwright "based his comedy on his observations of Hollywood and its television denizens during the past few years." Initially called *The*

Happy Medium, the satire on TV was first going to be directed by comedian Ernie Kovacs. Ultimately, the director turned out to be comedy ace Gene Saks, who was married to Bea Arthur, and directed Arthur, Ball, and Preston in *Mame* (1974).

Several preshow interviews revealed the behind-the-scenes nature of the show. A *N.Y. Herald Tribune* interview (November 4, 1963) noted that in the play, Preston would have a team of writers working for him on "what we will *not* call *The Lucy Show*. This disclaimer seemed necessary. The playwright recently spent three years in Hollywood, some of it working for Desilu productions, and as it happens Preston's boss in the play is the actress/head of the studio who is also the star of a top series."

Preston described his character, a television writer-producer with questionable morals: "He wants to maneuver himself into the position of taking all the credit if the show is a success, and ducking all the blame if it bombs."

The *N.Y. Journal American* reported, "Robert Preston's upcoming play, *Nobody Loves an Albatross*, satirizes people in the television industry. Of course, the authors will present the usual disclaimer, but even the most casual newspaper reader and TV viewer will recognize prototypes of many of the characters, including stars, agents, and producers. Example: One character is a comedian who owns a TV studio and stars in her own video series—but of course, she isn't Lucille Ball."

By that time, the show was getting ready for its pre-Broadway tryouts, first in New Haven, Connecticut at the Shubert Theater (November 27, 1963) and then in Boston (December 2, 1963). The reviews were largely favorable. Kevin Kelly, in the *Boston Globe*, wrote that "Constance Ford is sourly aggressive as a female producer, an aging star turned affluent executive, a television idol of millions." Elinor Hughes seconded him in the *Boston Herald*: "Ford plays the cold-eyed blond studio boss in decorative fashion."

The show opened at New York's Lyceum Theater on December 19, 1963. Ticket prices ranged from $6.90 to $7.50, and *Variety* noted, *Albatross* garnered "three favorable notices and three qualified approvals."

The actors were uniformly praised, down to the smallest player, with Preston garnering most of the kudos. In fact, Preston was so naturally charming that it presented a problem for the narrative structure of the play (he had just finished filming his most famous role, that of another con man: Harold Hill in *The Music Man*). Critic John Simon, writing in the *Hudson Review*, put it best: "The play is funny and sharp, but it has serious limitations as satire: The victims are all, ultimately, less attractive and intelligent than the hero-villain, so that his villainy becomes" less of an issue.

In pictures from the production, we see Ford clowning around and doing some very Ball-like physical shtick with Preston. She was apparently so convincing in the role that at least one reviewer, Creighton Peet of *The Virginian-Pilot*, thought she had red hair, though Ford was blonde: "Nat's studio is run by a violently animated red-haired person (suggesting Lucille Ball), who suspects him for a phony but nevertheless pays him $75,000 a year for his 'creative writing.'" Another reviewer concurred, adding that Hildy Jones could "countenance any deception as long as she's party to it."

Frank Harris, in the *Jackson* (Wyoming) *Daily News*, wrote that, "When the Lucille Ball character who is head of the studio recognizes the plagiarism [in the script Nat has presented her] and fires him, he immediately cons himself into a bigger and better job.... The aforesaid caricature of Lucille Ball is raucously played by Constance Ford."

Frederick Guidry of *The Christian Science Monitor* described Ford's Hildy Jones as, "a hard-boiled woman executive who gets a perverse kind of pleasure out of buttering up a victim before applying the truth."

Richard P. Cooke of *The Wall Street Journal* said the play contained "several genuinely poisonous types ... including Marian Winters as a hard-boiled, thick-skinned script writer and Constance Ford as a blonde tornado who runs a TV studio, [who] appear to be reproductions of people Mr. Alexander has met."

Norman Nadel praised Ford's portrayal of "a ruthless, flinty television tycoon. Her girl-baby face and soft eyes sharpen, by contrast, her witchy ways," in the *N.Y. World Telegram*.

Howard Taubman in *The New York Times* (December 20, 1963) called Ford "capital" as a "gal tough enough and shrewd enough to head up her own studio." Her "iceberg of a studio head" shines among the "behind-the-scenes maneuvering in TV-Land."

Alexander had done his homework well, but in casting the likeable Preston as the lead, the producers undercut some of the writer's bite. Still, the show was a modest hit with the public, running for 213 performances until June 20, 1964. Barry Nelson eventually replaced Preston toward the end of the run.

Unfortunately, the show wasn't as kind to its backers, who lost an estimated $25,000 of its $125,000 investment, *Variety* reported on June 24, 1964. Several days earlier, *Variety* noted the screen rights to *Nobody Loves an Albatross* were purchased "by MGM, for no more than $200,000," according to an associate of Alexander's. Unfortunately, no movie was ever made. (See the next entry.)

One can assume Alexander never wrote for TV again; he noted, in an interview with the *Boston Herald* weeks before *Albatross* opened that, "I hope that I shall never, not even hardly ever, return to television. It is a most frustrating medium for a writer, far more than film, for you have absolutely no control over your material."

Why has this play remained so obscure? Is it possible that Ball, her family, and friends, were never aware of the show? It seems unlikely that no one would have brought it to her attention. More likely, Ball was powerful and secure enough in herself, her image, and her career to not give *Albatross* a second thought. That excuses her. What about everyone else who's ever written about her? Surely, *Nobody Loves an Albatross* deserves at least a mention in any Ball retrospective, if only to note that she was indeed so powerful and well-known at the time to merit her own very public satire.

NOBODY LOVES AN ALBATROSS: THE SCREENPLAY

Despite its small success on Broadway, the motion picture rights to the play *Nobody Loves an Albatross* were purchased by MGM. Sixteen months after the sale was announced, a script was produced. Max Shulman wrote the screenplay, dated October 20, 1965. It was sold to MGM Inc. under the auspices of Bentwood Productions Inc.

Shulman (1919-'88) was a logical choice to do the screenplay; the novelist, playwright (*The Tender Trap*), and Hollywood screenwriter is perhaps best remembered for *The Many Loves of Dobie Gillis* (1951), which was a movie (1953's *The Affairs of Dobie Gillis*) and then a successful TV series (1959-'63). He was a well-known and respected humorist in the middle of a long career in 1965, when he submitted the script for *Nobody Loves an Albatross*.

The script is the definitive product of a mid-1960s conventional Hollywood comedy mindset. Now, it reads like a period piece, one of the fluffy, Technicolor comedies produced anywhere from the late 1950s to the early 1960s, only this one is trying to pretend it has a bit more bite.

The situations follow the action of the play, telling what happens as Nat Benson (in the stage production he was "Nat Bentley"), our hero, is ground up by the television production machine, specifically his boss, producer Hildy Jones, and then turns it all around to come out on top. Hildy is the character based on Lucille Ball, and in this script, she comes across as a mercenary with little respect for the audience, who'll do anything to make 'em laugh, as long as it makes money.

The tone of the script is set at the start, in a Senate hearing room, where network executive Mike Harper (described as a "roughneck") is testifying about why there are few cultural or educational programs on television. Harper tells the senators, "You go back to your home state and tell the voters that you decided for their own good they're going to get *Hamlet* instead of *Gomer Pyle* from now on. What do you think would happen to you?" A Senator Gordon replies, "I'd be hung from the highest antenna in the state." Harper agrees. Then Gordon asks Harper why, if he feels that way, does he put *any* cultural programs on TV at all? Harper's pat reply: "Frankly, Senator, to keep guys like you off my back."

Boy, those TV guys really have no respect, right? Cue laugh track and fade to next scene. Oops, this is a movie.

We meet Hildy Jones soon after the screenplay begins. She's described as a "baggy-pants comedienne turned executive, and her office looks it. The room is a jumble of styles, periods, decors, and colors. A big streamer at the top of a wall announces Hildy Jones Productions Inc." Posters of Hildy's five shows surround her. They are *Hildy, Emergency Ward, Grand Hotel, Rocky Gibraltar*, and *Daddy-O*.

Hildy is further described as "A ripe, handsome woman, somewhere between 30 and 40." When we first see her she is on the phone lamenting the end of her production company; the majority of her shows aren't doing well, and she needs a hit: "Last year I had one show … just one little, tiny smash-hit gold mine, *Hildy*, No. 1 on the tube. I was rich, famous, loved. Why, why did I have to become a big producer?" In the play, Hildy was clearly the owner of a TV studio.

In any case, Hildy is a supporting character in the movie, basically a plot device to get Nat into the TV action. He is a producer on one of her series, and she demands he come up with a winner. His initial concept of doing *David Copperfield* for TV (and adding a singing, dancing chimp for the title character to pal around with) is made much of, but is funnier in thought than on paper.

The one clear Ball reference comes in a short scene in which we see the filming of her hit show, *Hildy*. Hildy is wearing an apron and in her kitchen with her friend Maud, described in the script as "A Vivian Vance type." You see, Hildy and Maud have been trying to bake a soufflé, it's been in the oven for three hours, and when Hildy opens the oven door, what do you think happens? According to Shulman's script, "… slowly, like a big dough balloon, the soufflé comes out of the oven door and starts to expand in the kitchen."

Sound familiar? I doubt that scene—so reminiscent (*too* reminiscent) of Lucy and Ethel in the "Pioneer Women" episode (March 31, 1952), when the huge load of bread shoots out of the oven thanks to the extra yeast Lucy had put in the dough—would have made the final cut.

The script goes out its way to portray those involved in the TV industry as crass and unconcerned with the audience's taste. Several of the female characters, and an entire segment concerning a lisping gay commercial actor who looks rugged but has to have his voice dubbed by someone else, are throwbacks to an uglier era, and the script suffers as a result.

The character of Benson has been softened for the movie; he is portrayed as a loving father and somewhat of a scoundrel but nothing like the con artist he was in the play. In fact, his biggest crime is stealing the plot of *Rebecca of Sunnybrook Farm* for the TV pilot he is producing for Hildy.

The script fails as a satire of the TV industry because too much time is spent on scenes with Nat and his daughter Diane, Nat and his new secretary Jean Hart, Nat with his ex-wife Maggie, and resolving the Nat/Jean/Maggie triangle. Nat ends up with his ex, and his secretary marries his bookish assistant, who exists only for this plot turn.

It reads much like a situation comedy, and a stale one at that. Speaking of which, running through the action are riffs about the laugh track—its inventor is a character—and how it influences what you see on TV. The laugh track machine is in fact the linchpin of a major plot twist at the end; it's used as a *deus ex machina* to convince Mike Harper (the network executive) that others are interested in Nat, so Nat can sign a huge contract with Harper.

At least two reasons exist for this script being shelved:

—Nat had to be extremely likeable in order to be accepted as the hero of a movie, and as a result much of the play's sting was removed.

—Hollywood by this time was not as willing to spit on its younger stepsister, television, because many of the studios were profiting from TV.

In the end, though, the script just isn't funny enough or truly satiric enough to work. It remains a fascinating peek into what could have been the first and only big-screen portrayal of television's biggest star.

O

OBER, PHIL

Handsome stage and movie character actor who was Vivian Vance's third husband. He left his wife for Vance, and it was quite a scandal at the time. The Vance-Ober marriage was troubled, and even—according to published reports—abusive. Ober apparently had a problem with Vance's huge success and belittled her whenever possible. Ober guest-starred more than once on *I Love Lucy*, and appeared in one of Vance's few films, *The Secret Fury* (1950). He also had a supporting role in Ball's and Bob Hope's movie, *The Facts of Life* (1960).

He and Vance were divorced in 1959, at which time Vance told the court that Ober "wanted to live on a high scale on [my] earnings." She filed a cruelty complaint after Ober filed for divorce in March 1959. In granting the divorce, the judge noted, "It might be that I am very naïve, but if there ever was a case of killing the goose that laid a golden egg, this is it." Vance was awarded the couple's home in Pacific Palisades (at 629 Frontera Drive) as well as stocks and other properties. Ober retired from acting in the late '60s, and was working as a diplomat for the Mexico City U.S. Consulate when he died of a heart attack in 1982.

O'BRIEN, BOB

Also credited as Robert O'Brien, he was a television and film writer who wrote the screenplay for 1950's *Fancy Pants*, one of Ball's best movie showcases, and many of what are considered Ball's best *Lucy Show* episodes, including her favorite, 1966's "Lucy Dates Dean Martin." Equally adept at drama and musical comedy, O'Brien also wrote for *The Dick Powell Theatre* (1962-63); and the screenplays for the Deanna Durbin feature *Lady on a Train* (1945), and the 1959 Bing Crosby/Debbie Reynolds vehicle, *Say One for Me* (for which he was nominated for a 1960 Writer's Guild of America Screen Award). O'Brien died in November 2005 at age 86.

O'BRIEN, VIRGINIA

Deadpan musical comedienne best remembered for her roles in a dozen or so splashy MGM productions in the 1940s. O'Brien almost always played the "ugly duckling" sidekick to the glamorous star, or the second-banana comedy relief. She usually stole the show.

She co-starred with Lucille Ball in four films, but two of those—*Thousands Cheer* (1943) and *Ziegfeld Follies* (1946)—were star-filled extravaganzas in which MGM trotted out its roster of talent. Meatier roles came in Ball's *DuBarry Was a Lady* (1943) and *Meet the People* (1944). O'Brien also had supporting roles in Ann Sothern's *Panama Hattie* (1942) and Judy Garland's *The Harvey Girls* (1946), among others. O'Brien and her then-husband Kirk Alyn (the first movie Superman) were frequent guests at Ball and Arnaz's Chatsworth ranch. After her MGM contract ended, she toured the country performing in nightclubs and theater, and on TV in the 1950s. Her last film appearance was in 1976's *Gus*. She died at 81 in January 2001.

O'CONNOR, DONALD

O'Connor was the last of the great male Golden Age film dancers. He was in movies as a child in the late 1930s, and basically grew up onscreen, coming into his own in musicals like *Singing in the Rain* (1950), which features his riotous, acrobatic dancing to "Make 'Em Laugh," and *Call Me Madam* (1953), with Ethel Merman. He also had success in a series of comic films about a talking mule named Francis, in the 1950s. A friend of Lucille Ball's, he appeared in the 1980 special *Lucy Moves to NBC*, which made a big deal of Ball's leaving CBS, and followed her as she tried to get her first comedy show produced on NBC. The latter is a failed pilot called *The Music Mart* that ran within the hour-and-a-half special, starring O'Connor and Gloria DeHaven. O'Connor died in 2003 at the age of 78.

1,000 JOKES

A joke compendium/magazine published by Dell (which also put out the *I Love Lucy* Comic Books). Celebrities were often on the cover (in caricature), and Lucille Ball appeared at least three times, first in the Spring 1953 issue, with Desi Arnaz, busting out of a conga drum with the tagline "Dig That Crazy Lucy." On the March-May 1957 cover, Arnaz conducted while Ball sang. Finally, the June-August 1959 cover has a cartoon image of Lucy and Ricky Ricardo and the Mertzes stuffed into a plane. Lucy is piloting and the rest of the gang looks apprehensive, to say the least. A headline under the illustration says, "The Lucille Ball Game," and there is an article inside about Ball with the same title.

ON THE FARM

Ball and Arnaz both enjoyed time away from Hollywood once they had purchased a ranch in Chatsworth, California, in the San Fernando Valley, soon after they married. It was about 35 miles outside the city. A fan magazine article from the 1940s (source unknown) described the couple's life at the ranch:

"Citified kids who have 'gone country' for keeps, Lucille and Desi aren't kidding about farming. Whenever they're not at the studio they're in their truck garden (they'll talk your ear off about the miracles of their produce). Recently they spent six weeks planting 200 citrus trees, doing it all themselves.

"They are so impressed by the produce of the truck garden that they name everything. Desi is admiring José Cantaloupe [in the photo accompanying the article]; José was the first-born in the melon crop.

"No panic need arise in the farm belt because of this new competition, but the five acres are doing all they can. Lucille's greatest triumph was the day 24 hens laid 24 eggs, but by the time they called their friends to brag, [they realized] the eggs had cost 40 cents each [to produce]!"

OPPENHEIMER, JESS

The creator, head writer, producer, and guiding hand throughout the runs of the radio show *My Favorite Husband* and *I Love Lucy*. Brought on in 1948 to bolster the radio show, he hired two writers, Bob Carroll Jr. and Madelyn Pugh, and the classic comedy began to take shape. Oppenheimer was always self-effacing when describing his own reasons for being funny: "When I was a kid, I was so funny-looking that people only tolerated me because I was amusing," was one of the one-liners he fed to newspaper reporters.

His first big job came as a comedy writer on the Fred Astaire radio show in 1936. He briefly worked for Jack Benny and Edgar Bergen, and then became the head writer for Fanny Brice's *The Baby Snooks Show*. (Snooks became the inspiration for Lucy Ricardo.) When Brice quit over a salary dispute, Oppenheimer was out of work, but not for long; he got a call from

CBS to produce and direct *My Favorite Husband*, a radio sitcom he'd never heard. He took the job, and the rest, as they say, is history.

Lucille Ball and Desi Arnaz gave Oppenheimer credit for the success of *I Love Lucy*. He was the one who created the situation, supervised, shaped, and guided all the talent, and turned it into one coherent, classic mix. Oppenheimer stayed with the show until the end of the 1955-'56 season, when he left to become an NBC executive.

There were several reasons he left, including continuing friction with Arnaz over production credit on the show, of which Oppenheimer owned 20 percent, plus the fact that Oppenheimer's five-year contract with Desilu was up and he wanted to move on.

In 1962, he expounded on his and Ball's success to the *Albuquerque Journal*: "Glamor and sex appeal may be great at home and in the office but actresses who really rang the cash register were comics" the newspaper reported. "Sober-faced Jess Oppenheimer, chief brain for Lucille Ball, solemnly analyzed the chance of success in show business. He intoned: 'Great comediennes are rare. Yet they have always made more money, and had longer careers than the glamor girls.'

"Oppenheimer pointed at the few great funny women: Fanny Brice, Lucille Ball, Joan Davis, Cass Dailey, Beatrice Lillie, and Imogene Coca. Then he asked, 'Why aren't there more women comics? Can it be the physical demands of funny business, which is historically devoted to pratfalls and acrobatic antics?'

"Oppenheimer and his [writers], bearded Bob Carroll Jr. and vivacious Madelyn Pugh, argued out all the scripts for Desi Arnaz and Lucy. But they all agree that [Ball] is unique in never losing her beauty even under handicaps. No matter how rough the action called for in the script, Ball emerges with her charm intact.

"Jess grinned, 'Lucy was on the road to success the day she stepped out of the chorus line to volunteer for [some mud in the face].'"

Oppenheimer worked with Ball a few more times. During the run of her later shows he was given a substantial settlement (more than $200,000) covering the use of the "Lucy Ricardo" character in Ball's post-*I Love Lucy* shows. (The characters were called Lucy *Carmichael* and Lucy *Carter*, but nobody was fooling anybody into thinking they were anything else but continuations of Lucy Ricardo, though written, admittedly, without the warmth and style of the original. See The "Lucy" Character.)

In the mid-1960s Oppenheimer wrote, directed, and produced for the hit *Get Smart*, and in 1969 he produced an *I Love Lucy* clone (and flop), *The Debbie Reynolds Show*. Debbie was married to a sportswriter and she was dying to become a reporter, so she was constantly putting him on the spot with her crazy schemes to get a byline, aided by her older sister … sound familiar? His last showbiz work was as a writer on *NBC: The First 50 Years—A Closer Look* in 1976. He died in 1988.

Jess Oppenheimer with his solid-gold *I Love Lucy* **cast. Photofest**

Recommended Reading: *Laughs, Luck … And Lucy*, started by Jess and finished by son Gregg Oppenheimer.

OSBORNE, ROBERT

The former member of Lucille Ball's Desilu Workshop in the late 1950s started out wanting to be an actor, but claims Ball was the one who directed him toward writing in the early '60s. She suggested he combine his love of the Golden Age of Hollywood with his writing facility, and he produced his first book, *The Academy Awards Illustrated*. He kept writing and began working at *The Hollywood Reporter* in 1982; he still writes a column for the trade paper. He's best known for being the knowledgeable host of Turner Classic Movies since its inception in 1994, and sharing his often-juicy Hollywood trivia with the viewers. TCM is a cable network that shows films from the MGM, Universal, Warners, and many other film libraries uninterrupted, along with shorts, old musical clips, and interviews with Golden Age stars hosted by Osborne.

As Osborne reminded an evening audience during the summer 2006 Lucille Ball Birthday Bash in Jamestown, New York, those who only know Ball from her TV work might be surprised to see just what a gorgeous movie star she really was.

Osborne presented a two-film "series" Ball did at the end of her run at RKO Studios, called *The Affairs of Annabel* and *Annabel Takes a Tour* (both 1938). In them, Ball played a popular actress whose career needed a lift. Jack Oakie played her crazy publicist, willing to put her in any situation, no matter how bizarre. The films were successful and more would have made except, according to Osborne, Ball's star was growing beyond such B-picture roles and, more importantly, co-star Oakie asked for $50,000 for the third picture (the entire movie would have cost about $100,000 to make).

P

PALEY CENTER FOR MEDIA, THE

A museum with branches in New York and Los Angeles, the former Museum of Television and Radio. (its name changed in June 2007) preserves television and radio history via audio, video, and print archives. What is always interesting about my trips to the New York branch is the fact that you never know what you're going to find. You can come prepared and look through the catalog for specific programs to watch on individual video screens. But on every occasion there have been other Lucille Ball extras I found just walking around the museum: for example, Al Hirschfeld drawings (lithographs and some originals). There is one of Ball and Desi Arnaz framed in a heart; another of Ball and her fellow Kennedy Center honorees from 1986; and one time I walked in on a *TV Guide* exhibit featuring 400 covers displayed in panels of about 30-35 each, with an entire panel of 23 covers devoted to Ball. This is a highly recommended trip. Since 2005, the Paley Center has honored, on a yearly basis, "Women Creating Television and Radio" under the rubric She Made It. Ball was in the first group of honorees in 2005.

PALM SPRINGS, CALIFORNIA

This oasis in the California desert, a weekend playground of the stars, had a special place in the hearts and lives of Lucille Ball and Desi Arnaz. The Thunderbird Country Club in nearby Rancho Mirage was finished in 1951, the same year that *I Love Lucy* went on the air. When Ball and Arnaz decided to build a desert home, it was at the Thunderbird (Desi was a golfer). They built a ranch-style house (on land reportedly won by Arnaz in a poker game) near the 17th fairway of the Thunderbird Golf Club. The house at 40-241 Club View Drive was one of the first homes in the club, finished in 1954.

Writer Allene Arthur described the home in *Palm Springs Life* as a "mid-Century Modern" designed by "noted architect Paul Williams" with "sweeping stone and glass structure curves around emerald greens," and views of "a panorama of the desert mountains." The air-conditioned abode was about 4,400 square feet, and featured six bedrooms (there were separate bedrooms for their children, divided by a large nursery); a swimming pool; and a lanai. A glass wall separated the patio from the living-dining area, and in keeping with the region, it was furnished in desert colors, but a contemporary style.

Their neighbors included songwriter Hoagy Carmichael; and Desi's friend, bandleader and actor Phil Harris and his wife, actress Alice Faye. The Thunderbird's general manager at the time, Frank Bogert, told Arthur that Ball was a ferocious game-player, indulging every evening. Arnaz's evening activities were entirely different, and those who were there report that Ball had her agenda (games) and Arnaz had his (poker, golf, and women) and never the twain did meet.

I Love Lucy director Bill Asher, a frequent Palm Springs guest, has said that despite Ball and Arnaz's difficulties, no outsider would ever have known anything was out of the ordinary. Ball was no fool and knew what was going on; Bogert says she often dispatched him to "fetch" Arnaz after the latter's evenings of drunken abandon.

Eventually Arnaz bought some land along with a group of other investors in nearby Indian Wells; the Indian Wells Country Club opened in 1956, and once the golf course was completed, Arnaz saw the need for a hotel, so he built one. The Desi Arnaz-Western Hills Hotel opened the following year.

The hotel featured 42 rooms, a golf course, and a restaurant. It is located on what became the 11th and 12th fairways of the Indian Wells Country Club golf course. (On Highway 111 at Club Drive, the hotel, now called the Indian Wells Resort Hotel, has 155 rooms on three floors.)

Just a few years later, *I Love Lucy* had ended, the Arnazes were divorced, and both had remarried. By 1963, Arnaz and his new wife, Edith Hirsh, lived at the Thunderbird in a house near the one he had shared with Ball, who had married comedian Gary Morton. (That year, Lucy was the Palm Springs Desert Circus Parade Queen.)

Unfortunately, due to the Thunderbird's unstated policy of discouraging Jews from playing there (now vigorously denied) Morton initially could not play on the course that surrounded his home. This reportedly made Ball furious. Morton joined the Tamarisk Country Club, founded by a group of prominent Jewish men, as a solution.

As Ball and Arnaz grew older, Arnaz spent less time in the desert and more at his Del Mar home and especially at the track. He died in Del Mar in 1986. After Ball's death in 1989, Morton continued to live in the Thunderbird home, eventually bringing his last wife, Susie

McAllister (a golf pro he married in 1994), there to live, where she still resides. Morton died in Palm Springs in 1999.

A life-size bronze statue of Ball as Lucy Ricardo (see <u>Art</u>) sits on a bench on one of Palm Springs' main streets, testifying to the mutual love between the star and the town.

PARTING GLANCES

Watershed gay film in which popular character actor Steve Buscemi made his first big splash (1986). Buscemi's character Nick, a musician dying of AIDS, has an eclectic apartment dominated by a dozen or so televisions; leaning prominently against one of them is a Lucille Ball ad for Chesterfield cigarettes.

PATTERSON, ELIZABETH

Sturdy character actress in 100 movies from 1926 on, Patterson played the Ricardos' neighbor, Mrs. Trumbull, in 10 episodes on *I Love Lucy* from 1953 to 1956. Previously, she made one appearance as a different character, Mrs. Willoughby, in "The Marriage License," April 7, 1952. In movies, Patterson often played a neighbor, aunt, grandmother, or landlady, and her better-known films include *Dinner at Eight* (1933), the *Bulldog Drummond* movie series in the late 1930s, *My Sister Eileen* and *I Married a Witch* (both 1942), *Little Women* (1949), and *Pal Joey* (1957). She died in 1966.

♥ **Lucy Trivia** In "The Marriage License," Lucy discovers Ricky Ricardo's last name is incorrectly listed as *Bacardi*. In real life, Desi Arnaz's grandfather was one of the founders of the Bacardi Rum Co.

PEARCE, ALICE

Comic actress on stage, film (*On the Town*, 1949), and television best remembered for her Emmy-winning role as original nosy neighbor Gladys Kravitz on *Bewitched* (1964-1966). Pearce died of cancer on March 3, 1966, a few hours before William Frawley collapsed and died on Hollywood Boulevard. The result was their deaths being associated in the next day's obituaries. *The New York Times* placed their separate obituaries side by side, but other papers treated them as one, with headlines like "Two of TV's 'Good Neighbors' Die" and "Hollywood Loses Two Top Comedians."

PEPPER, BARBARA

One-time Goldwyn Girl who struck a friendship with Lucille Ball. She appeared in the chorus with Ball in movies like *Roman Scandals* and *Kid Millions*, and became a busy bit player, often credited as "Girl at Bar," "Flossie," or "Tavern Lady" in nearly 100 movies from the 1930s through her death in 1969. A vivacious and enthusiastic player, Pepper could handle bigger roles when she got them, which wasn't often, though she made an impression as one of the comically insane Fleagle family in the riotous *Murder, He Says* (1945).

Pepper and her career fell on hard times in the late 1940s and 1950s. The death of her husband, actor Craig Reynolds, in a motorcycle accident in 1949, left Pepper with two young children to raise alone, and contributed to a depression and subsequent alcohol problem. Ball helped by seeing she consistently got bit parts on *I Love Lucy*. She also had a small role in Ball's movie *The Fuller Brush Girl* (1950). Her last movie roles were small parts in big films like *Auntie Mame* (1958), *The Music Man* (1962), and *My Fair Lady* (1964).

Pepper made many TV appearances in the 1950s and 1960s, and repeatedly guest-starred on *Richard Diamond*, *Perry Mason*, and *Petticoat Junction*. It is on the latter sitcom she created the role she is best remembered for: Mrs. Ziffel, "mom" to Arnold the pig. She took the character over to *Green Acres*, where she was a semi-regular for four years (1965-'69); she died of heart failure during the run of the show on July 18, 1969, and was replaced by character actress Fran Ryan for the final two seasons.

PETE AND GLADYS

This modestly successful (1960-'62) sitcom was a spin-off of the <u>Desilu</u> series *December Bride* (1954-'59). In the latter, regular Harry Morgan (Pete) always joked about his impossible wife Gladys, but she never appeared onscreen. Morgan, a busy character actor, is best known as Colonel Potter on *M*A*S*H* (1975-'83). In this show, Oscar-nominated actress (for *The Defiant Ones*, 1959) and comedienne Cara Williams played Gladys.

There were several *I Love Lucy* connections here besides Desilu. Actress Verna Felton, a *Bride* regular, appeared as a regular on this show; she's remembered for two *I Love Lucy* appearances, as the cantankerous maid Ricky insists Lucy hire in "Lucy Hires a Maid" (April 27, 1953), and as Mrs. Simpson on the episode "Sales Resistance" (January 26, 1953). Gale Gordon played Morgan's uncle, and Shirley Mitchell (who played Lucy Ricardo's friend Marion Strong) was a semi-regular on *Pete & Gladys*. *I Love Lucy* scribe Bob Weiskopf wrote the show.

PETERSON, DESIRÉE "DEDE" HUNT BALL

Lucille Ball's mother, a complicated and important figure in Lucy's life, married Henry Ball at the age of 18 in 1910. A year later (August 6, 1911) Lucille Desirée Ball was born. Though born in Jamestown, in western New York State, Ball lived her earliest years in Montana and Michigan, as the family traveled due to her father's job as a telephone lineman. By the time Ball was 3½, DeDe was pregnant again, and Henry had contracted typhoid fever. He died in 1915, and Lucy never got over the loss and the upheaval it caused in her young life.

Moving back to the Jamestown area and into her parent's home, DeDe gave birth to a son, named Fred after her father, just before Lucy turned 4. A few years later, DeDe met a Swedish man named Ed Peterson, and married him in 1918. DeDe was described in Kathleen Brady's Ball biography (see Books) as a woman who did not try to juggle the various demands of family, career, and motherhood, but rather one did what needed to be done at the moment.

That might explain leaving her young children often while looking for work so the family could survive. She's also been called hard, sweet, sour, cagey, and cold as ice. Despite the fact it's been said she never really cared for Desi Arnaz, DeDe turned out to be her daughter's greatest fan.

Ball's stepfather, Ed, has been called a fun-loving guy (i.e., a drinker) with no real zeal for children, who wouldn't allow Fred or Lucy to call him "Daddy." Soon after the wedding, DeDe took off with Ed to Detroit, following his job, leaving Ball with his parents, and baby brother Fred with her own. DeDe didn't return until 1922, and the period she was gone instilled a loneliness (and a fear of being left alone) that haunted Ball the rest of her life. Grandma Peterson was stern and very Old World, and Ball couldn't help but feel isolated from her family. She vowed that once she had the money, she'd bring her family together, and that is what she did as soon as she began earning a steady paycheck in Hollywood.

Ed, who died in 1943, was a failure as a dad, and DeDe eventually left him and took a series of retail jobs, landing in Washington, D.C., which is where she was when Ball sent for her from California. DeDe was never too far from Ball for the rest of her life, and sat in the audience for the shooting of every television episode her daughter made. You can hear her distinctive laugh on the *I Love Lucy* soundtrack and many other sitcoms that "borrowed" *I Love Lucy*'s laugh track to sweeten their own audience reactions.

DeDe, who lived to her mid-80s, remained a plain-talking, formidable character all her life. She cautioned director Herbert Kenwith that her daughter could be a bitch to work with. But when she died in 1977, Lucy was devastated.

PHILIP MORRIS

One of the original sponsors of *I Love Lucy*, the tobacco giant eventually pulled out after several years. Ball and Arnaz were loyal employees and smokers, and plugged the product in print and TV ads, and whenever else they could.

PHOBIAS

The day Lucille Ball's father died, a bird got trapped in the house. Thereafter, Ball could not stand birds, anywhere, in any shape or form; she'd even remove pictures of birds in hotel rooms. She was known to be compulsive about cleaning, especially later in life. She also had a potentially career-wrecking fear: being too close to people. "I get numb," she told author Eleanor Harris in *The Real Story of Lucille Ball*. "The first day I went to Metro-Goldwyn-Mayer in 1942, I wasn't really aware of this phobia. But a new hairdresser spent 45 minutes working on the bangs on my forehead, leaning against me, breathing on me. At the end of that time, I had tears streaming down my face. My make-up was ruined, and I was paralyzed." Harris wrote that co-star Vivian Vance was aware of the phobia, and "always worked at a suitable distance from her."

But remember that Lucy and Ethel hugged each other a lot and were extremely physical in any number of other situations. Obviously, Ball did not let this fear interfere with her movie, radio, or TV careers. So either Ball was the best actress ever, or this fear couldn't touch her when she was acting. It does help explain why Ball tended to surround herself on her later series with people she knew, respected, and with whom she was very comfortable working.

PHONEBOOK

In 2001, Alltel published a special phonebook featuring a Jamestown, New York, tribute celebrating Ball and her 50 years on television. On the cover was a full-color photo of Ball (from the 1960s) talking on a phone, of course. It is now a collectible.

PHOTOGRAPHERS

Lucille Ball was one of the most photographed personalities of the 20th century. Film or television studio public relations departments took many of these photos, so that the actual photographer remained anonymous. However, here are a few of the more prominent photographers for whom Ball sat.

Sid Avery, born in 1918, was well-known for his Hollywood photographs. He took photos for *LIFE, Collier's,* and the *Saturday Evening Post,* among many others. According to one source, Avery's "natural candid capabilities" gained him the respect of the most reserved people in the entertainment industry, allowing him access to their private moments. He shot Ball dancing with a mannequin as Desi Arnaz and William Frawley watched, on the set of *I Love Lucy.*

Ernest A. Bachrach, one of the top studio photographers at RKO, shot Ball and Arnaz in 1941 with a Christmas theme. The pair were shown in front of a door with a wreath, both holding packages, Arnaz in a topcoat and Ball in a white fur. Separately, Ball was pictured in a full skirt, novelty cap (with braids), suspenders, and a white silk blouse.

Clarence Sinclair Bull, a noted Hollywood chronicler, photographed Ball in 1945; one color Cibachrome print contrasts Ball's red hair and lips with a navy dress that has a shaded heart pattern on it.

Ralph Crane, a photographer associated with *LIFE* magazine, shot the cover of January 5, 1962, proclaiming "Lucy Is Back!" and showing three head shots rotated at different angles.

Murray Garrett In his book *Hollywood Moments,* the celebrity photojournalist offers some of his favorite star subjects with his own commentary on how the stars behaved. A four-page spread on Ball and Arnaz is very revealing; two full-page pictures augment text in which Garrett characterizes Arnaz as an alcoholic and a bully (once *I Love Lucy* became a success), who apparently had no compunction about pushing the press around; Ball, on the other hand, is described as a total professional, "a great lady" who respected what the press could do for her career and never misbehaved during a professional shoot.

Irv Goodnoff, a movie and television cinematographer, photographed Ball during her 1974 American Film Institute seminar; one of his photos was used as the cover to the AFI document *Dialogue on Film: Lucille Ball,* May-June 1974.

Philippe Halsman photographed an airborne Ball for a September 29-October 5, 1962 *TV Guide* cover. Halsman, famed for his traditional final request that his subject jump, also shot an iconic photo of Ball in 1950, in which she, wide-eyed and with lips fully made up, stares at the viewer over her raised (and bare) right shoulder. This image of Ball became the one man fans remember when thinking of her.

George Hurrell was the photographer who turned black-and-white Hollywood glamour portraits into a sensuous art form. As head of still photography for such studios as MGM, Warner Bros., and Columbia, he created immortal images of almost all the screen's great stars, from the 1940s to the 1960s. Hurrell photographed Ball just once. His notes are telling: "… in probably one of her only glamour indulgences," Ball was shot wearing a fur, with her left hand resting on her right shoulder (her left is bare), and leaning slightly back with a faraway look in her eyes. Ball has never looked more sensuous, lush, or beautiful. This photo took me several years to track down; I have a copy, but could not get permission to print it from Hurrell's estate.

Gene Lester, a top photojournalist, remembered photographing Ball during the World War II era: "Early for my appointment, I walked into Lucille Ball's house in Beverly Hills to find her seated at a writing desk reading and answering Christmas cards. She wanted to brush them aside for our session, but I insisted that she continue while I included the incident in my photo series. Over the years, I found Lucy to be the most cooperative star I photographed."—*Los Angeles* magazine, December 1990

Walter McBride photographed Lucy later in her life, from the early 1980s on. You can see some of his paparazzi-style photos online at the Retna.com photo agency site.

Leonard McCombe, also a *LIFE* veteran, shot Ball and Arnaz at work and with their kids for the feature story, "The TV Production Empire of Lucy and Desi," in the October 6, 1958 issue.

Kenny Rogers, the singer, also dabbles in photography; a black-and-white picture he took of Ball is in his book, *Kenny Rogers: Your Friends and Mine*, 1987.

Walter Sanders, a prolific *LIFE* magazine photographer, shot some gorgeous photos of Ball lounging in a flaming red midriff outfit circa 1943. Sanders, in fact, was such a fine photographer he is often credited with making *LIFE* the unique photographic showcase it was in the '40s and '50s.

Peter Stackpole, one of the original photographers for *LIFE* magazine, captured decades of the "Hollywood" lifestyle during filmdom's Golden Age. The book of his black-and-white photographs, *Life in Hollywood 1936-1952*, published in 1992 by Clark City Press, features black-and-white shots of his favorites, including Ball, in many candid moments, at work, play, dinner with friends and families, and so on, along with Stackpole's often-humorous accounts of the sessions.

Harry Warnecke photographed Ball in 1945, and his original 14x18-inch Carbro print is in the National Portrait Gallery, part of the Smithsonian Institution in Washington, D.C. Warnecke ran the color lab and studio for the *New York Daily News* for 20 years, and produced a Carbro print each week for the cover of the paper's *Sunday Gravure* magazine. [Note: a Carbro print is defined online at the Laurence Miller Gallery collector resource page as "a combination of the carbon and silver-bromide process. The trichrome or color carbro involves superimposing three-color carbro prints in primary colors made from three separate negatives, on each other, to produce a full-color print. The carbro print has a slightly raised and waxy surface."] This gorgeous photo graces the cover of this volume, thanks to Nicholas Orzio, who worked for Warnecke and was left many of the original negatives by Warnecke's widow. **Laszlo Willinger** photographed many of the most important personages of this century. Born in Budapest, Hungary, he was already photographing celebrities when he went to Paris, where he managed the portrait studio of the Keystone Agency, also known as the Talbot Studios. At 23 he opened his own studio in Vienna, and again photographed the most important names of that period. With the political situation in Europe becoming too threatening, Willinger left for Hollywood in 1937. At MGM he shot Ball—and gave her his trademark sophisticated black-and-white glamour look—among many others for the studios' PR machine.

PIANO

A publicity item from the early 1940s noted that Lucille Ball "wanted to be a concert pianist, and Carnegie Hall may have lost a great attraction when she switched to a Ziegfeld chorus and modeling."

PIONEERS

As early as 1953, *TV Guide* recognized *I Love Lucy* as a groundbreaking show. In its fall preview issue dated September 18-24, 1953, an article titled "Situation Comedies Galore!" noted in a subhead that "Funny Families Replace Fast-Patter Comedians." The No. 1 funny family was, of course, The Ricardos, and *TV Guide* wrote, "Almost entirely responsible for the tremendous surge toward laughs arising from situations instead of gags is of course the fantastically successful *I Love Lucy*. Since its debut in 1951, *Lucy* has run up increasingly astonishing ratings, and there's no end in sight. The marital misadventures of Mr. and Mrs. Ricardo, as portrayed by Desi Arnaz and Lucille Ball, provide no end of joy to TV fans, and as a result the TV comedy scene has been entirely reshaped."

PREEMPTING *I LOVE LUCY*

Once *I Love Lucy* became a hit, basically after its first broadcast in October 15, 1951, people and even institutions adjusted their schedules so they could catch it on Monday nights. Stores hung signs in their windows that read, "We love Lucy, too, and so we'll be closed during the show." Water pressure spiked and dropped as people in a given city rushed to the bathroom during the commercials, so as not to miss one precious minute of the sitcom (remember, TV itself was still a relatively new medium at the time).

Is it possible the Democrats lost an election because of this dedication? The Canadian website Civilization.ca, on its "Timeline of Television History" page, reports that in 1952, "The first political ads appear on U.S. television networks, when Democrats buy a half-hour slot for Adlai Stevenson. Stevenson is bombarded with hate mail for interfering with a broadcast of *I Love Lucy*. Eisenhower, Stevenson's political opponent, buys only 20-second commercial spots, and wins the election." To illustrate that Ball was nonpartisan, note that in the following year, the birth of Little Ricky outshined the inauguration of Eisenhower on TV and in the papers.

"PROFESSOR" ARNAZ

Variety announced in its March 29, 1972 issue that Desi Arnaz was teaching film techniques and acting at San Diego State College.

"PROFESSOR" BALL

Ball enjoyed sharing her professional experience with a younger generation, so it's no surprise that later in life she occasionally held seminars and even taught comedy at various institutions of learning. These included the Museum of Television and Radio in New York (now known as The Paley Center for Media), Foothills College in Los Altos Hills, California, California State University at Northridge, and Sherwin Oak Experimental College in Hollywood.

PUBLICITY PLOY

The popularity of Ball and *I Love Lucy* leads many to use the name or image of Ball to hook the reader/viewer when the actual piece has no further mention of Ball. A case in point: a *New York Times* article from May 2, 2001, headlined "Where Lucy and Ricky Meet Bart and Lisa." Naturally, intrigued by the juxtaposition of the lead characters of the most successful sitcom ever (*I Love Lucy*) and the most successful modern sitcom (*The Simpsons*, 19 years and going strong in 2007) many readers would pore over the story. What they found was a profile of the Museum of Television and Radio in New York, now The Paley Center for Media, with nary a mention of Lucy or Ricky (or Bart and Lisa, for that matter) in it.

PUGH DAVIS, MADELYN

One of the first, and most successful, female comedy writers in television, Pugh was hired for Lucille Ball's radio show *My Favorite Husband*, along with partner Bob Carroll Jr. She wrote for Ball throughout that series and *I Love Lucy*, the first few seasons of *The Lucy Show*, and on and off until Ball's death in 1989, including Ball's final TV special and series. She remains at this writing one of the few original *I Love Lucy* creators still alive. For more, see <u>Carroll Jr., Bob and Madelyn Pugh Davis</u>.

Note that at various times in her career Madelyn has taken the surnames Davis, Martin, Pugh, Pugh Davis, and Pugh Martin.

Q

QUAGMIRE

A difficult or dangerous situation, i.e., what Lucy Ricardo invariably found herself in every week on *I Love Lucy*.

QUEEN ELIZABETH

An offscreen character in the January 13, 1956 episode of *I Love Lucy*; while in London, Lucy Ricardo is set to be presented to the Queen; she injures herself during rehearsals and ends up limping and clowning through the entire routine. It turns out the Queen loves her slapstick performance.

"QUITTING" TV

Lucille Ball and Desi Arnaz had had it ... after 180 half-hour episodes they felt they had run out of ideas and situations, so in the spring of 1957 they announced that *I Love Lucy* would no longer run on a weekly basis, but in an hour-long format.

Considering that *I Love Lucy* was rarely out of the No. 1 spot in the ratings during its six-year run, many might have been forgiven for thinking the Arnazes were a bit nuts. At the time, Arnaz said, "Lucy and I are not quitting like Rocky Marciano and Gene Tunney. We just aren't going to fight every Monday night. We'll fight five times a year. Among the reasons, he said, was, "We always tried to keep topping ourselves—getting out of the apartment, going to new places, bringing in new guest stars—anything that would keep the audience wondering what we would do next. The half-hour format is tough. All you have is 24½ minutes of playing time. You only have time to introduce one thread of a story and then resolve it. The hour show gives you time to develop several threads, and to present a well-rounded story."

Arnaz took umbrage at press indicating he and Ball were "quitting." He addressed the rumors as early as 1954 in a *TV Guide* article called "Who's Quitting!" with his byline. Among his comments: "In the first place, Lucy can't quit in two years even if she wanted to, which she doesn't. Our contract with Philip Morris runs until the end of the 1955-56 season. After that, CBS has the right to ask us to do two more years of the show, which would carry us through the end of the 1957-58 season."

Even then, the idea of a *Lucille Ball-Desi Arnaz Show* was one of the options on the table: "We might do any number of things," Arnaz said. "We might put *Lucy* into syndication. We might do another two years of *Lucy* for CBS. We might do a monthly hour-long version of *Lucy*. We might do nothing but a picture a year. We might just do five or six guest appearances—maybe as part of these new color extravaganzas, which are just getting started. We might do an entirely different series together, although I don't think that would be such a good idea. Or we might go fishing in Cuba."

The half-hour *I Love Lucy* played for the last time in its Monday night slot on June 24, 1957. *The Lucille-Ball Desi Arnaz Show* took over in the 1957-'58 season.

By 1960, Ball had divorced Arnaz and noted, "I filed for divorce the day after I finished my last piece of film under the Westinghouse [the hour-long shows] contract. I should have done it long ago." A reporter asked her—tastelessly—whether there would be any more Lucy-Desi specials. Her surprised but unsurprising reply was, "No. Even if everything were all right, we'd never work together again. We had six years of a successful series and two years of specials. Why try to top it? That would be foolish.

"We always knew that when the time came to quit, we'd quit. We were lucky. We quit while we were still ahead." They were indeed quitting at the top of their game, as far as ratings, popularity, and money were concerned. However, by that time, their marriage was beyond repair.

THE QUOTABLE LUCY

Straight from the horse's mouth, a compendium of Lucille Ball quotes (and some from her friends and co-stars):

"I don't have an epitaph for myself. You know, it's nice to have entertained five generations. I never expected to be around this long, and the length of time I've been around never occurred to me until one day recently I found out I was outliving my supply of henna."—*LIFE* magazine, January 1990, quoting Ball posthumously in a feature on famous people who had died in 1989

"You have to understand, I am from a suburb of Jamestown, N.Y. Not Jamestown itself, but a suburb, yet. You think Cleveland or Cincinnati is bad … Jamestown is only a place to be *from*. To be from *only*."—Ball, *Rolling Stone*, June 23, 1983

"… Though I've been around so many years, I've never really had any experience. I've still got a lot to learn about acting. The *Annabel* series has helped a lot, but my chief function at the studio [RKO] before that was taking pratfalls when nobody else would do it."—Ball, *Modern Screen*, April 1939

Though Ball may have been quoted otherwise, she did hold a special place in her heart for Jamestown, New York. Above, she arrives there on a war bonds trip during WWII. Photofest

"Every girl has some good points. I started with two; my eyes and an acceptable hairline. For the rest, either people told me or I thought it up myself. Take my word for it, a girl's best friend is a mirror."—Ball, *Hollywood Screen Life*, May 1938

"There's a need for an all-around comedienne, one who plays everything from slapstick to romance. I'm the girl, and I'm out to prove it."—Ball, *Cosmopolitan*, January 1953

"I'm a typical housewife at heart." —Ibid

"I don't know why, but I just love it when people laugh."—Ibid

"In Hollywood, I have everything a girl can ask for. I have a contract; I have producers letting me select my own plays and buying them for me, all the things I dreamed about when I managed my first Hollywood triumph. It was one line of dialogue in Goldwyn's *Roman Scandals* in which I played one of the chorus girls."—Ball, newspaper interview, 1947

"We were our own bosses, we could do as we pleased, and we did. There were no precedents set by anyone else, and we made our own mistakes, our own innovations, our own hours, and put our money back into our business. Didn't expect it to last five years, let alone twenty-five.

"I hadn't felt it before. I didn't even know how long it was, I never knew how many shows I made. I never knew how many hours I put in. I have never felt old, and I wasn't aware of being young. To me, it's been better than any party I ever went to. I always had the most fun when I was working.

"We always worked in front of an audience, so we had that shot of adrenaline every Thursday. And we had such a sense of accomplishment every day. That's a marvelous way to live. And you're making people happy at the same time …

"How could I be anything but grateful that it happened to me? I get the letters, I see the people, they come to me face-to-face and *thank* me for years of laughter and enjoyment. I've been babysitting for generations!"—Ball in 1976, reflecting on her 25th anniversary on television

"I've had stress in my life—recently quite a bit of it. The loss of my work … just quitting work was very stressful for me, and I missed it. I was in limbo. And then Vivian [Vance] died."—Ball, *Parade* magazine, January 13, 1980

"All you need to be an actress seems to be unbreakable bones and the ability to take a fall." —Ball, 1930s, commenting on her career

"Hunger brings out the genius in people. I like hungry people. You have to have a need of some sort."—Ball, *W*, February 4-11, 1977

"I wouldn't want to play anything but Lucy, and I'm too old to play her."—Ibid

"You don't know what time it is in Hollywood. Now you here [in New York] can figure on doing something next Tuesday. Out there they say, 'Now why don't you take a rest because we figure on doing this probably next July?"—Ball, 1939 New York newspaper interview

"I am very happy to have had this opportunity to reply to unfounded rumors and hope very much the Committee will see fit to release a complete transcript of the information I gave."—September 11, 1953 statement released by Ball through CBS, responding to the rumors that she had been interviewed by the House Un-American Activities Committee

"We both realize that it is important for each of us to make concessions. We are fully aware of the problem of having two careers in the same family. However, the most important thing in our lives is our marriage. We think that together we have worked out a very successful formula: Keep it a romance!"—Ball, magazine article circa 1949, "We Make Our Marriage a Romance!"

"Hi! Remember me? I used to work at Desilu!"—Ball's offhand comment to a friend after her 1960 divorce

"I go out because people ask me to. I have no love of nightclubs, unless there's an act I especially want to see."—Ball, 1960

"We try to make a game of our lives—but a game without any fixed or definite pattern. We believe that too many couples allow themselves to become 'settled' and prosaic, and as a result lose the fun which drew them together in the first place, and which keeps romance alive."—Ball, circa 1942

"I was never out of work. That's the astonishing thing. I always had a very well-paid apprenticeship."—Ball, *Drama-Logue*, September 25, 1986

"From the moment you begin to do comedy, you have to do it seriously, you don't try to be funny. I had to have a childish belief in everything that I did because it was so exaggerated, and I think that's very important in my type of comedy."—Ball, AFI *Dialogue on Film*, 1974

"I loathe people who come in and whisper at the first rehearsal, and are a little louder the second rehearsal, die the third rehearsal, and we're into Wednesday night—the show is on Thursday—and you don't know what they're going to do and neither do they. This is death. So long ago, I got strong about it, because I have a short space of time to do a show.... So I got the title of an ogre, and 'Oh, Jesus don't work with her,' growl, growl."—Ibid

"My best virtue was that I never thought the grass was greener anyplace else."—Ibid

"You have to have people around you who know how to do it, and you have to know whether or not they know their job. That was the only part I prided myself a little bit on: recognizing eventually—not on sight—eventually *that* was a good photographer, *that* was a good prop man, don't forget *that* name. Get him next time."—Ibid

"All I know is when you took brownies for last winter's bake sale, some kid took 'em for hockey pucks. [And] your potato salad tastes like yellow Play-Doh."—Vivian Vance, as "Viv," to Ball, as "Lucy Whittaker"
"Well, well, well … I noticed you managed to choke down three huge bites."—Ball to Vance, from the 1977 TV special *Lucy Calls the President*

"She came backstage to the dressing room, and I didn't know how to act, I mean, do I kiss her ring, or what … I needn't have worried because Lucy had that wonderful quality of putting people at ease in any circumstance, and she just sat down and we talked as if we'd been friends for a hundred years. She was complimentary, she was helpful, and she was encouraging. Later on I found out from many young actors and actresses that she was always that way, very nurturing to new talent."—Carol Burnett on the TV special *Funny Women of Television*, 1991

"First, you have to believe it, no matter how unbelievable it is. And I had great writers. Now you don't always have the greatest writers, but you still have to do it, and believe, no matter how absurd the situation is. As long as you've accepted the job and are going to stick with it, believe. *Believe*."—Ball, seminar at the Museum of Television and Radio (Now The Paley Center for Media), New York, 1984

"I'm not going to try alone now what I've done with my partners in the past. My partners are in heaven. No one could take the place of Vivian Vance in my life (*audience applause*). She was the greatest partner anyone could ever have."—Ibid

"When I think of great audience identification with *Lucy*, there always has been, even with a slight change of format, two or three times…. We've done domestic situation comedy with married people, that's with Bill and Vivian, and Desi and myself, and then the next change, without the husbands, that was certainly audience identification with millions of women, who try to go through life without a man, although not as bungling as I, of course…."—Ibid

"I've been playing like a rookie in rehearsals. 'Blank' Ball, they call me, 'Blank' Ball."—Ball to host Bert Convy on *Super Password*, 1986 (her partner was *Life with Lucy* daughter Ann Dusenberry)

"I got more out of my years with Lucy and Desi learning about timing—you can learn more from comedy than from action or adventure—and it was a great experience learning from all of them, particularly Lucy. Though Desi had great timing and a great memory, too. Desi could be his own worst enemy, but he was a talent that, in the history of TV, is not credited with all the things he did and all the chances he took."—Dann Cahn, film editor on *I Love Lucy*, to author, 2005

"She was a great gal and a great lady. As a comedian, she was a natural. Her instincts were sharp, and she loved to work. She worked to perfection in all she did."—Director William Asher (*I Love Lucy*), 2005

R

RADIO ROLES

Lucille Ball began her radio career in 1938 with a regular spot on comedian Phil Baker's Sunday night CBS radio show. She played Baker's wisecracking wife. When that gig ended, she joined actor (and friend) Jack Haley's show. From that point, she was "on the air" on a regular basis. Some of Lucy's guest appearances on radio before and during her show *My Favorite Husband* (1948-'51), include:

♥ *Campbell Playhouse:* "Dinner at Eight," with Orson Welles and Hedda Hopper, February 18, 1940

♥ *Screen Guild Theater:* "Tight Shoes" with Red Skelton, April 12, 1942

♥ *Suspense:* "A Dime a Dance," January 13, 1944

♥ *Suspense*: "The Ten Grand," June 24, 1944

♥ *Lux Radio Theater:* "Lucky Partners," with Don Ameche, September 25, 1944

♥ *Screen Guild Players:* "China Seas," with Clark Gable, December 4, 1944

♥ *Suspense:* "A Shroud for Sarah," October 25, 1945

♥ *The Jimmy Durante Show,* 1947

♥ *The Smiths of Hollywood:* "The Burglar," April 25, 1947

♥ *Reader's Digest Edition:* "The Lion and Mousie," with Quinton Moss and Les Tremayne, May 22, 1947

♥ *Lux Radio Theater:* "Dark Corner" with Mark Stevens, November 10, 1947 (Ball and Stevens also starred in the movie.)

♥ *The Martin and Lewis Show:* December 22, 1948

♥ *The Bob Hope Show:* also starring Doris Day, May 31, 1949

♥ *Suspense:* "The Red-Headed Woman," November 17, 1949

♥ *Suspense:* "Early to Death," April 12, 1951, with Desi Arnaz

RAT RACE

Movie released in 2001, directed by Jerry Zucker (executive producer of *Airplane!*, 1980), which owes a lot to the much better *It's a Mad, Mad, Mad, Mad World* (1963). An eccentric billionaire (John Cleese) in Las Vegas picks six people via a slot machine lottery to vie for a $2 million treasure hidden in Silver City, New Mexico, while a group of heavy rollers bets on the outcome.

As one of the contestants, Cuba Gooding Jr. ends up driving a bus filled with Lucille Ball look-alikes heading for a "Lucy" convention in Santa Fe. He steals the bus driver's clothes and takes off with the bus and its wacky, redheaded passengers. In one scene, with the *I Love Lucy* theme playing in the background, one of the gals accidentally sets her wig on fire, which the others put out with a jacket, which is smoldering, so they place it in the bus toilet, where some soap suds fall in, and … soon the bus is filled with soap suds. Kinda Lucy-ish, but it works better as a tribute to Ball's slapstick than as being outright funny.

When Gooding gets fed up with the antics of the conventioneers, who tend to spout "Lucy" dialogue all at once, and cry "Wahhhhhhhh!" when anything goes wrong, he confesses to not being the real driver, and the angry Lucys run after him for ruining their trip. The next scene shows Gooding in a barnyard, eyeing one of the horses as a way to get to Silver City. We never see how he actually got away from the red-haired mob.

On the DVD release is a scene cut from the movie that explains all: as Gooding is running from the group, another bus pulls up filled with … Rickys. One of them exclaims, "Lucys … you got some 'splainin' to do." With the Lucys' attention diverted, Gooding sneaks away. On the DVD, director Zucker claims the scene was cut because it was just too much. Considering what got into the final cut of the movie (including a prolonged scene with a cow dangling from a hot-air balloon and some "udder" nonsense), that's not a very convincing argument.

RATINGS

Television ratings services have been with the medium nearly as long as it has existed. An article in *Collier's* magazine dated October 29, 1954, dealt directly with the issue of ratings. In "Groucho, Dragnet, Lucy, Gleason: TV Ratings—Who *Knows* Who's on Top?" Bill Davidson notes that *I Love Lucy* is "consistently rated No. 1 by all pollsters." The article itself is long and somewhat technical, delving into how Nielsen and other companies actually determined the ratings. The chief caveat seemed to be that there was no consistency: "The darling of one ratings service may be the dud of another."

Lucy is mentioned chiefly in regard to comedian Red Buttons, whose show followed *I Love Lucy* on CBS and suffered a ratings drop from 60 to 40 (I assume the article refers to share of audience). It was subsequently canceled, even though Buttons noted that a 40 share was "better than some of the most successful shows on television." It didn't matter; his show was losing too substantial a share of the *Lucy* audience.

Ball's shows all did well in the ratings; see individual entries for specific numbers.

RED IS THE NEW EVERYTHING

According to Fox News online in November 2005, the color red was making a lipstick come-back. Noting that, "In the 1950s, comedian Lucille Ball and screen siren Veronica Lake were known for their signature cherry balms," a designer spokesperson tagged red as the "classic up-to-no-good color." That changed in the '70s, when red became a "power" color, though the '80s and '90s saw it turn pretty much vixenish. The article reported red had become more classy than trashy: "We're going back to a more elegant time, where people want to look like ladies." Ball would, no doubt, approve.

The redhead was also referenced in a *Baltimore Sun* article about the resurgence of red hair: "Flame-colored tresses are turning heads and pushing blondes out of the spotlight." "Red is the new blonde," adds Tim Rogers, editorial stylist and spokesman for Charles Worthington hair and beauty salons in London. "She is a head-turning hybrid between the moody brunette and the bubbly blonde. She's not afraid to have fun and get noticed." No matter the century, the *Sun* noted, redheads have always been eye-catchers, natural attention-getters. And what else—besides fame and money—do narcissistic celebrities crave more than attention?

"Redheaded women are portrayed as very strong, independent women," said Druann Heckert, associate professor of sociology at Fayetteville State University in North Carolina. "Or … the clown, like Lucy." Actually, if you look at some of the color shots of Ball from the 1940s, you'll see that she was much more than a clown—a great beauty, who excelled at comedy and was above average when given the chance in drama. Not to mention Hollywood's first, and to this day, only female studio owner. Sounds strong and independent to me.

RED SCARE REDUX

The wretched, sensational and rightwing *New York Post* was up to its old tricks on September 21, 2006. Cashing in on the release of previously never-seen celebrity files under the Freedom of Information Act, under the guise of "news," the *Post* filled a two-page spread spotlighting

John Lennon, Liberace, Marilyn Monroe, and Ball and Arnaz, among others. In the case of our favorite redhead, they brought up the old allegations that Lucy was a Communist. The paper absolves Arnaz of any Red leanings: he was too young, and his father supported a regime that was anti-Communist. But the piece ends on an appalling note: "But Arnaz's future wife did have political leanings that matched her hair."

One would think the least a reporter could do is some background checking that involved other sources than his primary one. If the *Post* had done this, it would have learned Lucy only registered as Communist to please her socialist-leaning grandfather (as did the rest of her family). She never intended to vote or do anything else as a Communist. The FBI discovered this and absolved her of any guilt in 1953. Too bad the *Post* decided to bring up an old lie and print it as the truth, but then, that's what this rag does best.

RICHARDS, RHONDA

See Medina, Rhonda.

RIDJANECK, GEORGE

Ridjaneck is a producer/director and Lucille Ball authority. Though he never met Ball, his knowledge of her life and career is truly exceptional. From his formative years as a member of both *We Still Love Lucy* and *Loving Lucy* fan clubs to the present, Ridjaneck has carefully documented the world's greatest clown. Along with producing associate Garret Boyajian he has spent years preserving the legacy of Ball, Desi Arnaz and Desilu. Together, they have conducted more than 200 interviews now preserved in the GAB Entertainment archive. Ridjaneck made his directorial debut in the upcoming holiday treat, *The Night Before Christmas*, featuring prolific actor and frequent Lucy-Desi player Charles Lane, then 101 years old. Along with Boyajian and fellow producer Jeff MacIntyre, Ridjaneck is producing both *You Know The Face*, a definitive Lane documentary, and a much-anticipated feature-length documentary on Ball and her fans. The producing/directing duo plan to contribute much more to the Lucille Ball legacy. Visit gabentertainment.com for more.

RITTER, JOHN

Comic actor Ritter, who could play comedy or drama, was best known for his "jiggle-com" *Three's Company* (for which he won an Emmy in 1984). Ritter was also a friend and fan of Lucille Ball, and the feeling was mutual. Ball hosted *The Best of Three's Company* retrospective (airing May 18, 1982), and Ritter returned the favor four years later by guest starring in Ball's final sitcom, *Life with Lucy* (in the second aired episode, "Lucy Makes a Hit with John Ritter," September 27, 1986, playing himself).

Ball loved the fact that Ritter was an accomplished slapstick comedian. The son of legendary singing cowboy Tex Ritter, John also distinguished himself in TV mini-series like *It* (1990) and movies like *Sling Blade* (1996). Ritter died unexpectedly in September 2003 of a heart attack; he collapsed on the set of his hit sitcom, *8 Simple Rules for Dating my Teenage Daughter*. Reports noted that Ritter died from a "dissection of the aorta"—the same rare defect that also claimed Lucy's life—which results from an unrecognized flaw in a main artery from the heart. He was 54.

ROBERTS, ROY

Blustery, familiar character actor in almost 100 movies since the early 1940s; he appeared with Ball in *Miss Grant Takes Richmond* (1949). Roberts was on TV from its inception, in such shows as *My Little Margie*, *Zane Grey Theater*, and *The Twilight Zone*.

He was a regular on the following series: *The Gale Storm Show* (1956-'60); *Gunsmoke* (1963-'70); *McHale's Navy* (1962-'66); *Petticoat Junction* (1963-'64, 1966-'67); *The Beverly Hillbillies* (1964-'67); and was the original Frank Stephens, father of Darrin, on *Bewitched* (1963).

In between all this, Roberts somehow found time to be a semi-regular on *The Lucy Show* from 1965 to 1968, when the format changed after Vivian Vance left. He played Mr. Cheever, Mr. Mooney's (Gale Gordon) boss, and was perhaps the only actor who could out-bluster Gordon. Roberts also made several *Here's Lucy* appearances in 1968, and had a small role in the classic film *Chinatown* (1974). He died in 1975.

S

SALARY NEGOTIATIONS

Just two days before he eloped with Lucille Ball in 1940, Desi Arnaz's mind was already on the future. Negotiating his contract at the Hurricane, a columnist reported, Arnaz was asked, "How much do you want?" by the proprietors of the café. His response: "Either $750 a week or $1,200—depending." "On what?" "On whether I'll have a wife to support at the time." See <u>Desilu</u> for information on what Ball and Arnaz earned in the 1950s.

SANDRICH, JAY

Sandrich is one of television's top sitcom directors—many consider him the finest TV comedy director, period—who first practiced his craft on *I Love Lucy* as a second assistant director, beginning in 1955. His father, director Mark, had helped Ball during one of her early bit parts in *Top Hat* (1935), and she never forgot the kindness, according to the book *Lucille*. Sandrich graduated to first assistant director by the time *I Love Lucy* morphed into *The Lucille Ball-Desi Arnaz Show* in 1957. He went to work as an AD on such shows as *Make Room for Daddy* and *The Dick Van Dyke Show* before directing series like *That Girl, Get Smart, Here's Lucy, Soap, Night Court*, and *The Golden Girls*, and perhaps his two biggest hits, *The Mary Tyler Moore Show* and *The Cosby Show*. Sandrich last practiced his craft, for which he's won four Emmys, in 2003, on an episode of the sitcom *Two And a Half Men*. Lately, he's appeared on two TV Land documentaries, in 2005 and 2007.

SCHILLER, BOB AND BOB WEISKOPF

Veteran comedy writers hired by producer/head writer Jess Oppenheimer for the fifth season (1955-'56) onward of *I Love Lucy*. The intent was to get new blood in the process, as scribes Bob Carroll, Madelyn Pugh and Oppenheimer had written every episode up to that time. The two Bobs (as they were known) continued writing for Ball on a regular basis through the second season (1963-'64) of *The Lucy Show*. Schiller and Weiskopf became Emmy-winners (for *All in the Family* and *The Flip Wilson Show*); Weiskopf died in February 2001 at the age of 86.

SEDGWICK, EDWARD

Classic Hollywood director from the 1920s to the early 1950s, Sedgwick was at MGM when Lucille Ball was under contract there and became a father figure to her. Sedgwick first saw Ball during her early Goldwyn Girl days, and was impressed with her; he was later introduced to her by director Alexander Hall. Thereafter, Lucy came to him for career and personal advice. Sedgwick had directed Buster Keaton in many of his shorts, and both of them worked with Lucy during her MGM days to enliven her craft.

Sedgwick died in 1953, a godfather to Ball's children, having lived to see Ball climb to the height of her success. Of him, Ball has said, "He did everything [for me].… Mr. Sedgwick was the mentor along with Mr. Keaton. He was very helpful to me in many ways—in helping me hold the line and have faith in myself at that point, because I didn't know what I wanted to do." Ball was devastated when he passed, and took care of his widow, Ebba, for many years after. The Sedgwick name occasionally popped up on *I Love Lucy* as a friend of the Ricardos.

SEEIN' STARS

A popular syndicated newspaper comic strip in the 1940s by Feg (Frederic) Murray, *Seein' Stars* took scenes and performers from movies of the day and pegged them to some interesting fact(s) about the production or stars. Illustrated by Murray, the style was reminiscent of the *Ripley's Believe it or Not!* strip. Ball was featured in several installments, and the text of each follows:

—"Lucille Ball, who was in a wheelchair 90 percent of the time in *Big Street*, actually spent three-and-a-half years of her life in a wheelchair."

Drawing is of Ball in a wheelchair. An auto accident that put her in a wheelchair was one story told by Ball, but there are other versions of her having been ill and/or paralyzed for several years, from about ages 17 to 19. According to Ball herself, she was indeed paralyzed, by an illness like rheumatic fever, had to wear special shoes and weights in order to walk and regain the shape of her legs; see my book *Lucy in Print* (2003) for the whole story.

—"It took Lucille Ball five times as long to dress for *Valley of the Sun* as it usually does, because she had to put on a bone-ribbed corset, a bustle, and six layers of petticoats and a billowy dress. (Lucille wore more clothes for this one costume than she did in her three previous pictures put together.)"

The drawing is of Ball being put into the corset.

—"In *Dance, Girl, Dance!* Lucille Ball did a hula that required the constant presence of a fire extinguisher! (Her costume was highly flammable.) Her skirt weighed less than one pound yet contained one-and-a-quarter miles of cellophane strips."

The drawing is of Ball doing the hula in the dress.

SENSE OF HUMOR

Although one of the *I Love Lucy* episodes made fun of Ball's inability to tell a joke correctly, that wasn't the case in real life, according to a New York newspaper item from the early 1940s headlined "Screwloose Item." It said that Ball, "RKO's glamour girl, who is in town ostensibly honeymooning with her Latin husband Desi Arnaz, is also knocking the brains out of her beautiful head making a round of personal appearances at every theater you can name. She appeared at five in the United chain on Tuesday and in six more last night.

"As well as being a reigning beauty, Lucille is famed as a wit. Her latest short story is about the two psychoanalysts who met on the street. One said to the other, 'You're fine today. How am I?'"

SET ACCIDENT

A newspaper item records a near miss on the set of Ball's movie *Panama Lady* (1939). Headlined "Lucille Ball Takes Unscheduled Dive," the article notes, "Quick-thinking Lucille Ball took a fully-clothed and unscheduled dive into a four-foot-deep pool when fire broke out on the *Panama Lady* set at RKO recently. Lucille was comfortably ensconced in a seaplane used in the picture when defective wiring high overhead sent down a shower of sparks onto the highly flammable wing covering. Without a moment's hesitation, Lucille flung open the cabin door and described [sic] a beautiful arc into the water."

SHAVELSON, MELVILLE "MEL"

Classic Hollywood comedy writer (with Bob Hope for many years), and television and film writer and director, Shavelson authored a 2007 memoir, *How to Succeed in Hollywood Without Really Trying: P.S. You Can't!* He wrote and directed one of Lucille Ball's best pictures—it certainly contains one of her best, most realistic performances—1968's *Yours, Mine and Ours*. In an article in the *Los Angeles Times* on May 2, 2007, Patrick Goldstein wrote that Shavelson said the filming was "fraught with tension," thanks to Ball's later-in-life habit of trying to wrest control from her directors; she felt she knew exactly what was needed to be funny, and no one need tell her ... or direct her.

Shavelson begged to differ. Once the final scene was in the can, Ball asked him how he'd felt about working with her, and whether he'd enjoyed it. "Lucy," he replied, "this is the first time I ever made a film with 19 children." [There were only 18 kids in the film.].... Ball burst into tears and wouldn't speak to Shavelson for a year, Goldstein noted. The 90-year-old director had a response for anyone who doubts the need for someone at the helm of a film: "There's a difference between being the performer and being outside, watching the performer do the performance," Shavelson said. "It just makes it easier for you to judge what's going on. It's not that you're trying to control the actor. You're just trying to do what you can to help get the best performance."

Among his other projects, Shavelson also wrote the screenplay for Lucy and Bob Hope's 1949 comedy *Sorrowful Jones*, and wrote the script and directed Vivian Vance in the well-received 1976 TV-movie biography, *The Great Houdini*. He died on August 8, 2007.

THE SIMPSONS

One of the most successful series in television history, and certainly the best animated sitcom ever produced, *The Simpsons* began its long run on Fox TV in 1989 and is still running as of this writing, in its 19th season. The wacky yet endearing characters of Homer, Marge, and their kids Bart, Lisa, and Maggie worked their way into the national consciousness, much like a certain dizzy redhead we all love. Indeed, *The Simpsons* has made more than a few references to Lucille Ball and *I Love Lucy* (see Krustylu). But perhaps the show's funniest tribute came in an episode that aired January 9, 2000, called "Little Big Mom."

Lisa is at her wit's end trying to take care of the household, specifically father Homer and brother Bart, while mom Marge is laid up with a broken leg. Ready to surrender, Lisa is visited by the (chain-smoking) ghost of Lucille Ball. Actually, when Lisa exclaims "Lucy?" at seeing the ghost materialize in her bedroom, the gravelly response is, "Lucy McGillicuddy Ricardo Carmichael. [Coughs] And I think there's some more." (The character's last names are those of Ball's characters from *I Love Lucy* and *The Lucy Show*. Left out were Lucy Carter of *Here's Lucy* and Lucy Barker of *Life with Lucy*.)

Lucy asks Lisa for an ashtray and then, in the best Lucy Ricardo tradition of scheming to get even with "the boys," tells Lisa what she can do to keep Homer and Bart in line: convince her brother and dad that they are lepers (!) because the house is so dirty … which she does. Prolific voice talent and *Simpsons* regular Tress MacNeille voiced Lucy.

Also in this episode: Homer and Bart are watching *I Love Lucy* loudly downstairs while Lisa is trying to sleep (it's a comically violent *I Love Lucy* in which Ricky slaps Lucy, she cries "Waaahhh!" and Fred notes, "Gee, Rick, you sure hit her hard that time."); the *Itchy & Scratchy* cartoon Bart and Homer watch is an (also violent) homage to the famous candy factory conveyor belt scene from the *I Love Lucy* episode "Job Switching" (September 15, 1952).

♥ **Lucy Trivia** Talented voice actress MacNeille actually voiced Lucy once before, on the "Weird Al" Yankovic version of "Ricky." (See Basil, Toni.)

SINATRA, FRANK

Ol' Blue Eyes was a pal of Lucille Ball's, though they only intermittently performed together. One of their earliest appearances together was on radio in a Screen Guild Theater play, *Too Many Husbands*, co-starring with Bob Hope; it aired on April 21, 1947 (noted in Nancy Sinatra's book, *Frank Sinatra, An American Legend*, 1995). Sinatra acquired a Nevada state gambling license in 1954 and became co-owner of Lake Tahoe's Cal-Neva Lodge from August 1961 through October 1963. Daughter Nancy noted Sinatra often chartered planes to fly in "friends like Lucille Ball to share his enjoyment at ringside," as well as buddies like Dean Martin and Lena Horne to entertain, all in the name of bringing more crowds to the resort. Sinatra himself reportedly signed Ball's son, Desi Jr., and his band mates Dino (Martin Jr.) and Billy (Hinsche) to his label, Reprise, after hearing them jam at Martin's house. As <u>Dino, Desi & Billy</u>, the teen trio outsold Sinatra himself for several months in the mid-1960s. When Sinatra celebrated 40 years in show business on his 64th birthday—December 12, 1979—at Caesar's Palace in Las Vegas, Lucy was in attendance. The event was taped for a two-hour NBC TV special that aired January 3, 1980, with Ball as one of the "guests." Sinatra taped an appearance to honor Ball on the Variety Clubs International TV special, *An All-Star Party for Lucille Ball*, on November 18, 1984, also for NBC (it aired December 9, 1984). Sinatra, in fact, sat next to Ball during the tribute. Ball co-chaired the January 7, 1989 Jewish Institute for National Security Affairs tribute to Nathan "Sonny" Golden (Frank's accountant), along with Sinatra and producer Jerry Weintraub, in Los Angeles. It was one of Ball's final public appearances.

SINGING VOICE

Lucille Ball could carry a tune, but through much of her movie career her singing voice was dubbed. That was the case in her MGM musicals, but it was the norm: unless stars had a distinctive voice of the caliber of Judy Garland, or Jeanette MacDonald, or they were doing a comic turn in which the timbre of the voice didn't really matter, they were invariably dubbed. Often even stars with solid singing voices were dubbed for various reasons.

I believe, however, that it is Ball singing in the "Friendship" finale of *DuBarry Was a Lady* (1943). I'm pretty sure that's Ball, too, singing "Breezin' Along with the Breeze" with husband Desi Arnaz in *The Long, Long Trailer* (1954); her daughter, Lucie, agrees. If not, both were near-perfect matches to Ball's real voice.

On *I Love Lucy*, a long-running joke was that Lucy Ricardo could *not* sing, and therefore Ball had to work hard to sing *off-key* when required. The fact that Ball could do this is evidence of her singing talent. By the time of *Mame* (1974), however, Lucy's voice was damaged from 40 years of acting, coupled with a heavy smoking habit, and it was rumored her singing was dubbed, or at least augmented, by actress Lisa Kirk.

SINGLETON, DORIS

Doris Singleton with Vivian Vance (left) and Lucille Ball filming the episode "Lucy Tells the Truth." It originally aired November 9, 1953. Photofest

A character comedienne who appeared on radio with Lucille Ball in *My Favorite Husband* and guested on *I Love Lucy* as Lucy Ricardo's "good friend" Carolyn Appleby, Singleton delivered her lines in a wry manner that made her a good foil to Ball's zany personality. Most memorably she appeared in the "Harpo Marx" episode (May 9, 1955), visiting the Ricardos and the Mertzes in California and expecting to see all the movie stars with whom Lucy had said she was friendly. Singleton also guest-starred on many dramas and sitcoms during the 1950s, 1960s, and 1970s, including a handful of appearances with Ball on *Here's Lucy* (on which she was initially supposed to be a regular: see my book, *Sitcom Queens: Divas of the Small Screen* for details).

When I met Doris in Jamestown, New York, she was as gracious, funny, and down-to-earth as I had hoped (and looked like a million bucks). In the introduction to *Sitcom Queens*, she noted that, "Working with Lucy was fun, but it *was* work: Learn your lines, hit your mark and so on. There wasn't any socializing between scenes, you were getting ready for the next one."

Of her performing history with Ball, she told me, "I started with Lucy in radio, but that was incidental, because I was doing all kinds of radio shows at that time ... and her show (*My Favorite Husband*) was just another situation comedy that came on. It was not [quite as big as] Jack Benny's show, or Burns & Allen. It was just a light, frothy show. But Lucy became fabulously successful on TV. Since I knew her from radio, I started on *I Love Lucy*. Then *The Lucy Show*, and *Here's Lucy*, and the specials.

"A lot of the time I worked with the top male comics: Jimmy Durante, Jack Paar, Benny, Hope, Alan Young, Walter Brennan, Red Skelton. Even on the one Bob Hope special I did, I was so glad to be working with a male comic for a change, and getting away from the other roles I played, and guess what? They cast me as Lucy's secretary!" [Note: this might be the special *Lucy Moves to NBC*, in which she played "Wanda Clark," the name of Lucy's real-life personal secretary. See Clark, Wanda.]

"So it was like, I can't get away from this. Though I enjoyed it, I did like doing all the other stuff as well. On *Hogan's Heroes*, I got to sing and play a sexy German spy, completely different things than I did on the *Lucy* shows."

Doris is resigned to the fact that she, tongue firmly in cheek, will just have to "settle" for being part of an immortal sitcom cast that will be remembered forever.

♥ **Lucy Trivia** Singleton played a character named Grace Munson on the episode of *Make Room for Granddaddy* that Ball also guested on (January 21, 1971). In fact, Grace Munson was a friend of Lucy's in real life, played by two actresses on *I Love Lucy*: Hazel Pierce in "The Club Election" (February 16, 1953), and Ruth Brady in "Country Club Dance" (April 22, 1957). Also, after Lucy Ricardo visits "Grace Munson" in Connecticut in the series' sixth season, Lucy decides she wants to move there.

SIX DEGREES OF KEVIN BACON

The game based on the premise of the John Guare play/movie *Six Degrees of Separation*; the idea is that we are all connected by no more than six links to other people. This was tailored to fit actor Kevin Bacon, possibly because his name substitutes nicely for "separation." Each of the *I Love Lucy* principals has a low Bacon number (2): Lucille Ball was in *Mame* (1974) with John Wheeler; Wheeler was in *Apollo 13* (1995) with Kevin Bacon. Desi Arnaz was in *The Escape Artist* (1982) with Tom Signorelli; Signorelli was in *Sleepers* (1996) with Bacon. Vivian Vance was in *The Great Race* (1965) with Jack Lemmon; Lemmon was in *JFK* (1991) with Bacon. William Frawley was in *Kill the Umpire* (1950) with Wally Rose; Rose was in *Murder in the First* (1995) with Bacon.

SIX DEGREES OF LUCILLE BALL

If Kevin Bacon (above) can be linked by six degrees to almost everyone in the world, then imagine how many people connect, directly or indirectly, to Ball. For example:

John Emery was a stage actor and a solid movie character player in about 30 films, as well as classic TV comedies and dramas. He made his second film with director <u>Alexander Hall</u>, a friend of Ball's who had dated her early in her career, and who, indeed, was reported to be engaged to Ball before she met Arnaz (in 1940).

♦ In Hall's classic *Here Comes Mr. Jordan* (1941), Emery helps set the plot in motion as a millionaire playboy's smarmy personal assistant who's out to kill his boss (with the help of his boss' wife). There are other Ball connections to *Jordan*: Edward Everett Horton played the novice heavenly messenger responsible for taking a prizefighter before his time. Horton toured in a popular stage vehicle, *Springtime for Henry*, that same year (1941) with future Ball co-star Vivian Vance. He also memorably guest-starred on *I Love Lucy* as a randy upstairs neighbor of the Ricardos.

♦ James Gleason, the fight promoter in *Jordan*, was nominated for Best Supporting Actor. He was considered to play Fred Mertz, but Gleason wanted too much money. Emery also played a shrink in Hall's final film, *Forever Darling*, which not so coincidentally starred Ball.

♦ Emery's TV connection: aside from guest starring on many of the top dramas of the 1950s and early 1960s, Emery acted in two episodes of *I Love Lucy*, in "The Quiz Show" (November 12, 1951) and "Little Ricky Gets a Dog" (January 21, 1957).

♦ Emery also co-starred in several summer stock productions with Vance, including *There Goes the Bride*, at the Lake Whalen Playhouse in Massachusetts in August 1960. For a partial review, see <u>Stage Career</u> under <u>Vance, Vivian</u>.

♦ But wait … there's more. Emery, a solid but second-tier star, hooked up with Tallulah Bankhead. The bawdy Bankhead was a favorite impersonation of Ball's (she did it on *I Love Lucy*) and had apparently met Emery doing summer stock. (They were married from 1937 to 1941. According to Robert Gottlieb of *The New Yorker* (May 16, 2005) it was more than Emery's good looks that kept Bankhead hooked: "One of Tallulah's party tricks was to escort guests to the master bedroom, fling back the covers from the bed in which Emery was sleeping, and crow, 'Did you ever see a prick as big as that before?'" Bankhead is remembered for a wild, comedic turn opposite Ball and company in one of the best of the 13 *Lucy-Desi Comedy Hour*s.

♦ Emery, who became one of those familiar film supporting faces that one would see and go, "Oh, yeah, I know him, what's his name?" died in 1964 at the age of 59.

Joan Davis is near the top of the list of the many other funny ladies who have touched my heart over the years (see my book, *Sitcom Queens: Divas of the Small Screen* for the whole list). The raucous, roustabout, slapstick movie, radio and TV comic Davis is often compared to Ball (and just as often unfairly accused of ripping off Ball's bits). My two favorite female clowns had more in common than making us laugh for generations.

♦ Bob Weiskopf wrote for the *Rudy Vallee Sealtest Radio* program in 1941, which co-starred Davis; he also wrote for *I Love Lucy* and *The Lucy Show*.

♦ Davis and Ball both worked with Rudy Vallee, Davis on radio and Ball on her series *The Lucy-Desi Comedy Hour* and *Here's Lucy*.

♦ Ray Singer, who wrote radio and film (*She Gets Her Man*) material for Davis, also wrote the "Lucy Wins Jack Benny's Account" episode of *The Lucy Show* and co-created *Here's Lucy* with Milt Josefsburg in 1968.

♦ Davis had a bit part (uncredited) as a phone operator in *Bunker Bean*; Ball had a small part (but larger than Davis') in this 1936 comedy.

♦ Two character actresses, <u>Mary Jane Croft</u> and <u>Sandra Gould</u>, who were regulars on Davis' sitcom *I Married Joan*, also appeared on *I Love Lucy* and *The Lucy Show*.

♦ On October 7, 1943, Ball and Davis both guest-starred on the *Kraft Music Hall*, a live radio broadcast hosted weekly by Bing Crosby. The shows went out live to the troops.

♦ Both were in films with Eddie Cantor; Ball as an "extra" at the beginning of her career, Davis in co-starring parts during the heyday of her film career. Both co-starred with swing bandleader Kay Kyser in films: Ball in 1939's *That's Right, You're Wrong*, and Davis in 1943's *Around the World*. And both appeared in films with Abbott & Costello (in Ball's case it was a literal cameo in 1945's *Abbott and Costello in Hollywood*; Davis had one of her best screen roles in the comedy team's 1941 hit, *Hold That Ghost*).

◆ In *Hold That Ghost*, Davis also co-starred with B-movie leading man Richard Carlson; Ball was Carlson's co-star in 1940's *Too Many Girls*.

◆ Female versions of "traveling salesman" comedies featured Davis, in 1950's *Traveling Saleswoman*, and Ball, in the same year's *The Fuller Brush Girl*. They each capped off their Golden Age film careers playing unlikely harem girls: Davis in the slapstick comedy *Harem Girl* (1952); and Ball in 1951's potboiler, *The Magic Carpet*.

◆ Davis worked with her daughter, Beverly Wills, in her 1950s sitcom, *I Married Joan*; Ball employed her daughter, Lucie, in the 1960s sitcom *Here's Lucy*.

◆ Both Ball and Davis died of heart-related ailments. (See also <u>Davis, Joan</u>.)

SKELTON, RED

Goofy, slapstick comedian born in 1913, Skelton could do it all: he was a mime, painter, and clown, whose red hair complemented Ball's, and whose career often intersected with hers. His film debut came in an early Ball clunker, *Having Wonderful Time* (1938) but Skelton went on to redeem himself in a score of successful comedies, many at MGM and one in particular, *DuBarry Was a Lady* (1943), in which he fought Gene Kelly for the lovely Ball's attentions.

Skelton went on to a long, successful TV career (his variety show was filmed at <u>Desilu Studios</u> and Vivian Vance made several guest appearances on it), and also guest-starred on one of the funnier hour-long *Lucy-Desi Comedy Hours*, called "Lucy Goes to Alaska." He died in 1997.

SLOT MACHINES

An article from Reuters on October 3, 2001, focused on the Global Gaming Expo in Las Vegas, featuring what's new and upcoming in the world of slot machines. That includes a group of machines honoring Hollywood icons, among them Ball. According to reporter Doug Young, "One innovative product [from International Gaming Technology] that breaks new ground on the sensory edge is a smell-producing Lucy machine, featuring the late comedian Lucille Ball. On tripping the bonus round, players can watch an animated Lucy in the famous chocolate assembly line scene desperately stuffing candy into her mouth. Players get to watch their bonus candy box fill up with point-labeled candies as the odor of chocolate wafts through an opening on the machine."

According to a 2005 article in the *Las Vegas Review-Journal*, "The company later removed the aroma option. 'The game is still (around). The scent machine just did okay, it wasn't overwhelming,' noted IGT's Ed Rogich, VP of marketing." Part of IGT's Game King series, "Lucy Grape-Stomping" and "Lucy in Hollywood" slot machines were introduced in 2004. So far, the biggest jackpot on the Ball slots has been $1,709,691.43, awarded on June 11, 2006, IGT reports. The slot machines can be found in casinos all over Nevada, including Las Vegas, Mesquite, Crystal Bay, Reno, and Stateline.

SMITH, CLEO (MANDICOS MORGAN)

Lucille Ball's first cousin, Cleo Mandicos grew up with Lucy in Celeron, New York (near Jamestown), after the Hunt clan consolidated into Grandma and Grandpa Hunt's house. DeDe (Ball's mom) had returned there in 1922 from Detroit (where she had gone with her second husband, Ed Peterson) to help with her mother, who had been diagnosed with cancer. Smith left the family to live with her father when her mother, Lola, died unexpectedly in 1930, but rejoined Ball in Hollywood after high school.

Smith had uncredited bit parts in two of Ball's movies (1938's *Having Wonderful Time* and 1947's *Two Smart People*), and one of Desi Arnaz's (1946's *Cuban Pete*.) Ball felt such a kinship with Smith she often referred to her as a sister, and Smith worked behind the scenes on both *I Love Lucy* and *The Lucy Show*. Her first husband, Ken Morgan, worked as a publicist for Ball and Arnaz, among other duties. Smith produced the 1966 special *Lucy in London* and in 1968 became a producer on *Here's Lucy*. By then Cleo had divorced Morgan and married Los Angeles journalist Cecil Smith. (See also <u>Morgan, Ken.</u>)

SOCIAL SECURITY NUMBERS

Desi Arnaz: 564-26-7086
Lucille Ball: 568-05-1624
William Frawley: 562-05-1177
Vivian Vance: 110-09-0642

SOME GIRLS

Rolling Stones album from 1978 features the hits "Miss You," "Beast of Burden," and the title song. Notorious for its cover, which featured a fake wig catalog page in which the model's faces were cut out and replaced by famous faces. One of these faces was Lucille Ball, and due to the unauthorized use of her image (along with those of Marilyn Monroe, Joan Crawford, and others) the record was pulled and reissued without the famous faces.

SOTHERN, ANN

Ann Sothern (born Harriette Lake) was in movies from the late 1920s on. The sassy comedienne tended to win the same type of roles as Lucille Ball; you could usually find her playing a resourceful, wisecracking dame. Sothern could also sing and act with the best of them, lifting herself above the often-routine material she was given. She and Ball became pals at RKO in the early 1930s, where Sothern graduated quickly to lead roles in musicals while Ball was stuck in a bit-player rut.

They worked together again at MGM in the 1940s, on more of an equal footing. Sothern had success in a series of movies throughout the decade about a plucky career gal named Maisie, and in the dramatic movies *Cry Havoc* (1943) and especially *A Letter to Three Wives* (1949). When her movie career waned, Ann filmed one of Desilu's successful sitcoms for almost a decade throughout the 1950s: *Private Secretary* (later reformatted and called *The Ann Sothern Show*).

Sothern was tired of being compared to Ball as early as 1953—specifically being referred to as competing with Ball for the title "Queen of Television." She told the *Galveston News* in November 1953 that, "I don't conflict with Lucille at all. We're different types of comediennes and there's no room for comparison. Besides, we're very good friends and I don't think we should be made to seem like rivals."

When pressed, Sothern opined, "I try to combine sex and comedy—and brother, that's not easy. Most men can't get excited about a girl who spends most of her time getting laughs. The two things just don't go together—no man likes to be the target of a joke." Sothern noted she had to "look sexy" on camera, but couldn't really dress that way: "Whoever heard of a secretary going to work in a low-cut gown or a bathing suit?"

Instead, Sothern strove to appear feminine, explaining there was a difference between sexy and feminine. "A sexy girl is sort of, you know, brazen about being a woman. Something of a show-off. But a girl can be feminine and still maintain good taste.... I try to dress and act the way a real secretary would. The laughs and sex, though, are a part of the show [in the simmering relationship between Sothern and boss Don Porter], and I don't think we overdo the glamour.

"And as far as Lucille's concerned, she plays a married gal with a family, and I'm the secretary trying to land the boss. Uh, uh. No comparison there at all."

As Ball looked ahead to a *Lucy Show* without longtime co-star Vivian Vance (who left after season three), Sothern was tested in a handful of episodes as Rosie Harrigan, the flamboyant but broke former Countess Framboise (by marriage). Though funny, the two performers were hampered by their slightly different wisecracking styles, Ball's focused on physical humor, with Sothern's more of a subtle, word-dependent approach.

When Vance left the show, Ball used Sothern intermittently, and then tried Joan Blondell (who left after experiencing Ball's strident on-set personality), before returning to old friend Mary Jane Croft.

Sothern did a handful of mostly routine movies in the 1960s and 1970s, as well as one of the best-remembered sitcoms ever made—remembered as god-awful, that is: *My Mother, the Car* (1965), as the voice of Jerry Van Dyke's mother who was reincarnated as a 1928 Porter).

Sothern and Ball kept in touch throughout the years, and Sothern's biographer, Colin Briggs, wrote that "Ann was saddened when Lucille Ball's [1986] show, *Life with Lucy*, was canceled." "I told her not to do it," Sothern noted, "but Gary Morton, her husband, wanted her to. She was crying when she told me, 'ABC has fired me, my series has been canceled after two months.'" Sothern tried to console Ball, telling her she was "greatly loved, and that something else will undoubtedly be on the horizon."

But Ball only made a handful of TV appearances until her death (game show and award-show appearances, and televised honors), while the plucky Sothern got to show her dramatic chops one last time in *The Whales of August* (1988), stealing scenes from Bette Davis, Lillian Gish, and Vincent Price. She was nominated for a Best Supporting Actress Oscar for her work in this, her final movie. Sothern died at the age of 92 in March 2001.

STAGE CAREER

Although Lucille Ball first dreamed of being a stage performer, her greatest fame came as a movie, radio, and then television star.

Throughout her 24-year sitcom television career Ball essentially performed a stage play every week, before a "live, studio audience," as they say. However, there are three legitimate theater experiences that prove Ball was at home treading the boards.

Hey, Diddle, Diddle, 1937

Through friend (some said boyfriend) and producer Pandro S. Berman at RKO, and with the backing of Lela Rogers, Ginger's mother and her dramatic coach at RKO, Ball was cast in this comedy about the movie industry and the roadblocks faced by several actresses trying to make it in motion pictures. The play opened at the McCarter Theater in Princeton, N.J. on January 21, 1937.

According to the Philadelphia program, director Anne Nichols was presenting the new comedy *Hey Diddle Diddle* by Bartlett Cormack, at the Locust St. Theater, Philadelphia's Most Beautiful Legitimate Theatre, prior to Broadway. The three-act play took place in the Casa Loma Apartments in Hollywood, California, in the afternoon.

The show centered on the amorous adventures of a trio of actress wannabes who date a temperamental movie director, an assistant director, and an associate producer in order to get ahead.

Tickets cost 50 cents to $1.50 for evening performances, and the matinee topped out at $1. The show featured Keenan Wynn, later one of Ball's best co-stars at MGM, as "A Man in White," and Ball played the role of Julie Tucker, a movie extra (or day player).

Audience response was positive; reviews were less so, though they praised the performers. *The Philadelphia Inquirer* noted, "There are more than a few laughs, but three acts pass by and one is still waiting for something interesting to happen." *Variety* didn't care for the play ("Whole yarn has a machine-made appearance that's against it") but made mention of Ball: "As the wisecracking extra girl, Lucille Ball, making her first stage appearance, fattens a fat part and almost walks off with the play."

Producer-director Nichols was famous for the long-running hit *Abie's Irish Rose*. *Hey, Diddle Diddle* would not follow suit; it was supposed to end up in New York, but never made it to Broadway. The play closed on February 13, 1937, in Washington, D.C. due to problems with its star, Conway Tearle, who was ill; and behind-the-scenes animosity between Nichols and one her colleagues. (Shades of the play's plot!)

The only positive experience taken from this production was Ball's interaction with a live audience; she liked it and the theatergoers liked her. It was a mode of performing (live, with feedback) that would cinch Ball's success in radio and, later, television.

Dream Girl, 1947
It took her a decade, but Ball finally starred in a hit, *Dream Girl*, written by Elmer Rice, taken on tour across the United States in 1947 (Boston, Detroit, Milwaukee, Oakland, and more). The show, directed by Herbert Kenwith—who would later direct Ball on television—opened at the McCarter Theater in Princeton, N.J. the week of June 23, 1947. It co-starred Hayden Rorke (later the excitable Dr. Bellows on *I Dream of Jeannie*), Scott McKay, and Philip Arthur.

Martha Scott, not Ball, was Kenwith's first choice to play the lead role of Georgina Allerton. According to the book *Desilu*, when Scott proved unavailable, Kenwith began a vigorous pursuit of Ball, who happened to be visiting New York at the time.

Dream Girl was included in John Glassner's *Best Plays of the Modern American Theater* (1947), Second Series. It is the story of Allerton, a dreamer, who lives her life as part of a series of fanta-sies she enacts. Rice wrote it for his wife, actress Betty Field, who played the part when the comedy opened at New York's Coronet Theatre (renamed the Eugene O'Neill Theater in 1959). Wendell Corey was featured. It ran for 348 performances, and June Havoc, baby sister of Gypsy Rose Lee, later played the lead role.

Georgina is a frustrated writer who works in a book-store. She has a "thing" for her soon-to-be-divorced brother-in-law. Pursuing her are a newspaper reporter who reviews books he doesn't read, and a well-off older man (a book distribu-tor) who wants to take her to a love nest in Mexico.

Lucy tangos with co-star Scott McKay in *Dream Girl,* **from the souvenir program. Author's collection**

One might think Georgina has it pretty good. But she's not happy. She's not sure her brother-in-law means it when he suggests moving West after his divorce. Her novel, in which the lead character spends much of her time in a fantasy world, is called "trash" by the reporter, after which she agrees to go to dinner and the theater with him. The older guy is nice but obviously after a roll in the hay. Truly, Georgina is one confused gal.

Eventually, during a long dinner with the reporter, she decides she can curb her dreaming long enough to take a chance on marrying him. The play ends with the two eloping to Greenwich, Connecticut, and getting married. Georgina's learned it's okay to dream, but that she shouldn't let her fantasies overtake her life.

Dream Girl is a play that works as a romantic comedy/fantasy only if the lead character is so likeable that we adore her despite her pretensions and fence sitting. Audiences adored Ball in the role and she spent almost half a year touring in it. (In its obituary of Ball, *The New York Times* noted, "On the stage, Miss Ball won favorable notices for a 22-week tour in the title role of Elmer Rice's fantasy *Dream Girl*.")

Harvey Taylor of the *Detroit Times* wrote that Ball, "… had a tasteful sense of comedy, the careful timing, and the sure-footed understanding to carry off the rich role of Georgina Allerton as deftly as she does. She is on stage every minute and dominates the play."

The fantasy sequences were made-to-order for Ball's innate sense of character and timing. They take Georgina to a balcony in Mexico; a maternity ward; the stage, where she plays Shakespeare's Portia; and a street corner, where she enacts a red-dressed "woman of the evening."

The play's sets (designed by Jo Mielziner) allow Georgina's fantasies to be blossom within the play. They suggest, rather than define. Mielziner built three units that glided smoothly across the stage.

The souvenir program notes the role of Georgina is "probably one of the most exacting ones ever written for the stage; to quote Lewis Nichols of *The New York Times*, it's a part that 'pales Hamlet's into polite insignificance.' In reality or dreams, Georgina is onstage just about all evening."

The fact that the character dreams of different lives is an interesting prelude to the character of Lucy Ricardo, who was always dreaming and scheming her way out of her New York apartment.

There are several other interesting real-world parallels or intersections between *Dream Girl* and Ball's real life. Ball and Desi Arnaz actually eloped to Greenwich to marry in 1940, and the incident was replayed in "The Marriage License" episode of *I Love Lucy* (April 7, 1952). Lucy discovers Ricky's name misspelled on their marriage license (as *Bacardi*) and refuses to acknowledge Ricky as her husband until he renews their vows, in Connecticut.

While Ball was touring in *Dream Girl* her husband was again touring with his band, and they were rarely together. Arnaz once surprised her with a visit during which his tour bus crashed, and the possibility of Arnaz being injured or even killed made the two more determined than ever to hang on to their marriage.

Dream Girl was made into a movie in 1948 starring Betty Hutton as Georgina. Judy Holliday starred in a limited run (15 performances) of *Dream Girl* beginning May 9, 1951, at the New York City Center of Music and Drama. Featured in the cast was Don DeFore, who later co-starred with Ball in *The Facts of Life* (1960).

Mielziner, who died in 1976, optioned *Dream Girl* for a musical production, in collaboration with Rice, for the 1956-'57 Broadway season. But Mielziner's option ran out before the show could be produced (according to his papers on file at the New York Public Library). Mielziner also did the sets for the Broadway production of *Best Foot Forward*; Ball would star in the movie version (the stage production was choreographed by Ball's future co-star and director Gene Kelly).

Dream Girl was finally adapted into a Broadway musical called *Skyscraper* that opened on November 13, 1965, starring Julie Harris, Peter L. Marshall, and Charles Nelson Reilly. A moderate hit, it ran for 241 performances.

In the program for Ball's *Dream Girl*, artist Hall Barnell did sketches of the play during rehearsal and noted, "The tall, very red-haired Miss Ball took time out from visualizing revolving stages, backdrops, and being involved in a dream to rumba over and give out with a big hello. She does one of the meanest rumbas I've ever seen. During a break she told a story about somebody's little boy, which I will be glad to repeat but which is not for publication. At 5:30 they broke so Miss Ball could keep an appointment with her hairdresser."

The program biography of Ball is as follows:

"By right of talent and public acclaim, Lucille Ball rises to the pinnacle as supreme comedienne. 'Queen of Comedy' is the recent accolade from the Associated Drama Guilds of America, and as such, the titian-haired star finds Hollywood preparing even greater roles for her.

"The picture that skyrocketed her to the highest honor was *Easy to Wed*, produced by Metro-Goldwyn-Mayer, to which studio she is under long-term contract."

Ball was soon to end that contract. She was still noted as having been born in <u>Butte, Montana</u>, and it is claimed her mother was "a concert pianist" and "started the wee daughter's music lessons at the age of five."

The rest of the bio is pretty much standard, combining truths, half truths, and outright fabrications, though it notes toward the end, "Sincerity is a keynote to Lucille Ball's character.

Kind of heart, she is generous in the extreme. She makes friends and holds them. Her rare, peppy personality has caused her to be titled 'Ball of Fire.'

"She likes dungarees, spicy dishes, makes pets even of her flock of chickens, and 'couldn't harm a mouse'! She insists on washing her own stockings, loves feathers, fussy negligees, small hats, slacks, steak, raw onions, and frilly nightgowns, and never wears white. She also likes blue, flowered wallpaper, old china, knitting, all animals including her three cocker spaniels, three-inch heels, and over-sized handbags."

Here's an equally revealing look at how Ball's career was described in the playbill biography from the McCarter Theater production:

"Lucille Ball (Georgina) was literally fired with ambition to succeed. Armed with high school and little theater experience, which she had acquired at Jamestown, New York, whence she had moved from her native Butte, Montana, she came to the great big city to work for John Murray Anderson and Robert Milton. In no time at all she had been hired, and fired, by Flo Ziegfeld, Earl Carroll, the Shuberts, and George White.

"Unfazed by the rebuffs, she took to modeling for Hattie Carnegie and Chesterfield Cigarettes, a task which took her to the West Coast. Goldwyn saw her and she made her screen debut in Eddie Cantor's *Roman Scandals* as one of the Goldwyn Girls. [Actually, it was her modeling that enabled her, by giving her somewhat of a "recognizable factor" in public, to sub for a Goldwyn Girl whose mother refused to allow the girl to trek to California.]

"Then RKO saw her and kept her under contract for the next seven years during which she did Damon Runyon's *The Big Street*, a picture which brought her into the big time and which she still regards as her favorite. Since that time, she has been seen in many of MGM's top features. A complete list of her film record would take more space than we have, but some of the highlights include *Stage Door, Five Came Back, A Girl, A Guy, and a Gob, Roberta, DuBarry Was a Lady, Best Foot Forward, Without Love* and *Easy to Wed*. [Interestingly, these films are always cited as among Ball's best roles.] She is shortly to be seen in United Artist's *Lured* with George Sanders, and in Columbia's *Her Husband's Affairs* with Franchot Tone.

"The McCarter Theater was the scene of her one and only [previous] stage appearance when she made a brief sally in *Hey, Diddle Diddle*, an opus which opened and closed here. Keenan Wynn also made a mistake by being in it."

That last paragraph is not the way in which, one would think, a performer would normally end a stage bio, but Ball was nothing if not frank in evaluating her own career. In any case, it's not true, as the play closed after its McCarter run, in the nation's capital.

Wildcat, 1960

In 1960, after the end of *I Love Lucy* and her marriage to Desi Arnaz, Lucille Ball decided she needed a change. After she did a movie with Bob Hope (*The Facts of Life*), she accepted the leading role in a new Broadway musical, despite the fact that what she *really* needed was rest and a complete break from show business for a while.

Ball said she had always wanted to appear on Broadway and loved the idea of a challenge.

In April 1960, it was announced that Ball would star in *Wildcat* the following season. Director and choreographer Michael Kidd staged the show. Co-star Keith Andes was hired on August 15. Chorus calls were made in August and dancer calls in September. The show cost about $400,000, all of it put up by Desilu.

Ball thought the lead character in *Wildcat,* Wildcat Jackson, had many similarities to Lucy Ricardo (well, both were dreamers). The unusual theme of the show concerned a lady oil-driller, and, as written by N. Richard Nash, the book ended with a big gusher. (Nash was best known for a previous hit, *The Rainmaker,* which ended with a huge rainstorm. Nash was ultimately taken apart by reviewers for what was called a boring, pedestrian, disconnected, derivative *Wildcat* book that even stole the basic plot from his previous hit show.)

Ball began rehearsing for what would prove to be her legitimate stage swan song on September 28, 1960. She threw herself into rehearsals, and by all accounts was the hardest-working person in the

Ball as Wildcat Jackson with her man, Joe Dynamite (Keith Andes). Behind Ball's right shoulder is a young Valerie Harper in her second Broadway show, billed as a Dancer. Photofest.

cast and crew. She was reportedly beloved by the cast and crew, and made a good friend in Paula Stewart, who played her younger sister.

The show opened October 29, 1960, for a sold-out six-week preview engagement at the Erlanger Theater in Philadelphia. It became apparent during the preview that the show would be a hit solely on the strength of its star, despite whatever shortcomings *Wildcat* had as a theater piece. Tickets sold well into the fall of 1961.

Wildcat opened in New York on December 1, 1960, at the Alvin Theatre (renamed the Neil Simon Theatre in 1983). It was an immediate hit, but, as many had suspected, the success was due largely to the fact that Ball starred in it, and her legions of fans were dying to see "Lucy Ricardo" onstage, in person.

One audience did get to see "Fred Mertz." William Frawley was in New York and went to see Ball in the play, reported AP's Cynthia Lowry in 1961. When "Lucy, at the end of show, introduced him from the audience, the reception was so warm Bill's gravelly, gruff voice actually became soft and sentimental just recalling it."

The reviews for *Wildcat* could basically be summed up in five words: "Loved Lucy, hated the show." Here are some excerpts:

"Everybody wanted to love Lucille Ball, but her new show didn't make it easy. *Wildcat* had as much spirit and excitement as a tame, old tabby. It was 45 minutes after the start of the overture before anything of consequence happened. This was a duet, 'What Takes My Fancy,' which Miss Ball sang with Don Tomkins, who played a dirty, engaging little landholder with rubbery animation. In their singing and dancing, these two finally woke up the somnolent *Wildcat*. Miss Ball worked hard, singing and dancing with zest and reading her lines with an expert's timing, but *Wildcat* did not seem to test her full capacities as a performer. *Wildcat* went prospecting for Broadway oil but drilled a dry hole. But don't you care, Miss Ball. They all still love Lucy—and you, too."—Howard Taubman, *The New York Times*

"Naturally, in the case of *Wildcat*, what you really want to know about is Lucille Ball. So do I. I want to know why that bonny and talented and ever so bright girl isn't present—in person—on the Alvin stage. Miss Ball is up there, all right, doing all of the spectacular and animated and energetic and deliriously accomplished things she can do. It's all done with gusto and skill and, I am sure, perfect honesty. But somehow, it's a ritual, a posture she's dived into for a demanding still photographer. Miss Ball is pouring her whole heart into a stencil. As one who has loved Lucy even before she was 'Lucy,' I'm deeply, deeply confused.

"Is it simply the unsmiling libretto of N. Richard Nash that makes her seem to be performing by proxy? Mr. Nash hasn't done much for anybody, as it happens. Can it be that director Michael Kidd hasn't been able to find, in so much quaint musing and doodling, a big enough outlet for Miss Ball's zanier talents? There's a moment in which we catch a glimpse of the pop-eyed clown we know best: she takes a big slug of tea and comes out of it with the spoon in her mouth. But these cartoon goodies are few."—Walter Kerr, *New York Herald Tribune*

"Seldom has a lady been hampered by so much excess luggage as Miss Ball in her emigration from the small screen to the large stage. Her finest achievement is her triumph over her role and a great deal of the surrounding action. The author of the book and the director, both of whom serve as producers, have envisioned Miss Ball as a lovable tomboy and have not permitted her to stray far from the confines of this narrow classification. What they have overlooked is that the lady is a brilliant comedienne and an actress of an ability way beyond the stereotyped carbon she is called upon to portray here. Cy Coleman, the composer, and to a lesser extent Carolyn Leigh, the lyricist, seem to realize this and have given her some rollicking and melodious songs. *Wildcat* is at is best in its musical numbers.

"A subplot that deals with Miss Ball's lame sister and her romance with a young Mexican is both intrusive and maudlin. It seems to me, even with her limited role, [Kidd] could have invented more variations for Miss Ball. The night I saw *Wildcat* Miss Ball had evidently hurt her leg and limped together with her sister and the plot. Nevertheless, she overcame this and other handicaps to give an ingratiating, warm performance, proving conclusively that, with the proper role, she can become one of our major musical comedy stars."—George Oppenheimer, *Newsday*

"It is good to see the handsome, talented, and vital Lucille Ball on the Broadway stage. It would be even better to see her in a good show. Her vehicle is a tremendous disappointment. [It is] weighed down by N. Richard Nash's cumbersome and amazingly uninteresting and unhumorous libretto, and staged with a surprising lack of imagination. It is fortunate there are Mr. Coleman's songs to fall back on…. They don't interrupt the plot frequently enough."—Richard Watts Jr., *The New York Post*

"*Wildcat* is a ball of fire when red-headed, lithe-limbed vital Lucille Ball is onstage. And it takes a great trouper to belt this one over. But our Lucy, reclaimed from the airwaves, is just the gal to do it. *Wildcat* has its faults, but it also has the one and only Lucille Ball to cover them with her terrific showmanship. We'll wager she spells money at the box-office."—Robert Coleman, *New York Mirror*

"The rich get richer, and a red-haired millionaire named Lucille Ball figures to make another bundle with a new musical, *Wildcat*, in which she is the star and solo backer. The extravaganza opened at the Alvin last week, and while it falls woefully short of expectations, it still exhibits enough of Miss Ball, blares forth moderately rousing music, and supplies sufficient hoopla and boffola to satisfy the millions who love Lucy.

"It's an increasing bore to be faced once more with a musical with no book. This mishmash could have been conceived on a TV-Western assembly line. But the pulling power of Miss Ball is overwhelming, and there is little doubt she has invested in herself wisely."—John McClain, *New York Journal-American*

"At the center of things, Miss Ball possesses abundantly that indispensable, magic blend of talent, personality and genuine warmth. [But] as a musical show romance, *Wildcat* often seems untidy, uncertain, and erratic."—John Beaufort, *Christian Science Monitor*

"Miss Ball ... shows glints of her comic prowess despite a suffocating book. Miss Ball remains one of the great stage beauties. *Wildcat* has a great deal of vivacity and action. There are also capital ingredients—but they are not integrated into a musical of any consistent quality."— Thomas R. Dash, *Women's Wear Daily*

"Miss Ball is her hearty self, strutting about happily, slapping people on the chest, cutting a caper when need be, pouting, laughing.... She never fails you. The audience loved every minute of it."—Richard P. Cooke, *Wall Street Journal*

"The ovation greeting the frisky lady threatened to reach into next month. And all evening affection ran so high that the last words and notes of specialties frequently were drowned in applause, a deserved compliment to Lucy and Lucille.... Her roguery and savvy, her energy and femininity stamps *Wildcat* as a hit that makes your ears ring."—Frank Aston, *New York World-Telegram & Sun*

"The best part of *Wildcat* ... is Lucille Ball, just as everyone hoped and expected. Miss Ball is a trouper who behaves as though she had been on the stage all her life. *Wildcat* is Miss Ball's show, and she is worth it. She is worth more, come to think of it."—John Chapman, *New York Sunday (Daily) News*

"*Wildcat* is Miss Ball's own show, lock, stock, and oil derrick. The strawberry blonde who left Broadway an unwanted chorine is a triumphant star a generation later, a hilarious hoyden in blue jeans, with a gravelly voice, a radiant personality, and a face that just can't stay composed. It's fortunate for all concerned that her rough, swivel-hipped Wildcat Jackson is on view during most of the entertainment at the Alvin, for the book provided by N. Richard Nash is a throwback to 1912, the year in which the carnival's action is set."—Edward Southern Hipp, *Newark* (New Jersey) *Evening News*

"I'm still in love with Lucy—always in love with Lucy—but I'm not in love with her show.... She riots and rowdies through the occasion ... as she tries to pump illusion, romance, spirit, and brio into the heavy-footed proceedings. Don Tomkins ... has a moment with Miss Ball in which they stop the show cold in a song called 'What Takes My Fancy.' The parched audience slaked itself on this sudden draught of good musical tune making.... It is no pleasure to me, who has admired so many of these assembled talents, to say that *Wildcat* doesn't ever really get off the ground."—Whitney Bolton, *New York Morning Telegraph*

Wildcat Postscript

Ball's press agent at the time, Harvey Sabinson, reflected on her time in *Wildcat* in an article in *The New York Post* in 1977. "Nobody worked harder during rehearsals than Lucille Ball," he said. "She was the complete professional—cooperative, cheerful, and totally attentive. The supporting cast and production staff adored her."

Sabinson continued: "*Wildcat* stepped immediately into the hit class, selling out at all performances, and Lucy worked herself into a frazzle trying to please her public. Daily she added to the show some hilarious shtick she had perfected over the years in television."

Yet the eight live performances each week "began to take their toll on the star. And less than two months after the opening, I was obliged to inform the press that *Wildcat* would suspend for two weeks because Lucille Ball was fighting a losing battle against a virus infection, and on doctor's orders had gone to Miami Beach to recover." The show shut down February 7 to 20, 1961.

On May 6, 1961, Sabinson wrote, Ball's divorce from Arnaz became final. "At a Wednesday matinee later that month, Lucy fainted onstage and was unable to continue. Was it more than a coincidence? A few days later I received a large envelope from her [containing] a color photograph of herself … inscribed, 'Harvey, please come fetch me before it's too late. Love, Lucy.' I knew then that *Wildcat* would close."

And indeed, after suffering a drastic box office drop when Ball was out sick for a week soon thereafter—from $63,000 a week with Ball to $24,000 a week without her—*Wildcat* closed on June 3, 1961, after a run of 22 weeks and nearly 200 performances. Sabinson said, "To leave the door open a little, I announced that the show would 'suspend' for nine weeks because of the star's need for recuperation from exhaustion. But nothing would bring Lucille Ball back to Broadway once she had escaped."

The show lost more than $300,000 of Desilu's money, close to its full investment. There were notices that *Wildcat* would reopen on August 7, but its failure to do so was blamed in the press on the "exorbitant demands of the musician's union," which would've added $50,000 to the cost of the show. No doubt Ball was very tired, and sad, and exhausted, and simply could not face the prospect of going back to the show. And without Ball there was no show.

The original cast recording is quite enjoyable, particularly "Hey, Look Me Over" and Ball's comedic duet with Tomkins, "What Takes My Fancy." It was recorded at Webster Hall, New York, December 18, 1960, and released in 1961.

The most interesting postscript of all is a tiny blurb that ran in *The New York Post* on January 7, 1966: it reported that Phil Feldman would produce a film version of *Wildcat*, to star Ann-Margret. What an intriguing idea … but, unfortunately, it never came to pass.

♥ **Lucy Trivia** Lucy became pals with *Wildcat* co-star Paula Stewart, who played her younger sister and was dating comedian Jack Carter at the time. Paula fixed her co-star up with the man who would become Ball's second husband, comedian Gary Morton. Stewart, who later became an interior decorator, designed Ball's New York apartment in the 1980s.

STANDARDS and PRACTICES

It's public knowledge that before CBS would allow Desi Arnaz to showcase his pregnant wife, Lucille Ball, on television, he had to jump through several hoops in order to please the censorship demons, a.k.a. Network Standards and Practices. Hell, *I Love Lucy* couldn't even use the word *pregnant* on the air; they had to say "expectant," or some other euphemism. It seems silly now, but Arnaz had to wrangle the participation of three ministers of different faiths to pore over the pregnancy scripts, and if they were okay with the language and presentation, the network would sign off on it.

These days, as Ball herself once noted, you can practically show the act of getting pregnant on TV. But according to a panel of industry executives put together by *Entertainment Weekly* for its May 11, 2007 issue, there would be other problems today for a show like *I Love Lucy*. The executives spoke on "condition of anonymity," according to reporter Lynette Rice. Along with the online text was a picture of Lucy and Ricky with the caption: "NO LOVE FOR LUCY Ball's digs at Arnaz's Cuban accent would raise a flag with standards and practices today, says one exec on our panel."

Specifically, when asked "whether *I Love Lucy* would air today, given how racist [sic] Lucy was with Ricky—like how she used to make fun of his Cuban accent," one executive responded, "Yeah, she definitely was. These are things that standards executives look for, even though they are not regulated by the FCC." The networks are to be applauded to for wanting to make sure everyone is portrayed fairly. However, there were, shall we say, extenuating circumstances.

It was brave of Ball to insist on doing the series with her Latin husband. The show certainly was the first to showcase an interracial marriage on television, and it did so without making a big deal of it. It helped that Ball and Arnaz were married in real life, and most everyone in the audience knew that. So when Ball made fun of Ricky's/Desi's accent, the audience laughed because they knew she was doing it out of love, not out of spite or hatred. Indeed, the show's writers have pointed out that they could not allow any of the other characters on the show, even the beloved Mertzes, to make fun of Ricky's accent, because if it wasn't Ball, it came across as mean-spirited, if not racist.

It must also be acknowledged that *I Love Lucy*, and its successor, *The Lucy-Desi Comedy Hour*, often went to great pains to show Lucy trying to learn Ricky's Cuban culture, or her desire to speak Spanish so that she could talk to his relatives when they were visiting. This sounds like the exact opposite of "racist" to me.

STAR TREK

One of the last series that studio chairwoman Lucille Ball green-lighted before selling <u>Desilu</u> to Paramount (the other was *Mission: Impossible*) was Gene Rodenberry's modest proposal for a "*Wagon Train* to the stars," called *Star Trek*. The cerebral science-fiction series limped along for three seasons (1966-'69) before cancellation. But when the 79 episodes were sold into syndication in the '70s, the idealistic plots (which championed diversity decades before it became a buzzword and even featured TV's first interracial kiss) became the industry's greatest beneficiary of Desilu's invention of the rerun with the classic <u>*I Love Lucy*</u>. Constant showings lodged

Captain Kirk and the crew of the starship Enterprise in the popular imagination powerfully enough to spawn four live-action and one (Emmy-winning) animated sequel series, 10 big-screen movie adaptations (with an 11th expected in 2008) and virtually every type of branded merchandise imaginable—indeed, its own universe. The original *Trek* employed a number of Desilu veterans in front of and behind the scenes (See entries for <u>Andes, Keith</u>, <u>Carmel, Roger C.</u>, <u>Daniels, Marc</u>, <u>Jefferies, Walter M.</u>, and <u>Kenwith, Herbert</u>), as well as Desilu Workshop veteran Majel Barrett, who played Nurse Chapel (Dr. Chapel in the films) and went on to voice the starship computers in all subsequent incarnations. Barrett married Rodenberry, eventually becoming guardian of the franchise when the "Great Bird of the Galaxy" passed away in 1991. In 1973, Leonard Nimoy, who played half-Vulcan/half human science officer Spock, told the Long Beach, California, *Independent-Press-Telegram* that his work on *Star Trek* would "follow me a long time." With Nimoy preparing to reprise his signature character in the latest film, Spock himself would no doubt cock an eyebrow and muse, "Fascinating."

STEVENSON, EDWARD

Creative movie and television costume designer Stevenson took over the costuming chores on *I Love Lucy* when <u>Elois Jenssen</u> left in 1955. He won an Oscar, along with Edith Head, for the black-and-white costumes of Lucy's 1960 movie, *The Facts of Life*, his final film assignment. He was Oscar-nominated for *The Mudlark* (1950) and *David and Bathsheba* (1951). He also designed the gowns and/or costumes for Ball in many of her RKO films, including *That Girl from Paris* (1936); *Joy of Living* and *Having Wonderful Time* (both 1938); *Beauty for the Asking*, *Panama Lady*, *Five Came Back*, and *That's Right—You're Wrong* (all 1939); *You Can't Fool Your Wife*, *Dance, Girl, Dance* and *Too Many Girls* (all 1940); *A Girl, A Guy and A Gob* and *Look Who's Laughing* (both 1941); *Valley of the Sun* (1942); and *Easy Living* (1949). Stevenson worked on over 200 movies starting in 1924, but his TV work centered on Ball from 1955 on, for *I Love Lucy*, *The Lucy-Desi Comedy Hour*, *The Lucy Show*, and various specials. In fact, from 1960 on, he worked exclusively for Ball, according to Trent Clegg, Stevenson's collection cataloguer at Idaho State University.

Edward Manson Stevenson was born in Pocatello, Idaho, May 13, 1906. "Edward lived in Pocatello," Clegg notes, "until 1922, when he moved permanently to Hollywood to gain relief from a chronic respiratory ailment." A neighbor introduced him to MGM designer André Andreive, whom Stevenson joined in 1925, where he designed for Greta Garbo.

Stevenson moved on to work at Fox; First National (where he was head of the costume department), which was purchased by Warner Bros. in 1930; Hal Roach Studios; Columbia; and RKO; Ball worked at the latter two studios from 1934 to 1942. According to Clegg, from 1931 to 1935 Stevenson also "designed clothes for the personal wardrobes of stars, partly through the Blakely House company, as well as for studios with no costume departments of their own."

In 1935, Clegg continues, "Stevenson started working as assistant to Bernard Newman at RKO. When Newman left RKO, he recommended that Stevenson be promoted into the top spot. Thus began one of the longest associations in Stevenson's career. From 1936 to 1949, Stevenson helmed the costume department of RKO, designing for such films as *Gunga Din*, *Love Affair*, *Citizen Kane*, *The Magnificent Ambersons*, *It's a Wonderful Life*, and *Cheaper by the Dozen*." Although he would occasionally return to RKO until 1956, Stevenson sought work elsewhere when his contract expired in 1949.

When Ball asked him to join her hit show *I Love Lucy*, he did, and stayed with her until the end of his life. "Television was an enjoyable challenge for Stevenson," Clegg says, "and he did some of his most imaginative work during this period. Ms. Ball reciprocated [his] devotion until the day he died of a coronary, December 2, 1968, fittingly while shopping for fabric on La Cienega Boulevard [in Los Angeles].

"Stevenson was an innovator: designing for the first two-strip Technicolor musicals, tak-

Lucille Ball in Black & White Floral Print with High Collar and Belted Waist: an undated sketch of Lucy by Edward Stevenson. Courtesy of the Edward Stevenson Collection, Special Collections Dept., Idaho State University.

ing part in the creation of a unique relationship between Hollywood designers and New York retail shops, and adapting design techniques to the unique parameters of television technology. He was also, by all accounts, a quiet man of good humor who touched the lives of those around him, most often for the better."

The Edward Stevenson Collection at Idaho State University fills 12 boxes with sketches and other renderings, three of which are devoted to Ball, Clegg notes. The cataloguing was finished in 2007, and much of it is online, including Stevenson's designs for Ball. You can view the gorgeous sketches of the Queen of Comedy and Queen of the B's at www.isu.edu/library/special/mc111.htm.

After Stevenson's death, fellow designer and friend Walter Plunkett (*Gone with the Wind* and *Singin' in the Rain*, among hundreds of other films) wrote to Ball, apparently looking for Stevenson items to auction. Ball's response [as seen in the *Profiles in History* Los Angeles auction house December 2002 catalog] on May 8, 1970, was:

Dear Walter:

Wonderful hearing from you. Needless to say, we miss Eddie very much and are most happy to try and give you any memorabilia that we can come up with. We are forwarding your letter to his family, who were the recipients of what little Eddie left around the office. Of his personal belongings I have no knowledge. Actually, Eddie lived as quietly as he died…without fuss or furbelows.

Of course, there is nothing left here at the studio, which is about to become a Jewish cemetery, that is even reminiscent of the old RKO—the publicity department long since gone. Only the ghost of Perry Leiber wanders the streets at night, occasionally joining Howard Hughes on a midnight trek through the archives.

Hope the family can be of some assistance to you. In the meantime, we shall keep looking, and will hang on to your address. —Love, Lucy

(By the way, a *furbelow* is defined by Webster's as "a pleated or gathered piece of material, *especially* a flounce on women's clothing; or something that suggests a furbelow in being showy or superfluous." Leiber was publicity director at RKO before Ball and Arnaz bought the studio.)

T

TELEVISION SPECIALS

This partial list gives you some idea of what Lucille Ball was doing on TV (other than her weekly series).

◆ *The Ed Wynn Show* (January 7, 1950) Ball and Desi Arnaz in their first network television appearance; Arnaz sings "The Straw Hat Song" (which he later performed on *I Love Lucy*), and Ball does a pantomime with Wynn.

◆ *Dinner with the President* (November 23, 1953) This black-tie affair celebrated the 40th anniversary of the Anti-Defamation League, with Walter Cronkite, <u>Ethel Merman</u>, Ball and Arnaz, Eddie Fisher, Helen Hayes, Rex Harrison, President Dwight D. Eisenhower and more.

◆ *The Bob Hope Chevy Show* (October 21, 1956) This special featured the cast of *I Love Lucy* in a spoof of the show, with Arnaz playing Fred Mertz.

◆ *The Good Years* (January 12, 1962) Little-seen since its first broadcast, this 90-minute special reunited Henry Fonda and Ball, and also fea-

**Ball hosting a segment during one of the many special appearances she made in the 1970s.
Photofest**

tured Mort Sahl and Margaret Hamilton in a series of vignettes celebrating American life between 1900 and World War I.

◆ *The Lucille Ball Comedy Hour: Mr. and Mrs.* (April 19, 1964) With <u>Bob Hope</u> and <u>Gale Gordon</u>. In the first half, Ball plays a studio owner trying to get a "big star" like Hope to appear in her next special. The second half was the actual show, *Mr. and Mrs.*, based on the Broadway play by Sherwood Schwartz (and distilled to 35 minutes by Desilu). Ball hired <u>Jess Oppenheimer</u> to produce, the first time they'd worked together since *I Love Lucy*. Jack Donahue, another Ball favorite, directed.

◆ *Lucy in London* (October 24, 1966) While filming this special, the script called for Ball to be dunked in the Thames after trying to negotiate it on an inflatable raft. Since the river at that time was quite polluted, Ball was advised that she would need various shots and a stomach pumping if she swallowed anything. Pooh-poohing advice to go shoot in a clean body of water, Ball marched into the Thames up to her lips.

◆ *Happy Anniversary and Goodbye* (November 19, 1974) Ball and Art Carney played a long-married couple who decide to try something different and end up realizing they still love each other. Also featuring Nanette Fabray and Peter Marshall, with future California governor (!) and *Terminator* Arnold Schwarzenegger making his TV debut as a masseur.

◆ *Lucy Gets Lucky* (March 1, 1975) With Dean Martin. Ball played a very "Lucy"-like character who sets Las Vegas on its ear.

◆ *Three for Two*, (December 3, 1975) Starring Ball and Jackie Gleason Featuring three short sketches with the two comedy titans, this special missed the mark. It was filmed without an audience, and canned laughter was added later.

◆ *Gypsy in My Soul* (1976) Salute to chorus line "gypsies" by star Shirley MacLaine, with special guest Ball, a former chorus girl herself. Watching Ball dance with the young chorus gals and guys is a pleasure.

◆ *A Lucille Ball Special: What Now Catherine Curtis?* (March 30, 1976) Ball's performance was delightful as she reteamed with Carney in the story of a divorced woman looking for romantic happiness. Joseph Bologna also co-starred.

◆ *CBS Salutes Lucy: The First 25 Years* (November 28, 1976) See separate entry.

◆ *Circus of the Stars II* (1977) Ball was a ringmaster in this special.

◆ *Lucy Calls the President* (November 21, 1977) When Ball, as civic-minded housewife Lucy Whittaker, calls President Carter about a domestic issue, he tells her he'll be in town and will discuss the matter personally. All of Lucy's friends want an invite to the meeting. This special featured Ball's final TV appearance with Vivian Vance, Mary Wickes, and Mary Jane Croft. Written and produced by longtime Ball scribes Bob Carroll and Madelyn Davis, and directed by original *I Love Lucy* director Marc Daniels. Believe it or not, this was the first special Vance had worked on with Ball. She said, "Shooting it was just a riot. The audience was so responsive you could hardly hear the lines for the laughs. And it was just wonderful working with dear Gale Gordon again. And with the rest of the gang."

◆ *An American in Pasadena* (March 13, 1978) Gene Kelly, Ball's old friend and former film co-star (*DuBarry Was a Lady*) did what he did best: sing and dance. In between, he staged a reunion of many of his leading ladies including Ball, Kathryn Grayson, Gloria de Haven, Betty Garrett, Janet Leigh, and Cyd Charisse. Gene returned the favor with a cameo on Ball's 1980 special, *Lucy Moves to NBC* (see below).

◆ *Lucy Comes to Nashville* (November 19, 1978) Taped at the Grand Ole Opry House, Ball introduces a number of country music performers.

◆ *Lucy Moves to NBC* (February 8, 1980) Pointless, overlong (90-minutes) special aimed at showing a pilot Ball has produced starring Donald O'Connor and Gloria DeHaven.

◆ *Bob Hope Buys NBC?* (September 17, 1985) A spoof of all the corporate takeovers that were happening at the time, Hope tries to take over the network with which he is most closely associated. Help comes from stars like Ball, Milton Berle, Phyllis Diller, and dozens of other stars in cameos.

◆ *The Kennedy Center Honors* (December 26, 1986) Soon after Desi Arnaz, the love of her life, passed away, Ball was honored (along with Ray Charles, Jessica Tandy and Hume Cronyn, and others), at this annual gala, the highest performing arts honor in the country. Paying tribute to Ball: Robert Stack, star of the Desilu series *The Untouchables*, who read a message from the gravely ill Arnaz that said, in part, "And by the way, *I Love Lucy* was never just a title"; Valerie Harper, Bea Arthur and Pam Dawber, who sang new lyrics to the *I Love Lucy* theme; and two Walters, legends themselves: Cronkite and Matthau.

◆ *Hollywood, the Golden Years: The RKO Story* (1987) One segment details Ball's tenure at the studio.

◆ *America's Tribute to Bob Hope* (1988) Ball sang and danced as a tribute to her old friend.

- *The Academy Awards* (March 1989) As a presenter with Bob Hope, this was Ball's final public appearance.
- *Bob Hope's Love Affair with Lucy* (September 23, 1989) Hope, a close friend and frequent co-star of Ball's, put together this clip-filled 90-minute show, highlighting Ball's appearances through the years in his TV specials.
- *The I Love Lucy Christmas Special* (December 18, 1989) This was the first airing of the holiday-themed episode since its original airdate, December 24, 1956. Basically a clip show, the Ricardos and Mertzes recall past events while decorating a Christmas tree. At the end, they all dress as Santa (unbeknownst to each other) to surprise Little Ricky, but a *fifth* Santa shows up.
- *I Love Lucy: The Very First Show* (April 30, 1990) This was the first airing of the "long-lost" pilot episode of *I Love Lucy*. Most interesting: no sign of the Mertzes.
- *PBS American Masters: Finding Lucy* (December 2000) Fine documentary looks for Ball behind the wacky character she portrayed on television.
- *The I Love Lucy 50th Anniversary Special* (November 11, 2001) See separate entry.
- *TV's 15 Greatest Comedians* (January 2002) Ball was the No. 1 television comic in this countdown that featured very brief profiles of the Top 15.

TERRAN, TONY

Terran is the last surviving Desi Arnaz Orchestra member at this writing. Born in 1926 in Buffalo, New York (a hop, skip, and a jump away from Lucille Ball's hometown, Jamestown), he was the first trumpet in Desi Arnaz's band from 1946, and later on the *I Love Lucy* and *Lucy Show* series. Terran came to Hollywood in the mid-1940s, where he went to work with Bob Hope and then Arnaz, who led Hope's in-house band at the time. He is described as "one of the most versatile trumpet players in the business" on the website LAstudiomusicians.com (and listed as a Studio Legend). For more information, visit Terran's MySpace page (myspace.com/tonyterran), where you can listen to his lead-trumpet version of the *I Love Lucy* theme.

"THEY LOVED LUCY"

The American Magazine, in a June 1953 article on Vivian Vance and William Frawley called "They Love Lucy," posed the question, "Do Vivian and Bill *really* love Lucy?" *AM* answered it this way: "Well, anyone watching these four actors clown around the set and listening to their good-natured ribbing when no cameras are around learns that they all have a very real affection for each other."

THIBODEAUX, KEITH

Also known as Richard Keith, the young drummer/actor was picked to play a more grown-up Little Ricky in the final half-hour season (1956-'57) of *I Love Lucy*. He later played Ron Howard's friend on *The Andy Griffith Show* from 1962 to 1966. His acting career ended with his parent's divorce in 1966, when he moved back to his native Louisiana. Thibodeaux wrote a book called *Life after Lucy* in 1994, describing his career, some darker periods on drugs afterward, and his subsequent religious rebirth.

THOMPSON, MAURY (MAURICE A.)

Thompson worked with Ball and Arnaz for 16 years (and later worked with Arnaz on his sitcom *The Mothers-in-Law* in the late 1960s). He joined Desilu as a script clerk in 1951 as *I Love Lucy* was beginning, and became camera coordinator in its second season. A script clerk makes sure that scenes follow each other in an understandable and smooth way, and fills in continuity sheets during production, which help the director match edits and put scenes together. The camera coordinator role was unique to Desilu, due to its three-camera filming technique, and a live audience responding to Lucy's antics.

He also was camera coordinator for other Desilu shows, and trained others for the job, according to Tom Gilbert (author of *Desilu*). Thompson also did bit parts on several *Lucy* episodes, including perhaps the most famous, "Lucy Does a TV Commercial" in which he played, appropriately, a script clerk. This let him subtly cue Ball using the actual script, during her extremely long scene.

He continued as camera coordinator for the first season of *The Lucy Show*, and was moved up to director in its second season.

Emmy-nominated for a *Lucy Show* episode, he moved on after the 1966-'67 season and retired after his stint on *The Mothers-in-Law*. Thompson died of cancer in August 2000 in Irvine, California, at the age of 83.

THREE STOOGES, THE

Raucous, violent slapstick trio from vaudeville that segued successfully into the movies in the 1930s and 1940s, making hundreds of shorts that later made them famous all over again in the 1950s and 1960s via television. Though the lineup changed through the years, the Stooges always delivered, whether it was a pie in the face or a sledgehammer on the noggin. Ball co-starred with the original trio (Moe Howard, Curly Howard, and Larry Fine) in an early short, *Three Little Pigskins* (1934) while at Columbia Studios, and was rewarded with seltzer in the face, among other indignities. She subsequently noted, "The only thing I ever learned from them was how to duck."

TRENDSETTER

According to *LIFE* magazine's August 5, 1940 issue, "Three pictures of snappy Lucille Ball shaking a cellophane-fringed skirt in RKO's new movie, *Dance, Girl, Dance*, signify more than meets the eye. They indicate a trend. They show how Hollywood responds when the public, weary of war news, demands to see more fun, more romance, more girls like Lucille Ball. In April over 30 anti-Nazi films were listed for production during the next year. Today all but half a dozen of them are shelved. Movie exhibitors complained that the public had enough of war in newspapers, radio, and dinner talk. Studios sent orders to their writers to be as lighthearted as possible without offending the Hays Office."

TRIBUTES, 1999

At the end of the millennium, Lucille Ball was everybody's favorite.

Here are some of the top honors given Ball and her landmark show, *I Love Lucy*, in 1999, a year that will be remembered for its lists as the new millennium approached and the media sought to put the 20th century in historical perspective.

TIME magazine started the party in 1998, celebrating Lucy as one of the top Entertainers of the Century. See Magazine Covers.

E! Online chose Ball as performing one of the century's funniest moments, and as one of its greatest innovators. In its online feature, "The Brightest Stars and Biggest Moments" of the century, Ball and Vivian Vance appeared in the logo, along with Marlon Brando, Fred Astaire, and Marilyn Monroe. Ball and her Vitameatavegamin pitch contributed moment No. 12 of the 12 top laugh-getters of the past 100 years. Even more impressive, since she was named the No. 4 (of 12) "Entertainment Innovator" (in such good company as Mary Pickford, Les Paul, and Louis Armstrong) it can be argued that nobody "gave better comedy" than Ball.

The wacky redhead also made an appearance (in statue form) in New York's Grand Central Terminal's Vanderbilt Hall, part of "The Turn of a Century: A Carousel Celebrating 100 years of Ups and Downs." Ball was situated behind Chuck Berry in a unique carousel created by current and former students of New York's School of Visual Arts. She and other important figures of the century turned for months in 1999 as part of the multimedia exhibition (featuring text, images, and video that explained more about the subjects).

Newsweek celebrated the "Voices of Entertainment" over the 20th century in its June 28, 1999 issue. Ball got two mentions, one in a photomontage that accompanied the introductory essay, and another, longer piece written by Keith Thibodeaux, on the joys and pains of being "Little Ricky."

TIME's sister magazine *LIFE*, no stranger to having Ball on the cover, put her there posthumously as it honored "The Shows That Changed America: 60 Years of Network Television." Inside, a full-page picture of Ball and Arnaz (and a smaller one of Ball and Vance at the candy factory conveyor belt) introduced the segment on the 1950s. Ball, according to the magazine, had a tonic effect on postwar America, giving us the gift of laughter.

TV Guide, in its Jan. 23, 1999 issue, celebrated "The 50 Funniest TV Moments of All Time." Ball made the list twice in the top 20 (for the candy factory and Vitameatavegamin episodes), but since she is perhaps the person most associated with the concept of TV sitcom humor, she is on the cover, with her friend and colleague Carol Burnett, and relative newcomer Jerry Seinfeld.

In a Valentine's Day salute to TV's most romantic couples, *TV Guide* celebrated Ball and Arnaz as No. 3. Not bad for a twosome whose marriage almost imploded any number of times before it finally self-destructed after 20 years. Still, there was obviously lots of love between the two, even after they separated, and Arnaz remained such a part of Ball's life that her second husband, Gary Morton, referred to Arnaz as his "husband-in-law."

In the October 16, 1999 issue of *TV Guide*, the cover story was "TV's 50 Greatest Characters Ever," and at No. 3 was Lucy Ricardo, the wacky redheaded every-person. She's between Henry Winkler's Fonz at No. 4 and Art Carney's Ed Norton at No. 2. (No. 1 is loudmouthed Louie De Palma from *Taxi*, played by Danny DeVito—a character, certainly, but No. 1? My vote would go to Mrs. Ricardo.) *TV Guide* wrote, "Lucy is [TV]'s DNA. Her uncanny and exuberant instincts for slapstick shaped everything that followed.... Any comic actor on TV today, male or female, who claims not to have been influenced by Lucy/Lucille is lying through his or her teeth." Or blackened teeth, as the case may be.

Entertainment Weekly published the first of its four issues celebrating the century on February 19, 1999: "The 100 Greatest Moments in Television." It was no surprise that Ball and company fared rather well, coming in at No. 5 with the "Birth of Little Ricky" episode.

In the accompanying poll, *I Love Lucy* was chosen as the fifth most popular sitcom of all time, and Lucy herself as the No. 1 "Best TV Actress/Sitcom" by a whopping 30 percent of those polled, nearly 20 percent ahead of her nearest rival, Carol Burnett.

When *EW* published its fourth issue celebrating the century, Ball also made the Top 10. As the No. 9 "greatest entertainer of the century," EW celebrated Lucy's looks (illustrated by a sultry black-and-white picture, from her early movie career), her impeccable comic timing, her "deliciously" subversive female character, her never-say-die attitude when it came to escaping the bonds of a 1950s housewife, and, above all, her commitment as an actress to the character.

As *I Love Lucy* producer and head writer <u>Jess Oppenheimer</u> noted, "She simply *was* Lucy Ricardo. And if you looked carefully, you would marvel that every fiber in the woman's body was contributing to the illusion. Her hands, her feet, her knees—every cell—would be doing the right thing."

TRIBUTES, 2000 AND BEYOND

In August of 2000, BBC News Online users voted for the funniest person of the last thousand years. While the list is heavily slanted toward British comedians, as might be expected, landing at No. 9 was none other than Lucille Ball. The list, in order: Spike Milligan, John Cleese, Billy Connolly, Charlie Chaplin, Rowan Atkinson, Peter Cook, Laurel and Hardy, Peter Sellers, Ball, and Eric Morecambe. Among those whose opinions were gathered was the comedy team of (Dawn) French and (Jennifer) Saunders, who put Ball at the top of their list. Saunders also wrote and starred in British TV's fabulous *Absolutely Fabulous*.

In September 2000, *Biography* magazine published a list of the Top 20 favorite television characters of all time, as voted on by its readers at its website. Coming in at No. 2 was Lucy Ricardo (No. 1 was Michael J. Fox's Alex Keaton from *Family Ties*). Janet Cawley noted, "The zany redhead who desperately wanted to break into show business kept the whole country laughing at her antics."

The TV series *Biography* placed Ball at No. 1 on its list of the Top 15 television comedians in a January 2002 episode. No. 4 four on its list of "TV's Top MVPs"—a "salute to television's most valuable and inspiring achievers"—in its March 9-15, 2002, issue. The stellar ratings performance of *The I Love Lucy 50th Anniversary Special* in November 2001 was noted, with *TV Guide* adding, "Our appetite for [Lucy's] delightfully boisterous brand of comedy only grows."

In December 2005, *TV Guide* and cable channel TV Land joined forces to present the "100 Most Unexpected TV Moments." Our favorite redhead is represented at No. 57 with the 1968 episode *Here's Lucy* episode, "Lucy Visits Jack Benny," in which Jackie Gleason made a surprise cameo as his alter ego, bus driver Ralph Kramden

That same month, an online poll by Yahoo Entertainment asking the question "Which sitcom character would you like to have as your wacky neighbor?" found the overwhelming favorites were neurotic Kramer from *Seinfeld* (No. 1) and "love-him-or-hate-him" Jack from *Will & Grace* (No. 2). Fortunately, cooler heads prevailed as *I Love Lucy's* Fred and Ethel Mertz came in at No. 3 with nine percent of the vote.

From an October 2005 interview with Omar Sharif on the UK Amazon.com site, comes this in the "Who knew?" category: When asked which leading lady, dead or alive, he wished he could have acted with, his answer was … Lucille Ball. I knew Sharif was a talented actor and bridge player, and now I know he has impeccable taste in leading ladies as well.

TIME magazine honored *I Love Lucy* (and put a postage-stamp-size picture of Ball on its cover) as one of the "17 Shows That Changed TV" in its September 17, 2007 issue. Its companion Web piece named *I Love Lucy* one of the Top 100 shows of all time (the shows were not ranked, but presented alphabetically). Critic James Poniewozik noted that the sitcom "by now is almost a synonym for classic," and added the show, "got that way by doing all the things that everyone at the time knew you weren't supposed to do. You couldn't have a female star who was both attractive and funny. You couldn't have her male lead be an urban Latino—playing those devil conga drums—whose Cuban accent was thicker than a platter of ropa vieja. You couldn't, for God's sake, build a storyline around a (gasp!) pregnancy. Lucille Ball's contributions to TV's past are so obvious—Vitameatavegamin, the Tropicana Club, the slapstick routines—that it's better to note sometimes the greatest sign of a future-classic TV show is that it doesn't look like classic TV."

TUCKER, TOMMY

Lucy's personal cue-card man starting in 1963. Filmmaker <u>Garret Boyajian</u> notes that Tucker was Ball's friend, as well: "Ball was introduced to Tucker by cue-card pioneer <u>Barney McNulty</u> during the second season of *The Lucy Show*. It was about this time that she began to lightly use cue cards." Tucker worked with Ball on all her series from then on, and carded various specials and guest appearances—such as *The Dean Martin Show* and *The Carol Burnett Show*, for which he worked regularly. "Lucy was enamored of those who had a college education," Boyajian adds, "and was immediately taken by Tucker, a recent UCLA grad who would spend countless hours playing games in her trailer. There was immediate chemistry between the two, and even though he was the last hired he immediately became the lead [cue-card] man." Tucker died in July 2006.

♥ **Lucy Trivia** A character played by Wally Cox in a 1972 episode of *Here's Lucy* was named Tommy Tucker, the Toy Tycoon.

TV GUIDE

TV Guide, a weekly digest-sized guide to programming (until October 2005, when it became a standard-size magazine) has had a unique relationship with Lucille Ball and her career since its first national issue, in 1953, which featured Ball and Desi Jr. with the headline, "Lucy's $50 Million Baby." Since that time Ball has appeared on the cover more times than any other star (34, according to the magazine's count; for our own meticulous count, see *TV Guide* Collectibles, below). Following is a list of *TV Guide* covers featuring Ball, Desi Arnaz, and others in the "Lucy" universe. Note that Ball and her co-stars were cover subjects on a handful of pre-national editions of *TV Guide*, too. Text in quotes is the cover line for that issue.

♦ April 3-9, 1953 "Lucy's $50 Million Baby" Ball, Desi Arnaz Jr. (the first national edition of *TV Guide*).

♦ April 17-23, 1953 Ball's at the top of a drawing of a TV star totem pole.

♦ July 17-23, 1953 "Lucy and Desi Tackle the Movies."

♦ April 23-29, 1954 "How TV Changed Lucille Ball."

♦ October 9-15, 1954 Full-cover picture of Ball, chin in hand.

♦ July 30-August 5, 1955 Ball, Arnaz, and the Whiting sisters.

♦ December 10-16, 1955 Full-cover Ball picture.

♦ January 12-18, 1957 Full-cover Ball picture, extreme close-up of face resting on hands.

♦ November 2-8, 1957 Al Hirschfeld color caricature of Ball.

♦ July 12-18, 1958 "Lucy Exposes Some Phony Publicity" Full-cover color picture of Ball.

♦ July 16-22, 1960 "Lucille Ball: Humiliated and Unhappy."

♦ September 29-October 5, 1962 Lucy jumping with flower, picture by Philippe Halsman.

♦ April 6-12, 1963 *TV Guide*'s 10th Anniversary, Ball alone on the cover.

♦ September 5-11, 1964 "The Change in Lucille Ball" Glamorous drawing.

- ◆ August 28-September 3, 1965 Ball and Splash, a dolphin at SeaWorld.

- ◆ April 30-May 6, 1966 Ronald Searle caricature of Ball (more inside).

- ◆ October 22-28, 1966 "Lucy Goes Mod in London."

- ◆ July 15-21, 1967 "Redhead With a Golden Touch" Ball in three caricature poses.

- ◆ March 30-April 5, 1968 "Four revealing Days with Lucille Ball" Ball in long coat, walking stick.

- ◆ March 1-7, 1969 *Here's Lucy*'s Lucie, Ball, and Desi Jr.

- ◆ September 5-11, 1970 Ball, Richard Burton, and Elizabeth Taylor.

- ◆ June 12-18, 1971 Child's-style drawing of Ball holding a flower.

- ◆ March 31-April 6, 1973 "Lucy and Her $50 Million Baby 20 Years Later."

- ◆ July 6-12, 1974 "End of an Era: Lucy Bows Out" Richard Amsel drawing of Ball.

In this issue of *TV Guide*, which tracked Ball as she prepared to exit the medium on a regular basis for the first time since 1951, the magazine noted that the redhead attained the following records:

Most Shows, Career: 495 (179 episodes of *I Love Lucy*, 156 of *The Lucy Show*, and 144 of *Here's Lucy*, plus 16 specials.

To which I would add: 13 *Lucy-Desi Comedy Hour*s, 13 episodes (five unaired) of *Life with Lucy*, and dozens more specials (her own and guest-star appearances) before and after the article was published. Not to mention the "Christmas Episode" of *I Love Lucy* and the show's pilot, both rediscovered in the 1990s.

Characters played: Over three dozen, including bricklayer, bullfighter, grape stomper, ballet dancer, Martian, cellist, clown, chorus girl, and front end of a horse.

Costumes worn: more than 1,500.

TV Guide added, "Unfortunately, complete records were not always kept in the early days of Lucy's career, and we must sadly report that such significant statistics as Most Blacked-Out Teeth, Career, and Custard Pies, Per Episode, Most Thrown, are lost to history."

- ◆ October 4, 1986 "Two Old Favorites Return" Ball in jogging outfit is half the cover; Andy Griffith as Matlock is the other half.

- ◆ March 12-18, 1988 "Is TV Getting Better or Worse?" Small picture of Ball and Arnaz.

- ◆ May 6-12, 1989 "TV Is 50" Small picture of Ball and Arnaz.

- ◆ December 16-22, 1989 "Lucy's Found Christmas Episode." Ball as Santa.

- February 9-15, 1991 "An Angry Family Speaks Out" Full-cover shot of Ball and Arnaz.
- Summer 1991 2000th Issue Commemorative Edition "TV's Legends Then & Now" Large-format magazine with a big photo of Ball in the center of the cover.
- December 18-24, 1993 "*TV Guide*'s 40th Anniversary" Small picture of Ball.
- April 4-10, 1998 "*TV Guide*'s 45th Anniversary" Tiny past cover reprints; Ball is shown on one.
- January 23-29, 1999 "The 50 Funniest TV Moments of All Time" Small pictures of Ball, Carol Burnett, Jerry Seinfeld.
- Canadian Edition: January 1, 2000 "TV's All-Time Greatest Shows" Small picture of Lucy.
- October 13-19, 2001 "The 50 Funniest Moments of *I Love Lucy.*" To celebrate the 50th Anniversary of television's most popular sitcom, *TV Guide* did something very special, putting out eight different black-and-white covers for its national edition. The pictures mostly spotlighted Ball in classic poses, including Vitameatavegamin, stomping grapes, at the candy factory assembly line, and one with her hugging Arnaz. In addition, a ninth cover was available exclusively online; it featured all four *Lucy* stars from the European trip Paris fashion episode.
- May 4-10, 2002 "Greatest Shows of All Time." Ball's next-to-last appearance (as of this writing) was this issue. *I Love Lucy* was chosen as the No. 2 all-time greatest show (*Seinfeld* was No. 1); Ball shared the cover with Johnny Carson, Bill Cosby, *The Simpsons*, Dick Van Dyke and Mary Tyler Moore, and James Gandolfini of *The Sopranos*. Of *I Love Lucy*, *TV Guide* wrote, "Loving Lucy still comes so very easily. Brilliantly polished in its frantic hilarity, *I Love Lucy* got there first and did what it did—and what so many other have tried to do—best. The legendary troupe of Lucille Ball, Desi Arnaz, Vivian Vance, and William Frawley set the standard for wacky antics, harebrained schemes, domestic humor, and outrageous shtick, pretty much inventing TV comedy on the spot."
- August 7, 2005 "The Ultimate TV Trivia Quiz" A silver bar across the top of the cover spotlighted the quiz inside and featured a small color photo of Ball and Arnaz.
- October 9-16, 2005 When *TV Guide* published its final digest-size issue, nine classic covers were recreated, including one of Ball as Lucy Ricardo stomping grapes as interpreted by singer/sitcom star Reba McEntire. Though I might have picked Debra Messing, the cover was tastefully done, including an interview between McEntire and Desi Jr., who, as a baby, graced the first national issue of the magazine. No new ground was broken, but in

one response, Arnaz made a slight gaffe. He noted, "Mom started doing physical comedy as a Ziegfeld Girl, for the extra money she got for taking a pie in the face." In fact, Ball's Hollywood career began as a *Goldwyn* Girl in 1933's *Roman Scandals*. Star Eddie Cantor and choreographer Busby Berkeley singled her out as the one chorus girl willing to get her hands (or any other part) dirty and unafraid to mask her beauty. For the record, Ball did contribute a novelty bit to the splashy, Technicolor MGM spectacular *Ziegfeld Follies* (1946), but Mr. Z was long dead by then.

***TV GUIDE* COLLECTIBLES: LUCILLE BALL ON THE COVER** Once upon a time, there was a new medium, called television, and nothing with which to guide viewers as to what was on which channel. This was the case for at least a month or so after the national debut of television. Newspapers began running schedules, and putting out their own weekly guides, a bunch of regional magazines (with names like *TV Digest* and *TV Forecast*), which were scooped up by Walter Annenberg in the early 1950s and made into one big national television guide, with a color cover and pictures: *TV Guide*.

With Lucille Ball being the biggest star of the new medium, it seemed only natural that she was on more covers than anyone else during TV's Golden Age, the 1950s. But even through the '60s and '70s, and '80s and '90s (to some degree), Ball kept showing up on the cover of the digest-sized collectible, to the point where she's become the entertainer most often on the cover of *TV Guide*. It's a fact.

That's not likely to change, especially since the magazine became standard-sized in 2005 and just isn't as much fun to collect. That being said, all of Ball's covers are eminently collectible (they sell for the most money on the collectibles market), especially the first national edition (with Desi Jr.), on up through the final digest-sized issue, which, fittingly, also featured a Lucy cover (see previous entry).

TV Guide, The Official Collectors Guide: Celebrating An Icon, is a wonderful book that pictures every single *TV Guide* cover through 2005. But even though the book rightly crowns Lucy as the *TV Guide* Cover queen, with 39 appearances, I count covers differently than the magazine does. For example, in 2001 it issued eight separate covers honoring *I Love Lucy*'s 50th Anniversary. The book counted them together as "one" cover. I count them as eight covers. Make that nine, as there was one special gatefold cover (featuring Ball, Arnaz, Vance and Frawley) only available for purchase on the Internet.

So, with special thanks to Rick Carl (see <u>Art</u>) for being part of the debate, my count is as follows:

1. Six pre-national issue covers (1951-'52)
2. Twenty-five national covers (1953-'74), when Lucy exited weekly series TV, including the first national edition cover
3. Twelve covers beginning with her last sitcom (*Life with Lucy*, 1986) and continuing after her death (1988-2005)
4. One regular-size magazine special cover celebrating the 2000th issue (July 1991: "TV's Legends Then & Now")
5. Nine special covers honoring her classic series' 50th anniversary (2001)

Add them up and you have a remarkable total of 53 Ball *TV Guide* covers.

♥ **Lucy Trivia** Desi Arnaz was featured on 12 *TV Guide* covers, six in the 1950s, and six from 1988 to 2005, after his death, with Ball and other performers. Vivian Vance, an icon herself, only made the cover twice: first on the next-to-last pre-national issue of the magazine, dated March 20, 1953. Vance is shown smiling up at William Frawley (it looks like two separate pictures put together) with the headline, "Lucy's Neighbors Exposed." The second and final time was on a special cover, part of the *I Love Lucy* 50th Anniversary celebration in 2001. In this foldout, all four lead characters were pictured, taken from one of the series' Paris-themed episodes. Frawley scored three covers; the two mentioned above plus one in the 1960s with Fred MacMurray for the sitcom *My Three Sons*.

TYPECASTING

Ball told an American Film Institute seminar in 1974, "I was in pictures and I didn't dig it too much because I wasn't typecast. I like to be typed. I'd always be playing someone else. But it wasn't a type—a real recognizable type so if you'd see me you could recognize me from pictures past. When television came along, I found a [way] to be typed. I could only find about three or four scenes [in my movies] that I cared anything about, and I put them all together and I found out they were domestic scenes, where I was a housewife—I don't know, maybe normal, natural, somewhat silly—but I loved the domestic scene. So [in television] I started from that."

U

THE UNTOUCHABLES

An action-packed <u>Desilu Studios</u> series that began life as a two-part show on the *Desilu Playhouse*, it was based on the memoirs of FBI agent Elliot Ness. ABC picked up the show as a series, and it was an immediate hit. Desi Arnaz personally took a lot of heat for it, from his boyhood chum Sonny Capone (gangster Al Capone's son, whom Arnaz knew from his youth in the Miami area) to FBI director J. Edgar Hoover, who liked to control how the FBI was portrayed. Setting new TV marks for portraying sex and bloody violence, the show ran for four years beginning in 1959. Protests from Italian Americans resulted in every ethnic group imaginable being portrayed as villains throughout the run of the show.

When Robert Stack (who played Elliott Ness) won an Emmy for Best Series Lead in 1960, producer Arnaz had a $12,000 Mercedes Benz waiting for Stack in the parking lot, claiming it was his win or lose, according to *The Big Book of Show Business Awards*. The *TV Guide TV Book* offers this roster of leading men who were offered the Elliott Ness part before Stack, proving just how mercurial casting is: Van Heflin, Van Johnson, Fred MacMurray, Jack Lord, and Cliff Robertson.

Once Arnaz sold his share of Desilu to his ex-wife, Lucille Ball, in 1962, he was quick to point out the series had eliminated much of the violence from the first seasons as a result of complaints from all sides. He termed it "one big mistake," and added, "The show has suffered by it." Arnaz, who was still producing it, claimed, "I'm going right back to the Mafia, the gangsters, the machine guns. I'm not gonna let any sentiment talk me out of it. We tried to please. We did not change the show because of network pressure: it was our own way of trying to comply with the overall atmosphere."

According to Joe Hyams of *Daily Variety*, "It was no secret that the network [ABC] as well as the sponsors were upset with [Arnaz's] candid—and to this viewer, at least—honest appraisal of the new *Untouchables*." The series left the air in 1963.

U.S. POSTAGE STAMPS

The first official U.S. Post Office *I Love Lucy* stamp debuted on May 26, 1999. The Postal Service used an image sure to please the most ardent Lucille Ball fan: a close-up of Ball circa 1953 being nuzzled by husband Desi Arnaz. The stamp was part of the USPS "Celebrate the Century" collection, a 33-cent series commemorating each decade of the 20th Century with a group of stamps spotlighting cultural, scientific, social, and sports achievements.

The subjects of the stamps were voted on by the public, which chose *I Love Lucy* (among others) to honor the 1950s.

News about a second stamp with Ball's likeness first broke July 21, 2000, at the "Loving Lucy" convention in Burbank, California: Ball would be honored in 2001 with a second postage stamp that would be part of the Legends of Hollywood series. This made Ball the only civilian so honored by the Postal Service (featured on two regular-issue stamps within the space of two years).

"As one of America's most admired, beloved, and talented actresses of the 20th Century, Lucille Ball's countless contributions to the entertainment industry endear her in the memories of millions of lives she touched," said actor Karl Malden at the "Loving Lucy" ceremony to unveil the stamp. Ball's cousin, Cleo Smith, joined Malden at the unveiling ceremony and noted, "What a wonderful honor for Lucy! I know she would be thrilled and very grateful, as are all of us in the Ball-Arnaz-Morton families."

The 2001 stamp (34-cents) featured a Ball portrait by Drew Struzan (see Art), based on a black-and-white photograph that dated to the mid-1950s. The stamp debuted August 7, 2001, and it is a beauty. My one disappointment: you could only buy it at the post office in groups of 20.

Ball, who died in 1989, was the seventh famous face in the "Legends of Hollywood" series joining Marilyn Monroe, James Dean, Humphrey Bogart, Alfred Hitchcock, James Cagney, and Edward G. Robinson; stamps honoring Cary Grant, Audrey Hepburn, John Wayne, Henry Fonda, Judy Garland, and James Stewart were issued after Ball's.

As of this writing (2007), both stamps are very collectible; try your local post office first, but you're more likely to find these in collector's markets, like eBay online. According to the USPS' postalnewsblog.com, the 2001 Lucy stamp currently ranks No. 25 on the list of the Top 25 Most Popular Commemoratives, with 38.7 million saved.

V

VANCE, VIVIAN

Birth name: Vivian Roberta Jones
Born: July 26, 1909, Cherryvale, Kansas
Died: August 17, 1979, Belvedere, California (of breast and bone cancer)
Cremated, ashes scattered in San Francisco Bay.

Born in 1909, Vivian Jones grew up in Independence, Kansas, of English, Irish, and Scottish heritage, the second of seven children born to Mae and Robert Jones. Apparently, almost from birth, she was dying to get out of Kansas; as she once put it, "Dorothy was so happy to wake up in Kansas. Not I! I'd have looked for another cyclone and stood right in its path!" She hated domestic life, had little use for school, yearned to get out and party, and by the time she graduated high school was striking enough

Vivian Vance in the early '60s, fresh off a flight during her coast-to-coast commute for *The Lucy Show*. **Photofest**

(5'7", blonde hair, blue eyes) to interest the producer of the touring Ziegfeld Follies. Her mother ended that possibility.

In fact, her family's lack of support, and her mother's brackish personality, instilled in her an inferiority complex that followed her all her life. She felt separate from her family, except for one younger sister, Dorothy, and though Vance adored her father, she didn't know how to please him, either. It's no wonder that blessed with a natural talent to perform, she got out of there as quickly as she could.

In short order, she got a job performing in a Tulsa, Oklahoma, amusement park, married a publicist (Joe Danneck) to gain further independence from her family, and took the last name Vance from a playwright she'd met in Kansas. She began touring in the chorus of several shows, one of which, *Cushman's Own Revue*, played Albuquerque, New Mexico, where her family had moved, at the KiMo, "America's Foremost Indian Theatre." An April 27, 1929 ad in the *Albuquerque Journal* listed Vance's name twice on the program, once as the title character in *The Circus Girl*, and again as "Twin Sister."

She divorced, rejoined her family in Albuquerque, and carved out a stage reputation at the Little Theater there. (She was "Albuquerque's Girl" forever more; the town went out of its way to make her feel at home when she returned to perform there after she became famous, and the *Journal* and its fellow paper, the *Albuquerque Tribune*, published every bit of Vance publicity it could find.)

Earlier, proceeds from a production there were used to send Vance to New York, where she sang in clubs to support herself until she landed her first Broadway chorus part. According to a Vance interview in the *Lima* (Ohio) *News* on September 9, 1962, "After a dismal two weeks of knocking on two doors, Vivian, drawing on the courage born of desperation, strolled past a doorman guarding an audition to Jerome Kern and Oscar Hammerstein's *Music in the Air*. It was for the chorus and the call was for voices trained in operetta.

"When Vivian's turn arrived, she cut loose with a loud version of 'After You've Gone.' She was being ushered to the nearest exit when Kern and Hammerstein called her back. She joined the cast in rehearsal the next day and the long run that followed."

In reality, it took Vance a bit longer than two weeks to jumpstart her career. Vance's stage career is covered in depth below.

She married a second time (a musician, George Koch), apparently for the security it gave her. Eventually, she met Philip Ober and divorced Koch. Soon after, Ober became her third husband (see <u>Divorce Scandal</u>, below). After the initial success of *I Love Lucy*, she told reporter Bob Thomas in 1952 that she was enjoying her newfound recognition, and that, "I've heard from dozens of people I hadn't heard from since school. I also heard from former G.I.s I had met when I was overseas with *Over 21*. My husband [Ober] and I toured North Africa and Italy with it; we were the first play to go overseas." Vance continued her stage career until felled in the mid-1940s by a nervous breakdown. It has been speculated that her WWII theatrical tour was a major contributor; she had a tough time dealing with the realities of war.

Vance went into analysis, didn't act for a while, and by the late 1940s was slowly easing her way back onto the stage. She appeared in several small movie roles in Hollywood, and periodically escaped to her and Ober's ranch in Cubero, New Mexico. That's where she got the call from friend Mel Ferrer to do *The Voice of the Turtle* at his La Jolla (California) Playhouse. She got excellent reviews, as always, and then, director Marc Daniels, whom Vance had known from her theater work, took Desi Arnaz and Jess Oppenheimer to see her on a summer weekend in 1951.

Daniels thought Vance would be perfect for the role of Ethel Mertz in their new sitcom. After seeing her, the others agreed. Lucille Ball took a little more convincing, but she changed her mind after seeing what an accomplished performer Vance was, and how committed Vance was to making the show a success. Those were qualities Ball admired. *Lucy* camera coordinator Maury Thompson once questioned how Vance could stand working with perfectionist Ball. Vance replied that if there were any chance that *I Love Lucy* might take off, she would "learn to love the bitch." By that time in her career, Vance was nothing if not pragmatic.

By the show's second season, Vance had already learned the power of TV: "When I do my Christmas shopping, people are always coming up to me and talking to me," she told the *Newport* (Rhode Island) *News* in January 1953. "They start talking, just as though we had met. They even put their hands on my arm, as an old friend would. There's one remark I get from nearly everyone: They always ask me why the show can't be on earlier than nine o'clock. They say their children are always sleepy Tuesday morning."

Some fans may have known about Vance's stage career, and that she sang in New York supper clubs and developed a pretty fair reputation as a torch singer. But it's a sure bet most didn't know that Vance lied about her age and many other circumstances of her real life, hiding behind a mask of humor and sarcasm. She had a contentious relationship with her mother—a repressed, fire-and-brimstone kind of gal—that colored her behavior. She loved men, marrying four times, and occasionally propositioned her co-stars. She also branded herself a sinner and experienced much guilt over her success. Most surprising of all, her final (and happiest) marriage was to a gay man who reputedly gave up his previous life (and lover of 20 years) for love of Vance.

The Other Side of Ethel Mertz covered her struggle to deal with how popular she had become as Ethel Mertz; several interesting might-have-been parts (including Vera Charles in *Auntie Mame* with Rosalind Russell); and her attempt to build a peaceful life out of the spotlight. She was mostly successful, and when she didn't work, it was because she didn't want to.

One exception, Vance noted, was a part in the blockbuster movie *Giant*. "I read Edna Ferber's novel," she said in a 1954 interview with *The Albuquerque Tribune*. "There was a part in it I was just dying to do in the movie. But they wouldn't give it to me—they were afraid the audience would see me and gasp, 'There's Ethel Mertz!' That's one thing about Hollywood—they're afraid to try things. In New York, they wouldn't be afraid."

Vivian Vance is excited about the new season of *The Lucy-Desi Comedy Hour*. **Author's collection**

Vance's success in varying theater projects probably cemented her feelings about Hollywood.

Vance spent nine years on *I Love Lucy* and *The Lucy-Desi Comedy Hour* (1951-'59). She came to believe that working on *I Love Lucy* helped cure her mental illness. When Vance started on the show, "She was unable to open doors because of her breakdown," UPI's Aline Mosby wrote in 1955 for a *San Mateo* (California) *Times* profile on Vance. "Being forced to open doors during the program pulled her over that hurdle. She also had been afraid to sing or play the piano—until the script called for it."

The *I Love Lucy* years made her a legend, but they inevitably came to an end.

In 1960, she made a pilot called *Guestward Ho!* (see <u>After Ethel</u>, below). She was offered a great deal of money to continue as Ethel Mertz in a *Lucy* spin-off centering on the Mertzes, but turned it down because she could not bear working with William Frawley any longer.

When she learned of Frawley's death in 1966, the popular story goes that she toasted colleagues at Sardi's, saying "Champagne for everyone!" Thereafter, whenever fans inquired about Fred Mertz's whereabouts, she told them simply, "He's dead." However, a UPI report after Frawley's death quoted Vance sounding mighty different: "Vivian Vance, who played Frawley's wife on I Love Lucy, praised the veteran performer. 'There's a great big amusing light gone out of this world,' she said."

Vance was very concerned with shedding the dowdy image of Ethel and that was no doubt responsible for her busy career in the early 1960s. Another reason was some advice she once got from Claudette Colbert, her *Secret Fury* (1950) co-star, who told her, "Always appear. Then people don't know you're changing and you won't grow older in their eyes." Vance guest-starred several times on Red Skelton's variety show—a 1960 review in the *Modesto* (California) *Bee* noted Vance played Clara, Skelton's wife in his continuing George Appleby sketches, and "she's a good one … funnier than many of the others [who've played the role]"—and co-hosted *The Mike Douglas Show* for a week in 1965.

Other shows she appeared on included *The Jack Paar Show, To Tell the Truth,* and *I've Got a Secret.* She made several appearances on *Candid Camera,* like one in July 1961, in which she portrayed "a salesgirl in a hosiery shop and a bakery customer who samples too much rum cake."

One unique potential project was reported by Cynthia Lowry in December 1963; it came as a result of Vance being tagged a "witty, urbane ad-libber" on her talk-show appearances: "[One of] the broadcasting chains that owned the stations on which Vance had appeared invited her to go to Europe—France, Germany, Italy, Denmark, and, most interesting, Russia—the following summer to talk to women of other countries in a series of taped interviews." But it never materialized.

Vance racked up more TV appearances and also did lots of regional theater during this period. She had divorced Ober in 1959 and married her fourth husband, literary agent John Dodds, on January 16, 1961, at the residence of author Babs Hooten (author of the book *Guestward Ho!*) in Santa Fe, New Mexico. The couple had met there two years earlier during a social event. The Santa Fe *New Mexican* reported the civil ceremony featured "a magnificent triptych placed before an arrangement of long-stemmed red rosebuds, and two white tapers in brass candlesticks," giving the appearance of an altar.

"The bride wore a Bergdorf-Goodman original," the paper noted, "of black faille, with tiny white faille yoke filling in the high neckline. A small crisp veil was attached to her tiny black hat," and the bridal bouquet consisted of orchids and pink rosebuds." Hooten was the matron of honor and husband Bill was the best man. Two of Vance's sisters were also in attendance.

"To be married to a man in the book business is heaven," Vance noted in 1966. "Our house is full of writers all the time and I've always loved writers. As an actress I'm so beholden to writers. Without the word, we are nothing."

By all accounts, it was her most successful marriage, despite the fact that Vance reportedly had a strong sexual appetite, and her husband was gay—or at the very least bisexual (see Dodds, John).

Ultimately, Vance was contacted by a persistent Ball to return to weekly TV in 1962's *The Lucy Show*. In it, Vance played TV's first divorced woman and made sure her contract stipulated she would look or sound nothing like Ethel; her character would be called Vivian and her clothes would be modern and not frumpy.

A December 20, 1963 article in the *Sheboygan* (Wisconsin) *Press* by Vernon Scott noted that Vance "is probably the only woman in this country who commutes 3,000 miles each week from home to work. It's true." Vance lived in Old Long Ridge Village, Connecticut at the time with Dodds, whose own commute was comparatively shorter (about 35 miles to New York).

"After we film the show on Thursday nights I catch the 12:30 (a.m.) flight to New York," Vance told Scott, "without a trace of fatigue." She continued: "I fall asleep right away, and when I wake up it's 8:30 a.m. in New York. John meets me at the airport and we drive home. The trip really isn't as bad as it sounds."

Vance calculated, with the time changes, that "it is only seven hours from Desilu studios to her house. Some Californians have been known to spend more time trying to get off the Hollywood Freeway," Scott wrote, only half joking. "Her schedule allows Vivian to spend Friday, Saturday, and Sunday with her husband. She hops aboard the last plane on Sunday night, or an early flight Monday morning, to arrive at the studio before noon.

"Vance's poodle, Boofie, has logged as many transcontinental miles as any pooch in the country. He flies back and forth between work and home every weekend with his mistress."

Vance stayed at the <u>Chateau Marmont</u> while in Hollywood, a fancy, Euro-style hotel and apartment house that catered to performers (and still does). "After a day at the studio she fixes herself a snack and goes right to bed," Scott wrote. "She does keep two wardrobes, however."

"I never know which sweater or dress is where," Vance said. "It's really bad during the winter because I get on the plane in New York wearing a heavy suit and arrive in Los Angeles in 80-degree weather. Or I wear a light dress on the plane from Hollywood and freeze to death when we arrive in New York." Vance tired of commuting after three years, and quit *The Lucy Show* in after the 1964-'65 season to enjoy her bucolic Connecticut life. It has been alleged that Vance asked Ball for a ton of money plus the opportunity to direct and other perks in order to continue on the show, which, given the show's budget, Ball could not have met. Other reports state that the stars' respective agents did the negotiations and there were a number of miscommunications as a result.

The Lincoln, Nebraska *Sunday Journal and Star* reported in June 1965 that, "… Whether Lucille Ball will miss the nicely balanced support of her old partner in comedy is still to be discovered. If so, shrewd Miss Ball will send out a hurry up call to [Connecticut]. There are those who, in spite of Miss Vance's protestations, believe she would respond—if Lucy would reward her with a percentage interest in the series."

Whatever the case, Vance was just as happy to live a comfy life in the suburbs with Dodds. A New York *Daily News* magazine feature on October 13, 1963, noted that Dodds and Vance "were apartment dwellers before they married in 1961. But once they wed, they decided they wanted to live in a good old-fashioned house. So recently the Dodds bought a frame house which was built in the 1820s in Old Long Ridge Village, Conn. [near Stamford]."

The main part of the house was built before the Civil War, with extensions added throughout the years. It was described as having four bedrooms, three baths, a roomy kitchen and an "enormous" living room. The Dodds did a lot of entertaining there.

"We have a swimming pool, too [which the Dodds added], which is something I never had in 10 years of living in Hollywood," Vance told AP reporter Vernon Scott. "She describes the decor of her home as 'casual elegance.' It is a mixture of furniture from Vivian's previous homes in Hollywood and John's home in San Francisco."

Vance was evidently quite content there. "Vivian's free time in Connecticut is devoted to gardening, raising an old-fashioned flower garden. She reads a great deal, too, inasmuch as John's work requires him to read endless manuscripts at home," Scott noted. And though Vance hardly ever entertained when she was in Hollywood, "'We visit back and forth a lot right in the neighborhood,' Vivian said. 'I have [help] in the house, but when we entertain I do all the cooking.' She and John are social butterflies in Old Long Ridge Village. They are particularly friendly with their neighbors, including the Josh Logans, the Benny Goodmans and actress Mildred Dunnock." Add actress Eileen Heckart to that group.

Vance sparked a friendship with Heckart after viewing one of her TV performances in the '50s and sending her a short but sweet fan letter, calling Heckart "… without a doubt, the greatest actress I ever saw." They started a correspondence that became a friendship. Vance and Dodds lived two towns away from Heckart and her family in Connecticut, and the actresses socialized when they could. They also gabbed on the commuter train to and from New York, according to Heckart's son, Luke Yankee, in his wonderful book about his mother's career, *Just Outside the Spotlight*.

Yankee recalls Vance as "a warm, caring sincere lady," and devoted a chapter to her in the book called "Our Neighbor, Ethel Mertz." By 1968, the Dodds had moved to a ranch in Sante Fe, but Vance kept in touch and ended up doing something very touching for the family, helping Heckart's husband through a mid-life crisis.

Ball and Vance appeared in nearly 300 TV episodes/specials together, making them one of the medium's most-watched and most popular comedy teams. Vance revealed one of their secrets to reporter Charles Witbeck of the Charleston, West Virginia, *Sunday Gazette Mail* in 1964: When they were having trouble with a scene, "They simply play it like children and it works. Lucy cries or stamps her foot, Viv sulks or sticks out her tongue, and whips back a caustic remark with slow burns if needed.

"Adults in a temper act like children," Vance said. "Watching them become juveniles is funny, and not mean or insulting. This is one reason why children like the series so much." Witbeck added, "The two ladies always make up, which is another child pleaser." Actually, it was a crowd pleaser.

Vance had a supporting role in the 1965 movie *The Great Race* (see Film Career, below). She regretted that a movie career never developed after that, but if she needed an audience, or a new living-room set, she would go on tour or do summer stock.

In the mid-1960s, she also voiced the desire to become a director. "I wish a playwright would write me a show for Eileen Heckart," she told Witbeck. "And I'd direct." Vance said she could tell by reading a script whether or not it would be a success, and had received good training from legendary theater producers like George Abbott. Ball often referred to Vance as the best script doctor she knew.

Vance deferred to someone else: "I'll tell you something that may be a surprise. Outside of Abbott, Desi Arnaz is the most knowing man around on what is right and wrong with a script. We need him back in the business." Vance never did get to direct Heckart.

She was most proud of her work with the mentally ill, and did whatever she could to publicize depression as an illness. That included talking to patients, something at which she excelled and enjoyed. She was also a mentor to many young performers, teaching them what she knew about comedy. And she managed to fit in a Broadway play during this period as well (*My Daughter Your Son*, 1969).

Vance was featured in a TV production of *The Front Page* (1970). She acted in several early made-for-TV movies, like the fluffy *Getting Away From It All* (1972), and played Harry Houdini's nurse in the meatier and well-received *The Great Houdinis* (1976, directed by Melville Shavelson, who directed Ball's 1968 movie, *Yours, Mine and Ours*).

She guest-starred regularly on Ball's series (including *Here's Lucy*), other TV shows (*Love, American Style*; *Rhoda*), and did several specials with Lucy: a Dean Martin roast, a taped appearance honoring Ball's 25 years in TV (1976), and their final appearance together, *Lucy Calls the President* (1977). She acted regularly in local and regional theater. The theater was where her heart was, and her name was always an audience draw.

Commenting on that in 1975, Vance noted, "Do you know I'm a bigger draw now—you know, at colleges and universities—than I was seven years ago? It's not to be believed. Now I thought that was because the people who grew up with *Lucy* were coming to see me. But the ones in college now … the younger ones … [saw the reruns]." She stressed to her students that "stumbling blocks, such as the incident with a Hollywood press agent who told me to 'Go home, your eyes are too close together,' can hurt a good actor if he doesn't have determination and confidence in himself…. If there's something you want badly enough, go out and fight for it if you have to."

Vance was also aware that it was unlikely she would ever top *I Love Lucy*. When an interviewer in the early 1970s asked her why she'd never done another series, her response was "Why, honey, what series would I do? I did the best one they ever had in *I Love Lucy*. Why settle for second best?"

Performing on TV as Maxine, the Maxwell House coffee lady, in a series of TV commercials in the 1970s that played off her natural warmth and effusiveness, delighted Vance. (A typical spot had Maxine bantering with a window washer, convincing him to try the coffee. It began with her crowing, "Taste, Birdman.") As she matured, Vance said all she ever wanted was a commercial that would allow her enough income to enjoy her later years, and if *Lucy* gave her that, then she had made her peace with Ethel Mertz. She dryly added, "When I die, people will send Ethel flowers."

In the 1970s, she suffered a mastectomy and a series of small strokes. Eventually, when the cancer returned, Vance decided enough was enough, but she did have one last get-together with the red-haired clown with whom she would always be associated.

When Vance died, her good friend, columnist Liz Smith, was on vacation. Smith covered Vance's death in her August 31, 1979 column, a few weeks later. Smith wrote, "Viv stuck out a tough illness for a long time, but one day put on her best make-up, had her hair done, and summoned her beloved husband, John Dodds, to her bedroom. 'Darling, you've just got to let me go.' So the life-support systems were dismantled. Well, so long, girl—you were the greatest."

Vance's popularity, like Ball's, has only grown since her death. *Premiere* magazine reported that 8,000 fans phoned the Hollywood Chamber of Commerce to protest when they discovered Vance did not have a star. In 1992 she was finally given her own star on Hollywood's Walk of Fame (sponsored by Lucie Arnaz).

She has been mimicked and aped by every other best friend/neighbor to come along since *I Love Lucy*. Vance's creation, the best-loved sidekick of all time, Ethel Mertz, has become a pop touchstone, and any time it is referenced, there is a smile and laughter accompanying it.

ADS FEATURING VIVIAN VANCE: Vance did several ads in the 1950s, and then nabbed a spokesperson role in the 1970s.

◆ Jell-O butterscotch pudding, TV, 1950s.

◆ Schaeffer pens, TV, 1950s, in *I Love Lucy* character.

◆ July 15, 1960, an ad ran in a show-business trade magazine, with the headline: "As Vivian or Ethel, She's Still a Madcap." The ad ran once and was placed by the William Morris Agency (Vance's agency) promoting Vance, with reviews of her experience on *I Love Lucy* plus a stage performance of *Here Today*. It measured 9.25x12.25 inches.

◆ Maxwell House Coffee, as "Maxine," print ads and TV, 1970s.

◆ AIDS Project LA, 1992: "Be a Buddy, Help Someone Out" was the headline for this ad featuring a picture of Lucy and Ethel wrangling with a huge fish, from the *I Love Lucy* Florida episode "Deep Sea Fishing," which aired November 19, 1956.

For a more recent ad with Vance, see <u>Ads Featuring William Frawley</u> under the entry <u>Frawley, William</u>.

AFTER ETHEL: A public relations article circa 1960 reports Vance's frame of mind regarding her career immediately following *I Love Lucy*. Vance was well off thanks to residuals from more than 200 *Lucy* shows; in fact, *I Love Lucy* made her financially independent for life, but the actress nonetheless wanted to continue her career on her own.

"In all the nine years I was with Lucy, I never appeared in [another] movie or TV show. [Vance did make several mostly 'Lucy'-related guest appearances on variety shows.] Toward the end, I thought I was getting tired of acting, but I was just weary of the same role. From now on I hope never to be seen wearing a marcel [her hair style as Ethel Mertz] and house dress."

She had just filmed a dramatic role in a Western series, *The Deputy*, in which the character she played was "A far cry from that biddy Ethel," Vance laughed. "The woman I portray is a strong individual who rides horses and drives buggies. It's given me a new lease on life."

She also mentioned she hoped to star in her own series, having just filmed the pilot for *Guestward Ho!* with Leif Erickson, about a married couple that forsakes the city and opens a dude ranch in New Mexico. Based on a book by Vance's friend Babs Hooten, the pilot was not picked up. A different version starring Joanne Dru aired during the 1960-'61 TV season.

One intriguing possibility Vance mentions is an hour-long musical for TV, which she and Ball were planning, with Vance again as the second banana. That would be her Ball swan song, she said. Though that project never materialized, she did return to TV with Lucy in *The Lucy Show* for three years (1962-'65), and spent most of the rest of her performing life on her first love, the stage.

At the time of her return to TV (1962), Vance told AP writer Bob Thomas that she'd been doing "everything she could" since *I Love Lucy* ended. "I played the Jack Paar show, summer stock; I kept as busy as possible. There was a special reason for this. I had to find my own identity. I was so submerged in Ethel Mertz that I was afraid I would never again be recognized for my own self.

"Oh, I was grateful to her for the biggest success I had ever known. But, being a creative person, I was worried that I would be stuck doing the same role for the rest of my life." Indeed, similar thoughts had driven Vance to long-term analysis, which she championed whenever she could. Instead, post-Lucy, Vance said, "I found people to be amazingly receptive: Many critics said of my summer-theater work: 'I went expecting to see Ethel Mertz, but after the first two minutes I wasn't aware that she was anyone but Vivian Vance.'"

In 1965, nearing the end of her run on *The Lucy Show*, Vance noted the part of Vivian Bagley was much more to her liking than Ethel Mertz. "She is nearer to my own personality and my own age. As Ethel, I was always asked to make the down remark. I got bored with that. I like to smile. Also, I get to dress up more."

Her main ambition in life, she said, was semi-retirement, a luxury she used to view more as a threat. "My drive hasn't been as great as a lot of people's. I'd always rather have stayed home and read a book or mended the curtains or fixed the flowers. And the nice thing is, now I can." Since this was the girl who couldn't wait to get out of Kansas, left home to be in show business, got married in defiance of her mother, and persevered in supper clubs in New York until she landed on Broadway, we can probably take her comments about her "lack of drive" with a grain of salt.

In 1976, Vance noted, "[*I Love Lucy*] has nothing to do with me now. My life has gone on. But it's hard for the public to realize that when they keep seeing me in reruns." Adding that she couldn't escape Ethel even when she traveled, Vance said, "People [in Europe] keep coming up to me and chattering away. They cannot understand why I don't know what they're saying because they've heard me [dubbed] speaking German or French or Italian.

"I have had to make my peace with it. I understand this happens to all stars on hit situation comedies, and when you've made as much money as I have it's hard to cry the blues. One gets to a certain place in life where you are much more content to take it easy. Now I have my blessed commercial [as Maxine, the Maxwell House coffee lady]. That's the goal of most people in this business."

Vance at the time was enjoying the acting seminars she gave for college students. She liked young people because, "They all grew up with me, so it's not difficult for us to talk. I'm like a good friend or an aunt or older sister. I tell them it should be a joy to act and not to be afraid. It's rewarding to be able to kind of mother the young people in the profession and get them started. People did that for me all my life."

AUTOBIOGRAPHY: In a July 15, 1974, *New Yorker* piece, Vance spoke of her autobiography, which, she said, was going to be called *Viv*.

"You know who thought that up?" she said. "It was Bart Howard, who wrote *Fly Me to the Moon*. He said all my other titles sounded like soap operas.

"I was thinking of calling it *Both Ends of the Rainbow*, or *There's a Hill, Beyond a Hill, Beyond a Hill*. I put everything in my book. Everything you ever saw in a Warner Bros. movie, I did. Honey, when I first arrived in New York from Albuquerque, I carried my own bags."

Also in 1974, Ed Sullivan wrote in his February 23 *On the Town* column, "Vivian Vance said at Joe's Pier 52 she has almost finished her book. It deals largely with her winning battle against cancer."

The next year, in an interview with the *Memphis Press Scimitar* on Nov. 5, 1975, titled "Viv's Back and Rhoda's Got Her," the author noted, "The actress is working on her own first book at present, entitled *Go Home, Your Eyes Are Too Close Together*. That piece of advice was actually given to [her] by an agent in Hollywood. 'He said I couldn't possibly be photographed, and for years that complex stayed with me,' Vance said."

Vance said, "I loved writing," in 1977. "Even if you usually find writing difficult, you'd be surprised at how easy it is when you're writing about yourself. Putting it to paper was actually very healthy for me. But then I decided I didn't want the book published. My husband tells me, 'Someday, Viv, you'll get it out.' And maybe someday parts of it will be published, but whether they are or not, I had a good time writing."

Her autobiography didn't see the light of day, until 1989—10 years after her death.

Over several weeks beginning in late August of 1989 the *National Enquirer* published what it purported to be excerpts from Vance's autobiography. The paper said Vance decided against publishing it because she did not want to hurt anyone. The manuscript was in the hands of Serge Matt, an antique dealer who had been the best friend and heir of Vance's husband, John Dodds. He said he had no plans to publish the manuscript. Nothing has surfaced of it since then.

BOOKS: There was scarcely much available on the life of Vivian Vance except for what was written in various books about Lucille Ball, Desi Arnaz, and *I Love Lucy* until 1998-'99, when two bios of Vance surfaced.

The first was *The Other Side of Ethel Mertz: The Life Story of Vivian Vance*, by Frank Castelluccio and Alvin Walker (1998). See <u>Vance, Vivian</u> for more. The authors write with a great deal of love and respect for their subject. Vance was way overdue for such treatment, considering her influence on TV comedy.

Meet the Mertzes, by Rob Edelman and Audrey Kupferberg followed in 1999. This dual biography of Vance and William Frawley is not as incisive as one might like, but it's a quick, enjoyable read. The book details Vance and Frawley's antagonism during the run of *I Love Lucy* and their careers after the show ended. Any biography split in two is bound to be missing information about its subjects; there's more to cover and less space in which to say it. But since there was so little written on Vance and Frawley to begin with, this book was a welcome addition.

BREAST CANCER: The most interesting thing about the text of a short postcard Vance wrote to a friend in the mid '70s is how cavalierly she handled having breast cancer. This card was sold on eBay in 2006.

"My dear Helen … So good to hear from you. We spend part of the year in San Francisco now & will leave Saturday for a 3-month stay. Now that I have a nice big commercial for Maxwell House Instant Coffee I don't [have to] work in the theater any more. I never did like to leave John. We love northern California & will eventually live there. [They did, in tiny Belvedere, near San Francisco.] I've done *Rhoda* and *Dinah!* lately and may do some more *Rhoda* [episodes]. I had a mastectomy, too. Horrible!! Love to you, Vivian Vance"

DIVORCE SCANDAL: It sure doesn't sound like Ethel Mertz! But Vance and Phil Ober began to play house while her second marriage, to musician George Koch, was not yet over, and Ober was still married to the former Phyllis Roper. This was the late 1930s, when scandals like this, especially involving "show" people, got big press. And Vance's relationship with Ober was no exception.

The United Press reported, under a headline, "Songstress Named in Divorce Suit," that, "Mrs. Philip Ober charged in [New York] Supreme Court today that her husband, a star in the Broadway hit *Mr. and Mrs. North*, found so much after-theater relaxation in the apartment of Vivian Vance, blonde musical comedy singer, that he forgot to come home several nights."

In a response, of sorts, to some of the publicity, a New York paper headlined "Answers Actor's Wife" wrote the following under a head shot of Vance: "Vivian Vance yesterday characterized as 'ridiculous' charges by Mrs. Phyllis Roper Ober that husband Philip N. Ober was paying Miss Vance's rent at 1 University Place. Ober, actor in play *Mr. and Mrs. North*, called the friendship platonic, and said he can't pay $200 a month wife asks."

As the inevitable happened, papers ran the final chapter, "Actor's Wife Gets Divorce and 35 Percent." The UP wrote it this way: "Actor Phil Ober, who happened to be in the apartment of the beautiful Vivian Vance when the lights went out, will receive official notification on two subjects today. He will be informed he is divorced and that he must henceforth pay his socially prominent wife, the former Phyllis Roper, 35 percent of his income."

"The decree was signed without any fuss or fanfare by Supreme Court Justice Philip J. McCook. Under it Mrs. Ober is also given custody of their 7-year-old daughter, Emily, although the father will have the right to visit.

"Ober, the amiable homicide squad detective of *Mr. and Mrs. North*, did not contest the action. Mrs. Ober produced private detectives who said Ober made a visit to the Greenwich Village apartment of Miss Vance, musical comedy singer, last Feb. 6, and that after a while the lights went out—but Ober didn't."

Oops. Vance must have hated this publicity in light of the image she tried to maintain on the home front to her very religious mother. In any case, Vance and Ober were married in 1941.

FILM CAREER: Of all the *I Love Lucy* principals, Vance had the fewest big-screen roles, literally a handful. They are:

1. *The Secret Fury*, 1950 (Leah). The first of two films Vance appeared in before accepting the part of Ethel Mertz. It's been said she hesitated to join the *Lucy* cast because she thought she might have a movie career ahead of her. It's hard to say, based on this minor role. A psychological mystery directed by Vance's friend Mel Ferrer and co-starring then-husband Phil Ober, the plot revolved around a distressed Claudette Colbert. In the midst of marrying Robert Ryan, Colbert informed she's

This picture of Vance ran under the headline "Songstress Named in Divorce Suit" in a New York paper. Author's collection

already been married. This leads to a mental collapse, and Ryan tries to find out who's trying to "gaslight" Colbert. Vance plays a small role as a tough hotel maid who's mixed up in the scheme. She does her part well, and it's fascinating to see her in this film noir setting, but her part is almost of the "blink and miss her" variety.

2. *The Blue Veil*, 1951 (Alicia). A tearjerker directed by Curtis Bernhard. Jane Wyman plays a woman fresh from the loss of her own baby who becomes governess/nurse to a series of children (the title refers to her nursing habit), eventually leaving them as they get too old to need her anymore. Vance is in the first segment of the movie, in which Charles Laughton hires Wyman to take care of his child, becomes fond of her, proposes to her, is turned down, and ends up marrying his crisp, efficient secretary Alicia. Vance is fine in the small role, and is shown in three scenes, including a brief phone conversation with Laughton; one in which she is introduced; and a second, longer scene, after her marriage, in which she has a "heart-to-heart" with Wyman about how long it'll take to teach Vance the duties of motherhood. Alicia exists to kick-start the love/abandonment theme of the movie. Based on a French movie called *Le Voile Bleu* from 1942, *The Blue Veil* is a sentimental "woman's picture" of the kind they rarely make anymore—somewhat dated in its plot and portrayals, but nonetheless enjoyable.

3. *The I Love Lucy Movie*, 1953 (Ethel Mertz) See separate entry.

4. *The Great Race*, 1965 (Hester Goodbody). This overlong but enjoyable comedy starred Tony Curtis, Natalie Wood, and Jack Lemmon. Vance played the wife of a newspaper owner (Arthur O'Connell) covering the race of the title. Of the role, she quipped, "I had more costumes than lines." Hester is a suffragette, and after stressing out her husband, ends up taking over the paper. In her final scene, we see Hester sitting in her husband's desk chair, smoking his cigar, feet up on the desk. It's a small part, but Vance is in her element (comedy) and does it well.

NERVOUS BREAKDOWN: In the May 1955 issue of *McCall's* magazine Vance publicly confronted the events and emotions that led to her nervous breakdown in the mid-1940s. In "I Don't Run Away Anymore," she recalls that her first symptoms showed up while playing on Broadway in *Hooray For What!* opposite Ed Wynn, in 1939.

She couldn't hold down food. Tired all the time no matter how much sleep she got, and developing pains in her arm she couldn't account for, Vance was told by a fellow actor her symptoms were "psychosomatic." Though she wasn't sure, all she knew was that, mental or not, the pain was real. She got unwanted (and wrong) advice from well-meaning friends, and was told by others, "You don't want to get well!"

Eventually, after a nervous breakdown that manifested while she was appearing onstage in 1945—Vance found she simply could not move or speak—she retired to her home in New Mexico and ultimately sought help. Four months of intensive therapy helped begin her healing process. She became a staunch advocate of mental health thereafter, and of all the awards and honors she had won in her lifetime, she said she was most proud of the national award given to her by the National Association of Mental Health.

"I do wish you'd mention the NAMH," she told a reporter in 1966. "I do a lot of work with them. I started out going to hospitals and I found I had a rapport with the patients because I knew what they were talking about, and they all knew me from *I Love Lucy*. When I was doing the show I was never conscious that comedy could help people forget their troubles. It was a wonderful thing to be told the show had meant a lot to them."

ON ACTING: "I hate to hear actors talk about themselves," Vance told a reporter in 1965. "Actors can go on and on. If you want the truth, it's all I can do to get my foot out of the mud and go out there and play the part. I don't have any time to think *who* I am or if I'm a tree."

She mentioned that she and Lucille Ball had taught a comedy course in Los Angeles in 1964, and was "astounded at the lack of interest young actors have in comedy. Comedy embarrasses them. It's beneath them. Like one fellow said, 'You want me to *overplay* everything, like you do on TV?' They want to toss the lines away! You can't toss a line away until you can overplay it.

"So we put 'em on their feet. They were all sitting there taking a lot of notes. I told 'em, you can't get through a producer's door taking notes."

Vance says her stage cohorts, including Gertrude Lawrence, Ed Wynn, writer Russel Crouse, and Ethel Merman, were "magnificent teachers. Well, they all became a part of me.

"My hands were a problem. Every actor has the same trouble. Your hands feel like four pounds of nothing. So I watched what Paul Muni did with his hands. He had the most expressive hands in the world. I practiced copying Mr. Muni's hands. Now I could never play *Counselor-at-Law* but at least I learned what to do with my hands."

Vance said producer George Abbott taught her more about comedy than anyone else did. "He once had me do a scene 47 times. Then he finally said, 'Viv, you're being funny in a funny part.' At last I knew what he meant: if the writer has done his job, all you have to do is [play] it. It was a flop show, but think of what I'd learned."

Sam: Mark Harmon starred in this short-lived TV series (it lasted one month in 1978) about a Labrador retriever (Sam) assigned to the Los Angeles Police Department. The final episode, aired April 18, 1978, starred Vivian Vance and George Gobel as a bickering couple whom the canine star tames. Vance and Gobel had previously appeared together in a *Love American Style* segment called "Love and the Medium," which aired December 29, 1969.

Second Banana Supreme: In a cleverly titled salute to second bananas from all areas of show business ("We're No. 2!"), *Entertainment Weekly* listed the top 50 sidekicks in its June 19, 2006 issue. At No. 5 is … you betcha, Vance as Ethel Mertz (the top four, in order: Ed McMahon; Robin, of Batman & Robin; George Costanza (aka Jason Alexander) of *Seinfeld*; and *Star Wars'* Chewbacca). *EW* writes about our beloved "dishwater" blonde: "Without Ethel to bail her out of trouble each week on *I Love Lucy*, original desperate housewife Lucy would have been nothing more than an overbearing harpy. But as cannily played by Vivian Vance, Mrs. Mertz—whose spats with hubby Fred hinted at dysfunction when TV rarely even acknowledged marital discord—was a perfectly exasperated partner in crime: happy to play along, even happier to put the kibosh on her pickle-prone friend's worst impulses."

In 2004, Vance was honored as one of "the best sidekicks ever," on the TV special *TV's Greatest Sidekicks*. That same year she and William Frawley were voted No. 9 on cable network TV Land's Top Ten list of TV's Wacky Neighbors. This kind of recognition almost 60 years after the first broadcast of *I Love Lucy* is further evidence of the iconic status all four major characters on the show have achieved. (See also my book, *The Comic DNA of Lucille Ball: Interpreting the Icon*.)

Stage Career: Vance, who came to New York to carve out a theater career for herself, struggled at first, and supported herself with cabaret gigs. But her persistence paid off, and she had done all right by the mid-1930s. She was in the chorus for her first big musical, *Music in the Air*, but it was a long run. By the time she made the chorus for *Anything Goes*, she was confident and noticeable enough (and had made enough important friends) to graduate to a bit part, and eventually became the understudy for the lead, Ethel Merman. Vance performed the lead in this classic show several times when Merman was out sick.

Vance's theater career can be divided into two "eras." The first would span her Broadway productions, beginning in 1932 and lasting through 1947. This period included several major tours as well. The second era, post-*I Love Lucy*, consisted largely of summer stock and touring productions, with one aborted stop and one short run on Broadway. The Broadway shows are first, followed by the stock productions, which are in general less well-documented, in chronological order.

Music in the Air November 8, 1932, Alvin Theatre, 342 performances.
Vance was in the chorus. (The Alvin Theatre, where Lucille Ball later starred in *Wildcat*, was renamed the Neil Simon Theatre in 1983.)

Anything Goes November 21, 1934, Alvin Theatre, 420 performances.
Vance was in the chorus, had a bit part, and was understudy to Ethel Merman, as Reno Sweeney.

Red, Hot & Blue October 29, 1936, Alvin Theatre, 183 performances.
Vance played Vivian, a reporter. She again understudied star Ethel Merman.

Hooray for What! December 1, 1937, Winter Garden Theatre, 200 performances.
The fact that Vance had performed a lead role on Broadway (even as an understudy) was not lost to the producers of her first real co-starring vehicle several years later, *Hooray for What!* Still it wasn't enough to get Vance her first co-starring role on the Great White Way … at first.

Vance was initially cast in the chorus of the show. Russel Crouse wrote the book for *Hooray for What!* and also penned an article that ran in the *N.Y. Herald Tribune* on December 26, 1937, a few weeks after the play opened to mostly positive reviews. In "An Author's Heart-Rending Tale of a Girl's Fight to Make Good," Crouse described his acquaintance with Vance, writing what he called a Cinderella story.

"A little more than a month ago, Vance was just the third girl from the left in the singing chorus of Ed Wynn's *Hooray for What!* Today she is playing one of the most important parts [in it] at the Winter Garden, with her name in lights, at least three film companies making inquiry as to her plans for the future—and even fan mail!"

Vance assumed the role of Stefania Stevanovich "on seven-hour notice one hectic day in Boston [during tryouts, after actress Kay Thompson had walked out] and after only one somewhat sketchy rehearsal," Crouse noted. Vance's history with Crouse gave him and the other creative forces involved in the show the idea she could handle it. He first noticed her in the chorus of *Anything Goes* (1934). Needing to "throw some lines" to the chorus, Crouse was reluctant because, as he wrote, "… while chorus girls are perhaps the most efficient and hardest working and even most charming element in the theater, they rarely know how to read lines. Give a chorus girl a line, and as often as not she doesn't even know what she has to say—let alone mean it.

"We found out immediately that whenever Miss Vance had anything to say she said it as though she meant it. And so she got four lines in *Anything Goes*." That led to Vance understudying Ethel Merman and actually performing the lead role several times. Nevertheless, when Merman left for Hollywood, Vance was not the choice to take her place. The producers wanted a "name." Crouse intended to reward Vance with a small part in his next show, *Red, Hot and Blue* (1936, also written with Howard Lindsey). The part became, thanks to rewrites, a bit part, literally one word: "Who?"

Still, she understudied for Merman again, and again went on to perform the lead several times, to acclaim. Crouse writes that Vance wasn't initially even considered for the part of Stefania because he and his partner knew that a "name" performer would be cast. He says her response when he finally told her was, "All right, I'll go into the chorus again."

Vivian Vance as she appeared in a newspaper drawing from 1939. Author's collection

She did, working "as hard as any of the principals," Crouse wrote. "Then came her chance to step into a leading role. She took the role that day [in Boston] with the rather heart-rending understanding that she was to play it only until a 'name' could be found. And she proceeded to defend herself against all comers. At almost every performance she played in the remaining weeks of the tryout, there sat out front a star eager to take over the role. Miss Vance knew of the presence of the star.

"And yet her performance on each of these occasions was such that the star went back to New York and Miss Vance continued in the part. New York was only two days away when she learned she had won the part." Vance's response: "I suppose I should cry, but I'm not going to."

Before her first performance in a leading role on Broadway, Crouse went to Vance's dressing room, figuring she'd be nervous, to try and calm her down: "The curtain was about to go up. It was probably the most important moment in her theatrical life. Suddenly she reached over and patted me on the shoulder. 'Now Russel,' she said, 'don't you be nervous.' There, ladies and gentlemen, is a trouper!"

Opening on December 1, 1937, and starring legendary stage comedian Ed Wynn, *Hooray for What!* was a saucy send-up of the spy game, patriotism, fascism, and making a profit from war. Wynn has invented the ultimate weapon and whoever gets it will be able to take over the world. Naturally, every spy in town wants it. That included Vance, who, as Stefania Stevanovich (no subtleties in this show), vamped her way into Wynn's confidence to get the weapon.

Howard Lindsay and Russel Crouse wrote the show's book, with music and lyrics by the legendary team of Harold Arlen and E.Y. (Yip) Harburg. Arlen (1905-'86) also wrote "It's Only a Paper Moon" and many other standards, and with Harburg (1896-1981) collaborated on *The Wizard of Oz*, producing their most famous tune, "Over the Rainbow." The production was "staged and supervised" by Vincente Minnelli (1903-'86), who would become better known for his film directing, including some of MGM's top musicals and the Lucille Ball/Desi Arnaz comedy *The Long, Long Trailer* (1954). Of Minnelli's work on *Hooray for What!*, John Anderson wrote in the *New York Journal American* that, "Mr. Minnelli has given [the show] the dash and taste we have come to expect from [him]. The settings are gay and amusing."

Songs included "Moanin' in the Mornin'," "Down With Love," "God's Country," and "In the Shade of the New Apple Tree." "Down With Love," a flip response to every love song ever written, was one of Vance's songs, and is perhaps the best-remembered tune to come out of the show, having been rediscovered in recent years as a cabaret staple.

Hugh Martin, who appeared in the cast, was a multitalented singer, arranger, and songwriter. He found later success writing for the show *Best Foot Forward* (1941, with partner Ralph Blane) and doing the vocal arrangements for *DuBarry Was a Lady* (1942). Both of the latter were made into films starring Lucille Ball. Martin was also the vocal director on the film *Too Many Girls* (1940), the movie on which Lucy and Desi met. His songs include "Buckle Down Winsocki," "Have Yourself a Merry Little Christmas," and "The Trolley Song," the latter two from the film *Meet Me In St. Louis* (1944, directed by Minnelli and starring his then-wife Judy Garland).

Hooray for What! was greeted with generally positive reviews, and most saw it for what it was: a vehicle for Wynn. Vance's personal reviews were almost always favorable; the first two clips are rare exceptions:

"June Clyde and Vivian Vance sing as well as they can … which is nothing remarkable and cannot compare to the singing of [co-star] Robert Shafer."—Brooks Atkinson, *The New York Times*

"Vivian Vance is the torch lady, hailing, I suspect, from the nightclub circuits. Her voice is a nightclub voice, at any rate. You get used to it after a while. About four in the morning I have an idea it is quite effective."—Burns Mantle, *New York Daily News*

"Miss Vivian Vance, a blues singer of the Ethel Merman school, is handsome and lively as a beautiful international spy."—Richard Watts, *New York Herald Tribune*

"… with Vivian Vance completing the necessary triangle as a beautiful spy who is, perhaps, in love with June Clyde's boyfriend. Miss Vance also has beauty and she did her big number, 'The Night of the Embassy Ball,' with impressive naughtiness."—Sidney Whipple, *New York World-Telegram*

"Some mention, however hasty and inadequate, must be made of … Vivian Vance's colorful performance as Stephanie."—John Mason Brown, *The New York Post*

"Robert Shafer, June Clyde, Vivian Vance, and Roy Roberts attend pleasantly and efficiently to such important matters as the love interest, dramatic suspense, and the Harburg-Arlen tunes."—Robert Coleman, *The Daily Mirror*

"Vivian Vance put over her songs well as the lady spy-menace."—Robert Francis, *The Brooklyn Daily Eagle*

"Vivian Vance plays a Mata Hari with a dialect that is dropped now and then. She duals pleasantly on 'Down with Love' with Roy Roberts."—*Variety*

Kiss the Boys Goodbye 1939

Vance toured through much of 1939, in Chicago; Detroit; Maine, the Erlanger Theater, Buffalo, New York; Saratoga Springs, New York; and more, as Myra Stanhope. This was Vance's first nonmusical role. The play, by Clare Booth (who also wrote *The Women*), was a hit on Broadway and then on tour. Produced by Brock Pemberton, a former critic, it revolved around the search for an actress to play the lead role of "Velvet O'Toole" in what was obviously a parody of *Gone with the Wind* and the real-life search for Scarlett O'Hara, which had happened the previous year in Hollywood. Vance's part, Myra Stanhope, was a fading movie star who grasps at any straw to land the coveted role of Velvet.

Incidentally, the play opened in New York in 1938 featuring Phil Ober (Vance's future husband), and actor and future producer Sheldon Leonard. Roy Roberts, also in the cast of a William Frawley Broadway show (*20th Century*), played Lloyd Lloyd in at least one of the productions of *Kiss the Boys Goodbye*. Lloyd is the scheming director who discovers Cindy Lou, the actress who will play Velvet.

An article in the *Cleveland Press* on May 11, 1939, by Jack Warfel was a playful interview with Vance. Titled "Some Notes on Kissing," he wrote, "… Miss Vivian Vance was approaching her 200th performance in *Kiss the Boys Goodbye*, and estimated that she was thereby due her 1,000th legitimate kiss, at the rate of five per show."

All that clinching meant Vance had to deposit lipsticks "in vases, ashtrays, and books around the stage, repairing her decorations between sessions.

"'I kiss five different men in each show. They're all nice friends. Offstage, we don't even call each other by first names." … 'Of course, that doesn't include rehearsals,' Vance added. 'It was terribly embarrassing at first but now it's just a breeze. I suppose it's because I'm Spanish and by nature I'm affectionate. So they tell me.'"

That fascinating tidbit is a fabrication of course; the question is why Vance felt she had to make up a foreign lineage. In any case, as with most of her stage roles, audiences and critics loved her. Some reviews follow:

"I thought Miss Vance, in particular, was excellent. She's from Broadway's song and dance stage; you probably saw her in *Red, Hot and Blue*."—Ward Morehouse, *The New York Sun*, reviewing the Chicago production

"Vivian Vance, as Myra Stanhope, has a meaty part to which she does full justice. The characterization of the hard-boiled, worldly screen star (who started out as a chambermaid in

Brooklyn) who uses men as stepping-stones in gaining a Hollywood career appears to have been faithfully done. She is as licentious as a barnyard animal and dissembles only to keep a current admirer in line."—Rex J. Ballard, *Davenport* (Iowa) *Times*

"Vivian Vance did nicely with the part of Myra Stanhope, the Hollywood product who was willing to do any favor requested as long as she could be Velvet O'Toole."—G.G., *Des Moines Register*

"Vivian Vance plays the contrasting Hollywood tramp well without making her too much of a heavy."—Charles Gentry, *Detroit Times*

Skylark October 11, 1939, Morosco Theatre, 256 performances.
In this show—written by Samuel (Samson) Raphaelson—Vance played Myrtle Valentine, described in reviews as the "blonde menace" of the show. Gertrude Lawrence played a neglected wife of an advertising executive who attempts to have a fling but ends up back with her husband. The show was basically a star vehicle for Lawrence, who reportedly was very guarded about being upstaged, and did her best to divert attention from Vance's performance.

   Regardless, she couldn't stop Vance from getting some great reviews, like these:

"Vivian Vance serves the hell-cat admirably, standing up to her impulsive star bravely."— Burns Mantle, *The New York Daily News*

"Vivian Vance plays the unpleasant part of a blonde harpy with sleek venom."—Brooks Atkinson, *The New York Times*

"I liked Vivian Vance, a blonde who, not content with marrying a million dollars, covets [the drunken lawyer played by Glenn Anders] for unspeakable purposes of her own."—Wolcott Gibbs, *The New Yorker*

"Vivian Vance, as the flirtatious wife who dominates the firm's big client … is a standout."— Ibee, *Variety*

"In particular, Miss Vivian Vance gives excellent support."—*New York World-Telegram*

Vance also played the part in previews and on tour, including Pittsburgh (September 1939) and the Biltmore Theater in Los Angeles (July 1940). Here are excerpts from two reviews of the Cleveland production:

"Vivian Vance is outstanding as the plotting wench [about whom] Miss Lawrence uses another somewhat and more graphic word to describe [the word was "bitch," apparently too titillating for the paper to publish]. Miss Vance, incidentally, will be remembered for her fine work here last spring in *Kiss the Boys Goodbye*."—Winsor French

"A vivid and acid portrayal of a hussy by Vivian Vance."—William F. McDermott

A short Vance playbill biography published at the time reads:

"Vivian Vance (*Myrtle*) is a native New Mexican. [We know she was actually from Kansas but adopted the more exotic New Mexico as home.] In the course of some Little Theater work in Albuquerque, she so impressed her hometown audience with her dramatic ability that they raised funds to send her to New York for a theatrical career. At first she did chorus work, played a bit in *Music in the Air*, and did a single act in smart night clubs, including Mon Paree, House of Lords, the Biltmore Roof, and the Club Simplon.

"Later she understudied Ethel Merman in *Red, Hot and Blue* and *Anything Goes*, playing the Merman role on the road. She was then featured with Ed Wynn in the Broadway production of *Hooray for What!* after which she joined *Kiss the Boys Goodbye*, in which she made the long trek to the Pacific Coast and back [on tour]."

♥ **Lucy Trivia** *Skylark* was playing in New York at the same time Desi Arnaz made his stage debut in *Too Many Girls*.

Out From Under May 4, 1940, Biltmore Theater, 9 performances.

Vance played Clair James. An item in a New York theater column on May 6, 1940, noted, "Vivian Vance is the little Albuquerque bombshell who just concluded a long engagement in support of Gertrude Lawrence in *Skylark*. This is her second appearance in a [Brock] Pemberton production, the first having been as Myra Stanhope in *Kiss the Boys Goodbye*."

Let's Face It October 29, 1941, Imperial Theater, 547 performances.

Eve Arden, Edith Meiser, and Vivian Vance in the WWII musical Broadway hit, *Let's Face It*. **Photofest**

Vance was Nancy Collister. This wartime musical comedy was Vance's biggest Broadway hit. It has a number of connections to *I Love Lucy* besides Vance. Vance, <u>Eve Arden</u>, and Edith Meiser played wives who missed their husbands and contemplated having affairs. In Vance's biography, she is quoted as saying that all the other actors stole bits from her and were extremely competitive. Arden later starred in Desilu's *Our Miss Brooks*, had a cameo on *I Love Lucy*, and starred in Desi Arnaz's sitcom *The Mothers-in-Law* (1967); Meiser played Mrs. Littlefield, wife of the Tropicana nightclub owner (played by <u>Gale Gordon</u>) on *I Love Lucy*. Danny Kaye, the male star of *Let's Face It*, would later guest on *The Lucy Show* and have Ball guest-star on his own variety hour.

Voice of the Turtle, 1945
In 1945, Vance played Olive Lashbrooke in the touring production at Chicago's Selwyn Theater; she repeated the role in San Francisco in March 1946, and in La Jolla, California, in

1951, among other venues. John Van Druten wrote this play about a soldier and his romantic entanglements. He also wrote *Bell, Book and Candle* and *I Am a Camera*, the basis for *Cabaret*.

The three-character play opened on Broadway in 1943 (starring Margaret Sullavan) and ran for 1,557 performances (four years), becoming one of the longest-running nonmusicals in Broadway history. Its success was due largely to its wartime-era plot, a time during which audiences were delighted to see romantic entertainment that reminded them what the country was fighting for. In its day, the subject of premarital sex was an explosive one.

These days, the play might seem outdated, slow moving, and stiff, but with the right players *Turtle* exuded charm and laughs, things that were in short supply when it debuted. It is set during a weekend in April in a small Manhattan apartment in the East Sixties, near Third Avenue, during World War II. (Vance would "return" to that neighborhood as a landlord in *I Love Lucy*.)

A young actress, Sally Middleton, has been burned by love and sworn off both sex and romance, deciding to concentrate on her career. Olive Lashbrooke, Sally's older, more libertine (i.e., she sleeps around) friend drops her current beau, Sgt. Bill Page, for a higher-ranking officer, leaving Bill in Sally's care. Left to spend a weekend together, Bill and Sally develop feelings for each other, and Sally must choose between giving into love or remaining cool and detached.

The bite in this romantic comedy is largely thanks to the character of Olive, a sarcastic "other woman" role. This was a part perfect for Vance's trademark sarcastic delivery, and she played it many times.

It was during a performance of this role in Chicago that Vance suffered a nervous breakdown and had to quit show business after finishing the engagement. She took on the role in a touring production after returning from entertaining U.S. troops in Europe in the play *Over 21*. Seeing wartime horrors close-up was a harrowing experience for her.

She was inactive professionally for several years; psychiatric treatment helped her overcome her varied fears during four months of intense therapy. It was her friend, actor Mel Ferrer, who persuaded Vance to come and play the role of Olive again at his playhouse in La Jolla, California, in the summer of 1951. Ferrer also cast her in a small role in his movie *The Secret Fury* (1950).

Gregory Peck, Dorothy McGuire, and Ferrer founded the La Jolla Playhouse in 1947. (It's currently a not-for-profit, professional theater in residence on the campus of the University of California, San Diego.) It was there that future *I Love Lucy* director Marc Daniels took Desi

<u>Arnaz</u> and Jess <u>Oppenheimer</u> for a look at Vance, after which they decided she'd be perfect for the part of Ethel Mertz.

Vance's biography in the showbill for *Turtle* revealed a modesty not usually associated with performers. After listing her Broadway successes, Vance is quoted as saying, "I was a very lucky actress, for all these plays were hits. I didn't have anything to do with that, of course, but it was fine to be able to sing and dance one year and do a legit play the next." It's difficult to imagine any performer these days being so self-effacing.

Voice of the Turtle was made into a movie in 1947 starring future President Ronald Reagan and Eleanor Parker, with Eve Arden in the Olive Lashbrooke role.

It Takes Two February 3, 1947, Biltmore Theater, 8 performances.
Vance played Bee Clark. Directed and produced by George Abbott, the cast also included Martha Scott; character actress Reta Shaw (who made a trio of *Here's Lucy* appearances, in 1968, 1972, and 1973); Hugh Marlowe (best remembered as Lloyd Richards in *All About Eve*, 1950); and John Forsythe, an underrated movie star who conquered TV (*Bachelor Father*, 1957-'62, and *Dynasty*, 1981-'89).

The Cradle Will Rock December 26, 1947, Mansfield and Broadway Theatres, 34 performances. The show played half its run at the Mansfield Theatre and moved to the Broadway Theatre on January 28, 1948.

Vance played Mrs. Mister in the revival of this politically charged show. The action happens in a place called Steeltown on the eve of a union meeting. Book, music, and lyrics were by Marc Blitzstein, and Howard Da Silva directed. Da Silva (who played Jud in the original 1943 stage production of *Oklahoma*) was blacklisted in the late 1940s after being "outed" as a communist sympathizer by actor Robert Taylor. His career was effectively ended for more than decade. He is perhaps best known for a role later in his career, as Benjamin Franklin in *1776* (1972). Others in the cast included Jesse White (who guest-starred on *Here's Lucy* in 1972), Will Geer (who later played Grandpa on *The Waltons*), Alfred Drake, the musical comedy star, and Leonard Bernstein, who conducted and played a clerk in the first three performances.

In the program for the production, there's an interesting credit: "Miss Vance's hat by Harold Green." Drake gets star billing, but Vance is next in the cast list.

Her biography notes, "Albuquerque behind her, in her New York initiation had Vinton Freedley's *Anything Goes* for a professional frame, and received a vote of confidence from that producer with an assignment in his *Red, Hot and Blue*. Following a musical fling in Ed Wynn's *Hooray for What!* she again caroled under the Freedley banner in *Let's Face It*. Her first dramatic role was in the Chicago company of Clare Booth's *Kiss the Boys Goodbye*, and New York first saw her in nonmusical emotions with Gertrude Lawrence in *Skylark*. Last season she was in *It Takes Two*, this on the heels of a long engagement in the Chicago variation of *The Voice of the Turtle*."

Don't Drink the Water, 1966

Vance played Marion Hollander. Produced by the legendary David Merrick, and written by standup comedian Woody Allen, this Iron Curtain farce was dated even for its day.

Nearly 20 years after her previous Broadway appearance, Vance finally headed back to the Great White Way. At first she exuded genuine excitement: "When I first came back [East] to stay, [legendary producer] David Merrick asked me when 1 was going to do a show. I wasn't ready then. I just wanted to have a good time for a while. Of course, I did [some TV] panel shows…. Merrick asked me to go into one of the *Hello, Dolly* companies, but I wasn't really ready until he offered me this play," she told the *Ada* (Oklahoma) *Evening News* in September 1966.

"It's a very funny play about a Newark caterer (Lou Jacobi) and his wife (me) and what happens to them when they visit an Iron Curtain country. I'm happy to be working with David Merrick because I feel secure with him."

Unfortunately, Vance chose to bail out of the show, reportedly due to the bullying behavior of co-star Jacobi (it's been reported Jacobi was nervous taking on his first starring role on Broadway). By then, Vance had opened the show at Philadelphia's Walnut Street Theater, and the critics liked her, but the show got mediocre reviews.

A Boston *Playbill* from the Colonial Theatre dated October 17, 1966, shows Vance on the cover at the center surrounded by Jacobi, Tony Roberts, and ingénue Lee Lawson. Vance has top billing inside; her name is top left above the title, and Jacobi's is on the right. Her bio quotes her as saying, "I'm back to my first love, the theater, after 14 years of happy association with Lucille Ball." It also notes Vance is "getting ready for her next [career], singing. 'I have wanted to sing more than anything else, so I'm studying singing.'" The latter is an interesting comment, considering that Vance had been singing professionally since the early 1930s.

By the time of the Broadway premiere, November 17, 1966, Kay Medford had replaced Vance; Medford is best known for playing Barbra Streisand's mother in the film *Funny Girl* (1968). The better-known Anita Gillette had replaced Lawson; Lawson subsequently played

Vance's daughter in the 1969 Broadway show *My Daughter, Your Son*; see below. Interestingly, the *Playbill* cover featured a drawing of the cast, also used as a poster, showing caricatures of the cast along the top, with Vance, not Medford, clearly pictured next to Jacobi. The billing of course was different now; Jacobi's name had the coveted top left above-the-title position, with Roberts' name next to his, and Medford's name centered beneath the two.

Perhaps the "billing wars" also contributed to the problems that made it intolerable for Vance to continue in the role. *Don't Drink the Water* was made into a forgettable movie with Jackie Gleason and Estelle Parsons in 1969, and an equally forgettable television movie, starring author Woody Allen and Julie Kavner in 1994.

In Eric Lax's 2000 biography of Woody Allen, there's another hint as to why Vance was, perhaps, not working out. Lax reports that Lou Jacobi was "the only person" Allen saw playing the father in the show. Producer David Merrick wanted "a more commercial, less pronouncedly ethnic actor." Allen won that battle, but then Merrick "… cabled him that he wanted Vivian Vance (of *I Love Lucy* fame) for the female lead, even though Woody had written the part 'with a more Jewish character in mind.' Merrick was adamant that she would play comedy perfectly and have great marquee value. Woody finally agreed, although he later said it was a mistake, not because there was anything wrong with Vivian Vance as an actress, 'just that she was the wrong person for the character. It was a crass attempt at commercialism rather than correct casting. It would have been just as wrong to cast Kim Stanley. David was trying too hard to Anglicize it.'"

Vance ultimately offered a different reason for leaving the show. One of the reasons she originally retired from *The Lucy Show* was that she wanted more of a home life. She subsequently returned to the theater after *The Lucy Show* and found that plays were more limiting, in terms of time off for home life, than television. "I've discovered that I wouldn't like playing Broadway [anymore]," she said. "I was in Philadelphia with *Don't Drink the Water* and we were headed for Broadway when I decided the part wasn't right for me. Producer David Merrick was wonderful in giving me my release. Working seven days a week with no time off is too much. Television isn't nearly so confining," she told the Long Beach, California *Independent* on January 9, 1967.

My Daughter, Your Son, May 13, 1969, Booth Theatre, 47 performances.
Vance played Maggie Gordon in this situation comedy of a play, and it was the only one of her sturdy touring vehicles in which she had created her role on Broadway. It was written by Phoebe and Henry Ephron and directed by Larry Arrick. Her fellow cast members on

Broadway included Robert Alda, Dody Goodman, Bill McCutcheon, Lee Lawson (see *Don't Drink the Water*), and juvenile Don Scardino, who went on to star in a number of soap operas and films. Scardino is now a TV director.

In a *New York Times* ad for the show that appeared after its opening (May 22, 1969), Vance wrote a "memo" to "Every Person Who Has Ever Laughed" and included snippets from the various reviews of the show:

"We finally saw a play about young people who are not hippies and it has many big, fat laughs. It has all the ingredients for lively entertainment. Vivian Vance, for example, after so many years on TV as Lucille Ball's sidekick, returns to Broadway with full exposure focused on her sparkling comedic talents, and she's a pleasure. Miss Vance handles her part in a breezy style, with double takes and an easy wit. Welcome back, lady, and do stay around."—Ethel Colby, *Journal of Commerce*

"All those gags produce a lot of laughs, and all those laughs produce a very nice play to see. You expect Vivian Vance to be wonderful, and she is. If you really feel like laughing, and want to enjoy several hundred laughs, buy a couple of tickets."—John Tucker, ABC-TV

"Vivian Vance is the major asset. This is an audience show, and should be a bonanza. Miss Vance makes familiar situations seem fresh with her perfect timing, her complete naturalness, her warmth, and her charm. She is aided greatly by Robert Alda as her loving and ingratiating husband."—George Oppenheimer, *Newsday*

"Playgoers are likely to collapse with laughter."—Hobe Morrison, *Variety*

"The jokes are swift, and come piling out one right on top of the other. Vivian Vance is completely fetching."—Leo Mishkin, *Morning Telegraph*

"The comedy is consistently funny. What makes it work is the ingenious timing techniques and character gimmicks of those two unique ladies, Vivian Vance and Dody Goodman."—Ted Hoffman, WINS radio

"Vivian Vance is split-second perfect. It is all delightfully engaging. If you want to rest your brain, and briefly escape from care, this comedy should do nicely."—William Glover, Associated Press

Vance's biography in the *Playbill* from the show is also worth a look:

"Vivian Vance (*Maggie Gordon*), after several successful years on the Broadway stage in musicals and straight plays, first received national recognition during her long association with Lucille Ball in both *I Love Lucy* and *The Lucy Show*. For her work in the latter she was the recipient of an Emmy Award. [Actually, it was for her work in the former.] Since leaving *The Lucy Show*, she has had many successful stock engagements, including appearances in *Here Today*, *Barefoot in the Park*, *Time of the Cuckoo*, and in John Patrick's new play, *Everybody's Girl*, which he wrote for Miss Vance and in which she appeared around the country for three years, including engagements in Palm Beach, Ogunquit and Westport, to name a few.

"Miss Vance's busy schedule does not preclude her important volunteer work with mental health societies and hospitals. Of the many awards she has received, she is most gratified by the National Award bestowed upon her by the National Association of Mental Health. In private life she is Mrs. John Dodds, who is the executive editor of Holt, Rinehart and Winston. She is a member of the Board of Directors of the Museum of the State of New Mexico, and is also an active supporter of the Santa Fe Opera. They live in New York and have homes in Santa Fe, New Mexico, and North Salem, New York."

Vance's stock and touring productions include the following:

Burlesque with Gypsy Rose Lee, Saratoga New York, summer 1939. Vance played Gypsy Rose Lee's best friend in this backstage look at the world of burlesque.

Springtime for Henry Spring 1941, San Francisco, Alcazar Theater, several months. Julia Jelliwell. Co-starring Marjorie Lord, later of TV's *Make Room for Daddy*, this play was a vehicle for comedy star Edward Everett Horton. According to a newspaper article at the time, the cast was headed for Los Angeles after this run to produce *George Washington Slept Here*, and was "planning a third production for use on the rural stages." Vance also appeared in this show during the summer of 1939 at Saratoga, New York.

Counselor-at-Law Vance co-starred with Paul Muni in Marblehead, Massachusetts. She played in this show for one month in the summer of 1947.

Over 21 At the El Teatro in Albuquerque, New Mexico, mid-August 1951, with husband Phil Ober. This is the same play in which the pair had toured Africa and Italy, entertaining the troops during World War II. It was the first stage production to tour a combat zone in WWII. She later toured with it in Chicago in December 1961 and February 1962, at the Drury Lane Theater, and in 1965. Of the second Chicago production, one critic noted, the "charming" Vance "… has shed her Ethel [Mertz] identity, and is a vivacious and lovely comedienne."

The play was written by actress Ruth Gordon, and concerned a newspaper editor past 40-years-old who is drafted into the army at the end of WWII, and his difficulties training to become an officer. Meanwhile, his wife takes over writing his editorials, but doesn't tell anyone. Its mix of army humor and changing gender roles made it a perfect vehicle to perform for the troops.

Over 21 premiered on Broadway in January of 1944, and was a modest hit with the female lead played by Gordon herself (she later played the role on TV in a December 1950 production for the *Prudential Family Playhouse*). Irene Dunne and Alexander Knox starred in the 1945 movie.

The Marriage-Go-Round Late 1950s through the early 1970s, at the Royal Poinciana Playhouse, Palm Beach, Florida; the Cherry County Playhouse; the Sombrero Theater in Phoenix (1960); and Traverse City, Michigan (August 1971); among other venues. Vance toured steadily in this sex farce, and one of the places it took her was Nassau, in the Bahamas, for the week of February 21-26, 1961. According to reviewer Jack Gordon on February 22, 1961, in the *Nassau Guardian*, "… Despite Miss Vance's vivacious sparkle and very adroit comedy style, I thought the soufflé was somewhat soggy last night. I must add that most of the rest of the audience didn't. They chuckled and chortled very cheerfully. She is a warm and wonderfully amusing woman.

"Vance, of all things, is most convincing in the tender and touching love scenes with her husband (played by John Baragrey) in which her wonderful smile and depth of feeling warm up the entire audience…. I believe she has tremendous dramatic abilities which have not been given a fair showing."

Here Today Vance played Mary Hilliard in this comedy, along with John Emery in May 1960 at Chicago's Drury Lane Theater and the Fayetteville (New York) Country Theater in July 1960, among other venues. She co-starred with Emery in another show, *There Goes the Bride*, that same year.

There Goes The Bride opened August 29, 1960, at Guy Palmerton's Lake Whalom Playhouse in Whalom, a northwest suburb of Boston, starring Vance, Phillip Terry and John Emery. A review in the *Fitchburg* (Massachusetts) *Sentinel* on August 30, 1960, called the show a "light and airy play" and noted, "This Vivian Vance has little resemblance to the character of Ethel Mertz she made indispensable on the *I Love Lucy* television show, with Lucille Ball and Desi Arnaz. She is younger, more attractive, and in this play, rather than being the follower to Lucy's wild schemes, *she* is the plotter.

The reviewer noted, "It was a good play for a hot summer night [that] wouldn't take any prizes for dramatic writing, but it was highly entertaining. Due to no fault of her own, Miss Vance's lines for the most part were flat, but she seemed to be [playing] straight man to John Emery, leading him into fast and funny comebacks. The audience was politely amused at the plot, which centered around a Boston matron and her daughter vacationing in Nassau." Vance and Emery played a conniving couple trying to break off the daughter's engagement.

"John Emery, with his long legs, dissipated countenance and beatnik beard has the prize lines of the play and he is in a constant state of wretched hangovers," the reviewer continued. "The three stars, Vance, Emery and Terry, all have long and credited dramatic careers on stage, in movies, and on television, but it was fun to see them in person give relaxed performances in a silly play."

Doing publicity for the play, the *Sentinel* published an interview that noted Vance was nothing like Ethel Mertz, which must have cheered her: "Vivian is vivacious and chatters like a magpie. She has much more sparkle than her television character and is taller, younger and slimmer than she appeared on TV."

Regarding the play, the paper noted, "She did insist [on doing] a good, fast, funny and clean play ... then the best supporting cast she could find. She feels one is only as good as the other, and no name-star can carry [an otherwise weak] production. She has the greatest admiration for John Emery and Philip Terry, her co-stars, as well as each member of her cast—all handpicked. She is proud to have taken this show all over the Midwest, New York State, and New Hampshire, and played to capacity audiences."

Barefoot in the Park Mid-1960s, as Ethel Banks, the "mother" role in this Neil Simon comedy about two newlyweds struggling to make it in a New York walk-up apartment. Vance's character gets most of the big laughs.

Time of the Cuckoo at the Ogunquit (Maine) Playhouse, August 1966; and the Corning (New York) Summer Theater, 1966; among other venues. *The Wellsboro* (Pa.) *Gazette* reported on July 21, 1966, that, "The first of four well-known and talented stars will be at the Corning Summer Theater this week. Miss Vivian Vance, long familiar as Lucille Ball's sidekick on television, will appear in *The Time of the Cuckoo* from Tuesday, July 19, through Sunday, July 24.... Now that the *Lucy* show is over [Vance left the show 1965], Miss Vance has returned to the theater. Her most recent engagements were in *The Marriage-Go-Round* and *Barefoot in the Park*, which broke box office records at the Cocoanut Grove Playhouse in Florida."

The article cited Vance's work within the mental health industry as her most "compelling interest" offstage. Also appearing in *Cuckoo* with her were William Roerick and future Oscar winner (for *Moonstruck*) Olympia Dukakis. Vance played the lead character, Leona Samish, a middle-aged woman who has an affair with a married man in Venice. The play originally starred Shirley Booth on Broadway, and Katharine Hepburn in the 1954 movie (which was called *Summertime*).

Everybody's Girl This play was written for Vance by author John Patrick. Born in 1905, Patrick wrote more than 30 plays, co-authored 19 films, adapted nine books and plays for the motion picture screen, and several works for television. Of his plays, the best known are *The Hasty Heart*, *The Teahouse of the August Moon*, and *Everybody Loves Opal*. *Teahouse*, adapted from Vern Sneider's novel, earned Patrick a Pulitzer Prize in 1954, and the Tony Award for Best Play.

Vance played *Girl's* title character, Beatrice Bundie, in Albuquerque, New Mexico, 1965-'66; at the Cherry County Playhouse, Traverse City, Michigan, July 4-9, 1967; the Royal Poinciana Playhouse, Palm Beach, Florida, January 29-February 3, 1968; and the Playhouse in the Mall, Paramus, New Jersey, October 8-20, 1968, among others.

A press release from the Cherry County Playhouse dated June 27, 1967, notes that Vance is "Starring in the first professional production of John Patrick's new comedy," and is making her third appearance at the Playhouse, having previously played there in *The Marriage-Go-Round* and *Over 21* in 1965.

Everybody's Girl deals with a likeable New England woman, Beatrice Bundie, promoted as "Mother of the Year" by an enterprising reporter. Bundie's five sons, prisoners of war, are released by the Viet Cong as a result, but complications result when it's revealed her Navy boys, patriotically named Washington, Jefferson, Jackson, Lincoln, and Grant Bundie, each had different fathers and that Beatrice never married. The President and Congress, having bestowed the title on Bundie, are wrathful until the final scene, in which it's revealed that the boys were all adopted.

A preview article about the Paramus production from October 1968 reported that Vance "last appeared at the Playhouse in the Mall a few years ago in *Marriage-Go-Round*. Her every performance was a sell-out." It went on to note that *Everybody's Girl* received "enthusiastic reviews by New England critics, where it was performed at several of the well-known summer theaters."

Though Vance's personal reviews, as always, were good, reviewers weren't quite so kind to the show itself. The *Newark Evening News'* Gunter David wrote of the Paramus production in October 9, 1968, "It is hard to believe a playwright of the stature of John Patrick is responsible for *Everybody's Girl*. The program describes itself as a 'new comedy,' which is one of the overstatements of the year. The play has been touring for some time, but has not been seen on Broadway, nor is it likely to.

"Vivian Vance, of television fame, a highly capable comedienne, deserves a better fate than stomping the provinces in this kind of vehicle. For [it] is a feeble attempt at a sermon on brotherhood, in the form of the flimsiest and most improbable of plots and witless humor. Except for a hilarious scene in which the mother films a commercial for a cigarette, the humor of the lines is on par with the plot."

Variety was slightly kinder. A review after the Poinciana Playhouse performance dated January 30, 1968, said, "John Patrick … has written a passable stock vehicle in *Everybody's Girl*, a comedy about a sort of Auntie Mame character. With Vivian Vance in the title role, it's okay for Frank Hale's spiffy Royal Poinciana Playhouse in Palm Beach and should satisfy in other such stands, but probably won't do for Broadway or regular tour bookings. The author staged the show here, but left immediately after the opening. Miss Vance scores as the star and the other performances are good enough."

Vance laughed all the way to the bank.

Butterflies Are Free Cape Cod, 1973; Pocono Playhouse, August 27-September 1, 1973; others. Vance played Mrs. Baker. A press release from the Pocono Playhouse (located in

Mountainhome, Pennsylvania) dated August 18 noted that the week of the play "was bound to be an 'I Love Vivian' week." Vance "last kept Playhouse patrons in stitches in the Silver Anniversary season [1971] in *My Daughter, Your Son* with Dody Goodman. She comes to the Poconos this summer from a tour of major summer theaters."

Vance played the overprotective mother (with a devastating wit) who tries to keep all young women away from her blind son. Gary Tomlin, who played the role of Vance's son in this production (and in the Pocono production of *My Daughter, Your Son*), was then appearing in the soap opera *Search for Tomorrow*, and later became a director, writer, and producer of soaps.

Eileen Heckart, Vance's friend and favorite actress, created this role on Broadway, and won a Best Supporting Actress Oscar for the 1972 movie.

Arsenic and Old Lace Florida, 1973. In this macabre farce, Vance played one of the Brewster sisters, a seemingly harmless pair of maiden aunts who in reality took in lonely older men, poisoned them, and had their mad brother bury them in the cellar.

Everybody Loves Opal, 1974. The tour included a stop at the Cherry County Playhouse in Traverse City, Michigan, August 20-25, 1974. *Opal* is a stock and regional staple played by many actresses of a certain type and age. Eileen Heckart—see Vance's bio—created the role on Broadway.

Several interesting items are mentioned in the playbill for the Michigan production. It notes, "This past winter [Vance] performed *Opal* in dinner theaters in Florida and New England, and completed work on her soon-to-be-published book, *Viv*."

That book was never published but apparently was retitled many times. See <u>Autobiography</u> for more details. Of greater interest, the bio states that Vance "is currently planning for a nationally syndicated talk show, and a production of *Fallen Angel* in which she will co-star with Lucille Ball at the Kennedy Center."

Unfortunately, neither of those projects ever materialized.

WEIGHTY ISSUES: Vivian Vance was apparently *not* required by contract to remain overweight so she would appear "frumpier" than Lucille Ball in *I Love Lucy*. When Ball was feted on an episode of Dinah Shore's syndicated talk show *Dinah!* in 1975, Vance surprised her friend with a visit, bringing along a "contract" that she read aloud to the audience.

Some sources have reported that Vance was reading aloud from her *I Love Lucy* contract, but a recent viewing of the episode reveals Vance stating the contract is "gag gift" penned by

Ball and presented to Vance in the 1950s. In it, Vance is admonished to never color her hair "within five shades in either direction" of Ball's, and to "gain five pounds a month for the duration of the show." And *that* is how rumors get started. Vance was made to look frumpier via makeup, lighting, and being costumed with undergarments and dresses that were too small.

Still, Ethel was shown to be an avid eater throughout the run of the show. There were times, due to endless takes, that Vance had to eat even more than she bargained for. One such event occurred during the 1957 season and was reported in the papers.

Vance, who, it was said, "was known to lose her appetite at the drop of a filet mignon," was shooting a scene that required her to taste some sandwiches Lucy Ricardo had made. "A 'taste,' according to the director's timing, meant enough bites to demolish a sandwich. The cameras were still rolling after Ethel had 'tasted' several sandwiches. 'Cut,' said director Jimmy Kern, 'let's try it again. Hand Ethel two more sandwiches.'

"Filming again, Ethel downed two more sandwiches. 'Hold it,' said Kern again. 'That's not quite right. Give Ethel a couple more of Lucy's tasty morsels.' (By this time, they weren't so tasty.) Four more sandwiches and four hundred feet of film later, the scene was right. 'Save the take on that one,' said Kern. 'Come on Ethel, I'll take you to dinner.'

"Ethel, who by that time had had more sandwiches than she knew what to do with, knew what to do with the one she had in her hand—but Kern ducked."

Vance did not always worry about her weight. Flush from her first Broadway co-starring role in 1938, a spy in *Hooray for What!*, L.L. Stevenson wrote, in his "Lights of New York" column dated March 9, "Having her name up in lights on Broadway—and thus seeing her dream come true—seemingly hasn't changed Albuquerque's Miss Jones in the slightest. Her favorite meal is still meat, mashed potatoes, gravy, pie, and coffee. Also she likes to cook and turns out a mean fried chicken.... There is this difference, however: When she left Albuquerque, she weighed 154 pounds. Now she weighs 120. And despite her favorite meals and love of cooking, has no trouble remaining at that weight."

WE HARDLY KNEW YE: A short article with this headline appeared in the *Charleston* (West Virginia) *Daily Mail* on March 7, 1954. It reported, "Vivian Vance set out to buy a new dress that she could wear on her Philip Morris *I Love Lucy* show. In talking with the salesgirl she explained its color would be important, since she wanted it for TV. Vivian made her selection and as she walked away with her purchase under her arm, the salesgirl called out cheerfully, 'Hope you get the job.'"

VAUDEVILLE

Lucille Ball and Desi Arnaz hit the stage together to convince CBS executives that audiences would accept them working together on *I Love Lucy*. They performed in the early 1940s at the Loew's State Theatre in New York, for example. A newspaper review notes the "two screen players, husband and wife in private, are heading the new State vaudeville presentation.

"Miss Ball and Mr. Arnaz have created an act made up of singing, dancing, and amusing dialogue, and their presentation of it is entertaining. They sing 'South American Way,' 'You and I,' and 'Cuban Pete'; they dance the rumba and conga; and Arnaz beats the conga drum and sings 'Babalu.'"

THE VICTOR BORGE COMEDY THEATER

The networks didn't pick up this <u>Desilu</u> pilot for the fall 1962 season. Borge hosted three sketches, one called "Flying L.A. to Paris," which featured Lucille Ball and Gale Gordon, was produced by Elliott Lewis, directed by Desi Arnaz, and written by *Lucy* scribes Bob Carroll Jr. and Madelyn Pugh Davis. Gordon was a stuffy executive and Ball played a passenger who feared flying. The bit was recycled for *The Lucy Show* by writer Bob O'Brien in the episode "Lucy Goes to London" (October 17, 1966); Carroll and Davis got story credit.

Also of interest: the first segment of the Borge pilot was called "Suzuki Beane" and featured Jimmy Garrett (soon to be cast as Ball's son in *The Lucy Show*) as a rich kid who befriends a downtown New York girl with Beatnik parents. The idea was to portray the culture clash between the two families.

Garrett was cast in *The Lucy Show* in the summer of 1962, and remembers doing this pilot a few months earlier; other sources speculate it may have been filmed in February or March of 1962. In any case, it shows that Arnaz was still professionally involved with his ex-wife, directing her more than a year after their divorce.

VIEW-MASTER

Ball appeared on a View-Master set in 1971, called "Lucy and the Astronauts," based on a *Here's Lucy* episode.

VINCENT, DIANE

Vincent is, as she told me, "honored to be officially licensed and authorized by CBS Worldwide and Desilu too llc to portray 'Lucy Ricardo' at Universal Studios Hollywood and throughout the world." Indeed, in 2000 Mayor Sam Teresi proclaimed her the "Official Lucille Ball Impressionist" for Jamestown, New York, a title she proudly continues to enjoy at the annual Lucy-Desi Days Festivals held by the Lucy-Desi Center. A seasoned actress with many credits on her résumé, Vincent goes beyond what is required of her when treating fans to a taste of Ball. I had the opportunity to befriend her during past festivals, and I can say without question her heart, talent, (and sense of humor) are all in the right place. "I don't become Lucy until I've got my Max Factor lipstick on," cracks Vincent, in the spirit of you-know-who. Like Lucy Ricardo, Vincent always "has to be in a show," she notes, and thus maintains a busy stage career. She's "had the privilege of sharing her musical theater talents" with, among others, Carol Burnett, Kaye Ballard, Tony Danza, Rachel York, Nanette Fabray, Adrienne Barbeau, Ken Berry, John Schneider, and Stefanie Powers. Vincent resides in Los Angeles with her "wonderfully supportive and talented husband," Sam Kriger. Her favorite *I Love Lucy* episodes are "L.A. at Last!" and "The Operetta." Look for her in Jamestown during Memorial Day and the Lucy's Birthday celebrations in August. See also Medina, Rhonda.

VITAMEATAVEGAMIN

"Health tonic" Lucy Ricardo sells (or tries to) during a commercial on one of Ricky's TV shows. Having wrangled her way into the role, Lucy is not aware that the tonic has a large percentage of alcohol in it, and gets steadily sloshed as she rehearses take after take for the director. This classic bit, perhaps the most famous of all Ball's work, is a primer in comic acting, use of props, facial expressions, and timing. Try to not laugh.

VIVIAN VANCE CREATIONS

There was a line of toiletries for women called Vivian Vance Creations from Preferred Toiletries of New York. Advertised in magazines from the early 1930s on, this collection had nothing to do with Vivian Vance, the actress.

VIVIAN VANCE IS ALIVE AND WELL AND RUNNING A CHINESE TAKE-OUT

Off-off-Broadway play from several years back written by John Wuchte illustrating the continued influence in the entertainment media of *I Love Lucy*, its lead players, and major characters. The plot details the lives of people who work in a Chinese take-out restaurant, and how their lives are influenced, affected, and defined by TV icons such as Ethel Mertz. For an interview with Wuchte, see my book, *Lucy in Print*.

VOICE OF THE TURTLE

Seminal play in the career of Vivian Vance. See <u>Stage Career</u> under <u>Vance, Vivian</u>.

W

WAAAAAAAAAAAAAAAHHHHHHHHHHHHHH!!!!!

Trademark Lucy Ricardo cry when things didn't go her way on *I Love Lucy*. Ball pulled the sob routine on *The Lucy Show*, as Lucy Carmichael, and *Here's Lucy*, as Lucy Carter, but it became less lovable as her characters matured.

WALLEY, DEBORAH

Pert, perky teen star of the 1960s who appeared as Gidget in the first sequel to that popular film and in a dozen more movies of that decade, many with the word "bikini" in the title, including the genre classic *Beach Blanket Bingo*. Deborah ended the decade with two seasons in the Desi Arnaz-produced sitcom *The Mothers-in-Law*, playing the daughter of Eve Arden and Herb Rudley. She continued in the business later in life as an actress, writer, and producer/director, founding two theater companies and working with underprivileged children. She died in May 2001 of cancer at 58.

WAYNE, JOHN

Wayne dominated the western/action film genres for four decades, starring in more movies than any other leading man. He was a friend of Lucille Ball's and appeared with her a handful of times on television, most notably in *I Love Lucy*, as the focus of a two-part Hollywood episode in which Lucy and Ethel steal Wayne's cement footprints from the front of Grauman's Chinese Theatre.

Wayne played himself in the second part (airing October 10, 1955) and was a great sport, showing he could handle comedy as well as drama. His massage scene with Lucy is a classic: Lucy gets trapped in his dressing room and he thinks she is his masseuse, so she plays along.

Wayne also guest-starred on *The Lucy Show*, on November 21, 1966, appropriately called "Lucy and John Wayne," in which Lucy Carmichael, trying to help Wayne during the filming of a movie scene, only makes things worse. When Wayne hosted a special praising the good things about America, *Swing Out, Sweet Land* (1970), Ball came aboard, playing it straight as, no kidding, the Statue of Liberty. And when CBS saluted Lucy for her 25 years in television (*CBS Salutes Lucy: The First 25 Years*, 1976), Wayne hosted one of the segments.

Wayne died of cancer in 1979.

WEISKOPF, BOB

One of the "two Bobs" who wrote steadily for Lucille Ball on television, beginning with *I Love Lucy*. See Schiller, Bob and Bob Weiskopf.

WESTINGHOUSE DESILU PLAYHOUSE

See Desilu Playhouse.

WHAT ABOUT THE '61 CHEVY'S?

A promotional film starring William Frawley as "Fred" (hmmm, wonder what association they were trying for?), a man trying to get information on the new Chevrolets for 1961. He enlists the aide of a detective agency. Also featured was Barbara Perry, who made an appearance on *The Lucy Show* in 1962.

WHAT ACTORS EAT WHEN THEY EAT

Book published in 1939 by Kenneth Harlan and Rex Lease featuring the recipes of hundreds of stars, along with their pictures and a short biography. Ball's bio notes she was born in Butte, Montana, and her recipes are for "Chicken Sauté Sec with Mushrooms and Artichokes" and "Brazil Nut Stuffing."

WHITE, BETTY

A durable, popular television and movie actor, her 1957 sitcom *Date with the Angels* was filmed at Desilu, and the *I Love Lucy* influence is clear.

White has been on the air for more than half a century in various roles, including her most famous: Sue Ann Nivens on *The Mary Tyler Moore* show (1973-'77) and Rose Nylund on *The Golden Girls* (1985-'92). She was married to *Password* host Allen Ludden from 1963 to his death in 1981. A multiple Emmy winner, White was inducted into the Television Hall of Fame in 1994.

White was very close to her mother, just as Ball was, and they both loved animals; as a result they become good friends. In fact, Ball was so bereft after her own mother died in 1977 that she would send flowers on the anniversary to White's mom.

WHO GETS THE DRUMSTICK?

Book by Helen Beardsley published in the 1960s about the union of two households with 10 and eight children. Became the basis for the Lucille Ball-Henry Fonda hit movie *Yours, Mine and Ours* (1968); a Bantam paperback was reissued that year to coincide with the movie's release. Ball and Fonda appeared on the cover. See <u>Film Career</u> for more.

WICKES, MARY

Born 1910 in St. Louis, Wickes appeared uncredited in a few films in the 1930s, but it was her turn as Miss Preen, the "take-no-prisoners" nurse in 1942's hilarious *The Man Who Came to Dinner*, that put her on the character actress map. Wickes found her niche—usually as a salty-tongued nurse, best friend, or companion to the movie's star—and parlayed it into 50 years of movie and television performances.

Among them was a famous guest-star appearance on *I Love Lucy* as Madame Lamand in "The Ballet" episode (February 18, 1952). Wickes, Lucille Ball's neighbor and friend in Los Angeles, was also a familiar face on *The Lucy Show* (where she made seven appearances) and *Here's Lucy* (nine appearances). It's been said that Wickes was briefly considered for the Ethel Mertz role on *I Love Lucy*, but turned it down, believing her friendship with Ball would suffer if she took the part. Wickes also appeared on Ball's last TV special, *Lucy Calls the President*, in 1977.

Wickes made more than 50 movies and lots of television appearances. She worked steadily up to her death in October 1995, at the age of 85. Some scenes for her final role, the voice of one of the gargoyles in Disney's 1996 version of *The Hunchback of Notre Dame*, were dubbed by another actress after Wickes' death.

♥ **Lucy Trivia** Wickes accompanied Ball on her final visit to Vivian Vance before her death in 1979.

WIGGED OUT

Lucille Ball's hairstylist Irma Kusely noted, in the Emmy ATS archive interview she did with Karen Herman, that the star's wigs "were handmade. They measured you from ear-to-ear, over the head, to the back of the nape of the neck, [and studied] the design of how your hair grows out. Each hair in the hair lace in the front [of the wig] is put in individually and on the lace there is an octagon shape. Whichever way you want the hair to fall, you tie it on that little side knot one at a time with a crochet hook. That's called ventilating.

"[When] I did Lucy in *Mame* [for which Kusely designed 15 period wigs and had a ball doing it, she said], she had definite ideas of what she did *not* want. She did not want that flat look. So I lifted it up a little bit and it worked out. It was still a passing period [look]. It looked the way it should but [it was] not flat.

The first time that Ball used wigs on TV was on *The Lucy-Desi Comedy Hour* episode "Lucy Hunts Uranium," with guest star Fred MacMurray. Said Kusely, "That's because she wanted her hair cut and so we had to try it with a wig, give it that artichoke cut, and it looked young and perky. And it made a different look from *I Love Lucy*. That was the idea—to get a different look."

In the 1960s, Ball began wearing wigs all the time, on the shows and in public, "because it was helpful," Kusely said. "It saved time.… You [didn't] have to wait until the end of the show to pick up some [scenes, or] have to curl her hair, get her under the dryer and all of that. You had none of that. Just take the wig off, the head [was] ready for another one to come on. And you do whatever has to be done on the pickups. So it was a time-saver for production, for the crew. Everybody got overtime if they were on [call], waiting for me."

But the wigs didn't necessarily save money, even if they did save production time. Kusely stressed that, "The wigs cost a lot of money," and she should know, since she "designed them all" for Ball and others.

Still, there were exceptions. One of the most famous *Lucy Show* episodes is "Lucy and Viv Put in a Shower" (January 28, 1963). Kusely pointed out, "That was not a wig show. It was just her [natural] hair, [it] got wet and that was it. Then you quickly take a towel and give it that Turkish look, bend over and wrap the towel and screw it up and then tuck it up under the back and it looks like a turban."

See also Guilaroff, Sidney, Hair Color, Henna Rinse, and Kusely, Irma.

WILDCAT

Musical comedy in which Ball made her Broadway debut in 1960. See the in-depth entry in Stage Career.

WORK ETHIC

Lucille Ball was not one to turn down any work, especially in the early years of her career. There were two reasons. First, that attitude could get you more work, and second, in taking a job that you might not necessarily want, you could meet someone who, down the line, would be of great help to you or your career. Both philosophies served her well.

No one loved to rehearse more than Lucy, but it looks like something's interrupted the process in this picture from the set of *I Love Lucy*. **Photofest**

On her first picture, 1933's *Roman Scandals*, she agreed to do some slapstick that none of the other Goldwyn Girls would do; Eddie Cantor, the star of the movie, remembered her and gave her more bits to do as a result. Ball's career is full of instances in which she met someone early on who ended up being a great influence on her career or life some time later (Ed Sedgwick, Buster Keaton, and Karl Freund, to name a few).

As a result of all she learned, coupled with her vast experience, Ball eventually became a hard-nosed perfectionist, a trait not beloved by all of her guest stars. Regarding her insistence on perfection, close friend and hairstylist Irma Kusely told Emmy archivist Karen Herman,

"Yes, she was always there [practicing routines] over and over and over, she wanted it absolutely right. And that was why the show was a success; let's face it. It came off with perfection."

X

XYLOPHONE

Parts of the vaudeville act that Ball and Desi Arnaz used to convince CBS executives the public would accept them working as a team were used in the *I Love Lucy* pilot episode. Never intended to be viewed by the public, and thought lost, it was discovered and finally aired in 1989.

Since the 1951 TV viewing audience had never seen these classic bits, taught to Ball by Arnaz's friend, a renowned Spanish clown named Pepito, they were used again in episode six, "The Audition" (November 19, 1951).

Lucy, ever-eager to break into show business, takes over for a sick clown in husband Ricky's act and plays a rigged cello; then she gets down on the floor, barking like a seal, and toots a specially rigged xylophone—set up by Pepito with horns in place of keys—that Lucy plays by honking them with her nose. When Ricky asks Lucy the name of instrument, she answers (this is as close as I could get), "A saxovibratronaphonovich."

Y

YEARNING

A persistent, often wistful desire or longing, as with Lucy Ricardo's urge to be in show business. Lucy would do anything to get out of the house, especially if it involved show business, something that struck a deep chord in the character, and which audiences could relate to as well. Some feminists see this aspect of Lucy Ricardo as presaging the women's movement of the next two decades, in which women were encouraged to be more than homemakers.

YEAST

A fermenting agent used in baking bread, featured in the *I Love Lucy* episode "Pioneer Women" (March 31, 1952), in which Lucy and Ethel make a bet with Ricky and Fred as to who will last longer living under the conditions of their pioneer ancestors. When Lucy realizes she has to make bread from scratch, she adds too much yeast to the mix, resulting in a superlong loaf that escapes from her oven, trapping her against the sink … at which point Ethel grabs a huge saw* and begins cutting.

Don't fence her in: Lucille Ball's Lucy character's insistent optimism in the face of all obstacles made her yearning for a bit more than her life in a tidy Manhattan apartment or Connecticut house something many housewives of the 1950s and 1960s could identify with. Photofest

*This and other similar occurrences throughout the run of *I Love Lucy* could make the viewer wonder what such items were doing lying around the Ricardo/Mertz households. It's to Ball and the cast's credit that their believable acting made such questions a moot point.

YEOMAN OF THE GUARD

A member of the ceremonial guard attending the British sovereign and royal family, e.g., stationed at Buckingham Palace. These guards are famous for not reacting to outside stimuli, so naturally Lucy tries to get one to laugh when the crew is visiting London as part of Ricky Ricardo's band's European tour in the episode "Lucy Meets the Queen" (January 30, 1956).

YOUNG, MARL

A self-taught arranger and jazz and classical pianist, Young worked with Desi Arnaz and Lucille Ball beginning in 1958. Coming from a jazz, blues and church background, Young was born in Bluefield, Virginia, in 1917, and ventured out to California in 1947. Ten years later he became the first black officer of the local musicians union. A year after that, accompanying Marilyn Lovell to a Desilu audition as her pianist, Young was asked back along with Lovell.

According to Young, as interviewed by Charles Walton on the Jazz Institute of Chicago website, "The next time we went, there were fewer people and Lucy was there. The singer and I still hadn't rehearsed. We did the same two numbers and when we got through everybody applauded. Lucy asked that we do something else and Marilyn informed her that we had not rehearsed anything. Lucy said, 'That piano player looks like he could play anything.'" Young was hired to do arrangements for the Desilu Workshop, Lucy's pet project. He also played piano and, eventually, was made assistant conductor.

After Ball and Arnaz split up, Young was called back for work on *The Lucy Show* in 1962, and, as he explains it, "I went in and everybody was there—Lever Bros., about 16 executives and Desi. Even though he and Lucy were [split], he was still at the studio and she really depended upon him to put the show together. Let me say right now, he was the best man in the business I had ever run into. She had the performance talent, but he had the business acumen. He knew what he was doing.

"After I played the number as it was written, which was a two-beat, show-type tune, Desi said, 'Marl, play that as a rhumba.' I played his rhumba. He said, 'Now play it as a samba.' He said, 'Now play it real funky.' And he called about six or seven styles and I was right there on the spot. When I got through, he said fine and we went into his office and they [said they] were getting together what they called the warm-up band. When they came to the piano they called some guy's name and Desi said, "We are going to present different singers in the show every week and we need a very flexible piano player up there." Then he said, almost offhand-edly, 'Wilbur [Hatch, the conductor], why don't you use Marl this time?"

Young went to work for Hatch and Desilu orchestra contractor Julian Davidson, and ended up writing special material and arrangements (as for the John Bubbles/Mel Tormé two-part episode in January 1967, "Main Street USA"), and eventually, around 1969, began taking over for Hatch, who was ill at the time, on *Here's Lucy*. When Hatch died in December 1969, Young took over as conductor. In February 1970, he was offered the job of musical director and took it, remaining with the show until Ball retired from the weekly grind in 1974. Young had become the first black musical director of a network series. One of the first things he did, with executive producer Gary Morton's blessing, was integrate the orchestra with three other black musicians.

YOUR TROPICAL TRIP
Short-lived radio show (1950-'51) hosted by Desi Arnaz just before the start of *I Love Lucy*.

Z

ZANRA PRODUCTIONS

Production company (the name is "Arnaz" spelled backwards) set up by Desi Arnaz in the mid-1950s to produce the film *Forever Darling* (1956). Arnaz and Ball owned 80 percent of it, with the rest going to <u>Desilu Studio</u> employees and their families and children. Unfortunately, Zanra never saw the success of the Arnaz's other, more famous venture, Desilu.

AFTERWORD

LUCILLE BALL IN THE NEW MILLENNIUM

The millennium hype is long over, and the Top Entertainer and Top Celebrity lists of the past century have come and gone. It might be logically assumed that Lucille Ball would not be so much in the public eye post-2000. As it turns out, nothing could be further from the truth.

The Internet auction house eBay is a good barometer of public taste. In 1999, a search for "Lucille Ball" brought up 500 to 600 items. On a random day in May 2007, the same search garnered 1,989 items for sale. In early October 2007, a similar search brought up 2,186 items. Images of Lucy, Ricky, Fred, and Ethel will be put on any surface that exists. And fans will buy the souvenirs. The number of Ball sites/tribute pages on the Internet also keeps growing, with no end in sight.

An icon for the ages. Photofest

429

The 50th Anniversary of *I Love Lucy* in 2001 brought a variety of celebrations and tributes. But you don't need a special anniversary to discover lots of Ball-related gems everywhere around you.

On television, *I Love Lucy* is broadcast every day, several times a day, on its cable home, TV Land, running with its original animated openings. Ball's movies are also plentiful on TV, and Turner Classic Movies designates Ball its "Star of the Month" every so often, which allows you to catch 30 or 40 of her flicks.

If you're a dedicated channel surfer, persistence will reward you. Once, within the space of a few hours, I saw Ball make an animated appearance on <u>The Simpsons</u>. A bit later, I was passing through VH-1 when I noticed a familiar drummer: Desi Arnaz Jr. Intrigued, I watched as <u>Dino, Desi & Billy</u> played a love song, and were congratulated by Ed Sullivan. Ready to keep surfing, I stopped as Sullivan introduced one of the trio's mothers from the audience ... none other than Ball herself.

But any medium can bring unexpected joy to the loyal fan. Recently, I read a newspaper review calling a stage production "a giddy farce worthy of Lucy and Ethel." Several hours later I watched *RV* (2006), and saw a scene in which the hapless lead played by Robin Williams does a sales pitch for soda while referencing *I Love Lucy* (indeed, the entire movie is basically one big homage—and that's putting it politely—to Ball's 1954 hit film, *The Long, Long Trailer*).

In 2007, as of this writing, Ball has already been honored with the first Legacy of Laughter award, to be given out annually by cable channel TV Land. Her children and Carol Burnett saluted her on the TV special with a series of Lucy clips. A book on her films, long overdue—*Lucy at the Movies*, by Cindy de la Hoz—debuted in Jamestown, late summer 2007. She was on the cover of *TIME* magazine in the fall as part of a salute to the Top 100 TV shows. And then ... ahem ... there are the steady sales of this book, which predicated the Fourth Edition you have in your hands.

The Ball phenomenon continues, nearly 20 years after her death. With the redhead firmly ensconced as a cultural icon, it's safe to say that as long as there are media, there will be Lucy sightings.

Ball often said she was just happy to know she had made people laugh. In the end, she did much more than that for America and, indeed, much of the world. She created a distinctly American character, one who was tolerant enough to marry a foreigner and create a loving (TV) marriage. Lucy Ricardo expressed the dreams, goals, and fantasies of many in the audience; she was someone who wasn't satisfied with her situation in life: she wanted *more*. Ball, as Lucys Ricardo, Carmichael, and Carter, clowned around in outrageous situations, but her zeal, and therefore her actions, were always just this side of believable, offering hope for many that they, too, could escape the more rigid confines of their lives. For others, merely watching *I Love Lucy*, *The Lucy Show*, and *Here's Lucy*, and *laughing*, became the escape they needed.

In our too-serious times, we routinely forget to stop and enjoy each precious moment of life, or to laugh as much as we should, because we're too "busy," or occupied with life's real burdens. Ball makes us laugh over and over and over again. What could be more important than that?

ABOUT THE AUTHOR

New York-based writer and editor Michael Karol has always loved Lucy. He watched *I Love Lucy* as a child growing up in New Jersey, where the show was rerun in the morning (never mind what he wasn't doing in school—he can't remember) with a trusted babysitter, laughing out loud and becoming entranced by the antics of Lucy and Ethel. Following this, when he discovered Lucille Ball and Vivian Vance were doing a new TV show, he forced the family to watch it on their only TV. Well, his mother may have held a grudge—years later, walking into his New York apartment, she noted dryly, "You have more pictures of Lucy here than you do of me"—but there were many other programs less worthy than *The Lucy Show* he might have watched.

As Michael grew up, the special fondness he held for Lucy and Viv (and various other sitcom queens, truth be told) only grew. When he graduated from Boston University with a Masters in Communications, he felt it was only prudent that he communicate, and began a quarter-century-plus career in publishing as a journalist and editor. Michael has written about everything from area rugs to pop music, from counterfeiting to colorization, but his favorite subjects are show-business-related, especially classic TV and golden-age movies. Several years ago, Michael finally landed his dream job: as copy chief at *Soap Opera Weekly*, he is mandated to watch TV during work hours.

While languishing in a previous job, circa 1999, Michael began writing a biography of Ball, based on everything he'd read and known. Once it got to be more than 10,000 words, he realized it might make a good book. His close friend and fellow author, Craig Hamrick, suggested the A to Z encyclopedic format (Craig was also a fine photographer; he took the author's photo on the back cover).

Thus began several years of intensive research during which Michael pored over the huge files at the New York Public Library for the Performing Arts at Lincoln Center and watched rare videos at the Museum of Television and Radio (now known as The Paley Center for Media). He even, during this period, got over his fear of the vastness of the New York Public Library and found it was quite user-friendly. Unearthing priceless Ball facts and pictures that hadn't been seen or written about in decades (or ever) struck Michael as being valuable and interesting to other fans.

Over the past 20 years, Michael has interviewed many celebrities, including such Lucille Ball associates as *I Love Lucy* film editor Dann Cahn, her personal secretary Wanda Clark, chauffeur Frank Gorey, and Lucy's surviving co-stars Doris Singleton (Carolyn Appleby) and Jane Connell (her *Mame* Gooch); and other celebrities like Susan Lucci, Johnny "Guitar" Watson, David Hedison, Denise Nickerson, Gale Storm, actors Jason-Shane Scott and Ignacio Serricchio, crooner Phyllis Hyman, and behind-the-scenes movers and shakers like *Wonderfalls* creator Bryan Fuller and *House MD*'s executive producer David Shore.

This Fourth Edition of *Lucy A to Z: the Lucille Ball Encyclopedia* is roughly three times the size of the first one. His other Ball-centric books include *Lucy in Print* (how the press dealt with Lucy and her TV co-stars, published in 2003); *The Lucille Ball Quiz Book* (2004); and *The Comic DNA of Lucille Ball: Interpreting the Icon* (2006).

[Michael does occasionally tackle subjects other than Lucymania, such as his current best-selling book, *The ABC Movie of the Week Companion*; his latest trivia collection, *The TV Tidbits Classic Television Book of Lists*; and the vampire novels *Kiss Me, Kill Me* and its prequel, *Sleeps Well With Others*.]

Michael has been an invited guest at various nostalgia conventions—including several Lucy Fests held in her hometown of Jamestown, New York and sponsored by The Lucy-Desi Center—and the Big Apple Con comic and nostalgia conventions, where he has served on author panels, provided unique insights and trivia as the "celebrity guest"on bus tours of Jamestown, and hosted *I Love Lucy* trivia events. He's also appeared on a half-dozen radio shows, including WCBS-FM New York, the biggest "oldies"/nostalgia station in the country. He's been quoted and reviewed in various national magazines, from niche market publications like *Classic Images* to mass-market magazines like the *Star*. He's also been quoted and referenced in other books about Lucy (like Stefan Kanfer's 2003 *Ball of Fire*) and comedy (Lawrence Epstein's 2004 *Mixed Nuts: America's Love Affair with Comedy Teams*). He will be featured in an upcoming documentary about the Lucy fan phenomenon.

Michael keeps a bottle of Vitameatavegamin next to his computer for good health and inspiration.

BIBLIOGRAPHY

As a happily obsessed fan of all things Lucy, I have read most of the books, and magazine and newspaper articles, about Lucille Ball, Desi Arnaz, Vivian Vance, and William Frawley over the past 40-plus years. I have watched, taped, and dissected hundreds of TV programs, movies, biographies, and interviews with Ball and those who knew her and worked with her. It is sometimes difficult to pinpoint where a specific kernel of information originated.

First, I recommend every book mentioned in *Lucy A to Z* (see Books).

In doing the research for this volume, I examined and read many articles from old newspapers, going back as far as the 1930s. Where possible I've mentioned the authors; but the condition of the newspapers, and in some cases the way the articles were clipped, has made it impossible to credit all the authors and reporters.

In the interest of easier reading, I have mostly eliminated ellipses (…) and use of "[sic]" in quotes and previously published copy, to indicate jumps in copy and misuse/misspelling of words, respectively (for example, back in the 1930s and 1940s rumba was invariably spelled "rhumba"). I left them in only when their elimination would have changed the meaning of a quote, or resulted in a grossly misspelled word.

Sometimes I have referenced magazine articles and books in individual entries in the main text of the book.

To those I would add:

Books

—*American Film Comedy, from Abbott & Costello to Jerry Zucker*, by Scott and Barbara Siegel, Prentice Hall, 1994.
A useful encyclopedic look at virtually everyone in film comedy.
—*Broadway Bound, A Guide to Shows that Died Aborning*, by William Torbert Leonard, The Scarecrow Press, 1983.
An indispensable guide to shows that previewed but never made it to Broadway.
—*Cordially Yours, Ann Sothern*, by Colin Briggs, BearManor Media, 2007.

Intimate biography of Ball's pal offers some juicy tidbits.

—*Crowning Glory, Reflections of Hollywood's Favorite Confidant*, by Sydney Guilaroff, as told to Cathy Griffin, General Publishing Group, 1996.

Hollywood remembered by the Golden Age's premier hairstylist.

—*Frank Sinatra, An American Legend*, by Nancy Sinatra, 1995.

—*The Golden Age of Television*, by Max Wilk, Moyer Bell Ltd., 1989.

Puts Ball and her show in historical perspective with her peers, such as Milton Berle, Jack Benny, George Burns, Sid Caesar, and Jackie Gleason.

—*Hedda and Louella*, by George Eels, Warner Books, 1973.

This is a fascinating dual memoir of the two queens of Hollywood gossip.

—*Just Outside the Spotlight*, by Luke Yankee, Watson-Guptil, 2006.

Yankee, son of actress Eileen Heckart, details the character actress' fabulous career; lots of showbiz dish, and a pearl of a chapter on Vivian Vance, the Heckarts' Connecticut neighbor.

—*Lucille Ball, First Lady of Comedy*, The Museum of Broadcasting (New York) circa 1985.

An odd-sized, slim, but wonderful paperback created to accompany an exhibit of the same title, with insightful essays by Molly Haskell, Jess Oppenheimer, TV critic Jack Gould, and others.

—*The Lucille Ball Story*, by James Gregory, Signet Paperback, 1974.

A lesser-known paperback biography of Lucy published around the time of the release of *Mame*.

—*Lucy & Desi: The Legendary Love Story of Television's Most Famous Couple*, by Warren G. Harris, Simon & Schuster, 1991.

A look at Lucy and Desi and their lives from the perspective of their passion for each other.

—*Max Factor's Hollywood: Glamour, Movies, and Makeup*, by Fred E. Basten, General Publishing Group, 1996.

—*The Real Story of Lucille Ball*, by Eleanor Harris, Farrar, Straus & Young/Ballantine Books, 1954.

One of the first in-depth biographies of Lucille Ball.

—*Total Television: The Comprehensive Guide to Programming from 1948 to the Present* (4th Ed), by Alex McNeil, 1996.

The chronicle of the TV age, from 1848 to 1995, featuring information and stats on 5,400 shows, including specials.

—*Valentines & Vitriol*, by Rex Reed, Delacorte Press, 1977.

—*Yes, Mr. Selznick*, Recollections of Hollywood's Golden Era, by Marcella Rabwin, Dorrance Publishing Co., 1999.

Executive assistant to David O. Selznick and close friend of Lucille Ball and Desi Arnaz, Rabwin's memoirs include separate chapters on Lucy and Desi, and there's a foreword by Lucie Arnaz.

Websites

—*The Internet Movie Database Pro*, pro.Imdb.com

Filled with information on Ball, her TV shows and movies, plus her co-stars and their careers.

—*NewspaperArchive.com*, www.newspaperarchive.com

This site can save you many trips to the library, searching through crumbling files and micro-film. There's a yearly subscription cost, but it's worth it.

Articles

—*LIFE*, October 5, 1942: "Lucille Ball Wins First Chance as Big-Time Star"

—*The New York Times*, December 24, 1950: "*Twentieth Century* Memoir," by Richard Maney

—*TV Guide*, March 20-26, 1953: "Lucy's Neighbors Exposed," by Katherine Pedell

—*The American Magazine*, June 1953: "They Love Lucy"

—*TV Fan*, October 1954: "How Do You Like Your TV Shows?" by Paul Marsh, and "Life with Lucy, On and Off Screen," by Vivian Vance

—*Collier's*, October 29, 1954: "Groucho … Lucy … Gleason … Dragnet: Those TV Ratings: Who *Knows* Who's on Top?" by Bill Davison

—*TV Guide*, November 20-26, 1954: "Honest, She's My Wife!"

—*Sunday Daily News* magazine, February 27, 1955: "Just Like the Folks at Home," by Florabel Muir

—*McCalls*, May 1955: "I Don't Run Away Anymore," by Vivian Vance

—*Cue*, May 14, 1955: "Young Man of Property," by Philip Minoff

—*TV Guide*, November 5, 1957: "You Can't Stand Still"

—*LIFE*, January 5, 1962: "Lucy Is Back!"

—*TV Guide*, February 9-15, 1963: "Vivian Vance Can Now Laugh Off-Camera, Too," by Leslie Radditz

—Sunday *New York News Coloroto Magazine*, October 13, 1963: "At Home with Vivian Vance"

—*Look*, September 7, 1971: "TV: Turn-on or Turn-off?" and "Lucille Ball: The Star that Never Sets," by Laura Bergquist

—The American Film Institute *Dialogue on Film* Volume, Number 6, May-June 1974: "Lucille Ball"

—*The New York Post*, 1977: "They Loved Lucy on the Stage, Too," by Harvey Sabinson

—*Parade*, January 13, 1980: "Conversation Piece: The *I Love Lucy* and Betty Show"

—*The Village Voice*, May 1 1984: "After the Ball: On Loving Lucy," by Guy Trebay

—*The Village Voice*, November 5, 1985: "Lucy on the Half-Shell," by Michael McWilliams

—*Television Quarterly*, Volume 24, No. 2, 1989: "A Fan of Lucy's," by Thomas J. Cottle

—*Emmy*, July-August 1989: "Everything Will Be for Lucy," by Ben Herndon

—*Cinema Journal* 29, No. 4, Summer 1990: "The Cabinet of Lucy Ricardo: Lucille Ball's Star Image," by Alexander Doty

—*The New York Times*, October 7, 2001: "America, Grandly Familiar," by Rick Lyman and others

—*The New York Times*, October 14, 2001: "The Good, The Bad, The Lucy: A Legacy of Laughs," featuring "Cooly Confident, Timelessly Funny," by Joyce Millman; "The Man Behind the Throne: Making the Case for Desi," by Douglas McGrath; and "Endlessly Lovable, But Damaging, Too" by Anita Gates.

—Vanity Fair, January 2002: "Magnificent Obsession," by David Kamp

—*Palm Springs Life*, January 2002: "How We Loved Lucy," by Allene Arthur

Finally, special nods to the New York Public Library for the Performing Arts—its copious performer files were a great source of information and inspiration (and thanks again, Craig, for bringing me there the first time)—and the staff at the Lucy-Desi Center in Jamestown, New York. No request was too small for staffers to try to answer, and a tired author really appreciates it.

INDEX

978-0-595-29761-0
0-595-29761-7

Made in the USA
Monee, IL
02 January 2020